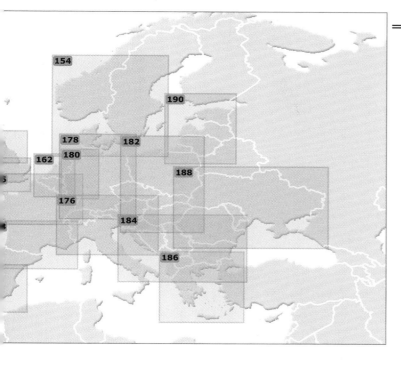

City plans

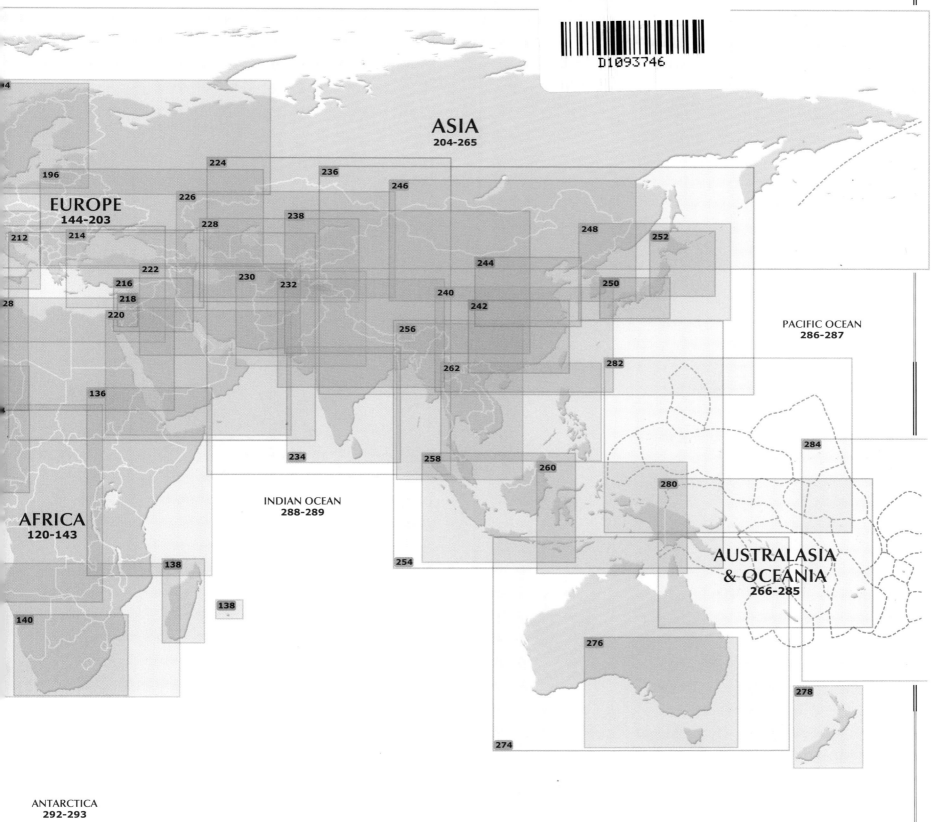

WORLD
BOOK

Third Edition
ATLAS OF THE WORLD

WORLD BOOK

Third Edition

ATLAS OF THE WORLD

World Book, Inc.
www.worldbook.com

Atlas of the World

An edition of this atlas is also published under the title
Complete Atlas of the World, Third Edition. Copyright © 2012, 2016
Dorling Kindersley Limited, 80 Strand, London WC2R 0RL

World Book, Inc.
180 North LaSalle Street
Suite 900
Chicago, Illinois 60601
USA

World Book edition reprinted with revisions 2017.
ISBN 978-0-7166-2659-6
Library of Congress Control Number: 2010925048

For information on other World Book publications, visit our
website at **www.worldbook.com** or call **1-800-WORLDBK
(967-5325)**. For information about sales to schools and libraries,
call **1-800-975-3250 (United States); 1-800-837-5365 (Canada)**.

Printed in Italy by L.E.G.O. S.p.A., Vicenza, Italy
1st printing April 2017

World Book:

President:
Jim O'Rourke

Vice President & Editor in Chief:
Paul A. Kobasa

Vice President, Finance:
Donald D. Keller

Vice President, International Sales:
Maksim Rutenberg

Vice President, Marketing:
Jean Lin

Senior Cartographer:
John M. Rejba

Senior Art Director:
Tom Evans

Manager, Contracts & Compliance:
Loranne K. Shields

Dorling Kindersley:

Publishing Director:
Jonathan Metcalf

Art Director:
Bryn Walls

Managing Editor:
David Roberts

Senior Cartographic Editor:
Simon Mumford

Digital Map Suppliers:
Advanced Illustration, Congleton, UK • Cosmographics,
Watford, UK

Encompass Graphics, Brighton, UK • Lovell Johns Ltd.,
Long Hanborough, UK

Netmaps, Barcelona, Spain

Digital Terrain Data:
Digital terrain data and continental panoramic images
created by Planetary Visions Ltd., Farnham, UK

Cartographers:
Paul Eames, Edward Merritt, John Plumer, Rob Stokes,
Iorwerth Watkins

Cartographic Editors:
Tony Chambers, John Dear, Ruth Hall, Andrew Johnson,
Belinda Kane, Lynn Neal, Ann Stephenson

Indexing and Database:
T-Kartor, Sweden
Francesca Albini, Eleanor Arkwright, Renata Dyntarova,
Edward Heelas, Britta Hansesgaard

Editor:
Robert Dinwiddie

Designers:
Nicola Liddiard, Yak El-Droubie

Picture Research:
Louise Thomas, Jenny Baskaya

Systems Coordinator:
Philip Rowles

Production Controllers:
Linda Dare, Melanie Dowland

Special Sales and Custom Publishing Manager:
Michelle Baxter

Flags courtesy of The Flag Institute, Cheshire, UK.

A WORLD OF IDEAS:
SEE ALL THERE IS TO KNOW
www.dk.com

Introduction

The world at the beginning of the 21st Century would be a place of unimaginable change to our ancestors. Since 1900, the human population has undergone fourfold growth, which has been combined with unparalleled development in the technology at humanity's disposal. The last vestiges of the unknown world are gone. The advent of aviation technology and the growth of mass tourism have allowed people to travel farther and more frequently than ever before.

Allied to this, the rapid growth of global communication systems means that world events have become more accessible than ever before, and their effects quickly ripple across the planet. News broadcasts and the Internet bring the far-flung corners of the world into everyone's lives and, with them, a view of the people and places that make up those regions. The mysteries of the world that once fueled global exploration and the quest to discover the unknown are behind us; we inhabit a world of mass transportation, a world where even the most remote regions have been mapped, a world with multifaceted viewpoints on every event, a world of communication overload.

It is increasingly important for us to have a clear vision of the world in which we live and such a deluge of information can leave us struggling to find some context and meaning. It has never been more important to own an atlas; the *Atlas of the World* has been conceived to meet this need. At its core, like all atlases, it seeks to define where places are, to describe their main characteristics, and to locate them in relation to other places. By gathering a spectacular collection of satellite imagery and combining these images with carefully selected and up-to-date geographic information, this atlas filters the world's data into clear, meaningful, and user-friendly maps.

The *Atlas of the World* works on many different levels. Readers can learn about global issues of many kinds, or they can probe in a little further for the continental context. Delving even further, they can explore issues at a regional, national, or even sub-national level. The very best available satellite data have been used to create topography and bathymetry that reveal the breathtaking texture of landscapes and sea-floors. These bring out the context of the places and features selected to appear on top of them. The full-spread map areas purposefully overlap to emphasize the connectivity and interdependence of our world.

This third edition of the *Atlas of the World* incorporates hundreds of revisions and updates, distilling the mass of information available via modern technology into an extraordinarily detailed and reliable view of our world.

The Editors

Contents

The atlas is organized by continent, moving eastward from the International Date Line. The opening section describes the world's structure, systems and its main features. The Atlas of the World which follows, is a continent-by-continent guide to today's world, starting with a comprehensive insight into the physical, political, and economic structure of each continent, followed by detailed maps of carefully selected geopolitical regions.

WORLD

NORTH AMERICA

SOUTH AMERICA

AFRICA

EUROPE

ASIA

AUSTRALASIA & OCEANIA

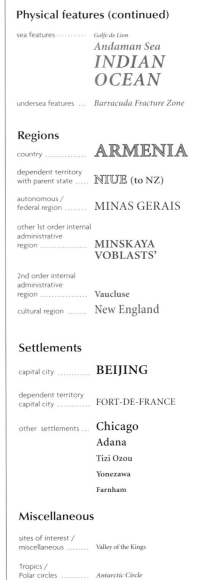

INDEX & GAZETTEER

Key to regional maps

Physical features

elevation

6000m / 19,686ft
4000m / 13,124ft
3000m / 9843ft
2000m / 6562ft
1000m / 3281ft
500m / 1640ft
250m / 820ft
100m / 328ft
sea level
below sea level

▲ elevation above sea level (mountain height)

▲ volcano

✕ pass

▼ elevation below sea level (depression depth)

sand desert

lava flow

coastline

reef

atoll

sea depth

sea level
-250m / -820ft
-2000m / -6562ft
-4000m / -13,124ft

▲ seamount / guyot symbol

▼ undersea spot depth

Drainage features

main river
secondary river
tertiary river
minor river
main seasonal river
secondary seasonal river
canal
waterfall
rapids
dam
perennial lake
seasonal lake
perennial salt lake
seasonal salt lake
reservoir
salt flat / salt pan
marsh / salt marsh
mangrove
wadi

○ spring / well / waterhole / oasis

Ice features

ice cap / sheet
ice shelf
glacier / snowfield
+ + + + summer pack ice limit
. . . . winter pack ice limit

Graticule features

lines of latitude and longitude / Equator

Tropics / Polar circles

45° degrees of longitude / latitude

Communications

motorway / highway
motorway / highway (under construction)
major road
minor road
tunnel (road)
main railroad
minor railroad
tunnel (railroad)

✈ international airport

Borders

full international border

undefined international border

disputed de facto border

disputed territorial claim border

indication of country extent (Pacific only)

indication of dependent territory extent (Pacific only)

demarcation / cease fire line

autonomous / federal region border

other 1st order internal administrative border

2nd order internal administrative border

Miscellaneous features

ancient wall

◇ site of interest

● scientific station

Settlements

built up area

settlement population symbols

■ more than 5 million

◉ 1 million to 5 million

◎ 500,000 to 1 million

⊚ 100,000 to 500,000

⊕ 50,000 to 100,000

○ 10,000 to 50,000

○ fewer than 10,000

■ ● ● country/dependent territory capital city

■ ● ● autonomous / federal region / other 1st order internal administrative center

■ ● ⊕ 2nd order internal administrative center

Typographic key

Physical features

landscape features ... *Namib Desert*
Massif Central
ANDES

headland .... *Nordkapp*

elevation / volcano / pass .... Mount Meru 4556 m

drainage features .... *Lake Geneva*

rivers / canals
spring / well /
waterhole / oasis /
waterfall /
rapids / dam .... *Mekong*

ice features .... *Vatnajökull*

Physical features (continued)

sea features .... *Golfe de Lion*
Andaman Sea
INDIAN OCEAN

undersea features ... *Barracuda Fracture Zone*

Regions

country .... ARMENIA

dependent territory with parent state ..... NIUE (to NZ)

autonomous / federal region .... MINAS GERAIS

other 1st order internal administrative region .... MINSKAYA VOBLASTS'

2nd order internal administrative region .... Vaucluse

cultural region .... New England

Settlements

capital city .... BEIJING

dependent territory capital city .... FORT-DE-FRANCE

other settlements ... Chicago
Adana
Tizi Ozou
Yonezawa
Farnham

Miscellaneous

sites of interest / miscellaneous .... Valley of the Kings

Tropics / Polar circles .... *Antarctic Circle*

The Solar System

The Solar System consists of our local star, the Sun, and numerous objects that orbit the Sun – eight planets, five currently recognized dwarf planets, over 165 moons orbiting these planets and dwarf planets, and countless smaller bodies such as comets and asteroids. Including a vast outer region that is populated only by comets, the Solar System is about 9,300 billion miles (15,000 billion km) across. The much smaller region containing just the Sun and planets is about 7.5 billion miles (12 billion km) across. The Sun, which contributes over 99 percent of the mass of the entire Solar System, creates energy from nuclear reactions deep within its interior, providing the heat and light that make life on Earth possible.

THE MOON'S PHASES

As the Moon orbits Earth, the relative positions of Moon, Sun and Earth continuously change. Thus, the angle at which the Moon's sunlit face is seen by an observer on Earth varies in a cyclical fashion, producing the Moon's phases, as shown at right. Each cycle takes 29.5 days.

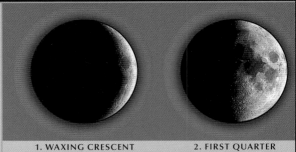

1. WAXING CRESCENT   2. FIRST QUARTER

The Moon

Earth's only satellite, the Moon, is thought to have formed 4.5 billion years ago from a cloud of debris produced when a large asteroid hit the young Earth. The Moon is too small to have retained an atmosphere, and is therefore a lifeless, dusty and dead world. However, although the Moon has only about 1 percent of the mass of the Earth, its gravity exerts an important influence on Earth's oceans, manifest in the ebb and flow of the tides.

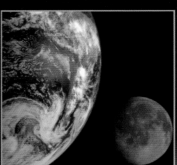

The Earth and Moon's relative sizes are clear in this long-range image from space.

What is a Planet?

The International Astronomical Union defines a Solar System planet as a near-spherical object that orbits the Sun (and no other body) and has cleared the neighborhood around its orbit of other bodies. A dwarf planet is a planet that is not big enough to have cleared its orbital neighborhood. Extra-solar planets are objects orbiting stars other than the Sun.

MERCURY   VENUS   EARTH   MARS

CERES (dwarf planet)

JUPITER

The Sun

The Sun is a huge sphere of exceedingly hot plasma (ionized gas), consisting mainly of the elements hydrogen and helium. It formed about 4.6 billion years ago, when a swirling cloud of gas and dust began to contract under the influence of gravity. When the center of this cloud reached a critically high temperature, hydrogen nuclei started combining to form helium nuclei – a process called nuclear fusion – with the release of massive amounts of energy. This process continues to this day.

SOLAR ECLIPSE

A solar eclipse occurs when the Moon passes between Earth and the Sun, casting its shadow on Earth's surface. During a total eclipse (below), viewers along a strip of Earth's surface, called the area of totality, see the Sun totally blotted out for a short time, as the umbra (Moon's full shadow) sweeps over them. Outside this area is a larger one, where the Sun appears only partly obscured, as the penumbra (partial shadow) passes over.

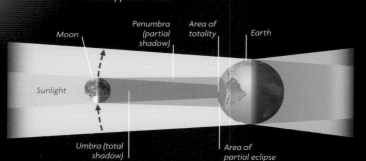

Moon

Penumbra (partial shadow)

Area of totality

Earth

Sunlight

Umbra (total shadow)

Area of partial eclipse

INSIDE THE SUN

The Sun has three internal layers. At its center is the core, where temperatures reach 27 million°F (15 million°C) and nuclear fusion occurs. The radiative zone is a slightly cooler region through which energy radiates away from the core. Further out, in the convective zone, plumes of hot plasma carry the energy towards the Sun's visible surface layer, called the photosphere. Once there, the energy escapes as light, heat and other forms of radiation.

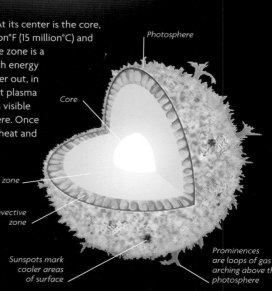

Photosphere

Core

Radiative zone

Convective zone

Sunspots mark cooler areas of surface

Prominences are loops of gas arching above the photosphere

3. WAXING GIBBOUS   **4. FULL MOON**   **5. WANING GIBBOUS**   **6. LAST QUARTER**   **7. WANING CRESCENT**   **8. NEW MOON**

PLANETS / MAIN DWARF PLANETS

	MERCURY	VENUS	EARTH	MARS	JUPITER	SATURN	URANUS	NEPTUNE	CERES	PLUTO	ERIS
DIAMETER	3029 miles (4875 km)	7521 miles (12,104 km)	7928 miles (12,756 km)	4213 miles (6780 km)	88,846 miles (142,984 km)	74,898 miles (120,536 km)	31,763 miles (51,118 km)	30,775 miles (49,528 km)	590 miles (950 km)	1432 miles (2304 km)	1429-1553 miles (2300-2500 km)
AVERAGE DISTANCE FROM THE SUN	36 mill. miles (57.9 mill. km)	67.2 mill. miles (108.2 mill. km)	93 mill. miles (149.6 mill. km)	141.6 mill. miles (227.9 mill. km)	483.6 mill. miles (778.3 mill. km)	889.8 mill. miles (1431 mill. km)	1788 mill. miles (2877 mill. km)	2795 mill. miles (4498 mill. km)	257 mill. miles (414 mill. km)	3675 mill. miles (5,915 mill. km)	6344 mill. miles (10,210 mill. km)
ROTATION PERIOD	58.6 days	243 days	23.93 hours	24.62 hours	9.93 hours	10.65 hours	17.24 hours	16.11 hours	9.1 hours	6.38 days	not known
ORBITAL PERIOD	88 days	224.7 days	365.26 days	687 days	11.86 years	29.37 years	84.1 years	164.9 years	4.6 years	248.6 years	557 years
SURFACE TEMPERATURE	-292°F to 806°F (-180°C to 430°C)	896°F (480°C)	-94°F to 131°F (-70°C to 55°C)	-184°F to 77 °F (-120°C to 25°C)	-160°F (-110°C)	-220°F (-140°C)	-320°F (-200°C)	-320°F (-200°C)	-161°F (-107°C)	-380°F (-230°C)	-405°F (-243°C)

DWARF PLANETS

In 2006 a new type of dwarf planet was defined in an attempt to classify the numerous smaller bodies within the solar system that behave like planets physically but which are only a fraction of the size of the major planets. Currently, there are five dwarf planets recognized under this system, Ceres, Pluto, Haumea, Makemake, and Eris.

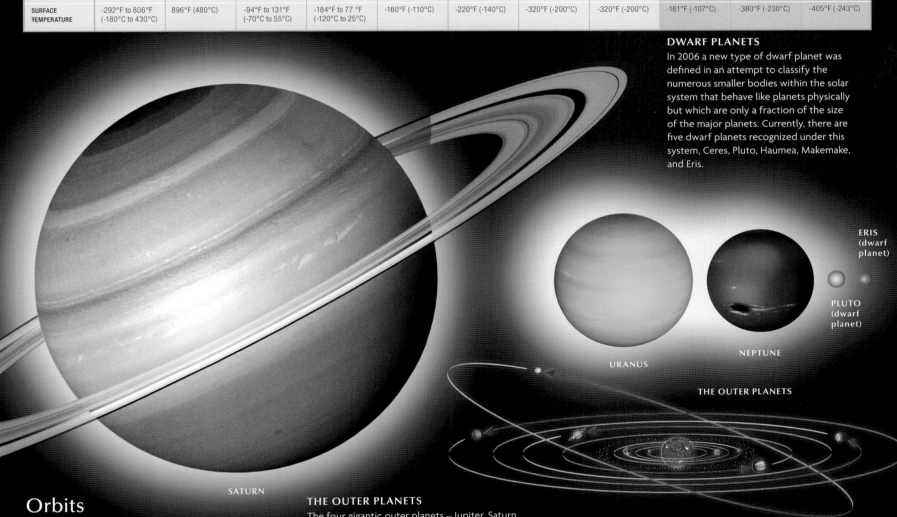

ERIS (dwarf planet)

PLUTO (dwarf planet)

NEPTUNE

URANUS

THE OUTER PLANETS

SATURN

Orbits

All the Solar System's planets and dwarf planets orbit the Sun in the same direction and (apart from Pluto) roughly in the same plane. All the orbits have the shapes of ellipses (stretched circles). However in most cases, these ellipses are close to being circular: only Pluto and Eris have very elliptical orbits. Orbital period (the time it takes an object to orbit the Sun) increases with distance from the Sun. The more remote objects not only have further to travel with each orbit, they also move more slowly.

THE OUTER PLANETS

The four gigantic outer planets – Jupiter, Saturn, Uranus and Neptune – consist mainly of gas, liquid and ice. All have rings and many moons. The dwarf planet Pluto is made of rock and ice.

THE INNER PLANETS

The four planets closest to the Sun – Mercury, Venus, Earth and Mars – are composed mainly of rock and metal. They are much smaller than the outer planets, have few or no moons, and no rings.

THE INNER PLANETS

AVERAGE DISTANCE FROM THE SUN

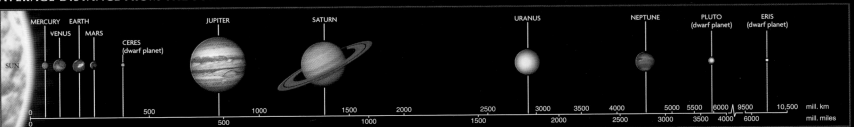

MERCURY EARTH   VENUS   MARS   JUPITER   SATURN   URANUS   NEPTUNE   PLUTO (dwarf planet)   ERIS (dwarf planet)

CERES (dwarf planet)

SUN

500   1000   1500   2000   2500   3000   3500   4000   4500   5000 5500   6000 9500   10,500 mill. km

500   1000   1500   2000   2500   3000   3500   4000   6000 mill. miles

The Physical World

Earth's surface is constantly being transformed. Movements of the rigid tectonic plates that make up this surface are continuously, if slowly, shifting its landmasses around, while the land itself is constantly weathered and eroded by wind, water, and ice. Sometimes change is dramatic, the spectacular results of earthquakes or floods. More often it is a slow process lasting for millions of years. A physical map of the world represents a snapshot of Earth's ever-evolving architecture. The maps below and at right show the planet's whole surface, including variations in ocean depth as well as the mountain-rippled texture of Earth's continents.

THE WORLD'S OCEANS
Earth's surface is dominated by water. The hemisphere shown here, centered around the southwest Pacific, is nearly all ocean, with the waters interrupted only by Antarctica, a part of South America, Australia, and the numerous islands of Australasia & Oceania, and southeast Asia.

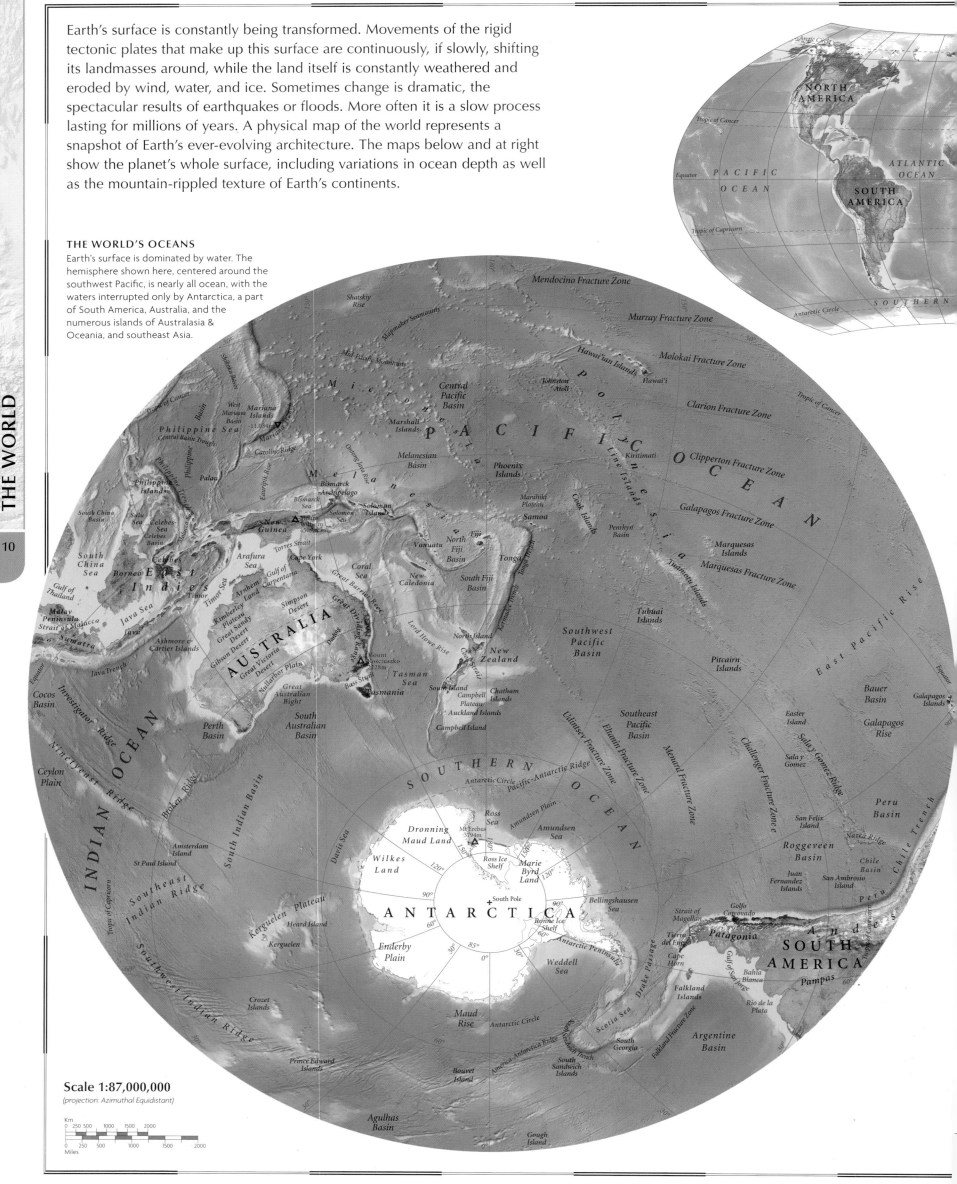

Scale 1:87,000,000

(projection: Azimuthal Equidistant)

Km
0 250 500 1000 1500 2000

0 250 500 1000 1500 2000
Miles

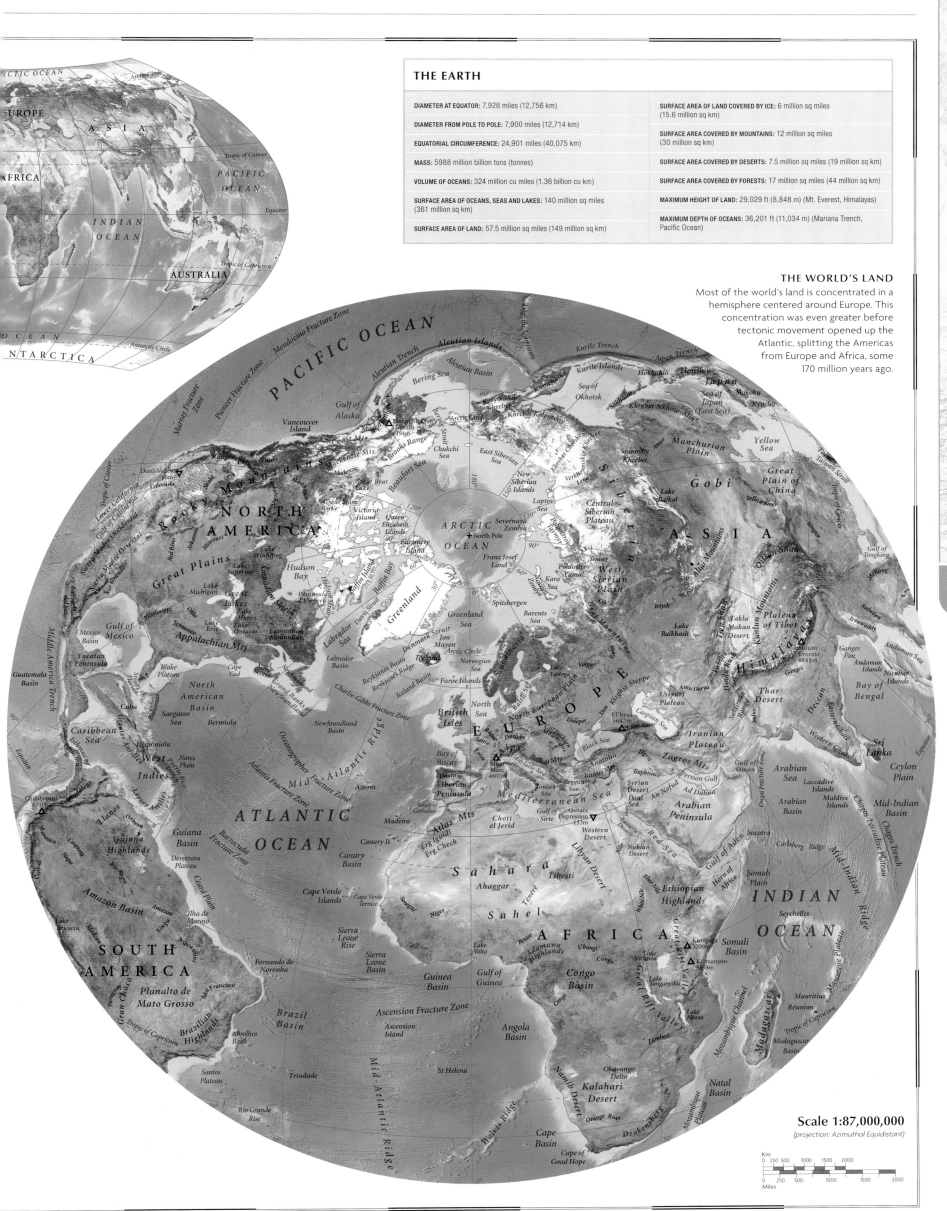

THE EARTH

DIAMETER AT EQUATOR: 7,926 miles (12,756 km)

DIAMETER FROM POLE TO POLE: 7,900 miles (12,714 km)

EQUATORIAL CIRCUMFERENCE: 24,901 miles (40,075 km)

MASS: 5988 million billion tons (tonnes)

VOLUME OF OCEANS: 324 million cu miles (1.36 billion cu km)

SURFACE AREA OF OCEANS, SEAS AND LAKES: 140 million sq miles (361 million sq km)

SURFACE AREA OF LAND: 57.5 million sq miles (149 million sq km)

SURFACE AREA OF LAND COVERED BY ICE: 6 million sq miles (15.6 million sq km)

SURFACE AREA COVERED BY MOUNTAINS: 12 million sq miles (30 million sq km)

SURFACE AREA COVERED BY DESERTS: 7.5 million sq miles (19 million sq km)

SURFACE AREA COVERED BY FORESTS: 17 million sq miles (44 million sq km)

MAXIMUM HEIGHT OF LAND: 29,029 ft (8,848 m) (Mt. Everest, Himalayas)

MAXIMUM DEPTH OF OCEANS: 36,201 ft (11,034 m) (Mariana Trench, Pacific Ocean)

THE WORLD'S LAND

Most of the world's land is concentrated in a hemisphere centered around Europe. This concentration was even greater before tectonic movement opened up the Atlantic, splitting the Americas from Europe and Africa, some 170 million years ago.

Scale 1:87,000,000
(projection: Azimuthal Equidistant)

The Structure of the Earth

Earth is an almost perfect sphere consisting of a partly liquid core overlain by a deep, semisolid layer, called the mantle, and two types of surface crust, known as continental and oceanic crust. Our planet has constantly evolved since it formed some 4.5 billion years ago. Its continents are neither fixed nor stable. Over the course of history, gradual movements of rocky material within Earth's mantle, resulting from massive internal flows of heat, have caused the great slabs of material that make up the planet's surface, known as tectonic plates, to shift around. The plates have moved, collided, joined together, and sometimes split apart. These processes continue to mold Earth's surface, causing earthquakes and volcanic eruptions, and creating oceans, mountain ranges, rift valleys, deep ocean trenches, and island chains.

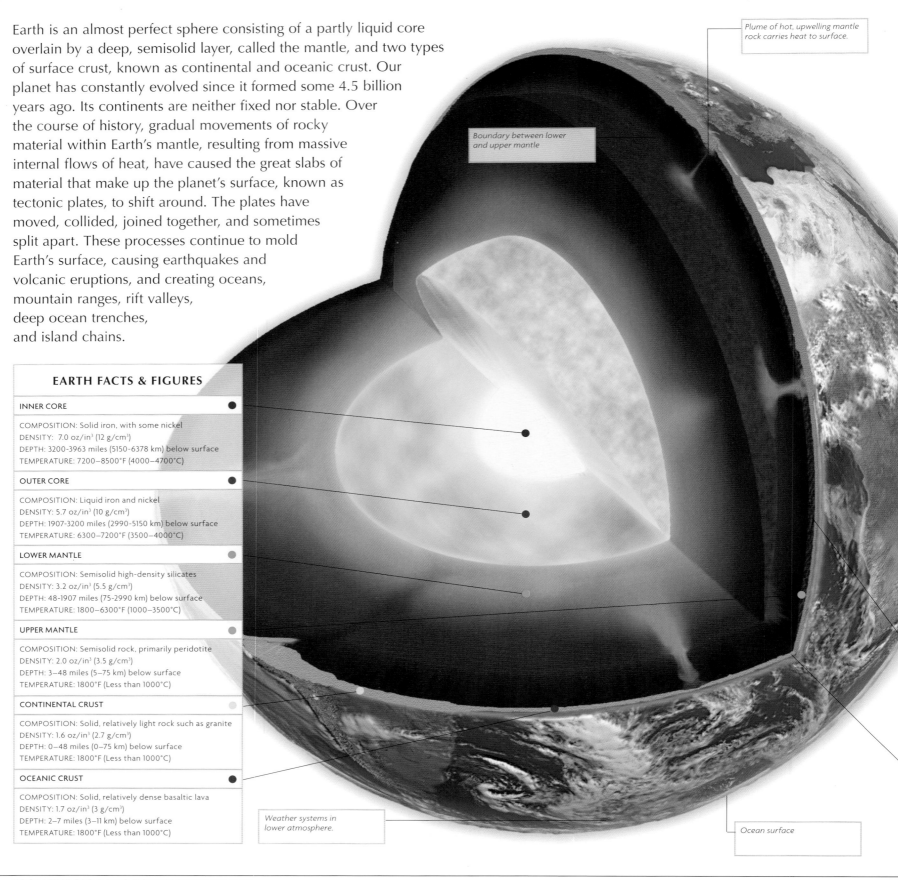

Plume of hot, upwelling mantle rock carries heat to surface.

Boundary between lower and upper mantle

Weather systems in lower atmosphere.

Ocean surface

EARTH FACTS & FIGURES

INNER CORE
COMPOSITION: Solid iron, with some nickel
DENSITY: 7.0 oz/in³ (12 g/cm³)
DEPTH: 3200–3963 miles (5150–6378 km) below surface
TEMPERATURE: 7200–8500°F (4000–4700°C)

OUTER CORE
COMPOSITION: Liquid iron and nickel
DENSITY: 5.7 oz/in³ (10 g/cm³)
DEPTH: 1907–3200 miles (2990–5150 km) below surface
TEMPERATURE: 6300–7200°F (3500–4000°C)

LOWER MANTLE
COMPOSITION: Semisolid high-density silicates
DENSITY: 3.2 oz/in³ (5.5 g/cm³)
DEPTH: 48–1907 miles (75–2990 km) below surface
TEMPERATURE: 1800–6300°F (1000–3500°C)

UPPER MANTLE
COMPOSITION: Semisolid rock, primarily peridotite
DENSITY: 2.0 oz/in³ (3.5 g/cm³)
DEPTH: 3–48 miles (5–75 km) below surface
TEMPERATURE: 1800°F (Less than 1000°C)

CONTINENTAL CRUST
COMPOSITION: Solid, relatively light rock such as granite
DENSITY: 1.6 oz/in³ (2.7 g/cm³)
DEPTH: 0–48 miles (0–75 km) below surface
TEMPERATURE: 1800°F (Less than 1000°C)

OCEANIC CRUST
COMPOSITION: Solid, relatively dense basaltic lava
DENSITY: 1.7 oz/in³ (3 g/cm³)
DEPTH: 2–7 miles (3–11 km) below surface
TEMPERATURE: 1800°F (Less than 1000°C)

FROM THE BIG BANG TO THE PRESENT DAY

The Big Bang   first galaxies form   Milky Way galaxy forms

13,700 million years ago (mya)   12,000 mya   11,000 mya   10,000 mya

1000 mya   2000 mya   3000 mya
first multi-celled organisms   first landmasses

Phanerozoic Eon

543 mya   present day

Phanerozoic Eon *(right)* has been enlarged to show geological eras, periods and epochs

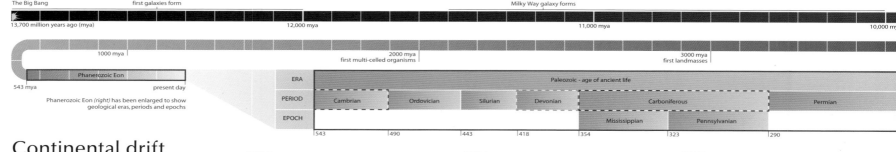

ERA		Paleozoic – age of ancient life						
PERIOD	Cambrian	Ordovician	Silurian	Devonian		Carboniferous		Permian
EPOCH						Mississippian	Pennsylvanian	

543   490   443   418   354   323   290

Continental drift

Although Earth's tectonic plates move only a few inches (centimeters) each year, over hundreds of millions of years, its landmasses have moved many thousands of miles (kilometers), to create new continents, oceans, and mountain chains.

Cambrian 543–490 million years ago

Devonian 418–354 million years ago

Carboniferous 354–290 million years ago

Dynamic Earth

Earth's surface is split up into several rigid, closely-fitting sections, called tectonic plates. Each of the plates contains some oceanic crust, and most also contain some continental crust. The plates constantly move relative to one another. Movements at different types of plate boundary produce various types of geological structure and activity.

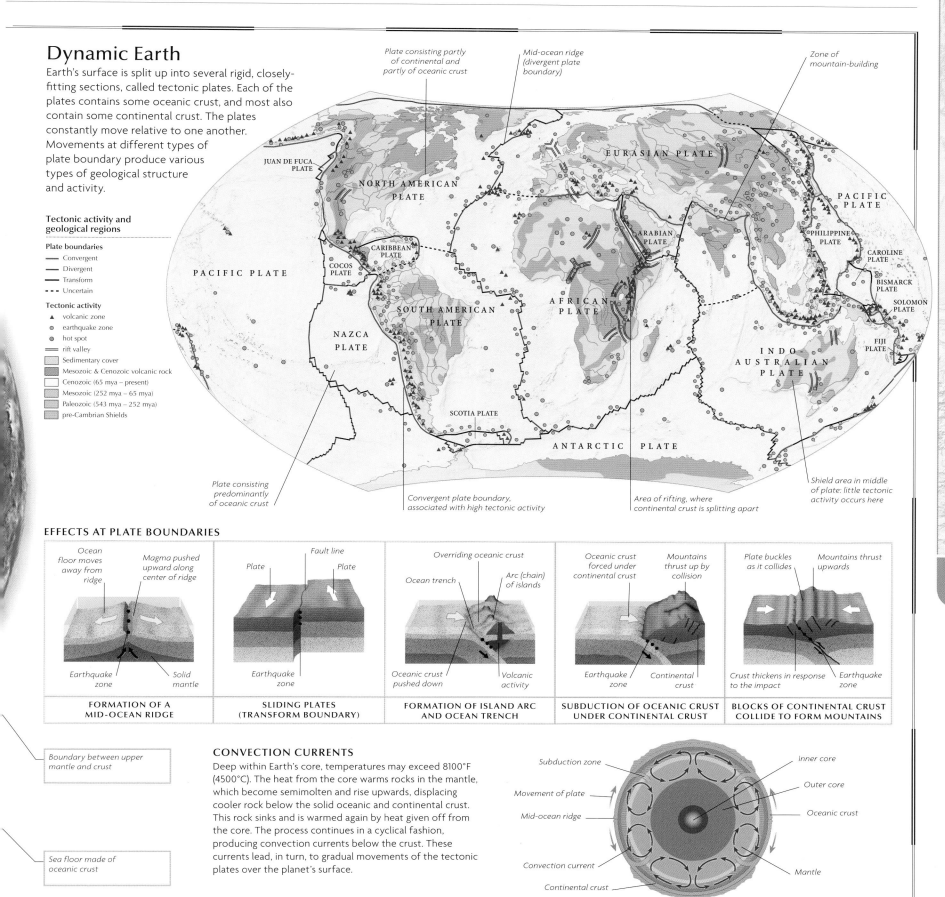

Plate consisting partly of continental and partly of oceanic crust

Mid-ocean ridge (divergent plate boundary)

Zone of mountain-building

JUAN DE FUCA PLATE

EURASIAN PLATE

NORTH AMERICAN PLATE

PACIFIC PLATE

PACIFIC PLATE

PHILIPPINE PLATE

CAROLINE PLATE

CARIBBEAN PLATE

COCOS PLATE

ARABIAN PLATE

BISMARCK PLATE

SOLOMON PLATE

SOUTH AMERICAN PLATE

AFRICAN PLATE

NAZCA PLATE

INDO AUSTRALIAN PLATE

FIJI PLATE

SCOTIA PLATE

ANTARCTIC PLATE

Tectonic activity and geological regions

Plate boundaries
— Convergent
— Divergent
— Transform
- - - Uncertain

Tectonic activity
▲ volcanic zone
● earthquake zone
● hot spot
═ rift valley

☐ Sedimentary cover
☐ Mesozoic & Cenozoic volcanic rock
☐ Cenozoic (65 mya – present)
☐ Mesozoic (252 mya – 65 mya)
☐ Paleozoic (543 mya – 252 mya)
☐ pre-Cambrian Shields

Plate consisting predominantly of oceanic crust

Convergent plate boundary, associated with high tectonic activity

Area of rifting, where continental crust is splitting apart

Shield area in middle of plate: little tectonic activity occurs here

EFFECTS AT PLATE BOUNDARIES

Ocean floor moves away from ridge — *Magma pushed upward along center of ridge*

Earthquake zone — *Solid mantle*

FORMATION OF A MID-OCEAN RIDGE

Plate — *Fault line* — *Plate*

Earthquake zone

SLIDING PLATES (TRANSFORM BOUNDARY)

Overriding oceanic crust — *Arc (chain) of islands*

Ocean trench

Oceanic crust pushed down — *Volcanic activity*

FORMATION OF ISLAND ARC AND OCEAN TRENCH

Oceanic crust forced under continental crust — *Mountains thrust up by collision*

Earthquake zone — *Continental crust*

SUBDUCTION OF OCEANIC CRUST UNDER CONTINENTAL CRUST

Plate buckles as it collides — *Mountains thrust upwards*

Crust thickens in response to the impact — *Earthquake zone*

BLOCKS OF CONTINENTAL CRUST COLLIDE TO FORM MOUNTAINS

Boundary between upper mantle and crust

Sea floor made of oceanic crust

CONVECTION CURRENTS

Deep within Earth's core, temperatures may exceed 8100°F (4500°C). The heat from the core warms rocks in the mantle, which become semimolten and rise upwards, displacing cooler rock below the solid oceanic and continental crust. This rock sinks and is warmed again by heat given off from the core. The process continues in a cyclical fashion, producing convection currents below the crust. These currents lead, in turn, to gradual movements of the tectonic plates over the planet's surface.

Subduction zone

Movement of plate

Mid-ocean ridge

Convection current

Continental crust

Inner core

Outer core

Oceanic crust

Mantle

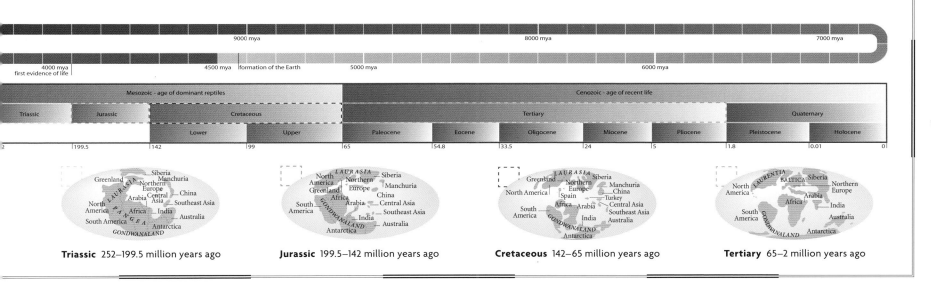

9000 mya

8000 mya

7000 mya

4000 mya
first evidence of life

4500 mya | formation of the Earth

5000 mya

6000 mya

| Mesozoic - age of dominant reptiles | | | Cenozoic - age of recent life | | | | | | | |

Triassic	Jurassic	Cretaceous		Tertiary						Quaternary	
		Lower	Upper	Paleocene	Eocene	Oligocene	Miocene	Pliocene		Pleistocene	Holocene

2 | 199.5 | 142 | 99 | 65 | 54.8 | 33.5 | 24 | 5 | 1.8 | 0.01 | 0

Triassic 252–199.5 million years ago

LAURASIA
Greenland — Siberia — Manchuria
North America — Northern Europe — China
Arabia — Central Asia
Africa — India — Southeast Asia
South America — Australia
PANGEA
Antarctica
GONDWANALAND

Jurassic 199.5–142 million years ago

LAURASIA
North America — Northern Europe — Siberia — Manchuria
Greenland — China
Africa — Central Asia
South America — India — Southeast Asia
GONDWANALAND — Australia
Antarctica

Cretaceous 142–65 million years ago

LAURASIA
Greenland — Northern Europe — Siberia — Manchuria
North America — Spain — China
Africa — Arabia — Central Asia
South America — Turkey — Southeast Asia
India — Australia
GONDWANALAND
Antarctica

Tertiary 65–2 million years ago

LAURENTIA — BALTICA
North America — Siberia
Northern Europe
Africa — Arabia
South America — India
Australia
GONDWANALAND
Antarctica

Shaping the Landscape

The basic material of Earth's surface is solid rock: valleys, deserts, soil, and sand are all evidence of the powerful agents of weathering, erosion and deposition that constantly transform Earth's landscapes. Water, whether flowing in rivers or grinding the ground in the form of glaciers, has the most clearly visible impact on Earth's surface. Also, wind can transport fragments of rock over huge distances and strip away protective layers of vegetation, exposing rock surfaces to the impact of extreme heat and cold. Many of the land-shaping effects of ice and water can be seen in northern regions such as Alaska *(below)*, while the effects of heat and wind are clearly visible in the Sahara *(far right)*.

● FJORD
A valley carved by an ancient glacier and later flooded by the sea is called a fiord.

Ice and water

Some of the most obvious and striking features of Earth's surface are large flows and bodies of liquid water, such as rivers, lakes, and seas. In addition to these are landforms caused by the erosional or depositional power of flowing water, which include gullies, river valleys, and coastal features such as headlands and deltas. Ice also has had a major impact on Earth's appearance. Glaciers—rivers of ice formed by the compaction of snow—pick up and carry huge amounts of rocks and boulders as they pass over the landscape, eroding it as they do so. Glacially-sculpted landforms range from mountain *cirques* and U-shaped valleys to fiords and glacial lakes.

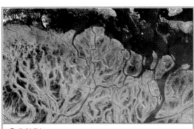
● DELTA
A delta, such as that of the Yukon River (above), is a roughly triangular or fan-shaped area of sediment deposited by a river at its mouth.

● PINGO
These blister-like mounds, seen in regions of Arctic tundra, are formed by the upward expansion of water as it freezes in the soil.

● TIDEWATER GLACIER
Glaciers of this type flow to the sea, where they calve (disgorge) icebergs. Like all glaciers, they erode huge amounts of rock from the landscape.

● LANDSLIDE
The freezing and later thawing of water, which occurs in a continuous cycle, can shatter and crumble rocks, eventually causing landslides.

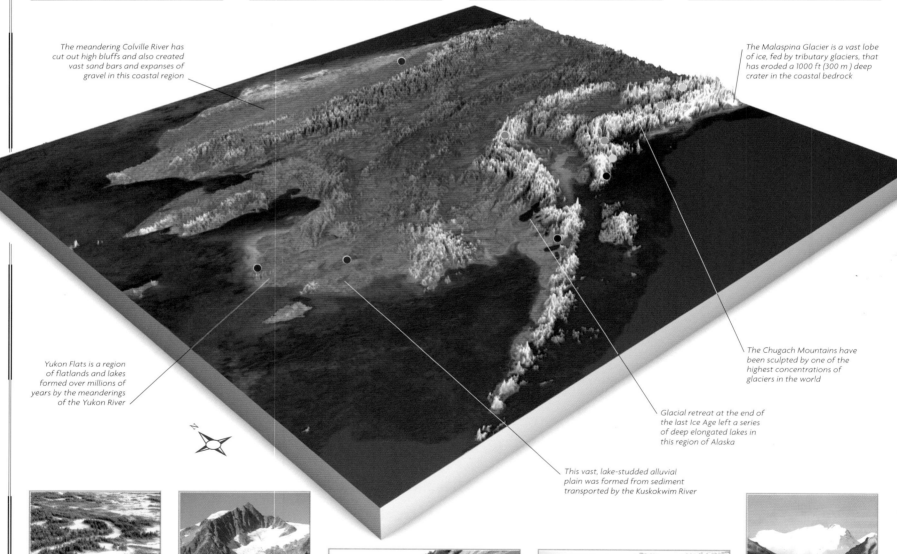

The meandering Colville River has cut out high bluffs and also created vast sand bars and expanses of gravel in this coastal region

The Malaspina Glacier is a vast lobe of ice, fed by tributary glaciers, that has eroded a 1000 ft (300 m) deep crater in the coastal bedrock

Yukon Flats is a region of flatlands and lakes formed over millions of years by the meanderings of the Yukon River

The Chugach Mountains have been sculpted by one of the highest concentrations of glaciers in the world

Glacial retreat at the end of the last Ice Age left a series of deep elongated lakes in this region of Alaska

This vast, lake-studded alluvial plain was formed from sediment transported by the Kuskokwim River

● MEANDERING RIVER
In their lower courses, some rivers carve out a series of looping bends called meanders.

● CIRQUE
A cirque is a hollow formed high on a mountain by glacial action. It may be ice-filled.

● POSTGLACIAL FEATURES
Glacially-polished cliffs like these are a tell-tale sign of ancient glacial action. Other signs include various forms of sculpted ridge and hummock.

● RIVER VALLEY
Over thousands of years, rivers erode uplands to form characteristic V-shaped valleys, with flat narrow floors and steeply-rising sides.

● GULLIES
Gullies are deep channels cut by rapidly flowing water, as here below Alaska's Mount Denali.

Heat and wind

Marked changes in temperature—rapid heating caused by fierce solar radiation during the day, followed by a sharp drop in temperature at night—cause rocks at the surface of hot deserts to continually expand and contract. This can eventually result in cracking and fissuring of the rocks, creating thermally-fractured desert landscapes. The world's deserts are also swept and scoured by strong winds. The finer particles of sand are shaped into surface ripples, dunes, or sand mountains, which can rise to a height of 650 ft (200 m). In other areas, the winds sweep away all the sand, leaving flat, gravelly areas called desert pavements.

DESERT LANDSCAPES

In desert areas, wind picks up loose sand and blasts it at the surface, creating a range of sculpted landforms from faceted rocks to large-scale features such as *yardangs*. Individually sculpted-rocks are called ventifacts. Where the sand abrasion is concentrated near the ground, it can turn these rocks into eccentrically-shaped "stone mushrooms." Other desert features are produced by thermal cracking and by winds continually redistributing the vast sand deposits.

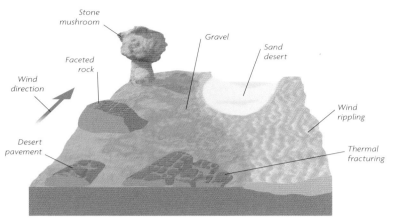

FEATURES OF A DESERT SURFACE

● **DUST STORM**
A common phenomenon in some deserts, dust storms result from intense heating of the ground creating strong convection currents.

● **LOESS DEPOSIT**
A deposit of silt that has been transported over long distances by wind, then compacted. Loess is found in a few marginal areas of the Sahara.

● **YARDANG**
A yardang is a ridge of rock produced by wind erosion, usually in a desert. Large yardangs can be many miles long.

● **DESERT PAVEMENT**
Dark, gravelly surfaces like this result from wind removing all the sand from an area of desert.

Part of the Grand Erg Oriental, this region is a vast wind-sculpted sea of sand, much affected by sand storms

This area of complex dune morphology has resulted from two different types of dunes overlapping and coalescing

Wind erosion of the sandstone rocks in this area (the Tassili n'Ajjer) has created nearly 300 natural rock arches

The Tefedest is an impressive, sun-baked, wind-eroded, granite massif located in southern Algeria

This highland region, called the Ahaggar Mountains, has largely been blasted free of sand and is heavily eroded throughout

● **TRANSVERSE DUNES**
This series of parallel sand ridges lies at right angles to the prevailing wind direction.

● **VENTIFACT**
A ventifact is a rock that has been heavily sculpted and abraded by wind-driven sand.

● **CRACKED DESERT**
Intensely heated and dried-out desert areas often developed geometrically-patterned surface cracking.

● **WADI**
Wadis are dried out stream beds, found in some desert regions, that carry water only during occasional periods of heavy rain.

● **BARCHAN DUNE**
This arc-shaped type of dune migrates across the desert surface, blown by the wind.

The World's Oceans

Two-thirds of Earth's surface is covered by the five oceans: the Pacific, Atlantic, Indian, Southern (or Antarctic), and Arctic. The basins that form these oceans, and the ocean floor landscape, have formed over the past 200 million years through volcanic activity and gradual movements of the Earth's crust. Surrounding the continents are shallow flat regions called continental shelves. These shelves extend to the continental slope, which drops steeply to the ocean floor. There, vast submarine plateaus, known as abyssal plains, are interrupted by massive ridges, chains of seamounts, and deep ocean trenches.

Ocean currents

Surface currents are driven by winds and by the Earth's rotation. Together these cause large circular flows of water over the surface of the oceans, called gyres. Deep sea currents are driven by changes in the salinity or temperature of surface water. These changes cause the water to become denser and sink, forcing horizontal movements of deeper water.

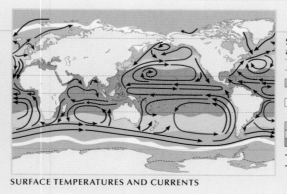

Surface temperature and currents

- - - - ice-shelf (below 32°F / 0°C)
  sea-ice* (average) below 28°F / -2°C
  sea-water 28–32°F / -2 to 0°C
  * sea-water freezes at 28.4°F / -1.9°C
  32–50°F / 0–10°C
  50–68°F / 10–20°C
  68–86°F / 20–30°C
→ warm current
→ cold current

SURFACE TEMPERATURES AND CURRENTS

DEEP SEA TEMPERATURES AND CURRENTS

The ocean floor

The ages of seafloor rocks increase in parallel bands outward from central ocean ridges. At these ridges, new oceanic crust is continuously created from lava that erupts from below the seafloor and then cools to form solid rock. As this new crust forms, it gradually pushes older crust away from the ridge.

Ages of the ocean crust

- 0–5 million years
- 5–21 million years
- 21–38 million years
- 38–65 million years
- 65–140 million years
- 140–190 million years
- continental shelf
- no data

Tides

Tides are caused by gravitational interactions between the Earth, Moon, and Sun. The strongest tides occur when the three bodies are aligned and the weakest when the Sun and Moon align at right angles

Strongest tides

Weakest tides

Gravitational pull from the Sun

Tidal bulges created by gravitational interactions

Earth

Moon

ASIA
Yellow River
Yangtze
Mekong
Gulf of Thailand
Strait of Malacca
Investigator Ridge
Java Trench
Wharton Basin
East Indiaman Ridge
Perth Basin
Carmania Harrot Ridge
Fremantle Fracture Zone
Great Australian Bight
AUSTRALIA
South Australian Basin
South Australian Plain
Indian Ridge
OCEAN
TICA
South Indian Basin

PACIFIC OCEAN
Arctic Circle
Bering Strait
Yukon
Bering Sea
ASIA
Sea of Okhotsk
Kuril-Kamchatka Trench
Aleutian Trench
Gulf of Alaska
NORTH AMERICA
Northwest Pacific Basin
Emperor Seamounts
Mendocino Fracture Zone
Izu Trench
Bonin Trench
Hawaiian Ridge
Murray Fracture Zone
Molokai Fracture Zone
Gulf de California
Cedros Trench
Middle America Trench
Tropic of Cancer
Mid-Pacific Mountains
Marshall Seamounts
Clarion Fracture Zone
Guatemala Basin
Mariana Trench
West Mariana Basin
East Mariana Basin
Central Pacific Basin
Clipperton Fracture Zone
Galapagos Fracture Zone
East Pacific Rise
Colón Ridge
Equator
Melanesian Basin
Nova Trough
Peru Basin
Bismarck Sea
Solomon Sea
Torres Strait
Arafura Sea
Vityaz Trench
North Fiji Basin
Samoa Basin
Penrhyn Basin
Marquesas Fracture Zone
Mendaña Fracture Zone
Peru-Chile Trench
SOUTH AMERICA
Coral Sea Basin
Coral Sea
New Hebrides Trench
Tuamotu Fracture Zone
Austral Fracture Zone
Sala y Gomez Ridge
Tropic of Capricorn
South Fiji Basin
Lord Howe Rise
Kermadec Trench
Tonga Trench
Southwest Pacific Basin
Agassiz Fracture Zone
Easter Fracture Zone
Challenger Fracture Zone
Peru-Chile Trench
Bass Strait
Tasman Sea
Chatham Rise
Campbell Plateau
East Pacific Rise
Bellingshausen Plain
SOUTHERN OCEAN
Antarctic Circle
Pacific-Antarctic Ridge
Ross Sea
Amundsen Sea
Bellingshausen Sea
ANTARCTICA

Temperature

| 0°C | 5 | 10 | 15 | 20 | 25 |
| 32°F | 41 | 50 | 59 | 68 | 77 |

North Atlantic Heat Conveyor

The North Atlantic Heat Conveyor is a system of heat flows in the Atlantic that keeps western Europe relatively warm. Surface currents, notably the Gulf Stream and its extension, the North Atlantic Drift, carry warm water from the tropical Atlantic into the northeastern Atlantic. There, the heat they supply is released, warming Europe, while the water itself cools and sinks. This cold water then returns at depth towards the equator.

A key part of the North Atlantic Heat Conveyor is the warm Gulf Stream, visible as the dark red ribbon in this Atlantic sea-surface temperature map.

Sinking regions

Winter sea-ice cover

Deep southerly return flow

North Atlantic flow

Subtropical recirculation

Gulf Stream

Deep sea temperature and currents

- ice-shelf (below 32°F / 0°C)
- sea-water 28–32°F / -2 to 0°C (below 16,400 ft / 5000 m)
- sea-water 32–41°F / 0–5°C (below 13,120 ft / 4000 m)
- → primary currents
- → secondary currents

Global Climate

The climates of different regions on Earth are the typical long-term patterns of temperature and humidity in those regions. By contrast, weather consists of short-term variations in factors such as wind, rainfall, and sunshine. Climates are determined primarily by the Sun's variable heating of different parts of Earth's atmosphere and oceans, and by Earth's rotation. These factors drive the ocean currents and prevailing winds, which in turn redistribute heat energy and moisture between the equator and poles, and between sea and land. Most scientists think that major changes are currently occurring in global climate due to the effects of rising carbon dioxide levels in the atmosphere.

The atmosphere

Earth's atmosphere is a giant ocean of air that surrounds the planet. It extends to a height of about 625 miles (1000 km) but has no distinct upper boundary. The Sun's rays pass through the atmosphere and warm Earth's surface, causing the air to move and water to evaporate from the oceans.

Global air circulation

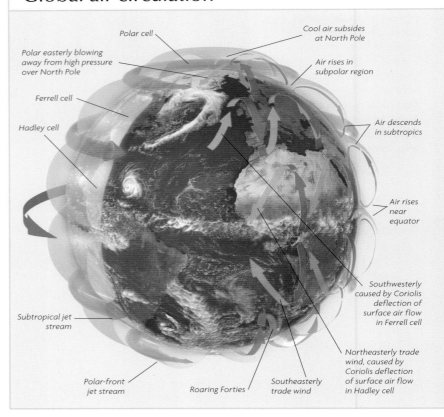

- Polar cell
- Polar easterly blowing away from high pressure over North Pole
- Ferrell cell
- Hadley cell
- Cool air subsides at North Pole
- Air rises in subpolar region
- Air descends in subtropics
- Air rises near equator
- Southwesterly caused by Coriolis deflection of surface air flow in Ferrell cell
- Northeasterly trade wind, caused by Coriolis deflection of surface air flow in Hadley cell
- Subtropical jet stream
- Polar-front jet stream
- Roaring Forties
- Southeasterly trade wind

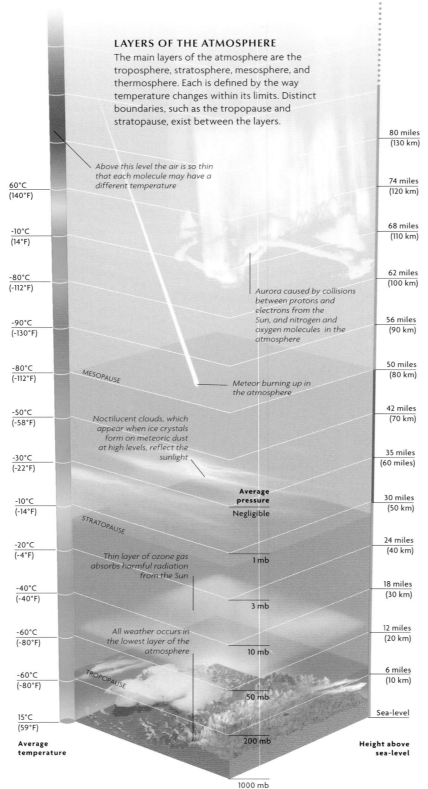

LAYERS OF THE ATMOSPHERE
The main layers of the atmosphere are the troposphere, stratosphere, mesosphere, and thermosphere. Each is defined by the way temperature changes within its limits. Distinct boundaries, such as the tropopause and stratopause, exist between the layers.

Above this level the air is so thin that each molecule may have a different temperature

Aurora caused by collisions between protons and electrons from the Sun, and nitrogen and oxygen molecules in the atmosphere

MESOPAUSE

Meteor burning up in the atmosphere

Noctilucent clouds, which appear when ice crystals form on meteoric dust at high levels, reflect the sunlight

STRATOPAUSE

Thin layer of ozone gas absorbs harmful radiation from the Sun

All weather occurs in the lowest layer of the atmosphere

TROPOPAUSE

Average temperature	Height above sea-level
60°C (140°F)	80 miles (130 km)
	74 miles (120 km)
-10°C (14°F)	68 miles (110 km)
-80°C (-112°F)	62 miles (100 km)
-90°C (-130°F)	56 miles (90 km)
-80°C (-112°F)	50 miles (80 km)
-50°C (-58°F)	42 miles (70 km)
-30°C (-22°F)	35 miles (60 miles)
-10°C (-14°F)	30 miles (50 km)
-20°C (-4°F)	24 miles (40 km)
-40°C (-40°F)	18 miles (30 km)
-60°C (-80°F)	12 miles (20 km)
-60°C (-80°F)	6 miles (10 km)
15°C (59°F)	Sea-level

Average pressure
- Negligible
- 1 mb
- 3 mb
- 10 mb
- 50 mb
- 200 mb
- 1000 mb

Winds, currents, and climate

Earth has 12 climatic zones, ranging from ice-cap and tundra to temperate, arid (desert), and tropical zones. Each of these zones features a particular combination of temperature and humidity. The effects of prevailing winds, ocean currents of both the warm and cold variety, as well as latitude and altitude, all have an important influence on a region's climate. For example, the climate of western Europe is influenced by the effects of the warm North Atlantic Drift current.

● **THERMOSPHERE**
This layer extends from a height of 50 miles (80 km) upward. Its temperature increases rapidly above a height of 60 miles (90 km), due to absorption of highly energetic solar radiation.

● **MESOSPHERE**
The temperature of the lower part of this layer stays constant with height; but above 35 miles (55 km), it drops, reaching -112°F (80°C) at the mesopause.

● **STRATOSPHERE**
The temperature of the stratosphere is a fairly constant -76° F (-60°C) up to an altitude of about 12 miles (20 km), then increases, due to absorption of ultraviolet radiation.

● **TROPOSPHERE**
This layer extends from Earth's surface to a height of about 10 miles (16 km) at the equator and 5 miles (8 km) at the poles. Air temperature in this layer decreases with height.

Arctic Circle January

Chinook Janua

Alaska Current

North Pacific Current

WESTERLIES

Ocea

Northern January

Tornadoes May-Ju

Tropic of Cancer

California Current

NORTH

EAST

Northern Equatorial Current

TRADES

Equatorial Counter Current

Equator Doldrums · El Niño

South Equatorial Current

SOUTH

EAST

TRADES

Tropic of Capricorn

WESTERLIES

West Wind Dr

Antarctic Circle

January

July

Air moves within giant atmospheric cells called Hadley, Ferrell, and polar cells. These cells are caused by air being warmed and rising in some latitudes, such as near the equator, and sinking in other latitudes. This north-south circulation combined with the Coriolis effect *(below)* produces the prevailing surface winds.

THE CORIOLIS EFFECT

Air moving over Earth's surface is deflected in a clockwise direction in the northern hemisphere and counterclockwise in the south. Known as the Coriolis effect, and caused by Earth's spin, these deflections to the air movements produce winds such as the trade winds and westerlies.

Direction of Earth's spin

Deflected clockwise

Deflected counterclockwise

Initial direction

Temperature and precipitation

The world divides by latitude into three major temperature zones: the warm tropics, the cold polar regions; and an intermediate temperate zone. In addition, temperature is strongly influenced by height above sea level. Precipitation patterns are related to factors such as solar heating, atmospheric pressure, winds, and topography. Most equatorial areas have high rainfall, caused by moist air being warmed and rising, then cooling to form rain clouds. In areas of the subtropics and near the poles, sinking air causes high pressure and low precipitation. In temperate regions rainfall is quite variable.

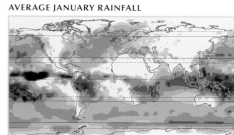

AVERAGE JANUARY TEMPERATURE

Arctic Circle
Tropic of Cancer
Equator
Tropic of Capricorn
Antarctic Circle

AVERAGE JANUARY RAINFALL

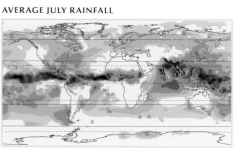

AVERAGE JULY TEMPERATURE

Arctic Circle
Tropic of Cancer
Equator
Tropic of Capricorn
Antarctic Circle

AVERAGE JULY RAINFALL

below -22°F (-30°C)	32 to 50°F (0 to 10°C)
-22 to -4°F (-30 to -20°C)	50 to 68°F (10 to 20°C)
-4 to 14°F (-20 to -10°C)	68 to 86°F (20 to 30°C)
14 to 32°F (-10 to 0°C)	above 86°F (30°C)

0–1 in (0–25 mm)	8–12 in (200–300 mm)
1–2 in (25–50 mm)	12–16 in (300–400 mm)
2–4 in (50–100 mm)	16–20 in (400–500 mm)
4–8 in (100–200 mm)	above 20 in (500 mm)

Ocean currents, winds and climatic regions

Climate zones

ice-cap	temperate
subarctic	warm temperate
tundra	mediterranean
continental	semi-arid
	arid
	hot humid
	humid-equatorial
	tropical

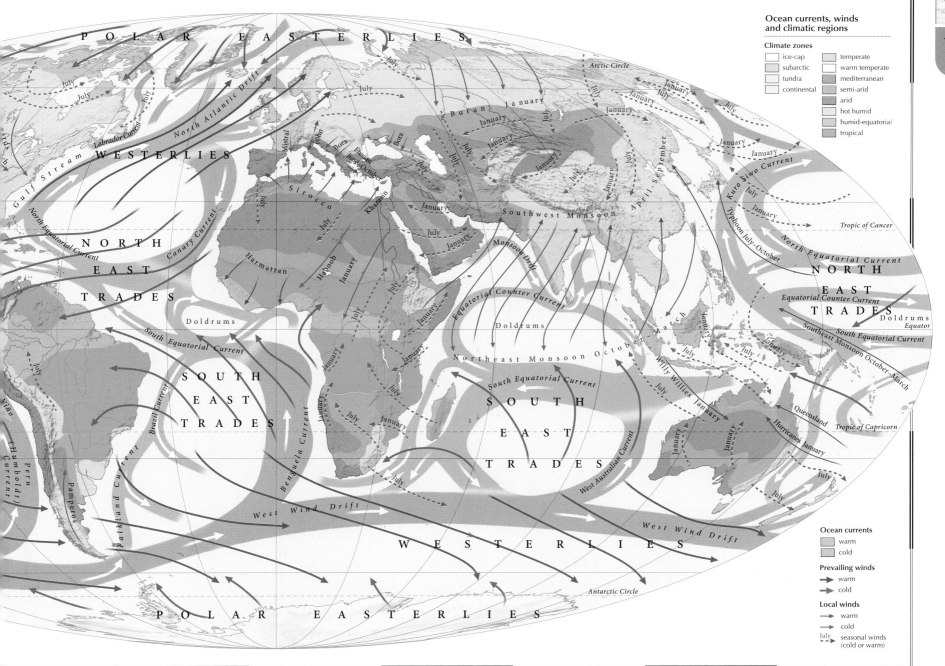

Ocean currents

warm
cold

Prevailing winds

warm
cold

Local winds

warm
cold
July seasonal winds (cold or warm)

Life on Earth

A unique combination of an oxygen-rich atmosphere and plentiful surface water is the key to life on Earth, where few areas have not been colonized by animals, plants, or smaller life-forms. An important determinant of the quantity of life in a region is its level of primary production—the amount of energy-rich substances made by organisms living there, mainly through the process of photosynthesis. On land, plants are the main organisms responsible for primary production; in water, algae fulfil this role. These primary producers supply food for animals. Primary production is affected by climatic, seasonal, and other local factors. On land, cold and aridity restrict the quantity of life in a region, whereas warmth and regular rainfall allow a greater diversity of species. In the oceans, production is mainly affected by sunlight levels, which reduce rapidly with depth, and by nutrient availability.

POLAR REGIONS
Ice restricts life in these regions to just a few species, such as polar bears in the Arctic.

Biogeographical regions

Earth's biogeographical regions, or biomes, are communities where certain species of plants and animals coexist within the constraints of particular climatic conditions. They range from tundra to various types of grassland, forest, desert, and marine biomes such as coral reefs. Factors like soil richness, altitude, and human activities such as deforestation can affect the local distribution of living species in each biome.

TEMPERATE GRASSLAND
Also known as steppe or prairie, grassland of this type occurs mainly in the northern hemisphere and in South America (the Pampas).

NEEDLELEAF FOREST
These vast forests of coniferous trees cover huge areas of Canada, Siberia, and Scandinavia.

TROPICAL GRASSLAND
This type of grassland is widespread in Africa and South America, supporting large numbers of grazing animals and their predators.

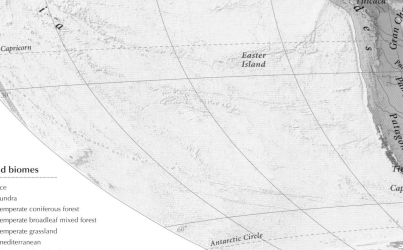

World biomes
- ice
- tundra
- temperate coniferous forest
- temperate broadleaf mixed forest
- temperate grassland
- mediterranean
- desert and shrubland
- boreal forest/taiga

Animal diversity

The number of animal species, and the range of genetic diversity within the populations of those species, determines the level of animal diversity within each country or other region of the world. The animals that are endemic to a region—that is, those found nowhere else on the planet—are also important in determining its level of animal diversity.

Number of animal species per country
- more than 2,000
- 1000–1999
- 700–999
- 400–699
- 200–399
- 100–199
- 0–99
- data not available

TUNDRA
With little soil and large areas of frozen ground, the tundra is largely treeless, though briefly clothed by small flowering plants in summer.

TEMPERATE RAIN FOREST
Occurring in mid-latitudes in areas of high rainfall, these forests may be predominantly coniferous or mixed with deciduous species.

CORAL REEFS
Occurring in clear tropical waters, coral reefs support an extraordinary diversity of species, especially fish and many types of invertebrate.

MOUNTAINS
In high mountain areas only a few hardy species of plant will grow above the tree-line.

TROPICAL RAINFOREST
Characterized by year-round warmth and high rainfall, tropical rainforests contain the highest diversity of plant and animal species on Earth.

HOT DESERT
Only a few highly adapted species can survive in hot deserts, which occur mainly in the tropics.

OPEN OCEAN
Earth's largest biome, the oceans are home to a vast diversity of fish, mammals, invertebrates, and algae.

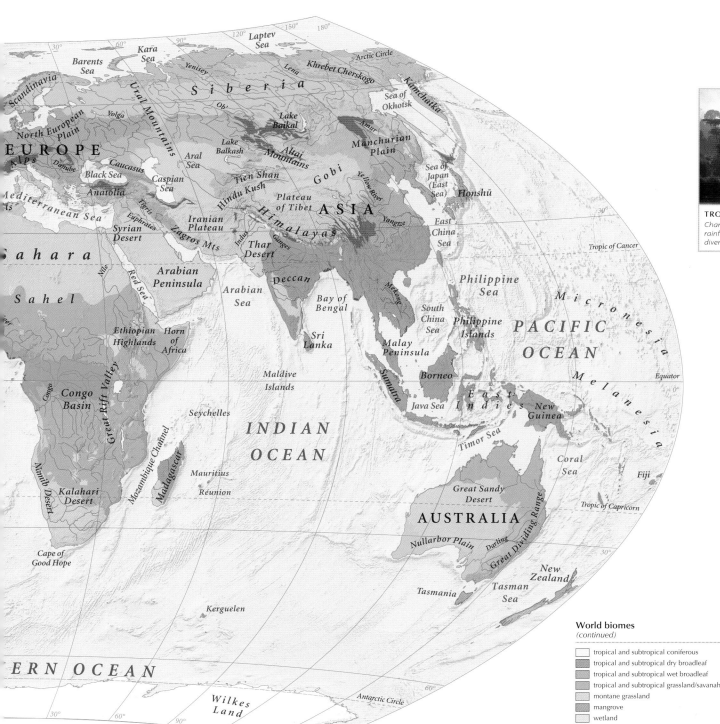

World biomes
(continued)

- tropical and subtropical coniferous
- tropical and subtropical dry broadleaf
- tropical and subtropical wet broadleaf
- tropical and subtropical grassland/savanah
- montane grassland
- mangrove
- wetland

Number of plant species per country

- more than 50,000
- 7000–49,999
- 3000–6999
- 2000–2999
- 1000–1999
- 600–999
- 0–599
- data not available

Plant diversity

Environmental conditions, particularly climate, soil type, and the extent of competition with other living organisms, influence the development of plants into distinctive forms and thus also the extent of plant diversity. Human settlement and intervention has considerably reduced the diversity of plant species in many areas.

Man and the Environment

The impact of human activity on the environment has widened from being a matter of local concern (typically over the build-up of urban waste, industrial pollution, and smog) to affect whole ecosystems and, in recent decades, the global climate. Problems crossing national boundaries first became a major issue over acid rain, toxic waste dumping at sea, and chemical spillages polluting major rivers. Current concerns center on loss of biodiversity and vital habitat including wetlands and coral reefs, the felling and clearance of great tropical and temperate forests, overexploitation of scarce resources, the uncontrolled growth of cities and, above all, climate change.

OZONE HOLE

Man-made chlorofluorocarbons (CFCs), used in refrigeration and aerosols, damaged the ozone layer in the stratosphere which helps filter out the sun's harmful ultraviolet rays. When a seasonal ozone hole first appeared in 1985 over Antarctica, a shocked world agreed to phase out CFC use.

1980   1985

CO$_2$ emissions in 2008
(million tons)

- over 4000
- 1000–4000
- 500–1000
- 100–500
- 50–100
- 10–50
- 2–10
- 0–2
- no data

Climate change

Global warming is happening much faster than Earth's normal long-term cycles of climate change. The consequences include unpredictable extreme weather and potential disruption of ocean currents. Melting ice-caps and glaciers, and warmer oceans, will raise average sea levels and threaten coastlines and cities. Food crops like wheat are highly vulnerable to changes in temperature and rainfall. Such changes can also have a dramatic affect on wildlife habitats.

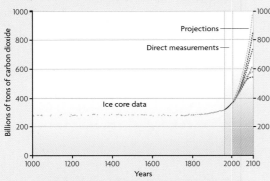

Since 1800 the amount of C0$_2$ in the atmosphere has risen sharply. Urgent worldwide action to control emissions is vital to stabilize the level by the mid 21st century.

THE GREENHOUSE EFFECT

Some solar energy, reflected from the Earth's surface as infra red radiation, is reflected back as heat by "greenhouse gases" (mainly carbon dioxide and methane) in the atmosphere. Nearly all scientists now agree that an upsurge in emissions caused by humans burning fossil fuel has contributed to making the resultant warming effect a major problem.

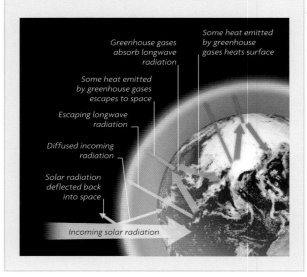

CO$_2$ emissions by country in 2014
(million tons)

TOTAL: 35,669

- Other 11,349
- China 10,540
- United States 5334
- Brazil 501
- Canada 565
- South Korea 610
- Iran 618
- Germany 767
- Japan 1278
- India 2341
- Russian Federation 1766

FOOD AND LAND USE

The world has about five billion hectares of agriculturally useful land, well under one hectare per person. The majority of this is pasture for grazing. Crops are grown on about 30 percent (and nearly a fifth of cropland is artificially irrigated). Mechanized farming encouraged vast single crop "monocultures," dependent on fertilizers and pesticides. North America's endless prairies of wheat and corn, huge soybean plantations, and southern cotton fields are mirrored in Ukraine (wheat), Brazil and Argentina (soya) and Uzbekistan (cotton). Elsewhere, scarce farmland can be squeezed by the housing needs of growing urban populations. Current interest in crop-derived "biofuels" means further pressure to grow food more productively on less land.

Intensive farming. Satellite photography picks up the greenhouses that now cover almost all the land in this Spanish coastal area southwest of Almeria.

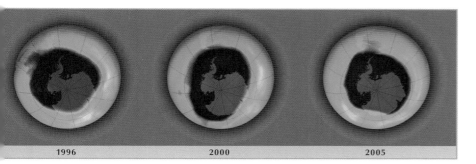

DEFORESTATION

At current rates of destruction, all tropical forests, and most old-growth temperate forest, will be gone by 2090. The Amazon rain forest is a valuable genetic resource, containing innumerable unique plants and animals, as well as acting as a crucial natural "sink" for absorbing climate-damaging carbon dioxide. Stemming the loss of these precious assets to logging and farming is one of the major environmental challenges of modern times.

Over 25,000 sq miles (60,000 sq km) of virgin rain forest are cleared annually by logging and agricultural activities, destroying an irreplaceable natural resource.

Deforestation
- frontier forest
- degraded forest
- frontier forest 8000 years ago

GLACIATION

The world's glaciers and ice sheets have been in retreat for decades, forming less new ice at high altitudes than they lose by melting lower down. The loss of ice from Greenland doubled between 1996 and 2005, with alarming implications for rising sea levels. Other dramatic evidence of global warming includes the rapid thinning of ice in the Himalayas, and the highly symbolic loss of the snowcap on Africa's Mount Kilimanjaro.

Helheim Glacier 2001
The Helheim glacier *(above)* almost completely fills this image, with the leading edge visible on the righthand side, and was in a relatively stable condition.

Helheim Glacier 2005
By 2005 *(right)* it had retreated by 2.5 miles (4 km).

Delhi 1971
In 1971 Delhi *(above)* occupied an area of about 190 sq miles (500 sq km).

Delhi 1999
By 1999 *(right)* it had sprawled to cover 500 sq miles (1300 sq km). It vies with Mumbai in the southwest to be the sub-continent's most populous city, fast approaching 20 million people.

CITY GROWTH

The world in 2015 had 15 cities with populations over 20 million. The number of cities with populations between 10 and 20 million has surpassed 20 and continues to rise. The search for work, and the hope of escape from rural poverty, drives migration from rural to urban areas across the developing world. Urban dwellers now amount to more than half the world's population, and consume more resources than their rural counterparts.

Population and Settlement

Earth's human population is projected to rise from its current level of 7.3 billion to between 8.1 and 11 billion by the year 2050. The distribution of this population is very uneven and is dictated by climate, terrain, and by natural and economic resources. Most people live in coastal zones and along the valleys of great rivers such as the Ganges, Indus, Nile, and Yangtze. Deserts cover over 20 percent of Earth's surface but support less than 5 percent of its human population. Over half the world's population live in cities—most of them in Asia, Europe, and North America—as a result of mass migrations that have occurred from rural areas as people search for jobs. Many of these people live in so-called "megacities"—sprawling urban areas that have populations higher than 10 million.

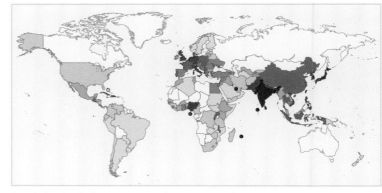

Population density by country (population per sq mile)

over 2600
775–2599
390–774

260–389
195–259
130–194

65–129
26–64
0–25

Population density

A few regions, including Europe, India, and much of eastern Asia, have extremely high population densities. Within these areas, a few spots, such as Monaco and Hong Kong, have densities of over 12,900 per sq mile (5000 people per sq km). Other regions (mostly desert, mountain, ice cap, tundra, or thickly forested areas) have densities close to zero –examples include large areas of Australia, western China, Siberia, North Africa, Canada, Greenland, and much of the Amazon rain forest region.

NORTH AMERICA

World population 8%   World land area 17.0%

EUROPE

World population 10%   World land area 7.1%

SOUTH AMERICA

World population 6%   World land area 11.8%

ANTARCTICA

World population 0.0%   World land area 8.9%

Million-person cities

In the year 1900 there were fewer than 20 cities in the world with a population that exceeded one million. By 1950 there were 83 such cities, and by the year 2015 there were more than 500 such cities, 100 of them in China alone, with another 54 in India, 20 in Brazil, and 14 in Japan.

Million-cities in 1900

• Cities over 1 million in population

Population density
(persons per sq mile)

520–2600
260–520
130–260
52–130
26–52
13–26
3–13
0–3

Million-cities in 1950

Million-cities in 2006

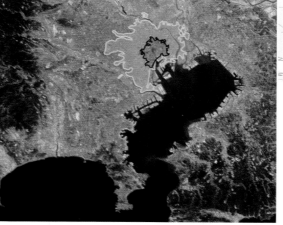

Tokyo urban sprawl

—— City boundary, 1860   —— City boundary, 1964

GREATER TOKYO

The Greater Tokyo Area is the most populous urban area in the world, with an estimated head count in 2015 of 37.8 million. It includes Tokyo City, which has a population of about 12 million, and adjoining cities such as Yokohama. This satellite photograph shows the Greater Tokyo Area today, and also the boundaries of Tokyo City in 1860 (red) and 1964 (yellow).

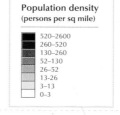

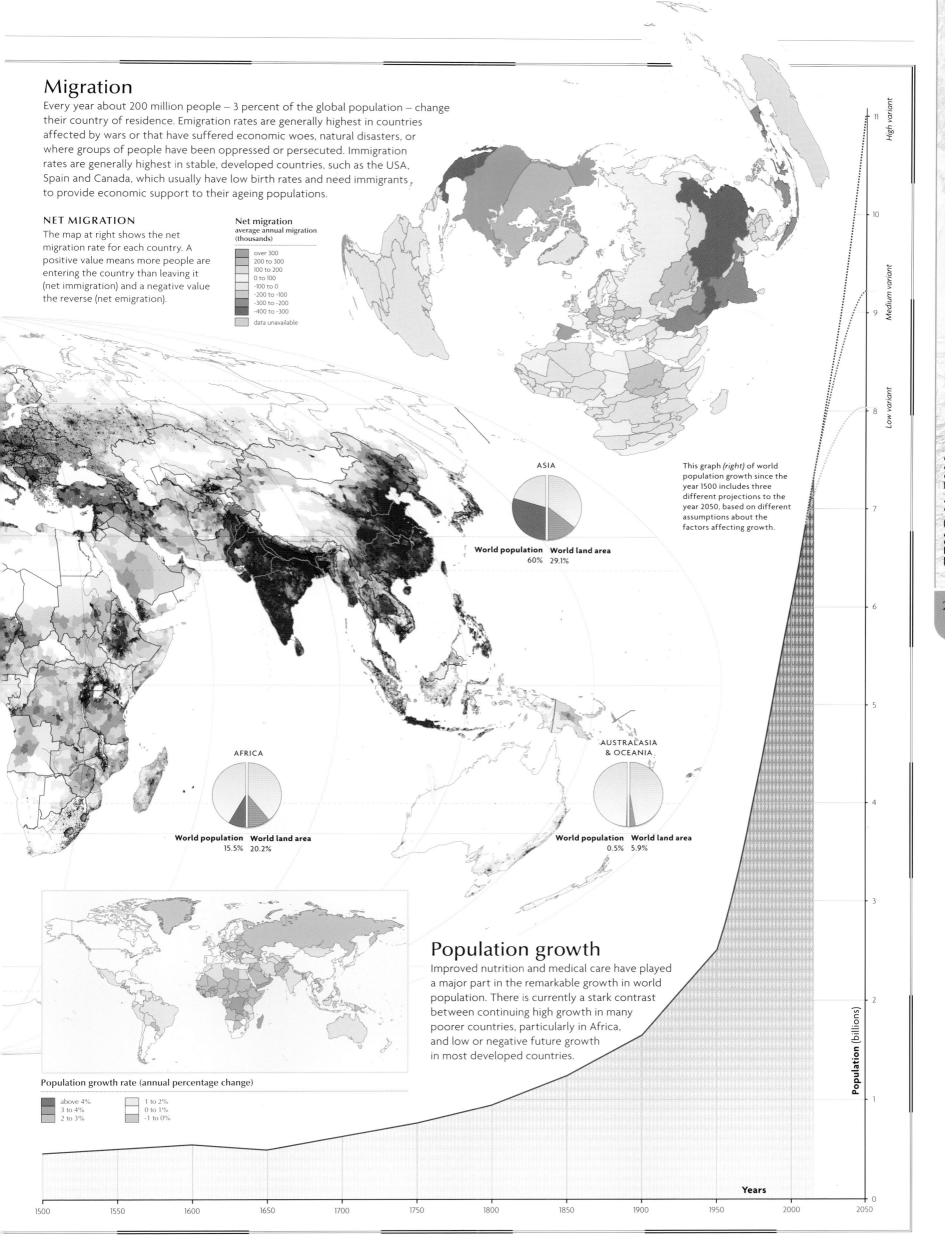

Migration

Every year about 200 million people – 3 percent of the global population – change their country of residence. Emigration rates are generally highest in countries affected by wars or that have suffered economic woes, natural disasters, or where groups of people have been oppressed or persecuted. Immigration rates are generally highest in stable, developed countries, such as the USA, Spain and Canada, which usually have low birth rates and need immigrants to provide economic support to their ageing populations.

NET MIGRATION

The map at right shows the net migration rate for each country. A positive value means more people are entering the country than leaving it (net immigration) and a negative value the reverse (net emigration).

Net migration
average annual migration (thousands)

- over 300
- 200 to 300
- 100 to 200
- 0 to 100
- -100 to 0
- -200 to -100
- -300 to -200
- -400 to -300
- data unavailable

This graph *(right)* of world population growth since the year 1500 includes three different projections to the year 2050, based on different assumptions about the factors affecting growth.

ASIA

World population 60% **World land area** 29.1%

AFRICA

World population 15.5% **World land area** 20.2%

AUSTRALASIA & OCEANIA

World population 0.5% **World land area** 5.9%

Population growth

Improved nutrition and medical care have played a major part in the remarkable growth in world population. There is currently a stark contrast between continuing high growth in many poorer countries, particularly in Africa, and low or negative future growth in most developed countries.

Population growth rate (annual percentage change)

- above 4%
- 3 to 4%
- 2 to 3%
- 1 to 2%
- 0 to 1%
- -1 to 0%

High variant

Medium variant

Low variant

Population (billions)

Years

1500 1550 1600 1650 1700 1750 1800 1850 1900 1950 2000 2050

Language

Over 6800 different languages exist throughout the world, each one with its own unique evolutionary history and cultural connotations. Most of these languages are spoken only by small groups of people in remote regions. Sadly these minority tongues are dying out—it is estimated that about a third will have disappeared by the year 2100. The relatively small number of widely-spoken languages have gained their current predominance and pattern of distribution through a variety of historical factors. Among these have been the economic, military, or technological success of certain peoples and cultures, differing population growth rates, and the effects of migrations and colonization.

The European Union (EU) embraces the diversity of its 28 countries and 24 official languages by providing a translation and interpretation service for the majority of its meetings and documentation. This costs around US$ 650 million per year, which equates to 1 percent of the EU budget.

Main international languages

- Chinese
- Spanish
- Arabic
- Hindi
- English
- French
- Russian
- Portuguese
- English/Spanish
- Spanish/other
- Arabic/French
- French/other
- English/other
- Arabic/other
- Hindi/English/other
- Chinese/other
- Russian/other
- English/French
- Portuguese/other
- other language

Bantu language group
Mari other language

- uninhabited land

The colonial powers

Colonialism between the 15th and 20th centuries had a major influence in establishing the world prevalence of various, mainly European, languages. Britain, for example, was the colonial power in Canada, the USA (until 1776), the Indian subcontinent, Australia, and parts of Africa and the Caribbean. Hence, English is still the main (or a major) language in these areas. The same applies to France and the French language in parts of Africa and southeast Asia, and to Spain and the Spanish language in much of Latin America. For similar reasons, Portuguese is the main language in Brazil and parts of Africa, and there are many Dutch speakers in Indonesia.

This dual language sign, written in both in Hindi and English, stands outside Shimla railway station in northern India. The sign reflects India's past—the British used Shimla as their summer capital during the colonial period.

TOP TEN LANGUAGES

About 45 percent of people speak one of just ten languages as their native tongue. Mandarin Chinese is spoken by far the largest number—a situation likely to persist, as minority language speakers in China are encouraged to switch to Mandarin. English usage is also increasing, as it is the most favored language on the internet and in business circles. Wherever English is not the mother tongue, it is often the second language.

THE TEN MOST SPOKEN LANGUAGES
(number of native speakers)

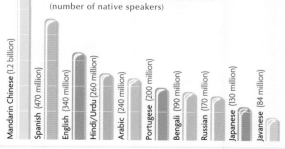

- Mandarin Chinese (1.2 billion)
- Spanish (470 million)
- English (340 million)
- Hindi/Urdu (260 million)
- Arabic (240 million)
- Portugese (200 million)
- Bengali (190 million)
- Russian (170 million)
- Japanese (130 million)
- Javanese (84 million)

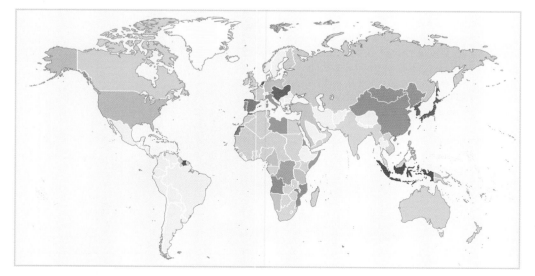

Colonial Empires in 1914

- Austro-Hungarian
- Belgian
- British
- Chinese
- Danish
- Dutch
- French
- German
- Italian
- Japanese
- Ottoman
- Portuguese
- Russian
- Spanish
- United States
- Independent
- Disputed

Religion

The spread of religion

By their nature, religions usually start off in small geographical areas and then spread. For Christianity and Islam, this spread was rapid and extensive. Buddhism diffused more slowly from around 500 BCE into a large part of Asia. The oldest religion, Hinduism, has always been concentrated in the Indian subcontinent, although its adherents in other parts of the world now number millions following migrations from India.

1ST–7TH CENTURY

During this period, Christianity spread from its origins in the eastern Mediterranean, while Hinduism and forms of Buddhism spread in Asia. Islam became established in Arabia.

Rise and spread of the classical religions to 650 CE

- Buddhist heartland
- Chinese Confucianism/ Daoism and indigenous primal traditions
- Converted to Christianity by 600 CE
- Hinduism
- Islam under Muhammad
- Mahayana Buddhism
- Shintoism
- Zoroastrianism
- → spread of Buddhism
- → spread of Christianity
- → spread of Hinduism
- → dispersion of Jews, to 500 CE

7TH–16TH CENTURY

Islam later spread further through Asia and into parts of Africa and Europe. Christianity diffused through Europe and was then carried to many other parts of the world by colonialists and missionaries. Buddhism spread further in Asia.

Each year millions of Muslims visit Mecca during the the Islamic pilgrimage known as the *Hajj*

World religions c.1500 CE

- Catholic Christianity
- area converted to Catholic Christianity
- Hinduism
- Islam
- Mahayana Buddhism and Confucianism, Daoism and Shinto
- Mahayana Buddhism and Confucianism, Daoism
- Russian Orthodoxy
- Theravada Buddhism
- Tibetan Buddhism
- Aztec Empire
- Inca Empire
- → spread of Catholicism
- → spread of Islam
- → spread of Protestantism
- → spread of Russian Orthodoxy

About 83 percent of the world's population adheres to a religion. The remainder adopt irreligious stances such as atheism. In terms of broad similarities of belief, there are about 20 different religions in the world with more than 1 million adherents. However, the larger of these are split into several denominations, which differ in their exact beliefs and practices. Christianity, for example, includes three major groupings that have historically been in conflict—Roman Catholicism, Protestantism, and Orthodox Christianity—as well as hundreds of separate smaller groups. Many of the world's other main religious, such as Islam and Buddhism, are also subdivided.

RELIGION AROUND THE WORLD

About 72 percent of humanity adheres to one of five religions: Christianity, Islam, Hinduism, Buddhism, and Chinese traditional religion (which includes Daoism and Confucianism). Of the remainder, many are adherents of primal indigenous religions (a wide range of tribal or folk religions such as shamanism).

Buddhist (0.36 billion)
Judaism (15 million)
Sikhism (23 million)
Chinese traditional (0.36 billion)
Christianity (1.9 billion)
Primal indigenous (0.36 billion)
Hindu (0.84 billion)
Islam (1.06 billion)
Not religious (0.96 billion)

Majority religions

- Protestant Christianity
- Catholic Christianity
- Orthodox Christianity
- Shi'a Islam
- Sunni Islam
- Hinduism
- Judaism
- Theravada Buddhism
- Mahayana Buddhism
- Tibetan Buddhism
- other
- Marxism / Maoism

State policy

- ▲ secular ideologies governing
- ● communist states during 20th century
- ■ non-pluralist states

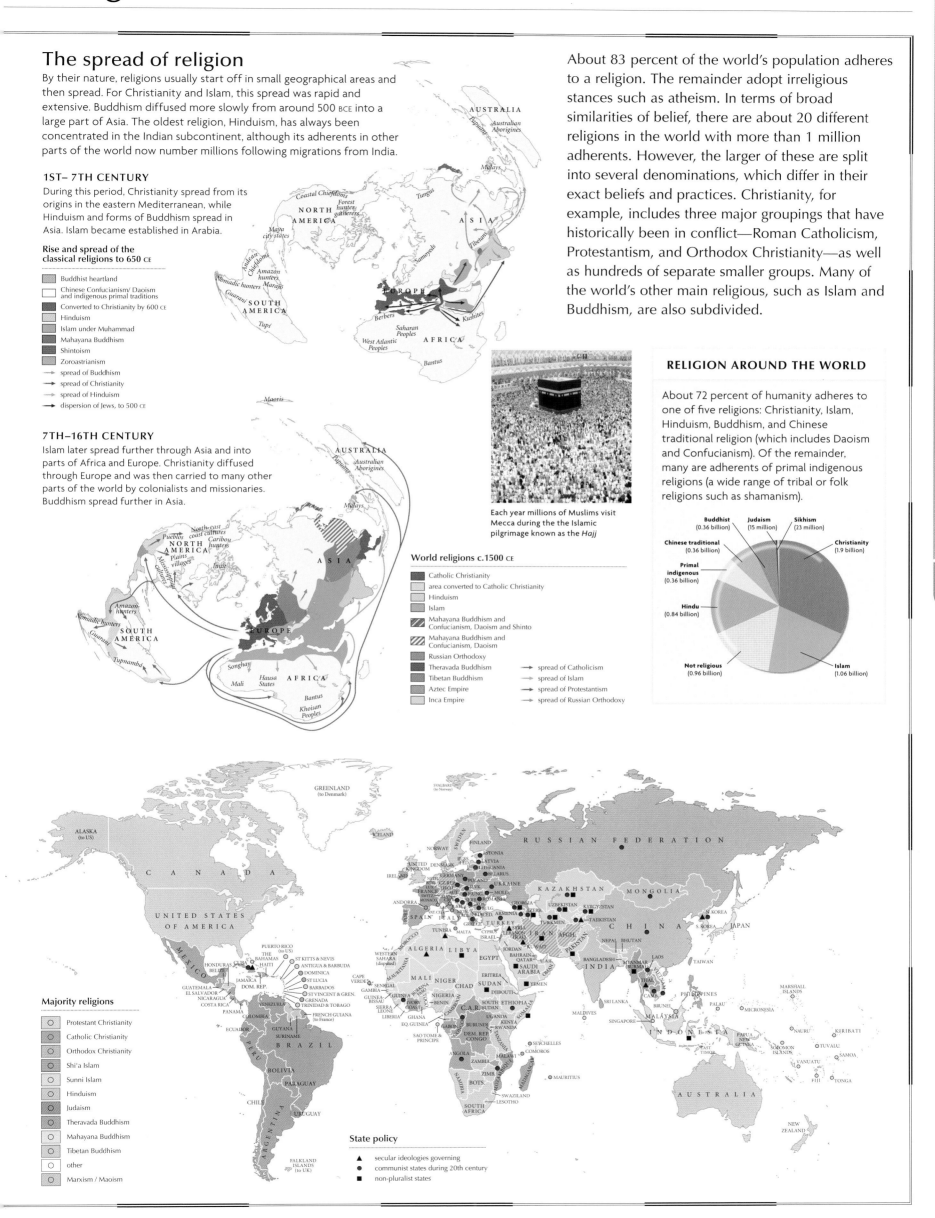

Health

On most health parameters, the countries of the world split into two distinct groups. The first of these encompass the richer, developed, countries, where medical care is good to excellent, infant mortality and the incidence of deadly infectious diseases is low, and life expectancy is high and rising. Some of the biggest health problems in these countries arise from overeating, while the two main causes of death are heart disease and cancer. The second region consists of the poorer developing countries, where medical care is much less adequate, infant mortality is high, many people are undernourished, and infectious diseases such as malaria are major killers. Life expectancy in these countries is much lower and in some cases is falling.

Life expectancy

Life expectancy has risen remarkably in developed countries over the past 50 years and has now topped 80 years in many of them. In contrast, life expectancy in many of the countries of sub-Saharan Africa has fallen well below 50, in large part due to the high prevalence of HIV/AIDS.

Many people in developed countries are now living for 15–20 years after retirement, putting greater pressure on welfare and health services.

Infant deaths and births

Infant mortality is still high in many developing nations, especially some African countries, due in part to stretched medical services. As well as lower infant mortality, the world's developed countries have much lower birth rates—greater female emancipation and easier access to contraceptives are two causative factors.

World infant mortality rates (deaths per 1000 live births)

above 125	75–124	35–74	15–34	below 15

Number of births (per 1000 people)

above 40	30–39	20–29	below 20

Nutrition

Two-thirds of the world's food is consumed in developed nations, many of which have a daily calorific intake far higher than is needed by their populations. By contrast, about 800 million people in the developing world do not have enough food to meet basic nutritional needs.

Daily calorie intake per capita

above 3000	2500–2999	2000–2499	below 2000

Healthcare

An indicator of the strength of healthcare provision in a country is the number of doctors per 1000 population. Some communist and former communist countries such as Cuba and Russia score well in this regard. In general, healthcare provision is good or adequate in most of the world's richer countries but scanty throughout much of Africa and in parts of Asia and Latin America.

The extensive public healthcare system in Cuba provides for around 6 doctors per 1000 people, one of the highest ratios in the world.

Medical doctors (per 1000 people)

above 5	4–5	3–4	1–3	0.5–1	below 0.5	no data

Life expectancy

above 80 years
75–80 years
70–75 years
60–70 years
50–60 years
below 50 years

USA
(Alaska)

CANADA

UNITED STATES
OF AMERICA

MEXICO

Greenland
(to Denmark)

ATLANTIC
OCEAN

THE BAHAMAS
CUBA HAITI DOMINICAN REPUBLIC
JAMAICA
BELIZE
GUATEMALA HONDURAS
EL SALVADOR NICARAGUA
COSTA RICA PANAMA
ANTIGUA & BARBUDA
DOMINICA
SAINT LUCIA
ST KITTS & ST VINCENT & THE GRENADINES
NEVIS GRENADA
BARBADOS
TRINIDAD & TOBAGO
VENEZUELA
COLOMBIA
GUYANA
SURINAME
French Guiana
(to France)
ECUADOR
PERU
BRAZIL
BOLIVIA
PARAGUAY
CHILE
ARGENTINA
URUGUAY

United States of America: has an average life expectancy of about 78 years, with women living about 5 years longer than men.

ATLANTIC
OCEAN

ICELAND

NORWAY
UNITED DENMARK
IRELAND KINGDOM NETH. POL.
BELG. GERMANY CZECH
LUX. LIECH. REP.
FRANCE SWITZ. AUS. HU
SLOVENIA CRO
MONACO SAN B-H
MARINO ITALY MON
PORTUGAL SPAIN ANDORRA ALBANIA GR
MALTA

MOROCCO

WESTERN SAHARA
(occupied by Morocco)
ALGERIA LIBY

CAPE VERDE
MAURITANIA MALI NIGER
SENEGAL
GAMBIA BURKINA CHA
GUINEA- FASO NIGERIA
BISSAU GUINEA BENIN
SIERRA LEONE IVORY GHANA CENTRI
COAST TOGO AFRIC
LIBERIA EQUATORIAL CAMEROON REPUB
GUINEA CONGO DE
SAO TOME & R
PRINCIPE GABON CON

ANGOLA
(Cabinda)

ANGOL
NAMIBIA

Liberia: currently has one of the lowest life expectancies in West Africa, at about 45 years, owing to factors such as high rates of infectious disease, recent conflict, and poverty.

Smoking

Cigarette smoking—one of the most harmful activities to health—is common throughout much of the world. Smoking prevalence is generally highest in the richer, developed countries. However, awareness of the health risks has seen cigarette consumption in most of these countries stabilize or begin to fall. By contrast, more and more people, especially males, are taking up the habit in poorer developing countries.

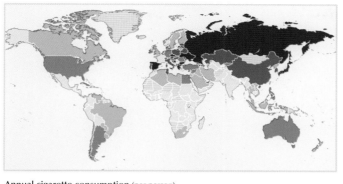

Annual cigarette consumption (per person)

- above 2000
- 1500–2000
- 1000–1499
- 500–999
- 0–499
- no data

Japan: has one of the world's highest life expectancies, at over 81 years—a fact commonly put down to the typical Japanese low-fat diet of rice, fish, and soy products.

Swaziland: currently has the lowest life expectancy in the world, at about 40 years, due to widespread HIV/AIDS.

Communicable diseases

Despite advances in their treatment and prevention, infectious diseases remain a huge problem, especially in developing countries. Three of the most common and deadly are tuberculosis (TB), HIV/AIDS, and malaria. Of these, active TB affects about 25 million people (often as a complication of AIDS), with a particularly high prevalence in parts of Africa. HIV/AIDS has spread since 1981 to become a global pandemic. Malaria affects about 225 million people every year.

Estimated tuberculosis cases (per 100,000 per year)

- above 300
- 100–300
- 50–100
- 10–50
- below 10

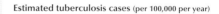

Adult (15-49) HIV prevalence rate (percent of population)

- 15–34
- 5–15
- 1–5
- 0.5–1
- 0.1–0.5
- below 0.1
- no data

Malaria cases (per 100,000 per year)

- above 25,000
- 10,000–25,000
- 1000–10,000
- 100–1000
- 10–100
- below 10
- low risk

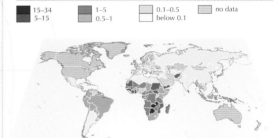

Preventive medicine

Throughout the world, doctors recognize that the prevention of disease and disease transmission is just as important as the treatment of illness. Preventive medicine has many aspects and includes advice about diet and nutrition; education about the avoidance of health-threatening behaviors such as smoking, excess alcohol consumption, and unprotected sex; and the use of vaccines against diseases such as typhoid, polio and cholera. In developing countries, some of the main priorities in preventive medicine are the provision of pure water supplies and proper sanitation, as well as measures against malaria, including the use of antimalarial drugs and mosquito nets.

The use of mosquito nets greatly reduces the transmission of malaria and the risk of infection.

TOP TEN KILLER DISEASES

The world's biggest killer diseases fall into two main groups. One group, which includes HIV/AIDS, malaria, tuberculosis, and childhood diseases such as measles, mainly kills people in poor countries. The other group includes cardiovascular diseases and cancer, the big killers in rich countries.

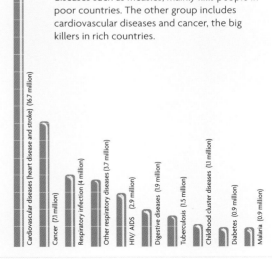

- Cardiovascular diseases (heart disease and stroke) (16.7 million)
- Cancer (7.1 million)
- Respiratory infection (4 million)
- Other respiratory diseases (3.7 million)
- HIV/ AIDS (2.9 million)
- Digestive diseases (1.9 million)
- Tuberculosis (1.5 million)
- Childhood cluster diseases (1.1 million)
- Diabetes (0.9 million)
- Malaria (0.9 million)

Water Resources

Water covers 71 percent of Earth's surface, but only 2.5 percent of this is fresh water, and two thirds of that is locked up in glaciers and polar ice sheets. Patterns of human settlement have developed around fresh water availability, but increasing numbers of people are now vulnerable to chronic shortage or interruptions in supply. Worldwide, fresh water consumption multiplied more than sixfold during the 20th century as populations increased and agriculture became more dependent on irrigation, much of it hugely wasteful because of evaporation and run-off. Industrial water demand also rose, as did use in the home, for washing, flushing, cooking, and gardening.

Amid the desert of Wadi Rum, Jordan, crops grow on circular patches of land irrigated with water from an underground aquifer.

Availability of fresh water
total renewable
(cubic yards/capita/per year)

- less than 1300 (**water scarcity**)
- 1300–2221 (**water stress**)
- 2222–3921 (**insufficient water**)
- 3922–12,999 (**relatively sufficient**)
- 13,000 or more (**plentiful supplies**)

▬ major drainage basin

▼ over 50% of water resource originating from outside country

Water withdrawal

Agriculture accounts for 70 percent of water consumption worldwide. Industry and domestic use each account for 15 percent. Excessive withdrawal of water affects the health of rivers and the needs of people. China's Yellow River now fails to reach the sea for most of the year.

Percentage of freshwater withdrawal by agriculture

| 79–100 | 66–79 | 47–66 | 31–47 | 16–31 | 0–16 |

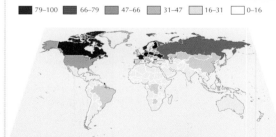

Percentage of freshwater withdrawal by industry

| 79–100 | 66–79 | 47–66 | 31–47 | 16–31 | 0–16 |

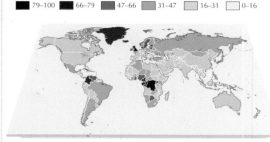

Percentage of freshwater withdrawal by domestic use

| 60–81 | 45–60 | 30–45 | 15–30 | 0–15 | no data |

Drought

The disruption of normal rainfall patterns can cause drought problems even in temperate zones,   with consequences ranging from domestic water usage restrictions to low crop yields to forest fires. In regions of the developing world where monsoon rains fail, or water is perennially scarce, drought is a life or death issue. Parts of central and east Africa, for instance, have suffered severe and recurring droughts in recent decades, with disastrous results including destruction of livestock, desertification, famine, and mass migration.

In a severe drought, river beds may dry up *(above left)*, leaving stranded fish to die, as here in Florida.

A Chinese farmer waters dry fields *(above)* in China's southern province of Guangdong. This picture was taken in May 2002, but the image is timeless; it could be August 2006 in Sichuan province, to the northwest of here—or almost any year in water-stressed northern China.

Water stress

A region is under "water stress" when the rate of water withdrawal from its rivers and aquifers exceeds their natural replenishment, so that people living there are subject to frequent shortages. Currently 1.7 billion people live in "highly stressed" river basins worldwide. This is a major potential cause of conflict, particularly when several countries share one river; the Euphrates, running through Turkey, Syria, and Iraq, or the rivers of southern China running south into Korea, are just two examples.

Freshwater stress in 1995 Water withdrawal (% of total available)

above 40   20–40   10–20   below 10

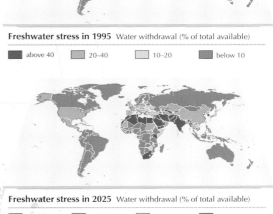

Freshwater stress in 2025 Water withdrawal (% of total available)

above 40   20–40   10–20   below 10

WATER AVAILABILITY

(by percentage of world's population)

relative sufficiency

Plentiful 16.3%

Water scarcity 7.8%

Water stress 24.5%

Relatively sufficient 24.5%

Insufficient 16.7%

insufficiency

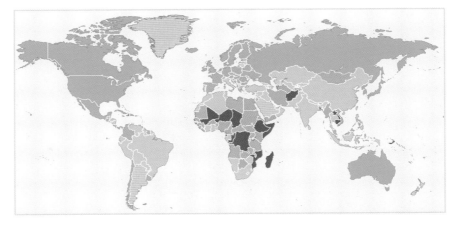

Mozambican children *(above)* fetch precious water in metal pans.

Gujarati villagers gather to draw water from a huge well *(above left)* in Natwarghad, western India. Many wells and village ponds ran dry in the severe drought of 2003, leaving local people to wait for irregular supplies brought in by state-run tankers.

Clean drinking water

Sub-Saharan Africa is among the most deprived regions for lack of access to safe drinking water. Worldwide, this terrible health hazard affects over a billion people—at least 15 percent of the population. One of the agreed United Nations "millennium goals" for international development is to halve this proportion by 2015, by tackling chemical pollution from agriculture and industry, and by introducing essential purification facilities and local supply systems. In the industrialized world, people have come to expect clean drinking water on tap, even if they face rising prices for its treatment and supply.

Access to safe drinking water source (percentage of population)

 91%–100%
76%–90%
50%–75%

 below 50%
no data

Economic Systems

The world economy is now effectively a single global system based on "free market" capitalist principles. Few countries still cling, like North Korea, to the "command economy" formula developed in the former communist bloc, where centralized state plans set targets for investment and production. In the West, state ownership of companies has greatly diminished thanks to the wave of privatization in the last 25 years. Major companies move capital and raw materials around the globe to take advantage of different labor costs and skills. The World Trade Organization (WTO) promotes free trade, but many countries still use subsidies, and protect their markets with import tariffs or quotas, to favor their own producers.

Enormous volumes of trade pass through the world's stock markets making them key indicators of the strength of the global economy.

Balance of trade

Few countries earn from their exports exactly as much as they spend on imports. If the imbalance is persistently negative, it creates a potentially serious problem of indebtedness. The European Union's (EU) external trade is broadly in balance, but the US balance of trade has been in deficit since the 1970s, partly because it imports so many consumer goods. This deficit now stands at around US$ 500 billion a year.

Balance of trade
(million US$)

over 30,000	
10,000–29,999	
1000–9999	Surplus
0–999	
0–999	
1000–9999	
10,000–29,999	Deficit
over 30,000	
data unavailable	

TOP TEN GLOBAL COMPANIES (2015)

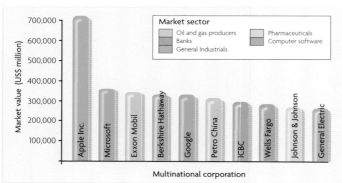

Market sector
- Oil and gas producers
- Banks
- General Industrials
- Pharmaceuticals
- Computer software

Market value (US$ million)

Multinational corporation

Apple Inc., Microsoft, Exxon Mobil, Berkshire Hathaway, Google, Petro China, ICBC, Wells Fargo, Johnson & Johnson, General Electric

Energy

Countries with oil and gas to sell (notably in the Middle East and Russia) can charge high prices; trade in fuel was worth US$ 1.4 trillion in 2005. The US and others are turning back to nuclear power (despite safety fears) for generating electricity. China relies heavily on (polluting) coal. Renewable technologies promise much, but so far make relatively minor contributions.

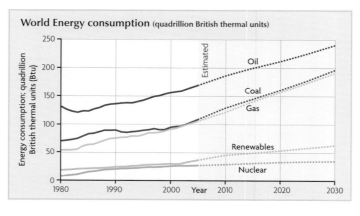

World Energy consumption (quadrillion British thermal units)

Energy consumption; quadrillion British thermal units (Btu)

Estimated

Oil
Coal
Gas
Renewables
Nuclear

1980 1990 2000 2010 2020 2030 Year

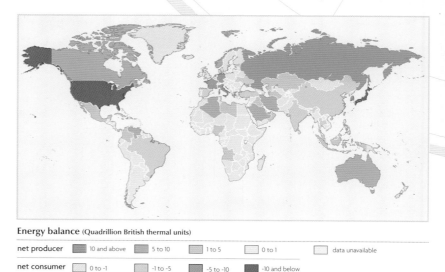

SOUTH AMERICA

New York

London

EUROPE

AFRICA

Energy balance (Quadrillion British thermal units)

net producer	10 and above	5 to 10	1 to 5	0 to 1	data unavailable
net consumer	0 to -1	-1 to -5	-5 to -10	-10 and below	

International debt
(as percentage of GNI)

- above 100%
- 75–100%
- 50–74%
- 25–49%
- 15–24%
- below 15%
- no data

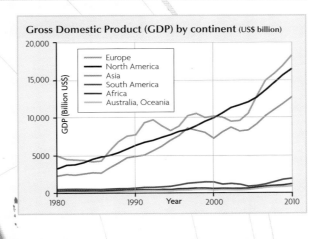

International debt

Saddled with crippling debts from past borrowing, the world's poorest countries are still paying off US $100 million a day. This is despite recent successful campaigns to get some of their debts cancelled to allow them to use their limited resources for development. Most international debt, however, is owed by developed countries to one another. The US owes just over a trillion dollars, around 7% of its total debt, to China.

Trade sector

World trade in merchandise tops US$ 10 trillion a year. The global pattern is uneven. Latin America, Africa, the Middle East, and Russia principally export "primary" goods (agricultural produce, mining and fuel). The "secondary" manufacturing sector includes iron and steel, machine tools, chemicals, clothing and textiles, cars and other consumer goods. The West still dominates the "tertiary" or non-merchandise sector, worth US$ 2.4 trillion, in services such as insurance and banking.

Gross Domestic Product (GDP) by continent (US$ billion)

- Europe
- North America
- Asia
- South America
- Africa
- Australia, Oceania

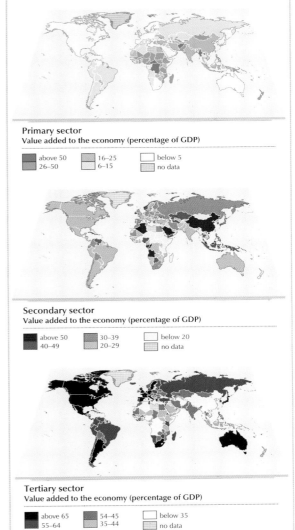

Primary sector
Value added to the economy (percentage of GDP)

- above 50
- 26–50
- 16–25
- 6–15
- below 5
- no data

Secondary sector
Value added to the economy (percentage of GDP)

- above 50
- 40–49
- 30–39
- 20–29
- below 20
- no data

Tertiary sector
Value added to the economy (percentage of GDP)

- above 65
- 55–64
- 54–45
- 35–44
- below 35
- no data

NORTH AMERICA

ASIA

AUSTRALIA

Tokyo

Gross Domestic Product (GDP*)
(nominal per capita US$)

- 40,001–90,000
- 10,001–40,000
- 6251–10,000
- 2501–6250
- 1501–2500
- 501–1500
- 251–500
- 0–250
- data unavailable

*Gross Domestic Product (GDP) is defined as the total market value of all final goods and services produced in a country.

Direct Foreign Investment

→ from USA
→ from Europe
→ from Japan

● major stock exchange
• stock exchange

Average monthly salary
(US$)

- above 3000
- 2000–3000
- 1000–2000
- 500–1000
- 250–500
- below 250
- no data

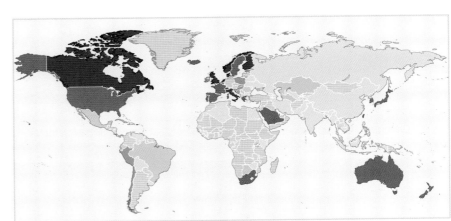

Labor

China's huge low-cost labor force promotes its conquest of world markets for manufactured goods. India's educated workforce attracts call centers and other service sector jobs, while the more economically developed countries's (MEDC) caring professions, and low-wage agriculture, draw in immigrant labor.

Travel

Mass travel is now a ubiquitous feature of all developed countries, and the provision of transport and tourism facilities one of the world's biggest industries, employing well over 100 million people. The travel explosion has come about, first, through major improvements in transportation technology; and second, as a result of increasing amounts of disposable income and leisure time in the world's wealthier countries. The main reasons for travel today include leisure pursuits and tourism (accounting for well over half of the total financial outlay), work and business, pilgrimage, migration, and visits to family and friends.

There are currently around 4.2 billion air travelers a year passing through over 1600 international and domestic airports. This figure is forecast to grow by 4 percent each year, leading to increased pressure on air traffic control and ground handling systems that, in many areas, are already close to maximum capacity.

Major modes of transportation

The major transport modes for people in the 21st century are road, rail, and air travel. The most popular air routes are highly concentrated within and between the USA, western Europe, and Asia. Major roads and railroads are more evenly spread, following the general distribution of the world's population.

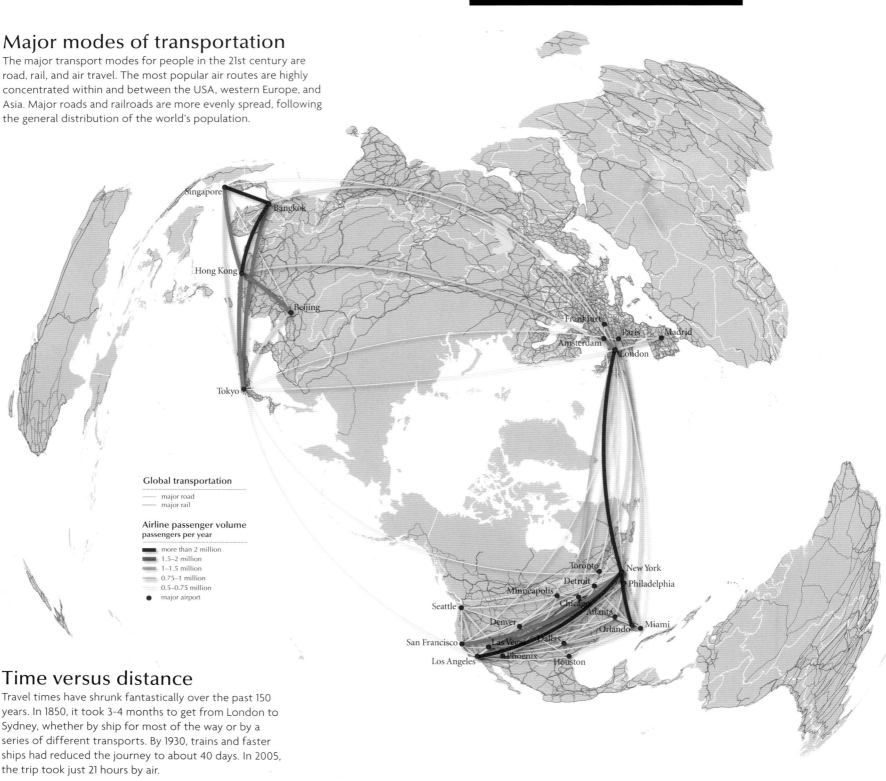

Global transportation

— major road
— major rail

Airline passenger volume
passengers per year

— more than 2 million
— 1.5–2 million
— 1–1.5 million
— 0.75–1 million
— 0.5–0.75 million
● major airport

Time versus distance

Travel times have shrunk fantastically over the past 150 years. In 1850, it took 3–4 months to get from London to Sydney, whether by ship for most of the way or by a series of different transports. By 1930, trains and faster ships had reduced the journey to about 40 days. In 2005, the trip took just 21 hours by air.

London
1850 ●
by coach to Portsmouth and thence ship around the Cape of Good Hope

1850 ●
Istanbul
Basra
coach . ferry . coach . horseback
horseback . river boat
river boat

1930 ●
Istanbul
Basra
Bombay
Calcutta
Singapore
Sydney
train . ferry . train
train . river boat
river boat . steamship
train
steamship
steamship

2005 ● I ● London–Sydney by air including one refueling stop

DAYS 1 2 3 4 5 6 7 8 9 10 11 12 13 14 15 16 17 18 19 20 21 22 23 24 25 26 27 28 29 30 31 32 33 34 35 36 37 38 39 40 41 42 43 44 45 46 47 48 49 50 51 52 53 54 55

Media and Communications

Over the past 50 years, the term "media" has come to denote various means of communicating information between people at a distance. These include mass media—methods such as newspapers, radio, and television that can be used to rapidly disseminate information to large numbers of people—and two-way systems, such as telephones and e-mail. Currently, the communication systems undergoing the most rapid growth worldwide include mobile telephony and various Internet-based applications, such as web sites, blogs, and podcasting, which can be considered forms of mass media.

Internet usage

Internet usage has grown extremely rapidly since the early 1990s, largely as a result of the invention of the World Wide Web. Usage rates are highest in the USA (where about 80 percent of people were using the Internet in 2006), Australia, Japan, South Korea, and Finland. They are lowest in Africa, where on average less than 5 percent of the population were Internet users in 2006.

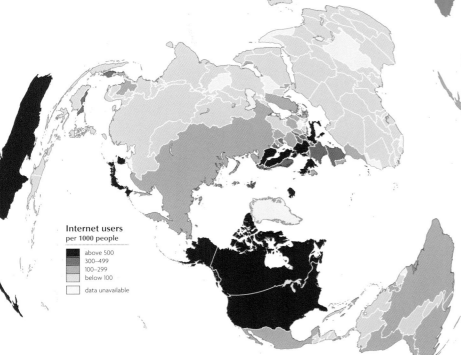

Internet users
per 1000 people

- above 500
- 300–499
- 100–299
- below 100
- data unavailable

Mobile phone usage

By 2006, there were more than 2.5 billion mobile phone users worldwide. In some parts of Europe, such as Italy, almost everyone owns and uses a mobile—many possess more than one phone. In contrast, throughout much of Southern Asia and Africa, less than 10 percent of the population are users. As well as utilizing them as telephones, most users now employ the devices for the additional functions they offer, such as text messaging and e-mail.

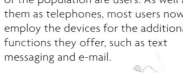

Mobile phone users
per 1000 people

- above 900
- 700–899
- 500–699
- 300–499
- 100–299
- below 100
- data unavailable

Satellite Communications

Modern communications satellites are used extensively for international telephony, for television and radio broadcasting, and to some extent for transmitting Internet data. Many of these satellites are deployed in clusters or arrays, often in geostationary orbits—that is, in positions that appear fixed to Earth-based observers.

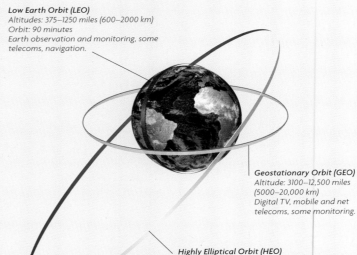

Low Earth Orbit (LEO)
Altitudes: 375–1250 miles (600–2000 km)
Orbit: 90 minutes
Earth observation and monitoring, some telecoms, navigation.

Geostationary Orbit (GEO)
Altitude: 3100–12,500 miles (5000–20,000 km)
Digital TV, mobile and net telecoms, some monitoring.

Highly Elliptical Orbit (HEO)
Altitude: 25,000 miles (40,000 km)
Orbit: 5–6 hours
Russian communications satellites

The internet emerged in the early 1990s as a computer-based global communication system. Since then massive growth has seen user numbers increase to around 1.1 billion people, or roughly 17 percent of the world's population.

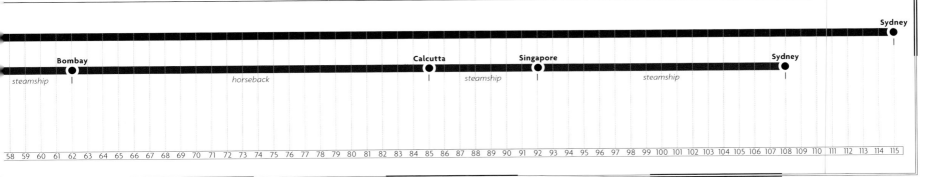

The Political World

Today's world map shows nearly 200 independent states, compared with about 80 after World War II. The transformation is mainly due to the withdrawal of European powers from huge colonial empires; their remaining overseas dependencies are tiny by comparison. The late 20th century also saw the collapse of communism, realignment in Europe, and fragmentation in former Yugoslavia. Globally, the Soviet Union's demise left the USA as the sole superpower, though with fast-growing China and India emerging as economic giants of the future. US security preoccupations switched to combating terrorism, while looming oil and other resource shortages, and environmental constraints, underlined the need for more effective international cooperation.

CONTINENTAL FACTFILE

	Total area: sq miles	Total area: sq km	Total population
North & Central America	9,358,340	24,238,000	565.3 million
South America	6,886,000	17,835,000	406.7 million
Africa	11,712,434	30,335,000	1110.6 million
Europe	4,053,309	10,498,000	742.4 million
Asia	16,838,365	43,608,000	4298.7 million
Australia & Oceania	3,285,048	8,508,238	38.3 million

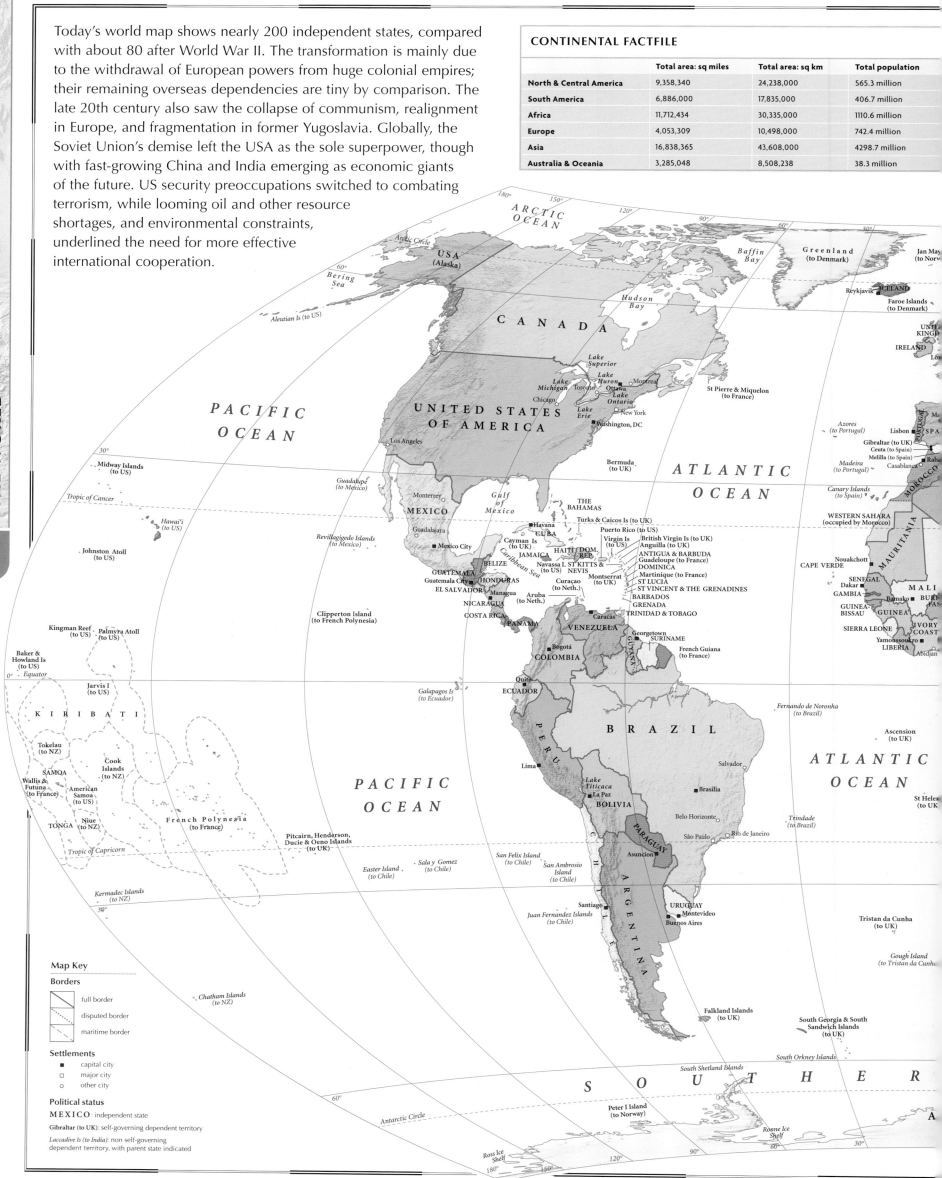

Map Key

Borders

full border

disputed border

maritime border

Settlements

■ capital city

□ major city

○ other city

Political status

MEXICO: independent state

Gibraltar (to UK): self-governing dependent territory

Laccadive Is (to India): non self-governing dependent territory, with parent state indicated

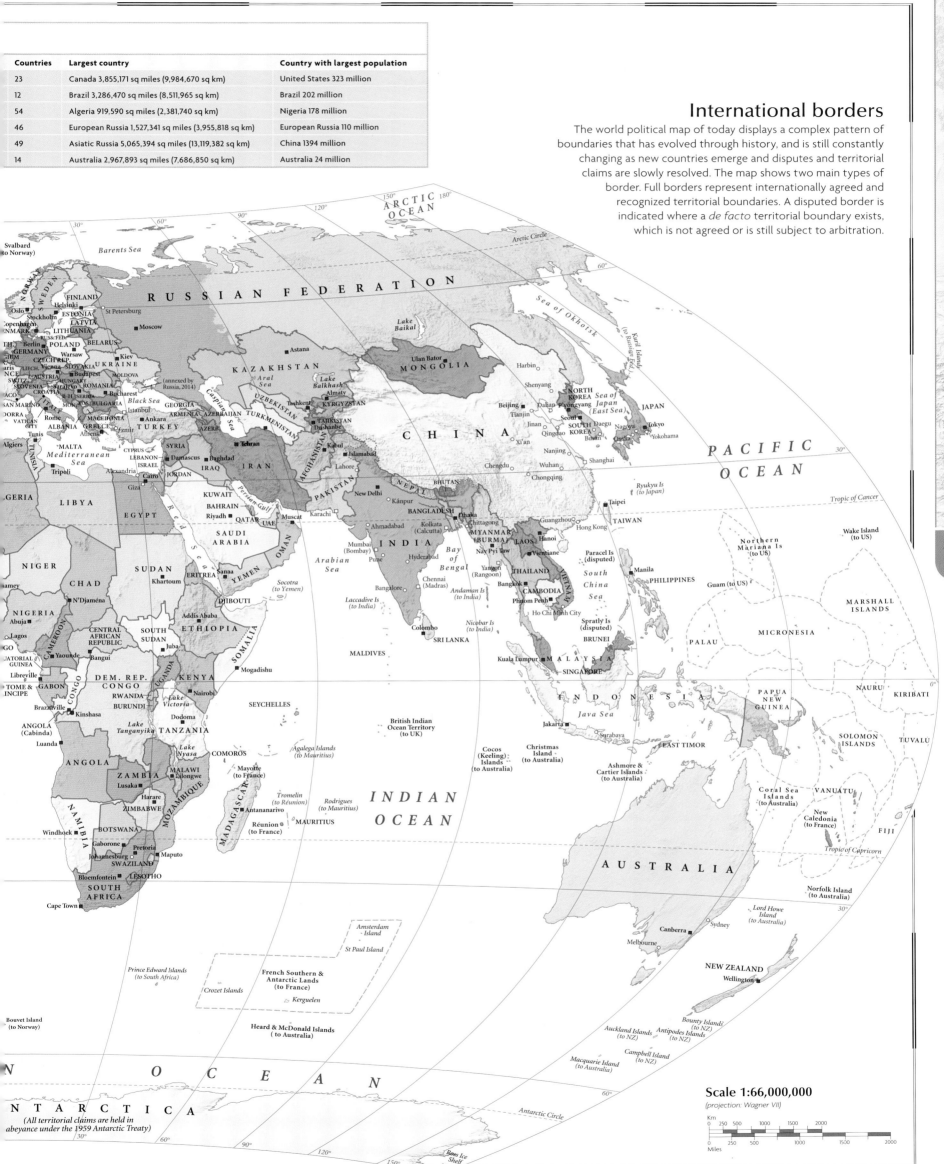

Countries	Largest country	Country with largest population
23	Canada 3,855,171 sq miles (9,984,670 sq km)	United States 323 million
12	Brazil 3,286,470 sq miles (8,511,965 sq km)	Brazil 202 million
54	Algeria 919,590 sq miles (2,381,740 sq km)	Nigeria 178 million
46	European Russia 1,527,341 sq miles (3,955,818 sq km)	European Russia 110 million
49	Asiatic Russia 5,065,394 sq miles (13,119,382 sq km)	China 1394 million
14	Australia 2,967,893 sq miles (7,686,850 sq km)	Australia 24 million

International borders

The world political map of today displays a complex pattern of boundaries that has evolved through history, and is still constantly changing as new countries emerge and disputes and territorial claims are slowly resolved. The map shows two main types of border. Full borders represent internationally agreed and recognized territorial boundaries. A disputed border is indicated where a *de facto* territorial boundary exists, which is not agreed or is still subject to arbitration.

Scale 1:66,000,000

(projection: Wagner VII)

Borders, conflicts and disputes

Conflict evolved in the 20th century from conventional land- or sea-based warfare to increasingly long-range airborne attacks. Nuclear arms from 1945 took this to the intercontinental scale. The Cold War presented a new type of conflict, underlined by the race for weapons capabilities between the US and the Soviet Union. In Korea, Vietnam, the Middle East and elsewhere, soldiers and civilians were exposed to deadly chemicals. International treaties aimed to prevent the spread of nuclear, biological and chemical "weapons of mass destruction". Intercommunal conflict and "ethnic cleansing" reminded the world that horror needed no sophisticated weaponry. After 9/11, the US-led "war on terror" perceived conflict in a new light, where international terrorism knew no borders.

THE PEACEKEEPERS

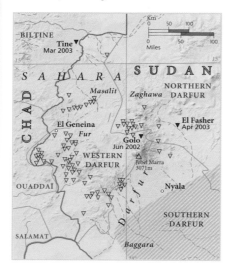

Over 130 countries have contributed around a million troops to UN missions to monitor peace processes and help implement peace accords since 1948. Regional alliances such as NATO and the African Union (AU) are increasingly deploying their own multinational forces in trouble-spots, while Australia has intervened in a similar manner in nearby Pacific island states. Peacekeepers oversaw East Timor's elections in 2001 and subsequent celebration of independence *(above)*. The US defines many of its activities as peacekeeping, despite the confrontational nature of some of its interventions.

DARFUR

African ethnic minorities in Darfur in western Sudan have suffered appalling violence since 2003 at the hands of genocidal Arab Janjaweed militias, for which the government in Khartoum denies responsibility. Displaced in their hundreds of thousands, refugees receive inadequate protection and aid from an international community unwilling to commit to full-scale intervention.

Darfur conflict

Fur ethnic group
⬚ arabic speaking area
▽ villages destroyed by Janjaweed
▼ towns that have been attacked by rebels opposing the Sudanese government

ISRAEL

Since its creation in 1948, Israel has been at war with its Arab neighbors. The Palestinians are fighting for a separate, viable state, comprising of at least East Jerusalem, and the West Bank and Gaza Strip, territories occupied by Israel in 1967. Their struggle *(intifada)* has attracted international support, but has been met by a hard-line response from Israel, which is backed by the US.

Arab-Israeli Wars 1947-2006

MAIN MAP: Arab-Israeli Wars
▪ Israel in 1949
▫ occupied by Israel after 1967 war
▫ occupied by Israel after 1973 war
▫ occupied by Israel after 1967 war reoccupied by Egypt after 1973 war
▭ demilitarized zone held by UN after Israel-Syria agreement, 1974, and 2nd Sinai agreement, 1975
▽ Hezbollah rocket attacks 2006
▼ Israeli rocket attacks 2006
- ·- disputed border

INSET MAP 1: UN Partition plan in 1947
— border of British mandate 1923
▪ proposed Arab State
▪ proposed Jewish State
▪ proposed international zone

INSET MAP 2: West Bank security
▪ Palestinian responsibility for civil affairs and internal security
▪ Palestinian responsibility for civil affairs; Israel responsible for security
— Security Wall (existing and planned)

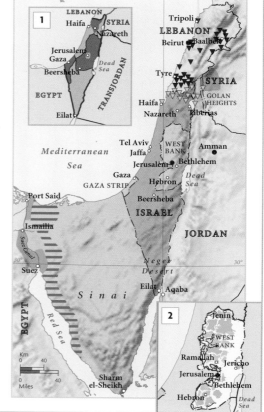

Conflicts and international disputes

- Major active territorial or border disputes
- Countries involved in internal conflict
- Active territorial or border disputes and internal conflict

Types of government

- Multiparty democracy for more than 10 yrs
- Multiparty democracy within last 10 yrs
- Single-party government
- Military regime
- Theocracy
- Monarchy
- Non-party system
- Transitional regime

Lines on the map

The determination of international boundaries can use a variety of criteria. Many borders between older states follow physical boundaries, often utilizing natural defensive features. Others have been determined by international agreement or arbitration, or simply ended up where the opposing forces stood at the end of a conflict.

WORLD BOUNDARIES

Dates from which current boundaries have existed

1990–present	1946–1965	1850–1914	Pre-1800
1966–1989	1915–1945	1800–1849	

POST-COLONIAL BORDERS

Independent African countries have largely inherited the earlier carve up of the continent by European colonial powers. These often arbitrarily divided or grouped differing ethnic and religious groups which has, in turn, contributed to the tensions that underlie the many civil conflicts that have plagued post-colonial Africa.

ENCLAVES

Changes to international boundaries occasionally create pockets of land cut off from the main territory of the country they belong to. In Europe, Kaliningrad has been separated from the rest of the Russian  Federation since the independence of the Baltic States. Likewise, when Morocco was granted independence, Spain retained the coastal enclaves of Ceuta and Melilla.

GEOMETRIC BORDERS

Straight lines and lines of longitude and latitude have occasionally been used to determine international boundaries: the 49th Parallel forms a large section of the Canada–US border, while the 38th Parallel roughly divides the Korean Peninsula. Internal administrative divisions within Canada, the US, and Australia also use geometric boundaries.

PHYSICAL BORDERS

Rivers account for one-sixth of the world's borders: the Danube forms part of the boundaries for nine European nations. Changes in a river's course or disruption of its flow can lead to territorial disputes. Lakes and mountains also form natural borders.

Lake border (right)
Mountain border (below left)
River border (below right)

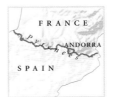

GULF CONFLICTS

Although the West armed Saddam Hussein in the brutal 1980s Iran-Iraq War, his unprovoked invasion of Kuwait in 1990 was decried the world over. A US-led coalition, including Arab states, repelled his troops but left him in power. A decade of sanctions followed until, in 2003, Saddam was finally toppled by US-led forces. Following elections in 2005, Iraq has struggled to contain a violent insurgency.

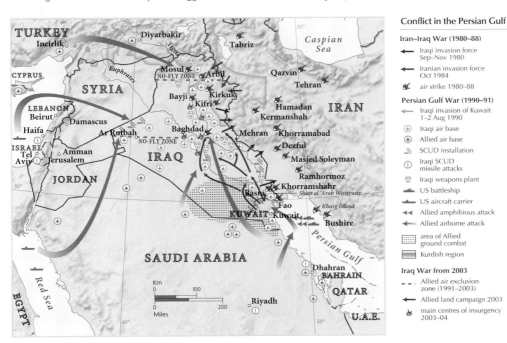

Conflict in the Persian Gulf

Iran–Iraq War (1980–88)
- Iraqi invasion force Sep–Nov 1980
- Iranian invasion force Oct 1984
- air strike 1980–88

Persian Gulf War (1990–91)
- Iraqi invasion of Kuwait 1–2 Aug 1990
- Iraqi air base
- Allied air base
- SCUD installation
- Iraqi SCUD missile attacks
- Iraqi weapons plant
- US battleship
- US aircraft carrier
- Allied amphibious attack
- Allied airborne attack
- area of Allied ground combat
- Kurdish region

Iraq War from 2003
- Allied air exclusion zone (1991–2003)
- Allied land campaign 2003
- main centres of insurgency 2003–04

The World's Standard Time Zones

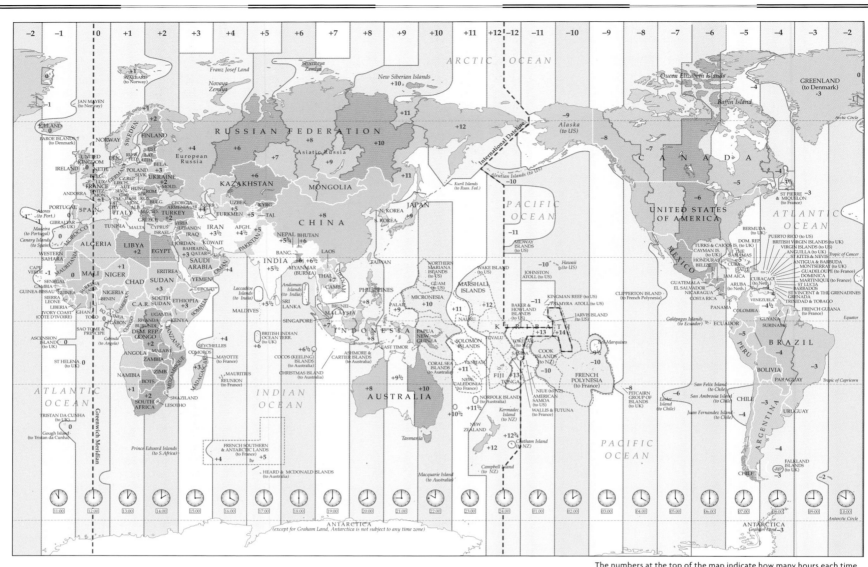

The numbers at the top of the map indicate how many hours each time zone is ahead or behind Coordinated Universal Time (UTC). The row of clocks indicate the time in each zone when it is 12:00 noon UTC.

TIME ZONES

Because Earth is a rotating sphere, the Sun shines on only half of its surface at any one time. Thus, it is simultaneously morning, evening and night time in different parts of the world (see diagram below). Because of these disparities, each country or part of a country adheres to a local time. A region of Earth's surface within which a single local time is used is called a time zone. There are 24 one hour time zones around the world, arranged roughly in longitudinal bands.

STANDARD TIME

Standard time is the official local time in a particular country or part of a country. It is defined by the time zone or zones associated with that country or region. Although time zones are arranged roughly in longitudinal bands, in many places the borders of a zone do not fall exactly on longitudinal meridians, as can be seen on the map (above),

but are determined by geographical factors or by borders between countries or parts of countries. Most countries have just one time zone and one standard time, but some large countries (such as the USA, Canada and Russia) are split between several time zones, so standard time varies across those countries. For example, the coterminous United States straddles four time zones and so has four standard times, called the Eastern, Central, Mountain and Pacific standard times. China is unusual in that just one standard time is used for the whole country, even though it extends across 60° of longitude from west to east.

COORDINATED UNIVERSAL TIME (UTC)

Coordinated Universal Time (UTC) is a reference by which the local time in each time zone is set. For example, Australian Western Standard Time (the local time in Western Australia) is set 8 hours ahead of UTC (it is UTC+8) whereas Eastern Standard Time in the United States is set 5

hours behind UTC (it is UTC-5). UTC is a successor to, and closely approximates, Greenwich Mean Time (GMT). However, UTC is based on an atomic clock, whereas GMT is determined by the Sun's position in the sky relative to the 0° longitudinal meridian, which runs through Greenwich, UK.

In 1884 the Prime Meridian (0° longitude) was defined by the position of the cross-hairs in the eyepiece of the "Transit Circle" telescope in the Meridian Building at the Royal Observatory, Greenwich, UK.

DAY AND NIGHT AROUND THE WORLD

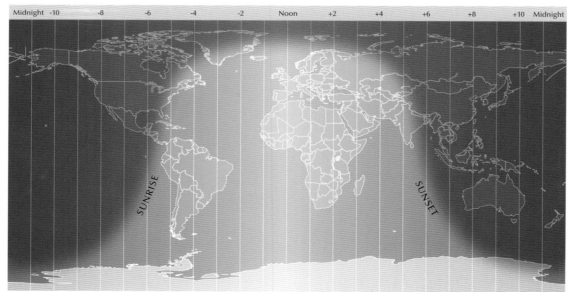

THE INTERNATIONAL DATELINE

The International Dateline is an imaginary line from pole to pole that roughly corresponds to the 180° longitudinal meridian. It is an arbitrary marker between calendar days. The dateline is needed because of the use of local times around the world rather than a single universal time. When moving from west to east across the dateline, travelers have to set their watches back one day. Those traveling in the opposite direction, from east to west, must add a day.

DAYLIGHT SAVING TIME

Daylight saving is a summertime adjustment to the local time in a country or region, designed to cause a higher proportion of its citizens' waking hours to pass during daylight. To follow the system, timepieces are advanced by an hour on a pre-decided date in spring and reverted back in the fall. About half of the world's nations use daylight saving.

COMPLETE ATLAS OF THE WORLD

THE MAPS IN THIS ATLAS ARE ARRANGED CONTINENT BY CONTINENT, STARTING FROM THE INTERNATIONAL DATE LINE, AND MOVING EASTWARD. THE MAPS PROVIDE A UNIQUE VIEW OF TODAY'S WORLD, COMBINING TRADITIONAL CARTOGRAPHIC TECHNIQUES WITH THE LATEST REMOTE-SENSED AND DIGITAL TECHNOLOGY.

North America is the world's third largest continent with a total area of 9,358,340 sq miles (24,238,000 sq km) including Greenland and the Caribbean islands. It lies wholly within the Northern Hemisphere.

FACTFILE

N **Most Northerly Point:** Kap Morris Jesup, Greenland 83° 38′ N
S **Most Southerly Point:** Peninsula de Azuero, Panama 7° 15′ N
E **Most Easterly Point:** Nordostrundingen, Greenland 12° 08′ W
W **Most Westerly Point:** Attu, Aleutian Islands, USA 172° 30′ E

Largest Lakes:
1. Lake Superior, Canada/USA 31,151 sq miles (83,270 sq km)
2. Lake Huron, Canada/USA 23,436 sq miles (60,700 sq km)
3. Lake Michigan, USA 22,402 sq miles (58,020 sq km)
4. Great Bear Lake, Canada 12,274 sq miles (31,790 sq km)
5. Great Slave Lake, Canada 10,981 sq miles (28,440 sq km)

Longest Rivers:
1. Mississippi-Missouri, USA 3710 miles (5969 km)
2. Mackenzie, Canada 2640 miles (4250 km)
3. Yukon, Canada/USA 1978 miles (3184 km)
4. St Lawrence/Great Lakes, Canada/USA 1900 miles (3058 km)
5. Rio Grande, Mexico/USA 1900 miles (3057 km)

Largest Islands:
1. Greenland 849,400 sq miles (2,200,000 sq km)
2. Baffin Island, Canada 183,800 sq miles (476,000 sq km)
3. Victoria Island, Canada 81,900 sq miles (212,000 sq km)
4. Ellesmere Island, Canada 75,700 sq miles (196,000 sq km)
5. Newfoundland, Canada 42,031 sq miles (108,860 sq km)

Highest Points:
1. Mount McKinley (Denali), USA 20,332 ft (6194 m)
2. Mount Logan, Canada 19,550 ft (5959 m)
3. Volcán Pico de Orizaba, Mexico 18,700 ft (5700 m)
4. Mount St Elias, USA 18,008 ft (5489 m)
5. Popocatépetl, Mexico 17,887 ft (5452 m)

Lowest Point:
▼ Death Valley, USA -282 ft (-86 m) below sea level

Highest recorded temperature:
⊕ Death Valley, USA 135°F (57°C)

Lowest recorded temperature:
⊖ Northice, Greenland -87°F (-66°C)

Wettest Place:
≋ Vancouver, Canada 262 in (6650 mm)

Driest Place:
⊖ Death Valley, USA 2 in (50 mm)

Cross-section from San Francisco to Washington DC

line of cross-section

Political

Democracy is well established in some parts of the continent but is a recent phenomenon in others. The economically dominant nations of Canada and the USA have a long democratic tradition but elsewhere, notably in the countries of Central America, political turmoil has been more common. In Nicaragua and Haiti, harsh dictatorships have only recently been superseded by democratically-elected governments. North America's largest countries—Canada, Mexico, and the USA—have federal state systems, sharing political power between national and state or provincial governments. The USA has intervened militarily on several occasions in Central America and the Caribbean to protect its strategic interests.

Transportation

In the 19th century, railroads were used to open up the North American continent. Air transport is now more common for long distance passenger travel, although railroads are still extensively used for bulk freight transport. Waterways, like the Mississippi River, are important for the transport of bulk materials, and the Panama Canal is a vital link between the Pacific Ocean and the Caribbean. In the 20th century, road transportation increased massively in North America, with the introduction of cheap, mass-produced cars and extensive highway construction.

Transportation
- major roads and motorways
- major railroads
- major canals
- international borders
- • transport intersections
- ⊕ international airports
- ⊥ major ports

Standard of living
(UN human development index)

high

low

Standard of living

The USA and Canada have one of the highest overall standards of living in the world. However, many people still live in poverty, especially in inner city ghettos and some rural areas. Central America and the Caribbean are markedly poorer than their wealthier northern neighbors Haiti is the poorest country in the western hemisphere.

UNITED STATES OF AMERICA

Scale 1:13,000,000

Km
0   50 100 150 200

Miles
0   50   100   150   200

HAWAII

UNITED STATES OF AMERICA

Ni'ihau · Kaua'i · O'ahu · Honolulu · Moloka'i · Lana'i · Maui · Kaho'olawe · Hawai'i

PACIFIC OCEAN

ASIA · ARCTIC · Beaufort Sea · Bering Strait · Brooks Range · UNITED STATES OF AMERICA · ALASKA · Anchorage · Gulf of Alaska · Aleutian Islands · Aleutian Range · Bering Sea · Mackenzie · Great Bear Lake · YUKON · Whitehorse · NORTHWEST TERRITORIES · Yellowknife · Juneau · Great Slave Lake · Lake Athabasca · BRITISH COLUMBIA · CANADA · ALBERTA · SASKATCHEWAN · Queen Charlotte Islands · Prince George · Edmonton · Calgary · Saskatoon · Vancouver Island · Vancouver · Victoria · Seattle · Olympia · Tacoma · WASHINGTON · Portland · Salem · Eugene · OREGON · IDAHO · MONTANA · Helena · Boise · WYOMING · UNITED · Santa Rosa · Reno · Carson City · Salt Lake City · Cheyenne · Oakland · Sacramento · NEVADA · UTAH · Denver · San Francisco · Stockton · San Jose · Salinas · Fresno · CALIFORNIA · Las Vegas · Colorado · Colorado Springs · Pueblo · Bakersfield · Simi Valley · OF AM · Los Angeles · Riverside · Santa Fe · Oceanside · San Diego · ARIZONA · Albuquerque · Tijuana · Mexicali · Phoenix · NEW MEXIC · Tucson · El Paso · Ciudad Juárez · Hermosillo · Gulf of California · Chihuahua · Tropic of Cancer · Lower California · Durango · Mazatlán · M · Guadalajara · Manzanillo · PACIFIC OCEAN

Fairbanks · Dutch Harbor · Tuktoyaktuk · Anchorage · Skagway · Hay River · Prince Rupert · Prince George · Edmonton · Nanaimo · Calgary · Vancouver · Seattle · Thunder Bay · Québec · St.John's · Portland · Spokane · Winnipeg · Halifax · Coos Bay · Butte · Duluth · Sault Ste. Marie · Montréal · St.John · Fargo · Minneapolis · Toronto · Albany · Boston · Salt Lake City · Sioux Falls · Chicago · Detroit · Newark · New York · Oakland · Cheyenne · Omaha · Toledo · Philadelphia · San Francisco · Denver · Kansas City · Saint Louis · Washington DC · Baltimore · Los Angeles · Long Beach · Oklahoma City · Memphis · Nashville · Norfolk · San Diego · Phoenix · Albuquerque · Atlanta · Charleston · Wilmington · El Paso · Dallas · Birmingham · Savannah · Chihuahua · Houston · Mobile · Jacksonville · San Antonio · New Orleans · Orlando · Corpus Christi · Tampa · Miami · Mazatlán · Monterrey · Havana · San Juan · Tampico · Mérida · Kingston · Manzanillo · Mexico City · Toluca · Coatzacoalcos · Salina Cruz · Guatemala City · San Salvador · Corinto · Balboa · Panama Canal · Panama City

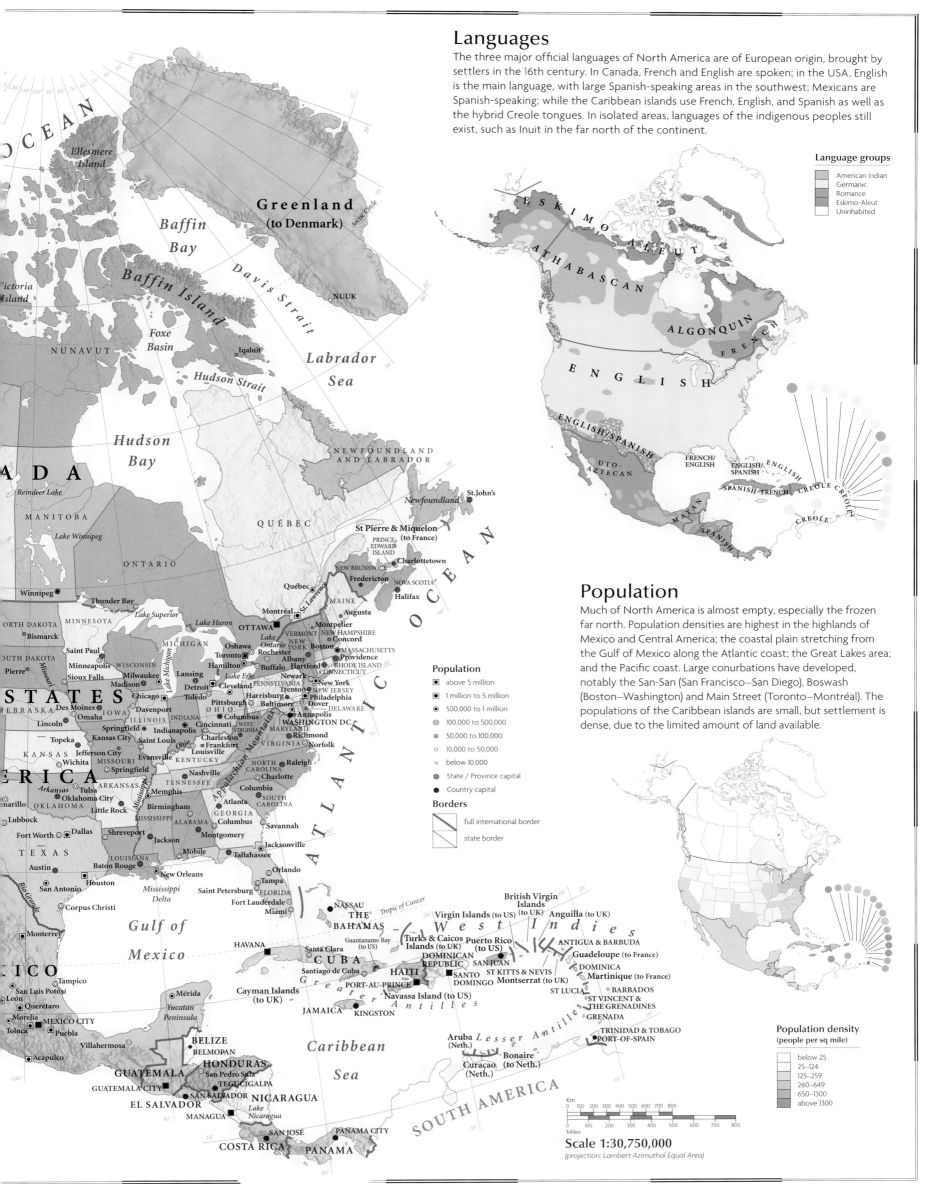

Languages

The three major official languages of North America are of European origin, brought by settlers in the 16th century. In Canada, French and English are spoken; in the USA, English is the main language, with large Spanish-speaking areas in the southwest; Mexicans are Spanish-speaking; while the Caribbean islands use French, English, and Spanish as well as the hybrid Creole tongues. In isolated areas, languages of the indigenous peoples still exist, such as Inuit in the far north of the continent.

Language groups
- American Indian
- Germanic
- Romance
- Eskimo-Aleut
- Uninhabited

Population

Much of North America is almost empty, especially the frozen far north. Population densities are highest in the highlands of Mexico and Central America; the coastal plain stretching from the Gulf of Mexico along the Atlantic coast; the Great Lakes area; and the Pacific coast. Large conurbations have developed, notably the San-San (San Francisco–San Diego), Boswash (Boston–Washington) and Main Street (Toronto–Montréal). The populations of the Caribbean islands are small, but settlement is dense, due to the limited amount of land available.

Population
- ▣ above 5 million
- ◙ 1 million to 5 million
- ◉ 500,000 to 1 million
- ◎ 100,000 to 500,000
- ⊕ 50,000 to 100,000
- ○ 10,000 to 50,000
- ○ below 10,000
- ● State / Province capital
- ● Country capital

Borders
- full international border
- state border

Population density
(people per sq mile)
- below 25
- 25–124
- 125–259
- 260–649
- 650–1300
- above 1300

Scale 1:30,750,000
(projection: Lambert Azimuthal Equal Area)

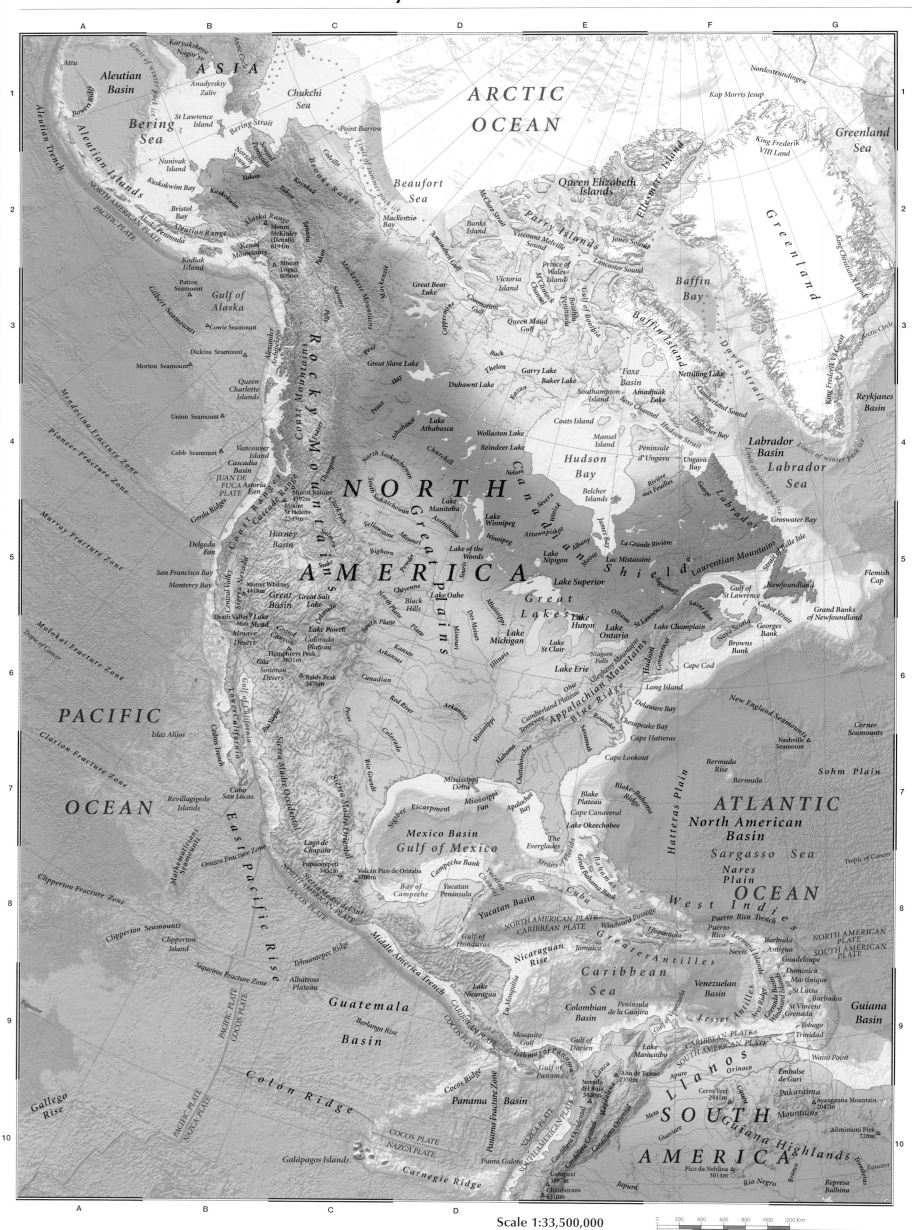

Scale 1:33,500,000
(projection: Lambert Conformal Conic)

0	200	400	600	800	1000	1200 Km
0	200	400	600	800	1000	1200 Miles

Environmental Issues

Many fragile environments are under threat throughout the region. In Haiti, all the primary rain forest has been destroyed, while air pollution from factories and cars in Mexico City is among the worst in the world. Elsewhere, industry and mining pose threats, particularly in the delicate arctic environment of Alaska where oil spills have polluted coastlines and decimated fish stocks.

Climate

North America's climate includes extremes ranging from freezing Arctic conditions in Alaska and Greenland, to desert in the southwest, and tropical conditions in southeastern Florida, the Caribbean, and Central America. Central and southern regions are prone to severe storms including tornadoes and hurricanes.

Average Rainfall

January rainfall *July rainfall*

Rainfall

- 0–1 in (0–25 mm)
- 1–2 in (25–50 mm)
- 2–4 in (50–100 mm)
- 4–8 in (100–200 mm)
- 8–12 in (200–300 mm)
- 12–16 in (300–400 mm)
- 16–20 in (400–500 mm)
- more than 20 in (500 mm)

Average Temperature

January temperature *July temperature*

Temperature

- below -22°F (-30°C)
- -22 to -4°F (-30 to -20°C)
- -4 to 14°F (-20 to -10°C)
- 14 to 32°F (-10 to 0°C)
- 32 to 50°F (0 to 10°C)
- 50 to 68°F (10 to 20°C)
- 68 to 86°F (20 to 30°C)
- above 86°F (30°C)

Environmental issues

- national parks
- risk of acid rain
- tropical forest
- forest destroyed
- desert
- risk of desertification
- polluted rivers
- radioactive contamination
- marine pollution
- heavy marine pollution
- poor urban air quality

Climate

- ice cap
- tundra
- subarctic
- cool continental
- warm humid
- semi-arid
- arid
- humid equatorial
- tropical
- daily hours of sunshine, January
- daily hours of sunshine, July
- direction of hurricanes
- tornado zones

Land use

Abundant land and fertile soils stretch from the Canadian prairies to Texas creating North America's agricultural heartland. Cereals and cattle ranching form the basis of the farming economy, with corn and soybeans also important. Fruit and vegetables are grown in California using irrigation, while Florida is a leading producer of citrus fruits. Caribbean and Central American countries depend on cash crops such as bananas, coffee, and sugar cane, often grown on large plantations. This reliance on a single crop can leave these countries vulnerable to fluctuating world crop prices.

Using the land and sea

- cropland
- forest
- ice cap
- mountain region
- pasture
- tundra
- wetland
- desert
- major conurbations
- cattle
- goats
- pigs
- poultry
- reindeer
- sheep
- bananas
- citrus fruits
- coffee
- corn (maize)
- cotton
- fishing
- fruit
- maple syrup
- peanuts
- rice
- shellfish
- soya beans
- sugar cane
- timber
- tobacco
- vineyards
- wheat

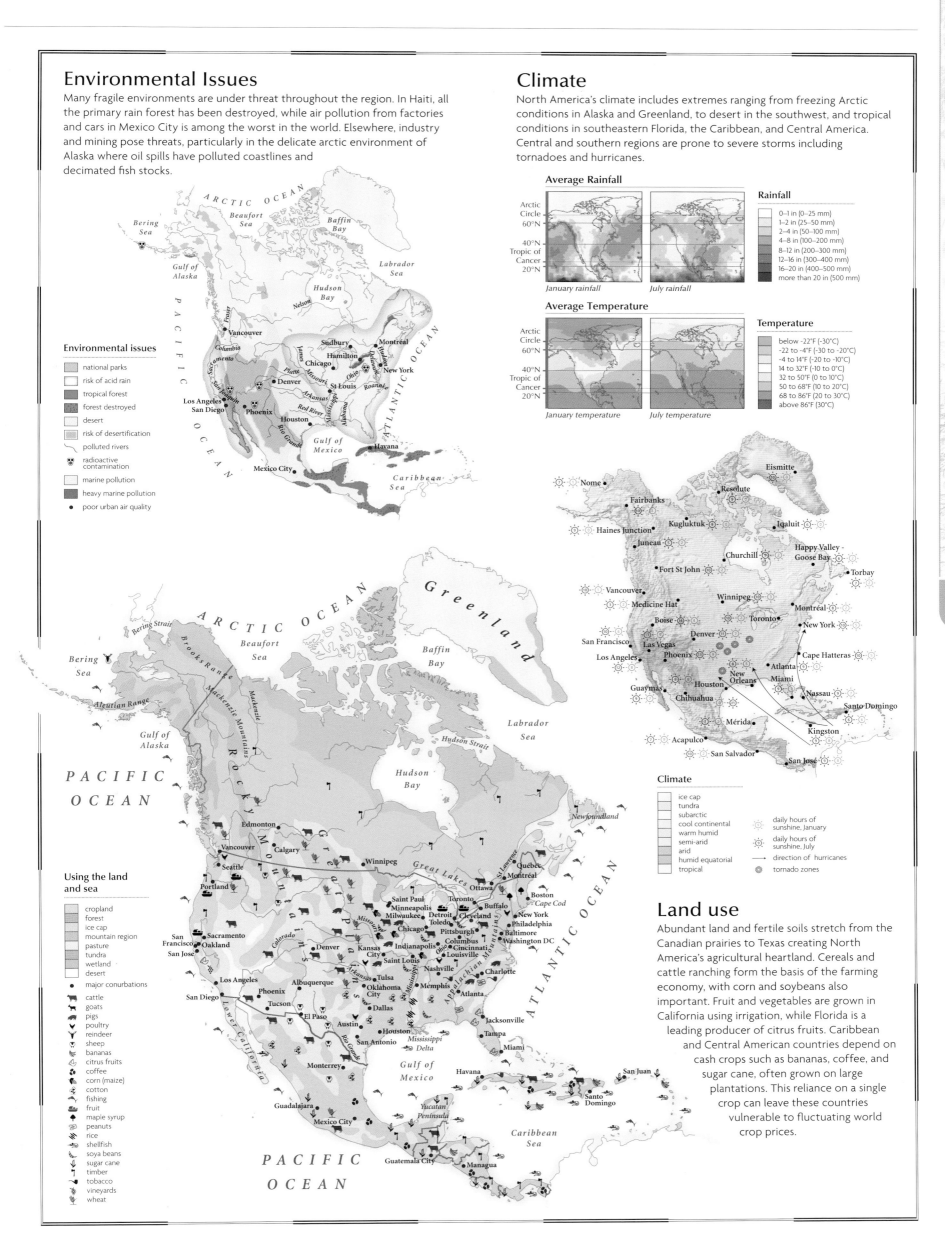

1 VANCOUVER, BRITISH COLUMBIA, CANADA
Canada's premier west coast city occupies the delta of the Fraser river, formed among the Coast Mountains.

2 MOUNT SAINT HELENS, WASHINGTON, USA
In 1980, this volcano's catastrophic eruption devastated 270 sq miles (700 sq km) of forest almost instantly.

3 GREAT SALT LAKE, UTAH, USA
A causeway carries a railroad, blocking circulation between the northern and southern parts, the water reddened by bacteria in the more saline north.

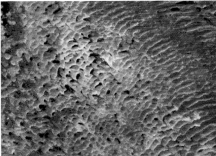

4 SAND HILLS, NEBRASKA, USA
Forming the largest sand sea in the Western Hemisphere, these hills are not classified as desert because today's relatively wet climate has allowed grasses to take hold.

9 LOS ANGELES AND LONG BEACH, CALIFORNIA, USA
Taken together, these west coast cities constitute the busiest seaport in the United States.

10 ISLA GUADALUPE, MEXICO
The volcanic island, 186 miles (300 km) off the west coast of Mexico, is a protected wildlife reserve.

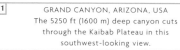

11 GRAND CANYON, ARIZONA, USA
The 5250 ft (1600 m) deep canyon cuts through the Kaibab Plateau in this southwest-looking view.

12 DENVER, COLORADO, USA
Colorado's state capital nestles under the Rocky Mountains with the South Platte River running through its center.

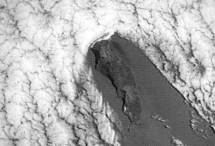

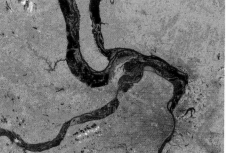

BELCHER ISLANDS, NUNAVUT, CANADA [5]
These low-lying, treeless, and sparsely-populated islands lie icebound in Hudson Bay for much of the year.

MISSISSIPPI, MISSOURI, AND ILLINOIS RIVERS, USA [6]
This Infrared image shows how these rivers burst their banks in many places after heavy rains in the summer of 1993, leading to the area's worst floods on record.

RÉSERVOIR MANICOUAGAN, QUÉBEC, CANADA [7]
This unusual 62 mile (100 km) diameter annular lake occupies the low ground between the rim and central uplift of an ancient meteorite crater.

NEW YORK CITY, USA [8]
The largest city in the United States, with a population of over 8 million, it is also the country's main financial center.

MISSISSIPPI RIVER DELTA, LOUISIANA, USA [13]
This delta has developed a "bird's foot" shape due to the shifting course of the river over the last 6000 years.

FLORIDA, USA [14]
This low-lying, subtropical peninsula is home to thousands of lakes that have formed among its limestone "karst" topography.

HAVANA, CUBA [15]
Cuba's capital city is home to 2 million people and was founded by the Spanish in 1519 around a natural harbor.

BARRIER REEF, BELIZE [16]
The world's second-longest barrier reef lies about 12 miles (20 km) off the coast of Belize.

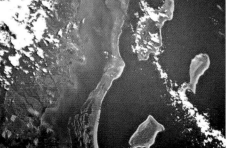

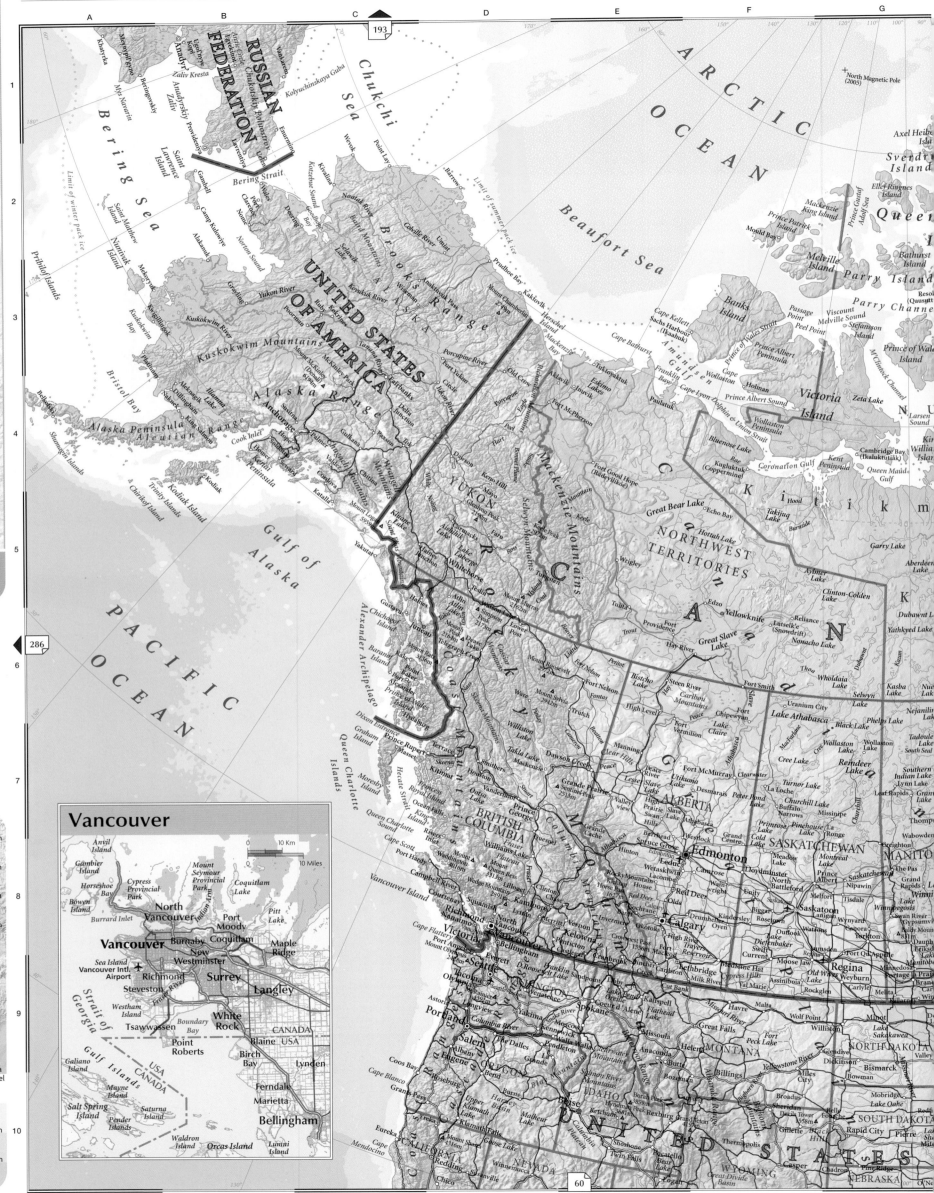

A R C T I C   O C E A N

Beaufort Sea

Chukchi Sea

RUSSIAN FEDERATION

UNITED STATES OF AMERICA

ALASKA

Brooks Range

Kuskokwim Mountains

Alaska Range

Bering Sea

Limit of winter pack ice

Gulf of Alaska

P A C I F I C   O C E A N

YUKON

NORTHWEST TERRITORIES

Great Bear Lake

Great Slave Lake

Victoria Island

Banks Island

Melville Island

Parry Islands

Queen

North Magnetic Pole (2005)

Mackenzie Mountains

C A N A D A

BRITISH COLUMBIA

ALBERTA

SASKATCHEWAN

MANITO

Edmonton

Calgary

Regina

Saskatoon

Vancouver Island

Victoria

Vancouver

WASHINGTON

OREGON

IDAHO

MONTANA

NORTH DAKOTA

SOUTH DAKOTA

WYOMING

NEBRASKA

NEVADA

CALIFORNIA

U N I T E D   S T A T E S

Portland

Salem

Seattle

Spokane

Helena

Billings

Bismarck

Rapid City

Vancouver

Anvil Island

Gambier Island

Horseshoe Bay

Bowen Island

Cypress Provincial Park

Mount Seymour Provincial Park

North Vancouver

Burrard Inlet

Vancouver

Burnaby

New Westminster

Coquitlam

Port Moody

Pitt Lake

Coquitlam Lake

Indian Arm

Maple Ridge

Sea Island

Vancouver Intl. Airport

Richmond

Steveston

Surrey

Langley

Strait of Georgia

Westham Island

Boundary Bay

Tsawwassen

White Rock

Point Roberts

Birch Bay

CANADA

USA

Blaine

Lynden

Ferndale

Marietta

Bellingham

Galiano Island

Mayne Island

Salt Spring Island

Pender Islands

Saturna Island

Waldron Island

Orcas Island

Lummi Island

0   10 Km

0   10 Miles

Sea Level

6000m
4000m
3000m
2000m
1000m
500m
250m
100m
Sea Level
-250m
-2000m
-4000m

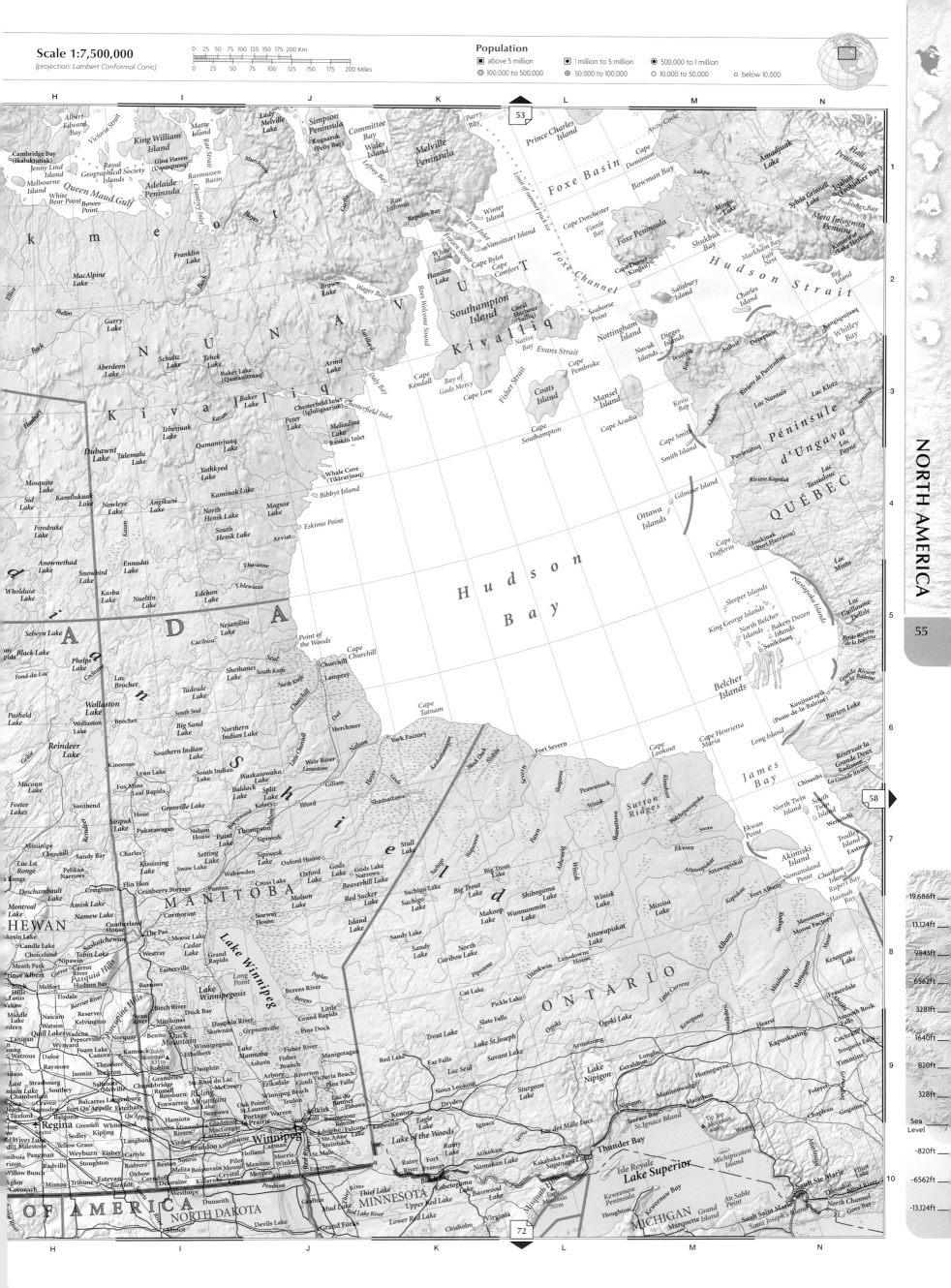

54

A   B   C   D   E   F   G

USA
ALASKA

Wrangell

Revillagigedo
Island

Ketchikan
Mountain Point
Annette
Island

Metlakatla

Duke
Island

Hyder
Stewart

Mount Pattullo
2739m

Meziadin
Junction

Skeena   Mountains

Coast

Finlay

Ware

Sustut Peak
2470m

Omineca   Mountains

Finlay

Trutch

Great Snow Mountain
2896m

Sikanni Chief

Sikanni Chief

Pink
Mountain

Beatton River

Beatton

Chinchaga

Twin

Clear Hills

Manning

Williston
Lake

Wonowon

Cameron

Fort
St.John

Taylor

Peace

Hines
Creek

Grimshaw

Fairview

Fall

Hudson's Hope

Chetwynd

Dawson
Creek

Spirit
River

Rycroft

Prince Rupert
Port
Edward

Porcher
Island

Skeena

Cranberry
Junction

Nass

Kitwanga

Hazelton
New Hazelton

Seven Sisters Peaks
2755m

Terrace

Kitimat

Takla Lake

Granisle
Smithers
Telkwa

Babine Lake

Houston

Mackenzie
McLeod
Lake

Pine Pass
869m

Sentinel Peak
2515m

Tupper

Hythe

Beaverlodge

Wembley

Sexsmith

Grande Prairie

Tumbler
Ridge

Wapiti

Banks
Island

Pitt
Island

Keimano

Burns
Lake

Stuart Lake

Fort
St.James

Stuart

Fraser
Lake
Vanderhoof

Nechako

Prince
George

Sinclair Mills

Mount Sir Alexander
3274m

Grande Cache

Smoky

Little Smo

Princess
Royal
Island

Ocean
Falls

Eutsuk Lake

Ootsa Lake

Nazko

Quesnel

Barkerville

Likely

Marguerite

Williams
Lake

McBride

Mount Robson
3954m

Tête Jaune
Cache

Yellowhead Pass
1131m

Mount Sir
Wilfrid Laurier
3505m

Valemount

Jasper

Jasper
National Pa

Columbia

Aristazabal
Island

Bella Bella

King Island

Hagensborg
Bella Coola

Mount Saugstad
2908m

Anahim Lake

Fraser

Plateau

BRITISH

COLUMBIA

Alexis
Creek

Cariboo
Mountains

Kinbasket Lake

Mount
Columbia
3741m

Mica Creek

Queen

Charlotte Sound

Burke
Channel

Namu

Rivers
Inlet

Dawsons Landing

Rivers Inlet

Monarch Mountain
3533m

Kleena Kleene

Tatla Lake

Hanceville

100 Mile
House

Clearwater

Blue River

Selkirk
Mountains

Rogers Pass
1327m

Glaci

Cape Caution

Mount Waddington
4016m

Mount Queen Bess
3313m

Little Fort

Columbia

Columbia

Mountains

Cape
Scott

Queen Charlotte Strait

Cape
Cook

Port Hardy

Winter Harbour

Port
McNeill
Port
Alice

Telegraph Cove

Knight
Inlet

Bute
Inlet

Mount Gilbert
3109m

Clinton

Barrière

Cache Creek
Thompson

Ashcroft

Lillooet

Logan
Lake

Kamloops

Chase

Salmon
Arm

Sicamous

Revelstoke

Enderby

Armstrong

Coldstream

Mica Creek

Sayward

Campbell
River

Tahsis

Gold River

Courtenay
Comox

Strait of Georgia

Powell
River

Pemberton

Whistler

Wedge Mountain
2891m

Lytton

Boston Bar

Merritt

Vernon

Okanagan
Lake

Nakusp

New Denver

Nootka Sound

Vancouver
Island

Parksville

Nanaimo

Sechelt

Gibsons

North
Vancouver

Squamish

Westbank
Peachland
Summerland

Kelowna

Okanagan

Tofino

Port
Alberni

Ladysmith
Lake Cowichan

Richmond

Vancouver
Burnaby
Langley

Hope

Princeton

Penticton

Ucluelet

Barkley Sound

Bamfield

Duncan
Swartz Bay

Blaine
Ferndale
Lynden
Sumas

Abbotsford

Chilliwack

Columbia River

Oliver
Osoyoos

Grand
Forks

Castlegar

Rossland

Nels

Port Renfrew

Cape Flattery
Neah Bay

Clallam Bay

Victoria

Esquimalt

San Juan
Islands

Friday
Harbor

Anacortes

Bellingham

Newhalem

Oroville

Tiffany Mountain
2512m

Tonasket

Republic

Grand
Forks

Trail

Kettle
Falls

Colville

Northport

Orient

P A C I F I C

O C E A N

Strait of Juan de Fuca

Olympic
Mountains

Mount Olympus
2428m

Port
Angeles

Sequim

Port
Townsend

Oak
Harbor

Coupeville

Mount Vernon

Stanwood

Arlington

Darrington

Glacier Peak
3213m

Skagit River

Rockport

Newhalem

Winthrop

Mazama

Methow River

U N I T E D

Paterson

Lake Chelan

Grand
Coulee

Franklin D.
Roosevelt Lake

Chewelah

Deer
Park

New

Forks

Queets

Taholah

Quinault

Quinault River

Moclips
Pacific Beach
Copalis Beach

Humptulips

Bremerton
Port
Orchard

Puget Sound

Edmonds
Redmond
Bellevue

Seattle

Seattle-Tacoma

Kent
Auburn

Tacoma

Puyallup

Shelton

Monroe

Everett

Marysville

Snohomish

Skykomish

Leavenworth

Entiat

Wenatchee

Grand
Coulee

Banks
Lake

Coulee City

Wilbur

Davenport

Odessa

Spokane River

Spokane

Crab Creek

Sprague

Che

W A S H I N G T O N

Roslyn

Cle Elum

Ellensburg

Ephrata

S T

76

A   B   C   D   E   F   G

Scale 1:3,750,000
(projection: Lambert Azimuthal Equal Area)

0 20 40 60 80 100 Km
0 20 40 60 80 100 Miles

Population
■ above 5 million ▣ 1 million to 5 million ◉ 500,000 to 1 million
◎ 100,000 to 500,000 ⊕ 50,000 to 100,000 ○ 10,000 to 50,000 ∘ below 10,000

CANADA

ALBERTA

SASKATCHEWAN

UNITED STATES OF AMERICA

MONTANA

IDAHO

Great Plains

Birch Mountains

Reindeer Lake
Cree Lake
Foster Lakes
Macoun Lake
Southend
Turnor Lake
Frobisher Lake
Churchill Lake
Buffalo Narrows
Ile-à-la-Crosse
Pinehouse Lake
Missinipe
Churchill
Pelikan Narrows
La Ronge
Lac La Ronge
Deschambault Lake
Beauval
Peter Pond Lake
La Loche
Clearwater
Fort MacKay
Fort McMurray

Primrose Lake
Doré Lake
Green Lake
Montreal Lake
Waskesiu Lake
Candle Lake
Tobin Lake
Meadow Lake
Big River
Choiceland
Nipawin
Carrot River
Meath Park
Prince Albert
Birch Hills
Melfort
Tisdale
St.Louis
Rosthern
Waldheim
Wakaw
Middle Lake
Naicam
Watson
Quill Lakes
Lanigan
Wynyard
Watrous
Dafoe
Raymore
Strasbourg
Last Mountain Lake
Davidson
Chamberlain
Craven
Lumsden
Southey
Regina Beach
Balgonie
Regina
Moose Jaw
Tuxford
Chaplin
Stewart Valley
Herbert
Swift Current
Gull Lake
Tompkins
Maple Creek
Cypress Hills
Eastend
Shaunavon
Mankota
Val Marie
Climax
Robsart
Rockglen
Coronach
Minton
Willow Bunch
Assiniboia
Lafleche
Gravelbourg
Hodgeville
Old Wives Lake
Ardill
Milestone
Pangman
Horizon
Ponteix
Cadillac
Cabri
Leader
Elrose
Outlook
Lake Diefenbaker
Elbow
Riverhurst
Cut Knife
Battleford
North Battleford
Hafford
Blaine Lake
Duck Lake
Borden
Martensville
Aberdeen
Saskatoon
Biggar
Delisle
Kerrobert
Rosetown
Kindersley
Smiley
Dundurn
Allan
Young
Watrous
Eston
Eatonia
Alsask
Oyen
Leader
South Saskatchewan
Unity
Wilkie
Macklin
Provost
Consort

Cold Lake
Grand Centre
Bonnyville
Piercleland
St.Walburg
Turtleford
Glaslyn
Spiritwood
Shellbrook
Lloydminster
Marwayne
Maidstone
Lashburn
North Saskatchewan
Marsden
Vermilion
Mannville
Vegreville
Mundare
Two Hills
St.Paul
Elk Point
Willingdon
Smoky Lake
Redwater
Fort Saskatchewan
St.Albert
Sherwood Park
Edmonton
Spruce Grove
Stony Plain
Devon
Leduc
Morinville
Wetaskiwin
Camrose
Daysland
Viking
Killam
Wainwright
Hardisty
Ponoka
Rimbey
Bentley
Lacombe
Sylvan Lake
Red Deer
Stettler
Castor
Coronation
Delburne
Innisfail
Bashaw
Sundre
Olds
Trochu
Three Hills
Didsbury
Carstairs
Crossfield
Drumheller
Morrin
Hanna
Youngstown
Beiseker
Airdrie
Cochrane
Calgary
Strathmore
Banff
Canmore
Okotoks
Turner Valley
Black Diamond
High River
Nanton
Vulcan
Bassano
Brooks
Bow City
Leader
Rosetown

Athabasca
Boyle
Lac La Biche
Smith
Honda
Calling Lake
Conklin
Nipin
Cold Lake
Desmarais
Sandy Lake
Utikuma Lake
Gift Lake
Lesser Slave Lake
Kinuso
Faust
Slave Lake
Swan Hills
Wallace Mountain 1259m
Fox Creek
Whitecourt
Mayerthorpe
Barrhead
Westlock
Edson
Evansburg
Drayton Valley
Little Smoky
Nordegg
Rocky Mountain House
Kicking Horse Pass 1627m
Lake Louise
Golden
Mount Assiniboine 3618m
Radium Hot Springs
Invermere
Purcell Mountains
Elkford
Sparwood
Crowsnest Pass 1356m
Coleman
Fernie
Kimberley
Cranbrook
Creston
Kingsgate
Roosville
Eureka
Moyie Springs
Libby
Whitefish
Columbia Falls
Kalispell
Somers
Bigfork
Snowshoe Peak 2665m
Cabinet Mountains
Thompson Falls
Plains
Ronan
Polson
Flathead Lake
Hungry Horse Reservoir
Rocky Mountain 2863m
Fairfield
Choteau
Teton River
Fort Benton
Winifred
Jordan
Missouri River
Piney Buttes
Circle
Vida
Poplar
Wolf Point
Glasgow
Nashua
Fort Peck Lake
Fort Peck
Malta
Milk River
Dodson
Saco
Loring
Opheim
Scobey
Wild Horse
Sweetgrass
Sunburst
Babb
Cut Bank
Shelby
Conrad
Lothair
Chester
Rudyard
Gildford
Havre
Chinook
Harlem
Big Sandy
Baldy Mountain 2018m
Lake Elwell
Marias River
Browning
Mount Brown 2121m
Mount Cleveland 3190m
Logan Pass 2026m
Kicking
Lethbridge
Fort Macleod
Coaldale
Taber
Pincher Creek
Raymond
Magrath
Cardston
Milk River
Foremost
Claresholm
Vauxhall
Bow Island
Taber
Medicine Hat
Redcliff
Walsh
Suffield
Travers Reservoir
Big Sandy

North Saskatchewan
South Saskatchewan
Red Deer
Bow River
Battle
Athabasca
Richardson
Beaver
Nipin
Milk River
Poplar River
Missouri River
Kootenay River

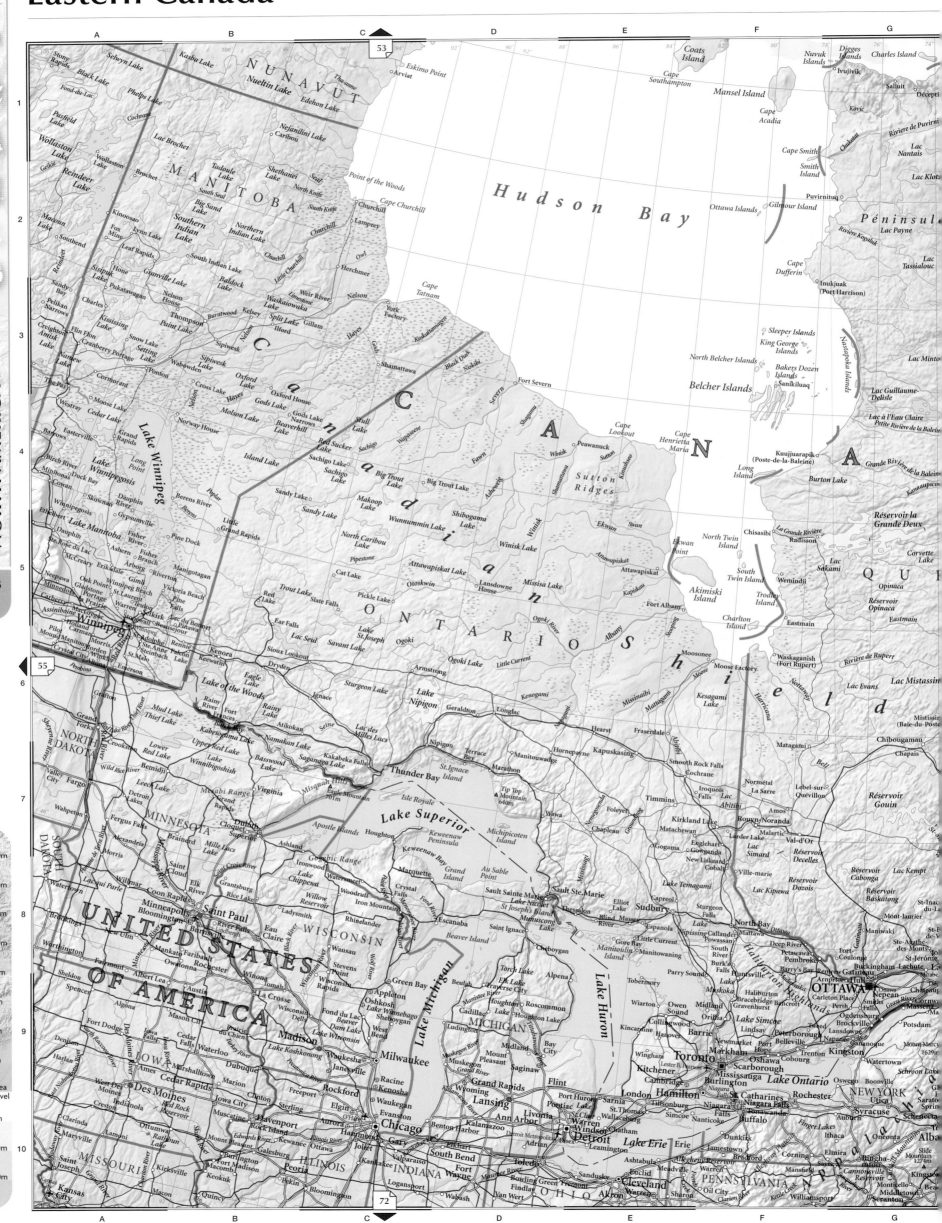

The United States of America

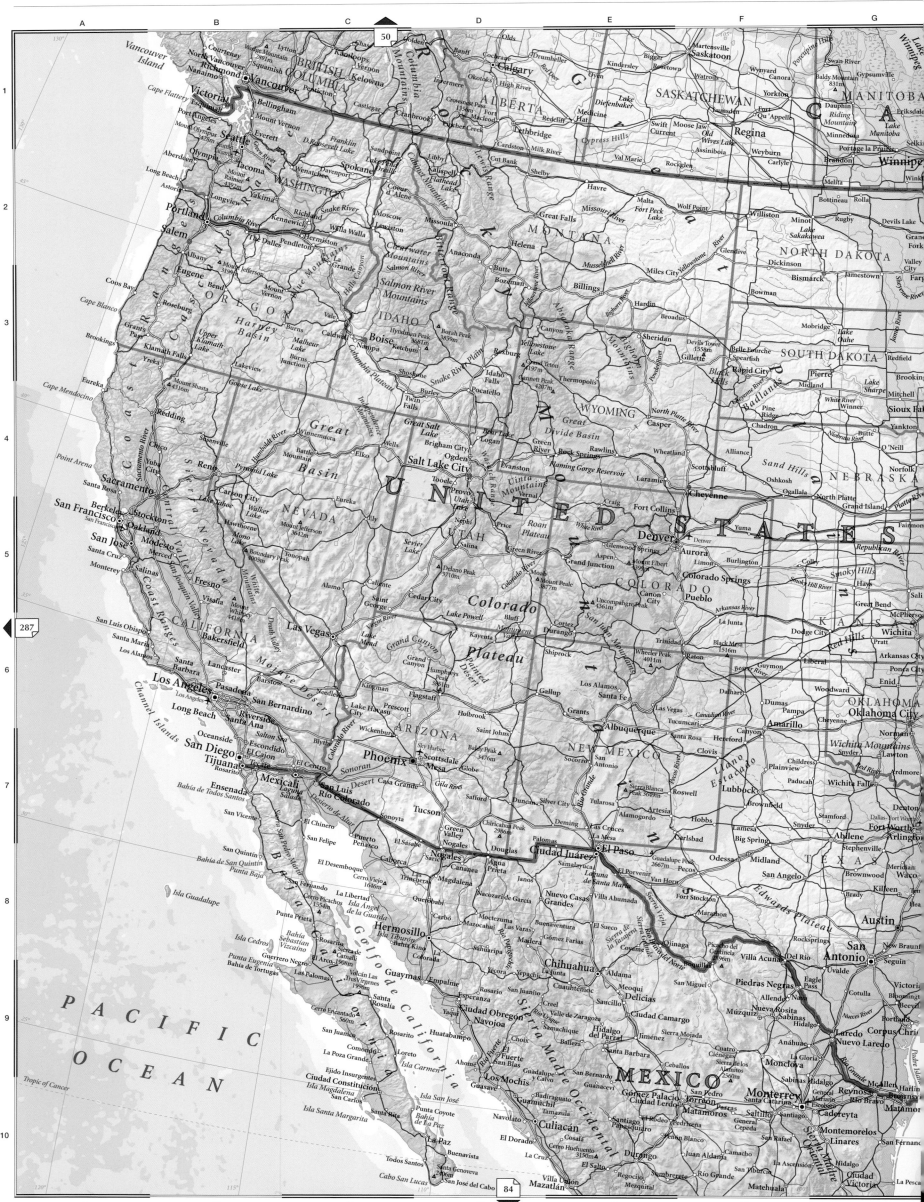

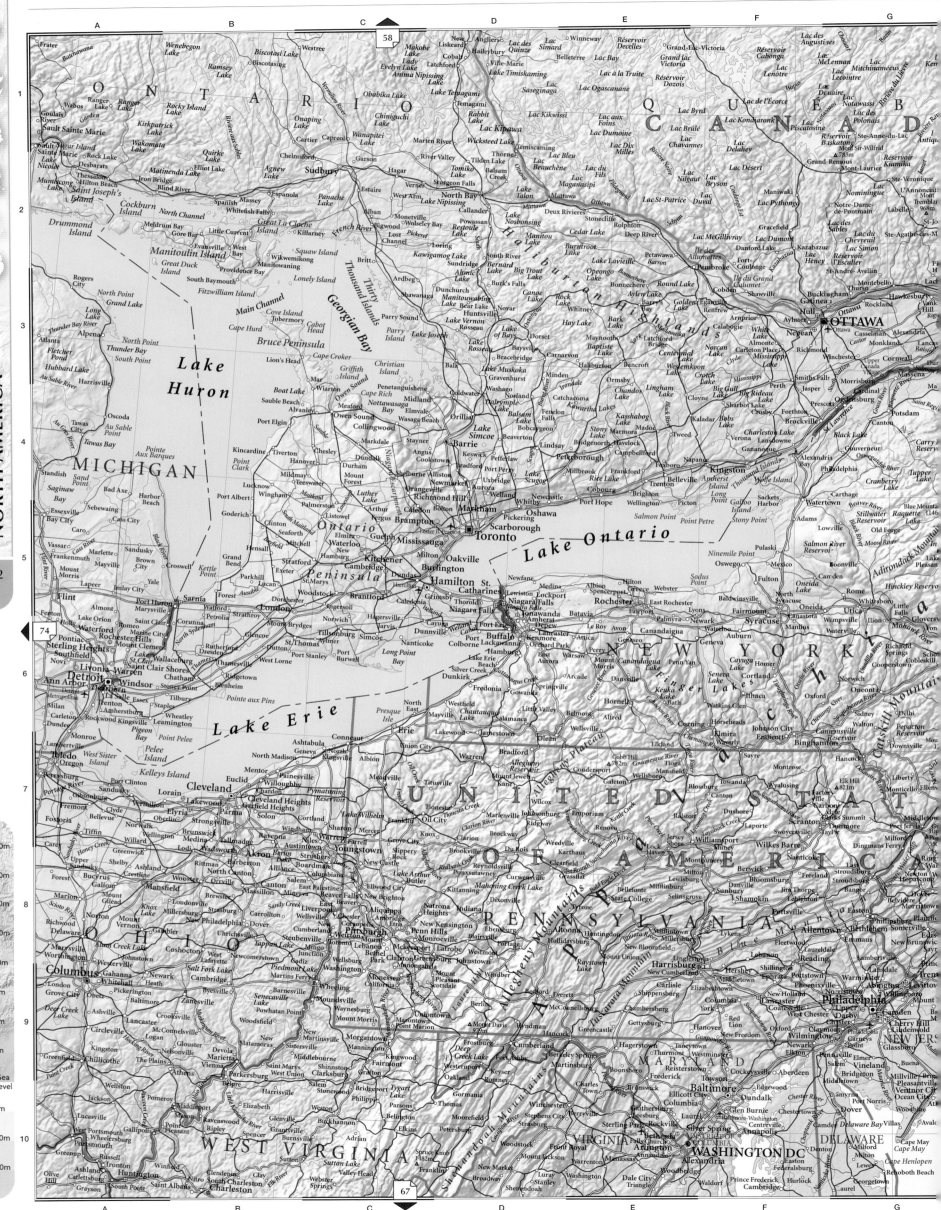

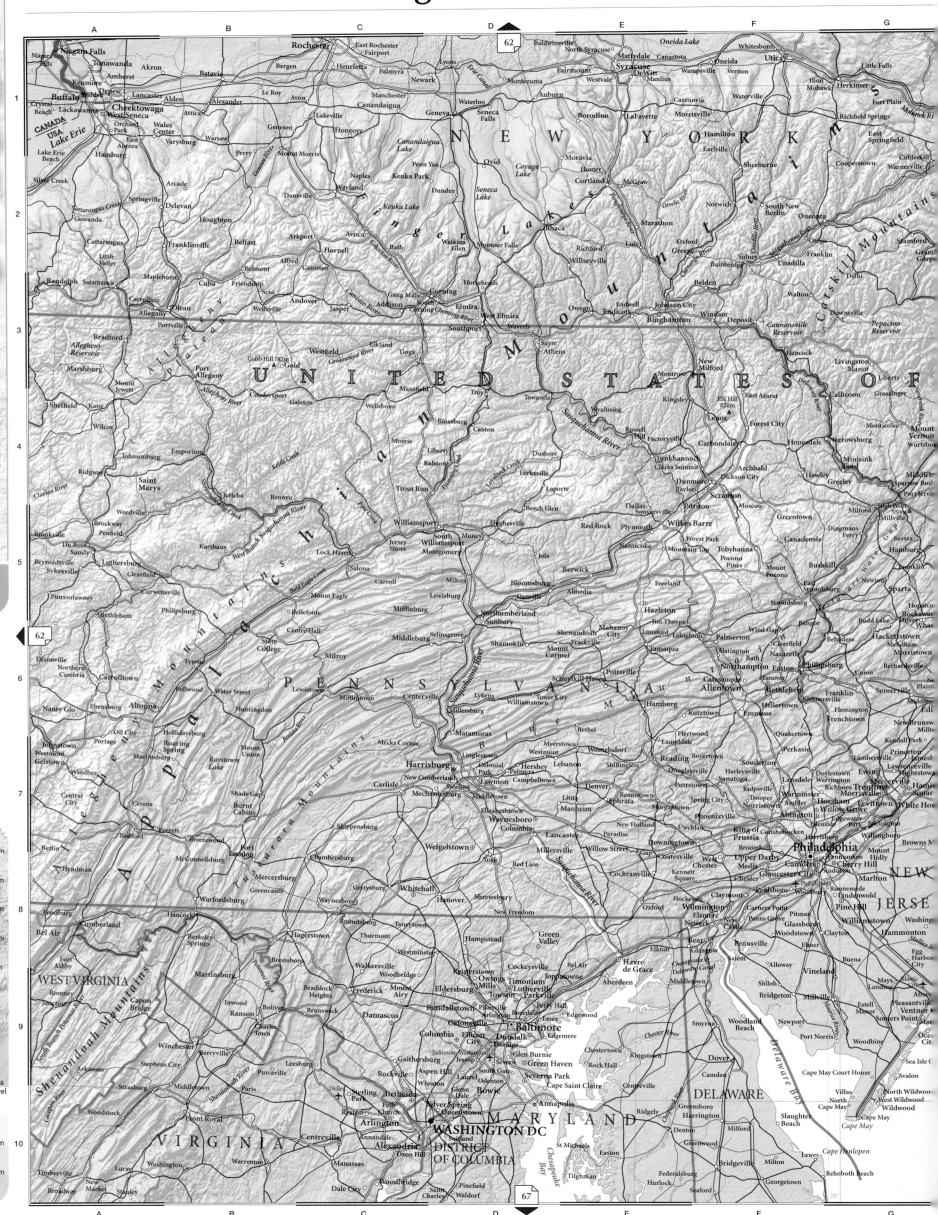

Scale 1:3,000,000
(projection: Lambert Conformal Conic)

0 20 40 60 80 100 Km
0 20 40 60 80 100 Miles

Population
- ■ above 5 million
- ◙ 1 million to 5 million
- ◉ 500,000 to 1 million
- ◎ 100,000 to 500,000
- ⊕ 50,000 to 100,000
- ○ 10,000 to 50,000
- ∘ below 10,000

PENNSYLVANIA

WEST VIRGINIA

VIRGINIA

MARYLAND

DELAWARE

NEW JERSEY

WASHINGTON DC

DISTRICT OF COLUMBIA

NORTH CAROLINA

SOUTH CAROLINA

UNITED STATES OF AMERICA

Pittsburgh
Harrisburg
Philadelphia
Baltimore
Washington DC
Richmond
Norfolk
Virginia Beach
Charlotte
Raleigh
Greensboro
Winston Salem
Durham
Columbia
Charleston
Savannah

ATLANTIC OCEAN

Chesapeake Bay
Albemarle Sound
Pamlico Sound
Cape Hatteras
Cape Lookout
Cape Fear
Onslow Bay
Raleigh Bay
Long Bay
Delaware Bay
Cape May

BERMUDA (to UK)
HAMILTON
St George's Island
St Catherine Point
St George
St David's Island
Tucker's Town
Flatts Village
Somerset Island
Ireland Island North
Ireland Island South
Great Sound
Little Sound
Spanish Point
Harrington Sound
Commissioner's Point
Kindley Field
Castle Harbour
Gibbs Hill 73m

Scale 1:500,000
0 2.5 5 Km
0 2.5 5 Miles

ATLANTIC OCEAN

19,686ft
13,124ft
9843ft
6562ft
3281ft
1640ft
820ft
328ft
Sea Level
-820ft
-6562ft
-13,124ft

New Orleans

0 5 Km
0 5 Miles

6000m
4000m
3000m
2000m
1000m
500m
250m
100m
Sea Level
-250m
-2000m
-4000m

Scale 1:3,000,000
(projection: Lambert Conformal Conic)

0 20 40 60 80 100 Km
0 20 40 60 80 100 Miles

Population
■ above 5 million
▣ 1 million to 5 million
◉ 500,000 to 1 million
◎ 100,000 to 500,000
⊕ 50,000 to 100,000
○ 10,000 to 50,000
○ below 10,000

ATLANTIC OCEAN

ALABAMA

GEORGIA

S OF AMERICA

FLORIDA

Montgomery

Columbus

Macon

Tallahassee

Jacksonville

Gainesville

Orlando

Tampa

Saint Petersburg

Lakeland

Lake Okeechobee

Big Cypress Swamp

The Everglades

Ten Thousand Islands

Cape Sable

Florida Bay

Key Largo

Florida Keys

Straits of Florida

Dry Tortugas

Marquesas Keys

Key West

Miami

Miramar
Hallandale
Carol City
Norland
North Miami Beach
Golden Glades
Westview
Hialeah
West Little River
Miami Shores
Hialeah Park
Gladeview
North Bay Village
Virginia Gardens
Miami International Airport
Brownsville
West Miami
Miami Beach
Streetwater
Florida Intl. University
Westchester
Miami
Virginia Key
Miami Seaquarium
Olympia Heights
Coral Gables
Key Biscayne
Westwood Lake
Kendall
Cape Florida
Weeks Air Museum
Pinecrest
Richmond Heights
South Miami Heights
Perrine
Goulds
Cutler Ridge
Redland
South Allapattah
Naranja
Leisure City
Homestead
Florida City

Atlantic Ocean

Biscayne Bay

Sands Key

Elliot Key

0 5 Km
0 5 Miles

NORTH AMERICA

69

19,686ft
13,124ft
9843ft
6562ft
3281ft
1640ft
820ft
328ft
Sea Level
-820ft
-6562ft
-13,124ft

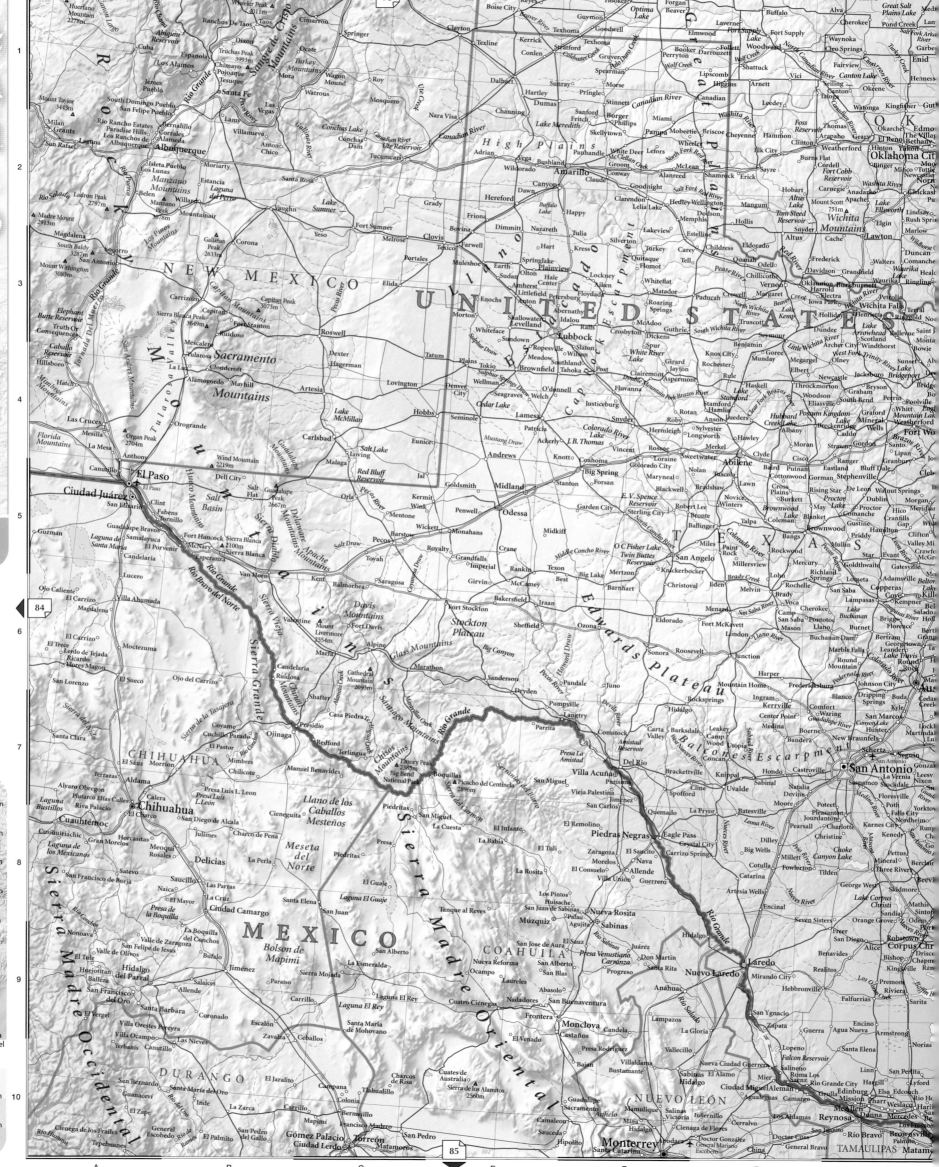

Scale 1:3,750,000
(projection: Lambert Conformal Conic)

0 20 40 60 80 100 Km
0 20 40 60 80 100 Miles

Population
■ above 5 million
◨ 1 million to 5 million
◉ 500,000 to 1 million
⊚ 100,000 to 500,000
⊕ 50,000 to 100,000
○ 10,000 to 50,000
· below 10,000

Houston

Gulf of Mexico

19,686ft
13,124ft
9843ft
6562ft
3281ft
1640ft
820ft
328ft
Sea Level
-820ft
-6562ft
-13,124ft

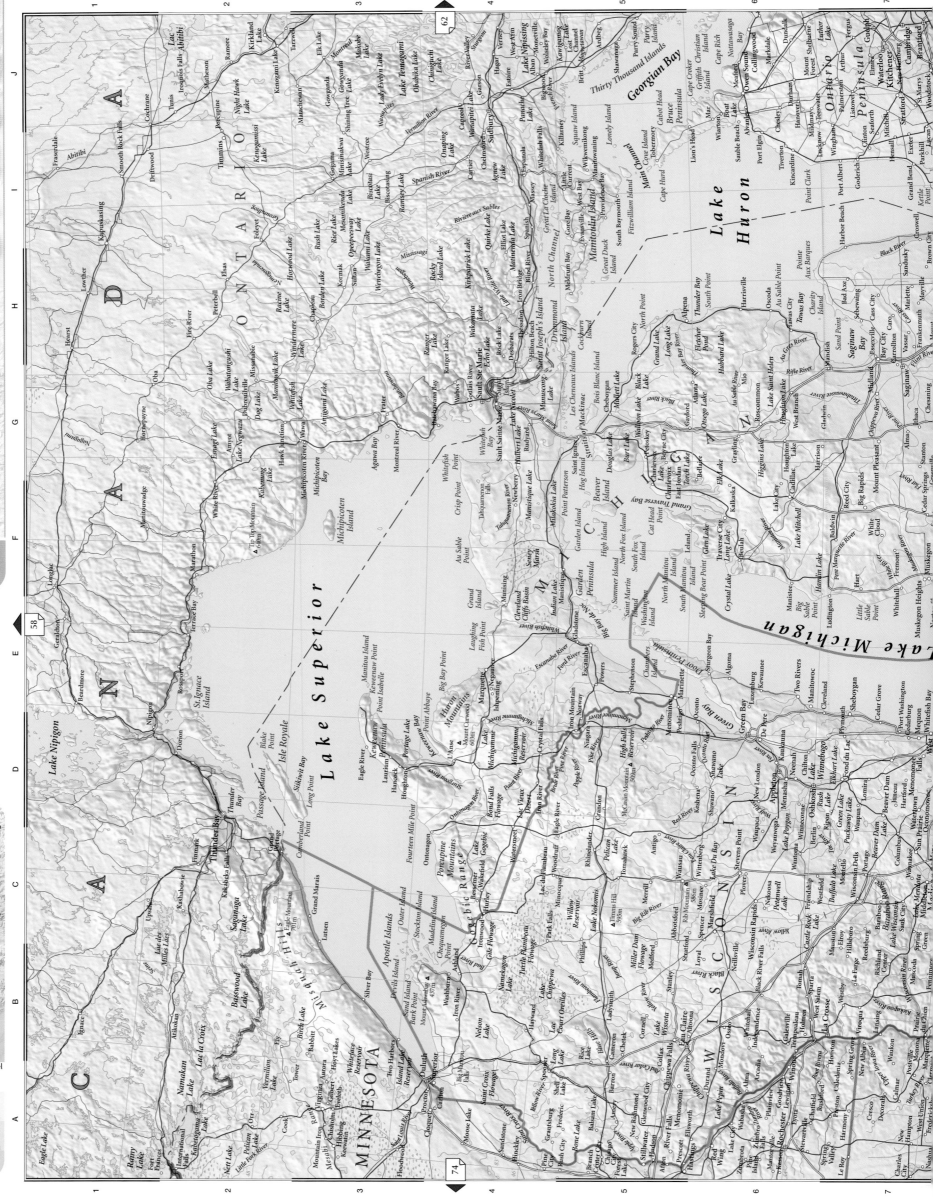

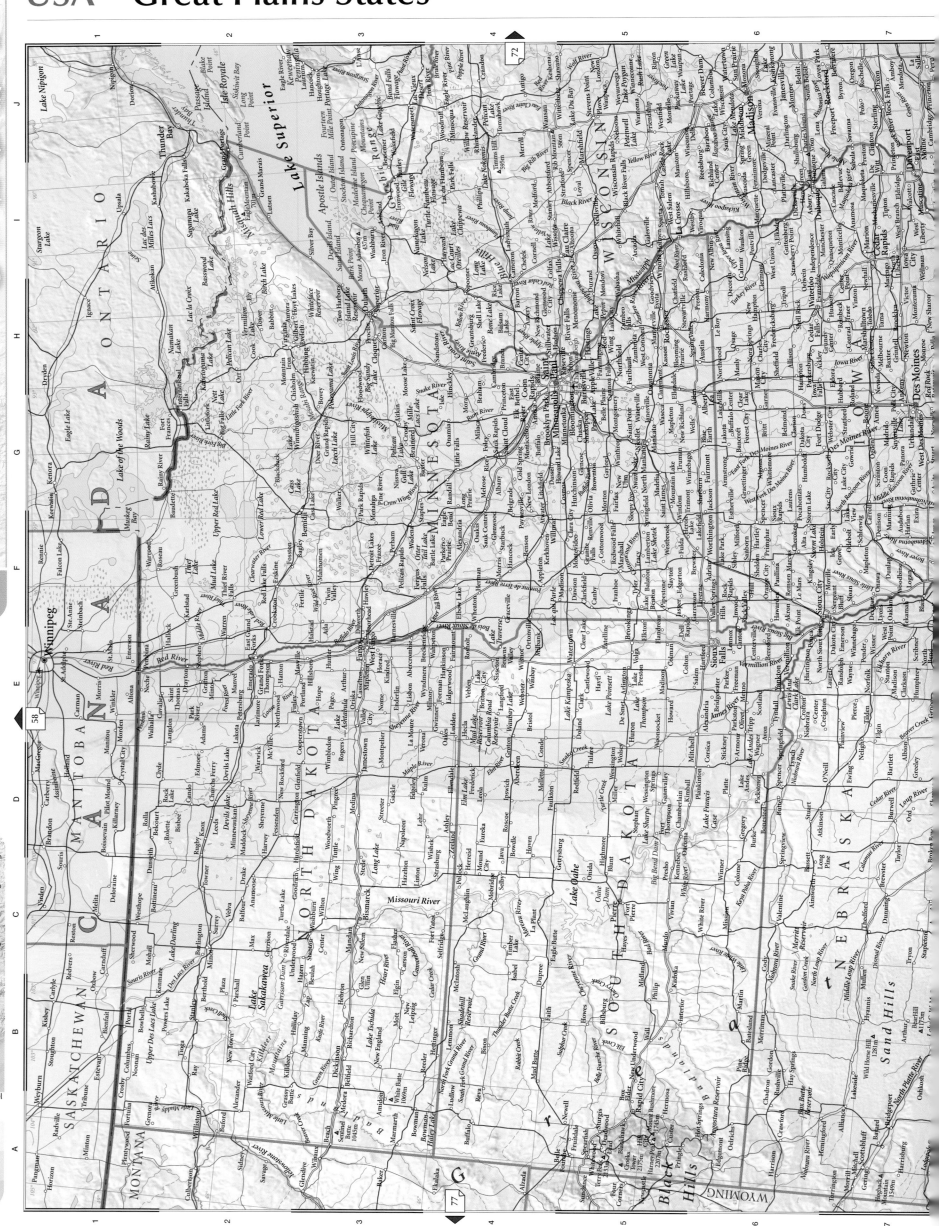

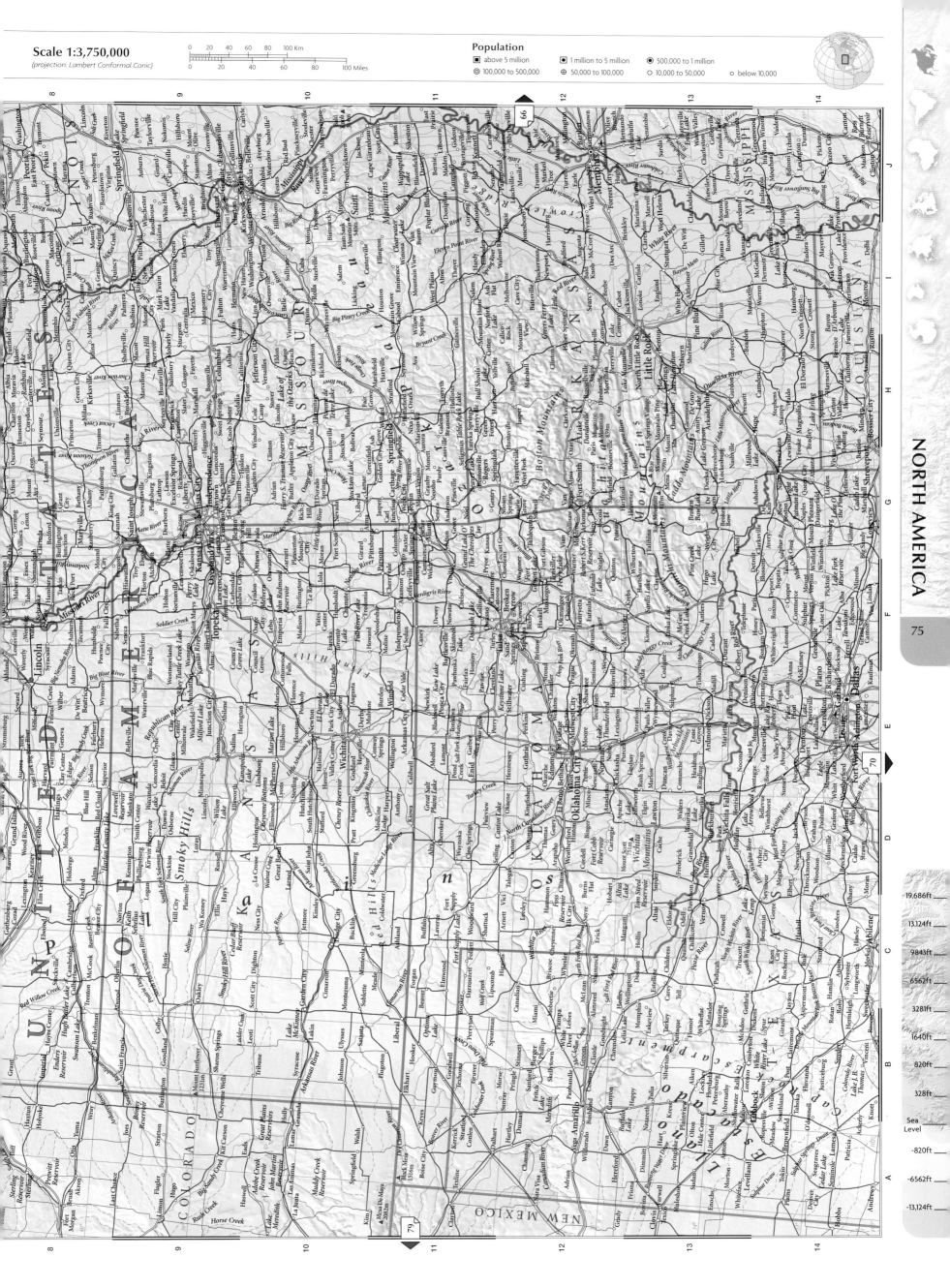

56

287

Scale 1:3,750,000
(projection: Lambert Conformal Conic)

0 20 40 60 80 100 Km
0 20 40 60 80 100 Miles

Population
- ■ above 5 million
- ■ 1 million to 5 million
- ◉ 500,000 to 1 million
- ◎ 100,000 to 500,000
- ⊕ 50,000 to 100,000
- ○ 10,000 to 50,000
- ○ below 10,000

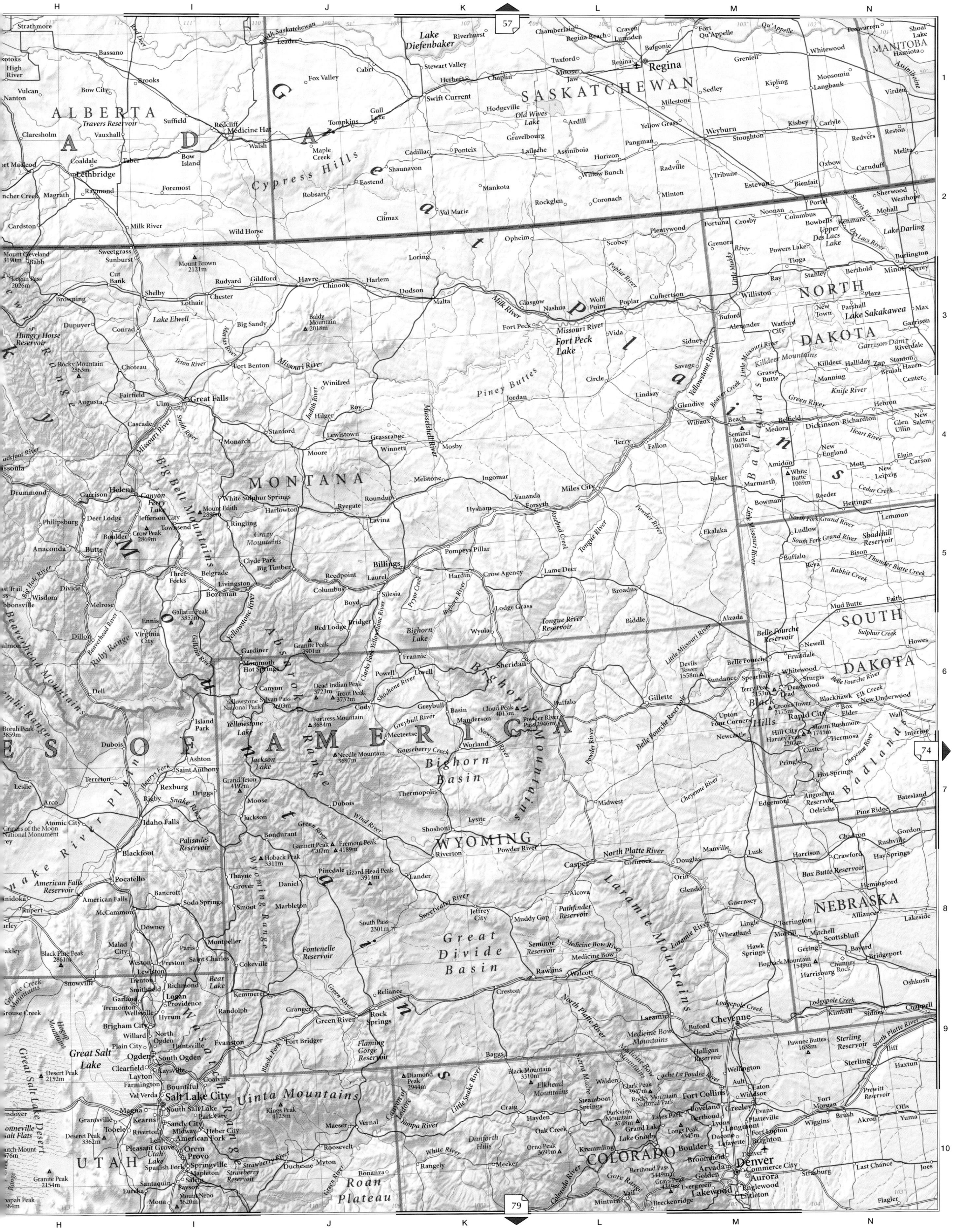

Elevation scale (right margin):
19,686ft
13,124ft
9843ft
6562ft
3281ft
1640ft
820ft
328ft
Sea Level
-820ft
-6562ft
-13,124ft

Grid references: H I J K L M N across top and bottom; 1–10 down sides.

Page/panel markers: 57 (top), 79 (bottom), 74 (right), 77 (right tab)

Major regions and provinces/states
- ALBERTA
- SASKATCHEWAN
- MANITOBA
- MONTANA
- NORTH DAKOTA
- SOUTH DAKOTA
- WYOMING
- NEBRASKA
- IDAHO
- UTAH
- COLORADO
- CANADA
- UNITED STATES OF AMERICA
- Great Plains
- Cypress Hills
- Bighorn Basin
- Great Divide Basin
- Black Hills
- Badlands
- Uinta Mountains
- Wyoming Range
- Wasatch Range
- Laramie Mountains
- Medicine Bow Mountains
- Bighorn Mountains
- Absaroka Range
- Big Belt Mountains
- Ruby Range
- Beaverhead Mountains
- Lemhi Range
- Snake River Plain
- Roan Plateau

Selected cities and towns
Regina, Moose Jaw, Swift Current, Medicine Hat, Lethbridge, Weyburn, Estevan, Williston, Minot, Dickinson, Great Falls, Havre, Helena, Butte, Bozeman, Billings, Miles City, Glendive, Sidney, Bismarck area towns, Rapid City, Sturgis, Deadwood, Gillette, Sheridan, Buffalo, Casper, Douglas, Cheyenne, Laramie, Rawlins, Rock Springs, Green River, Evanston, Idaho Falls, Pocatello, Blackfoot, Salt Lake City, South Salt Lake, Ogden, Provo, Orem, Denver, Aurora, Lakewood, Boulder, Fort Collins, Greeley, Longmont, Loveland, Scottsbluff, Alliance, Chadron

Physical features (selected peaks and waters)
- Missouri River
- Yellowstone River
- Milk River
- Musselshell River
- Bighorn River
- Tongue River
- Powder River
- North Platte River
- Green River
- Snake River
- Wind River
- Sweetwater River
- Cheyenne River
- Little Missouri River
- Fort Peck Lake
- Lake Sakakawea
- Bighorn Lake
- Yellowstone Lake
- Jackson Lake
- Flaming Gorge Reservoir
- Pathfinder Reservoir
- Seminoe Reservoir
- Bear Lake
- Great Salt Lake
- Great Salt Lake Desert
- Lake Diefenbaker
- Gannett Peak 4207m
- Fremont Peak 4189m
- Grand Teton 4197m
- Cloud Peak 4013m
- Kings Peak 4123m
- Borah Peak 3859m
- Gallatin Peak 3857m
- Lizard Head Peak 3914m
- Francs Peak area
- Granite Peak 3901m
- Longs Peak 4345m
- Hoback Peak 3311m
- Hoback Peak 3311m
- Mount Cleveland 3190m
- Logan Pass 2026m
- South Pass 2301m
- Yellowstone National Park

Scale 1:3,750,000
(projection: Lambert Conformal Conic)

0 20 40 60 80 100 Km
0 20 40 60 80 100 Miles

Population
- ■ above 5 million
- ■ 1 million to 5 million
- ◉ 500,000 to 1 million
- ◎ 100,000 to 500,000
- ⊕ 50,000 to 100,000
- ○ 10,000 to 50,000
- ∘ below 10,000

WYOMING

UTAH

COLORADO

NEBRASKA

ARIZONA

NEW MEXICO

TEXAS

SONORA

CHIHUAHUA

Great Salt Lake

Great Divide Basin

Rocky Mountains

Wasatch Range

Uinta Mountains

Roan Plateau

Roan Cliffs

Book Cliffs

Sangre de Cristo Mountains

San Juan Mountains

Colorado Plateau

Grand Canyon

Coconino Plateau

Kaibab Plateau

Kaibito Plateau

Painted Desert

Mogollon Rim

Sacramento Mountains

Tularosa Valley

Plains of San Agustin

Salt Lake City
South Salt Lake
Sandy City
West Valley City
Ogden
Provo
Orem
Denver
Aurora
Lakewood
Arvada
Wheat Ridge
Englewood
Littleton
Boulder
Longmont
Loveland
Fort Collins
Greeley
Colorado Springs
Pueblo
Phoenix
Mesa
Tempe
Scottsdale
Glendale
Tucson
Albuquerque
Rio Rancho Estates
Santa Fe
Los Alamos
El Paso
Ciudad Juárez
Cheyenne
Laramie
Rock Springs
Green River
Evanston
Grand Junction
Durango
Cortez
Farmington
Gallup
Flagstaff
Sedona
Prescott
Casa Grande
Nogales
Las Cruces
Roswell
Carlsbad
Hobbs

Kings Peak 4123m
Humphreys Peak 3851m
Blanca Peak 4372m
Pikes Peak 4300m
Mount Elbert 4399m
Mount Massive 4395m
Mount Harvard 4395m
Mount Wilson 4342m
Wheeler Peak 4011m
Baldy Peak 3476m

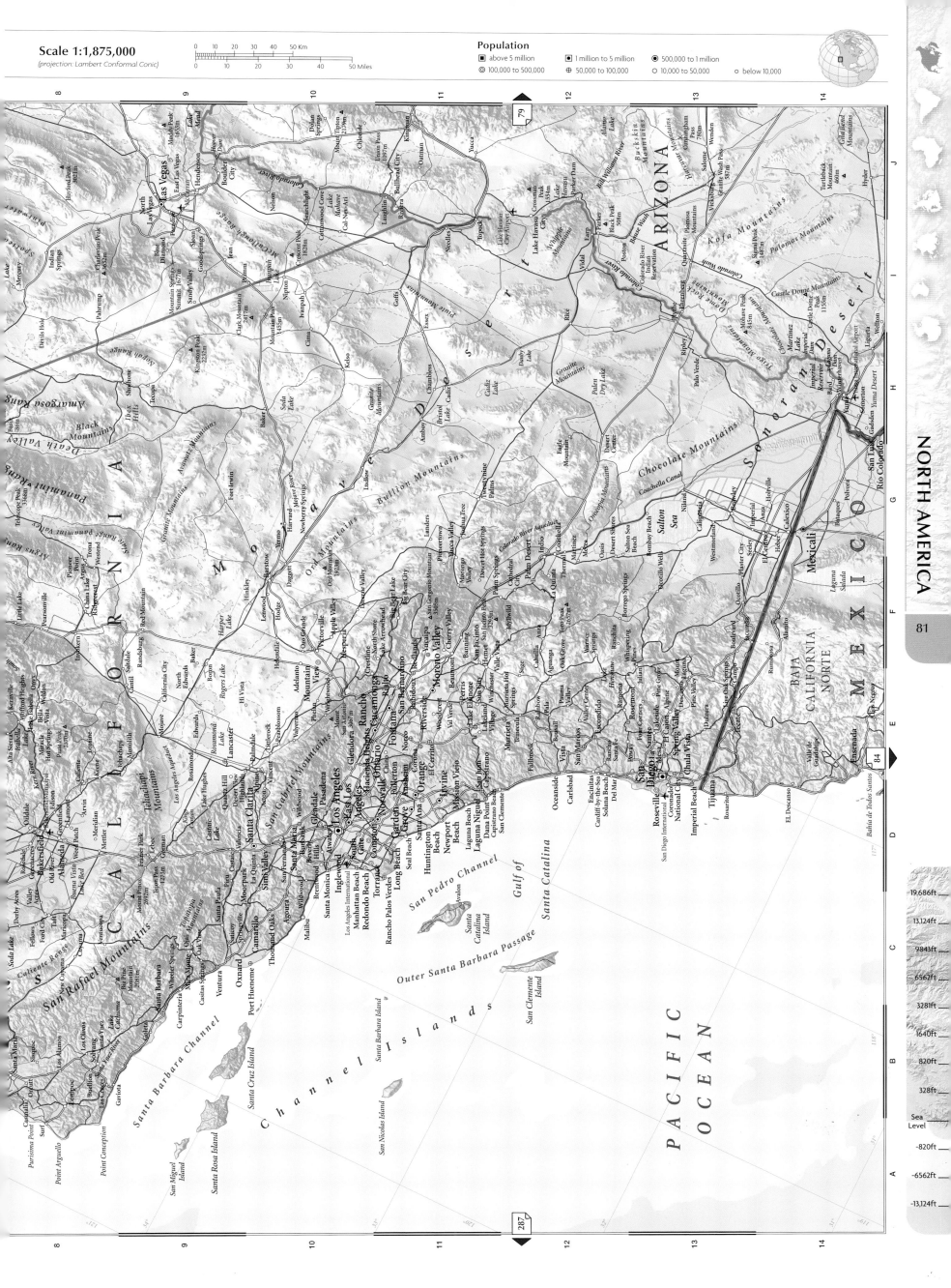

Scale 1:8,000,000
(projection: Lambert Conformal Conic)

0 25 50 75 100 125 150 175 200 Km
0 25 50 75 100 125 150 175 200 Miles

Population
■ above 5 million　■ 1 million to 5 million　◉ 500,000 to 1 million
◎ 100,000 to 500,000　⊕ 50,000 to 100,000　⊙ 10,000 to 50,000　∘ below 10,000

NORTH AMERICA

83

Scale 1:4,250,000
(projection: Lambert Conformal Conic)

0 20 40 60 80 100 Km
0 20 40 60 80 100 Miles

Population
■ above 5 million
■ 1 million to 5 million
◉ 500,000 to 1 million
◎ 100,000 to 500,000
⊕ 50,000 to 100,000
○ 10,000 to 50,000
∘ below 10,000

UNITED STATES OF AMERICA

NEW MEXICO

T E X A S

Edwards Plateau

Stockton Plateau

Davis Mountains

El Paso
Ciudad Juárez

Chihuahua

C H I H U A H U A

Meseta del Norte

C O A H U I L A

Monterrey

N U E V O L E Ó N

M E X I C O

D U R A N G O

Z A C A T E C A S

T A M A U L I P A S

S A N L U I S P O T O S Í

Durango

Mazatlán

N A Y A R I T

A G U A S C A L I E N T E S

J A L I S C O

G U A N A J U A T O

Q U E R É T A R O

H I D A L G O

V E R A C R U Z - L L A V E

San Luis Potosí

Guadalajara

León

Austin

San Antonio

Corpus Christi

Laredo
Nuevo Laredo

Reynosa
Matamoros

Brownsville

Tampico
Ciudad Madero

Saltillo

Torreón
Gómez Palacio

Gulf of Mexico

Tropic of Cancer

Padre Island

Laguna Madre

Sierra Madre Occidental

Sierra Madre Oriental

Ciudad Victoria

19,686ft
13,124ft
9843ft
6562ft
3281ft
1640ft
820ft
328ft
Sea Level
-820ft
-6562ft
-13,124ft

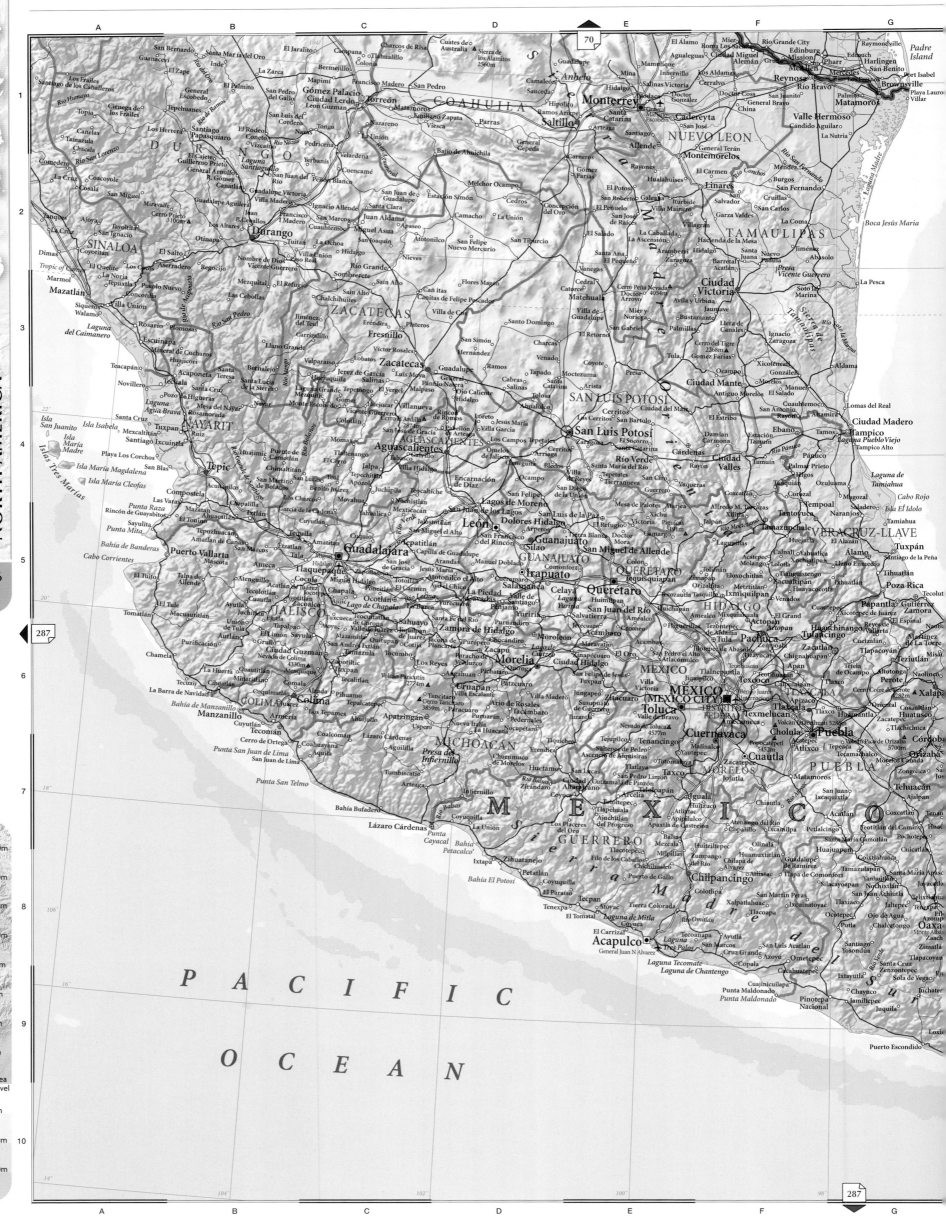

Central America

GUATEMALA:
ADMINISTRATIVE REGIONS:

① RETALHULEU   ⑨ GUATEMALA
② QUEZALTENANGO   ⑩ BAJA VERAPAZ
③ TOTONICAPÁN   ⑪ EL PROGRESO
④ SOLOLÁ   ⑫ ZACAPA
⑤ SUCHITEPÉQUEZ   ⑬ CHIQUIMULA
⑥ ESCUINTLA   ⑭ JALAPA
⑦ CHIMALTENANGO   ⑮ SANTA ROSA
⑧ SACATEPÉQUEZ   ⑯ JUTIAPA

EL SALVADOR:
ADMINISTRATIVE REGIONS:

① AHUACHAPÁN   ⑧ CABAÑAS
② SANTA ANA   ⑨ LA PAZ
③ SONSONATE   ⑩ SAN VICENTE
④ CHALATENANGO   ⑪ USULUTÁN
⑤ LA LIBERTAD   ⑫ SAN MIGUEL
⑥ SAN SALVADOR   ⑬ MORAZÁN
⑦ CUSCATLÁN   ⑭ LA UNIÓN

Guatemala City

The Caribbean

UNITED STATES OF AMERICA

Saint Petersburg
Bradenton
Sarasota
Wauchula
Venice
Port Charlotte
Fort Myers
Cape Coral
Bonita Springs
Naples

FLORIDA
Big Cypress Swamp
The Everglades
Everglades City
Cape Romano
Cape Sable
Florida Bay
Key Largo
Marathon
Florida Keys
Key West
Marquesas Keys
Dry Tortugas

Lake Wales
Avon Park
Okeechobee
Lake Okeechobee
Belle Glade
Immokalee
Punta Gorda
La Belle

Sebastian
Vero Beach
Fort Pierce
Jensen Beach
Stuart
Hobe Sound
Indiantown
West Palm Beach
Lake Worth
Boynton Beach
Boca Raton
Pompano Beach
Fort Lauderdale
Hollywood
North Miami
Miami Beach
Miami
Hialeah
Kendall
Homestead

Gulf of Mexico

Tropic of Cancer

Bimini Islands

Grand Bahama Island
West End
Freeport
Eight Mile Rock
Great Sale Cay
Little Abaco
Coopers Town
Pelican Point
Marsh Harbour
Great Abaco
Cherokee Sound
Moores Island

Northwest Providence Channel
Southwest Point

Berry Islands
Nicholls Town
Current
Eleuthera Island
Governor's Harbour
Northeast Providence Channel
Linden
Pindling
Adelaide
NASSAU
New Providence
Rock Sound

THE BAHAMAS

Andros Town
Behring Point
Andros Island
Bannerman Town
Arthur's Town
Cat Island
Cockburn Town
San Salvador
Columbus Point
Conception Island
George Town
Rum Cay
Santa Maria
Great Exuma Island
Little Exuma
Long Island
Deadman's Cay
Clarence Town
Samana Cay
Colonel Hill
Crooked Island
Northeast Point
Plana Cays
Mayaguana
The Carlton
Snug Corner
Acklins Island
Salina Point
Southeast Point
Caicos Passage

Cay Sal
Anguilla Cays
Kemp's Bay
Great Guana Cay
Great Exuma Cays
Exuma Sound
Tongue of the Ocean
Santaren Channel
Nicholas Channel
Archipiélago de Sabana
Old Bahama Channel
Crooked Island Passage
Ragged Island Range
Mayaguana Passage

Straits of Florida

La Habana (Havana)
Mariel
Guanabacoa
Artemisa
San Cristóbal
Guanajay
Güira de Melena
Güines
Cárdenas
Jovellanos
Matanzas
Archipiélago de los Colorados
Minas de Matahambre
Sierra de los Órganos
Consolación del Sur
Los Palacios
Pinar del Río
Golfo de Guanahacabibes
Cabo de San Antonio
Cabo Corrientes
Cayos de San Felipe
Nueva Gerona
Santa Fé
Isla de la Juventud
Archipiélago de los Canarreos
Cayo Largo

Pasajeros
Santo Domingo
Cruces
Placetas
Santa Clara
Caibarién
Cayo de Buena Vista
Sagua la Grande
Cayo Fragoso
Cayo Coco
Morón
Esmeralda
Cayo Romano
Cayo Guajaba
Nuevitas
Puerto Padre
Gibara
Banes

Archipiélago de Camagüey

CUBA
Cienfuegos
Pico San Juan 1156m
Trinidad
Sancti Spíritus
Cabaiguán
Ciego de Ávila
Florida
Camagüey
Vertientes
Santa Cruz del Sur
Golfo de Ana María
Archipiélago de los Jardines de la Reina
Golfo de Guacanayabo
Campechuela
Manzanillo
Cabo Cruz
Pilón
Sierra Maestra
Pico Turquino 1944m
Bahía de Guantánamo (to US)
Las Tunas
Holguín
Cueto
Mayarí
Moa
Cauto
Jiguaní
Bayamo
Palma Soriano
La Maya
Santiago de Cuba
Guantánamo
Baracoa
Maisí
Punta de Quemado
Sierra del Cristal
Sagua de Tánamo
Cabo Lucrecia
Punta Guarico
Great Inagua
Matthew Town
Lake Rosa
Little Inagua
Northeast Point

Peninsula Aguada de Zapata

Golfo de Batabanó

G r e a t e r

CAYMAN ISLANDS (to UK)
Little Cayman
Cayman Brac
Owen Roberts
Bodden Town
GEORGE TOWN
Grand Cayman

Windward Passage
Port-de-Paix
Jean-Rabel
Môle-St-Nicolas
Gros-Morne
Gonaïves
St-Marc
Golfe de la Gonâve
Île de la Gonâve
HAITI
Jérémie
Corail
Miragoâne
Léogâne
Cap Dame Marie
Dame-Marie
Chardonnières
Port Salut
Cayes
Pointe à Gravois
Île à Vache
Massif de la Hotte
Canal de la Gonâve
Canal de St-Marc

JAMAICA
Montego Bay
Sangster
Port Maria
Port Antonio
Christiana
Spanish Town
Mandeville
Blue Mountain Peak 2256m
Savanna-La-Mar
May Pen
KINGSTON
Port Royal
Norman Manley
Morant Bay
Black River
South Negril Point
Portland Point
Jamaica Channel

A n

ISLAS DE LA BAHÍA
Roatán
Isla de Guanaja
Isla de Roatán
Punta Caxinas

HONDURAS
Trujillo
Limón
Iriona
Balfate
Río Aguán
COLÓN
Savá
Brus Laguna
Río Patuca
Laguna de Caratasca
GRACIAS A DIOS
Puerto Lempira
San Esteban
Gualaco
Sico
Dulce Nombre de Culmí
Catacamas
Juticalpa
OLANCHO
Río Coco
Cabo de Gracias a Dios
Arrecifes de la Media Luna
Arrecife Edinburgh
Boom
Bocay
Waspam
Ulmukhuás
Jalapa
Wina
Siuna
Bonanza
La Rosita
Sadiuna
Cerro Chachagón 1690m
REGIÓN AUTÓNOMA ATLÁNTICO NORTE
Cayos Miskitos
Río Prinzapolka
Río Coco
Yablis
Dakura
Tuapí
Cayos Londres
Wounta
Laguna Bismuna
Puerto Cabezas
JINOTEGA
Jinotega
Río Tuma
Matagalpa
MATAGALPA
Muy Muy
Río Grande de Matagalpa
La Sirena
Prinzapolka
Barra de Río Grande
Isla Santa Catalina
Isla de Providencia

NICARAGUA
BOACO
Boaco
CHONTALES
Juigalpa
Muelle de los Bueyes
El Rama
Río Escondido
REGIÓN AUTÓNOMA ATLÁNTICO SUR
Kara
Barra de Río Grande
Cayos King
Bluefields
Lago de Nicaragua
Santo Tomás
Río San Juan
Morrito
RÍO SAN JUAN
Volcán Concepción
Isla de Ometepe
Monkey Point
Punta Gorda
Rivas
Cayos de Perlas
Isla de San Andrés
San Andrés y Providencia (to Colombia)
Islas del Maíz
Cayos de Albuquerque
Cayos del Este Sudeste

Caribbean Sea

San Juan del Sur
San Miguelito
San Carlos
La Cruz
Upala
Volcán Miravalles 2028m
El Castillo de la Concepción
San Juan del Norte
Barra del Colorado
Liberia
Cañas
Río San Juan

GUANACASTE
Santa Cruz
Volcán Arenal 1610m
Quesada
Puerto Viejo
Limón
LIMÓN
ALAJUELA
HEREDIA
Alajuela
Heredia
COSTA RICA
Puntarenas
PUNTARENAS
Volcán Irazú 3432m
Volcán Turrialba 3329m
Cartago
Siquirres
Guápiles
SAN JOSÉ
Limón

COLOMBIA
Riohacha
Dibulla
Santa Marta
MAGDALENA
Ciénaga
Pueblo Viejo
Ernesto Cortissoz
Barranquilla
Soledad
Sabanalarga
ATLÁNTICO
Santa Catalina
Salamina
Cartagena
Turbaco
BOLÍVAR
Pivijay
Plato
Fundación
Sierra Nevada de Santa Marta
Pico Cristóbal Colón 5775m
Valledupar
Villanueva
San Juan del Cesar
LA GUAJIRA
CESAR

C a r i b b e a n   S e a

JAMAICA (inset)

Caribbean Sea
Montego Bay
Sangster
Falmouth
Discovery Bay
St Ann's Bay
Port Maria
Don Christophers Point
Jamaica Channel
North East Point
Lucea
Birchs Hill
Clark's Town
Browns Town
Ocho Rios
Annotto Bay
Buff Bay
Port Antonio
Dolphin Head 545m
Grange Hill
Negril
Little London
Savanna-La-Mar
The Cockpit Country
Cambridge
Alexandria
Clarendon
Ewarton
Highgate
Maggotty
Mount Denham 986m
Frankfield
Linstead
Bog Walk
Port Maria
Crab Pond Point
Black River
Christiana
Mandeville
Spanish Town
Blue Mountain Peak 2258m
Santa Cruz
Chapelton
May Pen
Old Harbour
Port Royal
KINGSTON
Golden Grove
Malvern 725m
Alligator Pond
Lionel Town
Portland Ridge
Bath
Yallahs Hill 730m
Port Morant
Morant Bay
Great Pedro Bluff
Long Bay
Wreck Point
Portland Point
Portland Bight

Caribbean Sea

Scale 1:2 500 000
0 5 10   20 Km
0 5 10   20 Miles

6000m
4000m
3000m
2000m
1000m
500m
250m
100m
Sea Level
-250m
-2000m
-4000m

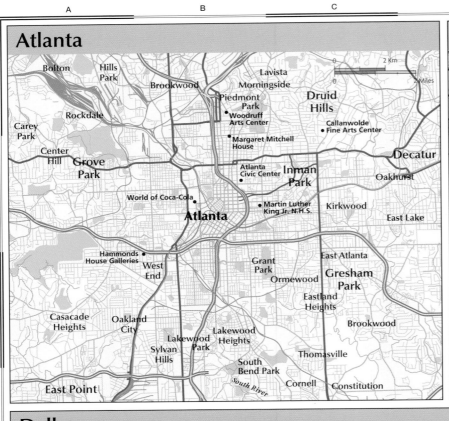

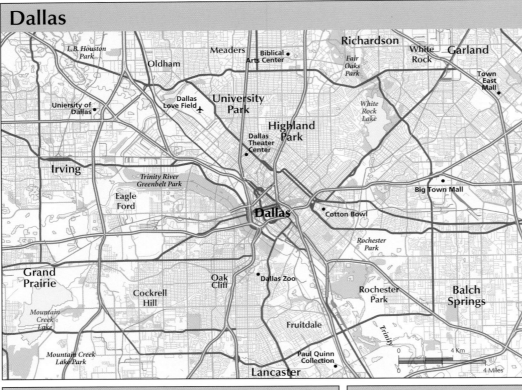

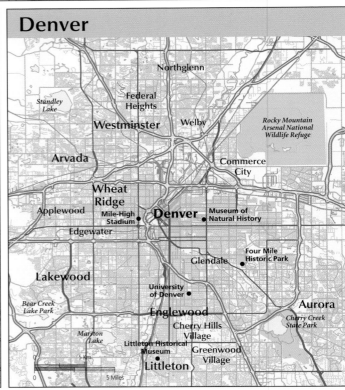

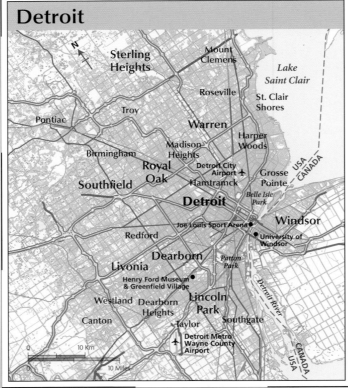

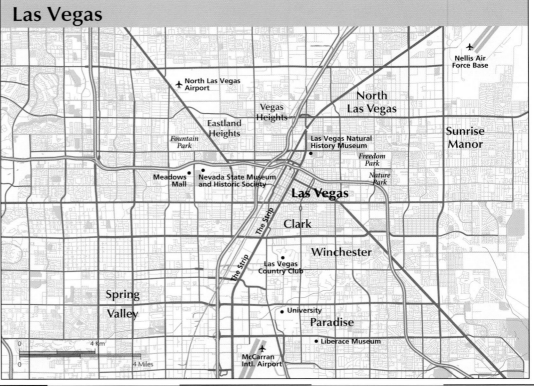

Los Angeles

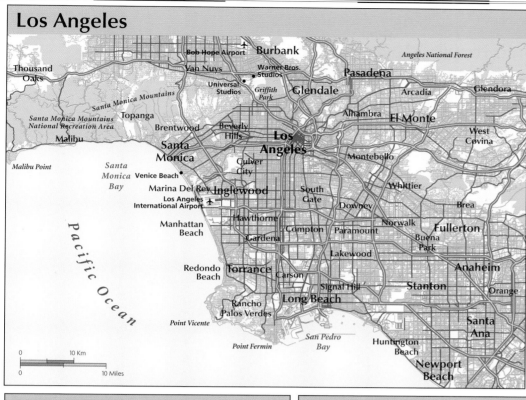

Thousand Oaks · Bob Hope Airport · Burbank · Warner Bros. Studios · Van Nuys · Angeles National Forest · Pasadena · Arcadia · Glendora · Santa Monica Mountains · Universal Studios · Griffith Park · Glendale · Alhambra · El Monte · West Covina · Topanga · Brentwood · Beverly Hills · Los Angeles · Montebello · Whittier · Brea · Santa Monica · Culver City · Downey · Norwalk · Fullerton · Venice Beach · Inglewood · South Gate · Compton · Paramount · Buena Park · Anaheim · Marina Del Rey · Los Angeles International Airport · Hawthorne · Gardena · Lakewood · Stanton · Santa Ana · Manhattan Beach · Torrance · Carson · Signal Hill · Long Beach · Orange · Redondo Beach · Rancho Palos Verdes · Huntington Beach · Newport Beach · Pacific Ocean · Santa Monica Bay · Malibu · Malibu Point · Santa Monica Mountains National Recreation Area · Point Vicente · Point Fermin · San Pedro Bay

0 10 Km
0 10 Miles

Montréal

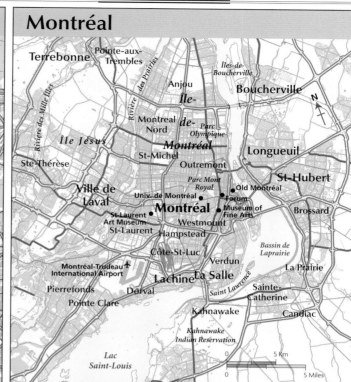

Terrebonne · Pointe-aux-Trembles · Îles-de-Boucherville · Anjou · Boucherville · Île-de-Montréal · Montréal Nord · Parc Olympique · Longueuil · St-Michel · Outremont · St-Hubert · Ste-Thérèse · Ville de Laval · Parc Mont Royal · Univ. de Montréal · Old Montréal · Brossard · St-Laurent Art Museum · Montréal · Forum · Museum of Fine Arts · St-Laurent · Westmount · Hampstead · Montréal-Trudeau International Airport · Côte-St-Luc · Verdun · Bassin de Laprairie · Pierrefonds · Dorval · Lachine · La Salle · La Prairie · Pointe Claire · Saint Lawrence · Sainte-Catherine · Kahnawake · Candiac · Kahnawake Indian Reservation · Lac Saint-Louis · Rivière des Mille Îles · Rivière des Prairies

0 5 Km
0 5 Miles

Philadelphia

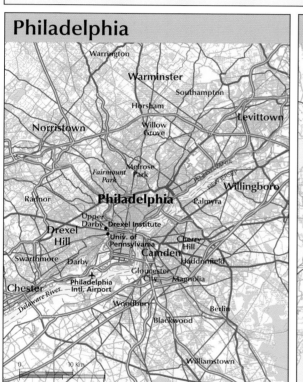

Warrington · Warminster · Southampton · Horsham · Levittown · Norristown · Willow Grove · Melrose Park · Fairmount Park · Willingboro · Radnor · Philadelphia · Palmyra · Upper Darby · Drexel Institute · Cherry Hill · Drexel Hill · Univ. of Pennsylvania · Camden · Haddonfield · Swarthmore · Darby · Gloucester City · Magnolia · Chester · Philadelphia Intl. Airport · Woodbury · Berlin · Delaware River · Blackwood · Williamstown

0 10 Km
0 10 Miles

Seattle

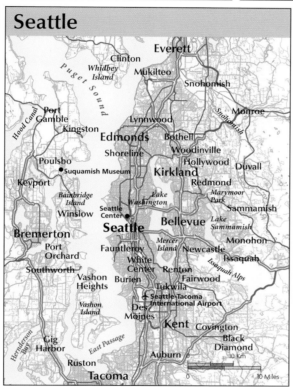

Clinton · Everett · Whidbey Island · Mukilteo · Snohomish · Port Gamble · Monroe · Hood Canal · Kingston · Lynnwood · Edmonds · Bothell · Woodinville · Duvall · Poulsbo · Shoreline · Hollywood · Suquamish Museum · Kirkland · Redmond · Keyport · Bainbridge Island · Lake Washington · Marymoor Park · Sammamish · Winslow · Seattle Center · Seattle · Bellevue · Lake Sammamish · Bremerton · Mercer Island · Monohon · Issaquah · Port Orchard · Fauntleroy · Newcastle · Fairwood · Southworth · White Center · Renton · Issaquah Alps · Burien · Tukwila · Vashon Heights · Seattle-Tacoma International Airport · Vashon Island · Des Moines · Kent · Covington · Black Diamond · Gig Harbor · East Passage · Ruston · Auburn · Tacoma · Puget Sound

0 10 Km
0 10 Miles

Toronto

Buttonville · Cherrywood · Pickering · Richmond Hill · Markham · Vaughan · Willowdale · Agincourt · Scarborough · Woodbridge · North York · Don Mills · Dentonia Park · Leaside · Ontario Science Centre · Downsview · York · East York · Rexdale · Weston · Toronto · Parliament · University of Toronto · CN Tower · Toronto City Airport · Brampton · Lester B. Pearson Intl. Airport · High Park · Humber Bay · Island Park · Islington · Mimico · Cooksville · Lake Ontario · Mississauga

0 6 Km
0 6 Miles

San Francisco

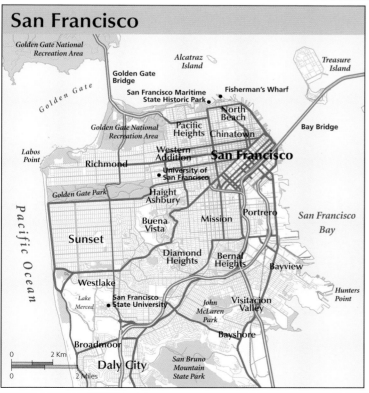

Golden Gate National Recreation Area · Alcatraz Island · Treasure Island · Golden Gate Bridge · San Francisco Maritime State Historic Park · Fisherman's Wharf · North Beach · Golden Gate · Golden Gate National Recreation Area · Pacific Heights · Chinatown · Bay Bridge · Labos Point · Western Addition · San Francisco · Richmond · University of San Francisco · Golden Gate Park · Haight Ashbury · Mission · Portrero · San Francisco Bay · Sunset · Buena Vista · Diamond Heights · Bernal Heights · Bayview · Westlake · Lake Merced · San Francisco State University · John McLaren Park · Visitacion Valley · Hunters Point · Pacific Ocean · Broadmoor · Bayshore · San Bruno Mountain State Park · Daly City

0 2 Km
0 2 Miles

Washington D.C.

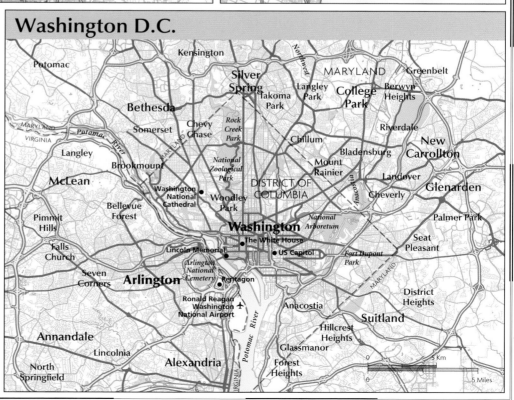

Kensington · Potomac · Silver Spring · MARYLAND · Greenbelt · Takoma Park · Langley Park · College Park · Berwyn Heights · Bethesda · Chevy Chase · Rock Creek Park · Chillum · Riverdale · MARYLAND · Somerset · Mount Rainier · New Carrollton · VIRGINIA · Potomac River · National Zoological Park · Bladensburg · Langley · Brookmount · DISTRICT OF COLUMBIA · Landover · McLean · Washington National Cathedral · Woodley Park · National Arboretum · Glenarden · Pimmit Hills · Bellevue Forest · Washington · Palmer Park · Falls Church · Lincoln Memorial · The White House · US Capitol · Fort Dupont Park · Seat Pleasant · Seven Corners · Arlington National Cemetery · Pentagon · Arlington · Ronald Reagan Washington National Airport · Anacostia · District Heights · Annandale · Lincolnia · Suitland · Hillcrest Heights · North Springfield · Alexandria · Glassmanor · Forest Heights · Potomac River

0 5 Km
0 5 Miles

SOUTH AMERICA

South America reaches from the humid tropics down into the cold South Atlantic, with a total area of 6,886,000 sq miles (17,835,000 sq km). It comprises 12 separate countries, with the largest, Brazil, covering almost half the continent.

FACTFILE

N **Most Northerly Point:** Punta Gallinas, Colombia 12° 28′ N
S **Most Southerly Point:** Cape Horn, Chile 55° 59′ S
E **Most Easterly Point:** Ilhas Martin Vaz, Brazil 28° 51′ W
W **Most Westerly Point:** Galapagos Islands, Ecuador 92° 00′ W

Largest Lakes:
1 Lake Titicaca, Bolivia/Peru 3141 sq miles (8135 sq km)
2 Mirim Lagoon, Brazil/Uruguay 1158 sq miles (3000 sq km)
3 Lago Poopó, Bolivia 976 sq miles (2530 sq km)
4 Lago Buenos Aires, Argentina/Chile 864 sq miles (2240 sq km)
5 Laguna Mar Chiquita, Argentina 695 sq miles (1800 sq km)

Longest Rivers:
1 Amazon, Brazil/Colombia/Peru 4049 miles (6516 km)
2 Paraná, Argentina/Brazil/Paraguay 2920 miles (4700 km)
3 Madeira, Bolivia/Brazil 2100 miles (3379 km)
4 Purus, Brazil/Peru 2013 miles (3239 km)
5 São Francisco, Brazil 1802 miles (2900 km)

Largest Islands:
1 Tierra del Fuego, Argentina/Chile 18,302 sq miles (47,401 sq km)
2 Ilha de Marajo, Brazil 15,483 sq miles (40,100 sq km)
3 Isla de Chiloé, Chile 3241 sq miles (8394 sq km)
4 East Falkland, Falkland Islands 2550 sq miles (6605 sq km)
5 Isla Wellington, Chile 2145 sq miles (5556 sq km)

Highest Points:
1 Cerro Aconcagua, Argentina 22,831 ft (6959 m)
2 Cerro Ojos del Salado, Argentina/Chile 22,572 ft (6880 m)
3 Cerro Bonete, Argentina 22,546 ft (6872 m)
4 Monte Pissis, Argentina 22,224 ft (6774 m)
5 Cerro Mercedario, Argentina 22,211 ft (6768 m)

Lowest Point:
▼ Laguna del Carbón, Argentina -344 ft (-105 m) below sea level

Highest recorded temperature:
✚ Rivadavia, Argentina 120°F (49°C)

Lowest recorded temperature:
⊖ Sarmiento, Argentina -27°F (-33°C)

Wettest Place:
≋ Quibdó, Colombia 354 in (8990 mm)

Driest Place:
⌒ Arica, Chile 0.03 in (0.8 mm)

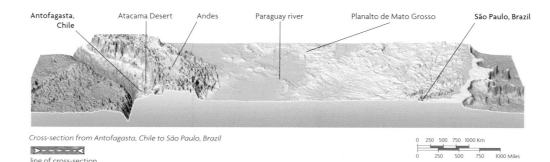

Cross-section from Antofagasta, Chile to São Paulo, Brazil

line of cross-section

0 250 500 750 1000 Km
0 250 500 750 1000 Miles

SOUTH AMERICA

95

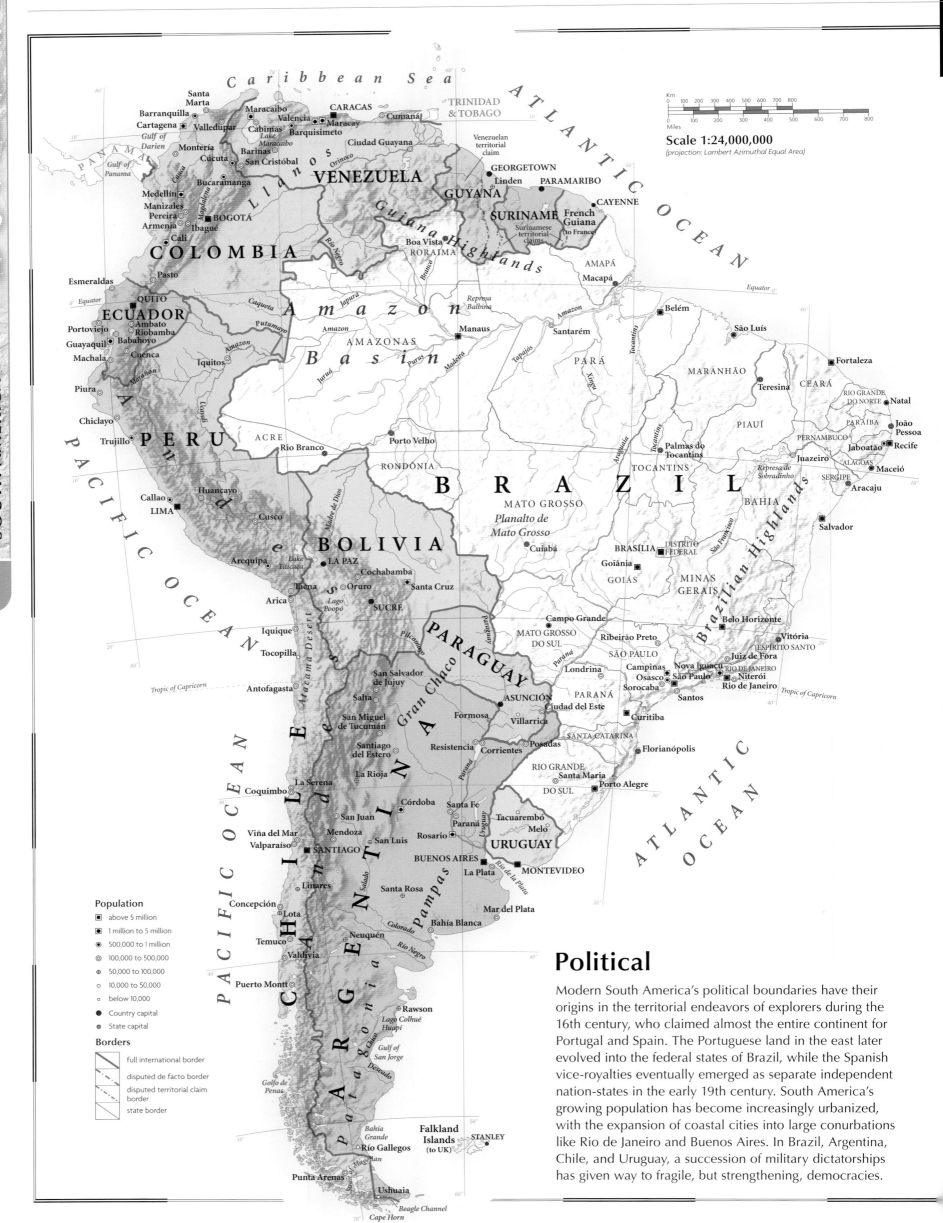

Scale 1:24,000,000
(projection: Lambert Azimuthal Equal Area)

Km 100 200 300 400 500 600 700 800

Miles 100 200 300 400 500 600 700 800

Population

- ◼ above 5 million
- ◾ 1 million to 5 million
- ◉ 500,000 to 1 million
- ◎ 100,000 to 500,000
- ⊕ 50,000 to 100,000
- ○ 10,000 to 50,000
- ∘ below 10,000
- ● Country capital
- ⊙ State capital

Borders

- full international border
- disputed de facto border
- disputed territorial claim border
- state border

Political

Modern South America's political boundaries have their origins in the territorial endeavors of explorers during the 16th century, who claimed almost the entire continent for Portugal and Spain. The Portuguese land in the east later evolved into the federal states of Brazil, while the Spanish vice-royalties eventually emerged as separate independent nation-states in the early 19th century. South America's growing population has become increasingly urbanized, with the expansion of coastal cities into large conurbations like Rio de Janeiro and Buenos Aires. In Brazil, Argentina, Chile, and Uruguay, a succession of military dictatorships has given way to fragile, but strengthening, democracies.

Languages

Prior to European exploration in the 16th century, a diverse range of indigenous languages were spoken across the continent. With the arrival of Iberian settlers, Spanish became the dominant language, with Portuguese spoken in Brazil, and Native American languages, such as Quechua and Guaraní, becoming concentrated in the continental interior. Today this pattern persists, although successive European colonization has led to Dutch being spoken in Suriname, English in Guyana, and French in French Guiana, while in large urban areas, Japanese and Chinese are increasingly common.

Language groups

American Indian
Germanic
Romance

Standard of living

Wealth disparities throughout the continent create a wide gulf between affluent landowners and those afflicted by chronic poverty in inner-city slums. The illicit production of cocaine, and the hugely influential drug barons who control its distribution, contribute to the violent disorder and corruption which affect northwestern South America, destabilizing local governments and economies.

Standard of living
(UN human development index)

low

high

Population

Almost half of South America's population lives in Brazil but, due to the large uninhabited expanses of the Amazon Basin, its overall population density is much lower than in other countries. During the 20th century the most important population trend was the movement from rural to urban areas, giving rise to great population concentrations in cities like São Paulo, Rio de Janeiro, Caracas, Lima, Bogotá, and Buenos Aires.

Population density
(people per sq mile)

below 10
11–23
24–36
37–49
50–75
above 75

Transportation

Most major road and rail routes are confined to the coastal regions by the forbidding natural barriers of the Andes mountains and the Amazon Basin. Few major cross-continental routes exist, although Buenos Aires serves as a transport center for the main rail links to La Paz and Valparaíso, while the construction of the Trans-Amazon and Pan-American Highways have made direct road travel possible from Recife to Lima and from Puerto Montt up the coast into central America. A new waterway project is proposed to transform the Paraguay river into a major shipping route, although it involves considerable wetland destruction.

Transportation

major roads and motorways
major railroads
international borders
transport intersections
international airports
major ports

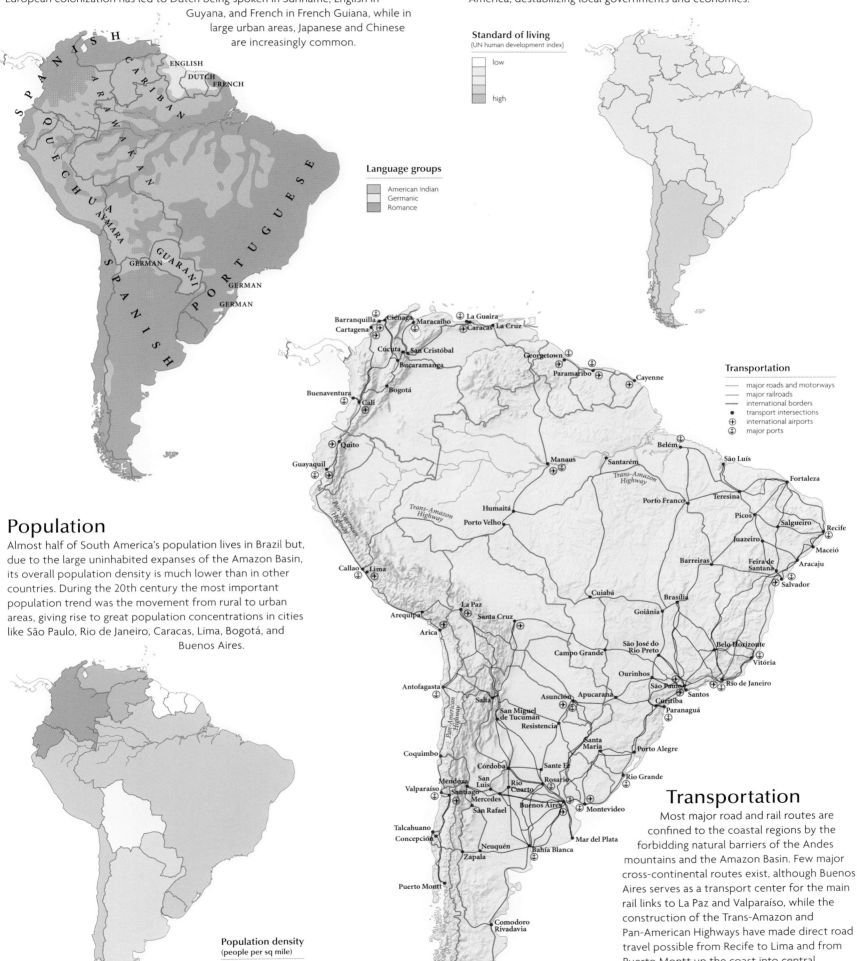

SOUTH AMERICA – Physical

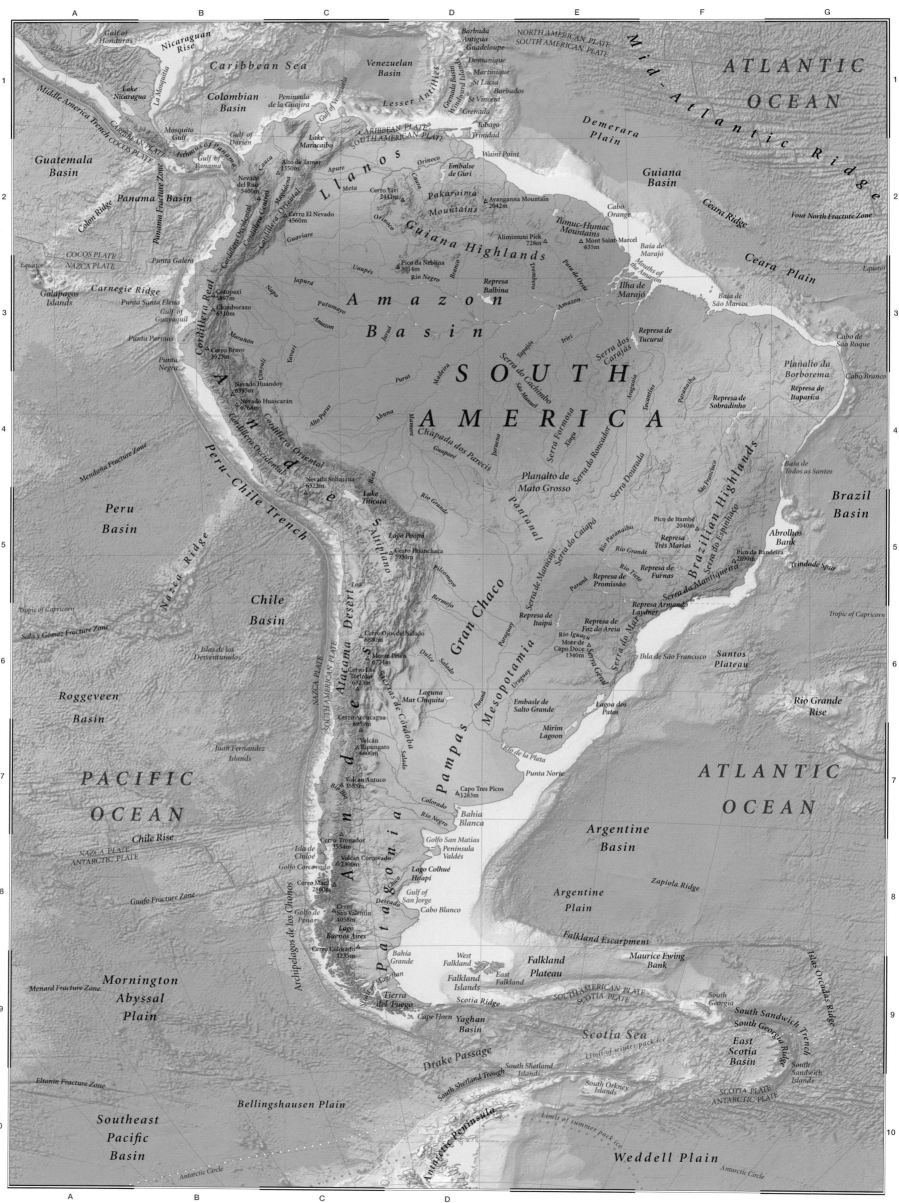

Scale 1:29,000,000

(projection: Lambert Azimuthal Equal Area)

Climate

The climate of South America is influenced by three principal factors:
the seasonal shift of high pressure air masses over the tropics, cold ocean currents
along the western coast, affecting temperature and precipitation, and the mountain
barrier produced by by the Andes, which creates a rain shadow over much of the south.

Average Rainfall

Equator
20°S
Tropic of
Capricorn
40°S

January rainfall

July rainfall

Rainfall

0–1 in (0–25 mm)
1–2 in (25–50 mm)
2–4 in (50–100 mm)
4–8 in (100–200 mm)
8–12 in (200–300 mm)
12–16 in (300–400 mm)
16–20 in (400–500 mm)
more than 20 in (500 mm)

Average Temperature

Equator
20°S
Tropic of
Capricorn
40°S

January temperature

July temperature

Temperature

below -22°F (-30°C)
-22 to -4°F (-30 to -20°C)
-4 to 14°F (-20 to -10°C)
14 to 32°F (-10 to 0°C)
32 to 50°F (0 to 10°C)
50 to 68°F (10 to 20°C)
68 to 86°F (20 to 30°C)
above 86°F (30°C)

Climate

tundra
cool continental
warm humid
semi-arid
arid
humid equatorial
tropical
daily hours of
sunshine, January
daily hours of
sunshine, July
cold wind

Land use

Many foods now common worldwide originated in South America.
These include the potato, tomato, squash, and cassava. Today, large
herds of beef cattle roam the temperate grasslands of the Pampas,
supporting an extensive meat-packing trade in Argentina, Uruguay and
Paraguay. Corn (maize) is grown as a staple crop across the continent
and coffee is grown as a cash crop in Brazil and
Colombia. Coca plants grown in Bolivia, Peru and
Colombia provide most of the western world's
cocaine. Fish and shellfish are caught off
the western coast, especially
anchovies off Peru, shrimps off
Ecuador and sardines
off Chile.

Environmental Issues

The Amazon Basin is one of the last great wilderness areas
left on Earth. The tropical rainforests which grow there are a
valuable genetic resource, containing innumerable unique
plants and animals. The forests are increasingly under threat
from new and expanding settlements and "slash and burn"
farming techniques, which clear land for the raising of beef
cattle, causing land degradation and soil erosion.

Environmental Issues

national parks
tropical forest
forest destroyed
desert
desertification
polluted rivers
marine pollution
heavy marine pollution
poor urban air quality

Using the Land and Sea

barren land
cropland
desert
forest
mountain region
pasture
major conurbations

cattle
pigs
sheep
bananas
corn (maize)
citrus fruits

cocoa
cotton
coffee
fishing
oil palms
peanuts
rubber
shellfish
soya beans
sugar cane
vineyards
wheat

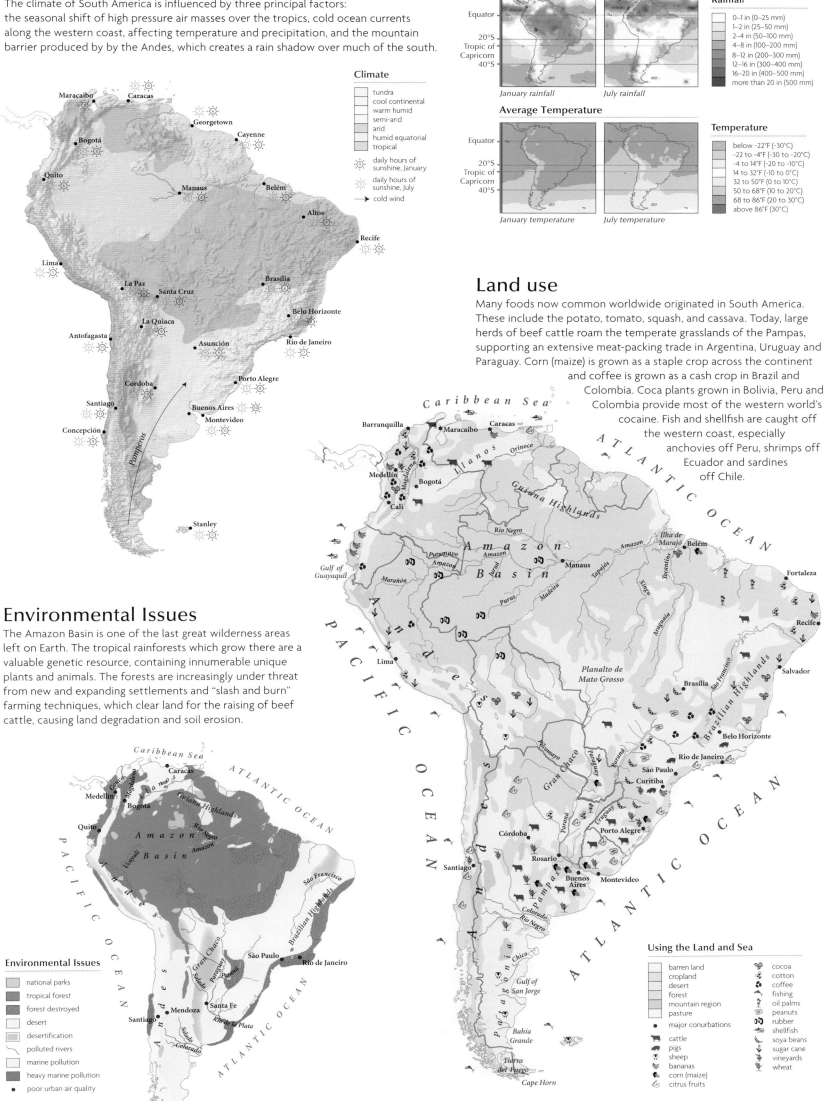

1 SANTIAGO, CHILE
Chile's capital city was founded in 1541 by Pedro de Valdivia who chose the location because it had a Mediterranean climate and was easy to defend.

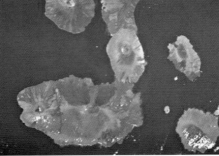

2 GALAPAGOS ISLANDS, ECUADOR
These islands are a collection of volcanoes rising from the ocean floor 621 miles (1000 km) west of the South American mainland.

3 SALAR DE UYUNI, BOLIVIA
Occupying a depression high up on the Altiplano between the volcanoes of the western Andes and the fold belts of the eastern Andes, this is the world's largest salt flat.

4 MACHU PICCHU, PERU
Perched precariously above the Urubamba valley, the lost Inca retreat was rediscovered in 1911 by Hiram Bingham, an American archaeologist.

9 LAGO VIEDMA, ARGENTINA
Lago Viedma enjoys a milky-blue appearance due to the glacial sediment suspended in its waters.

10 LOS LAGOS, CHILE
A region of many lakes at the foothills of the Andes in south-central Chile, this area is an attraction for many tourists.

11 ROSARIO, ARGENTINA
Located on the west bank of the Paraná river, Rosario lies at that heart of Argentina's industrial corridor, centered on the river.

12 RIVER PLATE, ARGENTINA/URUGUAY
Fed by the Paraná and Uruguay rivers, this Atlantic Ocean inlet separates Argentina and Uruguay.

RONDÔNIA, BRAZIL ⑤
Pale strips of forest clearance can be
seen along perpendicular tracks in this
region of the Amazon Basin.

MARACAIBO, VENEZUELA ⑥
Maracaibo is the center of Venezuela's oil
industry and its second largest city with a
population of 1.6 million.

AMAZON RIVER/RIO NEGRO, BRAZIL ⑦
The dark, plant debris-stained waters of
the Rio Negro join the beige Amazon near
the city of Manaus.

EMBALSE DE GURI, VENEZUELA ⑧
This enormous reservoir, on the Caroni river, was
completed in 1986 and its hydroelectric plant was the
first to produce more than 10 gigawatts of electricity.

FOREST CLEARANCE IN SANTA CRUZ STATE, BOLIVIA ⑬
This infrared image shows the distinctive radial
clearance patterns of original tropical dry forest
with a small settlement at each center.

LAGOA DOS PATOS AND MIRIM LAGOON, ⑭
BRAZIL/URUGUAY
These two lagoons are separated from the Atlantic
Ocean by 248 miles (400 km) of sandbar.

ITAIPU DAM, BRAZIL/PARAGUAY ⑮
With an installed capacity of 14 gigawatts this is the world's
largest hydroelectric power scheme, delivering 95% of
Paraguay's energy needs and 24% of Brazil's.

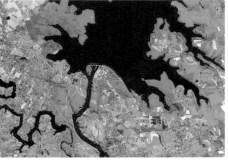

POINT BALEIA, BRAZIL ⑯
This headland has built up through steady
accumulation of silt and sediment, shaped by
tides and ocean currents.

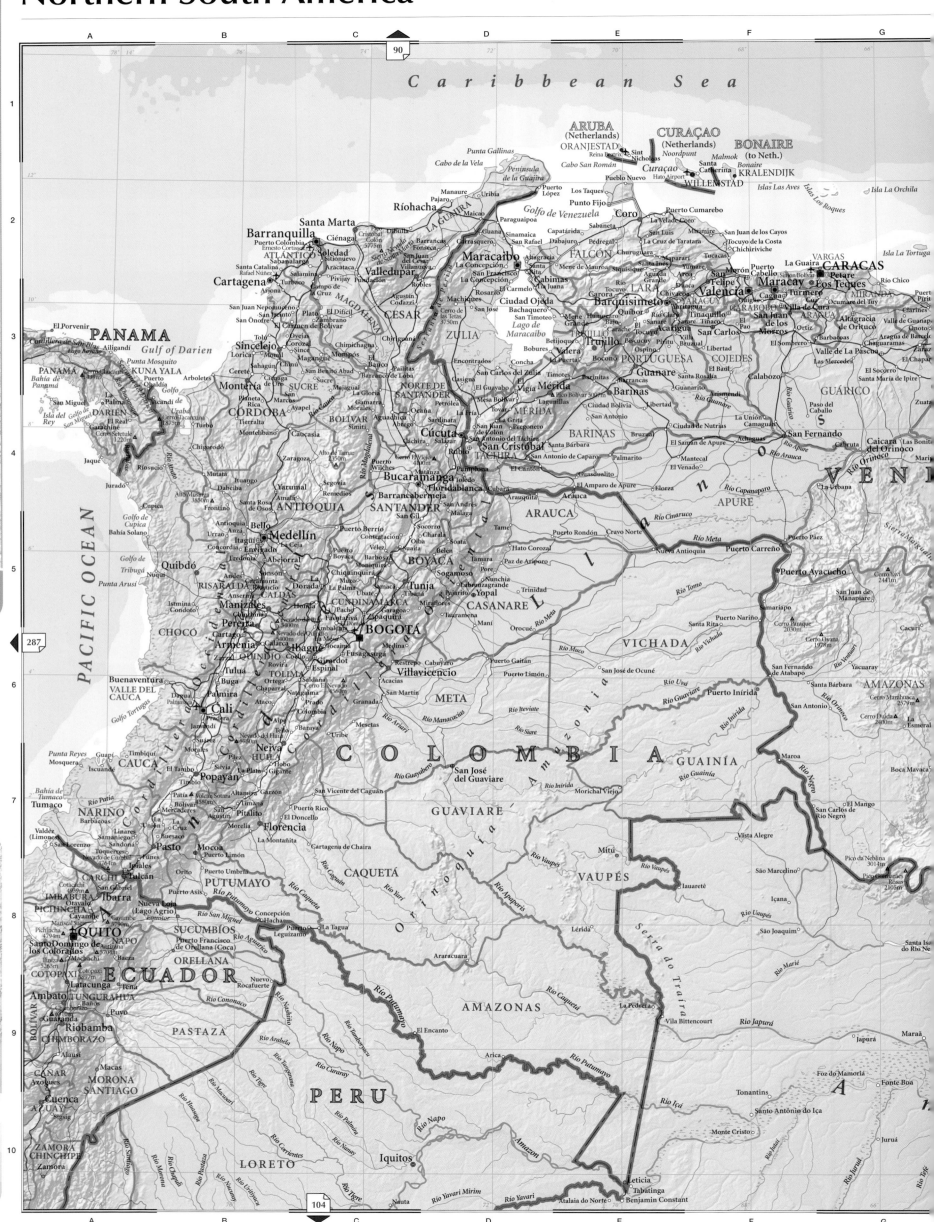

Caribbean Sea

ARUBA
(Netherlands)
ORANJESTAD

CURAÇAO
(Netherlands)

BONAIRE
(to Neth.)
KRALENDIJK

WILLEMSTAD

Islas Las Aves

Isla La Orchila

Islas Los Roques

Isla La Tortuga

VARGAS
La Guaira CARACAS

Maracay
Valencia Los Teques

MIRANDA

Barquisimeto

PORTUGUESA

COJEDES

GUÁRICO

BARINAS

APURE

V E N I

Barranquilla

Santa Marta

Cartagena

PANAMA

Gulf of Darien

PANAMÁ

DARIÉN

KUNA YALA

PACIFIC OCEAN

Maracaibo

Lago de
Maracaibo

ZULIA

CESAR

CÓRDOBA

SUCRE

BOLÍVAR

NORTE DE
SANTANDER

Cúcuta

San Cristóbal

MÉRIDA

TÁCHIRA

ARAUCA

CASANARE

Valledupar

Sincelejo

Montería

ANTIOQUIA

Medellín

Bello

Quibdó

CHOCÓ

RISARALDA

CALDAS

Manizales

Pereira

Armenia

QUINDÍO

Buenaventura

VALLE DEL
CAUCA

Cali

Palmira

Buga

Tuluá

TOLIMA

Ibagué

BOGOTÁ

CUNDINAMARCA

Girardot

Fusagasugá

Villavicencio

META

Granada

SANTANDER

Bucaramanga

Floridablanca

Barrancabermeja

BOYACÁ

Tunja

Sogamoso

Yopal

Puerto Carreño

VICHADA

Puerto Inírida

AMAZONAS

GUAINÍA

Río Negro

CAUCA

HUILA

Neiva

Popayán

Pasto

NARIÑO

Tumaco

CARCHI

IMBABURA

PICHINCHA

QUITO

ECUADOR

COTOPAXI

Latacunga

Ambato TUNGURAHUA

Riobamba

CHIMBORAZO

BOLÍVAR

CAÑAR

Cuenca

AZUAY

ZAMORA
CHINCHIPE

Zamora

MORONA
SANTIAGO

PASTAZA

PUTUMAYO

Mocoa

SUCUMBÍOS

ORELLANA

NAPO

Tena

CAQUETÁ

Florencia

GUAVIARE

San José
del Guaviare

C O L O M B I A

VAUPÉS

Mitú

AMAZONAS

Leticia
Tabatinga

P E R U

LORETO

Iquitos

Río Putumayo

Río Napo

Río Caquetá

Río Japurá

*Pico da Neblina
3014m*

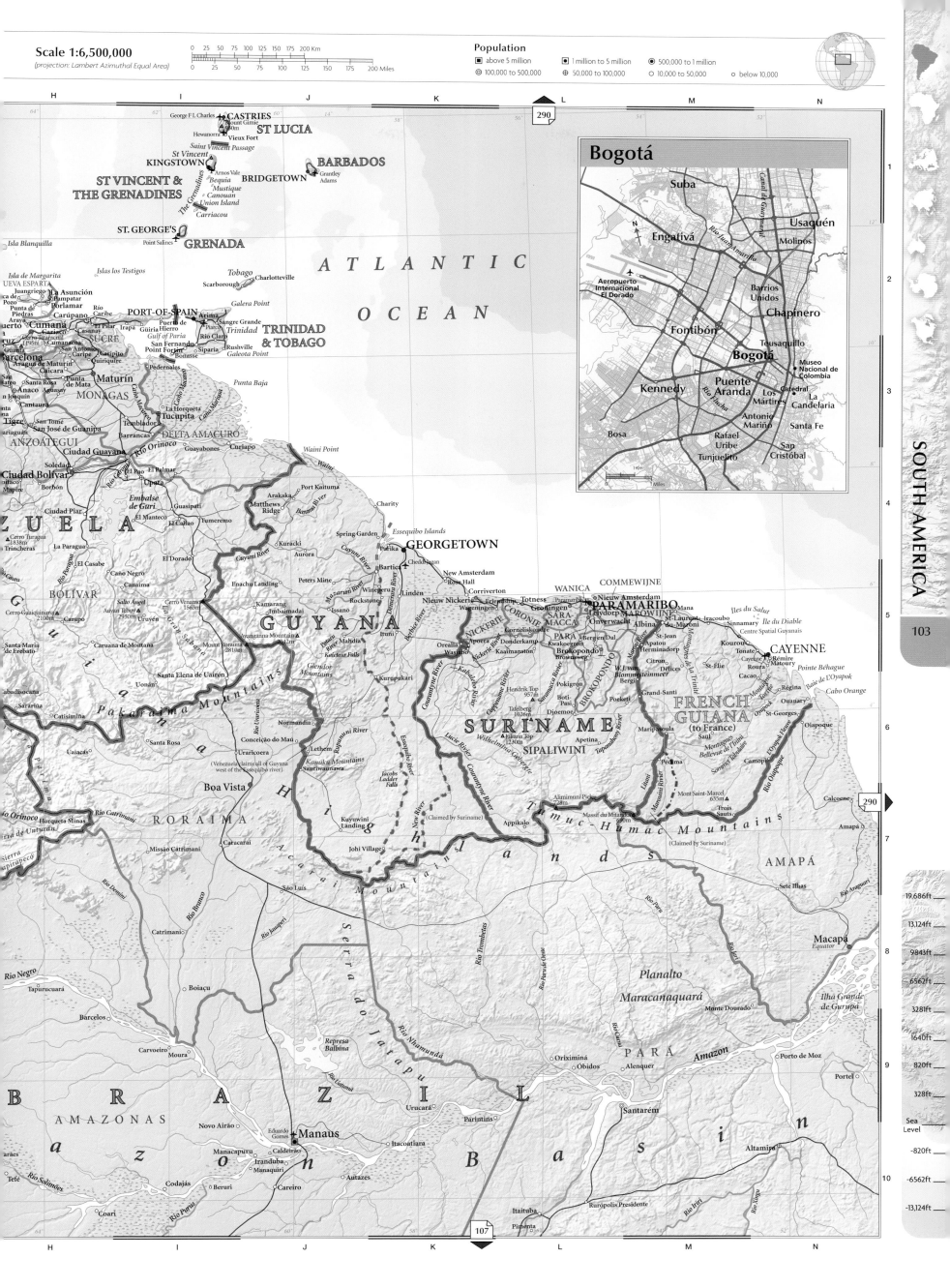

Western South America

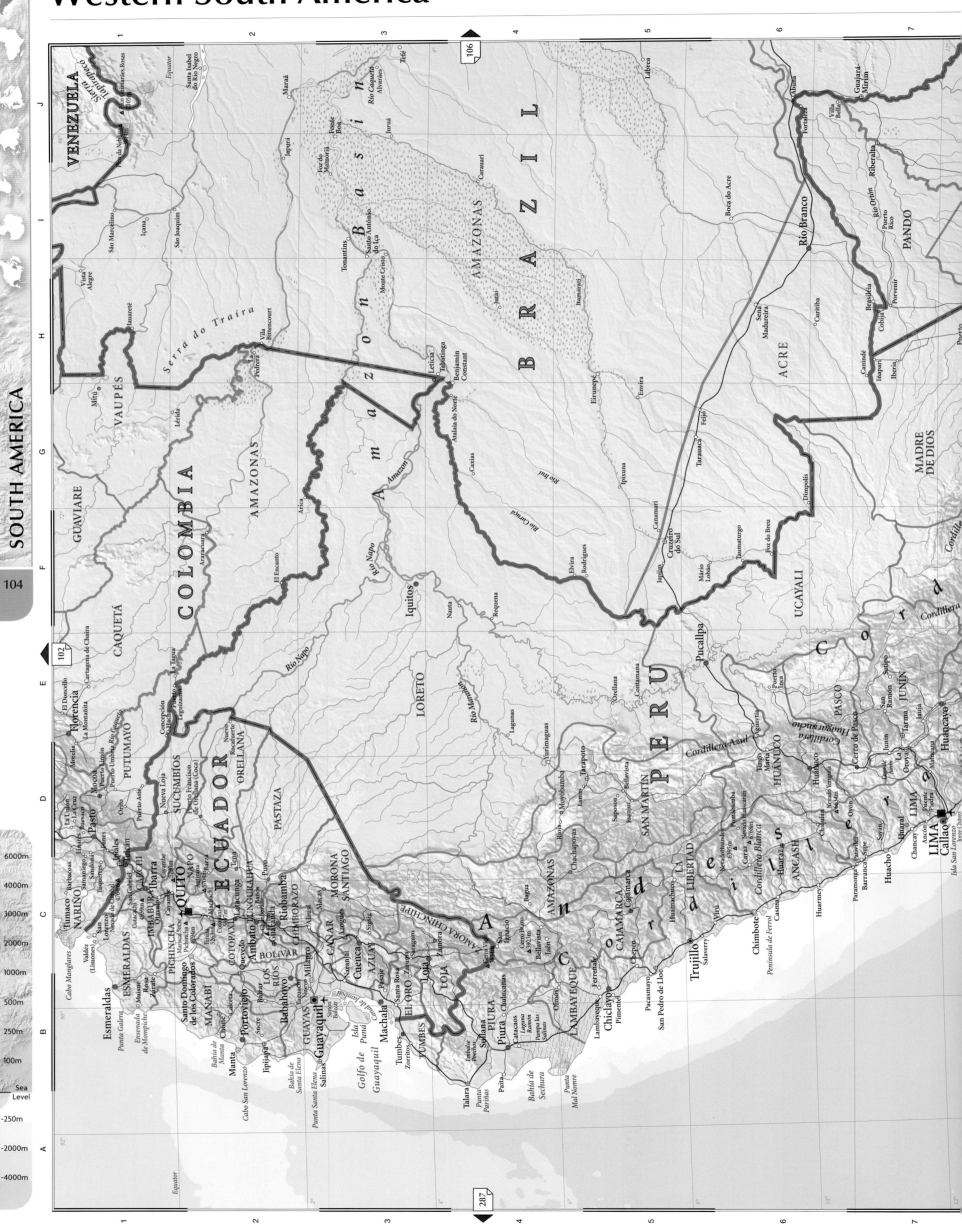

Scale 1:6,500,000
(projection: Lambert Azimuthal Equal Area)

0 25 50 75 100 125 150 175 200 Km
0 25 50 75 100 125 150 175 200 Miles

Population
■ above 5 million
■ 1 million to 5 million
◉ 500,000 to 1 million
◎ 100,000 to 500,000
⊕ 50,000 to 100,000
◌ 10,000 to 50,000
○ below 10,000

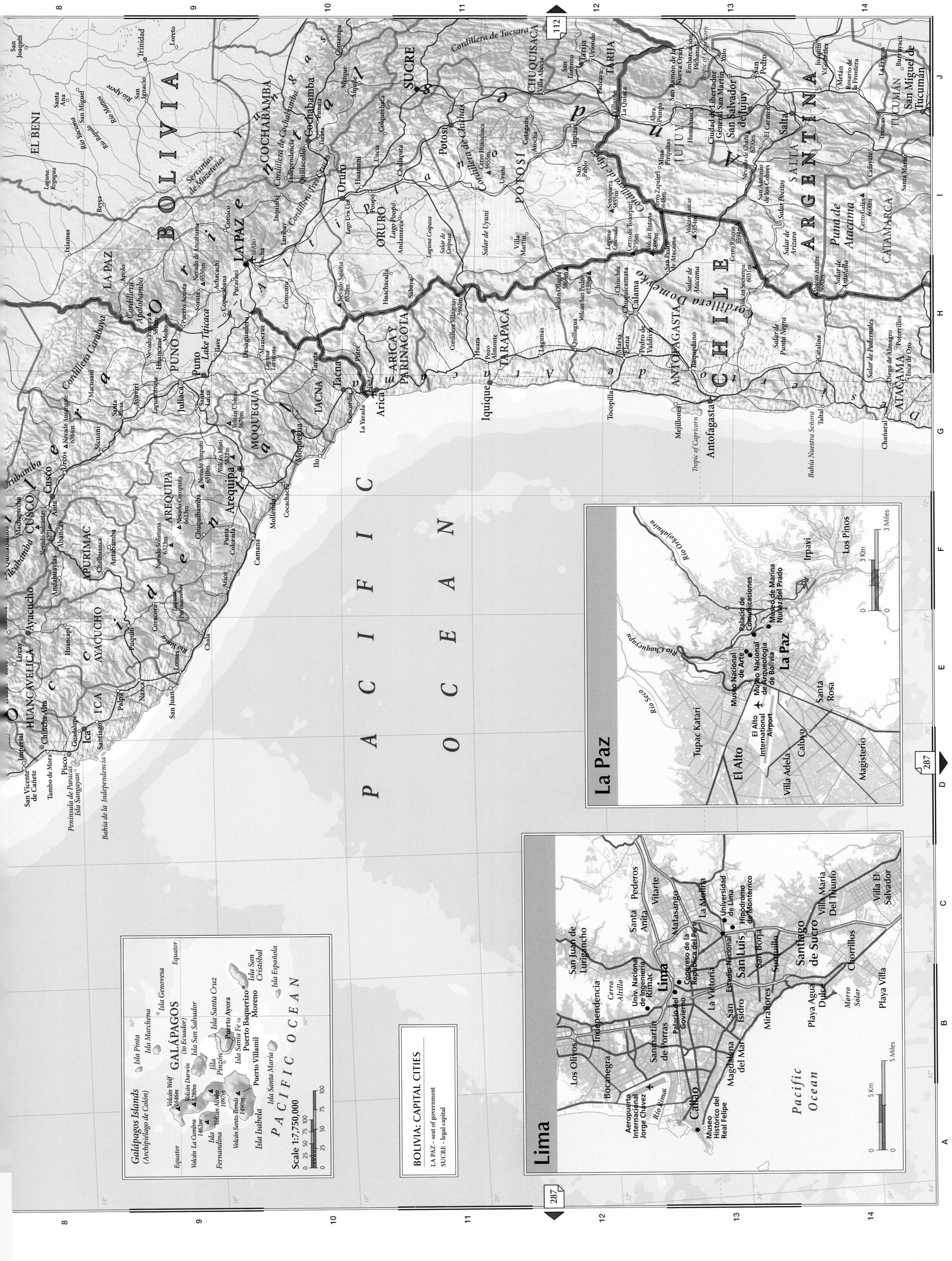

112
287

BOLIVIA
PERU
CHILE
ARGENTINA

PACIFIC OCEAN

La Paz

Lima

Galápagos Islands
(Archipiélago de Colón)
GALÁPAGOS
(to Ecuador)
Scale 1:7,750,000

BOLIVIA: CAPITAL CITIES
LA PAZ – seat of government
SUCRE – legal capital

19,686ft
13,124ft
9843ft
6562ft
3281ft
1640ft
820ft
328ft
Sea Level
-820ft
-6562ft
-13,124ft

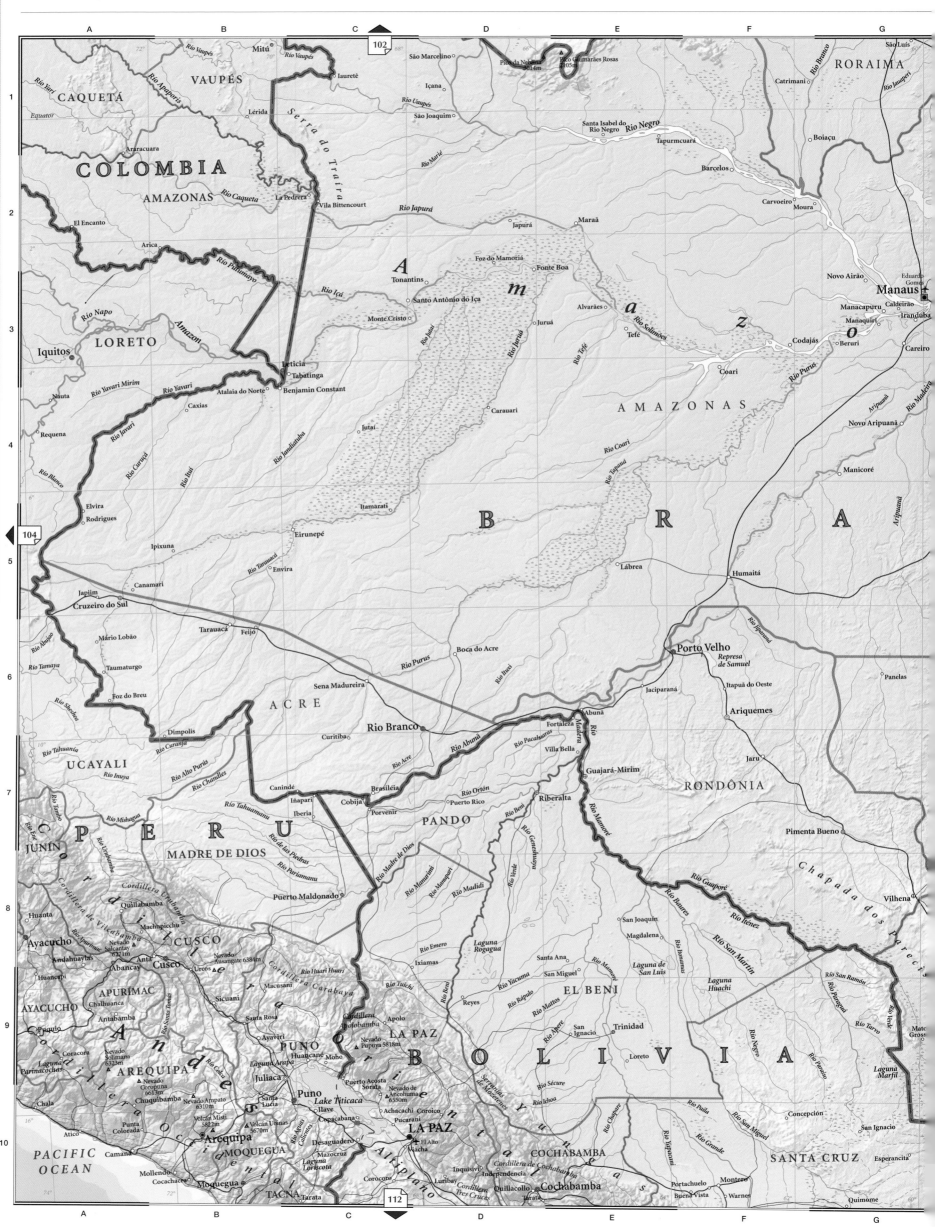

Scale 1:6,500,000
(projection: Lambert Azimuthal Equal Area)

0 25 50 75 100 125 150 175 200 Km

0 25 50 75 100 125 150 175 200 Miles

Population

■ above 5 million   ▪ 1 million to 5 million   ◉ 500,000 to 1 million

◎ 100,000 to 500,000   ○ 50,000 to 100,000   ○ 10,000 to 50,000   ○ below 10,000

103

113

108

ATLANTIC OCEAN

Equator

AMAPÁ

Macapá

Sete Ilhas

Rio Paru

Rio Araguari

Ilha Bailique

Ilha do Curuá

Ilha Janaucu

Ilha Caviana de Fora

Ilha Mexiana

Mouths of the Amazon

Planalto Maracanaquará

Monte Dourado

Rio Trombetas

Rio Paru de Oeste

Rio Nhamundá

Serra do Jatapu

Represa Balbina

Rio Jari

Rio Uatumã

Oriximiná

Óbidos

Alenquer

Amazon

Porto de Moz

Ilha Grande de Gurupá

Ilha de Marajó

Baía de Marajó

Belém

Castanhal

Capanema

Viseu

Carutapera

Turiaçu

Marudá

Vigia

Urucará

Parintins

Itacoatiara

Autazes

Santarém

Portel

Ilha Sirituba

Tomé-Açu

Alto Bónito

Rio Tocantins

Serra do Tiracambu

Rio Gurupi

Rio Gurupi

Altamira

BASIL

Z

B

R

I

L

PARÁ

Itaituba

Pimenta

Rurópolis Presidente Medici

Rio Iriri

Rio Tapajós

Rio Jamanxim

Tucunaré

Jacaré-a-Canga

Araras

Bom Futuro

Manuel Zinho

José Rodrigues

Serra dos Carajás

Parauapebas

São Félix do Xingu

Rio Xingu

Rio Jurunaí

São Félix

Marabá

Açailândia

Dom Eliseu

MARANHÃO

Imperatriz

Grajaú

Estreito

São Raimundo das Mangabeiras

Carolina

Balsas

Represa de Tucuruí

Barra do São Manuel

Serra do Cachimbo

Recreio

Pereirinha

Rio São Manuel

Colniza

Bandeirantes

Cachimbo

Paranaíta

Araguaína

Craolândia

Tasso Fragoso

Conceição do Araguaia

Serra dos Gradaús

Rio Araguaia

Rio Tocantins

Chapada das Mangabeiras

PIAUÍ

Alto Parnaíba

Santa Filomena

Corrente

Vila Rica

Peixoto de Azevedo

Juruena

Rio Juruena

Juará

Novo Horizonte

Porto dos Gaúchos

Marcelândia

Campo de Diauarum

Sinop

Serra Formosa

Pôsto Jacaré

Rio das Mortes

São Félix do Araguaia

Ilha do Bananal

Gurupi

Serra do Roncador

TOCANTINS

Palmas do Tocantins

Porto Nacional

Serra Geral de Goiás

Espigão Mestre

Taguatinga

Campos Belos

BAHIA

Rio da Sangue

Rio Arinos

Cocalinho

Porangatu

MATO GROSSO

Arenápolis

Nobres

Rosário Oeste

Rio Manso

Planalto de Mato Grosso

Itacaiu

Uruaçu

Tupiraçaba

Alto Paraíso de Goiás

Pontes e Lacerda

Cáceres

Várzea Grande

Cuiabá

Jaciara

Ceres

Rialma

Barro Alto

Goianésia

GOIÁS

Pirenópolis

BRASÍLIA

Planaltina

DISTRITO FEDERAL

San Matías

Rio Santo Corazón

Laguna Uberaba

Pantanal

Rondonópolis

Rio Piquiri

Rio Cuiabá

Alto Araguaia

Santa Rita de Araguaia

Mineiros

Piranhas

Aragarças

Goiás

Indiara

Goiânia

Anápolis

Cristalina

Unaí

MINAS GERAIS

Paracatu

Rio São Francisco

Planalto Central

Serra Dourada

19,686ft

13,124ft

9843ft

6562ft

3281ft

1640ft

820ft

328ft

Sea Level

-820ft

-6562ft

-13,124ft

SOUTH AMERICA

ATLANTIC OCEAN

Scale
6000m
4000m
3000m
2000m
1000m
500m
250m
100m
Sea Level
−250m
−2000m
−4000m

Mouths of the Amazon

Ilha de Marajó

Baía de Marajó

A m a z o n   B a s i n

AMAPÁ

Macapá

Equator

Ilha de Maracá
Sete Ilhas
Calçoene
Amapá
Sucurijú
Ilha Bailique
Ilha do Curuá
Ilha Caviana de Fora
Ilha Janaucu
Ilha Mexiana
Rio Araguari
Porto de Moz
Altamira
Rio Xingu
José Rodrigues
São Félix do Xingu
Ilha do Bananal
Vila Rica
Rio Araguaia
São Félix do Araguaia
Gurupi

PARÁ

Serra dos Carajás
Parauapebas
Represa de Tucuruí
Rio Tocantins
Portel
Tomé-Açu
Castanhal
Vigia
Capanema
Bragança
Curuçá
Turiaçu
Viseu
Belém
Ilha Sirituba

TOCANTINS
Palmas
Porto Nacional

Marabá
Conceição do Araguaia
São Félix
Araguaína
Estreito
Carolina
Imperatriz
Açailândia
Dom Eliseu
Alto Bonito
Rio Gurupi

BRAZIL

Serra dos Gradaús
Espigão
Serra Geral de Goiás
Chapada das Mangabeiras

MARANHÃO
São Luís
Ilha de São Luís
Baía de São Marcos
Recife Manuel Luís
Recife do Silva
Ilha do Caju
Rio Parnaíba
Parnaíba
Itapecuru-Mirim
Rio Itapicuru
Bacabal
Caxias
Codó
Chapadinha
Timon
Colinas
Presidente Dutra
Grajaú
Balsas
Barra do Corda
Serra do Tiracambu
Rio Grajaú
Rio Mearim
Roncador
Floriano
Tasso Fragoso
Alto Parnaíba
Santa Filomena
Corrente
São Raimundo das Mangabeiras
São João dos Patos
Caroliná

CEARÁ
Fortaleza
Caucaia
Cascavel
Aracati
Itapipoca
Camocim
Acaraú
Sobral
Arara
Granja
Crateús
Quixadá
Senador Pompeu
Açude Banabuiú
Açude Orós
Tauá
Serra Grande
Serra Grande do Piauí

PIAUÍ
Teresina
Piripiri
Campo Maior
Barro Duro
Oeiras
Valença do Piauí
Canto do Buriti
Picos
São João do Piauí
Simplício Mendes
São Raimundo Nonato
Rio Gurguéia
Corrente

RIO GRANDE DO NORTE
Natal
Ceará Mirim
Touros
Cabo de São Roque
Atol das Rocas
Mossoró
Areia Branca
Macau
Açu
Currais Novos
Caicó

PARAÍBA
João Pessoa
Campina Grande
Planalto da Borborema

PERNAMBUCO
Recife
Olinda
Jaboatão
Caruaru
Arcoverde
Garanhuns
Salgueiro
Ouricuri
Afrânio
Petrolina
Juazeiro
Represa de Sobradinho
Sento Sé
Santa Rita de Cássia
Remanso
Xique-Xique
Barra
Campo Alegre de Lourdes

ALAGOAS
Maceió
Arapiraca
Rio São Francisco
Propriá

SERGIPE
Aracaju
São Cristóvão
Estância
Serrinha
Quebrangulo
Monte Santo
Tucano
Camuros
Paulo Afonso
Juazeiro do Norte
Campos Sales
Marcolândia
Açude Poço da Cruz
Represa de Itaparica
Catuário

Equator

Scale 1:6,500,000
(projection: Lambert Azimuthal Equal Area)

0 25 50 75 100 125 150 175 200 Km

0 25 50 75 100 125 150 175 200 Miles

Population

- above 5 million
- 1 million to 5 million
- 500,000 to 1 million
- 100,000 to 500,000
- 50,000 to 100,000
- 10,000 to 50,000
- below 10,000

ATLANTIC

OCEAN

Salvador

Baía de Todos os Santos

Valença

Ilha de Boipeba

Ponta do Mutá

Maraú

Ilhéus

Itabuna

Comandatuba

Canavieiras

Belmonte

Santa Cruz Cabrália

Porto Seguro

Prado

Caravelas

Ilha Caçumba

Feira de Santana

Itaberaba

Jequié

Itapetinga

Itabuna

Rio Jequitinhonha

Eunápolis

Itamaraju

São Mateus

Nanuque

Vitória

Guarapari

Bom Jesus de Itabapoana

Cachoeiro de Itapemirim

ESPÍRITO

SANTO

Linhares

Vitória da Conquista

Brumado

Caetité

Bom Jesus da Lapa

Chapada Dia...

Lençóis

Itabira

Monte Azul

Espinosa

Teófilo Otoni

Itaobim

Araçuaí

Pedra Azul

Ponte Nova

Barra Mansa

Colatina

Santa Teresa

Rio Doce

Governador Valadares

Aimorés

Miracema

São Fidélis

Campos

Macaé

Conceição

Nova Friburgo

RIO DE JANEIRO

Arraial do Cabo

Cabo Frio

Montes Claros

Diamantina

Serro

Rio de...

Guanhães

Ipatinga

Itabira

MINAS GERAIS

Pirapora

Curvelo

Ipatinga

Ouro Preto

Conselheiro

Lafaiete

Barbacena

Juiz de Fora

Três Rios

Petrópolis

Teresópolis

São Gonçalo

Niterói

Rio de Janeiro

Represa

Três Marias

Paraopeba

Sete

Lagoas

Betim

Belo Horizonte

Divinópolis

Abaeté

São João del Rei

Três Pontas

Volta

Redonda

Resende

Barra do Piraí

Nova Iguaçu

Angra

dos Reis

Ilha Grande

Pouso Alegre

Poços de Caldas

Guaratinguetá

Taubaté

São José dos Campos

Caraguatatuba

Ubatuba

Ilha de São Sebastião

Ilha de Santo Amaro

Brazilian Highlands

Serra do Espinhaço

Planalto Central

Rio São Francisco

Brasília

Planaltina

DISTRITO

FEDERAL

Cristalina

Unaí

Paracatu

Patos de Minas

Araxá

Passos

Franca

Ribeirão Preto

Represa

de Furnas

Campinas

Bragança Paulista

Jundiaí

São Paulo

Osasco

São Bernardo do Campo

Santos

São Vicente

Peruíbe

Registro

Iguape

Ilha Comprida

Ilha do Mel

Paranaguá

Anápolis

Goiânia

GOIÁS

Goiás

Pirenópolis

Anhanguera

Araguari

Uberlândia

Uberaba

SÃO PAULO

Barretos

Bebedouro

São Joaquim

da Barra

Igarapava

Jaboticabal

Araraquara

São Carlos

Rio Claro

Limeira

Americana

Piracicaba

Sorocaba

Itu

Itapetininga

Capão

Bonito

Serra de Paranapiacaba

Curitiba

Ponta Grossa

Campo Largo

Lapa

Rio Negro

Mafra

MATO

GROSSO

Campos

Belos

Alto Paraíso de Goiás

Barro Alto

Goianésia

Pirangatu

Ceres

Rialma

Itumbiara

Rio Verde

Indiara

Caçu

Serra Dourada

Taguatinga

Porangatu

Uruaçu

Mineiros

Jataí

Ilha Solteira

Represa de

Água Vermelha

São José do

Rio Preto

Votuporanga

Fernandópolis

Catanduva

Novo

Horizonte

Lins

Bauru

Marília

Assis

Ourinhos

Londrina

Apucarana

Maringá

Campo Mourão

PARANÁ

Serra Geral

Tropic of Capricorn

MATO GROSSO

DO SUL

Três

Lagoas

Andradina

Araçatuba

Presidente

Prudente

19,686ft

13,124ft

9843ft

6562ft

3281ft

1640ft

820ft

328ft

Sea
Level

-820ft

-6562ft

-13,124ft

Scale 1:2,000,000
(projection: Lambert Conformal Conic)

0 10 20 30 40 50 60 70 80 Km
0 10 20 30 40 50 60 70 80 Miles

Population
■ above 5 million
■ 1 million to 5 million
◉ 500,000 to 1 million
◎ 100,000 to 500,000
⊕ 50,000 to 100,000
○ 10,000 to 50,000
∘ below 10,000

109

291

H I J K L M N

1 2 3 4 5 6 7 8 9 10

Congonhas
Guanhães
Gonzaga Sardoa
Virginópolis
Santa Efigênia
São Geraldo da Piedade
Governador Valadares
Central de Minas
São João de Manteninha
Barra de S. Francisco
Nova Venécia
São Mateus

Dom Joaquim
Açucena
Itanhomi
Divino das Laranjeiras
São Geraldo do Baixio
Galiléia
Goiabeira
Alto Rio Novo
Águia Branca
São Gabriel da Palha
Barra Nova

Conceição do Mato Dentro
Carmésia
Dores de Guanhães
Periquito
Sobrália
Tarumirim
Conselheiro Pena
Rio Doce
Resplendor
Itueta
Pancas
Governador Lindenberg
Rio Bananal
Linhares

Morro do Filar
Santo Antônio do Rio Abaixo
Ferros
Joanésia
Mesquita
Naque
São João do Oriente
Iapu
Dom Cavati
Santa Rita do Itueto
São Domingos
Marilândia

Passabém
São Sebastião do Rio Prêto
Belo Oriente
Ipaba
Bugre
Baixo Guandu
Colatina
Rio Doce
Regência

Jaboticatubas
Coronel Fabriciano
Ipatinga
Santana do Paraíso
Vargem Alegre
Entre Fôlhas
Inhapim
Imbé
Pocrane
ESPÍRITO
Itaguaçu
Jacupemba

Itabira
Antônio Dias
Jaguaraçu
Marliéria
Bom Jesus do Galho
Piedade de Caratinga
Ipanema
Tuparubá
Mutum
João Neiva
São Roque
Aracruz

Santa Luzia
Vespasiano
São José da Lapa
Sabará
João Monlevade
Nova Era
São Domingos do Prata
Córrego Novo
Caratinga
Santa Rita de Minas
Conceição de Ipanema
Laranja da Terra
Itarana
SANTO
Santa Teresa
Fundão
Nova Almeida

Belo Horizonte
Raposos
Nova Lima
Barão de Cocais
Santa Bárbara
Rio Piracicaba
Dionísio
Córrego Novo
Vermelho Novo
Santa Bárbara do Leste
São José do Mantimento
Afonso Cláudio
Santa Maria
Serra

Itabirito
Rio Acima
Calas Altas
Alvinópolis
Dom Silvério
Rio Casca
Simonésia
Reduto
Martins Soares
Brejetuba
Domingos Martins
Cariacica
Vitória
Vila Velha

Belo Vale
Mariana
Ouro Preto
Acaiaca
Dom Silvério
Rio Doce
Matipó
Manhuaçu
Irupi
Ibatiba
Conceição do Castelo
Marechal Floriano
Aracatiba

Ouro Branco
Diogo de Vasconcelos
Guaraciaba
Urucânia
Santo Antônio do Grama
São João do Manhuaçu
Iúna
Pico da Bandeira 2890m
Caparaó Velho
Castelo
Jerônimo Monteiro
Iconha
Anchieta
Guarapari

Conselheiro Lafaiete
Itaverava
Catas Altas da Noruega
Piranga
Pôrto Firme
Ponte Nova
Oratórios
Jequeri
Pedra do Anta
Espera Feliz
Dores do Rio Prêto
Guaçuí
Castelo
Vargem Alta
Piúma

São Brás do Suaçuí
Lamim
Bras Pires
Senhora de Oliveira
Viçosa
Teixeiras
São Miguel do Anta
Araponga
Caiana
Faria Lemos
Cachoeiro de Itapemirim
Itapemirim

ZIL
Caranaíba
Rio Espera
Capela Nova
Cipotânea
Paula Candido
São Geraldo
Coimbra
Belisario
Carangola
Pedra Dourada
Tombos
Varre-Sai
Castelo
Muqui
Mimoso
Marataízes

Alto Rio Doce
Dores do Turvo
Rosário da Limeira
Guiricema
Vieiras
Porciúncula
São José do Calçado
Itaperuna

Barbacena
Mercês
Silveirânia
Tocantins
Ubá
Guidoval
Rodeiro
Miraí
Antônio Prado
Eugenópolis
Natividade
Bom Jesus do Itabapoana
Rio Itabapoana

Antônio Carlos
Ibertioga
Eubanque
Goiana
São João Nepomuceno
Laje de Muriaé
Muriaé
Itália

Barroso
Ressaquinha
Astolfo Dutra
Itamarati
Descoberto
Palma
Laranjal
Miracema
Cambuci
Cardoso Moreira
Barra de Itabapoana

Paiva
Piraúba
Tabuleiro
Rio Novo
Cataguases
Recreio
Santo Antônio de Pádua

Juiz de Fora
Lima Duarte
Coronel Pacheco
Chácara
Argirita
Leopoldina
Pirapetinga
Itaocara
São Fidélis
Travessão
São João da Barra

Bias Fortes
Bicas
Guarara
Maripá
Volta Grande
Campos dos Goytacazes

Pedro Teixeira
Matias Barbosa
Além Paraíba
Rio Paraíba do Sul

Santa Bárbara do Monte Verde
Santana do Deserto
Mar de Espanha
Carmo
Cantagalo
Santa Maria Madalena
Carapebus

Rio Preto
Comendador Levy Gasparian
Barra de São Francisco
Duas Barras
Santa Bárbara do Alto
São Sebastião do Alto
Trajano de Morais

Três Rios
Sapucaia
Sumidouro
Cordeiro
Bom Jardim

Rio das Flores
Paraíba do Sul
Areal
Bom Jardim

Yassouras
Pedro do Rio
Nova Friburgo
Macaé

Barra do Piraí
Miguel Pereira
Teresópolis
Cachoeiras de Macacu
Casimiro de Abreu
Rio das Ostras

Pinheiral
Engenheiro Paulo de Frontin
Petrópolis
Guapimirim
Silva Jardim
São Vicente de Paula
Armação dos Búzios

Mendes
Paracambi
Imbariê
Majé
Tanguá
Rio Bonito
São Pedro da Aldeia

Queimados
Belford Roxo
São Gonçalo
Itaborai
Iguaba Grande
Araruama
Cabo Frio

Seropédica
Nova Iguaçu
Nilópolis
Caxias
Galeão
Niterói
Maricá
Saquarema

Itaguaí
Rio de Janeiro
Mangaratiba
Arraial do Cabo
Cabo Frio

RIO DE JANEIRO
MINAS GERAIS
BRAZIL

ATLANTIC OCEAN

Tropic of Capricorn

Rio de Janeiro

Mesquita
Coelho da Rocha
Duque de Caxias
Ilha do Governador

Nilópolis
São João de Meriti
Rio de Janeiro Galeão
Galeão
Cocotá

Guadalupe
Cordovil
Olaria
Ramos

Bangu
Magalhães
Rocha Miranda
Inhaúma

Realengo
Praça Sêca
Rio de Janeiro
Engenho Novo
São Cristóvão
Museu Nacional
Vila Isabel
Gamboa
Baía de Guanabara
Neves
Niterói
Santos Dumont

Taquara
Pechincha
Jacarepaguá
Gruta Paulo e Virginia
Catedral Metropolitana
Tijuca
Parque Nacional da Tijuca
Botafogo
Pão de Açúcar (Sugarloaf Mt.)

Barra de Tijuca
Lagoa de Jacarepaguá
Monumento Cristo Redentor
Gávea
Niemeyer
Copacabana
Lagoa Rodrigo de Freitas
Ipanema

Atlantic Ocean

0 2 Km
0 2 Miles

19,686ft
13,124ft
9843ft
6562ft
3281ft
1640ft
820ft
328ft
Sea Level
-820ft
-6562ft
-13,124ft

Scale 1:6,500,000
(projection: Lambert Azimuthal Equal Area)

0 25 50 75 100 125 150 175 200 Km
0 25 50 75 100 125 150 175 200 Miles

Population
- ■ above 5 million
- ◉ 1 million to 5 million
- ◉ 500,000 to 1 million
- ◎ 100,000 to 500,000
- ◉ 50,000 to 100,000
- ○ 10,000 to 50,000
- ○ below 10,000

109

291

Pantanal

GOIÁS
Rio Verde
Jataí
Itumbiara
Anhangüera
Araguari
Uberlândia
Coxim
Aquidauana
Campo Grande
MATO GROSSO DO SUL
Água Clara
Três Lagoas
Andradina
Nova Alvorada
Víctor
Dourados
Bela Vista
Pedro Juan Caballero
Cordillera de Amambaí
Serra de Amambaí
Naviraí
Pôrto Camargo
Umuarama
Guaíra
Ciudad del Este
Foz do Iguaçu
Cataratas del rio Iguaçu
Puerto Iguazú
Toledo
Santa Helena
Cascavel
PARANÁ
Maringá
Apucarana
Londrina
Cornélio Procópio

BRAZIL

SÃO PAULO
Ribeirão Preto
Franca
Uberaba
Araxá
MINAS GERAIS
Belo Horizonte
Ouro Preto
Divinópolis
Sete Lagoas
Betim
Ipatinga
Governador Valadares
Guanhães
Itabira
Barbacena
Juiz de Fora
Três Rios
Petrópolis
Nova Friburgo
Teresópolis
Niterói
RIO DE JANEIRO
Rio de Janeiro
Nova Iguaçu
São Gonçalo
Cabo Frio

Bauru
Marília
Presidente Prudente
Presidente Venceslau
Araçatuba
Campinas
São Paulo
Osasco
Santo André
São Bernardo do Campo
São Caetano do Sul
São Vicente
Santos
Guarujá
São José dos Campos
Taubaté
Jacareí
Sorocaba
Itapetininga
Ponta Grossa
Curitiba
Campo Largo
Paranaguá
Joinville
São Francisco do Sul
SANTA CATARINA
Blumenau
Itajaí
Brusque
Florianópolis
São José
Lages
Chapecó
Concórdia
Erechim
Passo Fundo
Caxias do Sul
Novo Hamburgo
Canoas
Gravataí
Porto Alegre
RIO GRANDE DO SUL
Santa Maria
Pelotas
Rio Grande

Tropic of Capricorn

ATLANTIC

OCEAN

Ilha de São Francisco
Ilha de Santa Catarina

URUGUAY
MONTEVIDEO
Rivera
Melo
Rio Branco
Punta del Este
Maldonado

Rio de la Plata

Buenos Aires

Las Conchas
Tigre
Pilar
Garín
San Isidro
Vicente López
San Miguel
General San Martín
Belgrano
Palermo
Buenos Aires
Hippodrome
Zoo
Teatro Colón
Cathedral
Plaza de Mayo
Morón
Sáenz Peña
Floresta
Barracas
Moreno
Merlo
San Justo
Villa Madero
Villa Alsina
Avellaneda
Quilmes
Lanús
Pontevedra
González Catán
Lomas de Zamora
Berazategui
Mariano Acosta
Aeropuerto Internacional de Ezeiza
Longchamps
Florencio Varela

Rio de la Plata
Rectificación del Riachuelo

0   10 Km
0   10 Miles

291

19,686ft
13,124ft
9843ft
6562ft
3281ft
1640ft
820ft
328ft
Sea Level
-820ft
-6562ft
-13,124ft

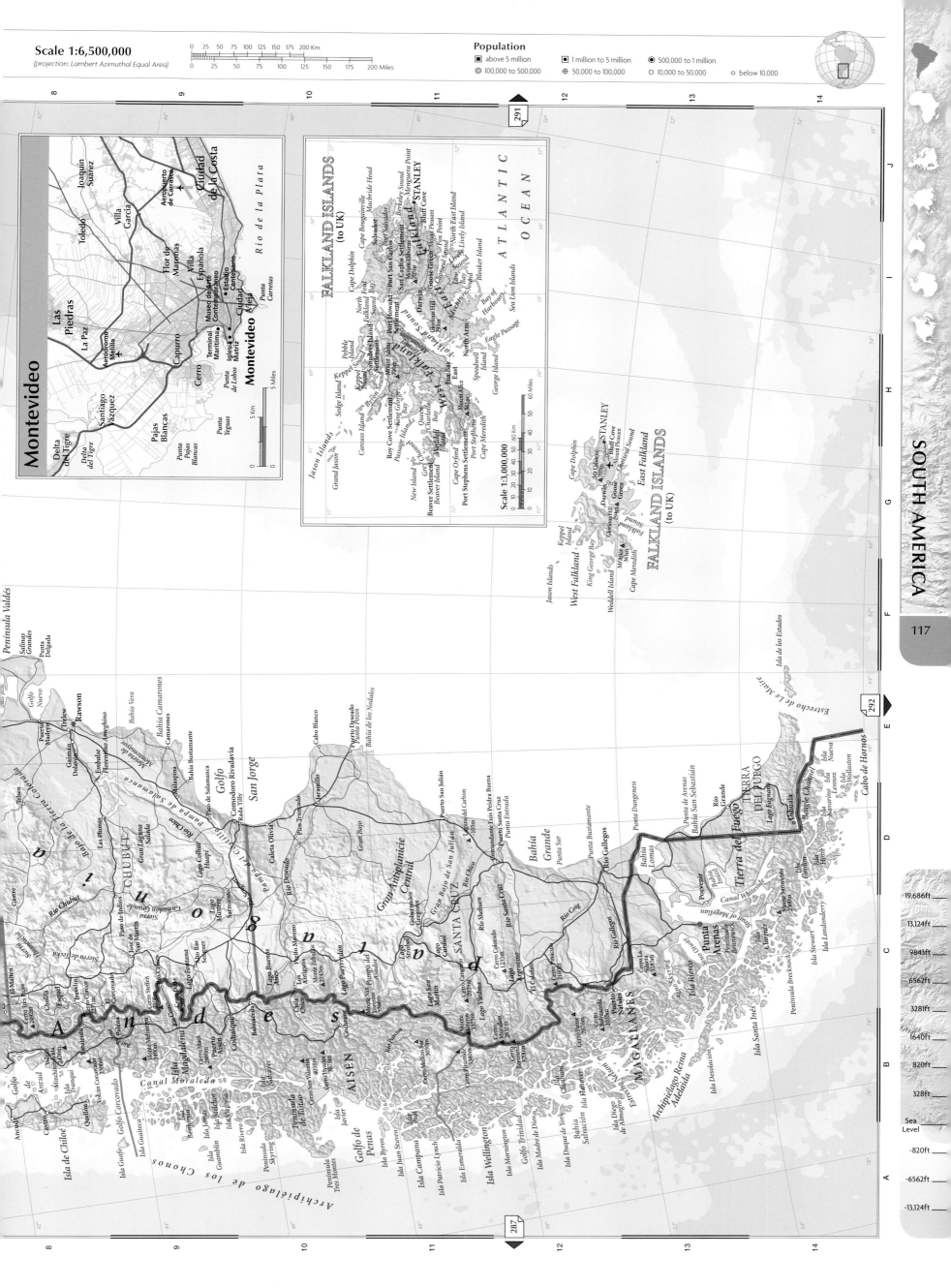

Central Chile & Argentina

Scale 1:2,600,000
(projection: Lambert Conformal Conic)

0 10 20 30 40 50 Km
0 10 20 30 40 50 Miles

Easter Island
(Isla de Pascua)
(to Chile)

Scale 1:500,000

PACIFIC OCEAN

PACIFIC

OCEAN

COQUIMBO

VALPARAÍSO

SANTIAGO

SANTIAGO

CHILE

LIBERTADOR

MAULE

BIO BIO

ARAUCANÍA

A n d e s

SAN JUAN

MENDOZA

ARGENTINA

LA
PAMPA

NEUQUÉN

Sierra del Nevado

6000m
4000m
3000m
2000m
1000m
500m
250m
100m
Sea
Level
-250m
-2000m
-4000m

SOUTH AMERICA – Cities

Brasília

Parque Nacional de Brasília
Peninsula Norte
Asa Norte
Estadio
Universida de Brasília
Retiro de Barra Alta
Lago do Paranoá
Brazlandia
Palacio de Justiça
Palacio de Alvorada
Brasília
Guará
Catedral Metropolitana
Rasgado
Taguatinga
Asa Sul
Cellândia
Jardim Zoológico de Brasília
Dom Bosco
Paranoá
Sto. Antonio do Descoberto
Aeropuerto Internacional do Brasília
Lago Sul
Nucleo Bandeirante
Recanto das Emas
Jardím Botânico do Brasília

4 Km
4 Miles

Caracas

Catia
La Mar
Maiquetía
Caribbean Sea
Mamo
Simón Bolívar Airport
Quebrada Tácagua
Macuto
Caraballeda
La Guaira
Rio Carabulleda
Parque Nacional Ávila
Cordillera de la Costa
Palacio Miraflores
Sarria
San Bernardino
Artigas
Capitolio Nacional
El Silencio
Jardin Botánico
Caracas
Los Dos Caminos
Antimano
Estadio Nacional
Las Acacias
Univ. Central de Venezuela
La Luz
El Valle
Las Mercedes
Cochecito
Petare
Baruta
El Hatillo
Rio Guaire

4 Km
4 Miles

Havana

N
Castillo de los Tres Reyes del Morro
Castillo de San Carlos de la Cabaña
Castillo de San Salvador de la Punta
Catedral
Bahía de la Habana
Havana (La Habana)
Regla
Guanabacoa
Castillo del Principe
Cerro
Straits of Florida
Vedado
Castillo de Atares
Jacomino
Miramar
Zoo
Diez de Octubre
San Miguel de Padrón
Nuevo Vedado
Jesus del Monte
Almendares
Lawton
Lucero
La Playa
Ciudad Libertad
La Vibora
Mantilla
Bello
La Lisa
Marianao
Rosario
El Calvario
Santa Fé
Siboney
Arroyo Arenas
Los Pinos
Collazo
Barlovento
Collazo
Punta Brava
Cantaranas
Arroyo Naranjo
Rio Almendares
Embalse Ejército Revelde
El Cano

2 Km
2 Miles

Quito

El Condado
Carcelen
Cordillera Pichincha
Cotocollao
Ronceano
Aeropuerto Mariscal Sucre
Concepcion
San Isidro de Inca
Volcán Guagua Pichincha 4794m
Cochapamha
Ilpijapa
Cumbaya
Rio de Guayllabamba
Rumipamba
Estadio Olimpico
Belisario Quevedo
Quito
Tumbaco
San Juan
Teatro Sucre
Museo de la Ciudad
Parque Metropolitano Chilibulo
Cerro Ilaló 3188m
Puengasi
Chillogallio
La Argelia
Conocoto
Quitumbe
La Ecuatoriana
Parque Metropolitano del Sur
Sangolqui
Guamani
Turubamba

5 Km
5 Miles

Santiago

El Carmen
Lo Barnechea
Quilicura
El Cortijo
Huechuraba
Conchali
Vitacura
Renca
Santa Emilia
Las Condes
Rio Mapocho
Recoleta
Cerro Navia
Carrascal
San Cristóbal
Sta. Rosa de Locobe
Quinta Normal
Congreso Nacional
Providencia
Barrancas
Palacio de la Moneda
Catedral
Lo Prado Arriba
Las Rejas
Universidad de Chile
Nunoa
Santiago
Club Hipico
Parque O'Higgins
Cerrillos
La Aguada
Maipu
San Miguel
Bellavista
Lo Espejo
La Blanca
Santa Julia
El Bosque
San Ramon
La Granja
San Bernardo
La Florida

4 Km
4 Miles

São Paulo

Congo
Pirituba
Itaberaba
Guarulhos
Mutinga
Limão
Jaguara
Santana
Jardim Brasil
Osasco
Lapa
Santa
Vila Guilherme
Adalgisa
Vila Madalena
Perdizes
Belènzinho
Tatuapé
Penha
Vila Ré
Butantã
Consolação
Brás
São Paulo
Jardim Ouro Preto
Instituto Butanta
Teatro Municipal
Jardim Europa
Vila Sonia
Moóca
Vila Formosa
Campo Belo
Estádio do Morumbi
Vila Mariana
Ipiranga
Cídade Líder
Pirajussara
Parque do Ibirapuera
Museo Ipiranga
Brooklin
Indianápolis
Vila Iguacu
Taboão da Serra
Jardim Sapopemba
Santo Amaro
São Paulo Congonhas
Parque do Estado
São Caetano do Sul
Itupu
Cupacé
Utinga
Jurubatuba
Zoológico
Interagos
Zuvuvús
Vila Oriental
Mauá
Pedreira
Diadema
Santo André
São Bernardo do Campo
Represa Billings

4 Km
4 Miles

19,686ft
13,124ft
9843ft
6562ft
3281ft
1640ft
820ft
328ft
Sea Level
-820ft
-6562ft
-13,124ft

Africa is the world's second largest continent with a total area of 11,712,434 sq miles (30,335,000 sq km). It has 54 separate countries, including Madagascar in the Indian Ocean. It straddles the equator and is the only continent to stretch from the northern to southern temperate zones.

FACTFILE

N **Most Northerly Point:** Jalta, Tunisia 37° 31′ N
S **Most Southerly Point:** Cape Agulhas, South Africa 34° 52′ S
E **Most Easterly Point:** Raas Xaafuun, Somalia 51° 24′ E
W **Most Westerly Point:** Santo Antão, Cape Verde, 25° 11′ W

Largest Lakes:
1. Lake Victoria, Kenya/Tanzania/Uganda 26,828 sq miles (69,484 sq km)
2. Lake Tanganyika, Dem. Rep. Congo/Tanzania 12,703 sq miles (32,900 sq km)
3. Lake Nyasa, Malawi/Mozambique/Tanzania 11,600 sq miles (30,044 sq km)
4. Lake Turkana, Ethiopia/Kenya 2473 sq miles (6405 sq km)
5. Lake Albert, Dem. Rep. Congo/Uganda 2046 sq miles (5299 sq km)

Longest Rivers:
1. Nile, NE Africa 4160 miles (6695 km)
2. Congo, Angola/Congo/Dem. Rep. Congo 2900 miles (4667 km)
3. Niger, W Africa 2589 miles (4167 km)
4. Zambezi, Southern Africa 1673 miles (2693 km)
5. Ubangi-Uele, C Africa 1429 miles (2300 km)

Largest Islands:
1. Madagascar, 229,300 sq miles (594,000 sq km)
2. Réunion, 970 sq miles (2535 sq km)
3. Tenerife, Canary Islands 785 sq miles (2034 sq km)
4. Isla de Bioco, Equatorial Guinea 779 sq miles (2017 sq km)
5. Mauritius, 709 sq miles (1836 sq km)

Highest Points:
1. Kilimanjaro, Tanzania 19,340 ft (5895 m)
2. Kirinyaga, Kenya 17,058 ft (5199 m)
3. Mount Stanley, Dem. Rep. Congo/Uganda 16,762 ft (5109 m)
4. Mount Speke, Uganda 16,043 ft (4890 m)
5. Mount Baker, Uganda 15,892 ft (4844 m)

Lowest Point:
▼ Lac 'Assal, Djibouti -512 ft (-156 m) below sea level

Highest recorded temperature:
⊕ Al'Aziziyah, Libya 136°F (58°C)

Lowest recorded temperature:
⊖ Ifrane, Morocco -11°F (-24°C)

Wettest Place:
≋ Cape Debundsha, Cameroon 405 in (10,290 mm)

Driest Place:
⊖ Wadi Halfa, Sudan <0.1 in (<2.5 mm)

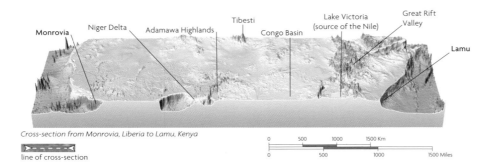

Cross-section from Monrovia, Liberia to Lamu, Kenya

▷ ─ ▪ ─ ▪ ◁
line of cross-section

AFRICA – Political

Political

The political map of modern Africa only emerged following the end of World War II. Over the next half-century, all of the countries formerly controlled by European powers gained independence from their colonial rulers—only Liberia and Ethiopia were never colonized. The post-colonial era has not been an easy period for many countries, but there have been moves toward multi-party democracy across much of the continent. In South Africa, democratic elections replaced the internationally-condemned apartheid system only in 1994. Other countries have still to find political stability; corruption in government and ethnic tensions are serious problems. National infrastructures, based on the colonial transportation systems built to exploit Africa's resources, are often inappropriate for independent economic development.

Scale 1:30,500,000
(projection: Lambert Azimuthal Equal Area)

Standard of living

Since the 1960s most countries in Africa have seen significant improvements in life expectancy, healthcare, and education. However, 28 of the 30 most deprived countries in the world are African, and the continent as a whole lies well behind the rest of the world in terms of meeting many basic human needs.

Transportation

African railroads were built to aid the exploitation of natural resources, and most offer passage only from the interior to the coastal cities, leaving large parts of the continent untouched—five land-locked countries have no railroads at all. The Congo, Nile, and Niger river networks offer limited access to land within the continental interior, but have a number of waterfalls and cataracts which prevent navigation from the sea. Many roads were developed in the 1960s and 1970s, but economic difficulties are making the maintenance and expansion of the networks difficult.

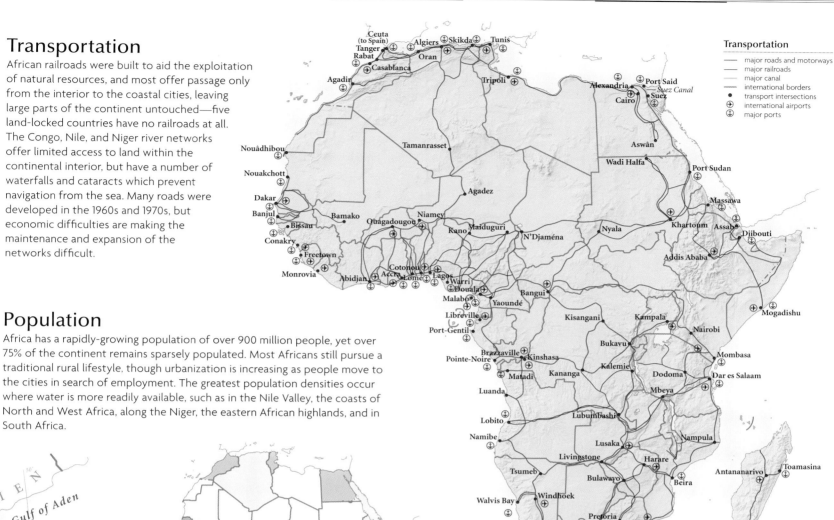

Transportation
— major roads and motorways
— major railroads
— major canal
— international borders
• transport intersections
⊕ international airports
⊕ major ports

Population

Africa has a rapidly-growing population of over 900 million people, yet over 75% of the continent remains sparsely populated. Most Africans still pursue a traditional rural lifestyle, though urbanization is increasing as people move to the cities in search of employment. The greatest population densities occur where water is more readily available, such as in the Nile Valley, the coasts of North and West Africa, along the Niger, the eastern African highlands, and in South Africa.

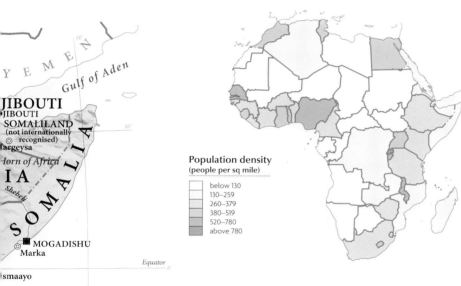

Population density
(people per sq mile)
- below 130
- 130–259
- 260–379
- 380–519
- 520–780
- above 780

Languages

Three major world languages act as *lingua francas* across the African continent: Arabic in North Africa; English in southern and eastern Africa and Nigeria; and French in Central and West Africa, and in Madagascar. A huge number of African languages are spoken as well—over 2000 have been recorded, with more than 400 in Nigeria alone—reflecting the continuing importance of traditional cultures and values. In the north of the continent, the extensive use of Arabic reflects Middle Eastern influences while Bantu languages are widely-spoken across much of southern Africa.

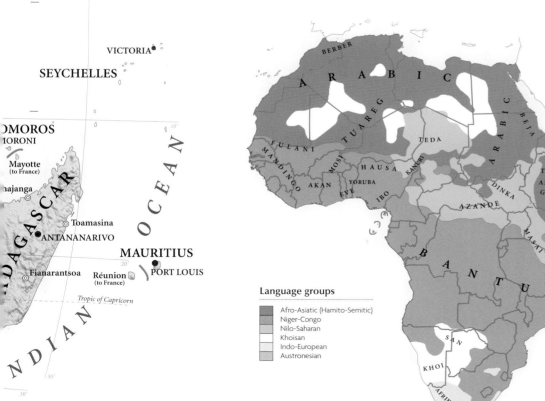

Language groups
- Afro-Asiatic (Hamito-Semitic)
- Niger-Congo
- Nilo-Saharan
- Khoisan
- Indo-European
- Austronesian

Official African Languages

- French
- English
- Arabic
- Portuguese
- Swahili
- Amharic
- Spanish
- French/English
- French/Arabic
- French/Malagasy
- English/Swahili
- Arabic/Somali

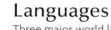

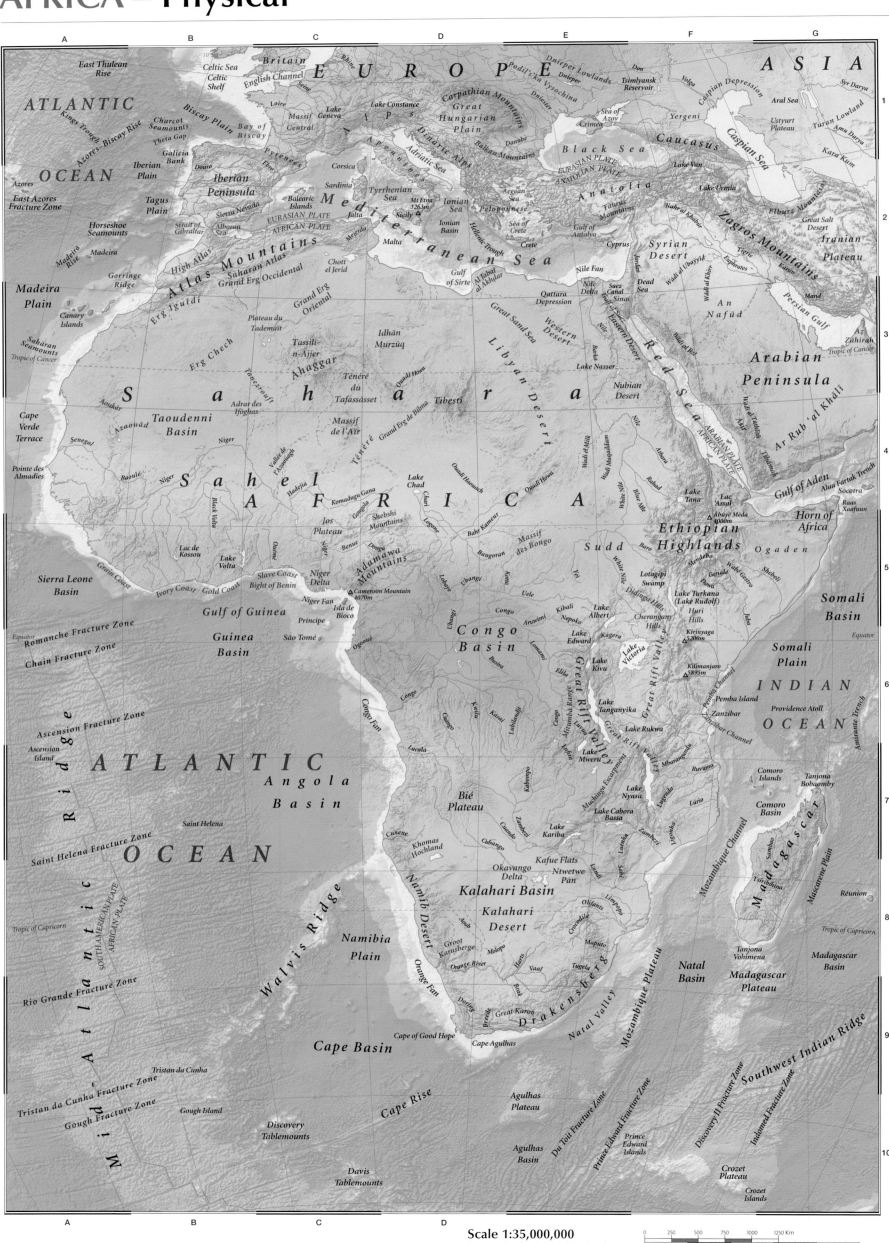

Scale 1:35,000,000
(projection: Lambert Azimuthal Equal Area)

0   250   500   750   1000   1250 Km

0   250   500   750   1000   1250 Miles

Climate

The climates of Africa range from mediterranean to arid, dry savannah and humid equatorial. In East Africa, where snow settles at the summit of volcanoes such as Kilimanjaro, climate is also modified by altitude. The winds of the Sahara export millions of tons of dust a year both northward and eastward.

Climate

- arid
- humid equatorial
- mediterranean
- semi-arid
- tropical
- warm humid
- ☼ daily hours of sunshine, January
- ☼ daily hours of sunshine, July
- → cold wind
- → hot wind

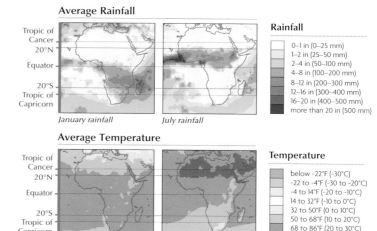

Average Rainfall

January rainfall *July rainfall*

Rainfall

- 0–1 in (0–25 mm)
- 1–2 in (25–50 mm)
- 2–4 in (50–100 mm)
- 4–8 in (100–200 mm)
- 8–12 in (200–300 mm)
- 12–16 in (300–400 mm)
- 16–20 in (400–500 mm)
- more than 20 in (500 mm)

Average Temperature

January temperature *July temperature*

Temperature

- below -22°F (-30°C)
- -22 to -4°F (-30 to -20°C)
- -4 to 14°F (-20 to -10°C)
- 14 to 32°F (-10 to 0°C)
- 32 to 50°F (0 to 10°C)
- 50 to 68°F (10 to 20°C)
- 68 to 86°F (20 to 30°C)
- above 86°F (30°C)

Land use

Some of Africa's most productive agricultural land is found in the eastern volcanic uplands, where fertile soils support a wide range of valuable export crops including vegetables, tea, and coffee. The most widely-grown grain is corn and peanuts (groundnuts) are particularly important in West Africa. Without intensive irrigation, cultivation is not possible in desert regions and unreliable rainfall in other areas limits crop production. Pastoral herding is most commonly found in these marginal lands. Substantial local fishing industries are found along coasts and in vast lakes such as Lake Nyasa and Lake Victoria.

Environmental issues

One of Africa's most serious environmental problems occurs in marginal areas such as the Sahel where scrub and forest clearance, often for cooking fuel, combined with overgrazing, are causing desertification. Game reserves in southern and eastern Africa have helped to preserve many endangered animals, although the needs of growing populations have led to conflict over land use, and poaching is a serious problem.

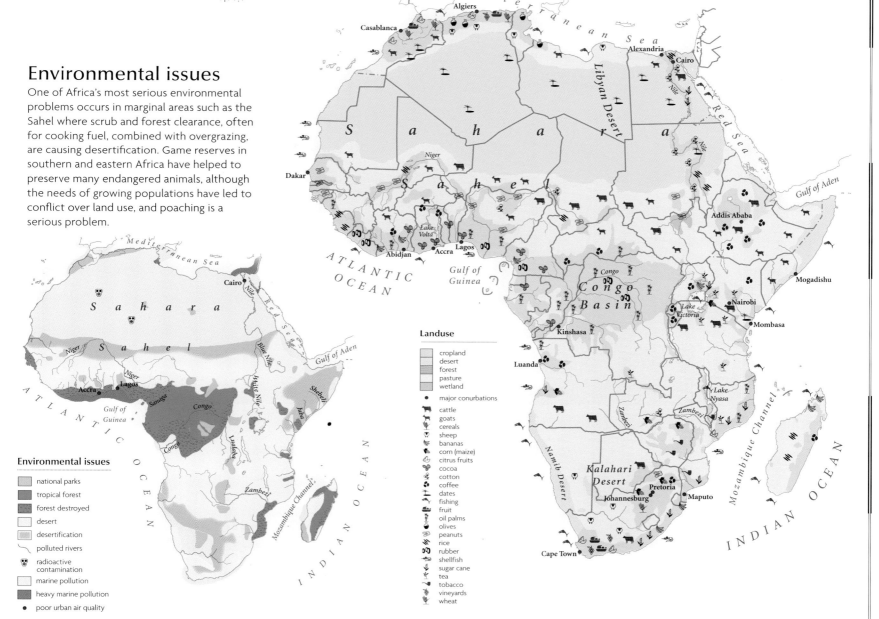

Environmental issues

- national parks
- tropical forest
- forest destroyed
- desert
- desertification
- polluted rivers
- ☢ radioactive contamination
- marine pollution
- heavy marine pollution
- • poor urban air quality

Landuse

- cropland
- desert
- forest
- pasture
- wetland
- • major conurbations
- cattle
- goats
- cereals
- sheep
- bananas
- corn (maize)
- citrus fruits
- cocoa
- cotton
- coffee
- dates
- fishing
- fruit
- oil palms
- olives
- peanuts
- rice
- rubber
- shellfish
- sugar cane
- tea
- tobacco
- vineyards
- wheat

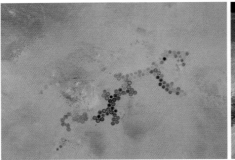

1 AL KHUFRAH, LIBYA
The circular irrigation patterns at this oasis have developed through the use of sprinkler units sweeping around a central point.

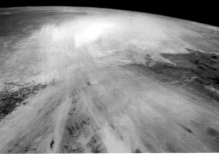

2 ERG DU DJOURAB, CHAD
Looking southwest, the pale area, just south of the darker Tibesti mountains on the right and the Ennedi plateau on the left, shows a desert sandstorm in motion.

3 ASWAN HIGH DAM, EGYPT
Completed in 1970 the dam controls flooding along the lower stretches of the Nile river.

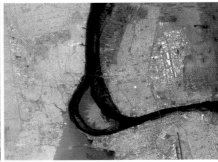

4 KHARTOUM, SUDAN
The capital of Sudan lies at the junction of the Blue Nile, flowing from the east, and the broad White Nile, flowing from the south.

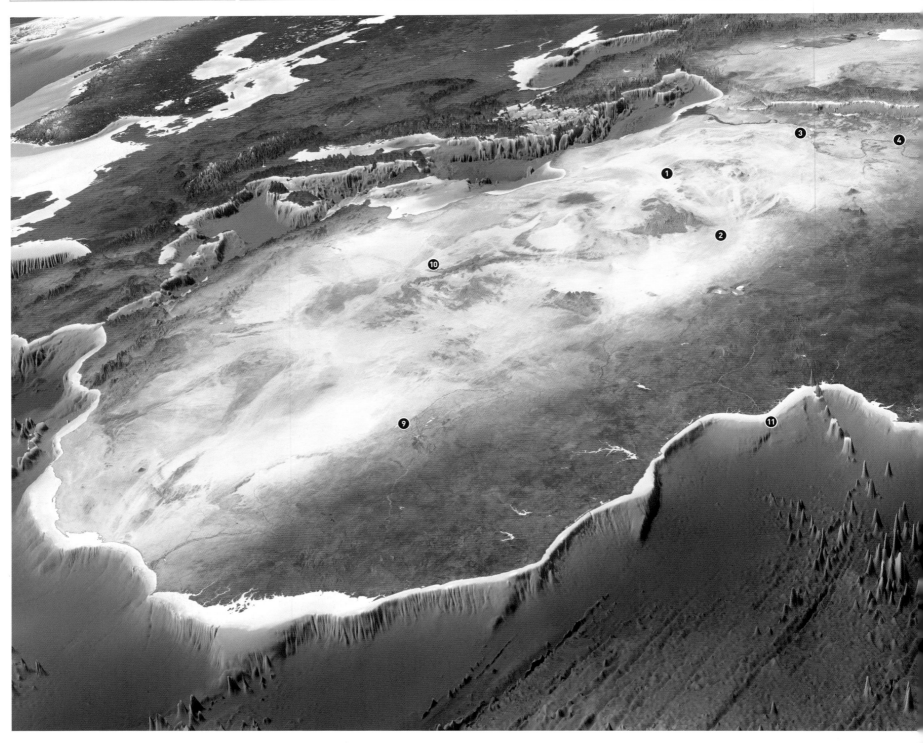

9 LAKE FAGUIBINE, MALI
Part of the Niger river's "inland delta," a region of lakes, creeks and backwaters near Tombouctou.

10 TASSILI-N-AJJER, ALGERIA
These sand dunes, one of a variety found in the Sahara, overlie the darker sandstone bedrock of the Tassili-n-Ajjer plateau.

11 NIGER DELTA, NIGERIA
At this point lies the vast, low-lying region through which the waters of the Niger river drain into the Gulf of Guinea.

12 CONGO/UBANGI RIVERS, DR CONGO
The confluence of these two rivers lies at the heart of the Congo Basin.

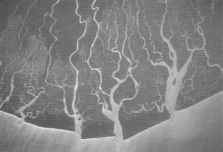

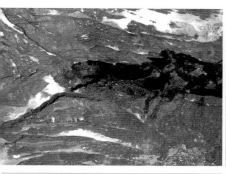

AFAR DEPRESSION, DJIBOUTI [5]
This low point is located at the junction of three tectonic plates—the Gulf of Aden to the east, the Red Sea to the north and the Great Rift Valley to the south.

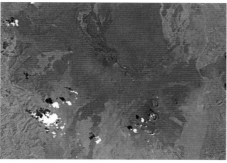

NYIRAGONGO AND NYAMURAGIRA VOLCANOES, [6]
DR CONGO
These two volcanoes, lying to the west of the Great Rift Valley, last erupted in 2002 and 2001 respectively.

KILIMANJARO, TANZANIA [7]
An extinct volcano, its great height modifies the local climate, forcing moist air streams from the Indian Ocean to rise, inducing rain and, higher up, snow.

BETSIBOKA RIVER, MADAGASCAR [8]
The waters of Madagascar's second longest river are red with sediment as it carries eroded topsoil from the interior and deposits it in the Indian Ocean.

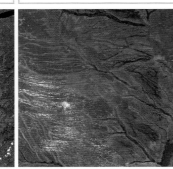

MALEBO POOL, CONGO/DR CONGO [13]
A lake in the lower reaches of the Congo river, it hosts two capital cities on its banks, Brazzaville, Congo to the north and Kinshasa, DR Congo to the south.

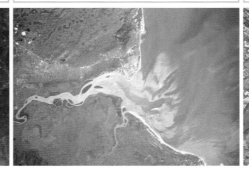

ZAMBEZI RIVER, ZAMBIA [14]
Seasonal flooding of the river and its tributaries turned the Mulonga and Liuwa plains on the Zambia-Angola border into a vast wetland in April 2004

BEIRA, MOZAMBIQUE [15]
This port and beach resort lies on the north side of the mouth of the Pungoé river.

CAPE TOWN, SOUTH AFRICA [16]
South Africa's third largest city with a population of 2.9 million, it is also the seat of the country's parliament.

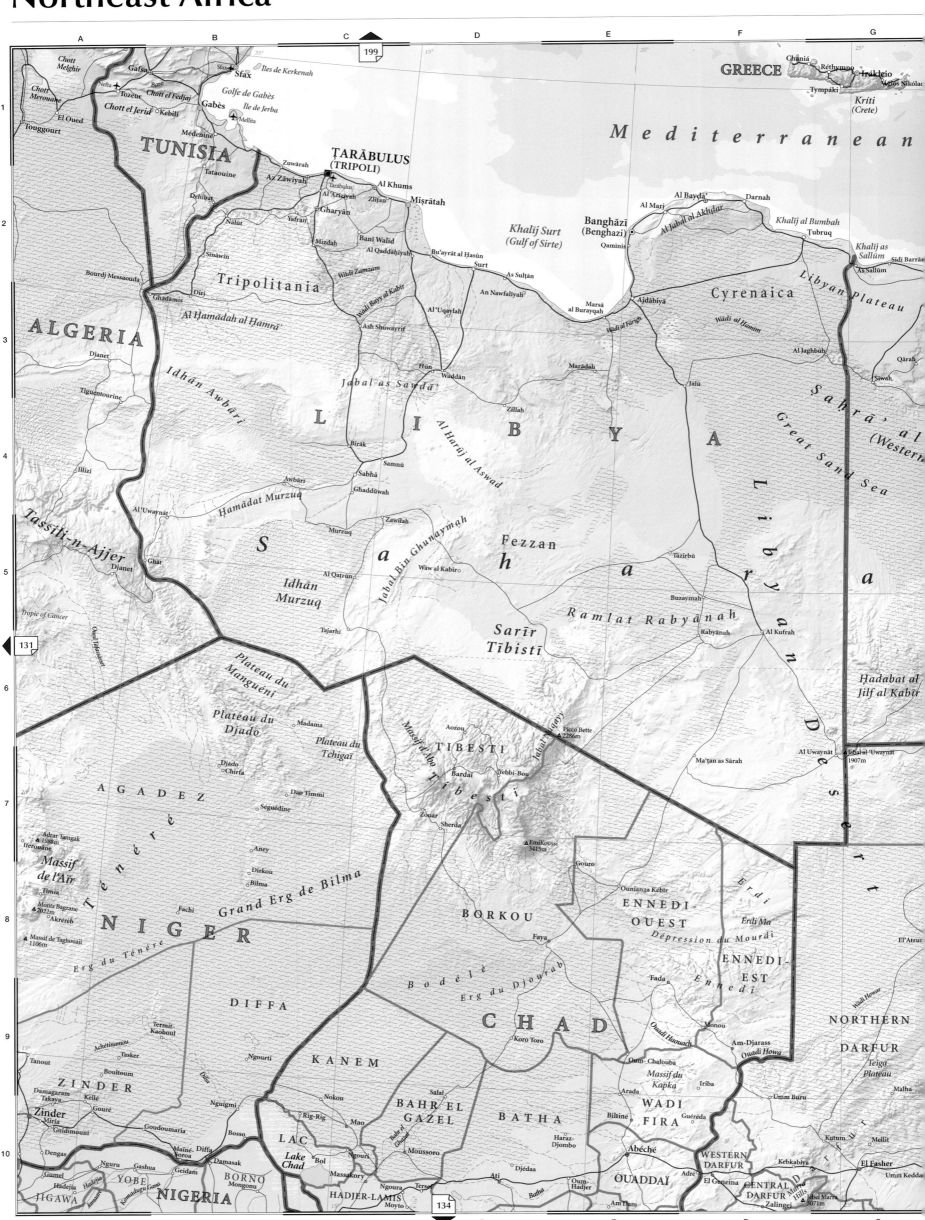

Scale 1:8,000,000
(projection: Lambert Azimuthal Equal Area)

0 25 50 75 100 125 150 175 200 Km
0 25 50 75 100 125 150 175 200 Miles

Population
- ■ above 5 million
- ◉ 100,000 to 500,000
- ▣ 1 million to 5 million
- ⊕ 50,000 to 100,000
- ● 500,000 to 1 million
- ○ 10,000 to 50,000
- ○ below 10,000

AFRICA

129

19,686ft
13,124ft
9843ft
6562ft
3281ft
1640ft
820ft
328ft
Sea Level
-820ft
-6562ft
-13,124ft

CYPRUS (TURKISH REPUBLIC OF NORTHERN CYPRUS recognized only by Turkey)
NICOSIA, Girne (Kyrenia), Gazimağusa (Ammóchostos, Famagusta), Lárnaca, Lemesós (Limassol), Páfos, Karpathos, Olympos

Al Lādhiqīyah (Latakia), Tartūs, Tripoli, Hamāh, Hims (Homs), Jabal Abū Rahbah

SYRIA — DIMASHQ (DAMASCUS), Syrian Desert, Al Jazīrah, Tigris, Tikrit

LEBANON — BEYROUTH (BEIRUT), Nahariyya, Hefa (Haifa), Dūma

ISRAEL — Tel Aviv-Yafo, Holon, Ashdod, JERUSALEM, Gaza Strip, Gaza, West Bank, Hebron, Rehovot, Be'ér Sheva

'AMMAN, Midabā, Madabā, Dead Sea, Al Karak, **JORDAN**, Ma'ān, Al Mafraq, Az Zarqā'

IRAN — Kermānshāh (Bākhtarān), KERMĀNSHĀH, LORESTĀN, ILĀM

IRAQ — BAGHDĀD, Al Fallūjah, Buḩayrat ath Tharthār, Ba'qūbah, Karbalā', An Najaf, Al Hillah, Al Kūt, Al 'Amārah, Ar Rahab, An Nāşirīyah, As Samāwah, Euphrates

Alexandria (Al Iskandarīyah), Al 'Alamayn, Al Nouzha, Marsá Matroûh, Rashid (Rosetta), Damanhūr, Kafr ash Shaykh, Tanta, Az Zaqāzīq, Shibin al Kawm, Banha, Dumyāt (Damietta), Bûr Sa'id (Port Said), Nile Delta

EGYPT — CAIRO (AL QĀHIRAH), Giza (Al Jīzah), Pyramids of Giza, Hilwān, Aş Şaff, Suez Canal (Qanāt as Suways), Al Ismā'īlīya, Suez (As Suways), Al 'Arīsh, Sinai (Sinā)

Al Fayyūm, Banī Suwayf, Al Fashn, Banī Mazār, Al Minyā, Mallawī, Dayrūt, Abnūb, Asyūt, Tahta, Sawhāj, Akhmīm, Jirja, Qinā, Luxor (Al 'Uqşur), Isnā, Idfū, Kom Ombo (Kawm Umbū), Aswān, Aswan Dam (Khazzān Aswān), Valley of the Kings

Al Qaşr, Mūt, Al Khārijah, Qaşr al Farāfirah, Bawīti, Baris, Abu Ballas 467m

Za'faranah, Abū Zenima, At Tūr, Ra's Ghārib, Al Ghurdaqah (Hurghada), Bûr Safāga, Al Quşayr, Marsá al 'Alam, Baranis, Ra's Banās

Jabal Mūsá 2285m, Jabal al Lawz 2580m, Jabal ash Shifa, Sharm ash Shaykh, Jazīrat Ra's Tīrān, Ra's Muhammad, Al Bad', Jabal al Dabbah 2550m, Ad Duwayhir, Al Muwayliḥ, Dubā, Al Wajh, Al 'Ulā, Wādī al Ḥisī, Al Ḥijāz

Gulf of Aqaba, Khalīj as Suways (Gulf of Suez), Şaḩārā ash Sharqīya (Eastern Desert), Red Sea

Lake Nasser (Buhayrat Nāşir), (Administrative border), (Hala'ib Triangle), Halaib, (Political border), Abu Simbel (Abū Sunbul), Wadi Halfa, Akasha, Selima Oasis, Laqiya Arba'in

NORTHERN (KORDOFAN / NORTHERN), Delgo, Argo, Dongola, El Khandaq, Merowe, Shereik, Abu Hamed, Kerma

Nubian Desert

SUDAN — KHARTOUM, Omdurman, Khartoum North, Umm Inderab, El Kamlin, Rufa'a, GEZIRA, Wad Medani, El Manaqil, El Hawata, Barakat, Sennar, SINNAR, Singa, Rabak, Kosti, WHITE NILE, Ed Dueim, Umm Ruwaba, Tendelti, El Obeid

NORTHERN KORDOFAN — Hamrat esh Sheikh, Sodiri, Khuwei, Wad Banda, **WESTERN KORDOFAN**

RIVER NILE — Ed Debba, Korti, Kabushiya, Shendi, Atbara, Ed Damer, Berber, Adarama, Musmar

Wadi Howar, Wadi 'Amur

RED SEA — Port Sudan, Sallom, Suakin, Sinkat, Ekowit, Tokar, Haiya, Derudeb, Musmar, Ras Shakal

SAUDI ARABIA — AL JAWF, Al Jawf, Adhfa', Sakākah, AL ḤUDŪD ASH SHAMĀLĪYAH, 'Ar'ar, Rafha', Nişāb, Hafar al Bātin, Al Mayyah, An Nafūd, Tabūk, TABŪK, Al Akhdar, Al Qalibah, Taymā', Ad Dār al Hamrā', Khaybar, Hā'il, HĀ'IL, Al Ghazālah, Al Ḥamūdīyah, Al Artāwīyah, Az Zilfī, Buraydah, 'Unayzah, Al Majma'ah, Jalājil, Shaqrā', Marāh, Durma, Ad Dawādīmī, Al Quwayyīyah, AL QASĪM, Najd, NAJD, AL MADĪNAH, Al Madīnah (Medina), Yanbu' al Bahr, Badr Ḥunayn, Rābigh, Jabal Radwā 1814m, Al Hanākīyah, Mahd adh Dhahab, Harrat Rahat, Al Mislah, Zalim, Budayyi'ah, Halabān, Tropic of Cancer, AR RIYĀḌ, Maqiah, Turabah, MAKKAH, Makkah (Mecca), King Abdul Aziz, Jiddah (Jedda), At Tā'if, Ar Rawdah, 'Aynīn, Al Khurmah, As Sulayyil, Wādī ad Dawāsir

Dungūnab, Ras Abu Shagara, Muhammad Qol

ERITREA — ASMARA, Keren, Massawa, Akurdet, Agordat, Nakfa, Eriba, Kassala, KASSALA, Teseney, Barentu, Mendefera, Mersa Fatma, Dahlak Archipelago, Massawa Channel, Engershatu 2576m

ETHIOPIA — TIGRAY, Mek'ele, AMHARA, Simēn, Ras Dashen 4620m, Aksum, Ādigrat, Ādwa, Gonder, Debark, AFAR, Danakil Desert, Korem, Sek'ot'a, Maych'ew

GEDAREF — Gedaref, Doka, Hag 'Abdullah, Metema, Āykel, Gallabat, Om Hajer

YEMEN — SAN'Ā (SANA), Amrān, Dhamār, Radā', Ibb, Ta'izz, Al Hudaydah (Hodeida), Zabid, Yarīm, Dhī as Sufāl, Qa'tabah, Al Bayt al Faqīh, Jabal an Nabī Shu'ayb 3760m, Al Mukhā, Mawza', Al Madīnah ash Sha'b, Madīnat ash Sha'b, Jazīrat al Hanīsh al Kabīr, Jazīrat Jabal Zuqar, Bāb al Mandab, Mocha, Lahij

'ASĪR — Al Bāḩah, AL BĀḤAH, Qal'at Bishah, Bishah, Tathlith, Khamis Mushayt, Abha, Jabal Sawda 3133m, Al Birk, Zahrān, Muhāyil, NAJRĀN, Najrān, Sabyā, JĪZĀN, Jīzān, Sa'dah, Midi, 'Abs, Hajjah, Kamarān, Al Luhayyah, Az Zaydīyah, Hūth, Khamir, Wādī Mawr, Wādī Māwiyah, Wādī Rima'

DJIBOUTI — Aseb, Beylul, Mouhoulé, Ed

King Abdul Aziz

Al Qunfudhah, Al Līth, Sāḩil 'Ulaya, Ad Darb, Wādī Bīshah, Wādī Tathlīth

IRAN

AFRICA

130

290

132

ATLANTIC

OCEAN

PORTUGAL

SPAIN

Sines · Baza
Azuaga · Montoro · Linares
Córdoba · Jaén
Cabo de São Vicente · Lagos · Faro · Huelva (Seville) · Dos Hermanas · Lucena · Guadix
Sevilla (Seville) · Osuna · Sierra Nevada · 3481m · Almería · Mojac
Lebrija · Granada · Motril
Jerez de la Frontera · Ronda · Málaga · Costa del Sol
Cádiz · San Fernando · Marbella
Vejer de la Frontera · Algeciras · **GIBRALTAR**
Strait of Gibraltar (to UK)
Cap Spartel · Ceuta (to Spain) · Cap des Trois Fourches
Boukhalef · Tanger · Melilla (to Spain)
Asilah · Tétouan · Al-Hoceima · Nador · Beni Ghazaouet
Larache · Chefchaouen
Ksar-el-Kebir · Rif · Oujda
Moulay-Bousselham · Ouazzane · El Aioun
Souk-el-Arba-Rharb · Taounate · Jerada
Kénitra · Sidi-Kacem · Taza
Salé · Sidi · Fès
RABAT · Salé · Bou
Casablanca · Khemisset · Meknès · Sefrou
Mohammed V · Mohammedia · Azrou · Ifrane
El-Jadida · Berrechid · Moyen Atlas
Settat · Oued-Zem · Khénifra
Khouribga · Tendrara
Sidi-Bennour · Beni-Mellal · Jbel Ayachi 3757m
Safi · El Kelâa Srarhna · Azilal · Er-Rachidia
Tensift · Haut Atlas · Béchar
Essaouira · Marrakech · Erfoud · Abadla
Menara · Jbel Toubkal 4165m · Ouarzazate · Hamada du Guir · Beni Ab
Cap Rhir · Imouzzer · Taroudannt
Agadir · Anti Atlas · Big er Raou
Sidi-Ifni · Tiznit · Bou-Izakarn · Hamada du Dra · Tabelbala
Tata · Hamada Tounassine
Guelmime · Draâ
Tan-Tan

Madeira (to Portugal)
Porto Santo
Funchal
Ilhas Desertas

La Palma · Santa Cruz de la Palma · Lanzarote
Tenerife · Santa Cruz de Tenerife · Arrecife
Gomera · Fuerteventura · Puerto del Rosario
Hierro · Islas Canarias (Canary Islands) (to Spain) · Las Palmas de Gran Canaria
Gran Canaria · Cap Juby

Tarfaya

LAÂYOUNE

Saguia al Hamra · Smara
Bou Craa
WESTERN SAHARA (occupied by Morocco)

Boujdour

Tindouf · Sebkha de Tindouf · **ALG**
El Mahbas · El Eglab
Aïn Ben Tili

Galtat-Zemmour · Bir Mogrein · Chegga
Tropic of Cancer

TIRIS · 'Ayoûn 'Abd el Mâlek
Ad Dakhla · Sebkhet Aghzoumal · **ZEMMOUR** · Erg el Ahmar
El Mreiti · 'Erg Ech Chech · **S**

Cap Barbas · Aousard · Zouérat · Kâghet · El Hank
Fdérik · El Hammâmi · Taoudenni
Bir-Gandouz · Aghouinit · Touril · Erg · El Guettâra
Techla · Tourine
Touâjil
Nouâdhibou · Boû Lanouâr · Azeffâl · Chār · Malqteïr
Lagouira · Ras Nouâdhibou · **Nouâdhibou** · Choûm · Ouarâne · El Mraÿer
Dakhlet Nouâdhibou · Akchâr · Atâr · Ouadâne · 'Erg Atouila
DAKHLET NOUÂDHIBOU · Oujeft · Chinguetti · **ADRAR** · 'Erg I-n-Sâkâ
Et Tîdra · **INCHIRI** · Araouane · 'Erîgât TOMBOUCTOU · 'Erg I-n-Échar
Nouâmghâr · Ras Timirist · Akjoujt · El Mreyyé · **MA**
Bennichâb

MAURITANIA

Boû Rjeïmât
Sebkhet Te-n-Dghâmcha · Rachid · Boû Djébéha
NOUAKCHOTT · Beita · Tidjikja · Tichit · **M**
Nouakchott · Idini · Araouane
TRARZA · **TAGANT** · Aoukâr · **HODH**
Tiguent · Boutilimit · Moudjéria · **ECH CHARGUI** · Azaou
Mederdra · Magta' Lahjar · Boûmdeid · Oualâta · Lac Faguibine
Rkiz · **BRAKNA** · Tâmchekket · Tombouctou
Rosso · Aleg · Guérou · Kiffa · Néma · Diré
Saint Louis · Dagana · Podor · Bogué · **ASSABA** · 'Ayoûn el 'Atroûs · Oudeïka
Richard Toll · Bababé · Kankossa · Qualâta
Lac de Guier · Kaédi · Mônguel · Kobenni · Goundam
Vallée du Ferlo · Mbout · **HODH EL GHARBI** · Niafounké
GORGOL · Timbedgha · Lac Niangay
Kébémer · Louga · Dara · Linguère · Maghama · Tintâne · Kobenni · Amoûrj · Lac Garou
DAKAR · Tivaouane · Ranérou · Matam · **GUIDIMAKA** · 'Adel Bagrou · Youvarou · Aougoundou
Pointe des Almadies · Mékhé · **SENEGAL** · Kaÿes · Vélingara · Ballé · **KOULIKORO** · Nampala · **MOPTI**
Dakar · Thiès · **KAYES** · Vioro · Sékou
Rufisque · Touba · Diourbel · Bambey · Bakel · **SEGOU**
Mbour · Fatick · Mbaké · Selibabi · Yélimané

20° · 15° · 10°

6000m
4000m
3000m
2000m
1000m
500m
250m
100m
Sea Level
-250m
-2000m
-4000m

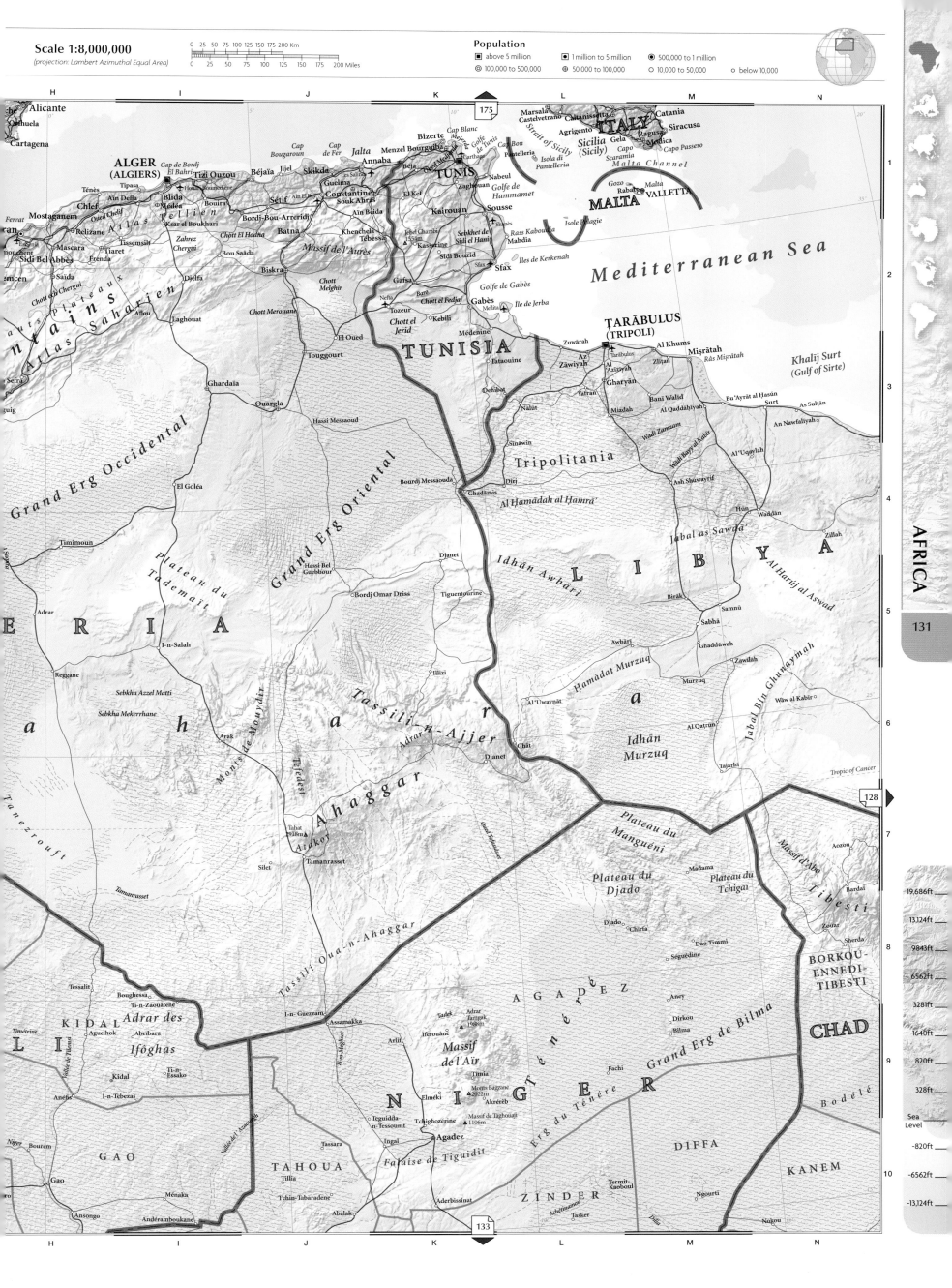

AFRICA

132

Map labels

Grid columns: A B C D E F G
Grid rows: 1–10

130

MAURITANIA

TIRIS ZEMMOUR

Cap Barbas · Bir-Gandouz · Techla · Aghouinit · Touâjîl · Tourine

Nouâdhibou · Lagouira · Râs Nouâdhibou · Dakhlet Nouâdhibou · Bou Lanouâr · Char · Choûm · El Mrâyer · El Guettâra

DAKHLET NOUÂDHIBOU · INCHIRI · Atâr · Chinguetti · Ouâdâne · ADRAR · Oujeft

Nouâmghâr · Râs Timirist · Bennichâb · Akjoujt · Akchâr · Azeffâl

El Mrêyyé · Ouarâne · 'Erg Atouila · 'Erg I-n-Sâkâne · I-n-Echaï · 'Erigât

Sebkhet Te-n-Dghâmcha · Beila · Nouakchott · Idini · Rachid · TAGANT · Tidjikja · Tichit · Aoukâr · HODH · Araouane · Boû Djébéha · TOMBOUCTOU

NOUAKCHOTT · TRARZA · Boutilimit · Moudjéria · Tâmchekket · 'Ayoûn el 'Atroûs · Oualâta · Néma · ECH CHARGUI · HODH · Azaouâd · Oudeïka

Tiguent · Magta' Lahjar · Boumdeïd · Guérou · Kiffa · Tintâne · Timbedgha · Amourj · Bassikounou

Mederdra · Rkîz · BRAKNA · Aleg · Bababé · Monguel · Kaédi · ASSABA · Kankossa · Kobenni · 'Adel Bagrou

Rosso · Dagana · Richard Toll · Bogué · Mbout · HODH EL GHARBI · Kébémer · Bababé · Amourj · Nampala

Saint Louis · Lac de Guier · Vallée de Ferlo · GORGOL · Magama · Sélibabi · Yélimané · Nioro · Ballé · Nara · Youvarou · Lac Faguibine · Tombouctou · Gourma-Rharous · Goundam · Diré · Niafounké · Lac Garou · Lac Niangay · Lac Aougoundou

SENEGAL · Louga · Linguère · Ranérou · Matam · Maghama · Yélimané · Sandaré · Diéma · Mourdiah · Sokolo · Niono · Ténenkou · Diaka · Konna · MOPTI · Douentza · Hombo

Pointe des Almadies · Dakar · Mékhé · Tivaouane · Touba · Dara · Vélingara · Bakel · Ambidédi · Kayes · Maréna · KAYES · KOULIKORO · SÉGOU · Mopti · Sévaré · Bandiagara

DAKAR · Thiès · Rufisque · Bambey · Diourbel · Mbaké · Kidira · Goudiri · Diamou · Sadiola · Bafoulabé · Didiéni · Banamba · Massina · Djénné · Bankass · Koro · Tiou · Djibo

Mbour · Fatick · Joal-Fadiout · Kaffrine · Koungheul · Maka · Tambacounda · Kita · Kolokani · Kati · Markala · Ségou · Bani · San · Tominian · Ouahigouya · Tikaré · Yako

Kaolack · Sokone · Nioro du Rip · Georgetown · Dialakoto · Médina Gounas · Saraya · Kédougou · Satadougou · Kokofata · Sebekoro · Koulikoro · Fana · BAMAKO · Ouéléssebougou · Yorosso · Bénéna · Bla · Ségou · Bobo-Dioulasso · Dédougou · Koudougou · OUAGADOUGOU

BANJUL · Brikama · Mansa Konko · Basse Santa Su · Vélingara · Diola · Koutiala · Sikasso · Sikass · Koutiala · Réo · Koudougou · BURKINA FASO

GAMBIA · Dioulouou · Bignona · Ziguinchor · Sédhiou · Farim · Bissora · Gabú · Bafatá · Koundara · Mali · Tamgué 1538m · Kolokani · SIKASSO · Kadiolo · Sindou · Orodara · Banfora · Sidéradougou · Gaoua · Loumbila

GUINEA-BISSAU · Cacheu · Mansôa · Bissau · Bolama · Fulacunda · Buba · Catió · Bolama · Koundara · Labé · Fouta Djallon · GUINEA · Siguiri · Kangaba · Lac de Sélingué · Bougouni · Niéna · Koloko · Koloko · Odienné · Boundiali · Korhogo · Ferkessédougou · Léo

Quinhámel · Bissau · Bolama · Bolama · Boké · Télimélé · Pita · Kavendou 1421m · Dalaba · Dinguiraye · Kouroussa · Yanfolila · Garalo · Kolondiéba · Manankoro · Kadiolo · Madinani · Boundiali · Tengréla · Niellé · Ouangolodougou · Ferkessédougou · Tafiré · Kong · Bouna

BISSAU · Kamsar · Fria · Dubréka · Kindia · Mamou · Dabola · Siguiri · Dabola · Faranah · Samatiguila · Odienné · Boundiali · Korhogo · Tehini

Cap Verga · Boffa · Konkouré · Kindia · Falaba · Kabala · Bintimani 1948m · Tokounou · Kankan · Mandiana · IVORY COAST

CONAKRY · Dubréka · Forécariah · Mongo · Kambia · Pendembu · Kissidougou · Kérouané · Bako · Boundiali · Katiola · Dabakala · Bondoukou

FREETOWN · Port Loko · Lunsar · Makeni · Magburaka · Koidu · Guéckédou · Macenta · Beyla · Touba · Séguéla · Mankono · Katiola · Bouaké · Sifié · Béoumi · Tanda

SIERRA LEONE · Pepel · Magburaka · Koidu · Kolahun · Voinjama · Pic de Tibé 1500m · Man · Blankouma · Kounahiri · Mbahiakro · Agnibilékrou

Shenge · Moyamba · Bo · Kenema · Kailahun · Zorzor · Lola · Mont Nimba · Zuénoula · Vavoua · Ouellé · Abengourou

Bonthe · Matru · Pujehun · Zimmi · Nzérékoré · Yomou · Nzo · Akpékro · Danané · Duékoué · Daloa · Issia · Bouaflé · Oumé · Toumodi · Bongouanou · Bibiani

Sulima · Tubmanburg · Gbanga · Ganta · Sanniquellie · Biankouma · Guiglo · Gagnoa · Lakota · Divo · Agboville · Adzopé · Awaso

Robertsport · LIBERIA · Kakata · Harbel · Tapeta · Toulépleu · Zwedru · Taï · Soubré · Gueyo · Tiassalé · Abidjan · Aboisso · Prestea · Enchi · Obuasi

MONROVIA · Marshall · Zwedru · Cavalla · Guétro · Dabou · Port-Bouet · Grand-Bassam · Half-Assini · Takoradi

Buchanan · River Cess · Grabo · San-Pédro · Fresco · Grand-Lahou · Cape Three Points

Greenville · Grand Cess · Plibo · Grand-Béréby · Sassandra · Sekondi

Harper · Tabou · Cape Palmas

YAMOUSSOUKRO · Dimbokro · GHANA · Goaso · Kumasi · Dunkwa

ATLANTIC OCEAN

AFRICA (spine)

Sea Level · 6000m · 4000m · 3000m · 2000m · 1000m · 500m · 250m · 100m · Sea Level · -250m · -2000m · -4000m

290

Inset: CAPE VERDE

Santo Antão · Pombas · Mindelo · Ilhas de Barlavento · Pedra Lume · Sal · São Vicente · Ribeira Brava · Amilcar Cabral · São Nicolau · Boa Vista · João Barrosa

ATLANTIC OCEAN · Tarrafal · Maio · Fogo · São Filipe · Santiago · PRAIA · Maio · Ilhas de Sotavento

Scale 1:8,000,000
0 50 100 Km
0 50 100 Miles

Inset: ASCENSION ISLAND (to UK)

North Point · Sisters Peak 446m · Porpoise Point · North East Bay · Clarence Bay · The Peak 859m · South East Point · South West Bay · **GEORGETOWN** · Portland Point · Mars Bay · Wideawake Airfield · South East Bay · Pillar Bay · South Point · ATLANTIC OCEAN

Scale 1:750,000
0 5 10 Km
0 5 10 Miles

Inset: TRISTAN DA CUNHA (to UK)

ATLANTIC OCEAN · Big Point · Rookery Point · Anchorstock Point · **EDINBURGH** · Queen Mary's Peak 2060m · Sandy Point · Longbluff · Lyon Point · Cave Point · Stonybeach Bay · Stonyhill Point · ATLANTIC OCEAN

Scale 1:750,000
0 5 10 Km
0 5 10 Miles

Inset: SAINT HELENA (to UK)

Sugar Loaf Point · Flagstaff Bay · **JAMESTOWN** · Horse Pasture Point · The Haystack 616m · Longwood · Egg Island · Diana's Peak 823m · Gill Point · South West Point · Long Range Point · Speery Island · Castle Rock Point · ATLANTIC OCEAN

Scale 1:750,000
0 5 10 Km
0 5 10 Miles

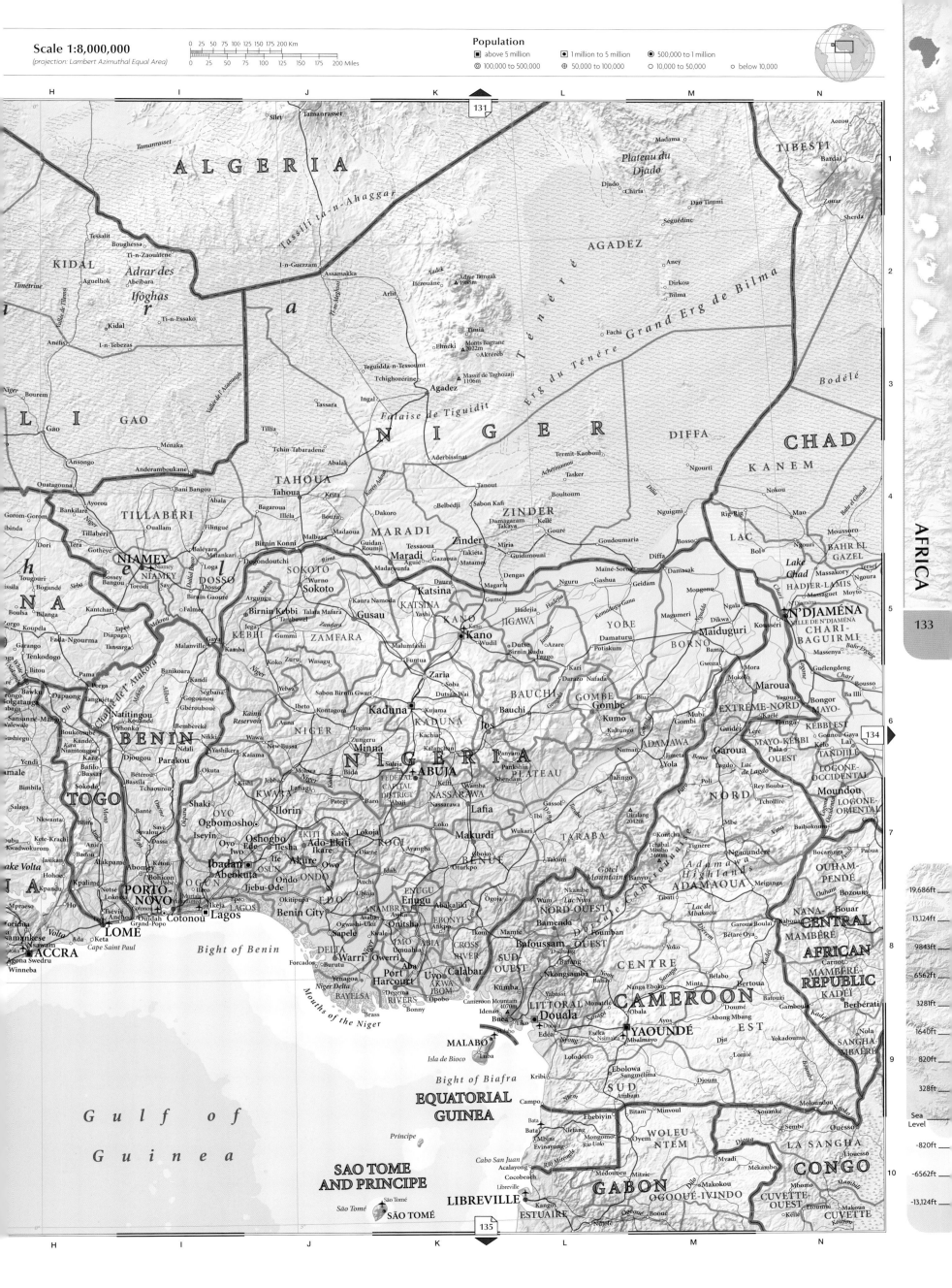

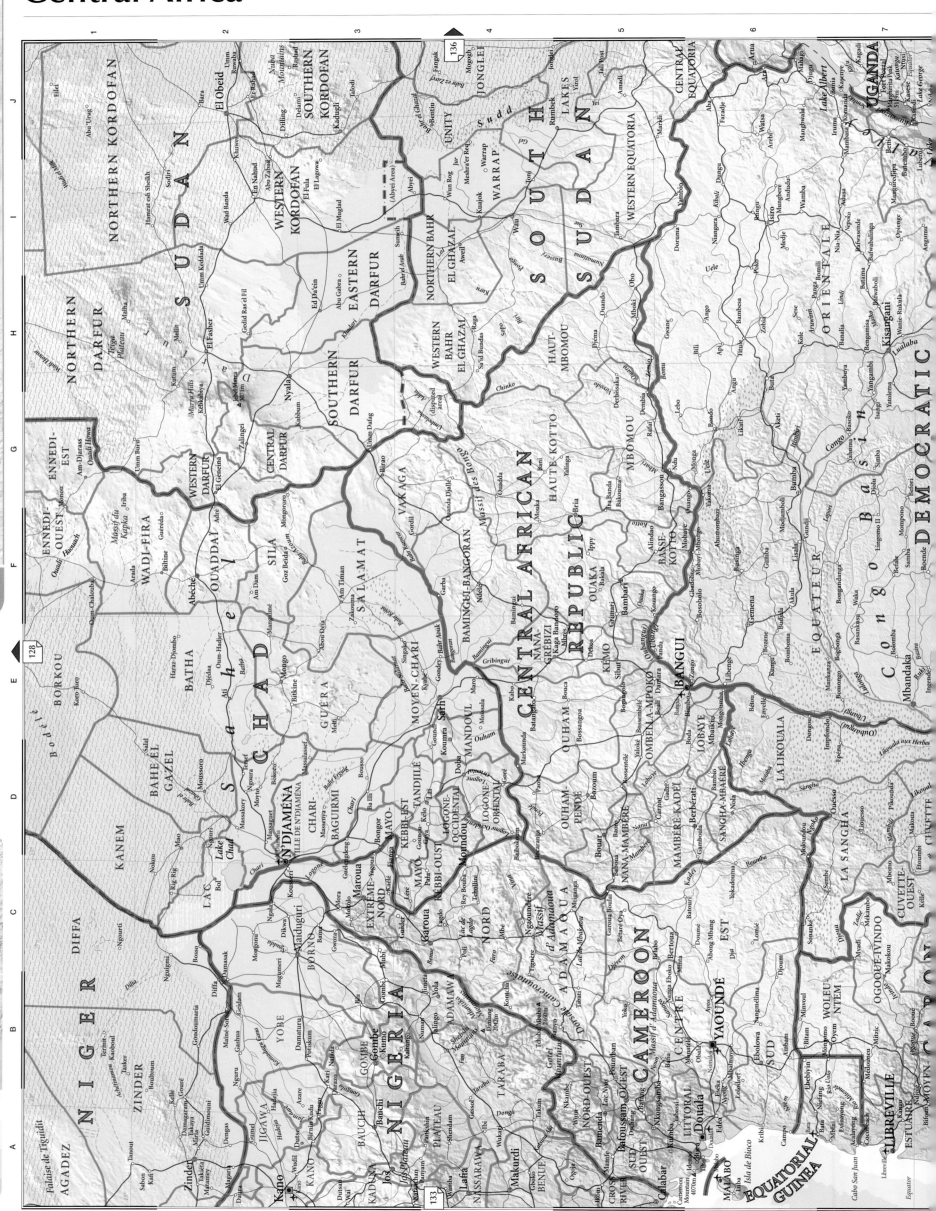

East Africa

288
129
134

KENYA: ADMINISTRATIVE REGIONS

1 NYAMIRA
2 BOMET
3 NAKURU
4 NYANDARUA
5 NYERI
6 MURANG'A
7 KIAMBU
8 NAIROBI CITY
9 KIRINYAGA
10 EMBU
11 THARAKA-NITHI
12 MACHAKOS
13 MAKUENI
14 MOMBASA

1 BUSIA
2 SIAYA
3 HOMA BAY
4 NYANDARUA
5 NYERI
6 BUNGOMA
7 KAKAMEGA
8 VIHIGA
9 KISUMU
10 WEST POKOT
11 TRANS NZOIA
12 ELGEYO/MARAKWET
13 UASIN GISHU
14 NANDI
15 KERICHO

Countries / Regions (labels)

SAUDI ARABIA
YEMEN
ERITREA
SUDAN
SOUTH SUDAN
ETHIOPIA
DJIBOUTI
SOMALILAND
SOMALIA
UGANDA
KENYA
DEM. REP. CONGO

Red Sea
Gulf of Aden

Ethiopian Highlands
Horn of Africa
Danakil Desert
Hadramawt

KHARTOUM
ADÍS ABEBA (ADDIS ABABA)
ASMARA
DJIBOUTI
MUQDISHO (MOGADISHU)
SAN'Ā' (SANA)
Hargeysa
Berbera
Boossaaso

Elevation scale

6000m
4000m
3000m
2000m
1000m
500m
250m
100m
Sea Level
-250m
-2000m
-4000m

Scale 1:8,000,000
(projection: Lambert Azimuthal Equal Area)

0 25 50 75 100 125 150 175 200 Km
0 25 50 75 100 125 150 175 200 Miles

Population
- ■ above 5 million
- ▣ 1 million to 5 million
- ◉ 500,000 to 1 million
- ◎ 100,000 to 500,000
- ⊕ 50,000 to 100,000
- ○ 10,000 to 50,000
- · below 10,000

SEYCHELLES

Inner Islands

Île Aride
Les Sœurs
Curieuse Grand Sœur
Praslin Félicité Marianne
Cousin La Digue
Cousine
Île du Nord ♦ Frégate
Mamelles
Silhouette Mahé North Point Île aux Recifs
Sainte Anne Île au Cerf
VICTORIA Île Thérèse Pointe Lazare Île au Cerf
Morne Seychellois 905m Mahé
Île Thérèse
Anse Boileau
Pointe Lazare Île Lazare
Quatre Bornes Pointe Police

INDIAN OCEAN

RÉUNION (to France)

Scale 1:2,000,000
0 10 20 30 Km
0 10 20 30 Miles

St-Denis
Le Port Ste-Marie Ste-Suzanne St-Benoît
St-Paul St-André
Pointe des Galets La Plaine-des-Palmistes
Trois-Bassins Salazie Ste-Rose
Aigrettes Pitons des Neiges 3070m Piton de la Fournaise
St-Leu 3070m 2631m
St-Louis La Rivière St-Philippe
Pointe au Sel St-Pierre St-Joseph
Pointe de la Table

INDIAN OCEAN

MAURITIUS

Scale 1:2,000,000
0 10 20 30 Km
0 10 20 30 Miles

Round Island
Flat Island
Gunner's Quoin
Île D'Ambre
Triolet Goodlands Rivière du Rempart
Pamplemousses Centre de Flacq
Canonniers Point Roce Hill Bel Air
Beau Bassin PORT LOUIS Mahébourg
Quatre Bornes Curepipe
Tamarin Mont du Rempart Rose Belle
Piton de la Petite Vacoas Chemin Grenier
Rivière Noire 828m Souillac
Pointe Sud
Ouest

INDIAN OCEAN

SEYCHELLES

Providence Atoll
Farquhar Group

Cosmoledo Group
Astove Island

Aldabra Group
Assumption Island

Nosy Glorieuses

COMOROS

Comoro Islands
Ngazidja MAMOUDZOU
MORONI Dembéni MAYOTTE (to France)
Le Kartala Matsamudu Pamanzi
2361m Nzwani Mwali

Mozambique Channel

MADAGASCAR

ANTSIRANANA
Ambilobe
Antalaha
TOAMASINA
MAHAJANGA
Mahajanga
Besalampy

KENYA

JUBBADA HOOSE
Kismaayo
Jumba
GARISSA
Garissa
Ngangerabeli Plain
LAMU Lamu
Pate Island
Malindi
Kilifi
KILIFI Mombasa
KWALE
NAIROBI
NAROK
KAJIADO
Lake Victoria
Kisumu

TANZANIA

Dar es Salaam
ZANZIBAR
Zanzibar
PEMBA NORTH
PEMBA SOUTH
Pemba
TANGA
Tanga
PWANI
DODOMA
Dodoma
MOROGORO
Morogoro
IRINGA
Iringa
SINGIDA
TABORA
Tabora
KIGOMA
Kigoma
MBEYA
Mbeya
RUKWA
RUVUMA
LINDI
Lindi
MTWARA
Mtwara
Lake Tanganyika
Great Rift Valley

ZAMBIA

NORTHERN
MUCHINGA
LUAPULA
CENTRAL
LUSAKA
Ndola
Kabwe

MALAWI

NORTHERN
Mzuzu
CENTRAL
LILONGWE
Lilongwe
SOUTHERN
Blantyre
Lake Nyasa

MOZAMBIQUE

CABO DELGADO
Pemba
NIASSA
NAMPULA
Nampula
ZAMBEZIA
TETE
MANICA

ZIMBABWE

MASHONALAND CENTRAL
MASHONALAND WEST

RWANDA
KIGALI
NORD
SUD
KIVU

BURUNDI
BUJUMBURA

INDIAN OCEAN

19,686ft
13,124ft
9843ft
6562ft
3281ft
1640ft
820ft
328ft
Sea Level
-820ft
-6562ft
-13,124ft

AFRICA

138

135

291

292

SOUTH AFRICA: CAPITAL CITIES

PRETORIA – administrative capital
CAPE TOWN – legislative capital
BLOEMFONTEIN – judicial capital

6000m
4000m
3000m
2000m
1000m
500m
250m
100m
Sea Level
-250m
-2000m
-4000m

ATLANTIC OCEAN

Tropic of Capricorn

ANGOLA
NAMIBIA
BOTSWANA
ZAMBIA
ZIMBABWE
SOUTH AFRICA
LESOTHO
MOXICO

Kalahari Desert

NORTH WESTERN
COPPERBELT
CENTRAL
WESTERN
SOUTHERN
CAPRIVI
NORTH-WEST
MATABELELAND NORTH
MATABELELAND SOUTH
CENTRAL
GHANZI
KWENENG
KGATLENG
SOUTHERN
SOUTH EAST
KGALAGADI
LIMPOPO (NORTHERN)
NORTH-WEST
FREE STATE
NORTHERN CAPE
EASTERN CAPE
WESTERN CAPE

HUILA
BENGUELA
CUNENE
NAMIBE
KUANDO KUBANGO
BIÉ
Planalto do Bié

OVAMBOLAND
OHANGWENA
OSHIKOTO
OKAVANGO
OSHANA
OMUSATI
KUNENE
OTJOZONDJUPA
OMAHEKE
ERONGO
KHOMAS
HARDAP
KARAS
Damaraland
Namaqualand

WINDHOEK
LUSAKA
LIVINGSTONE
GABORONE
JOHANNESBURG
PRETORIA
BLOEMFONTEIN
MASERU
CAPE TOWN
Port Elizabeth
East London

Okavango Delta

Cape of Good Hope
Cape Agulhas
Cape Seal
Cape St.Francis
Cape Recife
Algoa Bay

Scale 1:8,000,000
(projection: Lambert Azimuthal Equal Area)

0 25 50 75 100 125 150 175 200 Km
0 25 50 75 100 125 150 175 200 Miles

Population
- ■ above 5 million
- ■ 1 million to 5 million
- ◉ 500,000 to 1 million
- ◎ 100,000 to 500,000
- ⊕ 50,000 to 100,000
- ○ 10,000 to 50,000
- ∘ below 10,000

137

288

COMOROS

MAMOUDZOU
MAYOTTE
(to France)
Comoro Islands
Mwali
Nzwani
Mutsamudu
Pamandzi

CABO DELGADO

NIASSA

NAMPULA

ZAMBÉZIA

MOZAMBIQUE

SOFALA

MANICA

TETE

INHAMBANE

GAZA

MAPUTO

MAPUTO

Nampula
Quelimane
Beira
Inhambane
Xai-Xai
Matola

Lilongwe
LILONGWE
MALAWI
SOUTHERN
CENTRAL
NORTHERN
Blantyre
Lake Chilwa
Lake Nyasa

HARARE
Chitungwiza
Chimoio
BABWE
MANICALAND
MASHONALAND
MASVINGO

MBABANE
SWAZILAND
Manzini

KWAZULU/
NATAL
Pietermaritzburg
Durban

Mozambique Channel

**INDIAN
OCEAN**

Tropic of Capricorn

MADAGASCAR

Antsirañana
ANTSIRAÑANA
Nosy Be
Ambilobe
Iharaña
Sambava
Andapa
Antalaha
Ambohitralanana
Maroantsetra

MAHAJANGA
Mahajanga
Boriziny
Mandritsara
Soanierana-Ivongo
Nosy Sainte Marie

TOAMASINA
Toamasina
Moramanga
Ampasimanolotra

ANTANANARIVO
ANTANANARIVO
Antsirabe
Vatomandry
Mahanoro

Morondava
Miandrivazo
Belo Tsiribihina

FIANARANTSOA
Fianarantsoa
Manakara
Mananjary
Ikongo
Ifanadiana

TOLIARA
Toliara
Betroka
Ampanihy
Ambovombe
Tôlanaro
Beloha
Tsiombe
Tanjona Vohimena

Tropic of Capricorn

**INDIAN
OCEAN**

288

Ngazidja (Grande Comore)
Scale 1:4,500,000
0 20 40 60 80 Km
0 20 40 60 80 Miles

MORONI
Mitsamiouli
Saondzou 1087m
Hahaya
Mbéni
Koimbani
le Kartala 2361m
Mitsoudjé
Dembéni
Doumbouni

COMOROS

INDIAN
OCEAN

Nzwani (Anjouan)
Moutsamoudou
Ouani
Domoni
Fomboni Sima
Ouanani
Moya
Mramani

Mwali (Mohéli)
Miringoni
Nioumachoua

Comoro Islands
Mozambique Channel

MAYOTTE
(to France)
Dzaoudzi
Pamanzi
MAMOUDZOU
Bandrélé

Scale 1:8,000,000
0 25 50 75 100 125 150 Km
0 25 50 75 100 125 150 Miles

19,686ft
13,124ft
9843ft
6562ft
3281ft
1640ft
820ft
328ft
Sea Level
-820ft
-6562ft
-13,124ft

SOUTH AFRICA: CAPITAL CITIES

PRETORIA – administrative capital
CAPE TOWN – legislative capital
BLOEMFONTEIN – judicial capital

Algiers

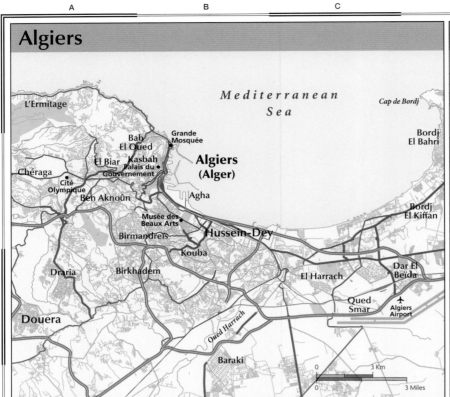

Mediterranean Sea

L'Ermitage
Cap de Bordj
Bab El Oued
Grande Mosquée
Bordj El Bahri
El Biar
Kasbah
Chéraga
Palais du Gouvernement
Algiers (Alger)
Cité Olympique
Ben Aknoûn
Agha
Musée des Beaux Arts
Bordj El Kiffan
Birmandreïs
Hussein-Dey
Draria
Kouba
Birkhadem
El Harrach
Dar El Beïda
Douera
Oued Smar
Algiers Airport
Oued Harrach
Baraki

0   3 Km
0   3 Miles

Cairo

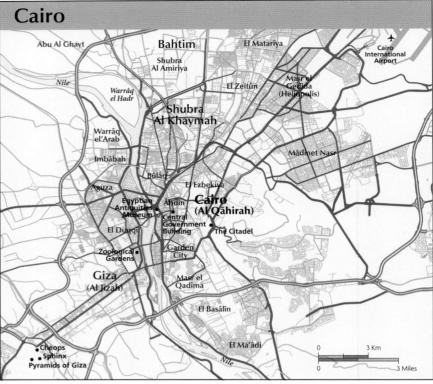

Abu Al Ghayt
Bahtim
El Matariya
Cairo International Airport
Shubra Al Amiriya
Nile
Warrâq el Hadr
El Zeitûn
Masr el Gedida (Heliopolis)
Shubra Al Khaymah
Warrâq el 'Arab
Imbâbah
Mâdinet Nasr
El Ezbekiya
Aguza
Bûlâq
Egyptian Antiquities Museum
Âbdin
Cairo (Al Qâhirah)
El Duqqi
Central Government Building
The Citadel
Zoological Gardens
Garden City
Giza (Al Jîzah)
Masr el Qadima
El Basâtin
Cheops
El Ma'âdi
Sphinx
Pyramids of Giza
Nile

0   3 Km
0   3 Miles

Cape Town

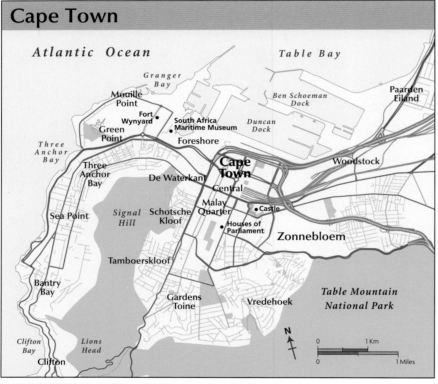

Atlantic Ocean
Table Bay
Granger Bay
Mouille Point
Ben Schoeman Dock
Paarden Eiland
Fort Wynyard
South Africa Maritime Museum
Green Point
Duncan Dock
Foreshore
Three Anchor Bay
Woodstock
Cape Town Central
Three Anchor Bay
De Waterkant
Sea Point
Signal Hill
Malay Quarter
Castle
Schotsche Kloof
Houses of Parliament
Zonnebloem
Tamboerskloof
Bantry Bay
Gardens Toine
Vredehoek
Table Mountain National Park
Clifton Bay
Lions Head
Clifton

N

0   1 Km
0   1 Miles

Casablanca

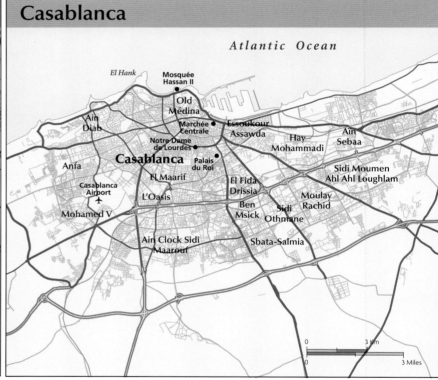

Atlantic Ocean
El Hank
Mosquée Hassan II
Old Médina
Aïn Diab
Marchée Centrale
Essoukour
Aïn Sebaa
Assawda
Notre Dame de Lourdes
Hay Mohammadi
Anfa
Casablanca
Palais du Roi
Sidi Moumen
El Maarif
Ahl Ahl Loughlam
Casablanca Airport
L'Oasis
El Fida Drissia
Moulay Rachid
Mohamed V
Ben Msick
Sidi Othmane
Aïn Clock Sidi Maarouf
Sbata-Salmia

0   3 km
0   3 Miles

Dakar

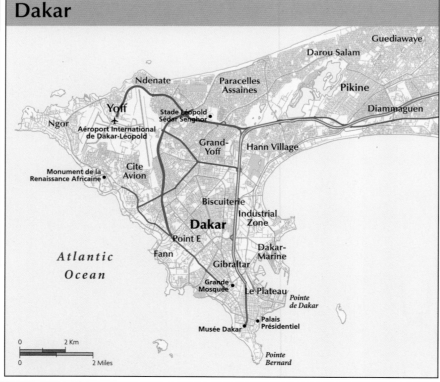

Guediawaye
Darou Salam
Ndenate
Paracelles Assaines
Pikine
Yoff
Stade Léopold Séder Senghor
Diammaguen
Ngor
Aéroport International de Dakar-Léopold
Grand-Yoff
Hann Village
Cite Avion
Monument de la Renaissance Africaine
Biscuiterie
Dakar
Industrial Zone
Point E
Fann
Dakar-Marine
Atlantic Ocean
Gibraltar
Grande Mosquée
Le Plateau
Pointe de Dakar
Musée Dakar
Palais Présidentiel
Pointe Bernard

0   2 Km
0   2 Miles

Harare

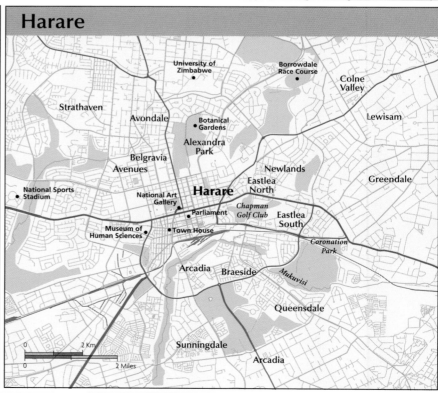

University of Zimbabwe
Borrowdale Race Course
Colne Valley
Strathaven
Avondale
Botanical Gardens
Lewisam
Belgravia
Alexandra Park
Avenues
Newlands
National Sports Stadium
National Art Gallery
Harare
Eastlea North
Greendale
Parliament
Chapman Golf Club
Eastlea South
Museum of Human Sciences
Town House
Coronation Park
Arcadia
Braeside
Mukuvisi
Queensdale
Sunningdale
Arcadia

0   2 Km
0   2 Miles

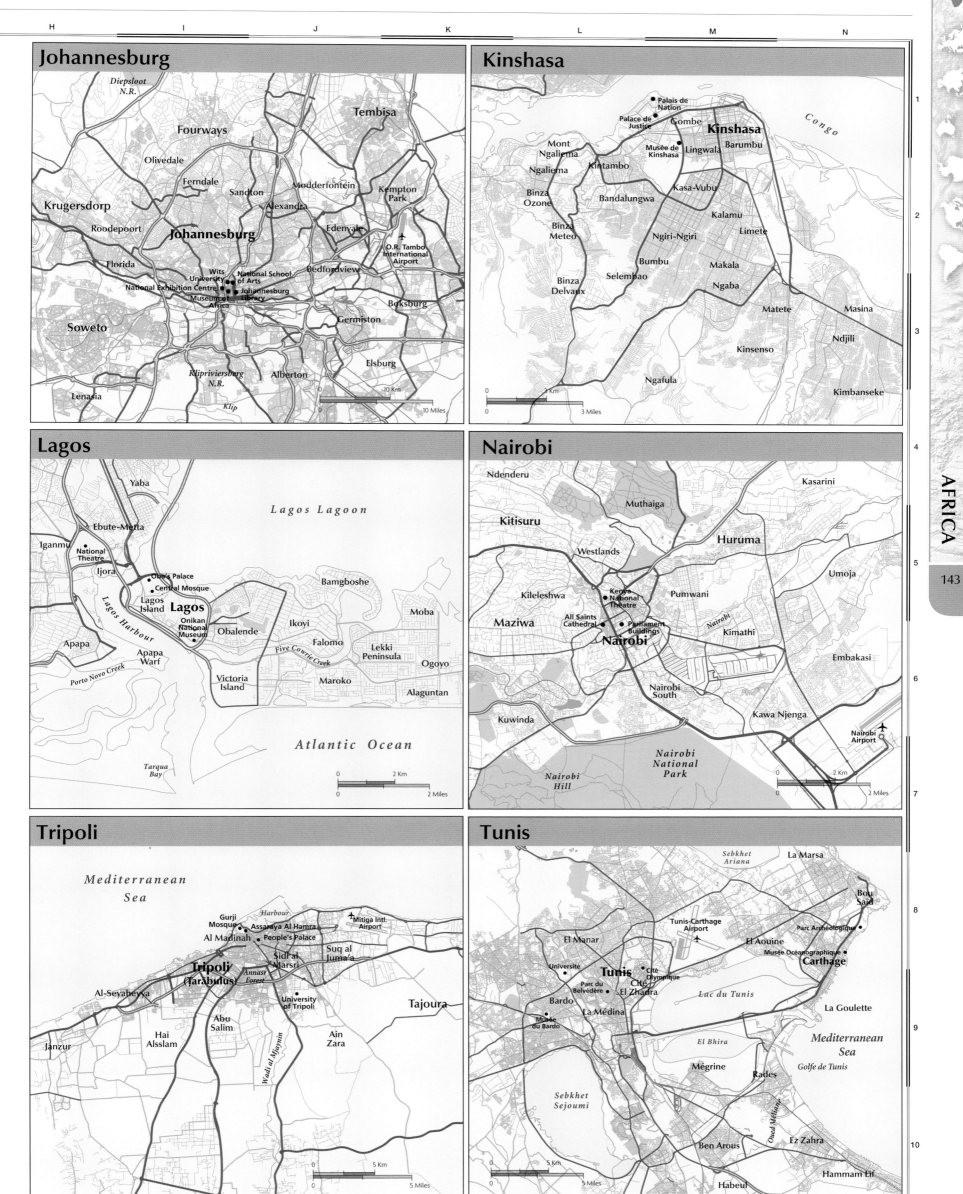

A B C D E F G

ARCTIC OCEAN

North Pole

Ellesmere Island

King Frederik
VIII Land

Greenland

King Christian X Land

Spitsbergen

Severnaya
Zemlya

Ostrov
Rudol'fa

Franz Josef Land

Kara Sea

Poluostrov Taymyr

Laptev Sea

Mys
Flissingskiy

Ostrov
Severniy

Novaya Zemlya

Greenland
Sea

Barents
Sea

Ostrov
Kolguyev

West Siberian
Plain

Yenisey

NORTH AMERICAN PLATE
EURASIAN PLATE

Jan Mayen
Jan Mayen Fracture Zone

Jan Mayen Ridge

Denmark Strait
Arctic Circle

Bjørnøya

Tromsøflaket
Fugløya Bank

North Cape
Nordkinn

Murmansk Rise

Kola Peninsula
Ozero Imandra

Poluostrov
Kanin

Pechora

Timanskiy Kryazh

Ural Mountains

A S I A

Iceland
Plateau

Bjargtangar

Iceland
Vatnajökull

Reykjanes Ridge

Iceland
Basin

Hatton Ridge

Rockall
Rise

Fenii Ridge

Rockall Trough

Kolbeinsey Ridge

Faroe-Iceland Ridge

Bill Baileys
Bank

Faroe-Shetland Trough

Norwegian Sea

Vøring Plateau

Norwegian
Basin

Vesterålen
Lofoten

Traena
Bank

Scandinavia

Kjølen
Kebnekaise
2117m

Inarijärvi

Torneälven

Komi

White Sea

Onega Bay

Severnaya Dvina

Mezen'

Gora Narodnaya
1895m

Ural

Unaäken

Oulujoki

Ozero
Vygozero

Northern Dvina

Vychegda

Kama

Chusovaya

Faroe Islands

Shetland
Islands

Viking Bank

Galdhøpiggen
2469m

Ljungan
Ljusnan

Gulf of Bothnia

Åland

Ozero
Onega

Lake
Onega

Ozero
Beloye

Volga

Vyatka

Belaya

Orkney Islands

Outer Hebrides

North Channel

Ben Nevis
1343m

Grampian
Mountains

Norwegian Trench

Jutland
Bank

Skagerrak
Kattegat

Vänern

Vättern

Gotland

Gulf of Finland

Gulf of
Riga

Lake
Peipus
Lake Pskov

Lake
Ladoga
Svir'

Lake
Onega

Rybinsk
Reservoir

Moskva

Gor'kiy
Reservoir

Volga Upland

Volga

Samara

North
Sea

Great
Fisher
Bank

Dogger
Bank

Jutland

Sjælland

Baltic Sea

Neman

Western Dvina

Lake Ilmen

E U R O P E

Central Russian Upland

Don

British
Isles

Ireland
Irish Sea

Shannon

Snowdon
1085m
Britain

Pennines

Trent

The
Fens
Thames

Frisian Islands

Elbe

Oder

Warta
Vistula

Bug

Pripet
Marshes

Desna

Seym

Khoper

Atlantic Ocean

Celtic Sea
Celtic
Shelf

St. George's
Channel

Bristol Channel

Land's End

English Channel

Channel Islands

Strait of Dover

Harz

Rhine

Ardennes

Meuse
Moselle

Seine

Marne

Loire

Vienne
Cher

Lake Constance

Danube

Black
Forest

Lake Geneva

Kiev
Reservoir

Dnieper Lowlands

Dniester
Podil's'ka
Vysochina

Kremenchuk
Reservoir

Pridnenny Buh

Donets

Dnieper

Tsimlyansk
Reservoir

Don
Manych

Kirghiz Steppe

Caspian
Depression

Porcupine
Plain

Azores-Biscay Rise

Charcot Seamounts

Theta Gap
Galicia
Bank

Biscay
Plain

Bay of
Biscay

Dordogne
Lot

Garonne

Massif
Central

Cévennes

Saône

Mont Blanc
4808m

Po

Alps

Carpathian
Mountains

Tisza

Bakony

Lake Balaton

Great
Hungarian
Plain

Drava
Sava

Transylvanian Alps

Danube

Balkan Mountains

Maritsa

Black Sea Lowland

Crimea

Sea of
Azov

Caucasus

Black Sea

Iberian
Plain

Miño
Douro

Cordillera Cantábrica

Aragón

Ebro

Aneto
3404m

Gulf of Lion

Ligurian
Sea

Arno

Corno Grande
2912m

Adriatic
Sea

Dinaric Alps

Apennines

Adriatic
Basin

Lake
Ohrid

Lake
Scutari

Rhodope Mountains

Sea of
Marmara

Anatolia

Iberian
Peninsula

Tagus Plain

Cabo
da Roca

Tagus

Guadiana

Sierra Morena

Guadalquivir

Duero

Sistema Central

Sistema Ibérico

Júcar

Segura

Gulf of
Valencia

Balearic Islands

Algerian Basin

Sardinia

Strait of Bonifacio

Tyrrhenian
Sea

Tyrrhenian
Basin

Gulf of
Taranto

Strait of Otranto

Lake
Prespa

Aegean
Sea

Mirtoan
Sea

Karpathos Strait

Taurus Mountains

Gulf of
Antalya

Cyprus

Cyprus
Basin

Horseshoe Seamounts

Gorringe
Ridge

Cape Saint Vincent

Punta de
Tarifa

Sierra Nevada

Sistemas Béticos

Alboran Sea

Strait of
Gibraltar

Mediterranean
Sea

Corsica

EURASIAN PLATE
AFRICAN PLATE

Mount Etna
3340m

Sicily

Malta

Ionian Sea

Ionian
Basin

Peloponnese

Crete

Sea of Crete

Gávdos

Mediterranean Ridge

Levantine Basin

Nile Fan

Dead
Sea

Suez Canal
Sinai

Nile

Madeira

Ampère Seamount

Seine Plain
Seine Seamount

Dacia Seamount

Canary Islands

Agadir Canyon

Oumer
Rbia

Middle Atlas
Moulouya

High Atlas

Atlas Mountains

Tell Atlas

Saharan Atlas

Chott el Jerid

Gulf of
Sirte

Qattara Depression
-133m

Western Desert

Libyan Desert

Erg Iguidi

Grand Erg Occidental

Grand Erg Oriental

S A H A R A

A F R I C A

Erg Chech

Europe is the world's second smallest continent with a total area of 4,053,309 sq miles (10,498,000 sq km). It comprises 46 separate countries, including Turkey and the Russian Federation, although the greater parts of these nations lie in Asia.

FACTFILE

N **Most Northerly Point:** Ostrov Rudol'fa, Russian Federation 81° 47′ N

S **Most Southerly Point:** Gávdos, Greece 34° 51′ N

E **Most Easterly Point:** Mys Flissingskiy, Novaya Zemlya, Russian Federation 69° 03′ E

W **Most Westerly Point:** Bjargtangar, Iceland 24° 33′ W

Largest Lakes:
1. Lake Ladoga, Russian Federation 7100 sq miles (18,390 sq km)
2. Lake Onega, Russian Federation 3819 sq miles (9891 sq km)
3. Vänern, Sweden 2141 sq miles (5545 sq km)
4. Lake Peipus, Estonia/Russian Federation 1372 sq miles (3555 sq km)
5. Vättern, Sweden 737 sq miles (1910 sq km)

Longest Rivers:
1. Volga, Russian Federation 2265 miles (3645 km)
2. Danube, C Europe 1771 miles (2850 km)
3. Dnieper, Belarus/Russian Federation/Ukraine 1421 miles (2287 km)
4. Don, Russian Federation 1162 miles (1870 km)
5. Pechora, Russian Federation 1124 miles (1809 km)

Largest Islands:
1. Britain, 88,700 sq miles (229,800 sq km)
2. Iceland, 39,315 sq miles (101,826 sq km)
3. Ireland, 31,521 sq miles (81,638 sq km)
4. Ostrov Severny, Novaya Zemlya, Russian Federation 18,177 sq miles (47,079 sq km)
5. Spitsbergen, Svalbard 15,051 sq miles (38,981 sq km)

Highest Points:
1. El'brus, Russian Federation 18,510 ft (5642 m)
2. Dykhtau, Russian Federation 17,077 ft (5205 m)
3. Koshtantau, Russian Federation 16,877 ft (5144 m)
4. Gora Kazbek, Georgia/Russian Federation 16,647 ft (5074 m)
5. Gora Dzhangitau, Georgia/Russian Federation 16,571 ft (5051 m)

Lowest Point:
▼ Caspian Depression, Russian Federation -92 ft (-28 m) below sea level

Highest recorded temperature:
⊕ Seville, Spain 122°F (50°C)

Lowest recorded temperature:
⊖ Ust'-Shchuger, Russian Federation -72.6°F (-58.1°C)

Wettest Place:
≋ Crkvice, Bosnia and Herzegovina 183 in (4648 mm)

Driest Place:
⊖ Astrakhan', Russian Federation 6.4 in (162.5 mm)

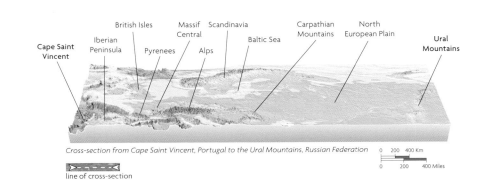

Cross-section from Cape Saint Vincent, Portugal to the Ural Mountains, Russian Federation

▷ – – – – –
line of cross-section

0 200 400 Km

0 200 400 Miles

Political

The political boundaries of Europe have changed many times, especially during the 20th century in the aftermath of two world wars, the break-up of the empires of Austria-Hungary, Nazi Germany, and, toward the end of the century, the collapse of communism in eastern Europe. The fragmentation of Yugoslavia has again altered the political map of Europe, highlighting a trend towards nationalism and devolution. In contrast, economic federalism is growing. In 1958, the formation of the European Economic Community (now the European Union or EU) started a move toward economic and political union and increasing internal migration. This process is still ongoing and the accession of Bulgaria and Romania in January 2007, and Croatia in 2013, brought the number of EU member states to twenty eight. Of these, nineteen have joined the Eurozone by adopting the Euro as their official currency.

Population
- above 5 million
- 1 million to 5 million
- 500,000 to 1 million
- 100,000 to 500,000
- 50,000 to 100,000
- 10,000 to 50,000
- Country capital

Borders
- full international border

EUROPE

146

Scale 1:17,250,000
(projection: Lambert Azimuthal Equal Area)

Km
0 100 200 300 400 500 600 700

Miles
0 100 200 300 400 500 600 700

ATLANTIC OCEAN
Denmark Strait
Arctic Circle
REYKJAVÍK
ICELAND
Norwegian Sea
Faroe Islands (to Denmark)
Shetland Islands
Outer Hebrides
Orkney Islands
Bergen
Trondheim
NORWAY
SWEDEN
FINLAND
Murmansk
Barents Sea
Kara Sea
Novaya Zemlya
Vorkut
White Sea
Archangel
Northern Dvina
RUSS
FEDERA
Kirov
Vologda
Yaroslavl'
Nizhniy Novgorod
Ul'yanovs
MOSCOW
Kazan
Tula
Saratov
Voronezh
Volgograd
Rostov-na-Donu
Stavropol'
Novorossiysk
Ca
Sea of Azov
Simferopol'
(annexed by Russia, 2014)
Black Sea
Istanbul
Turkey

Lake Onega
Lake Ladoga
Tampere
Åland
Turku
HELSINKI
St Petersburg
Gulf of Bothnia
Uppsala
Örebro
STOCKHOLM
TALLINN
ESTONIA
RIGA
LATVIA
Vitsyebsk
LITHUANIA
Kaunas
VILNIUS
MINSK
BELARUS
Babruysk
Homyel'
Brest
Baltic Sea
Gotland
Ventspils
Liepāja
RUSS. FED. (Kaliningrad)
Kaliningrad
Gdańsk
Bydgoszcz
Western Dvina
Vistula
WARSAW
Łódź
POLAND
Poznań
Wrocław
Kraków
L'viv
UKRAINE
KIEV
Kharkiv
Dnipropetrovs'k
Donets'k
Dniester
Dnieper
CHIŞINĂU
MOLDOVA
Odesa
Cluj-Napoca
ROMANIA
Braşov
BUCHAREST
Constanţa
Ruse
Danube
Varna
Burgas
Stara Zagora
BULGARIA
SOFIA
Salonica
GREECE
Aegean Sea
Larisa
Piraeus
ATHENS
Irákleio
Crete
Ionian Sea

Vänern
OSLO
Stavanger
Kristiansand
Gothenburg
Jönköping
Vättern
North Sea
SCOTLAND
Aberdeen
Glasgow
Dundee
NORTHERN IRELAND
Edinburgh
Belfast
IRELAND
DUBLIN
Newcastle upon Tyne
UNITED KINGDOM
Liverpool
Leeds
Manchester
Sheffield
Birmingham
WALES
Cardiff
ENGLAND
Southampton
Thames
LONDON
Channel Islands
English Channel
le Havre
Seine
Rennes
St-Nazaire
Nantes
PARIS
Loire
Orléans
FRANCE
Bay of Biscay
A Coruña
Porto
PORTUGAL
Duero
Valladolid
Ebro
LISBON
Setúbal
MADRID
SPAIN
Tagus
Seville
Córdoba
Valencia
Gibraltar (to UK)
Cádiz
Málaga
Ceuta (to Spain)
Melilla (to Spain)
Murcia
Ibiza
Palma
Majorca
Minorca
Balearic Islands
Mediterranean Sea
Zaragoza
Barcelona
Bilbao
Pyrenees
Bordeaux
Toulouse
Limoges
Marseille
Nice
Lyon
Rhône
Geneva
BERN
SWITZERLAND
Zurich
Alps
ANDORRA LA VELLA
ANDORRA
MONACO
Corsica
Sardinia
Cagliari
Palermo
Sicily
Catania
Messina
Cosenza
MALTA
VALLETTA
Denmark
Ålborg
DENMARK
COPENHAGEN
Odense
Helsingborg
Malmö
Hamburg
Bremen
Groningen
AMSTERDAM
NETH.
Hanover
Elbe
Oder
BELGIUM
BRUSSELS
Antwerp
Liège
Rotterdam
THE HAGUE
Nijmegen
Düsseldorf
LUXEMBOURG
Bonn
Rhine
GERMANY
BERLIN
Leipzig
Dresden
Frankfurt am Main
PRAGUE
CZECH REPUBLIC
Nuremberg
Stuttgart
Munich
Strasbourg
Salzburg
Danube
VIENNA
AUSTRIA
LIECHTENSTEIN
Innsbruck
Alps
Milan
Turin
Verona
Venice
SLOVENIA
LJUBLJANA
ZAGREB
CROATIA
Trieste
Genoa
Bologna
Florence
Pisa
SAN MARINO
ITALY
VATICAN CITY
ROME
Naples
Bari
Adriatic Sea
Tyrrhenian Sea
BRATISLAVA
SLOVAKIA
Győr
BUDAPEST
HUNGARY
Miskolc
Chernivtsi
Bosnia & Herzegovina
SARAJEVO
Mostar
MONTENEGRO
PODGORICA
BELGRADE
SERBIA
KOSOVO (disputed)
PRISTINA
SKOPJE
MACEDONIA
TIRANA
ALBANIA

Languages

There are three main European language groups: Germanic languages predominate in central and northern Europe; Romance languages in western and Mediterranean Europe and Romania; while Slavic languages are spoken in eastern Europe and the Russian Federation. Isolated pockets of local languages, such as Basque and Gaelic, persist and frequently provide a focus for national identity.

Language groups

- Turkic
- Albanian
- Finno-Ugric/Samoyed
- Germanic
- Slavic
- Romance
- Basque
- Baltic
- Celtic
- Greek
- Caucasian
- Iranian
- Mongol

Population

Europe is a densely populated, urbanized continent; in Belgium over 90% of people live in urban areas. The highest population densities are found in an area stretching east from southern Britain and northern France, into Germany. The northern fringes are only sparsely populated.

Population density
(people per sq mile)

- below 130
- 130–259
- 260–379
- 380–519
- 520–780
- above 780

Standard of living

Living standards in western Europe are among the highest in the world, although there is a growing sector of homeless, jobless people. Eastern Europeans have lower overall standards of living—a legacy of stagnated economies.

Standard of living
(UN human development index)

- low
- high
- data not available

Transportation

Despite its fragmented geography and many natural frontiers, communications in Europe are well developed. Extensive motorway links allow rapid road transportation, while high-speed rail connections like France's TGV *(Train à Grande Vitesse)*, and the Channel Tunnel have improved rail travel. Outdated communication infrastructures in parts of eastern Europe, and insufficient transport links across the Alps, however, remain weak parts of the network.

Transportation

- — major roads and motorways
- — major railroads
- — international borders
- • transport intersections
- ⊕ major international airports
- ⊕ major ports

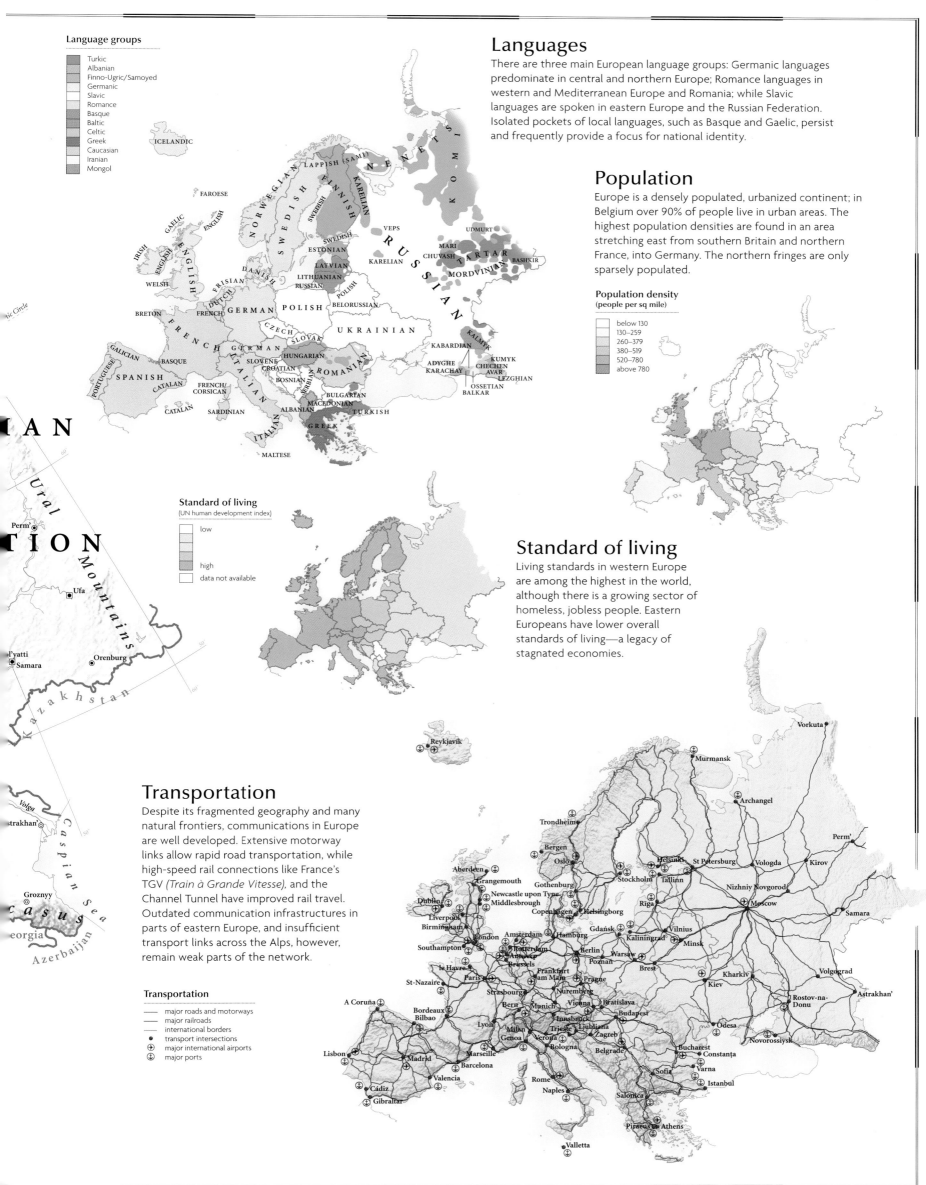

Scale 1:22,500,000
(projection: Lambert Conformal Conic)

| 0 | 200 | 400 | 600 | 800 | 1000 Km |
| 0 | 200 | 400 | 600 | 800 | 1000 Miles |

Climate

Europe experiences few extremes in either rainfall or temperature, with the exception of the far north and south. Along the west coast, the warm currents of the North Atlantic Drift moderate temperatures. Although east–west air movement is relatively unimpeded by relief, the Alpine Uplands halt the progress of north–south air masses, protecting most of the Mediterranean from cold, north winds.

Climate

☐ tundra	☀ daily hours of sunshine, January
☐ subarctic	
☐ cool continental	☀ daily hours of sunshine, July
☐ warm humid	
☐ mediterranean	→ cold wind
☐ semi-arid	→ hot wind

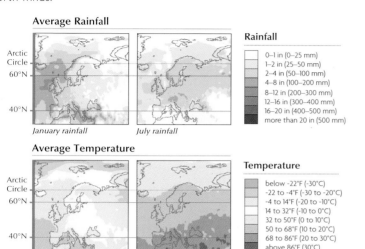

Average Rainfall

January rainfall *July rainfall*

Rainfall

☐	0–1 in (0–25 mm)
☐	1–2 in (25–50 mm)
☐	2–4 in (50–100 mm)
☐	4–8 in (100–200 mm)
☐	8–12 in (200–300 mm)
☐	12–16 in (300–400 mm)
☐	16–20 in (400–500 mm)
☐	more than 20 in (500 mm)

Average Temperature

January temperature *July temperature*

Temperature

☐	below -22°F (-30°C)
☐	-22 to -4°F (-30 to -20°C)
☐	-4 to 14°F (-20 to -10°C)
☐	14 to 32°F (-10 to 0°C)
☐	32 to 50°F (0 to 10°C)
☐	50 to 68°F (10 to 20°C)
☐	68 to 86°F (20 to 30°C)
☐	above 86°F (30°C)

Environmental issues

The partially enclosed waters of the Baltic and Mediterranean seas have become heavily polluted, while the Barents Sea is contaminated with spent nuclear fuel from Russia's navy. Acid rain, caused by emissions from factories and power stations, is actively destroying northern forests. As a result, pressure is growing to safeguard Europe's natural environment and prevent further deterioration.

Environmental issues

☐ national parks	☐ marine pollution
☐ risk of acid rain	☐ heavy marine pollution
~ polluted rivers	• poor urban air quality
☢ radioactive contamination	

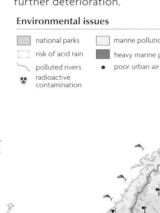

Land use

Europe's swelling urban population and the outward expansion of many cities has created acute competition for land. Despite this, European resourcefulness has maximized land potential, and over half of Europe's land is still used for a wide variety of agricultural purposes. Land in northern Europe is used for cattle-rearing, pasture, and arable crops. Towards the Mediterranean, the mild climate allows the growing of grapes for wine; olives, sunflowers, tobacco and citrus fruits. EU subsidies, however, have resulted in massive overproduction and a land "set-aside" policy has been introduced.

Using the land and sea

☐	cropland	☙	citrus fruits
☐	forest	🦗	cotton
☐	ice cap	🐟	fishing
☐	mountain region	☷	fodder
☐	pasture	🍎	fruit
☐	tundra	🫒	olive oil
☐	wetland	🥔	potatoes
•	major conurbations	🌾	rice
🐄	cattle	🌱	root crops
🐐	goats	🌹	roses
🐖	pigs	🦪	shellfish
🦃	poultry	🌻	sunflowers
🦌	reindeer	🌲	timber
🐑	sheep	🌿	tobacco
🌾	cereals	🍇	vineyards

1 VATNAJÖKULL, ICELAND
Europe's largest ice cap is located in the southeast of this Atlantic island.

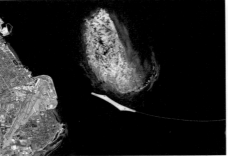

2 ORESUND LINK, DENMARK/SWEDEN
This link was opened to traffic in 2000, joining the Danish capital, Copenhagen, with the Swedish town of Malmö across the waters of the Oresund Strait.

3 BALSFJORD, NORWAY
Fjords were cut into Norway's west coast by glaciers during the last ice age but as the ice retreated rising sea-levels flooded the valleys left behind.

4 PRAGUE, CZECH REPUBLIC
In August 2002 some parts of the capital were still under water after the worst floods in living memory.

9 GIBRALTAR
A British colony since 1713, this rocky promontory commands a strategic position at the southern end of the Iberian Peninsula.

10 BORDEAUX, FRANCE
Famous for its wines, this city sits on the west bank of the Garonne river, which is joined from the east by the Dordogne river.

11 SOUTH FLEVOLAND, NETHERLANDS
This polder was reclaimed from the sea in the early 1970s and is now home to extensive farmland and small towns.

12 RHINE, GERMANY
The Rhine has been straightened in places, such as here, just south of Mannheim, to ease navigation.

HEL PENINSULA, POLAND 5
The long spit of this peninsula encloses Puck Bay and shelters the important port of Gdynia.

TALLINN, ESTONIA 6
The capital and main port of Estonia has become a popular tourist destination in recent years.

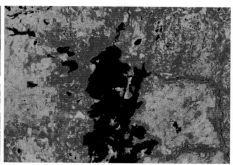

LAKE VODLOZERO, RUSSIAN FEDERATION 7
The lake lies within a national park, which protects one of the most untouched wilderness areas in Europe and encompasses plains, taiga forests, and wetlands.

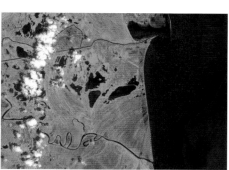

DANUBE DELTA, ROMANIA 8
The Danube river splits into several channels as it flows into the Black Sea, forming one of Europe's most important wetland ecosystems.

VENICE, ITALY 13
Occupying the largest island in a sheltered lagoon at the north end of the Adriatic, this city was founded in 452 CE and grew rich on an extensive trading network.

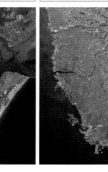

ISTRA PENINSULA, CROATIA 14
This triangular peninsula marks the northern extent of Croatia's Dalmatian coastline.

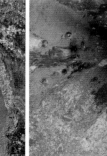

MOUNT ETNA, SICILY, ITALY 15
This combination of visible and thermal images shows the volcano erupting in July 2001 and clearly indicates the major lava flows.

KEFALLONIÁ, GREECE 16
The largest of the Ionian Islands off Greece's west coast, Kefalloniá is mountainous with relatively high rainfall.

Scandinavia, Finland & Iceland

Scale 1:4,750,000

(projection: Lambert Conformal Conic)

0 20 40 60 80 100 Km
0 20 40 60 80 100 Miles

Population

- ▣ above 5 million
- ◙ 1 million to 5 million
- ◉ 500,000 to 1 million
- ◎ 100,000 to 500,000
- ⊕ 50,000 to 100,000
- ○ 10,000 to 50,000
- ○ below 10,000

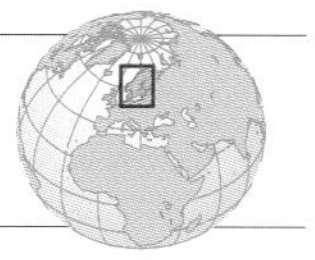

NORWAY
SWEDEN
FINLAND
ESTONIA
LATVIA
LITHUANIA
BELARUS
POLAND
GERMANY
DENMARK
RUSSIAN FED.
OSLO
STOCKHOLM
HELSINKI
TALLINN
RĪGA
KØBENHAVN (COPENHAGEN)
MINSK
VILNIUS
Sankt-Peterburg (Saint Petersburg)
Gulf of Bothnia
Gulf of Finland
Gulf of Riga
Baltic Sea
Skagerrak
Kattegat
North Sea
Gotland
Öland
Bornholm
Lake Peipus
Vänern
Vättern

EUROPE

19,686ft
13,124ft
9843ft
6562ft
3281ft
1640ft
820ft
328ft
Sea Level
-820ft
-6562ft
-13,124ft

Southern Scandinavia

Norwegian Sea

Atlantic Ocean

Gulf of Bothnia

Álands Hav

NORWAY

SWEDEN

NORDLAND

NORD-TRØNDELAG

SØR-TRØNDELAG

MØRE OG ROMSDAL

SOGN OG FJORDANE

OPPLAND

HEDMARK

BUSKERUD

HORDALAND

AKERSHUS

OSLO

JÄMTLAND

VÄSTERNORRLAND

VÄSTERBOTTEN

GÄVLEBORG

DALARNA

VÄSTMANLAND

UPPSALA

ÅLAND

Trondheim

Bergen

Gävle

Uppsala

Östersund

Sundsvall

Härnösand

Örnsköldsvik

Umeå

Lillehammer

Elverum

Molde

Kristiansund

Torshavn

FAROE ISLANDS (to Denmark)

Scale 1:2,500,000

Sea Level
6000m
4000m
3000m
2000m
1000m
500m
250m
100m
-250m
-2000m
-4000m

153

290

United Kingdom & Ireland

155

290

UNITED KINGDOM

North Sea

SCOTLAND

ATLANTIC OCEAN

Shetland Islands

Herma Ness
Unst
Fetlar
Yell
Out Skerries
Whalsay
Bressay
Lerwick
Sullom Voe
Yell Sound
Hillswick
Mainland
St Magnus Bay
Scalloway
West Burra
Papa Stour
Foula
Fitful Head
Sumburgh Head
Fair Isle

Orkney Islands
Papa Westray
Westray
The North / North Ronaldsay
Rousay
Eday
Sanday
Stronsay
Mainland
Shapinsay
Stromness
Hoy
Kirkwall
Burray
Scapa Flow
St Margaret's Hope
South Ronaldsay
Pentland Firth
Duncansby Head
John o'Groats
Noss Head
Wick

Dunnet Head
Strathy Point
Thurso
Halkirk
Helmsdale
Cape Wrath
Durness
Tongue
Bettyhill
Halladale
Kinbrace
Brora
Golspie
Dornoch Firth
Tarbat Ness
Loch Shin
Lairg
Dornoch
Moray Firth
Lossiemouth
Elgin
Buckie
Macduff
Banff
Kinnaird Head
Fraserburgh
Peterhead
Buchan Ness
Aberdeen
Girdle Ness
Stonehaven

Ben Klibreck 721m
Loch Naver
Bonar Bridge
Tain
Invergordon
Alness
Cromarty
Nairn
Forres
Keith
Turriff
Ellon
Inverurie

Ben More Assynt 998m
Loch Assynt
Lochinver
Inchnadamph
Beauly
Inverness
Loch Ness
Grantown-on-Spey
Aviemore
Huntly
Alford
Banchory
Deeside
Don

Edrachillis Bay
Enard Bay
Ullapool
Carn Eige 1183m
Glen Affric
Fort Augustus
Cairn Gorm 1245m
Grampian Mountains
Ben Macdui 1309m
Braemar
Ballater

Loch Maree
Loch Torridon
Inner Sound
Stromeferry
Kyle of Lochalsh
Glen More
Spean Bridge
Loch Lochy
Ben Nevis 1344m
Fort William
Loch Linnhe
Glen Coe
Schiehallion 1083m
Ben Lawers 1214m
Loch Rannoch
Loch Tay
Crieff
Perth
Dundee
Broughty Ferry
Carnoustie
Arbroath
Firth of Tay
Montrose
Brechin
Forfar
Blairgowrie
Kirriemuir
Pitlochry

The Minch
Rubha Reidh
Applecross
Broadford
Canna
Mallaig
Knoydart
Loch Hourn
Loch Nevis
Morar
Loch Shiel
Loch Eil
Loch Etive
Loch Awe
Ben More 966m
Crianlarich
Ben Lomond 974m
Loch Lomond
Callander
Stirling
Dunfermline
Kinross
Loch Leven
Cupar
St Andrews
Fife Ness
Firth of Forth
North Berwick
Haddington
Edinburgh
Musselburgh
Dalkeith
Bathgate

Eye Peninsula
Broad Bay
Port of Ness
Butt of Lewis
Carloway
Stornoway
Isle of Lewis
Harris
Tarbert
Scalpay
Loch Roag
Scarp
Taransay
Pabbay
Sound of Harris
North Uist
Monach Islands
Benbecula
South Uist
Lochboisdale
Eriskay
Barra
Barra Head
Flannan Isles
Shiant Islands
Raasay
Portree
Isle of Skye
Sea of the Hebrides
Rum
Eigg
Muck
Ben More 966m
Isle of Mull
Tobermory
Point of Ardnamurchan
Loch Linnhe
Oban
Firth of Lorn
Coll
Tiree
Iona
Colonsay
Jura
Sound of Jura
Gigha Island
Kintyre
Campbeltown
Mull of Kintyre
Islay
Port Askaig
Port Ellen
Mull of Oa

Sula Sgeir
Sula Sgeir
North Rona
Sule Skerry
Stack Skerry

St Kilda

Outer Hebrides
Inner Hebrides

Greenock
Glasgow
Paisley
Hamilton
Motherwell
East Kilbride
Kilmarnock
Irvine
Troon
Ardrossan
Prestwick
Ayr
Firth of Clyde
Rothesay
Isle of Bute
Gourock
Dumbarton
Dunoon
Helensburgh
Clyde
Cumnock
Merrick 843m
Girvan
Ailsa Craig
Ballantrae

North Channel
Rathlin Island
Giant's Causeway
Portrush
Portstewart
Coleraine
Ballycastle
Bushmills
Dunluce Castle
Inishtrahull
Malin Head
Sheep Haven
Tory Island
Bloody Foreland
Dunfanaghy
Errigal Mountain 752m
Lough Swilly
Carndonagh
Buncrana

Sea Level
6000m
4000m
3000m
2000m
1000m
500m
250m
100m
Sea Level
-250m
-2000m
-4000m

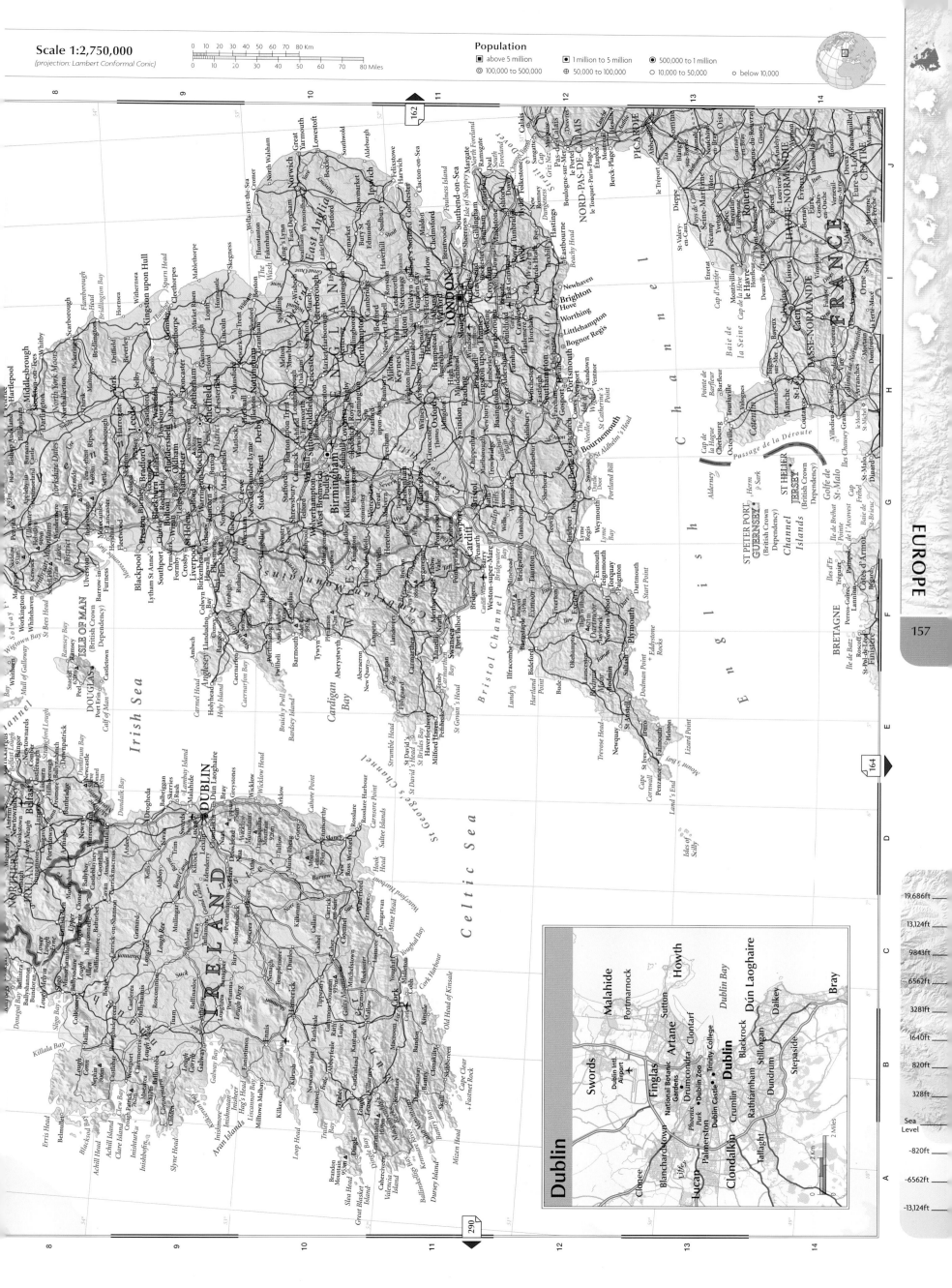

ATLANTIC

OCEAN

EUROPE

158

IRELAND

NORTHERN IRELAND

UNITED

Sea of the Hebrides

Inner Hebrides

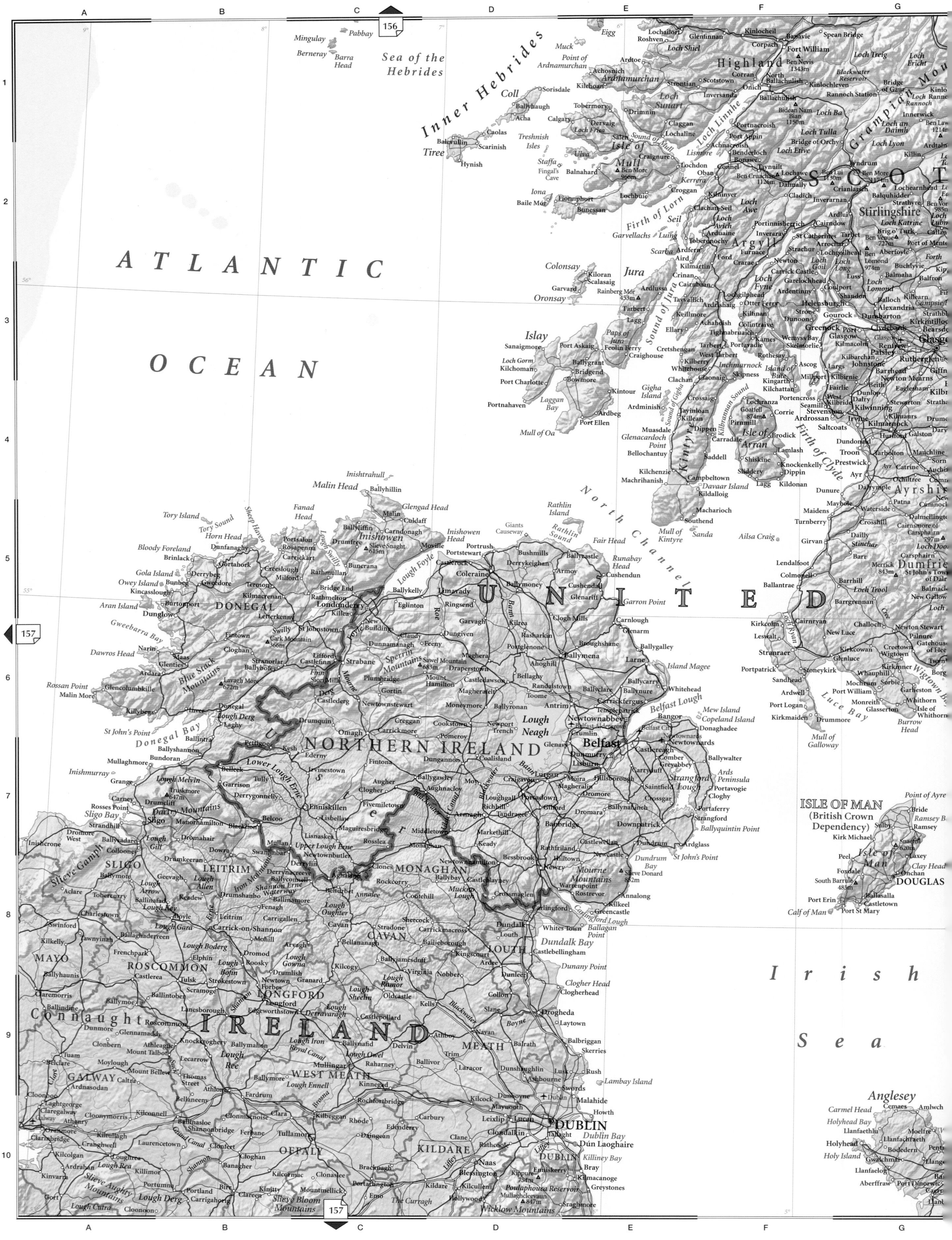

North Channel

Irish

Sea

ISLE OF MAN
(British Crown
Dependency)

DOUGLAS

DUBLIN

Belfast

Highland

SCOT

Connaught

MAYO

SLIGO

LEITRIM

ROSCOMMON

LONGFORD

WEST MEATH

OFFALY

KILDARE

MEATH

LOUTH

CAVAN

MONAGHAN

DONEGAL

GALWAY

Anglesey

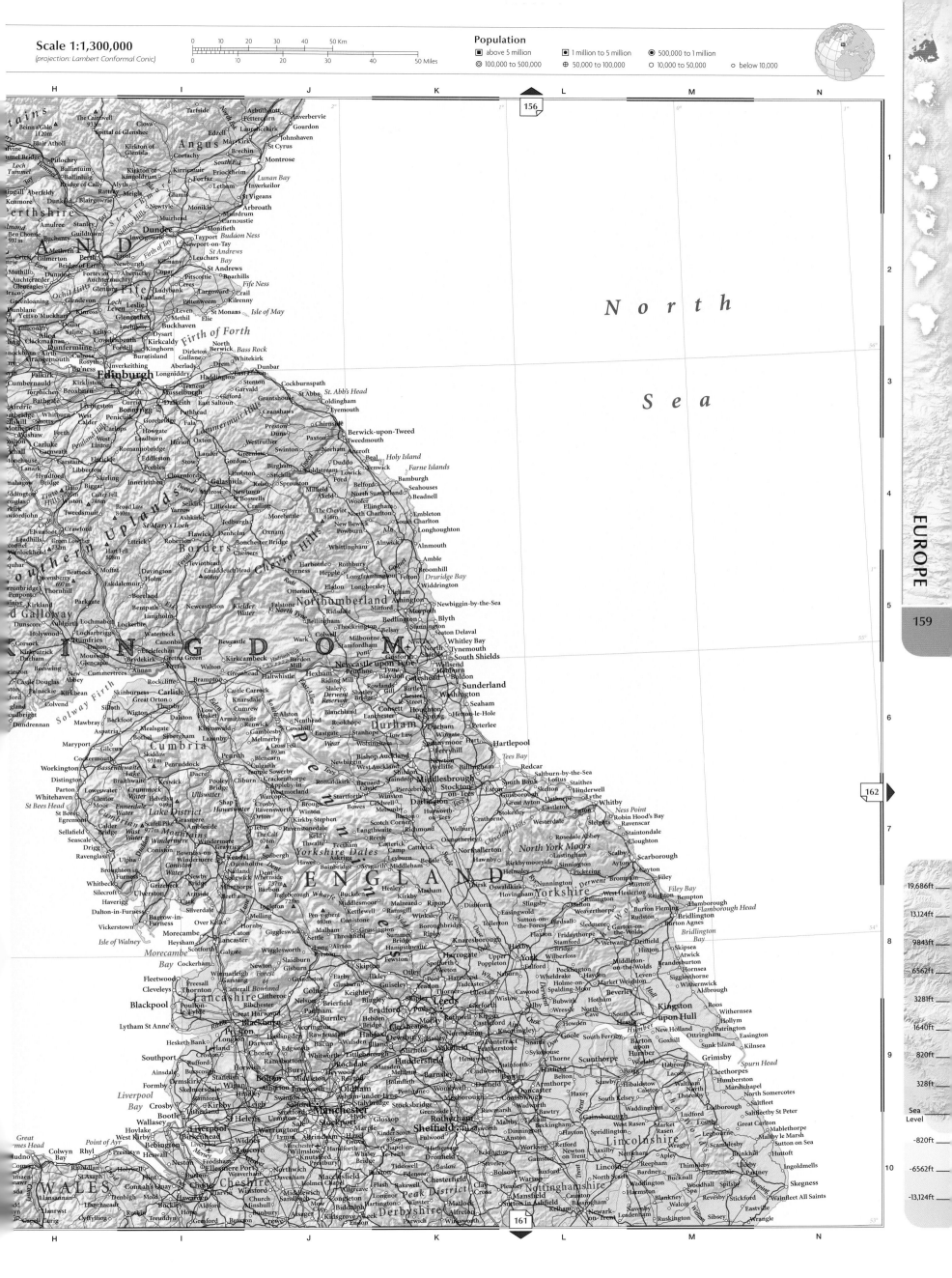

EUROPE

160

IRELAND

MEATH
WESTMEATH
OFFALY
KILDARE
DUBLIN
LAOIS
CARLOW
WICKLOW
KILKENNY
WEXFORD
WATERFORD

WALES
UNITED

Irish Sea

Caernarfon Bay

Cardigan Bay

St George's Channel

Celtic Sea

Bristol Channel

Bridgwater Bay

Lyme Bay

Cornwall

Devon

Dartmoor

Exmoor

Bodmin Moor

Anglesey

Snowdonia

Dublin
Dún Laoghaire

Cardiff
Swansea
Newport
Plymouth
Exeter

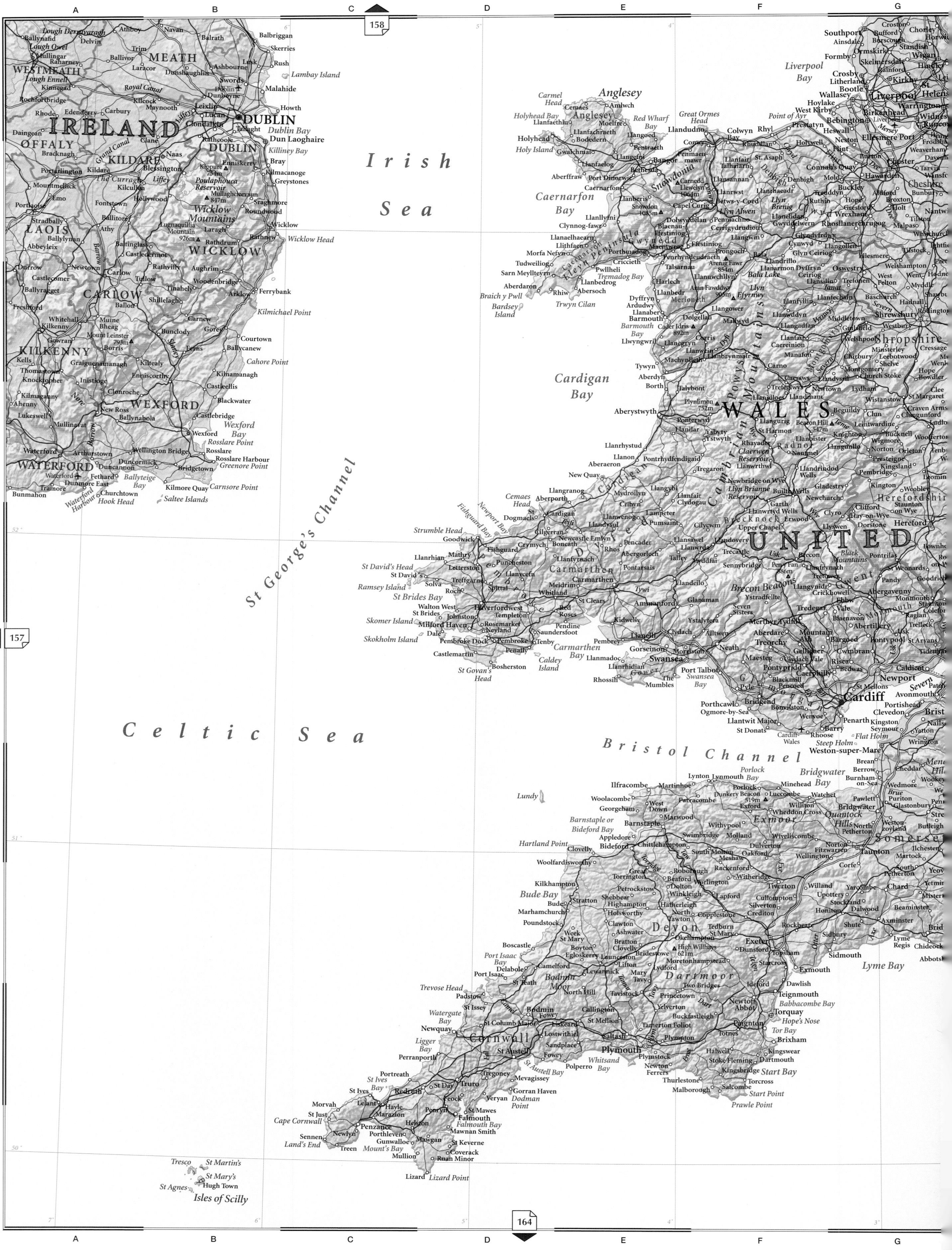

Land's End
Lizard Point

Isles of Scilly

158

157

164

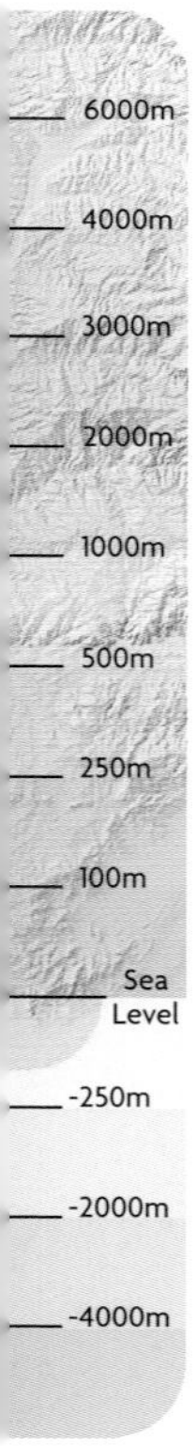

6000m
4000m
3000m
2000m
1000m
500m
250m
100m
Sea Level
-250m
-2000m
-4000m

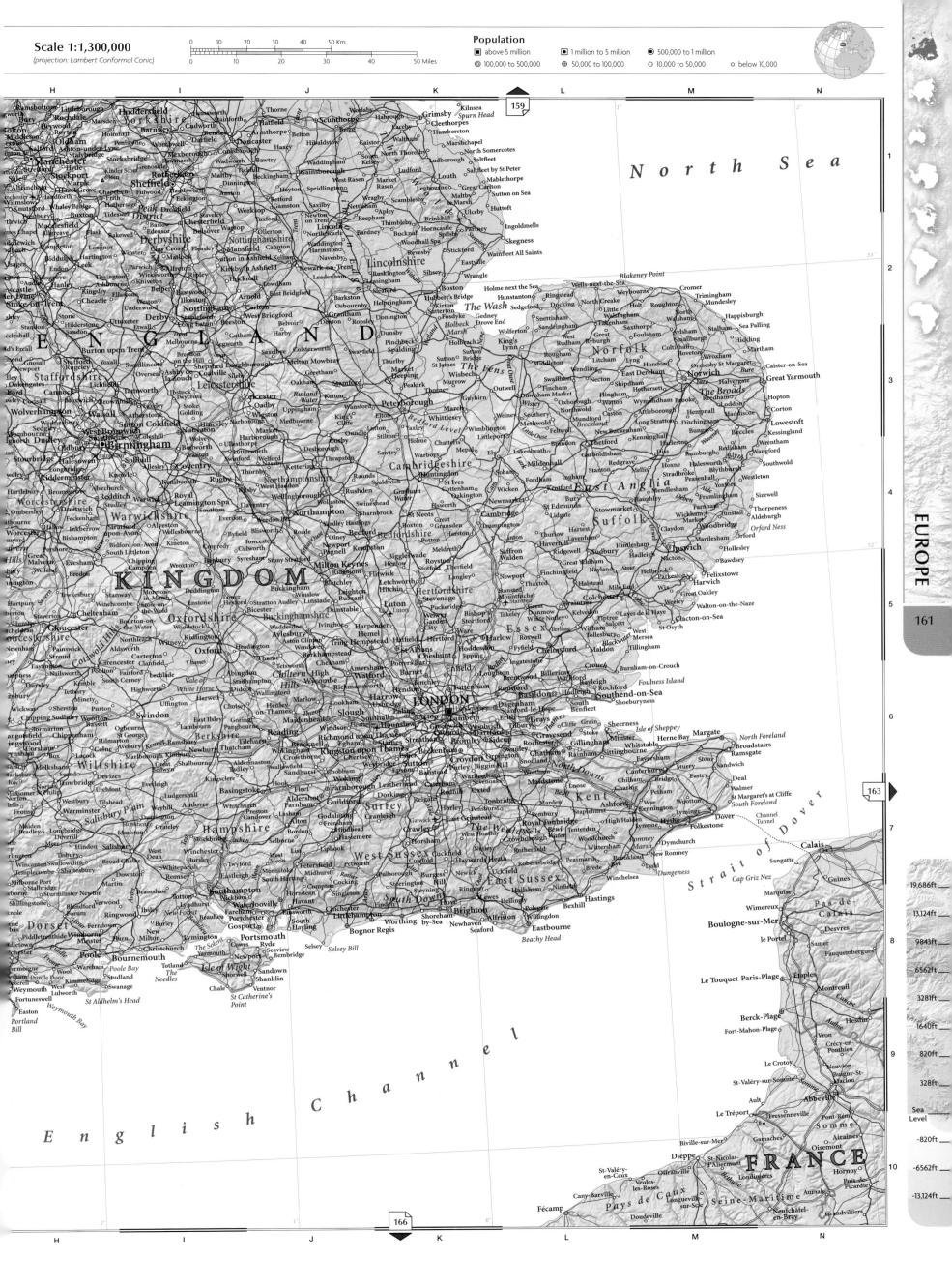

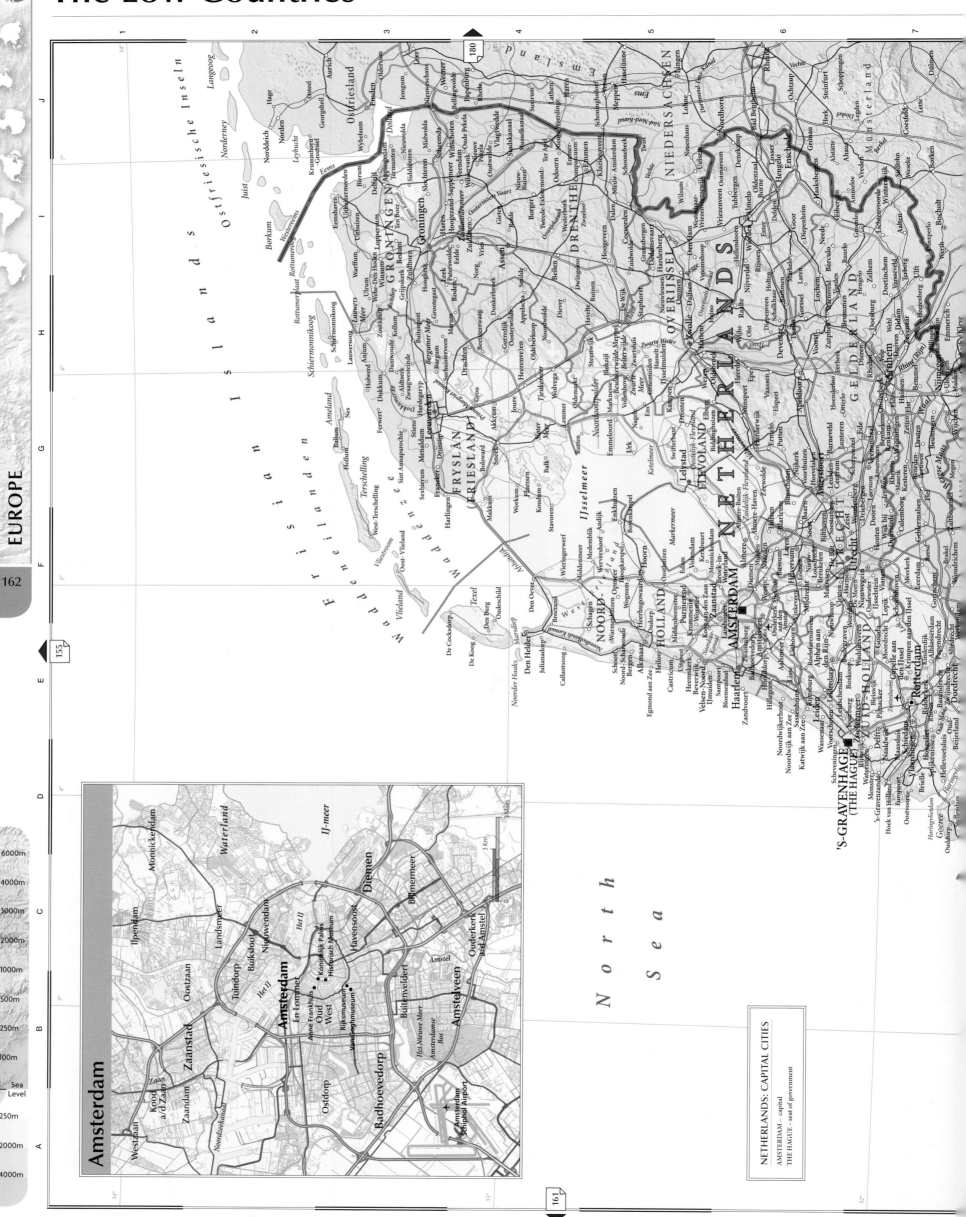

Amsterdam

NETHERLANDS: CAPITAL CITIES

AMSTERDAM – capital
THE HAGUE – seat of government

6000m
4000m
3000m
2000m
1000m
500m
250m
100m
Sea
Level
-250m
-2000m
-4000m

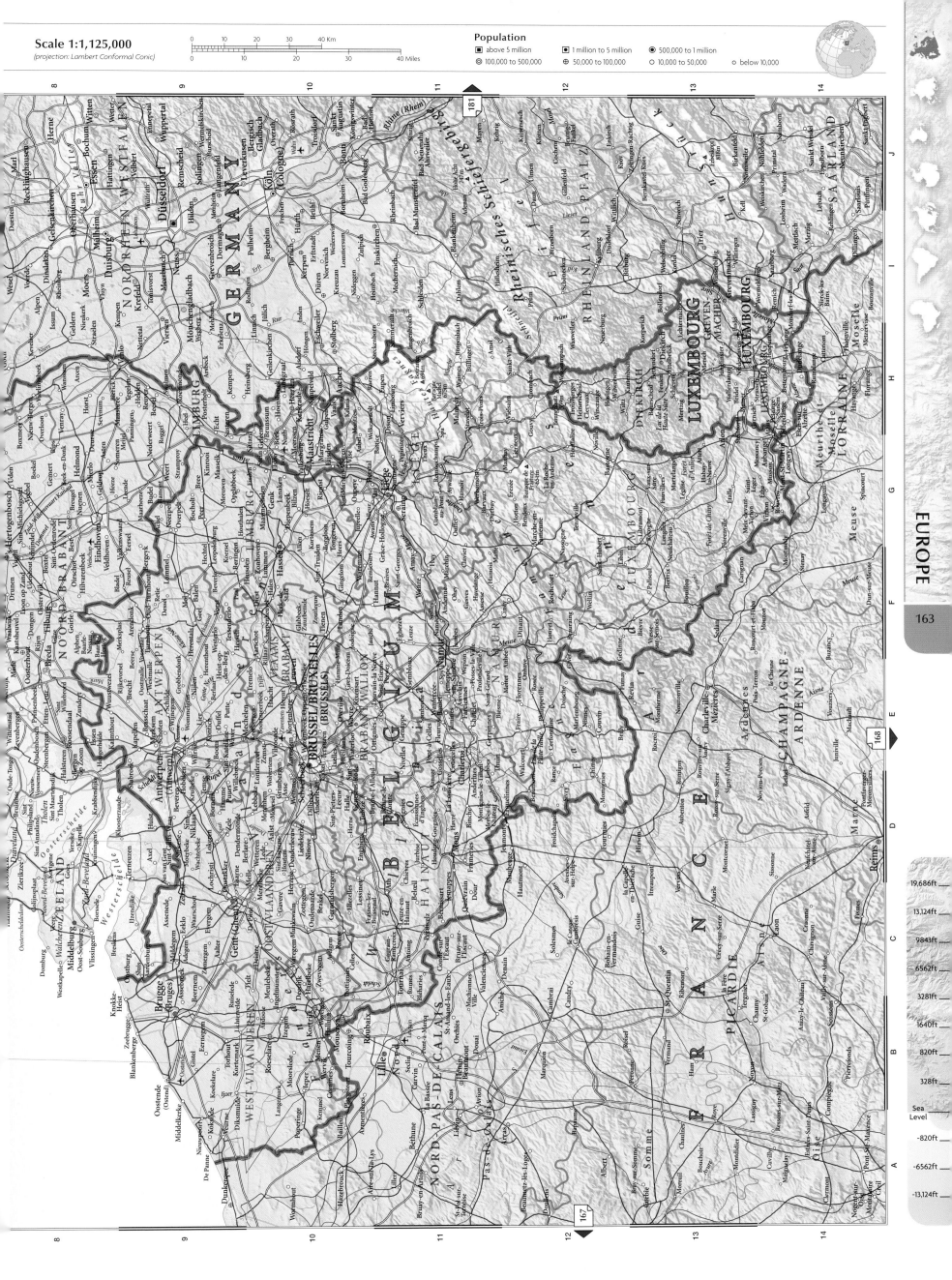

Scale 1:1,125,000
(projection: Lambert Conformal Conic)

0 10 20 30 40 Km
0   10   20   30   40 Miles

Population

■ above 5 million
◉ 500,000 to 1 million
⊙ 50,000 to 100,000
○ below 10,000

▣ 1 million to 5 million
◎ 100,000 to 500,000
○ 10,000 to 50,000

19,686ft
13,124ft
9843ft
6562ft
3281ft
1640ft
820ft
328ft
Sea Level
-820ft
-6562ft
-13,124ft

France

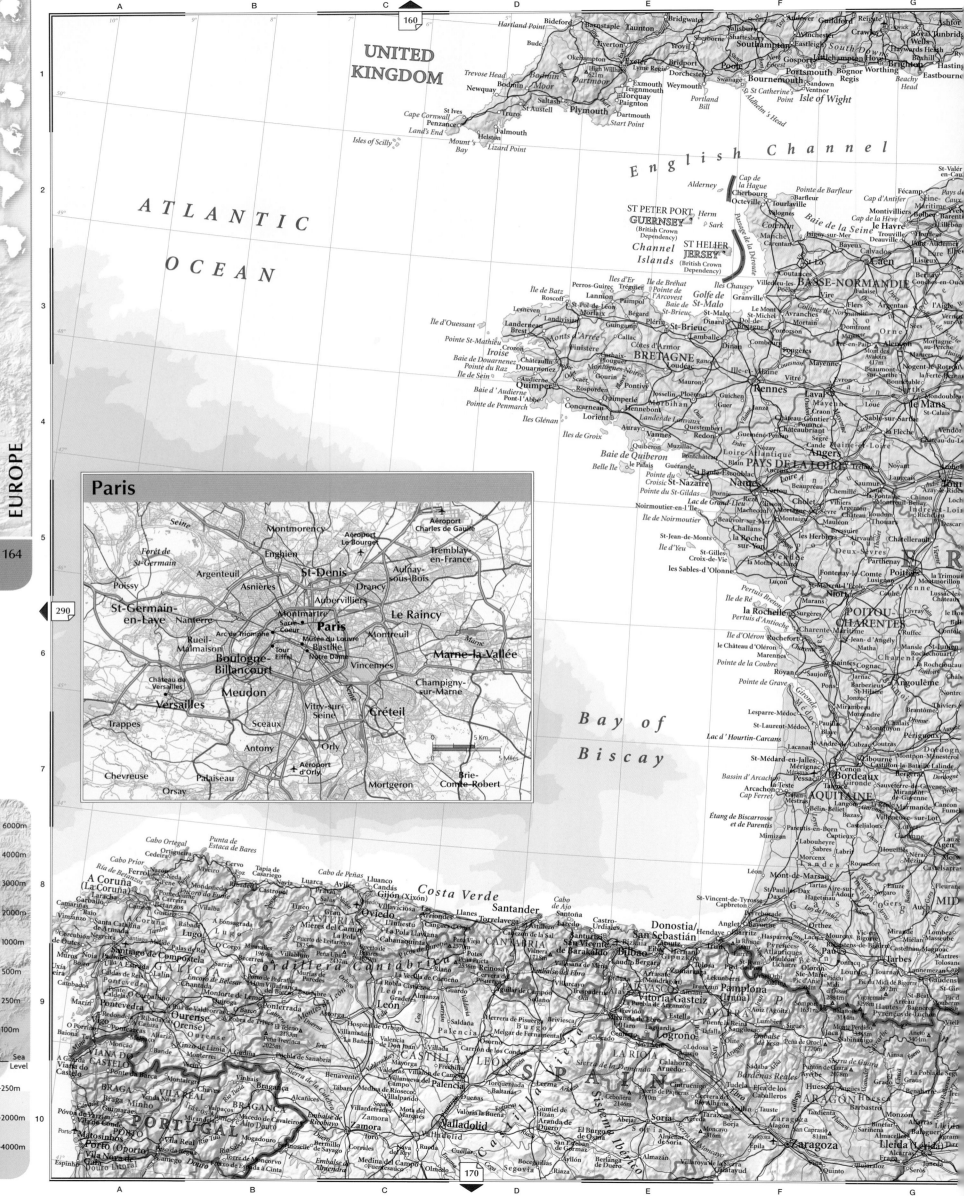

Scale 1:3,250,000
(projection: Lambert Conformal Conic)

0 20 40 60 80 100 Km

0 20 40 60 100 Miles

Population
- ■ above 5 million
- ■ 1 million to 5 million
- ◉ 500,000 to 1 million
- ◎ 100,000 to 500,000
- ⊕ 50,000 to 100,000
- ⊙ 10,000 to 50,000
- ○ below 10,000

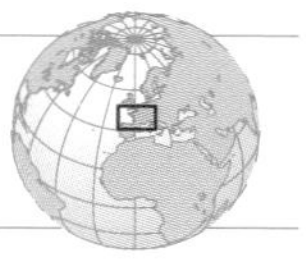

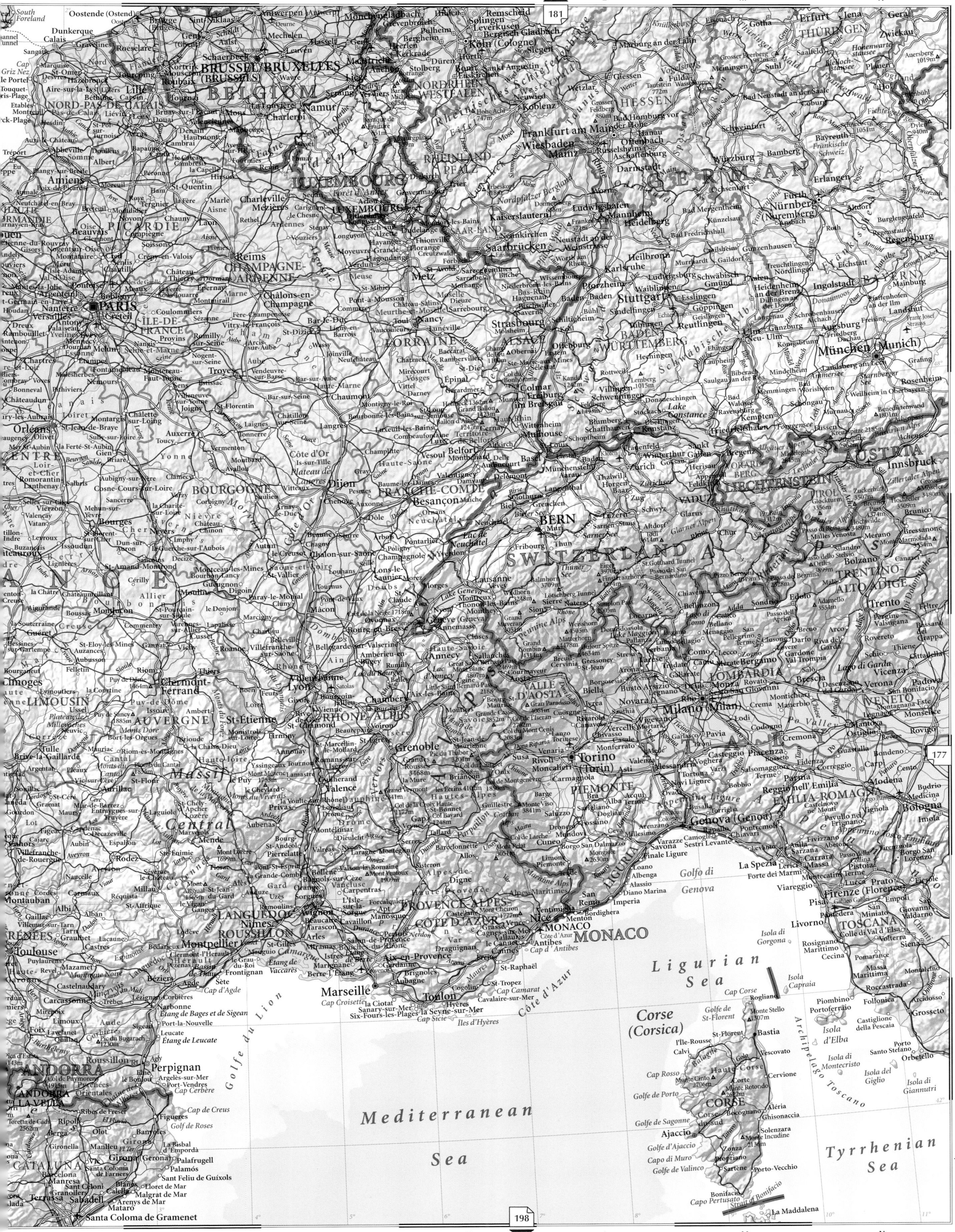

19,686ft
13,124ft
9843ft
6562ft
3281ft
1640ft
820ft
328ft
Sea Level
-820ft
-6562ft
-13,124ft

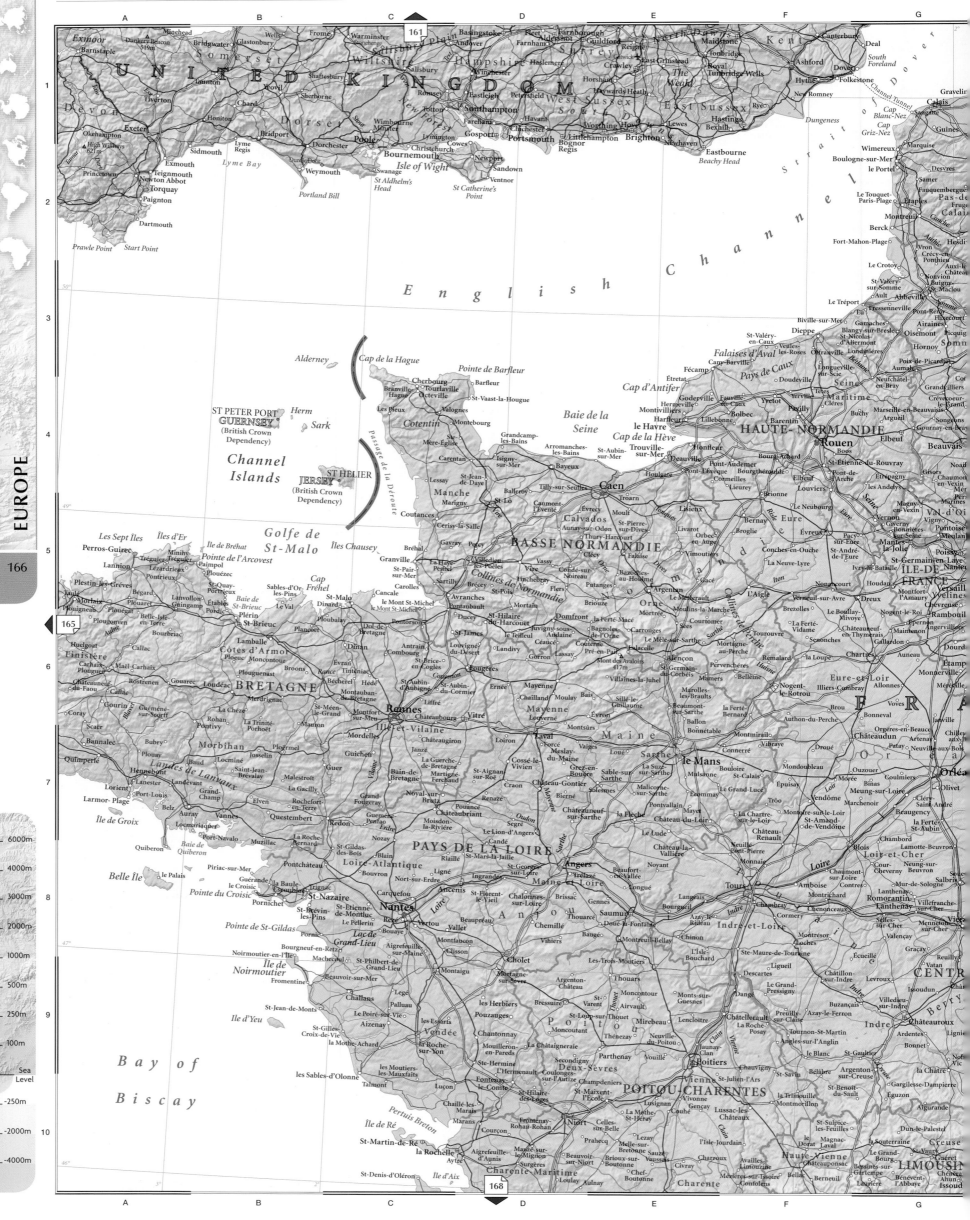

Scale 1:1,750,000
(projection: Lambert Conformal Conic)

0 10 20 30 40 50 Km
0 10 20 30 40 50 Miles

Population

■ above 5 million
■ 1 million to 5 million
◉ 500,000 to 1 million
◉ 100,000 to 500,000
⊕ 50,000 to 100,000
○ 10,000 to 50,000
· below 10,000

EUROPE

167

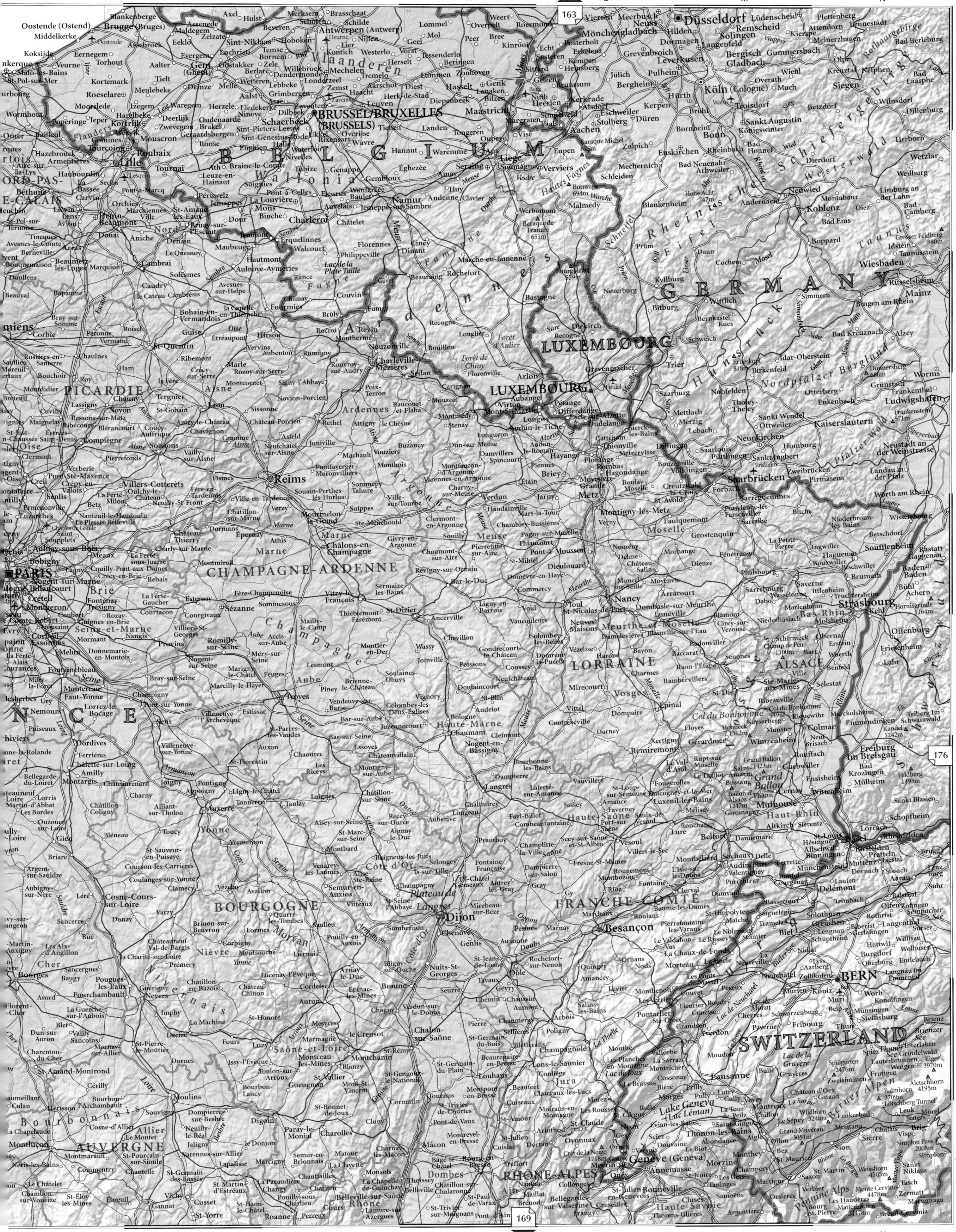

176

19,686ft
13,124ft
9843ft
6562ft
3281ft
1640ft
820ft
328ft
Sea Level
-820ft
-6562ft
-13,124ft

Scale 1:1,750,000
(projection: Lambert Conformal Conic)

```
0   10   20   30   40   50 Km
0   10   20   30   40   50 Miles
```

Population
■ above 5 million   ■ 1 million to 5 million   ◉ 500,000 to 1 million
◉ 100,000 to 500,000   ⊕ 50,000 to 100,000   ○ 10,000 to 50,000   ∘ below 10,000

Elevation scale:
19,686ft
13,124ft
9843ft
6562ft
3281ft
1640ft
820ft
328ft
Sea Level
-820ft
-6562ft
-13,124ft

Major labels:

Puy-de-Dôme Clermont-Ferrand **AUVERGNE** *Monts Dore* *Monts du Cantal* *Massif Central* Lyon Villeurbanne St-Étienne **RHÔNE-ALPES** *Haute-Savoie* Annecy Chambéry *Savoie* *Massif de la Vanoise* Grenoble *Vercors* Valence *Drôme* *Ardèche* *Hautes-Alpes* Gap **PROVENCE-ALPES-CÔTE D'AZUR** *Maritime Alps* *Ligurian Alps* **ITALY** Torino (Turin) Cuneo

LANGUEDOC-ROUSSILLON *Lozère* Mende *Aveyron* Rodez *Gard* Nîmes Montpellier *Hérault* Béziers Narbonne *Pyrénées-Orientales* Perpignan *Costa Brava* Girona (Gerona) Figueres *Golf de Roses* *Cap de Creus*

Marseille Toulon Aix-en-Provence *Bouches-du-Rhône* *Camargue* Arles *Étang de Berre* *Var* Draguignan Cannes Antibes Nice **MONACO** Menton San Remo *Côte d'Azur*

Golfe du Lion *Ligurian Sea* *Golfo di Genova* **Mediterranean Sea**

167   174   198   169

The Iberian Peninsula

290

EUROPE

170

ATLANTIC OCEAN

Bay of Biscay

Costa Verde

PORTUGAL

SPAIN

MADRID

LISBOA (LISBON)

GALICIA
ASTURIAS
CANTABRIA
CASTILLA Y LEÓN
MADRID
EXTREMADURA
ANDALUCÍA

Cordillera Cantábrica
Sistema Central
Sierra Morena
Sistemas Béticos

Sierra Nevada

Golfo de Cádiz
Strait of Gibraltar
Alboran Sea
Costa de la Luz
Costa del Sol

GIBRALTAR (to UK)
Europa Point

MOROCCO
Tanger
Ceuta (to Spain)
Tetouan

MADEIRA (to Portugal)
Funchal
Porto Santo
Madeira
ATLANTIC OCEAN
Scale 1:2,500,000
0 5 10   20 Km
0 5 10   20 Miles

ISLAS CANARIAS (CANARY ISLANDS) (to Spain)
Scale 1:6,500,000
0 25 50 75 Km
0 25 50 75 Miles
La Palma
Santa Cruz de la Palma
Tenerife
Santa Cruz de Tenerife
Gran Canaria
Las Palmas de Gran Canaria
Lanzarote
Arrecife
Fuerteventura
Puerto del Rosario
Hierro
Gomera
ATLANTIC OCEAN

6000m
4000m
3000m
2000m
1000m
500m
250m
100m
Sea Level
-250m
-2000m
-4000m

The Italian Peninsula

FRANCE
GERMANY
CZECH REPUBLIC
SLOVAKIA
AUSTRIA
HUNGARY
SWITZERLAND
LIECHTENSTEIN
SLOVENIA
CROATIA
BOSNIA AND HERZEGOVINA
ITALY
MONACO
SAN MARINO

BADEN-WÜRTTEMBERG
BAYERN
TIROL
LOMBARDIA
PIEMONT
VALLE D'AOSTA
LIGURIA
EMILIA-ROMAGNA
TRENTINO-ALTO ADIGE
FRIULI-VENEZIA GIULIA
VENETO
TOSCANA
MARCHE
UMBRIA
RHÔNE-ALPES
PROVENCE-ALPES-CÔTE D'AZUR
FRANCHE-COMTÉ
ALSACE
LORRAINE
PLZEŇSKÝ KRAJ
JIHOČESKÝ KRAJ
VYSOČINA
BRATISLAVA
WIEN
VIENNA
ZAGREB
LJUBLJANA
REPUBLIKA SRPSKA
FEDERACIJA BOSNE I HERCEGOVINE
SARAJEVO
SPLIT-DALMACIJA
ZADAR
GORSKI KOTAR
PRIMORJE
SOMOGY
VAS
VESZPRÉM
ZALA
BARANYA

München (Munich)
Wien (Vienna)
Budapest
Bratislava
Linz
Salzburg
Innsbruck
Bern
Zürich
Stuttgart
Genova (Genoa)
Torino (Turin)
Milano (Milan)
Venezia (Venice)
Bologna
Firenze (Florence)
Ancona
Zagreb
Ljubljana
Trieste

Adriatic Sea
Ligurian Sea
Gulf of Venice
Gulf of Trieste

Corse (Corsica)
Cap Corse
Isola d'Elba
Arcipelago Toscano

Côte d'Azur

Sea Level
6000m
4000m
3000m
2000m
1000m
500m
250m
100m
Sea Level
−250m
−2000m
−4000m

183
179
169

Scale 1:3,000,000
(projection: Lambert Conformal Conic)

| 0 | 20 | 40 | 60 | 80 | 100 Km |
| 0 | 20 | 40 | 60 | 80 | 100 Miles |

Population

- ■ above 5 million
- ◉ 500,000 to 1 million
- ⊕ 50,000 to 100,000
- ○ below 10,000
- ▣ 1 million to 5 million
- ◎ 100,000 to 500,000
- ⊙ 10,000 to 50,000

MALTA (inset)

Scale 1:900,000

| 0 | 5 | 10 Km |
| 0 | 5 | 10 Miles |

Gozo, Victoria, Kemmuna (Comino), San Pawl il-Baħar, Mellieħa, Mosta, San Ġiljan, Sliema, VALLETTA, Rabat, Paola, Marsaxlokk, Birżebbuġa, Il-Kullana, Mediterranean Sea

Malta, Il-Ponta ta' San Dimitri, Il-Ponta ta' Wardija

MONTENEGRO

NERETVA

Strait of Otranto

Ionian Sea

Adriatic Sea

PUGLIA — Bari, Brindisi, Lecce, Taranto, Foggia, Barletta, Molfetta, Monopoli, Manduria, Gallipoli, Otranto, Gagliano del Capo, Capo Santa Maria di Leuca

Golfo di Taranto

BASILICATA — Potenza, Matera

CALABRIA — Catanzaro, Cosenza, Crotone, Reggio di Calabria, Lamezia Terme, Capo Rizzuto, Capo Colonne, Capo Spartivento

Appennino Lucano

MOLISE — Campobasso, Isernia

ABRUZZO — Pescara, Chieti, Lanciano, Teramo, L'Aquila, Avezzano, Sulmona

CAMPANIA — Napoli (Naples), Salerno, Avellino, Benevento, Caserta, Sorrento, Torre del Greco, Pompei, Golfo di Napoli, Golfo di Salerno, Isola di Capri, Isola d'Ischia

LAZIO — ROMA (ROME), VATICAN CITY, Latina, Frosinone, Civitavecchia, Lido di Ostia

Appennino Campano

Isole Tremiti, Isole Ponziane, Isola di Ustica

Isole Eolie — Isola Stromboli 926m, Isola Salina, Isola Lipari, Isola Vulcano, Isola Filicudi, Isola Alicudi, Isola Panarea

Golfo di Gaeta, Golfo di Gioia, Golfo di Squillace, Golfo di Sant'Eufemia, Golfo di Policastro, Capo Palinuro, Capo Vaticano, Capo Spartivento

Tyrrhenian Sea

Sicilia (Sicily) — Palermo, Catania, Messina, Siracusa, Marsala, Trapani, Agrigento, Gela, Ragusa, Caltanissetta, Enna, Modica, Vittoria, Licata, Mazara del Vallo, Capo Passero, Capo San Vito, Golfo di Patti, Golfo di Castellammare, Golfo di Catania, Golfo di Noto, Stretto di Messina

Etna 3340m

Malta Channel

Strait of Sicily

Isole Egadi — Isola Marettimo, Isola Favignana, Isola Levanzo

Isole Pelagie (to Italy)

Pantelleria, Isola di Pantelleria (to Italy)

MALTA — VALLETTA, Rabat, Gozo, Victoria, Kemmuna (Comino), Sliema, Mellieħa, Paola

Sardegna (Sardinia) — Cagliari, Sassari, Oristano, Nuoro, Olbia, Alghero, Iglesias, Carbonia, La Maddalena, Golfo di Cagliari, Golfo di Oristano, Golfo di Palmas, Golfo di Orosei, Capo Carbonara, Capo Spartivento, Capo Caccia, Capo Comino, Capo Coda Cavallo, Isola di Sant'Antioco, Isola di San Pietro, Punta La Marmora 1834m

CORSE (to France) — Ajaccio, Bonifacio, Corscu-Sud, Strait of Bonifacio, Monte Incudine 2136m, Monte Cinto 2706m

Isola di Montecristo, Isola del Giglio, Isola di Giannutri

Mediterranean Sea

TUNISIA — TUNIS, Bizerte, L'Ariana, Kairouan, Sousse, Monastir, Mahdia, Nabeul, Hammamet, Cap Bon, Golfe de Tunis, Golfe de Hammamet, Carthage

ALGERIA — Annaba, Tébessa, El Kef

Ile de Zembra, Iles Kuriat

Elevation legend (right margin):
19,686ft
13,124ft
9843ft
6562ft
3281ft
1640ft
820ft
328ft
Sea Level
-820ft
-6562ft
-13,124ft

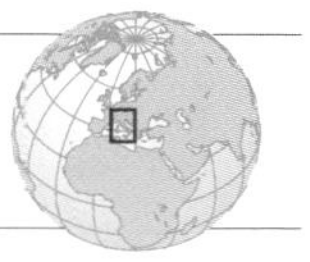

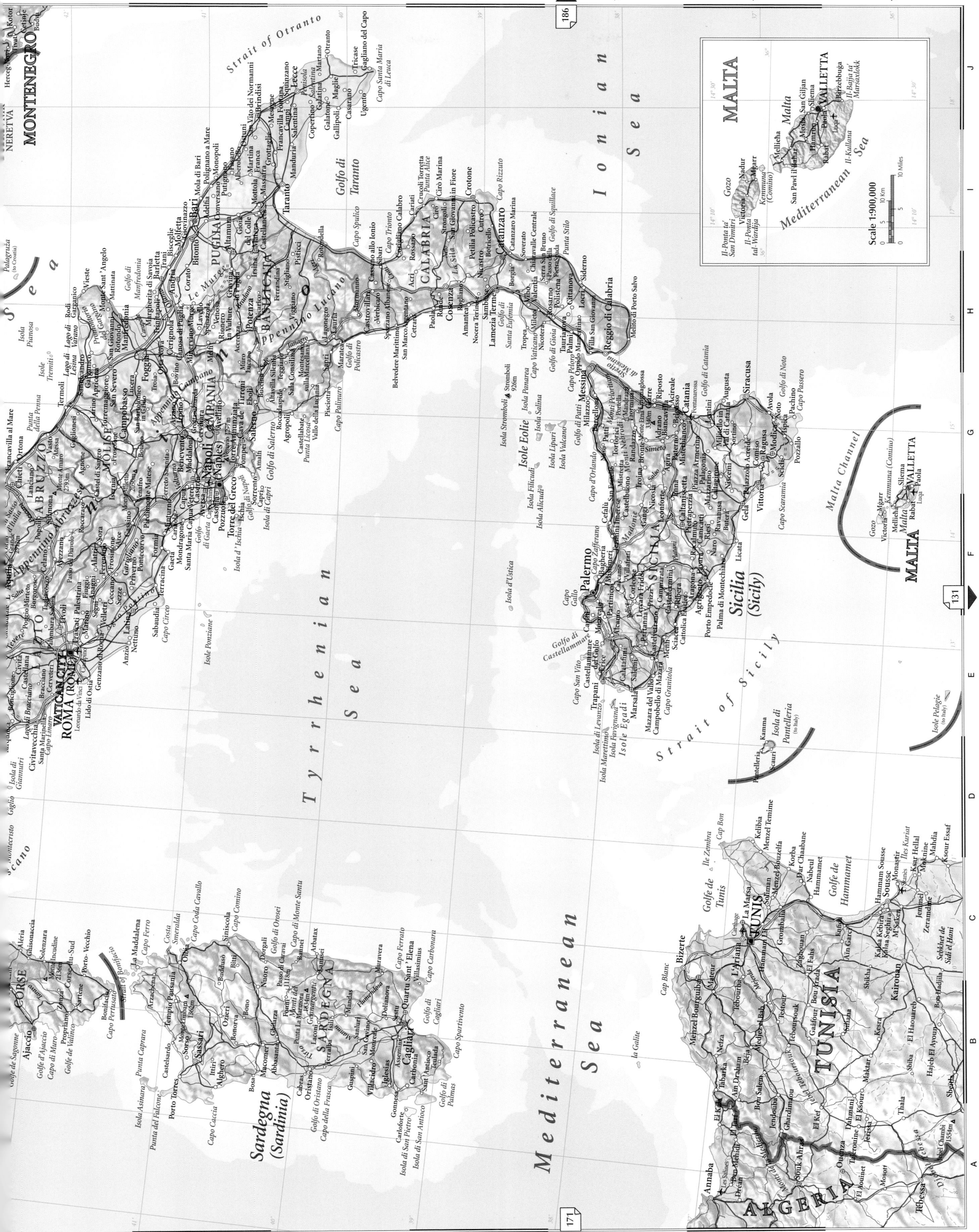

Germany

North Sea

Baltic Sea

Kattegat

SWEDEN

BLEKINGE
SKÅNE

DENMARK
MIDTJYLLAND
SYDDANMARK
Jylland
Sjælland
Fyn
Lolland
Falster
Møn
Langeland
Als

BORNHOLM
Bornholm

KØBENHAVN (COPENHAGEN)

Århus
Odense
Esbjerg
Kolding
Flensburg
Kiel
Lübeck
Hamburg
Bremen
Bremerhaven
Hannover
Wolfsburg
Braunschweig
Berlin
Potsdam
Magdeburg

SCHLESWIG-HOLSTEIN
MECKLENBURG-VORPOMMERN
NIEDERSACHSEN
BRANDENBURG
SACHSEN-ANHALT

Rostock
Wismar
Schwerin
Stralsund
Greifswald
Rügen
Usedom

POLAND
POMERANIA
ZACHODNIO-POMORSKIE
LUBUSKIE

Szczecin
Świnoujście
Frankfurt an der Oder

NETHERLANDS
GRONINGEN
DRENTHE
FRYSLÂN (FRIESLAND)
OVERIJSSEL
GELDERLAND
FLEVOLAND

North Frisian Islands (Nordfriesische Inseln)
Ostfriesische Inseln
Helgoländer Bucht
Helgoland

Kieler Bucht
Mecklenburger Bucht
Pomeranian Bay

Elbe
Weser
Havel
Oder/Odra

Scale 1:2,250,000
(projection: Lambert Conformal Conic)

0 10 20 30 40 50 60 70 80 Km
0 10 20 30 40 50 60 70 80 Miles

Population
- ■ above 5 million
- ■ 1 million to 5 million
- ● 500,000 to 1 million
- ◉ 100,000 to 500,000
- ⊕ 50,000 to 100,000
- ○ 10,000 to 50,000
- ∘ below 10,000

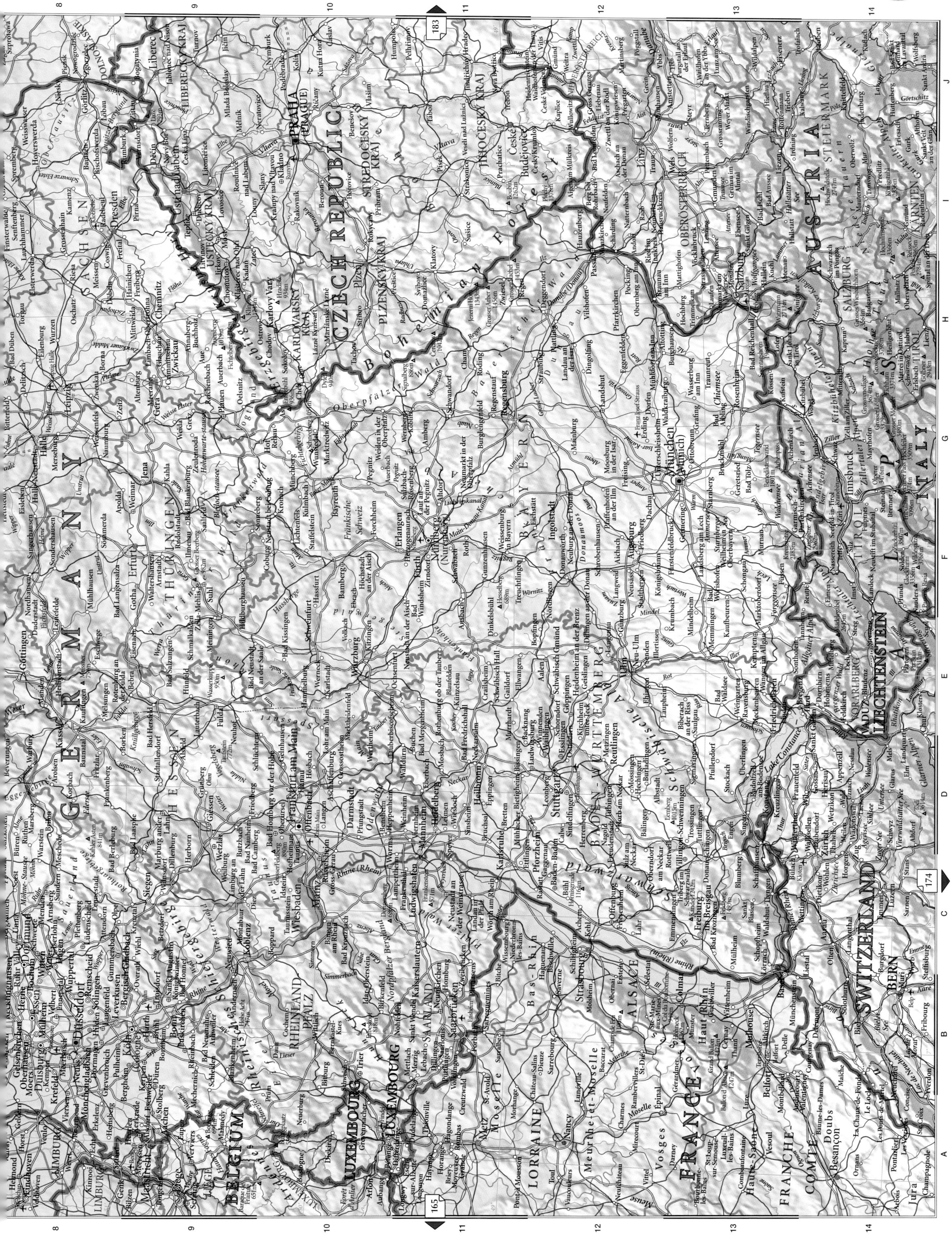

19,686ft
13,124ft
9843ft
6562ft
3281ft
1640ft
820ft
328ft
Sea Level
-820ft
-6562ft
-13,124ft

GERMANY

CZECH REPUBLIC

PRAHA (PRAGUE)

AUSTRIA

ITALY

SWITZERLAND

LIECHTENSTEIN

FRANCE

LUXEMBOURG

BELGIUM

THÜRINGEN

SACHSEN

HESSEN

BAYERN

BADEN-WÜRTTEMBERG

RHEINLAND-PFALZ

SAARLAND

ALSACE

LORRAINE

FRANCHE-COMTÉ

TIROL

OBERÖSTERREICH

STEIERMARK

SALZBURG

KÄRNTEN

VORARLBERG

 STŘEDOČESKÝ KRAJ

JIHOČESKÝ KRAJ

PLZEŇSKÝ KRAJ

KARLOVARSKÝ KRAJ

ÚSTECKÝ KRAJ

LIBERECKÝ KRAJ

DOLNOŚLĄSKIE

LIMBURG

München

Dresden

Stuttgart

Nürnberg

Frankfurt am Main

Würzburg

Regensburg

Bern

Innsbruck

Salzburg

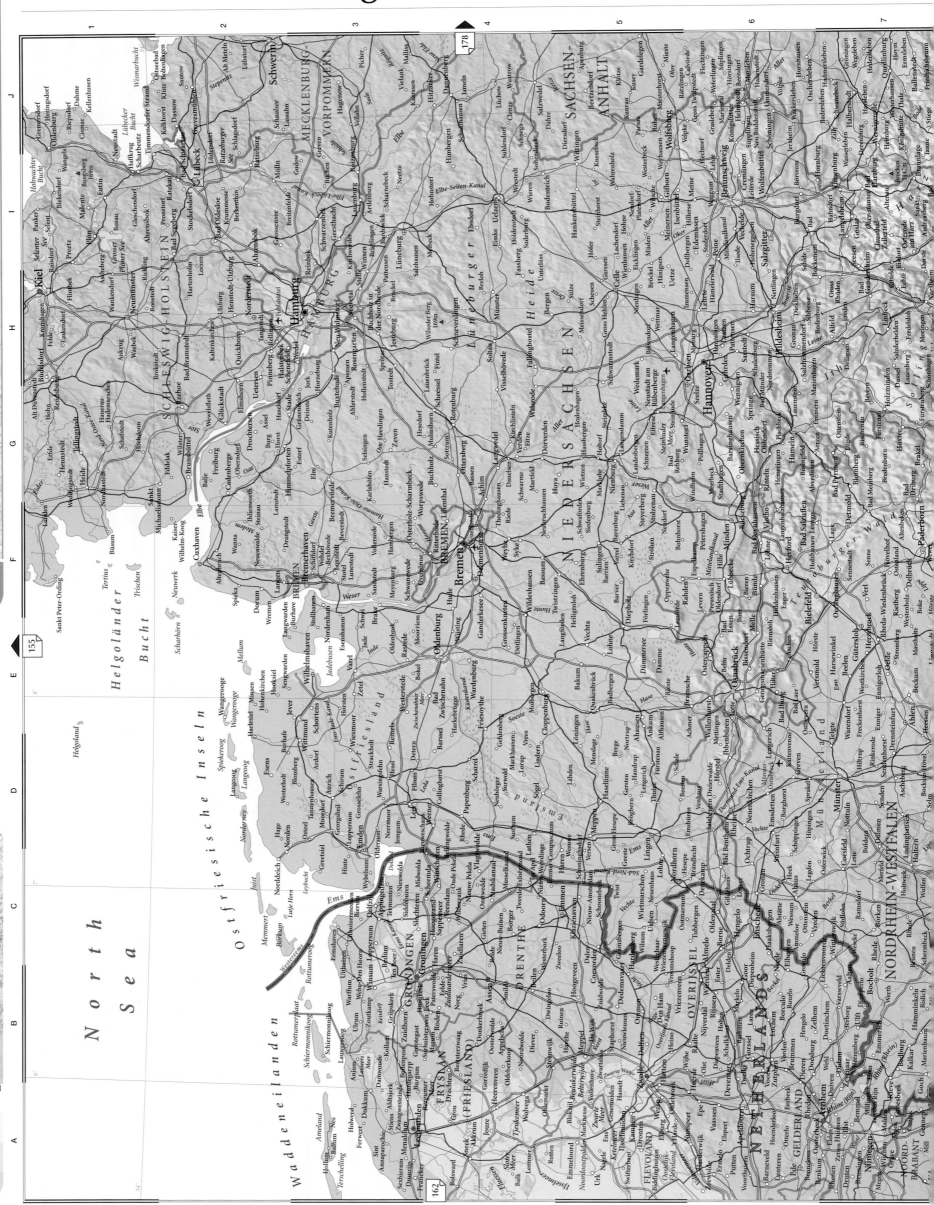

Central Europe

191
155
178

LATVIA

LITHUANIA

RUSSIAN FEDERATION

KALININGRADSKAYA OBLAST'

BELARUS

POLAND

GERMANY

DENMARK

SWEDEN

BALTIC SEA

Kattegat

Gulf of Danzig

Pomeranian Bay

Öland

Bornholm

Sea Level

6000m
4000m
3000m
2000m
1000m
500m
250m
100m
Sea Level
-250m
-2000m
-4000m

Scale 1:2,750,000

(projection: Lambert Conformal Conic)

0 10 20 30 40 50 60 70 80 Km

0 10 20 30 40 50 60 70 80 Miles

Population

◼ above 5 million
◻ 1 million to 5 million
◉ 500,000 to 1 million
◎ 100,000 to 500,000
⊕ 50,000 to 100,000
○ 10,000 to 50,000
∘ below 10,000

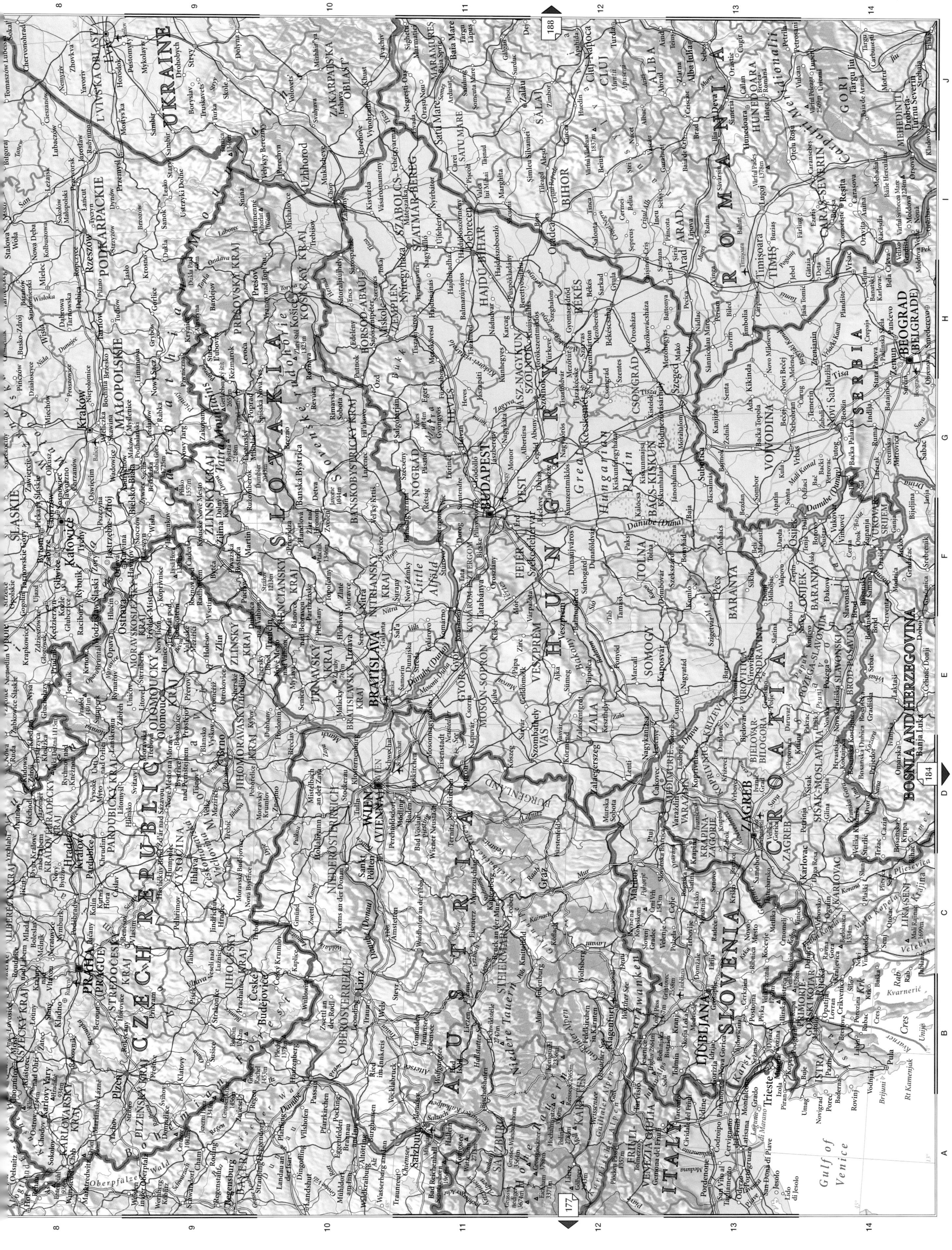

19,686ft
13,124ft
9843ft
6562ft
3281ft
1640ft
820ft
328ft
Sea Level
-820ft
-6562ft
-13,124ft

UKRAINE

POLAND

SLOVAKIA

CZECH REPUBLIC

AUSTRIA

HUNGARY

ROMANIA

SERBIA

CROATIA

SLOVENIA

BOSNIA AND HERZEGOVINA

ITALY

Budapest

Wien (Vienna)

Bratislava

Beograd (Belgrade)

Zagreb

Ljubljana

Praha (Prague)

Gulf of Venice

In February 2008, Kosovo (a UN Protectorate within Serbia since 1999) declared independence. Although now recognized by numerous countries, this decision has proved controversial with other states wary of setting a precedent for separatist groups within their own borders. It is therefore likely to be some time before Kosovo becomes universally recognized.

Scale 1:2,500,000
(projection: Lambert Conformal Conic)

0 10 20 30 40 50 Km
0 10 20 30 40 50 Miles

Population
■ above 5 million
■ 1 million to 5 million
◉ 500,000 to 1 million
◎ 100,000 to 500,000
⊕ 50,000 to 100,000
○ 10,000 to 50,000
· below 10,000

EUROPE
185

Countries and major regions

ROMÂNIA

BULGARIA

TURKEY

MOLDOVA

UKRAINE

GREECE

MACEDONIA

Seas

Black Sea

Aegean Sea

Thracian Sea

Marmara Denizi (Sea of Marmara)

Major cities and towns

BUCUREŞTI (BUCHAREST)

SOFIA

Plovdiv

VARNA / Varna

BURGAS

CONSTANŢA

Cluj-Napoca

Târgu Mureş

Braşov

Sibiu

Craiova

Ploieşti

Galaţi

Brăila

Buzău

Bacău

Thessaloníki

İSTANBUL / Istanbul

Bursa

EDIRNE / Edirne

TEKİRDAĞ / Tekirdağ

ÇANAKKALE

KIRKLARELİ

Lárisa

Romanian județe / regions

BIHOR, ALBA, CLUJ, MUREŞ, HARGHITA, NEAMŢ, BACĂU, VASLUI, COVASNA, BRAŞOV, SIBIU, HUNEDOARA, ARAD, CARAŞ-SEVERIN, VÂLCEA, ARGEŞ, DÂMBOVIŢA, PRAHOVA, VRANCEA, GALAŢI, BUZĂU, BRĂILA, IALOMIŢA, TULCEA, GORJ, MEHEDINŢI, DOLJ, OLT, TELEORMAN, GIURGIU, ILFOV, CĂLĂRAŞI

Bulgarian regions

VIDIN, MONTANA, VRATSA, PLEVEN, LOVECH, GABROVO, VELIKO TARNOVO, RAZGRAD, RUSE, SILISTRA, DOBRICH, SHUMEN, TARGOVISHTE, VARNA, BURGAS, SLIVEN, STARA ZAGORA, YAMBOL, HASKOVO, KARDZHALI, SMOLYAN, PLOVDIV, PAZARDZHIK, BLAGOEVGRAD, KYUSTENDIL, PERNIK, SOFIA GRAD

Mountains and physical features

Carpathian Mountains

Carpaţii Meridionali

Balkan Mountains / Stara Planina

Rhodope Mountains

Sredna Gora

Pirin

Dunavska Ravnina

Ludogorie

Dobrudja

Thracian Sea

Mt Olympus (Óros Ólymbos) 2917m

Moldoveanu 2544m

Omu 2506m

Musala 2925m

Botev 2376m

Vihren 2914m

Turkish regions

İSTANBUL, TEKİRDAĞ, KIRKLARELİ, EDİRNE, ÇANAKKALE, BALIKESİR, BURSA

Greek regions

KENTRIKÍ MAKEDONÍA, ANATOLIKÍ MAKEDONÍA KAI THRÁKI, THESSALÍA, CHALKIDIKÍ, ÁGION ÓROS, VÓREION AIGAÍON

Marmara Denizi (Sea of Marmara)

İstanbul Boğazı (Bosporus)

Çanakkale Boğazı (Dardanelles)

188
187
214

Elevation scale

19,686ft
13,124ft
9843ft
6562ft
3281ft
1640ft
820ft
328ft
Sea Level
-820ft
-6562ft
-13,124ft

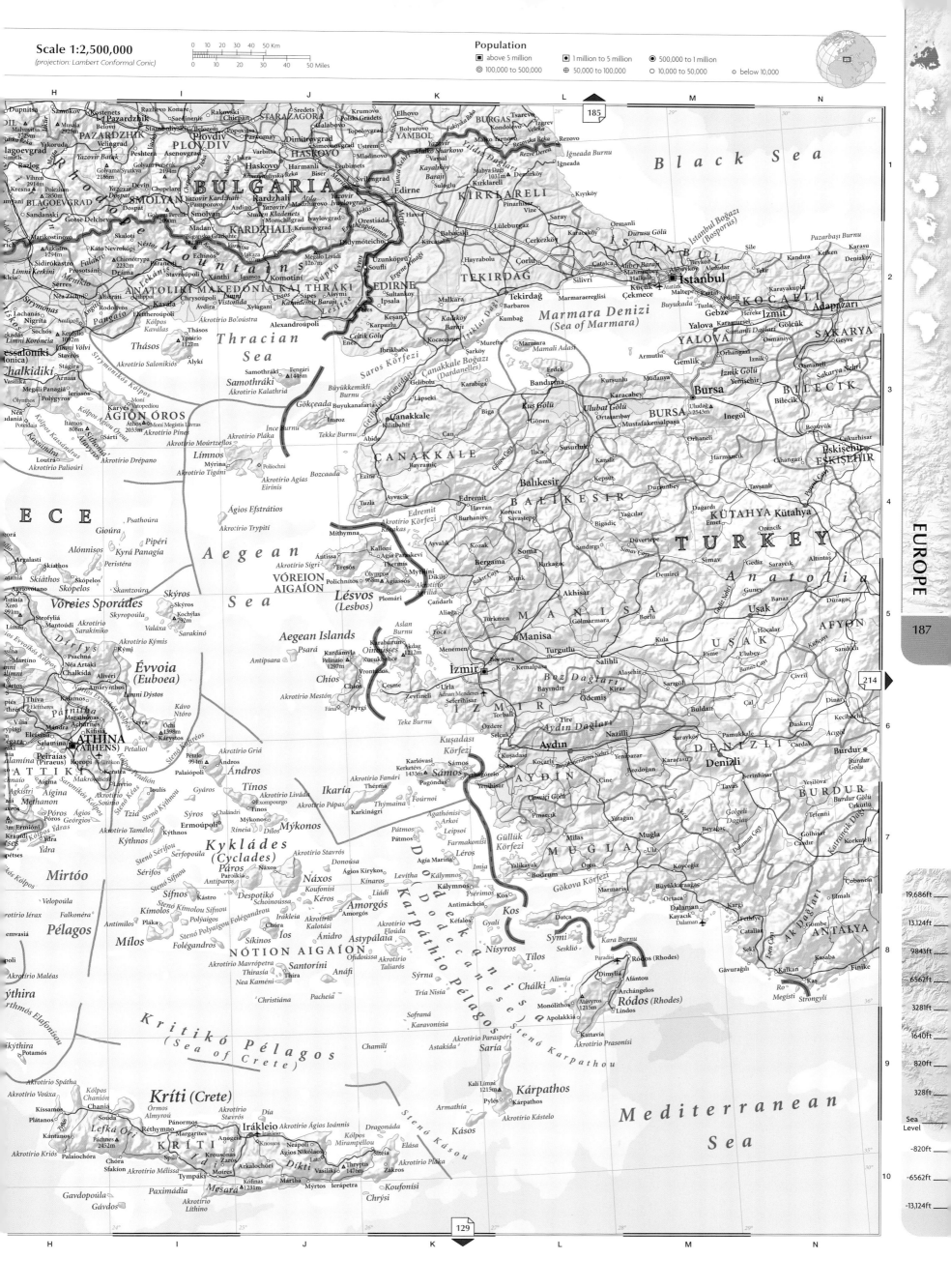

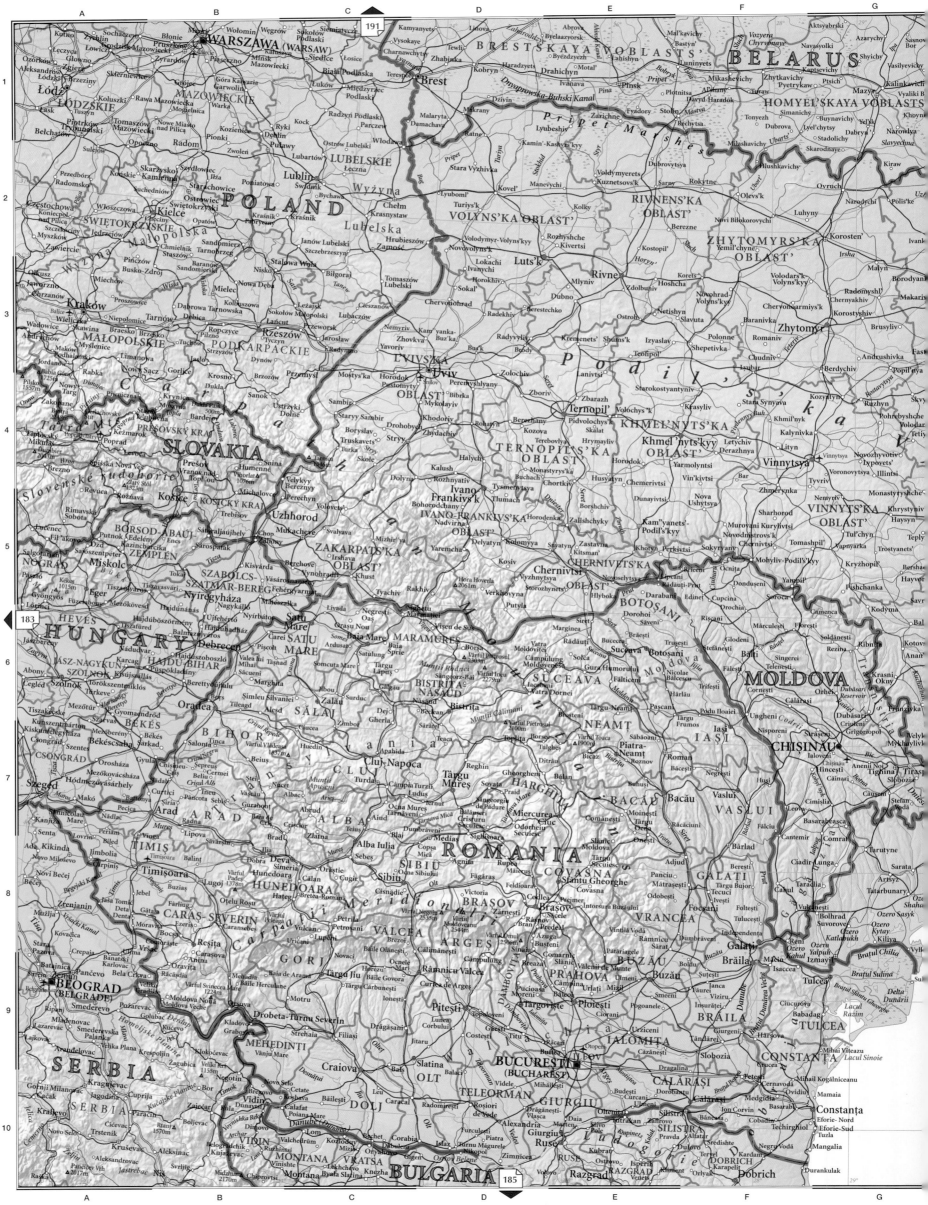

Scale 1:3,000,000
(projection: Lambert Conformal Conic)

Population
■ above 5 million
■ 1 million to 5 million
◉ 500,000 to 1 million
◎ 100,000 to 500,000
⊕ 50,000 to 100,000
○ 10,000 to 50,000
○ below 10,000

0   20   40   60   80   100 Km
0   20   40   60   80   100 Miles

196

H   I   J   K   L   M   N

EUROPE

189

RUSSIAN FEDERATION

ORLOVSKAYA OBLAST'
LIPETSKAYA OBLAST'
KURSKAYA OBLAST'
BELGORODSKAYA OBLAST'
VORONEZHSKAYA OBLAST'

Homyel'
Voronezh
Kursk
Belgorod
Kharkiv
Sumy
Chernihiv

CHERNIHIVS'KA OBLAST'
SUMS'KA OBLAST'
POLTAVS'KA OBLAST'
KHARKIVS'KA OBLAST'
LUHANS'KA OBLAST'

KYYIV (KIEV)
KYYIVS'KA OBLAST'
Cherkasy
CHERKAS'KA OBLAST'
Poltava
Kirovohrad
KIROVOHRADS'KA OBLAST'
UKRAINE
Dnipropetrovs'k
DNIPROPETROVS'KA OBLAST'
Luhans'k
Donets'k
DONETS'KA OBLAST'
Rostov-na-Donu

Kryvyy Rih
Zaporizhzhya
ZAPORIZ'KA OBLAST'
Mariupol'
Taganrog
Azov
Bataysk

Dnipropetrovs'k
MYKOLAYIVS'KA OBLAST'
Mykolayiv
Odesa
ODES'KA OBLAST'
KHERSONS'KA OBLAST'
Kherson
Melitopol'
Berdyans'k

Black   Sea

Gulf of Taganrog
KRASNODARSKIY KRAY
Krasnodar

Sea of Azov

Dnieper Lowland

AVTONOMNA RESPUBLIKA KRYM
(annexed by Russian Federation, 2014)
Kryms'kyy Pivostriv (Crimea)
Yevpatoriya
Simferopol'
Sevastopol'
Yalta
Kerch
Kerch Strait

Black   Sea

19,686ft
13,124ft
9843ft
6562ft
3281ft
1640ft
820ft
328ft
Sea Level
-820ft
-6562ft
-13,124ft

Scale 1:2,750,000
(projection: Lambert Conformal Conic)

0 10 20 30 40 50 60 70 80 Km
0 10 20 30 40 50 60 70 80 Miles

Population

■ above 5 million
■ 1 million to 5 million
◉ 500,000 to 1 million
◎ 100,000 to 500,000
⊕ 50,000 to 100,000
○ 10,000 to 50,000
○ below 10,000

19,686ft
13,124ft
9843ft
6562ft
3281ft
1640ft
820ft
328ft
Sea Level
-820ft
-6562ft
-13,124ft

LITHUANIA
BELARUS
POLAND
RUSSIAN FEDERATION
UKRAINE
KALININGRADSKAYA OBLAST'

VILNIUS
MINSK
WARSZAWA / WARSAW
KYIV (KIEV)

Vitsyebsk
Mahilyow
Homyel'/Gomel'
Chernihiv
Brest
Lublin
Rivne
Luts'k
L'viv
Ternopil'
Zhytomyr
Kaunas
Hrodna/Grodno
Bialystok
Smolensk
Kaliningrad

VITSYEBSKAYA VOBLASTS'
MAHILYOWSKAYA VOBLASTS'
MINSKAYA VOBLASTS'
HRODZYENSKAYA VOBLASTS'/GRODNENSKAYA OBLAST'
BRESTSKAYA VOBLASTS'
HOMEL'SKAYA VOBLASTS'/GOMEL'SKAYA OBLAST'
SMOLENSKAYA OBLAST'
BRYANSKAYA OBLAST'
CHERNIHIVS'KA OBLAST'
KYIVS'KA OBLAST'
ZHYTOMYRS'KA OBLAST'
RIVNENS'KA OBLAST'
VOLYNS'KA OBLAST'
L'VIVS'KA OBLAST'
TERNOPIL'S'KA OBLAST'
KHMEL'NYTS'KA OBLAST'
VINNYTS'KA OBLAST'
CHERKAS'KA OBLAST'
PODILLYA
POLISSYA
PODLASKIE
MAZOWIECKIE
LUBELSKIE
PODKARPACKIE
MALOPOLSKIE
SWIETOKRZYSKIE
WARMINSKO-MAZURSKIE
WYZYNA LUBELSKA
TAURAGE
UTENA
AUKŠTUMA

Pripet Marshes
Gulf of Danzig
Courland Lagoon

Dnieper (Dnyapro/Dnepr)
Bug
Wisla
Pripet
Styr
Horyn'

THE RUSSIAN FEDERATION: ADMINISTRATIVE REGIONS

The administrative area names in European Russia have been omitted west of the Ural Mountains. Please refer to pages 194-195 and 196-197 where these areas are shown at a larger scale.

EUROPE

192

6000m
4000m
3000m
2000m
1000m
500m
250m
100m
Sea Level
-250m
-2000m
-4000m

LATVIA

LITHUANIA

Kaliningrad
KALININGRADSKAYA OBLAST'

POLAND

WARSZAWA (WARSAW)

BELARUS

MINSK

Brest

Vitsyebsk/Vitebsk

Smolensk

SMOLENSKAYA OBLAST'

Mahilyow/Mogilev

TVERSKAYA OBLAST'

Tver'

MOSKOVSKAYA OBLAST'

MOSKVA (MOSCOW)

KALUZHSKAYA OBLAST'

Kaluga

R U S S I A

Tula

TUL'SKAYA OBLAST'

RYAZANSKAYA OBLAST'

Ryazan'

BRYANSKAYA OBLAST'

Bryansk

ORLOVSKAYA OBLAST'

Orel/Orl

LIPETSKAYA OBLAST'

Lipetsk

KURSKAYA OBLAST'

Kursk

Homyel'/Gomel

UKRAINE

KYYIV/KIEV

Pripet Marshes

Podil's'ka Vysochyna

L'VIV

BELGORODSKAYA OBLAST'

Belgorod

Kharkiv

VORONEZHSKAYA OBLAST'

Voronezh

Dnipropetrovs'k

Zaporizhzhya

Donets'k

ROSTOVSKAYA OBLAST'

Rostov-na-Donu

Taganrog

Mariupol'

Gulf of Taganrog

MOLDOVA

CHISINAU

ROMANIA

BUCURESTI (BUCHAREST)

Odesa

Mykolayiv

Kherson

Kryms'ky Pivostriv (Crimea) (annexed by Russian Federation, 2014)

Simferopol'

Sevastopol'

Yalta

Kerch

Novorossiysk

Krasnodar

KRASNODARSKIY KRAY

Maykop

RESPUBLIKA ADYGEYA

KARACHAYEVO-CHERKESSKAYA RESPUBLI...

Sochi

APKHAZIA

Sokhumi

Sea of Azov

Black Sea

BULGARIA

SOFIA

Balkan Mountains

Stara Gora

GREECE

Thásos

Límnos

Lésvos

TURKEY

Istanbul

İzmit Adapazari

Bursa

Köroğlu Dağlari

Zonguldak

Samsun

Trabzon

6000m
4000m
3000m
2000m
1000m
500m
250m
100m
Sea Level
-250m
-2000m
-4000m

Scale 1:5,750,000
(projection: Lambert Conformal Conic)

0 25 50 75 100 125 150 175 200 Km
0 25 50 75 100 125 150 175 200 Miles

Population
- ■ above 5 million
- ◉ 500,000 to 1 million
- ◎ 100,000 to 500,000
- ⊕ 50,000 to 100,000
- ○ 10,000 to 50,000
- ∘ below 10,000
- ▣ 1 million to 5 million

195

222

226

19,686ft
13,124ft
9843ft
6562ft
3281ft
1640ft
820ft
328ft
Sea Level
-820ft
-6562ft
-13,124ft

RUSSIAN FEDERATION

Nizhniy Novgorod, Dzerzhinsk, Murom, Arzamas, Saransk, RESPUBLIKA MORDOVIYA, Yoshkar-Ola, RESPUBLIKA MARIY EL, Cheboksary, RESPUBLIKA CHAVASH, Kazan', RESPUBLIKA TATARSTAN, Nizhnekamsk, Naberezhnyye Chelny, Izhevsk, UDMURTSKAYA RESPUBLIKA, Votkinsk, Sarapul, Neftekamsk, Ufa, RESPUBLIKA BASHKORTOSTAN, Yekaterinburg, Chelyabinsk, Zlatoust, Miass, Kopeysk, KURGANSKAYA OBLAST', CHELABINSKAYA OBLAST', KOSTANAY, Rudnyy, Magnitogorsk, Sterlitamak, Salavat, Ul'yanovsk, UL'YANOVSKAYA OBLAST', Tol'yatti, Samara, Syzran', Novokuybyshevsk, Chapayevsk, SAMARSKAYA OBLAST', Penza, PENZENSKAYA OBLAST', Saratov, SARATOVSKAYA OBLAST', Engel's, Balashov, Orenburg, ORENBURGSKAYA OBLAST', Orsk, Novotroitsk, Aktobe (Aktyubinsk), Kamyshin, VOLGOGRADSKAYA OBLAST', Volgograd, Volzhskiy, Volgodonsk, ASTRAKHANSKAYA OBLAST', Astrakhan', Elista, RESPUBLIKA KALMYKIYA, Stavropol', STAVROPOL'SKIY KRAY, Nevinnomyssk, Cherkessk, Pyatigorsk, Nal'chik, KABARDINO-BALKARSKAYA RESPUBLIKA, Vladikavkaz, RESPUBLIKA SEVERNAYA OSETIYA-ALANIYA, INGUSHSKAYA RESPUBLIKA, Grozny, CHECHENSKAYA RESPUBLIKA, Gudermes, Khasavyurt, Makhachkala, Kaspiysk, Buynaksk, DAGESTAN, Derbent

KAZAKHSTAN

ZAPADNYY KAZAKHSTAN, Ural'sk, AKTYUBINSK, ATYRAU, Atyrau, MANGYSTAU, Aktau, Caspian Depression, Ryn-Peski

UZBEKISTAN

QORAQALPOG'ISTON RESPUBLIKASI, Nukus, Ustyurt Plateau, Aral Sea

TURKMENISTAN

BALKAN WELAYATY, DAŞOGUZ WELAYATY, Garabogaz Aylagy

GEORGIA

TBILISI, Rustavi, Kutaisi

AZERBAIJAN

BAKI, Sumqayıt, Gäncä

ARMENIA

Caspian Sea

Scale 1:8,750,000
(projection: Lambert Conformal Conic)

0 25 50 75 100 125 150 175 200 Km
0 25 50 75 100 125 150 175 200 Miles

Population
- above 5 million
- 1 million to 5 million
- 500,000 to 1 million
- 100,000 to 500,000
- 50,000 to 100,000
- 10,000 to 50,000
- below 10,000

POLAND · BELARUS · UKRAINE · RUSSIAN FEDERATION · SLOVAKIA · HUNGARY · ROMANIA · MOLDOVA · CROATIA · BOSNIA AND HERZEGOVINA · SERBIA · MONTENEGRO · KOSOVO · MACEDONIA · ALBANIA · BULGARIA · GREECE · TURKEY · GEORGIA · CYPRUS · SYRIA · LEBANON · ISRAEL · JORDAN · IRAQ · SAUDI ARABIA · EGYPT · LIBYA

WARSZAWA (WARSAW) · KYYIV (KIEV) · BUDAPEST · BUCUREŞTI (BUCHAREST) · CHIŞINĂU · BEOGRAD (BELGRADE) · SARAJEVO · SOFIYA (SOFIA) · SKOPJE · TIRANË (TIRANA) · ATHINA (ATHENS) · ANKARA · ISTANBUL · NICOSIA · DIMASHQ (DAMASCUS) · BEYROUTH (BEIRUT) · AMMAN · JERUSALEM · CAIRO (AL QAHIRAH)

Black Sea · Sea of Azov · Aegean Sea · Mediterranean Sea · Ionian Sea · Red Sea · Kríti (Crete)

Elevation scale: 19,686ft · 13,124ft · 9843ft · 6562ft · 3281ft · 1640ft · 820ft · 328ft · Sea Level · -820ft · -6562ft · -13,124ft

Barcelona

Cerdanyola des Vallès
Ripollet
Montcada i Reixac
Santa Coloma de Gramenet
Horta
Sant Andreu
Badalona
Parc de Collserola
Guinardó
Sant Adrià Besàs
Ria Besòs
Parc Güell
Vallvidrera
Sagrada Familia
Sant Martí
Sant Gervasi
Gràcia
La Pedrera
Parc Zoologic
Sarrià
Barri Gòtic
L'Eixample
Catedral
Barcelona
Macba
Les Corts
Camp Nou
Museu Marítim
L'Aqàrium Barcelona
Esplugues de Llobregat
Sants
World Trade Centre
Cornellá de Llobregat
L'Hospitalet de Llobregat
Estadi Olimpic
Castell de Montjuïc
Montjuïc
Mediterranean Sea
El Prat de Llobregat
Zona Franca

0   2 Km
0   2 Miles

Berlin

Niederschönhausen
Malchow
Pankow
Heinersdorf
Wartenberg
Reinickendorf
Weissensee
Flughafen Berlin-Tegel
Wedding
Hohen-schönhausen
Siemensstadt
Prenzlauerberg
Prenzlauerberg
Moabit
Mitte
Schloss Charlottenburg
Tiergarten
Reichstag
Berlin
Lichtenberg
Spree
Brandenburger Tor
Charlottenburg
Tiergarten
Friedrichshain
Zoologischer Garden
Checkpoint Charlie
Friedrichsfelde
Halensee
Kreuzberg
Landwehrkanal
Spree
Wilmersdorf
Treptow
Schöneberg
Flughafen Tempelhof (disused)
Schmargendorf
Friedenau
Neukölln
Dahlem
Baumschulenweg
Tempelhof
Steglitz
Britz
Teltowkanal
Zehlendorf
Lichterfelde
Mariendorf
Lankwitz

0   2 Km
0   2 Miles

Belgrade

Borca
Bara "Veliko blato"
Kortež
Dunav (Danube)
Krnjaâa
Dunav (Danube)
Kozara
Zemun
Nebojsa Kula
Ada Huja
Belgrade (Beograd)
Veliko Ratno Ostrovo
Zoo
Karaburma
Kalemegdan
Stari Grad
Muzej Savremene Umetnosti
Palilula
Novi Beograd
Bežanija
Vraâar
Mirijevo
Sava
Senjak
Konjarnik
Ada Ciganlija
Âukarica
Voždovac
Brace Jerkovic
Savsko ezero
Banjica
Žarkovo
Kaluderica
Kanarevo Brdo
Kumodraž

0   2 Km
0   2 Miles

Bucharest

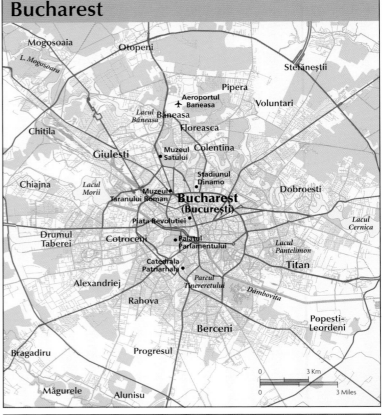

Mogosoaia
Otopeni
L. Mogosoara
Stefăneştii
Pipera
Aeroportul Baneasa
Voluntari
Chitila
Lacul Băneasa
Băneasa
Floreasca
Giulesti
Muzeul Satului
Colentina
Chiajna
Lacul Morii
Stadiunul Dinamo
Muzeul Taranului Roman
Bucharest (Bucureşti)
Dobroesti
Lacul Cernica
Piata Revolutiei
Drumul Taberei
Cotroceni
Palatul Parlamentului
Lucul Pantelimon
Catedrala Patriarhala
Titan
Alexandriej
Parcul Tinerertului
Dâmbovita
Rahova
Popesti-Leordeni
Berceni
Bragadiru
Progresul
Măgurele
Alunisu

0   3 Km
0   3 Miles

Budapest

Újpest
Pesthidegkút
Óbuda
Óbudai-sziget
Újpalota
Csömör
Angyalföld
Pestújhely
Rákos-szentmihály
Hüvösvölgy
Margit-sziget
Zugló
Sashalom
János-hegy 527m
Zugliget
Buda
Budapest
Mátyásföld
Budavári Palota
Dohány Zsinagógo
Pest
Rákos-patak
Magyar Nemzeti Galéria
Magyar Nemzeti Múzeum
Köbánya
Gazdagrét
Ferencváros
Rákos-keresztúr
Sasad
Kelenföld
Budaörs
Budapest Ferihegy Intl. Airport
Albert-falva
Kispest
Budafok
Csepel
Pesterzsébet
Pestlörinc
Duna (Danube)
Soroksári Duna
Csepelsziget
Soroksár

0   3 Km
0   3 Miles

Copenhagen

Vangede
Charlottenlund Slotspark
Gentofte
Charlottenlund
Øresund
Gladsakse
Hellerup
Herlev
Søborg
Gyngemosen
Østerbro
Utterslev Mose
Brønshøj
Copenhagen (København)
Islev
Nørrebro
Kastellet
Vanløse
Rosenborg Slot
Amalienborg
Rødovre
Frederiksberg
Charlottenborg
Christianshavn
Damhussøen
Tivoli
Frederiksberg Slot
Brøndbyøster
Valby
Sundbyerne
Sydhavnen
Amagerbro
Amager Fælled
Kastrup

0 2 Km
0 2 Miles

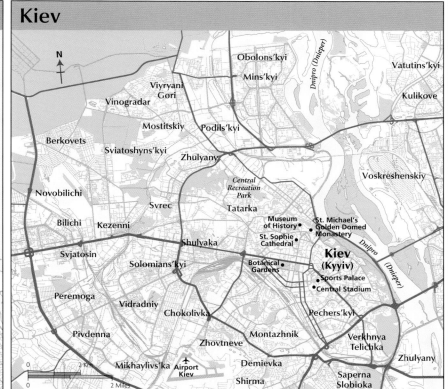

Kiev

N

Obolons'kyi
Dnipro (Dnieper)
Vatutins'kyi
Viyryani Gori
Mins'kyi
Kulikove
Vinogradar
Berkovets
Mostitskiy
Podils'kyi
Voskreshenskiy
Sviatoshyns'kyi
Zhulyany
Novobilichi
Svrec
Central Recreation Park
Bilichi
Kezenni
Tatarka
Museum of History
St. Michael's Golden Domed Monastery
Shulyaka
St. Sophie Cathedral
Dnipro (Dnieper)
Svjatosin
Kiev (Kyyiv)
Solomians'kyi
Botanical Gardens
Sports Palace
Peremoga
Vidradniy
Chokolivka
Central Stadium
Pechers'kyi
Pivdenna
Montazhnik
Verkhnya Telichka
Zhovtneve
Mikhaylivs'ka
Airport Kiev
Demievka
Zhulyany
Shirma
Saperna Slobioka

0 2 Km
0 2 Miles

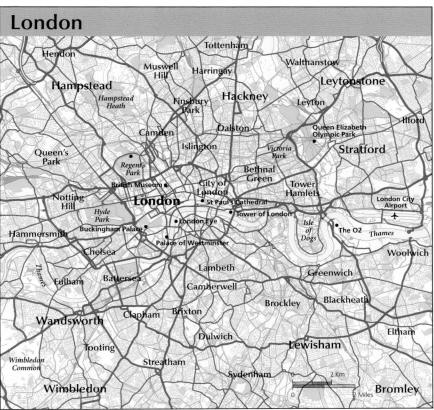

London

Hendon
Tottenham
Muswell Hill
Harringay
Walthanstow
Hampstead
Leytonstone
Hampstead Heath
Finsbury Park
Hackney
Leyton
Queen's Park
Camden
Dalston
Ilford
Regent's Park
Islington
Victoria Park
Stratford
Queen Elizabeth Olympic Park
Notting Hill
British Museum
City of London
Bethnal Green
Tower Hamlets
London
Hyde Park
St Paul's Cathedral
London Eye
Tower of London
London City Airport
Hammersmith
Buckingham Palace
Palace of Westminster
Isle of Dogs
The O2
Thames
Chelsea
Woolwich
Thames
Fulham
Battersea
Lambeth
Greenwich
Wandsworth
Camberwell
Blackheath
Clapham
Brixton
Brockley
Eltham
Tooting
Dulwich
Lewisham
Wimbledon Common
Streatham
Sydenham
Wimbledon
Bromley

0 2 Km
0 2 Miles

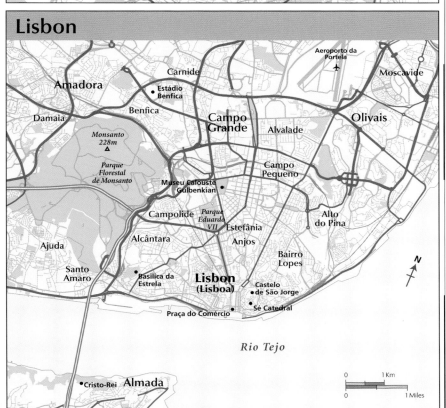

Lisbon

Aeroporto da Portela
Carnide
Amadora
Moscavide
Estádio Benfica
Damaia
Benfica
Campo Grande
Olivais
Monsanto 228m
Alvalade
Parque Florestal de Monsanto
Museu Calouste Gulbenkian
Campo Pequeno
Campolide
Parque Eduardo VII
Alto do Pina
Alcântara
Estefânia
N
Ajuda
Anjos
Bairro Lopes
Santo Amaro
Basílica da Estrela
Lisbon (Lisboa)
Castelo de São Jorge
Praça do Comércio
Sé Catedral

Rio Tejo

Cristo-Rei
Almada

0 1 Km
0 1 Miles

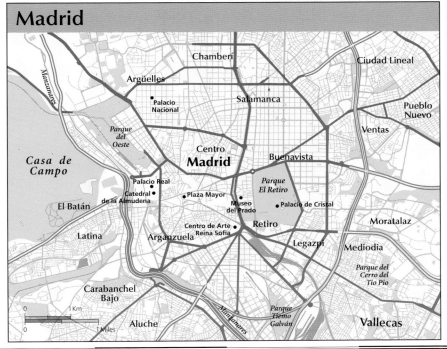

Madrid

Chamberí
Ciudad Lineal
Argüelles
Manzanares
Salamanca
Palacio Nacional
Pueblo Nuevo
Parque del Oeste
Ventas
Centro
Buenavista
Madrid
Casa de Campo
Palacio Real
Parque El Retiro
Catedral de la Almudena
Plaza Mayor
Palacio de Cristal
El Batán
Museo del Prado
Retiro
Moratalaz
Centro de Arte Reina Sofía
Latina
Arganzuela
Legazpi
Mediodía
Parque del Cerro del Tío Pío
Carabanchel Bajo
Manzanares
Parque Tierno Galván
Vallecas
Aluche

0 1 Km
0 1 Miles

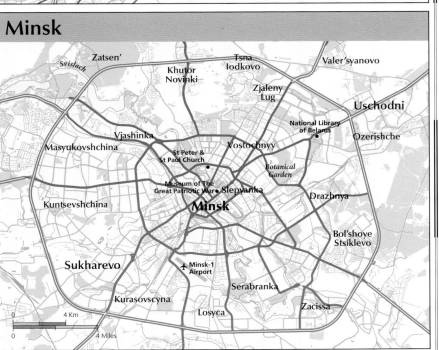

Minsk

Zatsen'
Tsna Iodkovo
Valer'syanovo
Svislach
Khutor Novinki
Zjaleny Lug
Uschodni
Vjashinka
National Library of Belarus
Masyukovshchina
Vostochnyy
Ozerishche
St Peter & St Paul Church
Botanical Garden
Museum of The Great Patriotic War
Slepyanka
Drazbnya
Kuntsevshchina
Minsk
Sukharevo
Bol'shoye Stsiklevo
Minsk-1 Airport
Serabranka
Kurasovscyna
Zacissa
Losyca

0 4 Km
0 4 Miles

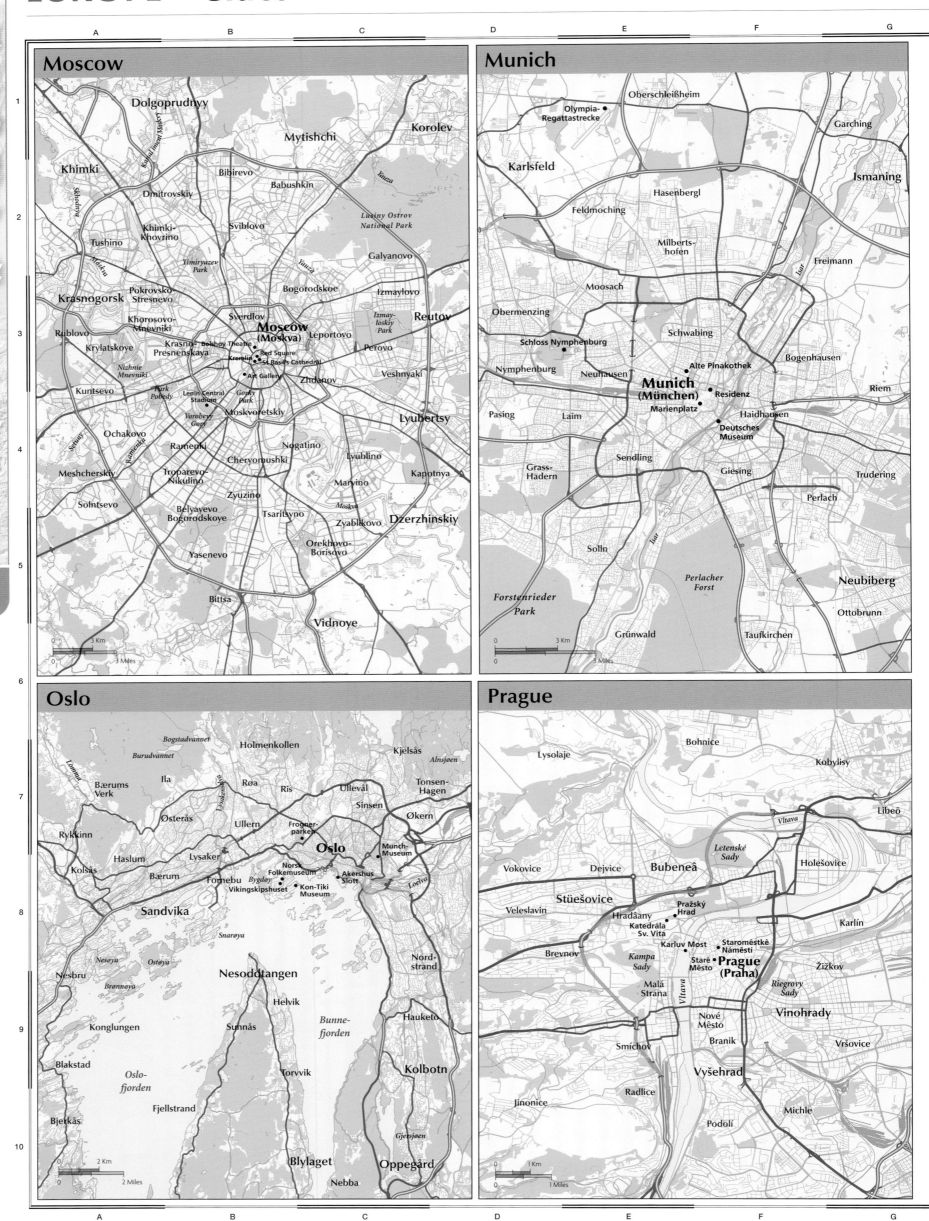

Rome

Tor di Quinto
Aeroporto di Roma - Urbe
Tufello
Torrevécchia
Stadio Olímpico
Flaminio
Villa Ada Savoia
Trieste
Monte Sacro
Primavalle
Trionfale
Parioli
Pietralata
Parco Regionale Urbano Pineto
Nomentano
Villa Borghese
Montespaccato
CITTÀ DEL VATICANO
Cappella Sistina
Rome (Roma)
Basilica di San Pietro
Castel Sant'Angelo
Piazza San Pietro
Fontana di Trevi
Aurelio
Pantheon
Palazzo di Quirinale
Tiburtino
Foro Romano
Valcamuta
Villa Doria Pamphili
Trastevere
Colosseo
Tor Pignattara
Fiumi Tevere
Tuscolano
Monteverde Nuovo
Cinecittà
Parco della Caffaerella
Corviale
Garbatella
Catacombe di Domitilla
Ostiense
Magliana

St Petersburg

Olgino
Ozero Lakhtinskiy Razliv
Grazhdanka
Vdelnoe
Rzhevka
0   3 Km
0   3 Miles
Ostrova Krestovskiye
Stoyka
Polyustrovo
Petrogradskaya Storona
Cruiser Aurora
Zhernovka
Finskiy Zaliv
Vasilyevskiy Ostrov
Hermitage and Winter Palace
Neva
Smolnyy Cathedral
Bolshaya-Okhta
Kirov Palace of Culture
Admiralty
Alexander Nevsky Abbey
Malaya-Okhta
St Isaac's Cathedral
St Petersburg (Sankt-Peterburg)
Ostrov Gutuyevskiy
Volynkina Derevnya
Volodanskoye
Vesolyy Posolok
Obukhovo
Utkina Zavod
Aytovo
Aleksandrovskoye
Neva
Ulyanka
Kupchino
Srednaya Rogatka
Ligovo
Novoaleksandrovskoye

Sofia

Vrybnitsa
Benkouski
0   2 Km
0   2 Miles
Nadezhda
Serdika
Iskŭr River
Lyulin
Vasil Levski
Vrazdebna
Ilinden
Sofia
Poduyane
Krasna Polyana
National Art Gallery
Cathedral
Sofia Airport
Sofia Art Gallery
Ovcha Kupel
National Stadium
National Palace of Culture
Borisova Gradina
Slatina
Krasno Selo
Lozenets
Izgrev
Iskyr
Knyazhevo
Triaditsa
Drouzhba Li
Bakston
Studentski
Vitosha National Park
Vitosha
Mladost

Stockholm

Kista
Inverness
Sundbyberg
Friends Arena
Solna
Lidingö
Stockholm-Bromma Airport
Lidingö
Bromma
Stockholm
Lilla Värten
Kärsön
Stadshuset
Vasamuseet
Ektorp
Mälaren
Kungliga Slottet
Skansen
Saltsjön
Älsten
Södermalm
Nacka
Hägersten
Enskede
Bagarmossen
Skärholmen
0   2 Km
0   2 Miles
Farsta

Warsaw

Marcelin
Ząbki
Tarchomin
Zacisze
Rembertów
Mlociny
Bródno
Wisla
Park Skaryszewski
Wawrzyszew
Praga
Grochów
Warsaw Babice Airport
Zoliborz
Zoo
Warsaw (Warszawa)
Górce
St John's Cathedral
Stadium
Saska Kępa
Goclaw
Royal Castle
Chopin Museum
Palace of Culture and Science
Wola
Park Lazienkowski
Wisla
Mokotów
Sadyba
Ochota
Raków
Augustówka
Wierzbno
Opacz
Okęcie
Sluzew
Wilanów
0   2 Km
0   2 Miles
Warsaw Frederic Chopin Airport

Zagreb

0   2 Km
0   2 Miles
Granešina
Maksimir
Sesvete
Črnomerec
Croatian History Museum
Cathedral
Croatian National Theatre
Zagreb
Tresnjevka
Sava
Jarun
Lake Jarun
Novi Zagreb
Botinec
Zagreb Airport

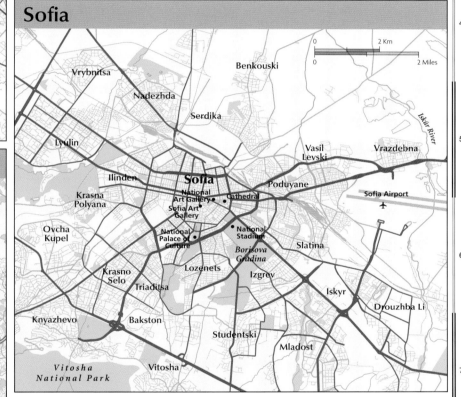
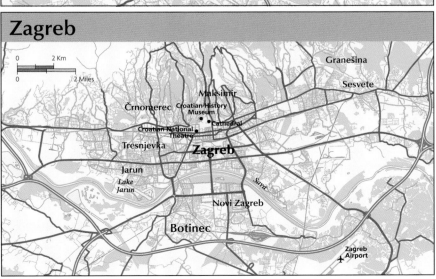

Asia is the world's largest continent with a total area of 16,838,365 sq miles (43,608,000 sq km). It comprises 49 separate countries, including 97% of Turkey and 72% of the Russian Federation. Almost 60% of the world's population lives in Asia.

FACTFILE

N **Most Northerly Point:** Mys Articheskiy, Russia 81° 12' N
S **Most Southerly Point:** Pulau Pamana, Indonesia 11° S
E **Most Easterly Point:** Mys Dezhneva, Russia 169° 40' W
W **Most Westerly Point:** Bozcaada, Turkey 26° 2' E

Largest Lakes:
1. Caspian Sea, Asia/Europe 143,243 sq miles (371,000 sq km)
2. Lake Baikal, Russian Federation 11,776 sq miles (30,500 sq km)
3. Lake Balkhash, Kazakhstan/China 7115 sq miles (18,428 sq km)
4. Aral Sea, Kazakhstan/Uzbekistan 6625 sq miles (17,160 sq km)
5. Tonlé Sap, Cambodia 3861 sq miles (10,000 sq km)

Longest Rivers:
1. Yangtze, China 3915 miles (6299 km)
2. Yellow River, China 3395 miles (5464 km)
3. Mekong, SE Asia 2749 miles (4425 km)
4. Lena, Russian Federation 2734 miles (4400 km)
5. Yenisey, Russian Federation 2541 miles (4090 km)

Largest Islands:
1. Borneo, Brunei/Indonesia/Malaysia 292,222 sq miles (757,050 sq km)
2. Sumatra, Indonesia 202,300 sq miles (524,000 sq km)
3. Honshu, Japan 88,800 sq miles (230,000 sq km)
4. Sulawesi, Indonesia 73,057 sq miles (189,218 sq km)
5. Java, Indonesia 53,589 sq miles (138,794 sq km)

Highest Points:
1. Mount Everest, China/Nepal 29,029 ft (8848 m)
2. K2, China/Pakistan 28,253 ft (8611 m)
3. Kangchenjunga I, India/Nepal 28,210 ft (8598 m)
4. Lhotse, Nepal 27,939 ft (8516 m)
5. Makalu, China/Nepal 27,767 ft (8463 m)

Lowest Point:
▼ Dead Sea, Israel/Jordan -1401 ft (-427 m) below sea level

Highest recorded temperature:
⊕ Tirat Zevi, Israel 129°F (54°C)

Lowest recorded temperature:
⊖ Verkhoyansk, Russian Federation -90°F (-68°C)

Wettest Place:
≋ Cherrapunji, India 450 in (11,430 mm)

Driest Place:
⊖ Aden, Yemen 1.8 in (46 mm)

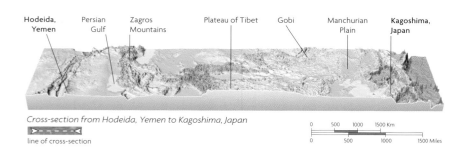

Cross-section from Hodeida, Yemen to Kagoshima, Japan

line of cross-section

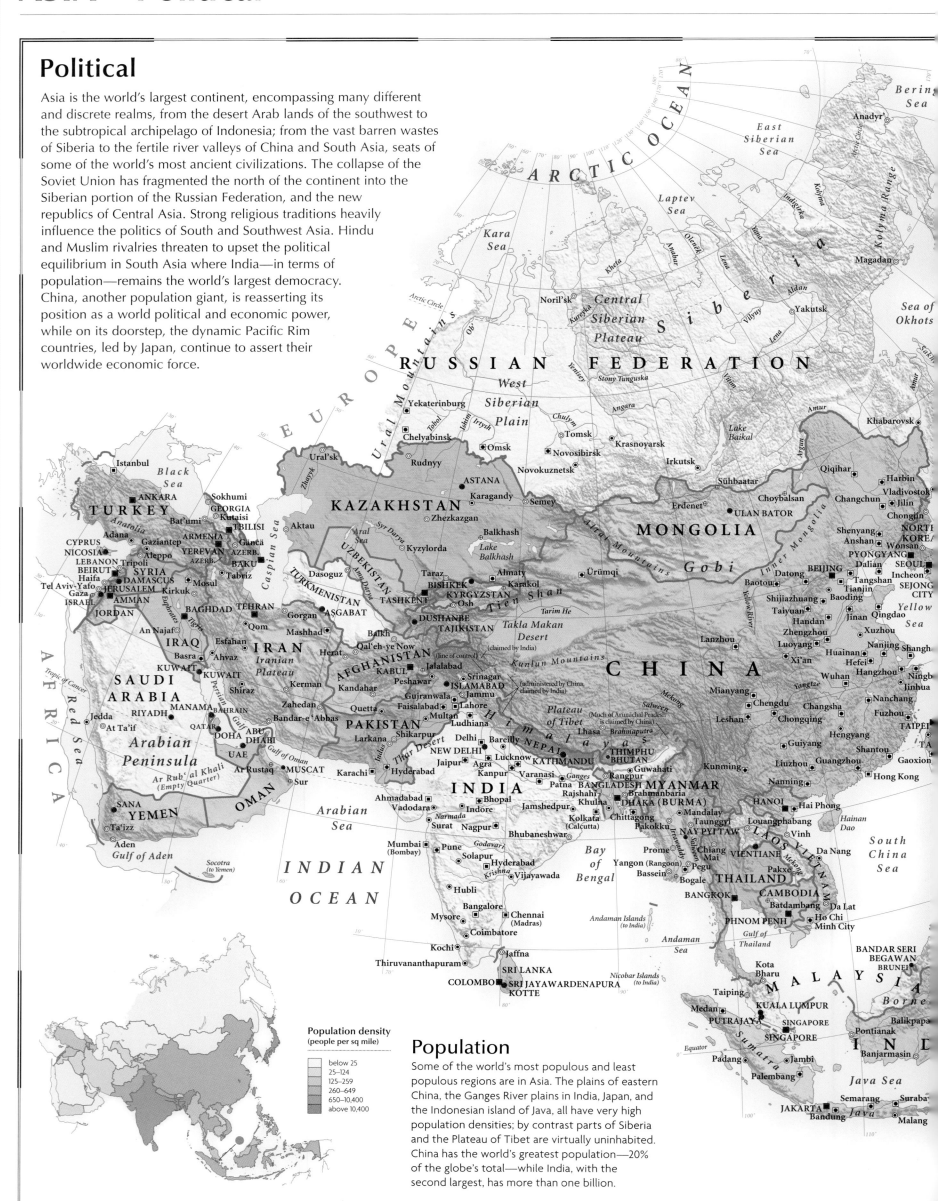

Political

Asia is the world's largest continent, encompassing many different and discrete realms, from the desert Arab lands of the southwest to the subtropical archipelago of Indonesia; from the vast barren wastes of Siberia to the fertile river valleys of China and South Asia, seats of some of the world's most ancient civilizations. The collapse of the Soviet Union has fragmented the north of the continent into the Siberian portion of the Russian Federation, and the new republics of Central Asia. Strong religious traditions heavily influence the politics of South and Southwest Asia. Hindu and Muslim rivalries threaten to upset the political equilibrium in South Asia where India—in terms of population—remains the world's largest democracy. China, another population giant, is reasserting its position as a world political and economic power, while on its doorstep, the dynamic Pacific Rim countries, led by Japan, continue to assert their worldwide economic force.

Population density
(people per sq mile)

- below 25
- 25–124
- 125–259
- 260–649
- 650–10,400
- above 10,400

Population

Some of the world's most populous and least populous regions are in Asia. The plains of eastern China, the Ganges River plains in India, Japan, and the Indonesian island of Java, all have very high population densities; by contrast parts of Siberia and the Plateau of Tibet are virtually uninhabited. China has the world's greatest population—20% of the globe's total—while India, with the second largest, has more than one billion.

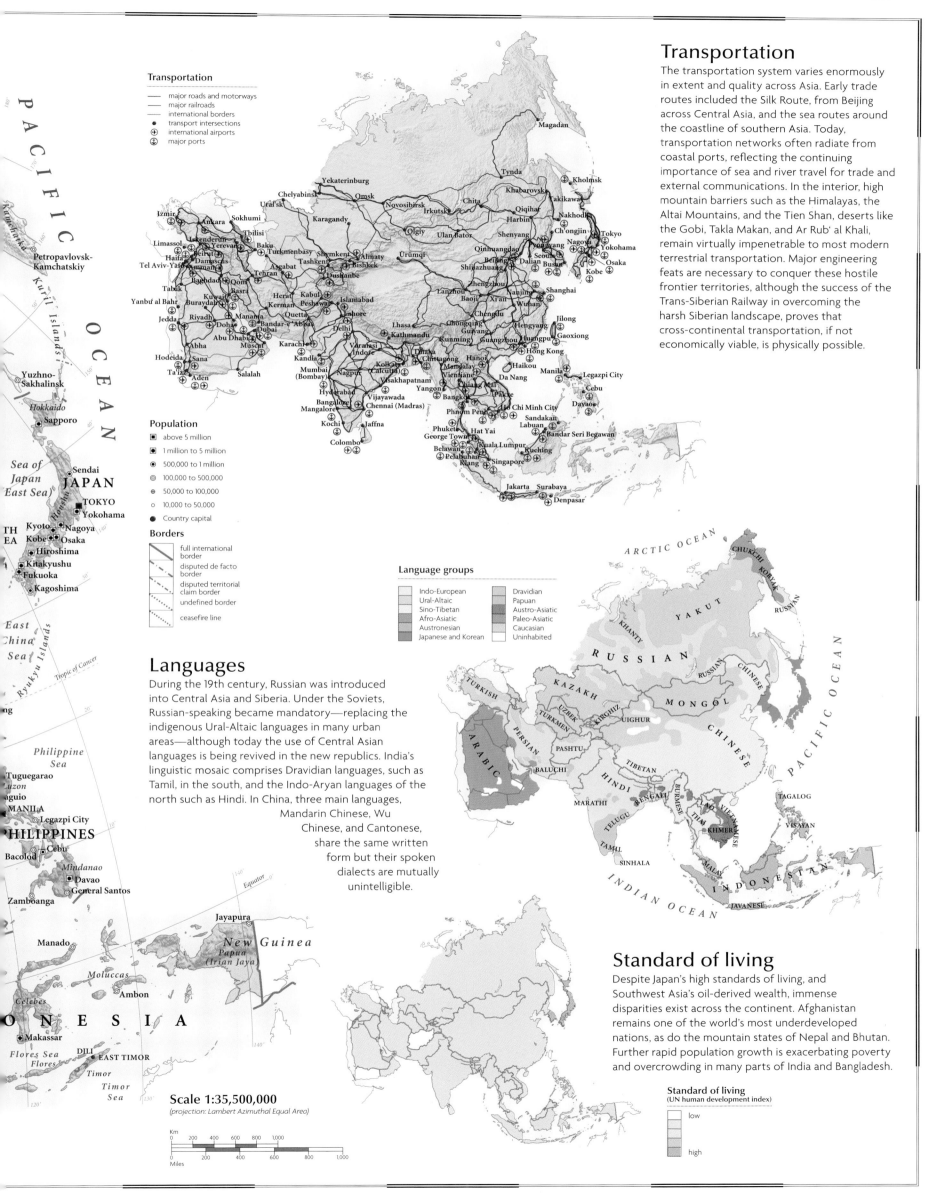

Transportation

The transportation system varies enormously in extent and quality across Asia. Early trade routes included the Silk Route, from Beijing across Central Asia, and the sea routes around the coastline of southern Asia. Today, transportation networks often radiate from coastal ports, reflecting the continuing importance of sea and river travel for trade and external communications. In the interior, high mountain barriers such as the Himalayas, the Altai Mountains, and the Tien Shan, deserts like the Gobi, Takla Makan, and Ar Rub' al Khali, remain virtually impenetrable to most modern terrestrial transportation. Major engineering feats are necessary to conquer these hostile frontier territories, although the success of the Trans-Siberian Railway in overcoming the harsh Siberian landscape, proves that cross-continental transportation, if not economically viable, is physically possible.

Transportation
- major roads and motorways
- major railroads
- international borders
- transport intersections
- international airports
- major ports

Population
- above 5 million
- 1 million to 5 million
- 500,000 to 1 million
- 100,000 to 500,000
- 50,000 to 100,000
- 10,000 to 50,000
- Country capital

Borders
- full international border
- disputed de facto border
- disputed territorial claim border
- undefined border
- ceasefire line

Language groups
- Indo-European
- Ural-Altaic
- Sino-Tibetan
- Afro-Asiatic
- Austronesian
- Japanese and Korean
- Dravidian
- Papuan
- Austro-Asiatic
- Paleo-Asiatic
- Caucasian
- Uninhabited

Languages

During the 19th century, Russian was introduced into Central Asia and Siberia. Under the Soviets, Russian-speaking became mandatory—replacing the indigenous Ural-Altaic languages in many urban areas—although today the use of Central Asian languages is being revived in the new republics. India's linguistic mosaic comprises Dravidian languages, such as Tamil, in the south, and the Indo-Aryan languages of the north such as Hindi. In China, three main languages, Mandarin Chinese, Wu Chinese, and Cantonese, share the same written form but their spoken dialects are mutually unintelligible.

Scale 1:35,500,000
(projection: Lambert Azimuthal Equal Area)

Km
0   200   400   600   800   1,000

Miles
0   200   400   600   800   1,000

Standard of living

Despite Japan's high standards of living, and Southwest Asia's oil-derived wealth, immense disparities exist across the continent. Afghanistan remains one of the world's most underdeveloped nations, as do the mountain states of Nepal and Bhutan. Further rapid population growth is exacerbating poverty and overcrowding in many parts of India and Bangladesh.

Standard of living
(UN human development index)
- low
- high

ASIA – Physical

ARCTIC OCEAN

NORTH AMERICA

PACIFIC OCEAN

INDIAN OCEAN

EUROPE

AFRICA

S i b e r i a

A S I A

Central Siberian Plateau

West Siberian Plain

North Siberian Lowland

Plateau of Tibet

Himalaya

Gobi Desert

Plateau of Mongolia

Kara Sea

Barents Sea

Laptev Sea

East Siberian Sea

Chukchi Sea

Bering Sea

Sea of Okhotsk

Sea of Japan (East Sea)

Yellow Sea

East China Sea

South China Sea

Philippine Sea

Bay of Bengal

Arabian Sea

Caspian Sea

Aral Sea

Lake Baikal

Lake Balkhash

Ural Mountains

Altai Mountains

Tien Shan

Kunlun Mountains

Hindu Kush

Zagros Mountains

Iranian Plateau

Arabian Peninsula

Red Sea

Persian Gulf

Gulf of Oman

NORTH AMERICAN PLATE

EURASIAN PLATE

INDO-AUSTRALIAN PLATE

Scale 1:47,500,000

(projection: Gall Stereographic)

0   500   1000   1500 Km

0   500   1000   1500 Miles

Climate

The climate of Asia exhibits marked differences from region to region, with freezing polar conditions in the north, hot and cold deserts in central regions and subtropical conditions throughout the south. Much of this variation can be attributed to enormous mountain barriers and internal depressions found across the continent. Monsoon winds, which reverse semi-annually, cause alternate wet and dry seasons across southern Asia. These air masses moving north from the ocean are stripped of their moisture over the Himalayas causing arid conditions across the Plateau of Tibet. Both the south and east are susceptible to tropical cyclones or typhoons.

Average Rainfall

January rainfall

July rainfall

Rainfall

- 0–1 in (0–25 mm)
- 1–2 in (25–50 mm)
- 2–4 in (50–100 mm)
- 4–8 in (100–200 mm)
- 8–12 in (200–300 mm)
- 12–16 in (300–400 mm)
- 16–20 in (400–500 mm)
- more than 20 in (500 mm)

Average Temperature

January temperature

July temperature

Temperature

- below -22°F (-30°C)
- -22 to -4°F (-30 to -20°C)
- -4 to 14°F (-20 to -10°C)
- 14 to 32°F (-10 to 0°C)
- 32 to 50°F (0 to 10°C)
- 50 to 68°F (10 to 20°C)
- 68 to 86°F (20 to 30°C)
- above 86°F (30°C)

Climate

- tundra
- subarctic
- cool continental
- warm humid
- mediterranean
- semi-arid
- arid
- humid equatorial
- tropical

- ☼ daily hours of sunshine, January
- ☼ daily hours of sunshine, July
- → cyclone
- → typhoon
- → cold/dry monsoon
- → warm/wet monsoon
- → cold wind

Environmental issues

The transformation of Uzbekistan by the former Soviet Union into the world's fifth largest producer of cotton led to the diversion of several major rivers for irrigation. Starved of this water, the Aral Sea diminished in volume by over 75% since 1960, irreversibly altering the ecology of the area. Heavy industries in eastern China have polluted coastal waters, rivers and urban air, while in Myanmar (Burma), Malaysia and Indonesia, ancient hardwood rainforests are felled faster than they can regenerate.

Environmental issues

- tropical forest
- forest destroyed
- desert
- desertification
- acid rain
- polluted rivers
- marine pollution
- heavy marine pollution
- ☢ radioactive contamination
- ● poor urban air quality

Using the land and sea

- cropland
- desert
- forest
- mountain region
- pasture
- tundra
- wetland
- ● major conurbations
- cattle
- pigs
- goats
- sheep
- coconuts
- corn (maize)
- cotton
- dates
- fishing

- fruit
- jute
- peanuts
- rice
- rubber
- shellfish
- soya beans
- sugar beet
- sugar cane
- tea
- timber
- wheat

Land use

Vast areas of Asia remain uncultivated as a result of unsuitable climatic and soil conditions. In favourable areas such as river deltas, farming is intensive. Rice is the staple crop of most Asian countries, grown in paddy fields on waterlogged alluvial plains and terraced hillsides, and often irrigated for higher yields. Across the black earth region of the Eurasian steppe in southern Siberia and Kazakhstan, wheat farming is the dominant activity. Cash crops, like tea in Sri Lanka and dates in the Arabian Peninsula, are grown for export, and provide valuable income. The sovereignty of the rich fishing grounds in the South China Sea is disputed by China, Malaysia, Taiwan, the Philippines and Vietnam, because of potential oil reserves.

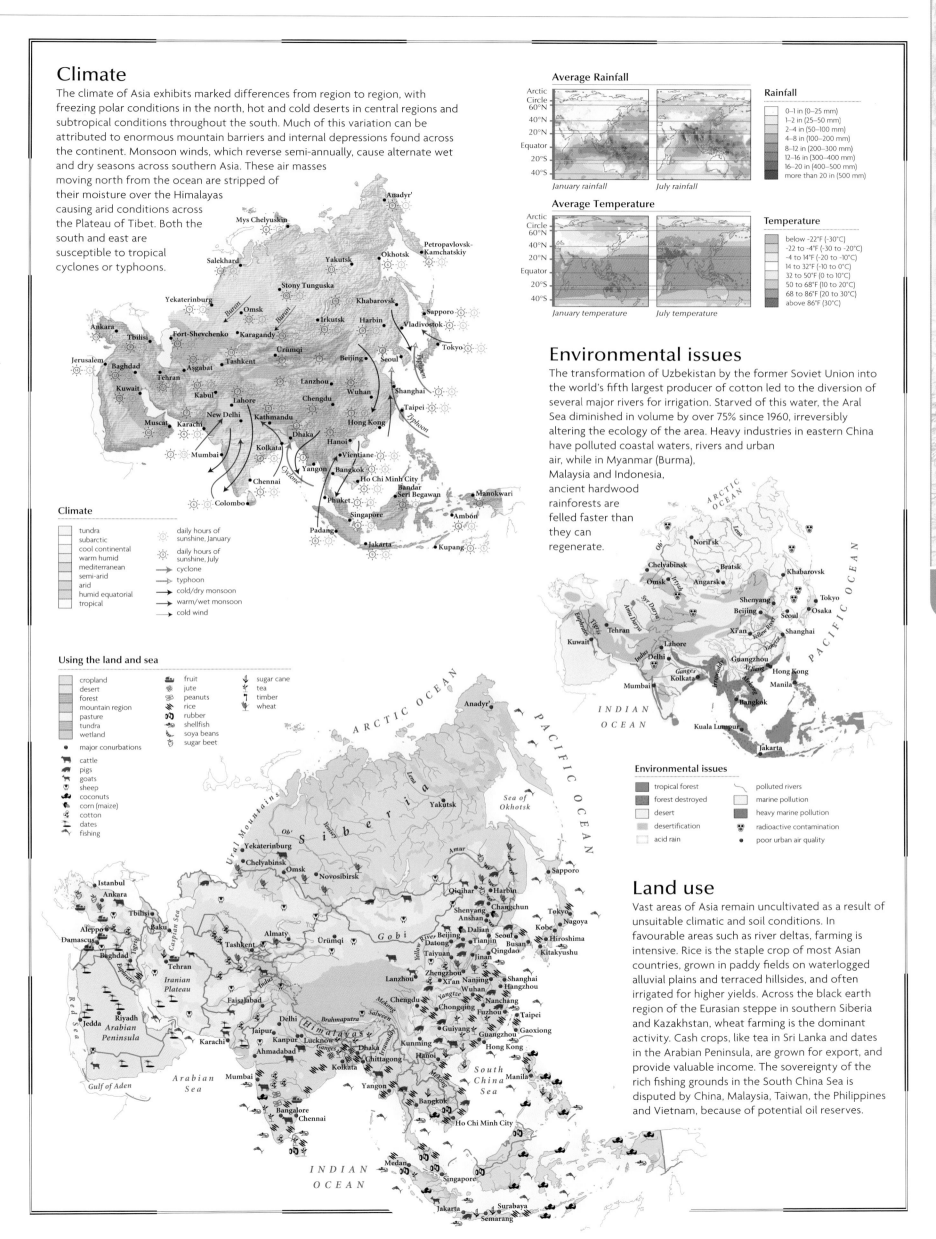

ASIA

1 BOSPORUS, TURKEY
The Bosporus provides the only outlet for the Black Sea, linking it with the Sea of Marmara to the south and then with the Mediterranean Sea via the Dardanelles.

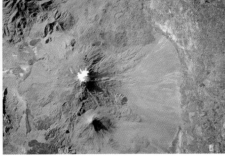

2 MOUNT ARARAT, TURKEY
Said to be the resting place for Noah's Ark, this extinct volcanic massif lies in the far east of Turkey.

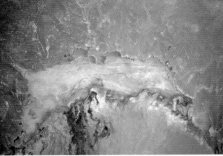

3 LAKE BALKASH, KAZAKHSTAN
Still covered in winter ice in this image, this lakes lies in a dry desert region and has no outlet.

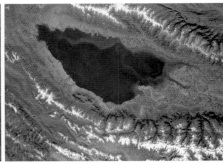

4 OZERO ISSYK-KUL', KYRGYZSTAN
Against the dry slopes of the Tien Shan mountains to the south this lake appears bright blue.

9 KUWAIT'S OILFIELDS, KUWAIT
The dark plumes are smoke rising from the 700 wells set alight by Iraqi forces during the Gulf War of 1991.

10 PALM ISLAND, UNITED ARAB EMIRATES
This luxury housing development and tourist resort, one mile (1.6 km) off the seafront of Dubai, is built from sediments dredged from the nearby port of Jebel Ali.

11 MALDIVES
The Maldives consist of 1300 coral formations in 19 atolls and stretch over 1491 miles (2400 km).

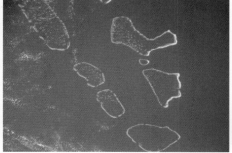

12 KARACHI, PAKISTAN
Pakistan's main seaport and former capital lies to the northwest of the delta of the Indus river.

THREE GORGES DAM, CHINA
Seen here during its construction in 2000, the world's largest dam is designed to tame the Yangtze river which has regularly flooded.

BEIJING, CHINA
China's ancient capital was laid out on a grid pattern centred on the Forbidden City and its streets are picked out in this winter image by snowfall.

MOUNT FUJI, JAPAN
The steep, symmetrical, snow-capped volcano last erupted in 1707.

VULKAN KLYUCHEVSKAYA SOPKA, RUSSIAN FEDERATION
The Kamchatka Peninsula's highest and most active volcano last erupted in 1994.

MOUNT EVEREST, CHINA/NEPAL
The world's highest mountain at 29,029 ft (8848 m) straddles the border between China and Nepal.

MOUTHS OF THE GANGES, BANGLADESH/INDIA
Stretching across the northern end of the Bay of Bengal, this river delta contains the Sundarbans, the world's largest mangrove forest, which appears as a rich green area.

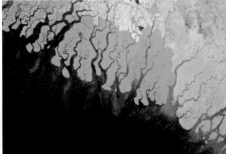

MEKONG DELTA, VIETNAM
The Mekong river flows over 2494 miles (4000 km) from the Plateau of Tibet before crossing Vietnam to reach the South China Sea.

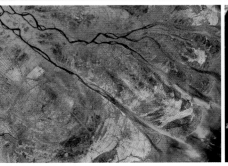

HONG KONG, CHINA
This image was taken around the time that Hong Kong was handed back to China by the British in 1997, this city remains east Asia's trade and finance center.

Southwest Asia

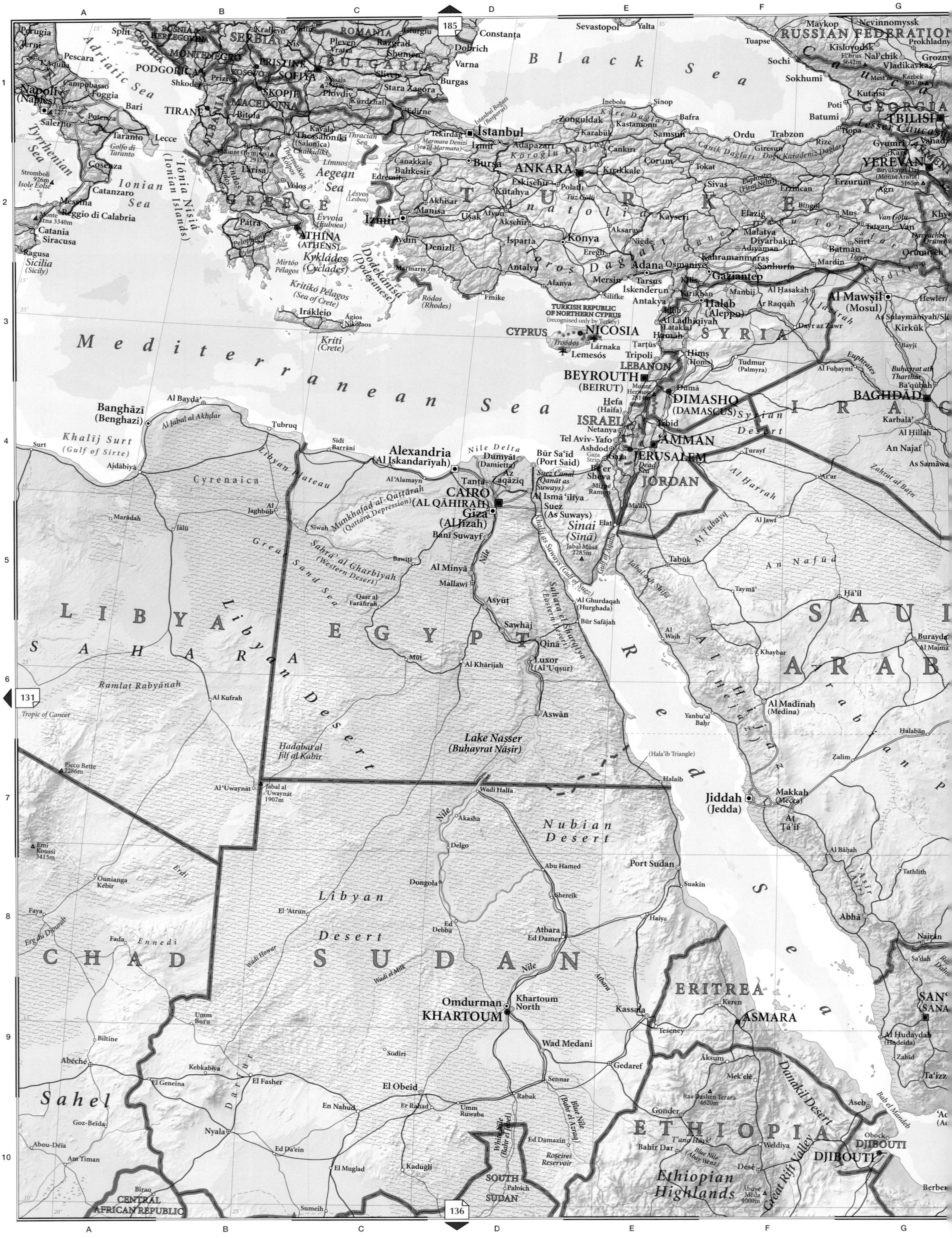

A B C D E F G
1 2 3 4 5 6 7 8 9 10
185
131
136
Black Sea
Mediterranean Sea
Adriatic Sea
Tyrrhenian Sea
Ionian Sea
Aegean Sea
Red Sea
TURKEY
GREECE
SYRIA
LEBANON
ISRAEL
JORDAN
IRAQ
CYPRUS
EGYPT
LIBYA
SUDAN
CHAD
ERITREA
ETHIOPIA
DJIBOUTI
SAUDI ARABIA
GEORGIA
RUSSIAN FEDERATION
SERBIA
BULGARIA
ROMANIA
MONTENEGRO
KOSOVO
MACEDONIA
ALBANIA
BOSNIA & HERZEGOVINA
CROATIA
SOUTH SUDAN
CENTRAL AFRICAN REPUBLIC
TURKISH REPUBLIC OF NORTHERN CYPRUS (recognised only by Turkey)
Anatolia
Sahara
Libyan Desert
Nubian Desert
Sahel
Ethiopian Highlands
Danakil Desert
Great Rift Valley
Syrian Desert
An Nafūd
Sinai (Sīnā)
Cyrenaica
Libyan Plateau
Great Sand Sea
Ramlat Rabyānah
Lake Nasser (Buḩayrat Nāşir)
Nile
Nile Delta
Suez Canal
Gulf of Suez
Gulf of Aqaba
Khalīj Surt (Gulf of Sirte)
Tropic of Cancer
Istanbul
Ankara
İzmir
Bursa
Konya
Adana
Gaziantep
Kayseri
Samsun
Trabzon
Erzurum
Sivas
Antalya
Mersin
Athina (Athens)
Thessaloniki (Salonica)
Pátra
Sofiya
Podgorica
Tiranë
Skopje
Prishtinë
Napoli (Naples)
Bari
Taranto
Messina
Catania
Reggio di Calabria
Varna
Burgas
Constanța
Sevastopol
Yalta
Sochi
Sokhumi
Batumi
Tbilisi
Yerevan
Nicosia
Lemesós
Lárnaka
Halab (Aleppo)
Ḩimş (Homs)
Ḩamāh
Al Lādhiqīyah (Latakia)
Ţarţūs
Tripoli
Beyrouth (Beirut)
Dimashq (Damascus)
Tudmur (Palmyra)
Al Mawşil (Mosul)
Kirkūk
Baghdād
Karbalā'
Al Ḩillah
An Najaf
Hefa (Haifa)
Tel Aviv-Yafo
Jerusalem
'Ammān
Irbid
Gaza
Be'er Sheva
Elat
Ma'ān
Dead Sea
Alexandria (Al Iskandarīyah)
Cairo (Al Qāhirah)
Giza (Al Jīzah)
Būr Sa'īd (Port Said)
Dumyāţ (Damietta)
Suez (As Suways)
Al Minyā
Asyūţ
Sawhāj
Qinā
Luxor (Al 'Uqşur)
Aswān
Al Khārijah
Sīwah
Banghāzī (Benghazi)
Ajdābiyā
Tubruq
Al Bayḑā'
Al Kufrah
Jālū
Marādah
Sirte
Wadi Halfa
Dongola
Atbara
Port Sudan
Suakin
Omdurman
Khartoum
Khartoum North
Kassala
Wad Medani
Gedaref
El Obeid
El Fasher
Nyala
Sennar
Abéché
Asmara
Aksum
Mek'ele
Gonder
Bahir Dar
Dessie
Djibouti
Jiddah (Jedda)
Makkah (Mecca)
Al Madīnah (Medina)
Tabūk
Ḩā'il
Abhā
Aţ Ţā'if
Halaib
(Hala'ib Triangle)
Mount Hermon 2814m
Trodos
Jabal Mūsā 2285m
Emi Koussi 3415m
Picco Bette 2286m
Jabal al 'Uwaynāt 1907m
Ras Dashen Terara 4620m
Stromboli 926m
Monte Etna 3340m
Kykládes (Cyclades)
Dodekánisa (Dodecanese)
Kríti (Crete)
Sicilia (Sicily)
Ródos (Rhodes)
Euphrates
Tigris
Blue Nile (Bahr el Azraq)
White Nile (Bahr el Jebel)

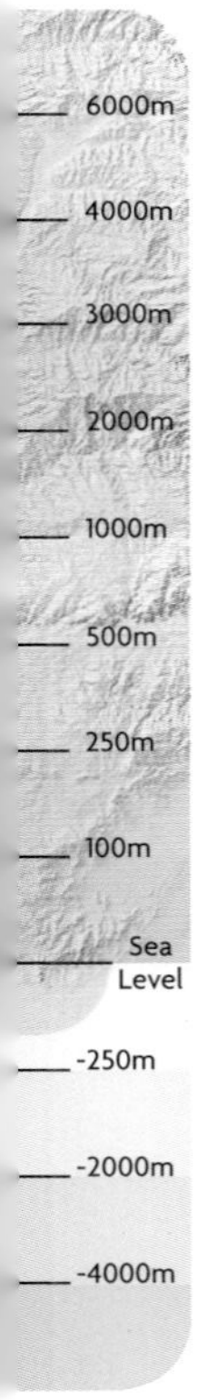

6000m
4000m
3000m
2000m
1000m
500m
250m
100m
Sea Level
-250m
-2000m
-4000m

Scale 1:11,750,000
(projection: Lambert Azimuthal Equal Area)

0 50 100 150 200 250 300 Km
0 50 100 150 200 250 300 Miles

Population
■ above 5 million
◙ 1 million to 5 million
◉ 500,000 to 1 million
◎ 100,000 to 500,000
⊕ 50,000 to 100,000
○ 10,000 to 50,000
○ below 10,000

226

KAZAKHSTAN
Aktau
Makhachkala
Zhanaozen
ynaksk
Derbent
Ustyurt Plateau
UZBEKISTAN
Nukus
Gubadag
Kyzyl Kum
Turkistan
Taraz
BISHKEK
Balykchy
Karakol
KAZAKHSTAN
Shymkent
KYRGYZSTAN
Talas
Kirghiz Range
Naryn
Kokshaal-Tau
Tien Shan
AZERBAIJAN
BAKI (BAKU)
Sumqayit
Sarygamys Köli
Daşoguz
Urganch
Üngüz Angyrsyndaky Garagum
Lebap
Uchquduq
TOSHKENT (TASHKENT)
Chirchiq
Angren
Namangan
Gora Ak-Tash 4718m
Dzhalal-Abad
CHINA
Kashi
Shache
Hacıqabal
Türkmenbaşy
Garabogaz Aylagy
TURKMENISTAN
Balkanabat
Buxoro
Navoiy
Aýdarko'l Ko'li
Guliston
Qo'qon
Andijon
Qsh
Kek-Art
Artux
Maraqheh
Rasht
Qazvin
Zanjan
Bābol
Sāri
Shāhrūd
Mashhad
Sabzevār
Serdar
Merkezi Garagumy
Seydi
Kattaqo'rg'on
Samarqand
Qarshi
Qatortirhi Zarafshon
Ayni
Kommunizm 7495m
Qullai
Qorako'l
DUSHANBE
TAJIKISTAN
Qullai Kommunizm 6974m
Murghob
Qatorkoh
Tabriz
Ardabīl
Lānkāran
Esenguly
Bojnūrd
Koppeh Dagh
Aşgabat
Mary
Yolöten
Atamyrat
Zeidskoye
Vodokhranilishche
Aqchah
Termiz
Konduz
Ishkashim
Denov
Qo'rqonteppa
Kūlōb
Khorugh
Pamir
Claimed by India
Karakoram Range
Gilgit
Indus
Rasht
Qazvin
Amol
Damghan
Semnān
Dasht-e Kavir
Sabzevār
Gonābād
Kushk
Qal'ah-ye Now
Herāt
Māimaneh
Margo
Mazār-e Sharīf
Balkh
Chārikār
KĀBUL (KABUL)
Jalālābād
Khyber Pass
Peshāwar
Srinagar
Barīkowt
Asnār
Saidu
Line of control
TEHRĀN
Qom
Hamadān
Malāyer
Arāk
Borūjerd
Kāshān
Robāt-e Khān
IRAN
Shahrak
AFGHANISTAN
Uruzgān
Skaran
Shīndand
Anār Darah
Baghrān
Dilārām
Qalāt
Arzow
Dera Ismāīl Khān
Mīānwāli
Jhelum
Jammu
Sanandaj
Kermānshāh (Bākhtarān)
Khorramābād
Najafābād
Esfahān
Shahreza
Yazd
Ābādeh
Kermānshāh
Rāvar
Anār
Iranian Plateau
Funāl Rūd
Dasht-e Lūt
Chakhānsūr
Dasht-e Mārgow
Darwēshān
Spin Boldak
Shaman
Kandahār
Gereshk
Gujrāt
Gujrānwāla
Amritsar
Faisalābād
Lahore
Al Kūt
Amārah
An Nāşiriyah
Masjed Soleymān
Ahvāz
Kāzerūn
Shīrāz
Sirjān
Bam
Kermān
Hāmūn-e Şāberi
Zābol
Daryā-ye Helmand
Dishū
Rēgestān
Quetta
Dera Ghazi Khān
Multān
Bahāwalnagar
Sāhīwāl
Okāra
Al Başrah (Basra)
Khorramshahr
Ābādān
Dezful
Kūh-e Shīb
Kūh-e Jebāl Barez
Zāhedān
Chāgai Hills
Dālbandin
Sūrāb
PAKISTAN
Jacobābād
Shikārpur
Rahīmyār Khān
Bīkāner
Bahāwalpur
KUWAIT
AL KUWAYT (KUWAIT)
An Nu'ayriyah
Būshehr
Bandar-e Kangān
Gaybandi
Bandar-e 'Abbās
Dārāb
Hāmūn-e Jaz Mūrīān
Īrānshahr
Siāhān Range
Central Makrān Range
Bela
Nawābshāh
Mīrpur Khās
Bārmer
Pāli
Jodhpur
INDIA
BAHRAIN
AL MANĀMAH (MANAMA)
Ad Dammām
Al Hufūf
Strait of Hormuz
OMAN
Ash Shāriqah
Dubayy (Dubai)
Konārak
Makran Coast
Gulf of Oman
Turbat
Lārkāna
Sukkur
Thar Desert
Hyderābād
R RIYĀD (RIYADH)
Al Dammām
Harad
QATAR
AD DAWHAH (DOHA)
ABŪ ZABY (ABU DHABI)
Tarif
Al'Ayn
UNITED ARAB EMIRATES
Şuhār
As Suwayq
MASQAT (MUSCAT)
Ar Rustāq
Ibri
Karāchi
Mouths of the Indus
Rann of Kachchh
Mahesāna
232
Layla
Al Fujaīrah
Al Gharbī
Adam
Şūr
Tropic of Cancer
Gāndhīdhām
Ahmadābād
Surendranagar
Vadodara
Jāmnagar
Rājkot
Bhāvnagar
Bharūch
Porbandar
Kāthiāwār Peninsula
Sūrat
Gulf of Kachchh
Gulf of Khambhāt
Ar Rub' al Khālī (Empty Quarter)
Al'Urūq al Mu'tariḍah
OMAN
Ramlat Āl Wahībah
Al Ghābah
Veraval
Duqm
Khalīj Maşīrah
Zufār
Jabal al Qamar
Jiddat al Harāsīs
Mughshin
Şawqirah
Thamarīt
Şalālah
Damqawt
Arabian
Sea
YEMEN
Ar Rawdah
Sanāw
Al Mahrah
Tarīm
Hadramawt
Ash Shihr
Sayhūt
Al Mukallā
Suquţrā (Socotra)
Gulf of Aden
Boosaaso
Caluula
SOMALIA
Shimbiris 2407m
Ceerigaabo
Raas Xaafuun
SOMALILAND
(internationally recognized)

Riyadh

Ad Dir'iyah
Al Marooj
Al Mursalat
Al Hamra
King Khaled Intl. Airport
Al Roudah Park
Al Ulayah
Al Ruwabi Park
Al Quds
Riyadh (Ar Riyad)
Al Murabba'
Al Malaz
Al Noor
Dhahal Badiah
Zoo
King Abdullah Park
Al Masmak Fortress
Al Nasiriyah Gate
Al Hamra'h Palace
King Abdul Aziz Manakh Park
Main Juma'a Mosque
Hijrat Laban
Al Madinah As Sinaiiyah
Yamamah
Al Masanya
Al Dar Al Baida
Nammar
Jiza

0 3 Km
0 3 Miles

288

19,686ft
13,124ft
9843ft
6562ft
3281ft
1640ft
820ft
328ft
Sea Level
-820ft
-6562ft
-13,124ft

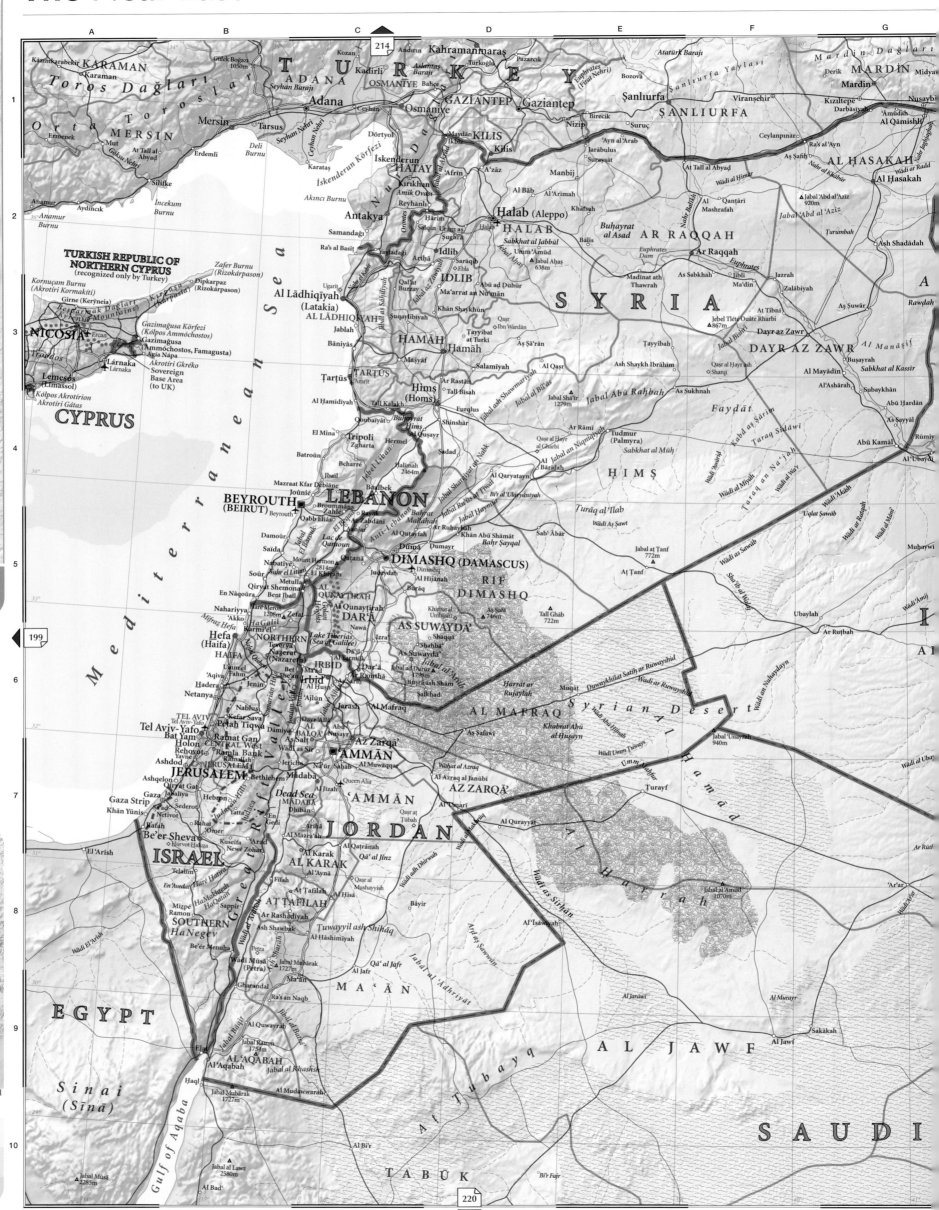

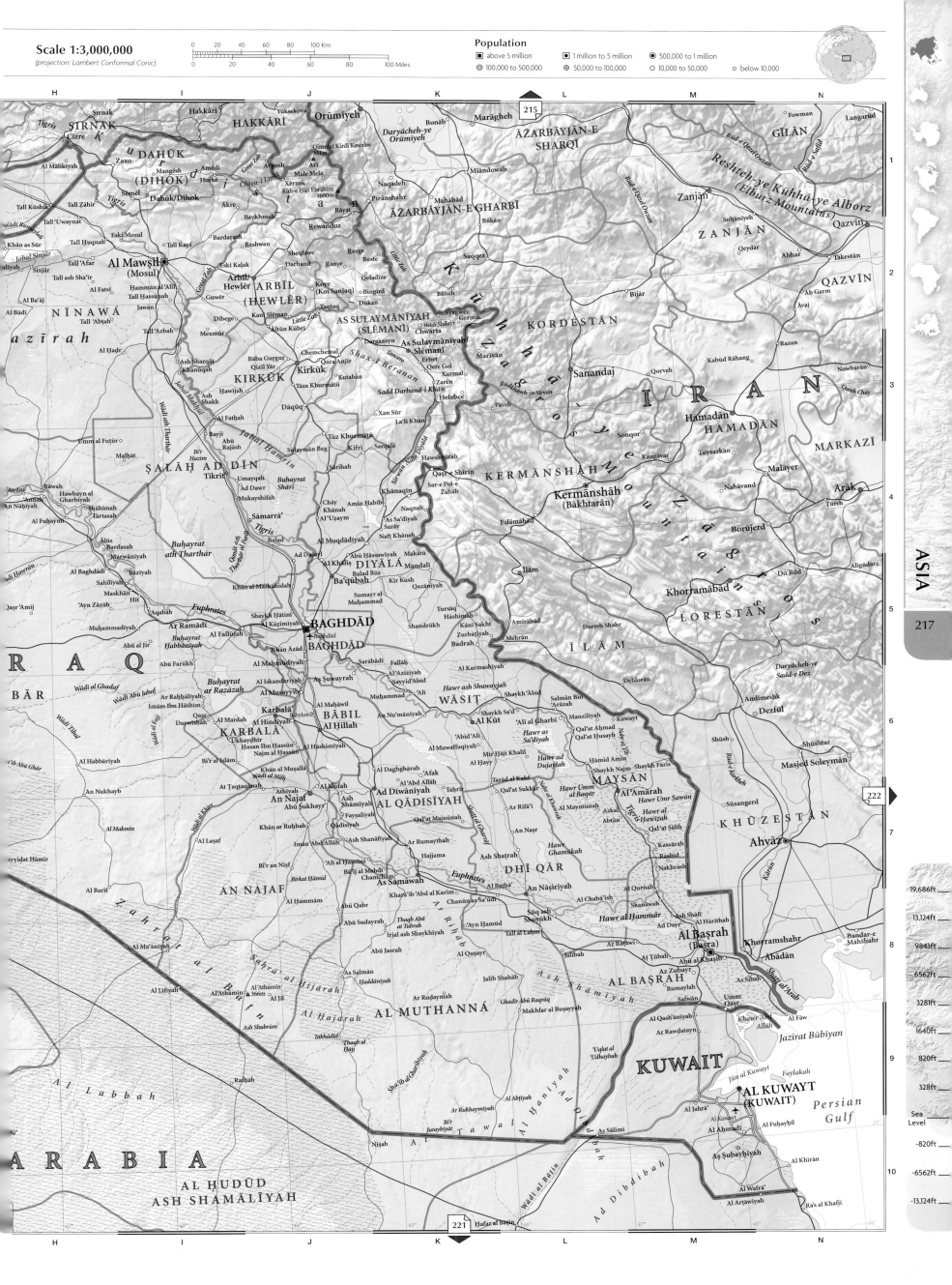

The Arabian Peninsula

Countries & regions: EGYPT, SAUDI ARABIA, SUDAN, SOUTH SUDAN, ETHIOPIA, ERITREA, YEMEN, IRAQ, KUWAIT, JORDAN, ISRAEL, DJIBOUTI, SOMALILAND, SUMALE, OROMIYA

Seas & deserts: Red Sea, RED SEA, SAHARA, Nubian Desert, An Nafūd, Syrian Desert, Libyan Plateau, Ethiopian Highlands, Danakil Desert, Afar Desert

Cities: CAIRO (AL QAHIRAH), Alexandria (Al Iskandariyah), Giza (Al Jizah), Luxor (Al Uqsur), Aswān, KHARTOUM, Omdurman, Port Sudan, Kassala, ASMARA, JERUSALEM, AMMAN, Tel Aviv-Yafo, Gaza, AR RIYĀD (RIYADH), Al Madinah (Medina), Makkah (Mecca), Jiddah (Jedda), At Tā'if, Abhā, Jīzān, Najrān, SAN'Ā' (SANA), Al Hudaydah (Hodeida), Ta'izz, 'Adan (Aden), DJIBOUTI, AN Najaf, KUWAIT, Tabūk, Hā'il, Buraydah, Al Bāhah

Features: Nile, Lake Nasser (Buhayrat Nāsir), Suez Canal (Qanat as Suways), Gulf of Aqaba, Gulf of Suez, Sinai (Sīnā), Tropic of Cancer, Bab el Mandeb, Golfe de Tadjoura, Massawa Channel, Dahlak Archipelago

Elevation scale: 6000m, 4000m, 3000m, 2000m, 1000m, 500m, 250m, 100m, Sea Level, -250m, -2000m, -4000m

Page refs: 216, 129, 136

Countries and major regions:

TURKEY — ARMENIA — AZERBAIJAN — BAKI (BAKU) — SYRIA — IRAQ — IRAN — SAUDI ARABIA — KUWAIT — BAHRAIN — QATAR — UNITED ARAB EMIRATES

Major cities:

YEREVAN — Tabrīz — Ardabīl — TEHRĀN — Karaj — Qazvīn — Rasht — BAGHDĀD — Kermānshāh — Khorramābād — Hamadān — Qom — Arāk — Esfahān — Ahvāz — Al Başrah (Basra) — Abādān — AL KUWAYT (KUWAIT) — Bandar-e Būshehr — Shīrāz — AL MANĀMAH (MANAMA) — AD DAWḤAH (DOHA) — AR RIYĀḌ (RIYADH) — ABŪ ZABY (ABU DHABI)

Seas and gulfs:

Caspian Sea — Persian Gulf — Gulf of Bahrain

Deserts:

Syrian Desert — An Nafūd — Najd

Provinces/regions:

ĀZARBĀYJĀN-E SHARQĪ — ĀZARBĀYJĀN-E GHARBĪ — GĪLĀN — MĀZANDARĀN — KORDESTĀN — HAMADĀN — QAZVĪN — ZANJĀN — TEHRĀN — QOM — MARKAZĪ — LORESTĀN — KERMĀNSHĀH — ĪLĀM — KHŪZESTĀN — ESFAHĀN — CHAHĀR MAḤĀL VA BAKHTĪĀRĪ — KOHGĪLŪYEH VA BOWYER AHMAD — FĀRS — BŪSHEHR — AL JAWF — AL ḤUDŪD ASH SHAMĀLĪYAH — ḤĀ'IL — AL QAṢĪM — AR RIYĀḌ — ASH SHARQĪYAH

Elevation scale:

6000m — 4000m — 3000m — 2000m — 1000m — 500m — 250m — 100m — Sea Level — -250m — -2000m — -4000m

Tropic of Cancer

197 — 220 — 220

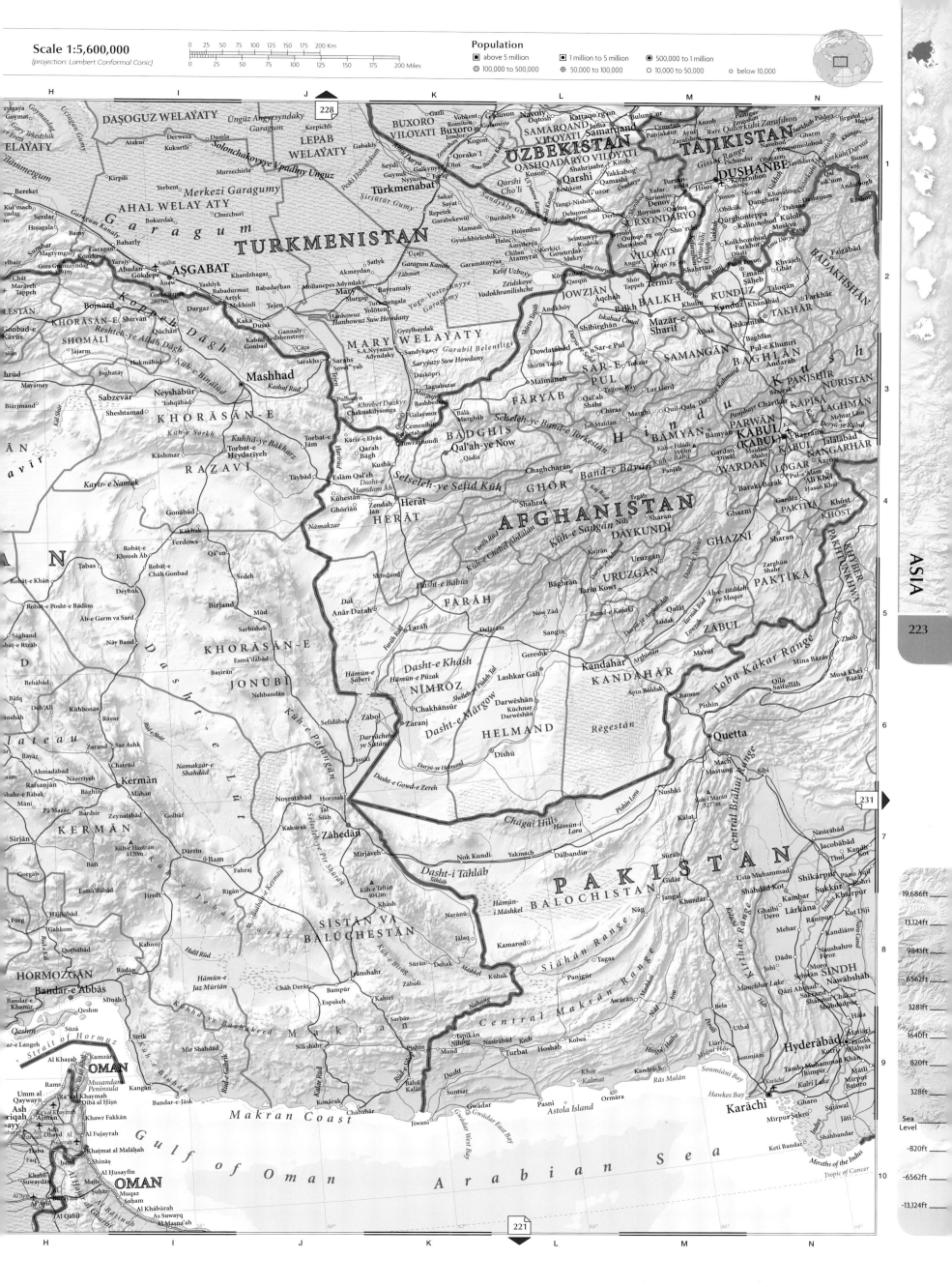

South & Central Asia

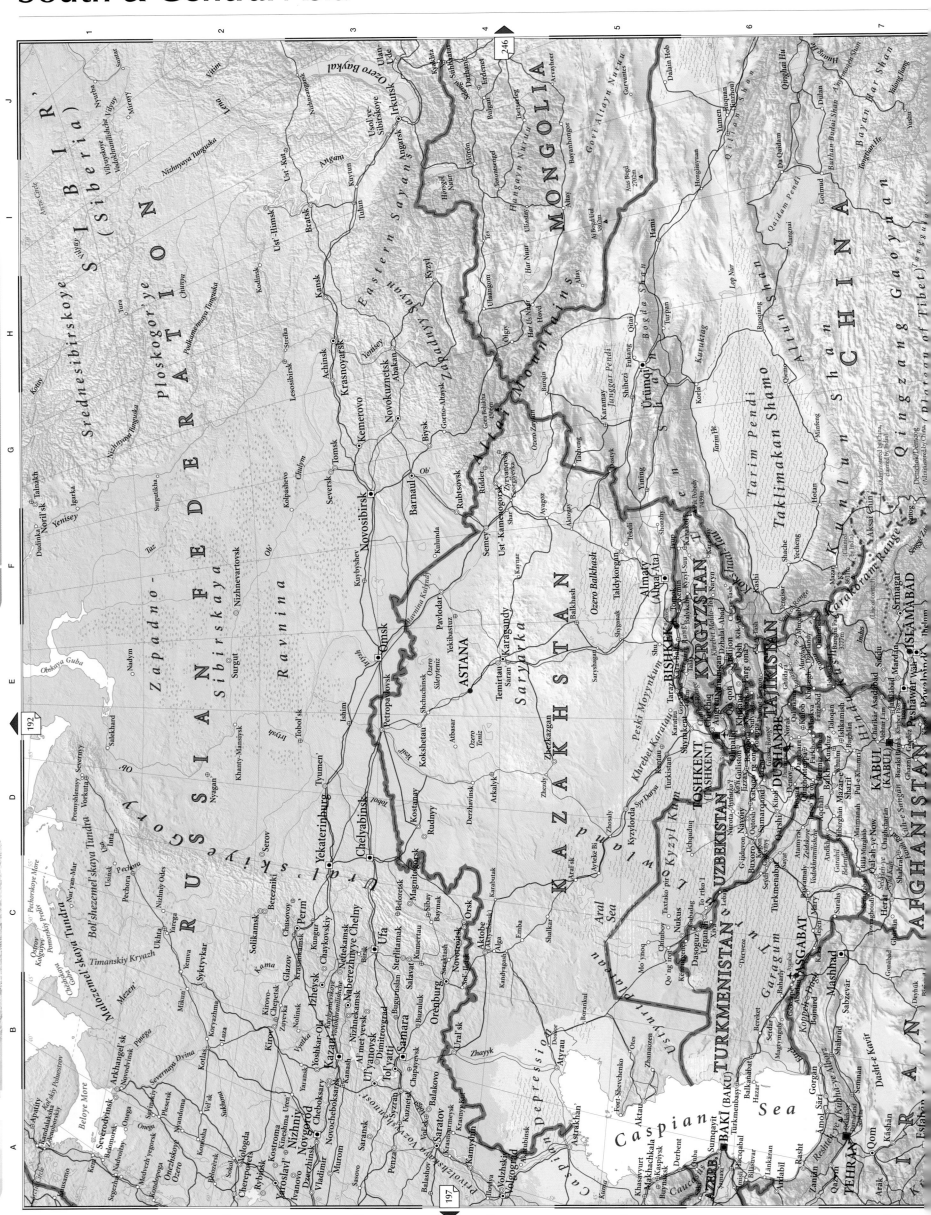

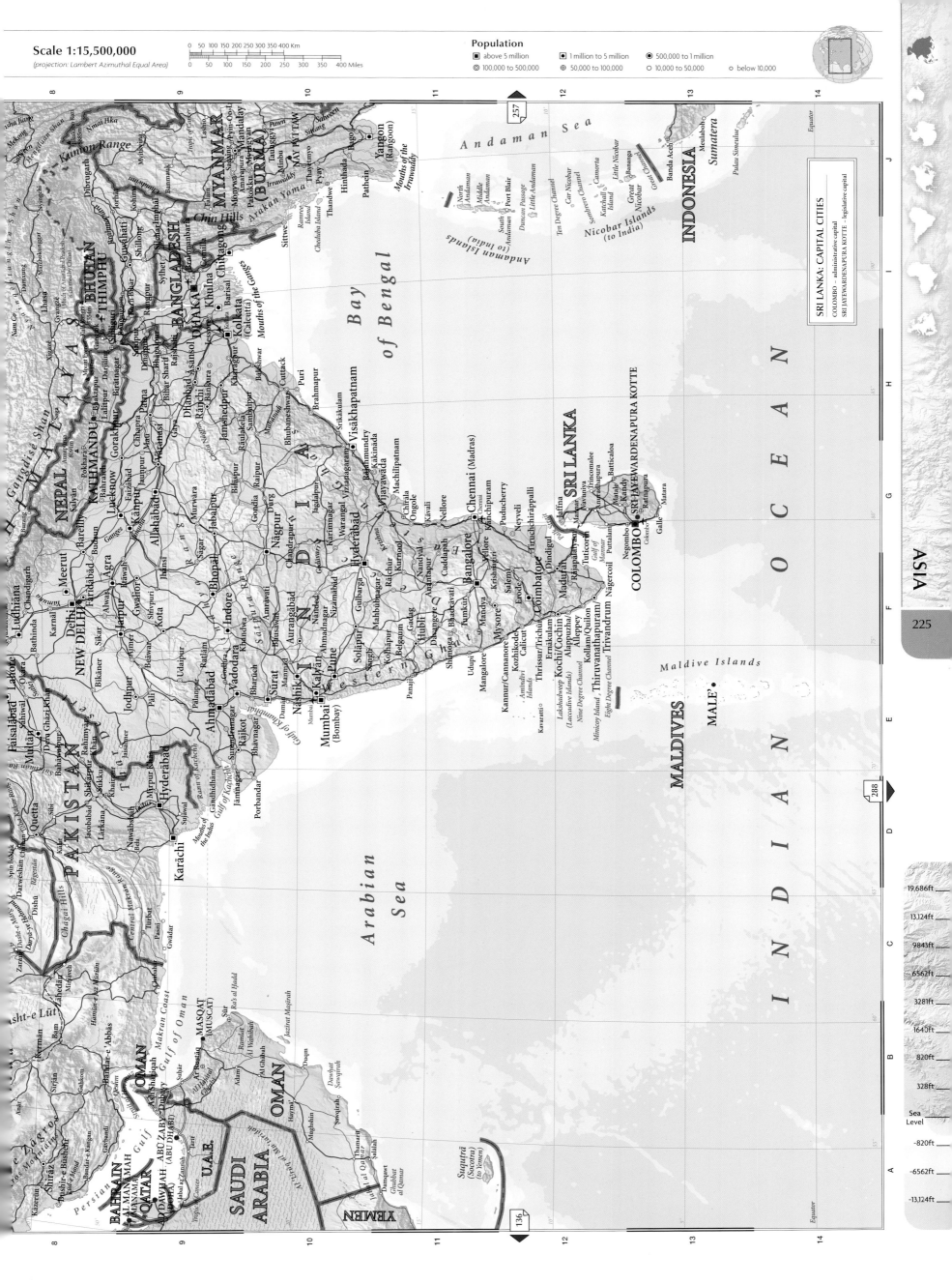

Kazakhstan

RUSSIAN

REPUBLIKA MORDOVIYA
PENZENSKAYA OBLAST'
UL'YANOVSKAYA OBLAST'
SAMARSKAYA OBLAST'
SARATOVSKAYA OBLAST'
VOLGOGRADSKAYA OBLAST'
ASTRAKHANSKAYA OBLAST'
REPUBLIKA KALMYKIYA
RESPUBLIKA DAGESTAN

REPUBLIKA TATARSTAN
RESPUBLIKA BASHKORTOSTAN
ORENBURGSKAYA OBLAST'
CHELYABINSKAYA OBLAST'
KURGANSKAYA OBLAST'

ZAPADNYY KAZAKHSTAN
ATYRAU
MANGYSTAU
AKTYUBINSK
KOSTANAY
KYZYLORDA

Ryn-Peski
Caspian Depression
Caspian Sea
Ustyurt Plateau
Aral Sea
Turgayskaya Stolovaya Strana
Plato Mangystau
Peski Bol'shiye Barsuki

AZERBAIJAN
BAKI (BAKU)

TURKMENISTAN
BALKAN WELAÝATY
DAŞOGUZ WELAÝATY
AHAL WELAÝATY
LEBAP WELAÝATY
MARY WELAÝATY
Garagum
AŞGABAT

UZBEKISTAN
QORAQALPOG'ISTON RESPUBLIKASI
Nukus
XORAZM VILOYATI
NAVOIY VILOYATI
BUXORO VILOYATI
QASHQADARYO VILOYATI
SAMARQAND VILOYATI
Kyzylkum
Buxoro

IRAN

195
197
223

Scale 1:6,250,000
(projection: Lambert Conformal Conic)

0 25 50 75 100 125 150 175 200 Km
0 25 50 75 100 125 150 175 200 Miles

Population
- ■ above 5 million
- ■ 1 million to 5 million
- ◉ 500,000 to 1 million
- ◎ 100,000 to 500,000
- ⊕ 50,000 to 100,000
- ○ 10,000 to 50,000
- ∘ below 10,000

192
238
231

FEDERATION

Ishim
TYUMENSKAYA OBLAST'
OMSKAYA OBLAST'
Trans-Siberian Railway
Tyukalinsk
Nazyvayevsk
Omsk
Petropavlovsk
Makusho
Mamlyutka
Bulayevo
Kuybyshev
Novosibirsk
Berdsk
Barabinsk
Kargat
Chulym
Iskitim
LENINSK-KUZNETSKIY
Belovo
KEMEROVSKAYA OBLAST'
Chernogorsk
Kiselevsk
Novokuznetsk
Mezhdurechensk
NOVOSIBIRSKAYA OBLAST'
Yelanka
Tatarsk
Kamen'-na-Obi
Prokop'yevsk
Osinniki
Abaza
Cherlak
Karasuk
Sibirskiy
Zarinsk
RESPUBLIKA KHAKASIYA
Barnaul
Novoaltaysk
Biya
Biysk
Gorno-Altaysk
RESPUBLIKA TYVA
Rubtsovsk
Zmeinogorsk
Gornyak
RESPUBLIKA ALTAY
Tuekta
Inya
Chemal

SEVERNYY KAZAKHSTAN
Kokshetau
AKMOLA
ASTANA
Temirtau
Karagandy
KARAGANDY
KARAZHAL
Zhezkazgan
Satpayev

ZAKHSTAN

VOSTOCHNY KAZAKHSTAN
Semey
Ust-Kamenogorsk
Altai Mountains
Gora Belukha 4506m
Tashanta
MONGOLIA
Khrebet Kalba
Khrebet Naryn
Ozero Markakol'
Ozero Zaysan
Zaysan

Saryarka
Betpakdala
Ozero Balkhash
Balkhash
Junggar Pendi
Gurbantünggüt Shamo

ALMATY
Taldykorgan
Zhetysuyskiy Alatau
Borohoro Shan
Karamay

Peski Saryyesik-Atyrau
Peski Taukum
Almaty (Alma-Ata)
Yining
Shihezi
Manas

BISHKEK
Taraz
Shymkent
YUZHNYY KAZAKHSTAN
Ozero Issyk-Kul'
Karakol
Tien Shan
CHINA

TOSHKENT (TASHKENT)
Namangan
Andijon
Osh
KYRGYZSTAN
Naryn
Kashi
XINJIANG UYGUR ZIZHIQU
Tarim Pendi
Tarim He
Taklimakan Shamo

Khujand
Guliston
Fargona
OSHSKAYA OBLAST'
BATKENSKAYA OBLAST'
Alai Range

DUSHANBE
TAJIKISTAN
Pamir

19,686ft
13,124ft
9843ft
6562ft
3281ft
1640ft
820ft
328ft
Sea Level
-820ft
-6562ft
-13,124ft

Central Asia

ASIA

228

KAZA
KYZYLORDA
Kyzylor

Aral
Sea

QORAQALPOG'ISTON RESPUBLIKASI

Ustyurt Plateau

MANGYSTAU

Caspian Sea

Aktau
Atyrau
ATYRAU

Nukus

Daşoguz
DAŞOGUZ WELAÝATY

Urganch
XORAZM VILOYATI

UZBEKISTAN
NAVOIY VILOYATI

BUXORO VILOYATI
Buxoro
Nayo

Garagum

TURKMENISTAN

Merkezi Garagumy

AHAL WELAÝATY

LEPAP WELAÝATY
Türkmenabat

MARY WELAÝATY
Mary

Aşgabat

Koppeh Dagh

BALKAN WELAÝATY
BALKANABAT
Türkmenbaşy

Bojnūrd
GOLESTĀN
Gorgān

KHORĀSĀN-E SHEMĀLĪ

Mashhad

IRAN

SEMNĀN

Dasht-e Kavīr

KHORĀSĀN-E RAŽAVĪ

KHORĀSĀN-E JONŪBĪ

Herāt
AFG
HERĀT
BĀDGHIS
FĀRYĀB
GHŌR

6000m
4000m
3000m
2000m
1000m
500m
250m
100m
Sea Level
-250m
-2000m
-4000m

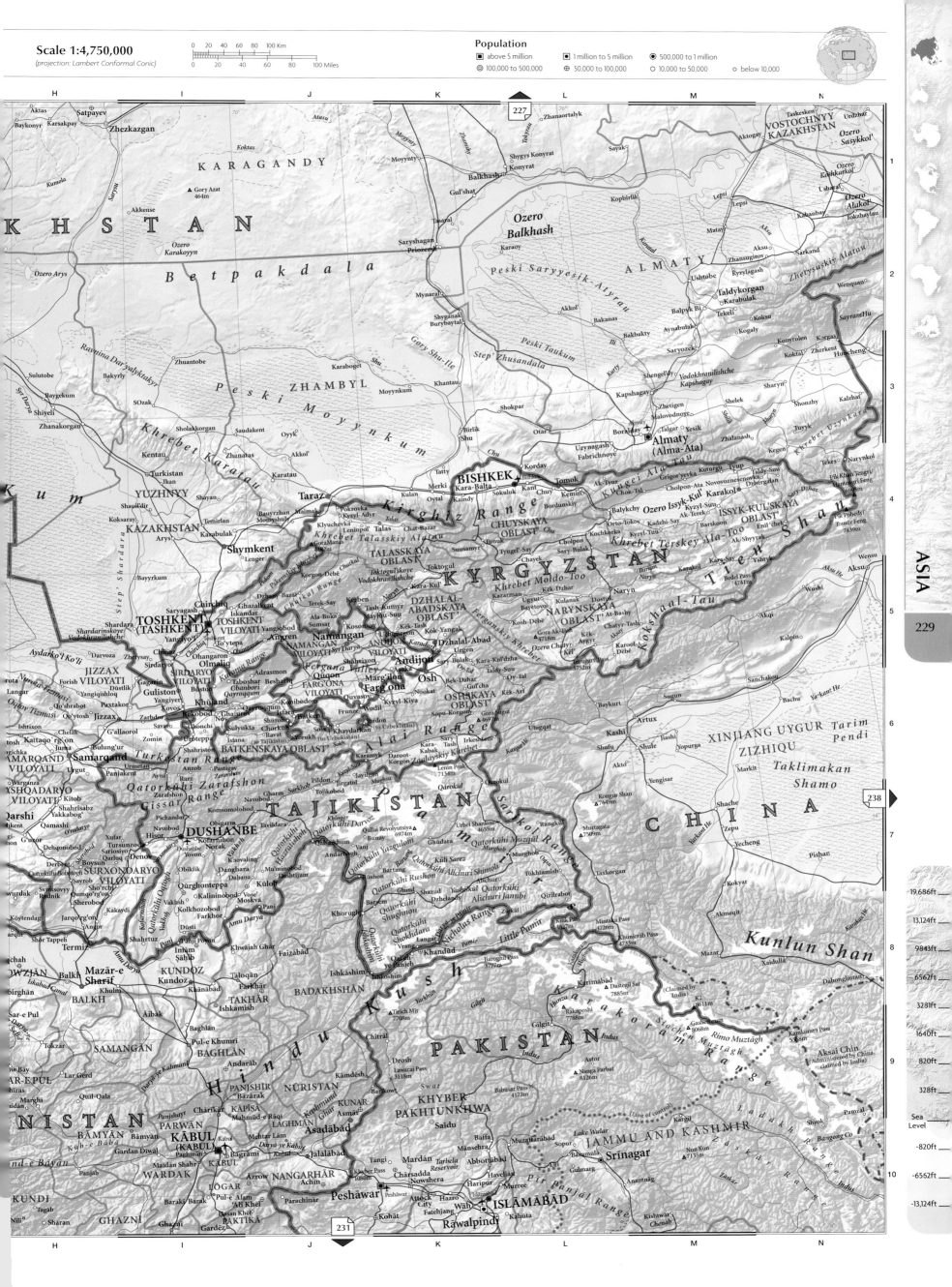

Afghanistan & Pakistan

TURKMENISTAN

UZBEKISTAN

DUSHANBE

AFGHANISTAN

IRAN

PAKISTAN

OMAN

U.A.E.

AŞGABAT

Mashhad

Herāt

Kandahār

Quetta

Zāhedān

Kermān

Bandar-e 'Abbās

MASQAT (MUSCAT)

Karāchi

Hyderābād

Mazār-e Sharīf

Kunduz

DUSHANBE

Qarshi

Mary

Regions / Provinces (Iran, Afghanistan, Pakistan):

GOLESTĀN, KHORĀSĀN-E SHEMĀLĪ, SEMNĀN, KHORĀSĀN-E RAŽAVĪ, KHORĀSĀN-E JANŪBĪ, YAZD, KERMĀN, HORMOZGĀN, SĪSTĀN VA BALŪCHESTĀN

HERĀT, GHOR, BĀDGHĪS, FARYĀB, SAR-E PUL, BALKH, SAMANGĀN, JOWZJĀN, BĀMYĀN, PARWĀN, WARDAK, DĀYKUNDI, GHAZNĪ, ZĀBUL, PAKTĪKĀ, URŪZGĀN, FARĀH, NĪMRŌZ, HELMAND, KANDAHĀR

BALOCHISTAN, SINDH

LEBAP WELAÝATY, MARY WELAÝATY, AHAL WELAÝATY

Physical features:

Koppeh Dagh, Dasht-e Kavīr, Dasht-e Lūt, Iranian Plateau, Kūh-e Jebāl Bārez, Kūh-e Taftān 4042m, Selseleh-ye Sefīd Kūh, Selseleh-ye Band-e Torkestān, Band-e Bayān, Dasht-e Mārgow, Dasht-e Khash, Régestān, Dasht-e Gowd-e Zereh, Chagai Hills, Toba Kākar Range, Central Brāhui Range, Kirthar Range, Central Makrān Range, Siāhān Range, Makran Coast, Gulf of Oman, Strait of Hormuz, Arabian Sea, Mouths of the Indus, Indus, Manchhar Lake, Astola Island, Hamūn-i Māshkel, Hāmūn-e Sābarī, Daryācheh-ye Sīstān

Cities and towns (selection):

Gorgān, Gonbad-e Kāvūs, Bandar-e Torkaman, Shāhrūd, Dāmghān, Sabzevār, Neyshābūr, Torbat-e Ḥeydarīyeh, Torbat-e Jām, Tāybād, Bīrjand, Qā'en, Ṭabas, Yazd, Kermān, Bam, Sīrjān, Zāhedān, Mirjāveh, Khāsh, Īrānshahr, Bampūr, Nīkshahr, Chābahār, Jāsk, Bandar-e 'Abbās, Mīnāb, Kahnūj, Qeshm

Mary, Tejen, Bayramaly, Kaka, Gyzylbaýdak, Dowlatābād, Andkhōy, Āqchah, Balkh, Khulm, Shibirghān, Maimanah, Qal'ah Shahr, Chaghcharān, Shahrak, Herāt, Ghōrīān, Shindand, Farāh, Delārām, Lashkar Gāh, Gereshk, Kandahār, Spīn Boldak, Chaman, Pishīn, Qalāt, Ghaznī, Sharan, Qal'ah-ye Now, Kushk, Dishū, Zaranj, Chakhānsūr, Zābol

Quetta, Nushki, Dālbandīn, Nok Kundi, Yakmach, Khuzdār, Kālat, Mastung, Surāb, Kharan, Panjgūr, Turbat, Gwādar, Pasni, Ormāra, Bela, Sonmiāni, Karāchi, Hyderābād, Shikārpur, Jacobābād, Sukkur, Lārkāna, Rohri, Nawābshāh

DUSHANBE, Hisor, Kofarnihon, Qŭrghonteppa

Elevation scale:
6000m, 4000m, 3000m, 2000m, 1000m, 500m, 250m, 100m, Sea Level, −250m, −2000m, −4000m

Northern India, Nepal & Bangladesh

229
230
234

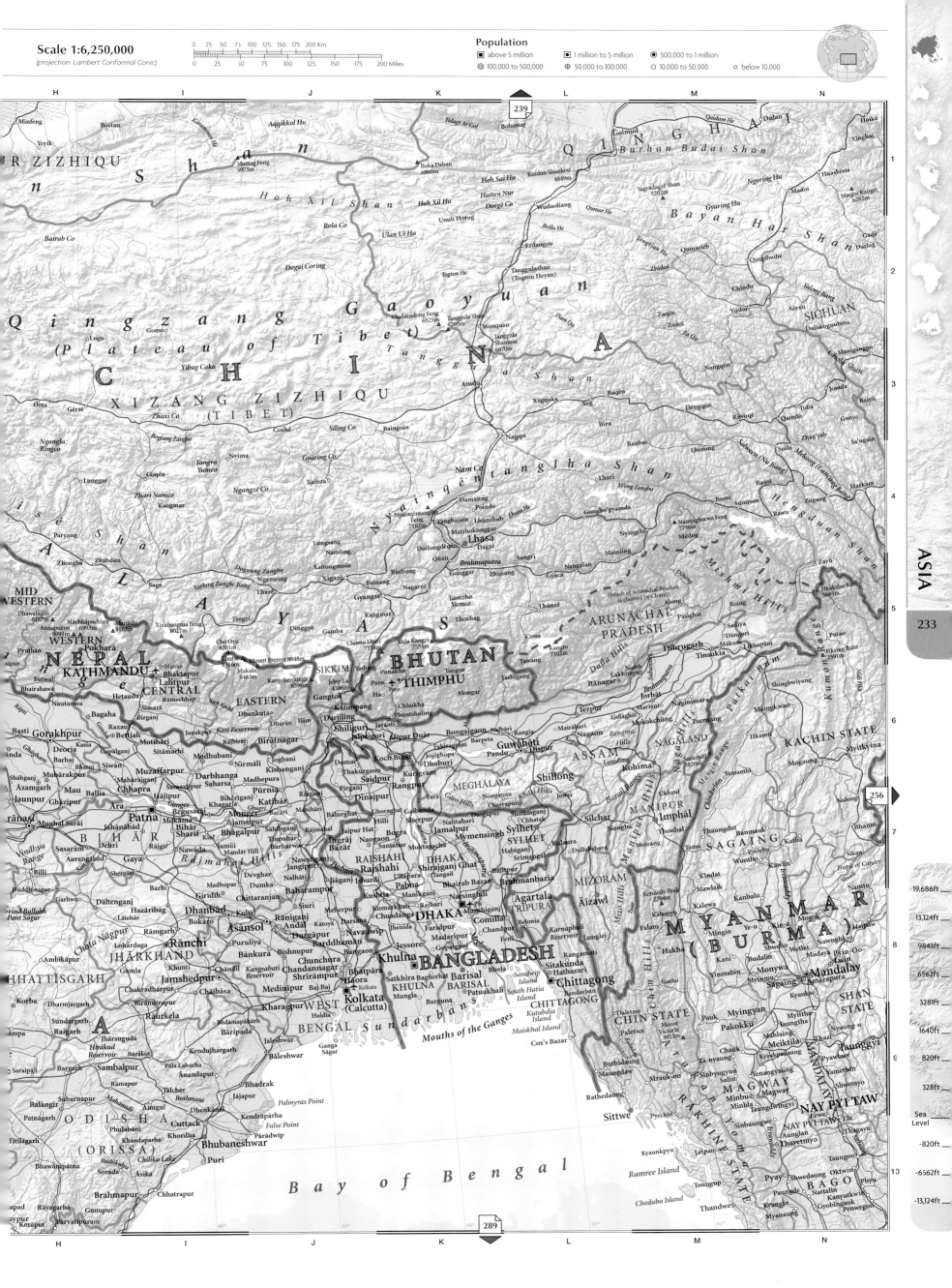

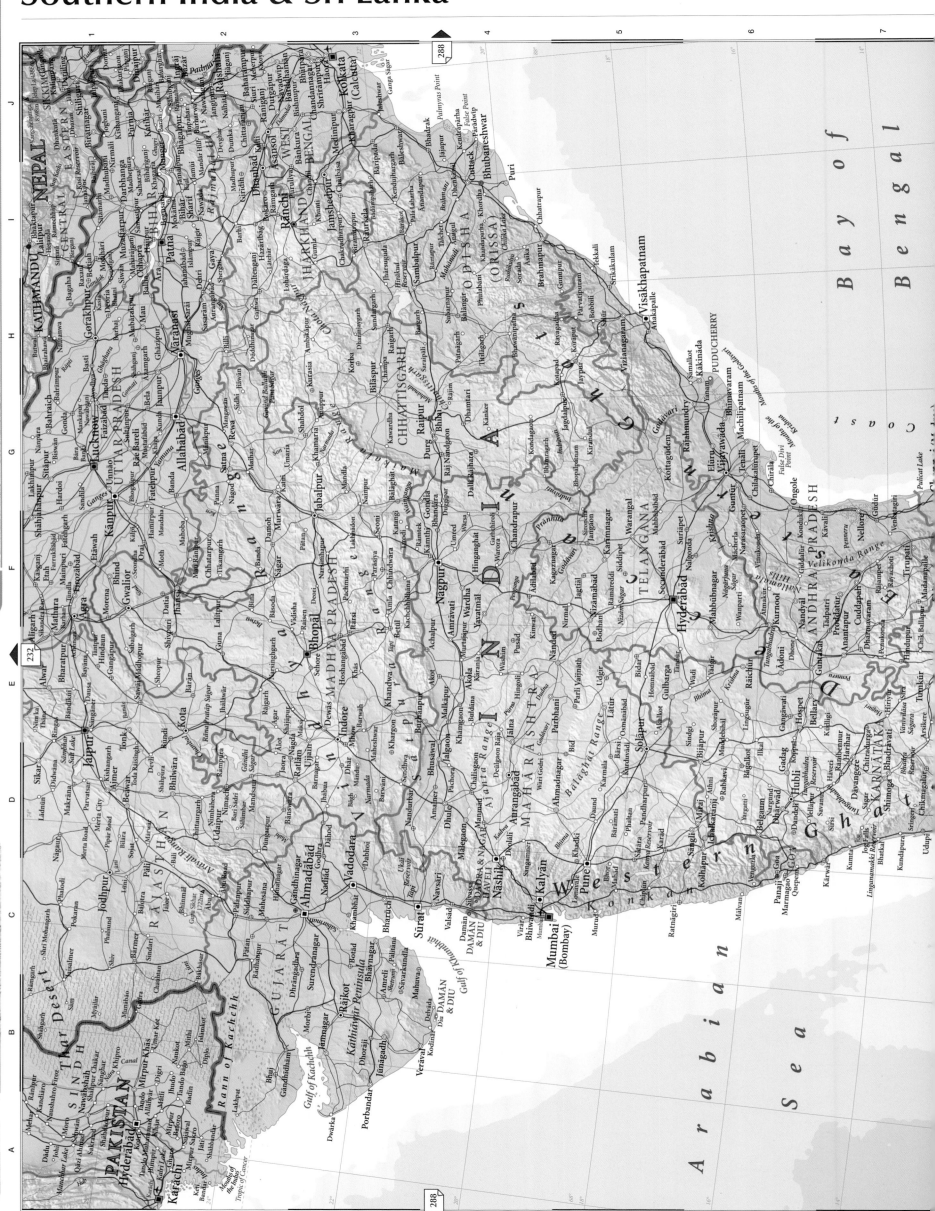

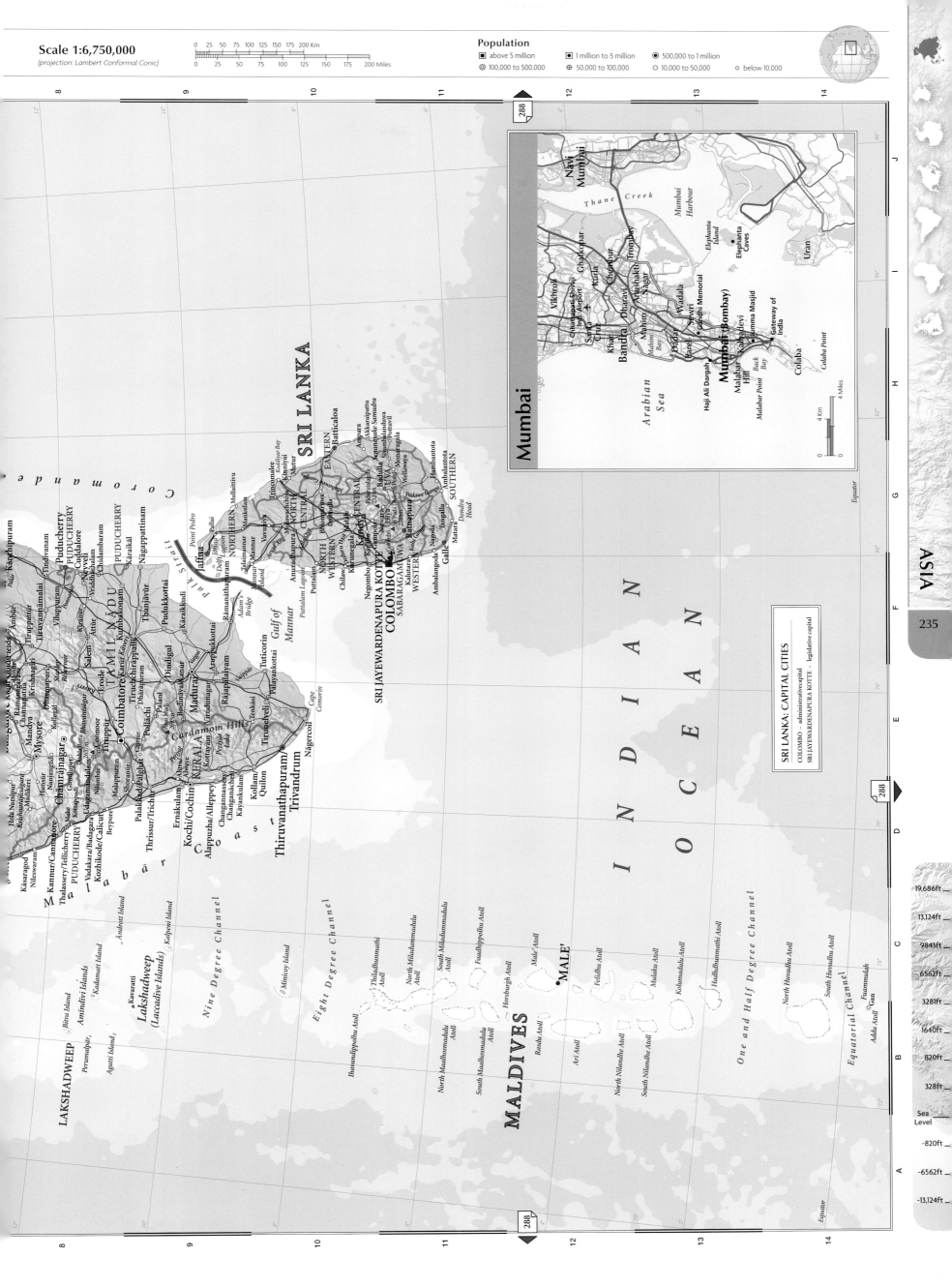

ASIA

236

231

192

256

RUSSIAN

KAZAKHSTAN

MONGOLIA

ULAANBAATAR (ULAN BATOR)

CHINA

XINJIANG UYGUR ZIZHIQU

Tarim Pendi

Taklimakan Shamo

Kunlun Shan

Altun Shan

Qingzang Gaoyuan (Plateau of Tibet)

QINGHAI

GANSU

NINGXIA

SICHUAN

SHAANXI

CHONGQING

GUIZHOU

YUNNAN

GUANGXI ZHUANGZU ZIZHIQU

HIMALAYAS

KYRGYZSTAN

BISHKEK

Tien Shan

Ürümqi

GOBI

Govi Altayn Nuruu

Hangayn Nuruu

Altai Mountains

Zapadnyy Sayan

Eastern Sayans

NEW DELHI

INDIA

NEPAL

KATHMANDU

BHUTAN

THIMPHU

BANGLADESH

DHAKA

MYANMAR (BURMA)

NAY PYI TAW

THAILAND

LAOS

VIANGCHAN (VIENTIANE)

HANOI

Bay of Bengal

Gulf of Tonkin

HAINAN

Hainan Dao

Elevation scale:
6000m
4000m
3000m
2000m
1000m
500m
250m
100m
Sea Level
-250m
-2000m
-4000m

ASTANA

Omsk

Novosibirsk

Krasnoyarsk

Bratsk

Irkutsk

Ulan-Ude

Kemerovo

Barnaul

Almaty

Lanzhou

Xining

Chengdu

Chongqing

Kunming

Nanning

Mandalay

Yangon (Rangoon)

Kolkata

Delhi

Lhasa

Mount Everest 8848m

Tropic of Cancer

Scale 1:14,500,000
(projection: Lambert Azimuthal Equal Area)

0 50 100 150 200 250 300 350 400 Km

0 50 100 150 200 250 300 350 400 Miles

Population
■ above 5 million
■ 1 million to 5 million
◉ 500,000 to 1 million
◎ 100,000 to 500,000
⊕ 50,000 to 100,000
⊙ 10,000 to 50,000
○ below 10,000

FEDERATION

Stanovoy Khrebet

Khrebet Dzhugdzhur

Sea of Okhotsk

Sea of Japan (East Sea)

JAPAN

Honshū

TŌKYŌ

PACIFIC

OCEAN

NORTH KOREA

P'YŎNGYANG

SOUTH KOREA

SEOUL

SEJONG CITY

Yellow Sea

Great Plain of China

East China Sea

Nansei-shotō
(Ryukyu Islands)

SHANGHAI SHI

Shanghai

TAIWAN

TAIBEI
(TAIPEI)

(China and Taiwan claim all
of each other's territory)

SOUTH KOREA: CAPITAL CITIES
SEOUL – capital
SEJONG CITY – administrative capital

South China Sea

Philippine Sea

Luzon

PHILIPPINES

MANILA

Paracel Islands
(disputed)

Shanghai

Baoshan

Kailu
Xincun

Gucun

Shanghai
University

Miaphang

Gaojing

Wujiao
Chang

Huangpu Jiang

Dachang

Pengpu

Jiangwan

Hongkou Stadium
Lu Xun Tomb

Hongkou

Yangpu

Gaohang

Zhenru

Yichuan

Zhabei

Tilan
Qiao

Huangshan
Xincun

Jinqiao

Putuo

Temple of the
Jade Buddha

Shanghai

Huangpu

Pudong

Jiaodong
University

Jing'an

People's Square

Shanghai
Museum

Zhangjiang

Beixinjing

Sun Yat Sen's
Former Residence

Dapu

Muamu

Humau
Zhen

Changning

Nanshi

Xujiahui

Luwan

Zhoujiadu

Yugiao

Beicai

Hongqiao

Qibao
Zhen

Caohe

Longua

Huangpu Jiang

Sanlin

Liuliqiao

19,686ft
13,124ft
9843ft
6562ft
3281ft
1640ft
820ft
328ft
Sea
Level
-820ft
-6562ft
-13,124ft

Western China

ASIA

238

227

230

232

Scale 1:7,750,000
(projection: Lambert Conformal Conic)

0 25 50 75 100 125 150 175 200 Km
0 25 50 75 100 125 150 175 200 Miles

Population
- ■ above 5 million
- ■ 1 million to 5 million
- ◉ 500,000 to 1 million
- ◎ 100,000 to 500,000
- ⊕ 50,000 to 100,000
- ○ 10,000 to 50,000
- ∘ below 10,000

Elevation scale:
19,686ft
13,124ft
9843ft
6562ft
3281ft
1640ft
820ft
328ft
Sea Level
-820ft
-6562ft
-13,124ft

246 · 244 · 256

Countries and regions

MONGOLIA · HÖVSGÖL · DZAVHAN · ARHANGAY · BULGAN · GOVI-ALTAY · BAYANHONGOR · ÖVÖRHANGAY · TÖV · DUNDGOVI · DORNOGOVI · ÖMNÖGOVI · SÜHBAATAR · HENTIY · DORNOD · GOVI-SUMBER

GOBI · NEI MONGOL ZIZHIQU · Nei Mongol Gaoyuan · Mu Us Shadi · Badain Jaran Shamo · Tengger Shamo

CHINA · QINGHAI · GANSU · NINGXIA · SHAANXI · SHANXI · HEBEI · HENAN · HUBEI · SICHUAN · Sichuan Pendi · CHONGQING SHI · GUIZHOU · YUNNAN · HUNAN · (Plateau of Tibet) · ARUNACHAL PRADESH · ASSAM · KACHIN STATE · MYANMAR (BURMA)

Major cities

ULAANBAATAR (ULAN BATOR) · Erdenet · Baotou · Hohhot · Datong · Zhangjiakou · Jining · Shijiazhuang · Taiyuan · Yinchuan · Lanzhou · Xining · Xi'an · Xianyang · Baoji · Tianshui · Zhengzhou · Luoyang · Nanyang · Xiangfan · Yichang · Wanzhou · Chengdu · Mianyang · Deyang · Nanchong · Chongqing · Leshan · Zigong · Yibin · Guiyang · Xichang · Panzhihua · Lijiang

Physical features

Hangayn Nuruu · Altayn Nuruu · Qilian Shan · Helan Shan · Qin Ling · Daba Shan · Micang Shan · Daxue Shan · Shaluli Shan · Hengduan Shan · Qionglai Shan · Burhan Budai Shan · Bayan Har Shan · A'nyemaqen Shan · Kunlun Shankou · Yellow River (Huang He) · Yangtze · Mekong (Lancang Jiang) · Salween (Nu Jiang) · Qinghai Hu · Har Hu · Qaidam Pendi · Gongga Shan 7556m · Atas Bogd 2695m

ASIA

240

Major labels:

QINGHAI · Qingzang Gaoyuan (Plateau of Tibet) · Bayan Har Shan · XIZANG ZIZHIQU (TIBET) · Nyainqentanglha Shan · Hengduan Shan · ARUNACHAL PRADESH (Much of Arunachal Pradesh is claimed by China) · INDIA · KACHIN STATE · GANSU · SICHUAN · SHAANXI · Qin Ling · HUBEI · Daba Shan · CHINA · HUNAN · GUIZHOU · Gaoyuan · YUNNAN · GUANGXI ZHUANGZU ZIZHIQU · MYANMAR (BURMA) · SHAN STATE · Shan Plateau · KAYAH STATE · KAYIN STATE · VIETNAM · LAOS · THAILAND · Gulf of Tonkin · HAINAN · Hainan Dao · NINGXIA · SHANXI

Cities/towns (selection):

Golmud · Xining · Huangzhong · Lanzhou · Linxia · Taiyuan · Luoyang · Xianyang · Xi'an · Weinan · Baoji · Tianshui · Hanzhong · Guangyuan · Mianyang · Chengdu · Deyang · Nanchong · Wanzhou · Yichang · Leshan · CHONGQING · Chongqing · Zigong · Yibin · Luzhou · Zunyi · Changsha · Xiangtan · Yiyang · Changde · Guiyang · Anshun · Kaili · Duyun · Liuzhou · Guilin · Kunming · Dali · Baoshan · Yuxi · Gejiu · Mengzi · Nanning · Beihai · Zhanjiang · Haikou · Myitkyina · Bhamo · Lashio · Taunggyi · Chiang Mai · Chiang Rai · HANOI · Hai Phong · Ha Long · Viangchan (VIENTIANE) · Louangphabang · Vinh · Mawlamyine

Physical features (selection):

Qinghai Hu · Huang He (Yellow River) · Chang Jiang (Yangtze) · Three Gorges Dam · Three Gorges Reservoir · Sichuan Pendi · Mekong · Salween · Red River (Yuan Jiang) · Dongting Hu · Tropic of Cancer · Gogga Shan 7556m · Hkakabo Razi 5885m · Fan Si Pan 3143m · Gulf of Tonkin

Elevation scale:
6000m · 4000m · 3000m · 2000m · 1000m · 500m · 250m · 100m · Sea Level · −250m · −2000m · −4000m

246 · 233 · 256

244

256

SHAANXI

HUBEI

SICHUAN

CHONGQING

C H I N A

GUIZHOU

HUNAN

YUNNAN

GUANGXI ZHUANGZU ZIZHIQU

VIETNAM

Chengdu
Mianyang
Deyang
Guangyuan
Nanchong
Chongqing
Leshan
Zigong
Yibin
Luzhou
Zunyi
Guiyang
Anshun
Duyun
Nanning
Liuzhou
Guilin
Changde
Huaihua
Hengyang
Yongzhou
Xiangfan
Yichang
Jingzhou

Longmen Shan
Min Shan
Daba Shan
Wu Shan
Dalou Shan
Wuling Shan
Fanjing Shan
Xuefeng Ling
Wumeng Shan
Yungui Gaoyuan
Miao Ling
Duyang Shan
Jiuwan Dashan
Shiwan Dashan
Darong Shan

Chang Jiang (Yangtze)
Three Gorges Reservoir
Three Gorges Dam

Han Shui

Tropic of Cancer

Sea Level

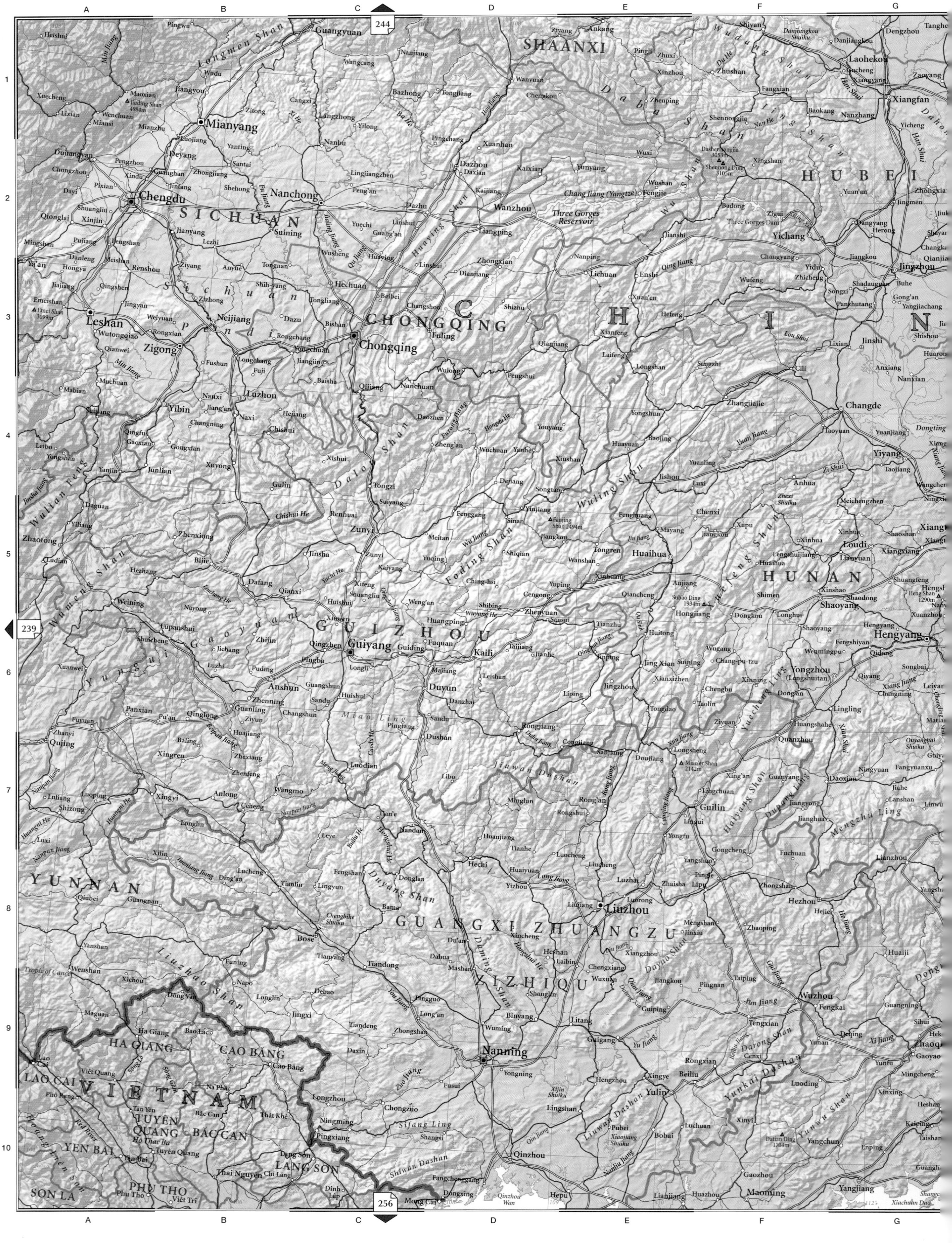

6000m
4000m
3000m
2000m
1000m
500m
250m
100m
-250m
-2000m
-4000m

Scale 1:3,750,000
(projection: Lambert Conformal Conic)

0 20 40 60 80 100 Km
0 20 40 60 80 100 Miles

Population
- ■ above 5 million
- ■ 1 million to 5 million
- ● 500,000 to 1 million
- ◉ 100,000 to 500,000
- ⊕ 50,000 to 100,000
- ○ 10,000 to 50,000
- ∘ below 10,000

ASIA

HENAN

Xincai
Funan
Fengtai
Jiangdu
Taizhou
Rugao
Jiangyan
Tongzhou

Zhengyang
Yingshang
Shouxian
Dingyuan
Chuzhou
Yangzhou
Yangzhong
Taixing
Jingjiang
Changlezhen
Qidong

Xinyang
Xixian
Huainan
Changfeng
Huoqiu
Yizheng
Zhenjiang
Haimen
Meili

Liuchia-ho
Huoshan
Gushi
Feixi
Lu'an
Lianyuan
Quanjiao
Zhuji
Nanjing
Danyang
Sheng
Jiangyin
Luyuan
Fushan

JIANGSU

ANHUI
Hefei
Chaohu
Ma'anshan
Dangtu
Wuhu
Changzhou
Jintan
Changshu
Wuxi
Taicang
Kunshan

Wuhan
Huangshi

Shanghai
SHANGHAI SHI

Suzhou
Huzhou
Jiaxing
Pinghu

Hangzhou

Ningbo

Shaoxing
Fenghua

ZHEJIANG

Jinhua

Quzhou

Jingdezhen

Nanchang

Shangrao

JIANGXI

Wenzhou

Fuzhou

FUJIAN

Sanming

Nanping

Fuzhou

Quanzhou

Xiamen

Zhangzhou

East China Sea

Taiwan Strait

Jilong

TAIBEI (TAIPEI)
Taoyuan
Pingzhen
Xinzhu
Xindian
Yilan

Miaoli

Fengyuan
Taizhong
Zhangua

Hualian

TAIWAN

Jiayi

Tainan

Gaoxiong
Fengshan
Pingdong
Taidong

(China and Taiwan claim
all of each other's territory)

GUANGDONG

Guangzhou
Foshan
Dongguan

Chaozhou
Shantou

Huizhou

Shenzhen

Kowloon
Hong Kong
(Special Administrative Region)

Macau
(Special Administrative Region)

Zhuhai

South China Sea

Bashi Channel

19,686ft
13,124ft
9843ft
6562ft
3231ft
1640ft
820ft
328ft
Sea Level
-820ft
-6562ft
-13,124ft

Tropic of Cancer

Yellow River Valley

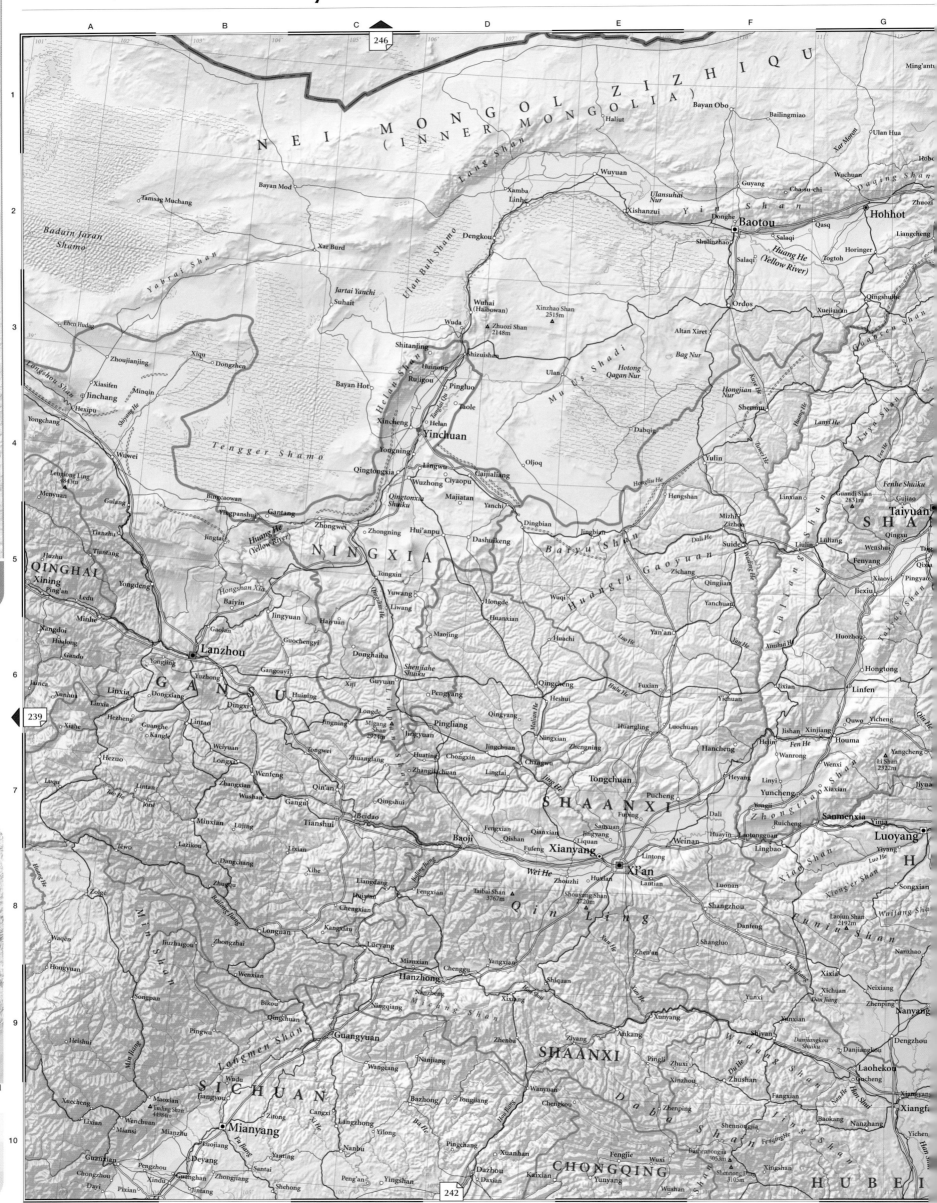

NEI MONGOL ZIZHIQU
(INNER MONGOLIA)

Badain Jaran Shamo

Yabrai Shan

Tengger Shamo

Ulan Buh Shamo

Mu Us Shadi

Helan Shan

QINGHAI

GANSU

NINGXIA

Lanzhou

SHAANXI

Xi'an
Xianyang

Qin Ling

SICHUAN

Mianyang

Min Shan

Longmen Shan

Daba Shan

CHONGQING

HUBEI

Hohhot

Baotou

Huang He
(Yellow River)

Taiyuan

Luoyang

246

242

239

Sea
Level

6000m
4000m
3000m
2000m
1000m
500m
250m
100m
-250m
-2000m
-4000m

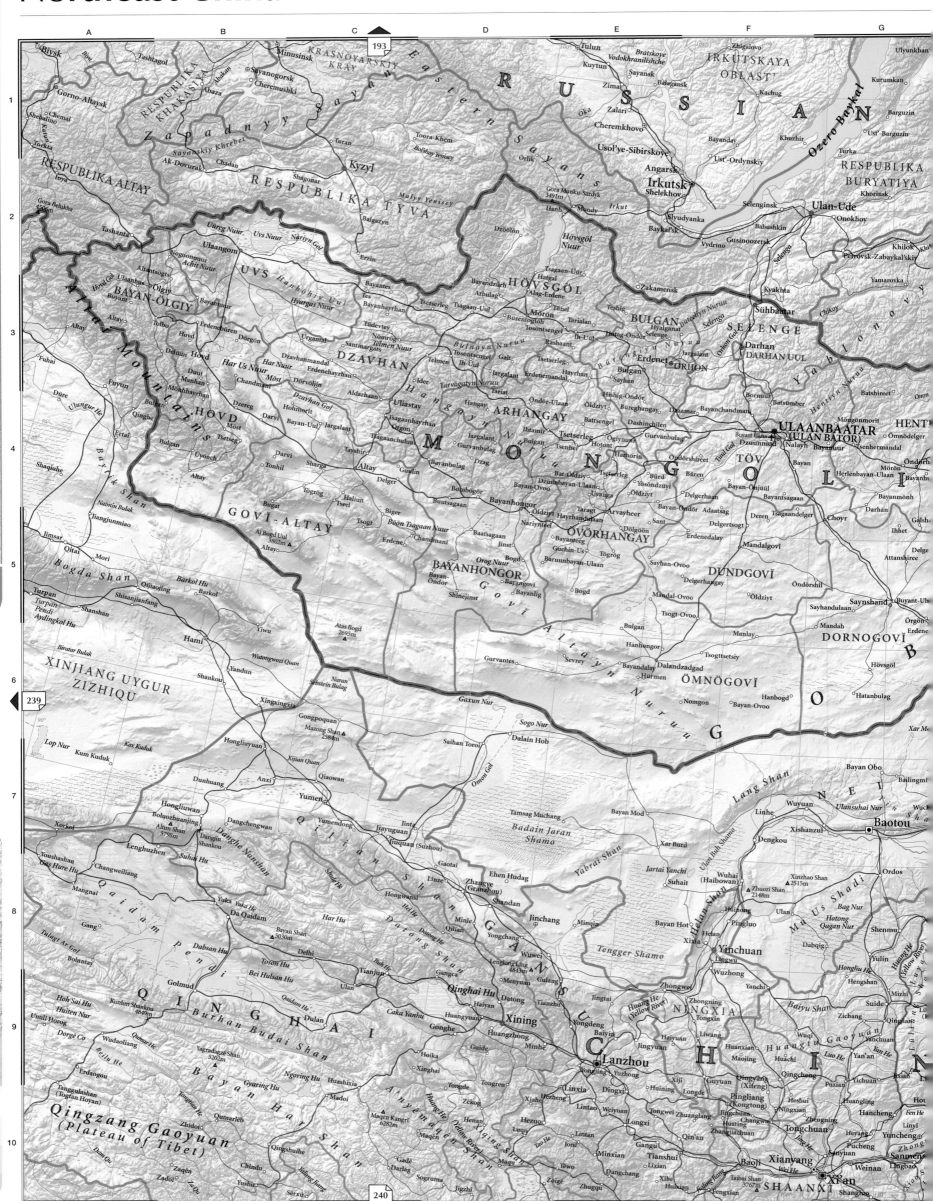

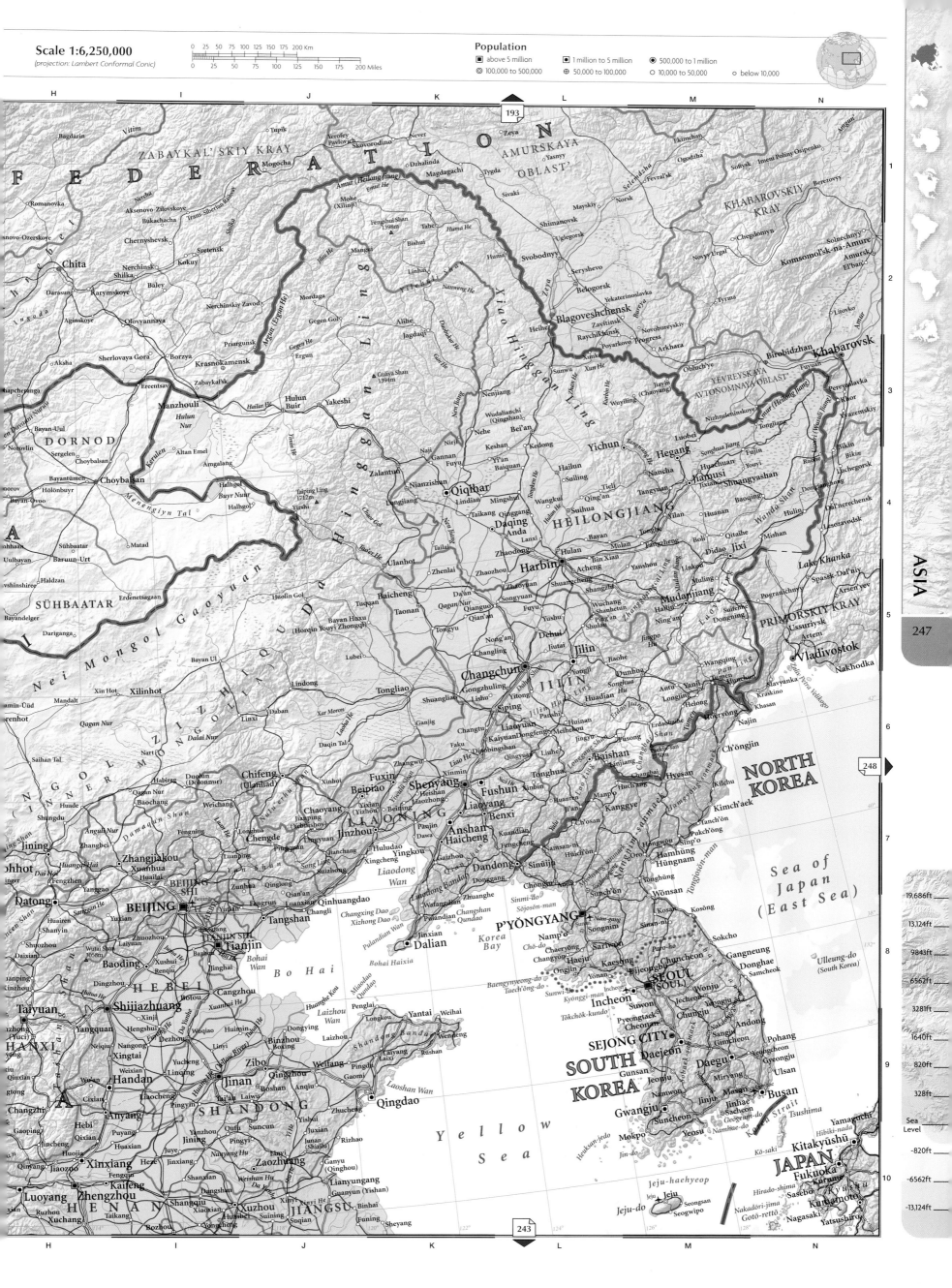

Korea & Japan

247

245

286

CHINA

NEI MONGOL ZIZHIQU (INNER MONGOLIA)

LIAONING

JILIN

HEILONGJIANG

PRIMORSKIY KRAY

RUSSIAN FEDERATION

NORTH KOREA

SOUTH KOREA

P'YŎNGYANG

SEOUL (SŎUL)

SEJONG CITY

Korea Bay

Yellow Sea

Sea of Japan (East Sea)

Korea Strait

East China Sea

Philippine Sea

JAPAN

Kyūshū

Shikoku

Place names

Changchun, Jilin, Siping, Liaoyuan, Tongliao, Shuangliao, Gongzhuling, Lishu, Jiutai, Yushu, Shulan, Shanhetun, Ping'an, Hailin, Mudan Jiang, Muling, Didao, Jixi, Misban, Linkou

Fuxin, Beipiao, Zhangwu, Kaiyuan, Tieling, Fushun, Shenyang, Anshan, Liaoyang, Benxi, Dandong, Sinŭiju, Chŏngju

Mudanjiang, Wangqing, Yanji, Tumen, Helong, Hoeryŏng, Najin, Ch'ŏngjin, Kimch'aek

Vladivostok, Nakhodka, Ussuriysk, Artem, Spassk-Dal'niy, Lake Khanka

P'yŏngyang, Namp'o, Sariwŏn, Kaesŏng, Haeju, Wŏnsan, Hamhŭng, Hŭngnam, Hyesan, Kanggye

Incheon, Seoul, Suwon, Uijeongbu, Chuncheon, Gangneung, Donghae, Samcheok, Sokcho

Ulleung-do

Daejeon, Cheonan, Cheongju, Chungju, Wonju, Jecheon, Gimcheon, Andong, Pohang, Yeongju, Gumi, Daegu, Miryang, Ulsan, Busan, Jinju, Masan, Jinhae, Sacheon, Jinju, Yeosu, Suncheon, Gwangju, Mokpo, Naju, Jeonju, Gunsan

Jeju, Seogwipo, Seongsan, Jeju-do, Jeju-haehyeop

Tsushima, Kami-Agata, Kami-Tsushima, Mitsushima

Fukuoka, Kitakyūshū, Shimonoseki, Yamaguchi, Hiroshima, Okayama, Kōbe, Ōsaka, Kyōto, Nagoya, Gifu

Nagasaki, Saga, Kurume, Ōita, Beppu, Kumamoto, Miyazaki, Kagoshima, Kōchi, Matsuyama, Tokushima, Takamatsu, Tottori, Matsue, Yonago

Sea Level
6000m
4000m
3000m
2000m
1000m
500m
250m
100m
-250m
-2000m
-4000m

ASIA

250

A B C D E F G

247

Sea of Japan (East Sea)

Liancourt Rocks
(Under South Korean control,
claimed by Japan)

Ulleung-do

SOUTH KOREA

GYEONGGI-DO
GANGWON-DO
CHUNGCHEONGBUK-DO
GYEONGSANGBUK-DO
GYEONGSANGNAM-DO
JEOLLABUK-DO

Gwangju · Pubal · Yeoju · Wonju · Pyeongchang · Jeongseon · Tonghae · Samcheok
Shindong · Yeongwol · Kohan · Taebaek · Wondeok
Keumkwang · Jecheon · Maepo · Taebaek-san 1568m · Uljin
Eumseong · Danyang · Punggi
Jeongpyeong · Chungju · Yeongju · Paegam-san 1003m
Cheongju · Yecheon · Pyeonghae
Daecheong-ho · Gaeun · Hamchang · Andong-ho · Yeongyang
Boeun · Sangju · Andong · Yeongdeok
Daejeon · Okcheon · Sangju · Seonsan
Gimcheon · Kumi · Bohyeon-san 1915m · Heunghae
Yeongdong · Waegan · Yeongcheon · Pohang
Muju · Gimcheon · DAEGU SI · Hayang · Gyeongju · Guryongpo
Jangsu · Deogyu-san 1614m · Goryeong · DAEGU · Gyeongsan · Oedong
Hamyang · Hapcheon · Cheongdo · Ulsan
Sancheong · Changnyeong · Miryang · Samnangjin · Yangsan
Jinyang-ho · Jiri-san 1915m · Uiryeong · Hanam · Jinyeong · Chang-an
Hadong · Jinju · Gaya · Changwon · Gimhae · Gijang
Gwangyang · Namhae · Sacheon · Masan · Jinhae · **Busan**
Yeosu · Yeocheon · Namhae-do · Goseong · Tongyeong · Geoje · Geoje-do
Toisan · Geumo-do · Geumpo · Geogeum-do
Sori-do

Korea Strait

Kami-Agata · Kami-Tsushima
Mitsushima · *Tsushima*
Kō-saki · Izuhara

Higashi-suidō

Matsue · Oki-shotō · Dōgo · Saigō · Dōzen · Nakano-shima · Chiburi-jima
Oki-kaikyō

Shimane-hantō · Jizō-zaki · Sakaiminato · Nakano-tori · Hamasaka · Aoya
Hino-misaki · Hirata · Taisha · Shinji-Ko · Yasugi · Yonago · Dai-sen 1729m · Kurayoshi · **TOTTORI** · Totto
Izumo · Kisuki · Yokota · Kōfu · Katsuyama · Hyōno-sen 1510m · Wakasa
Gōtsu · Oda · Sanbe-san 1126m · Tombara · Dōgo-yama 1269m · Tsuyama · Chizu
Hamada · Gō-gawa · **SHIMANE** · Miyoshi · Shōbara · Niimi · **OKAYAMA** · Takahashi · Tsuyama · Yamaza
Masuda · Susa · Abu · Kake · Garyū-san 1223m · HIROSHIMA · Ibara · Okayama · Kurashiki · Bizen · Tatsu
Tsuwano · Kanmuri-yama 339m · Higashi-Hiroshima · Fuchū · Fukuyama · Tamano · Tonosho · Takamatsu
Nagato · YAMAGUCHI · Ōtake · **Hiroshima** · Mihara · Onomichi · Saidai · KAGAWA · Hiketa · Na
Yamaguchi · Mine · Ogōri · Shin-nanyō · Tokuyama · Kure · Takehara · Imabari · Hōjō · Marugame · Zentsuji · **Tokushima**
Shimonoseki · Onoda · Hofu · Kudamatsu · Hikari · Yanai · Naga-shima · Niihama · Kawanoe · Ikeda · Tsurugi-san 1955m
Kitakyūshū · Ube · Hikari · Ya-shima · Heigun-jima · Matsuyama · Kanega-mori 1896m · **TOKUSHIMA** · Komatsushima
Nakama · Nōgata · Yukuhashi · Nakatsu · Ōzu · EHIME · KŌCHI · Tosa · Kōchi · Aki
Fukuoka · Mizuka · Tagawa · Buzen · Usa · Kitsuki · Iyo · Kuma · Yawatahama · Yusuhara · Nankoku · Mu
Karatsu · Kasuga · FUKUOKA · Amagi · Hiko-san 1200m · Hita · Beppu · **Ōita** · Uwajima · Onogara-yama 1151m · Nakamura · Kaina
Genkai-nada · Onojō · Ogōri · Kurume · Kurogi · ŌITA · Bungo-Ono · Usuki · Tsukumi · Sukumo · Tosa-Shimizu
Iki · Iki-suidō · Matsubara · Yame · Yamaga · Kikuchi · Takamori · Taketa · Sobo-san 1757m · Saiki · Inano-yama 865m · Ashizuri-misaki
Katsumoto · SAGA · Taku · Kashima · Yanagawa · Kumamoto · Kunimi-dake 1739m · Kyūshū-sanchi · Okino-shima

Fukuoka · Yobuko · Imari · Takeo · Ariake-kai · Ōmuta · KUMAMOTO · Nobeoka
NAGASAKI · Sasebo · Isahaya · Shimabara · **Kumamoto** · Ichifusa-yama 1727m · Hyūga
Arikawa · Ōmura · Minamishimabara · Uto · Yunomae · Tsuno
Nagasaki · Kuchinotsu · Misumi · Minamata · Saito · Takanabe
Nomo-zaki · Shimo-jima · Ushibuka · Izumi · Isa · MIYAZAKI · Kobayashi · Miyazaki
Amakusa-nada · Naga-shima · Akune · Hitoyoshi · Kirishima-yama 1700m
Satsuma-Sendai · Miyanojō · Kokubu · Miyakonojō · Nichinan
Kami-Koshiki-jima · Kushikino · KAGOSHIMA · Miyakonojō
Kagoshima · On-take 1117m · Tarumizu · Shibushi · Kushima
Shimo-Koshiki-jima · Noma-zaki · Mainamisatsuma · Shibushi-wan
Makurazaki · Ibusuki · Kanoya · Uchinoura
Yamagawa · Satsuma-hantō · Tōi-misaki

Kyūshū

East China Sea

Gotō-rettō · Nakadōri-jima · Narao · Fukue · Fukue-jima · Ōse-zaki
Uku-jima · Ojika-jima · Hirado-shima

Philippine Sea

Sata-misaki · Ōsumi-kaikyō
Uji-guntō · Kusagaki-guntō · Kuro-shima · Iō-jima · Take-shima · Mage-shima · Nishinoomote · Tanega-shima · Minamitane
Kuchinoerabu-jima · Kamiyaku · Minamitane · Yaku-shima

Seto-naikai

Suō-nada · *Iyo-nada* · *Hōyo-kaikyō* · *Bungo-suidō* · *Tosa-wan*

Inset:
1 *East China Sea* · Sakishima-shotō · Miyako-shotō · Irabu-jima · Minna-jima · Hirara · Miyako-jima · Tarama-jima
Yonaguni · Yonaguni-jima · Yaeyama-shotō · Hirakubo-saki · **OKINAWA** · Ishigaki-jima
Iriomote-jima · Ishigaki · Kuro-shima · *Philippine Sea*
Paimi-saki · Hateruma-jima

Scale 1:3,250,000
0 10 20 40 Km
0 10 20 40 Miles

245

6000m
4000m
3000m
2000m
1000m
500m
250m
100m
Sea Level
−250m
−2000m
−4000m

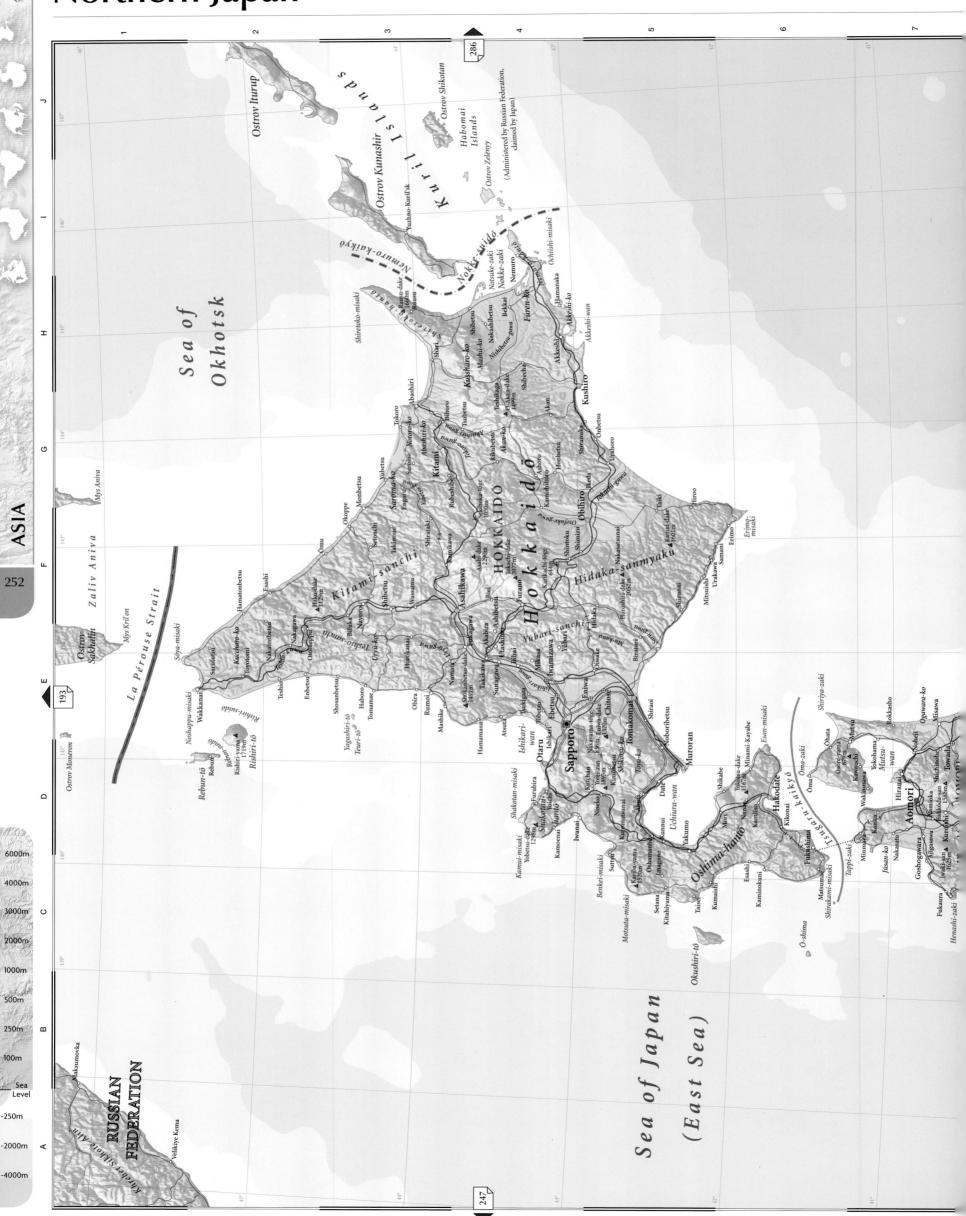

ASIA

252

Sea of
Okhotsk

Sea of Japan
(East Sea)

RUSSIAN
FEDERATION

HOKKAIDŌ

Sapporo

Hakodate

Aomori

Kuril Islands

Ostrov Iturup

Ostrov Kunashir

Ostrov Shikotan

Habomai
Islands

Ostrov Zelëny

(Administered by Russian Federation,
claimed by Japan)

Zaliv Aniva

La Pérouse Strait

Ostrov
Sakhalin

Ostrov Moneron

Mys Aniva

Mys Krilon

Kitami-sanchi

Teshio-sanchi

Yūbari-sanchi

Hidaka-sanmyaku

6000m
4000m
3000m
2000m
1000m
500m
250m
100m
Sea
Level
-250m
-2000m
-4000m

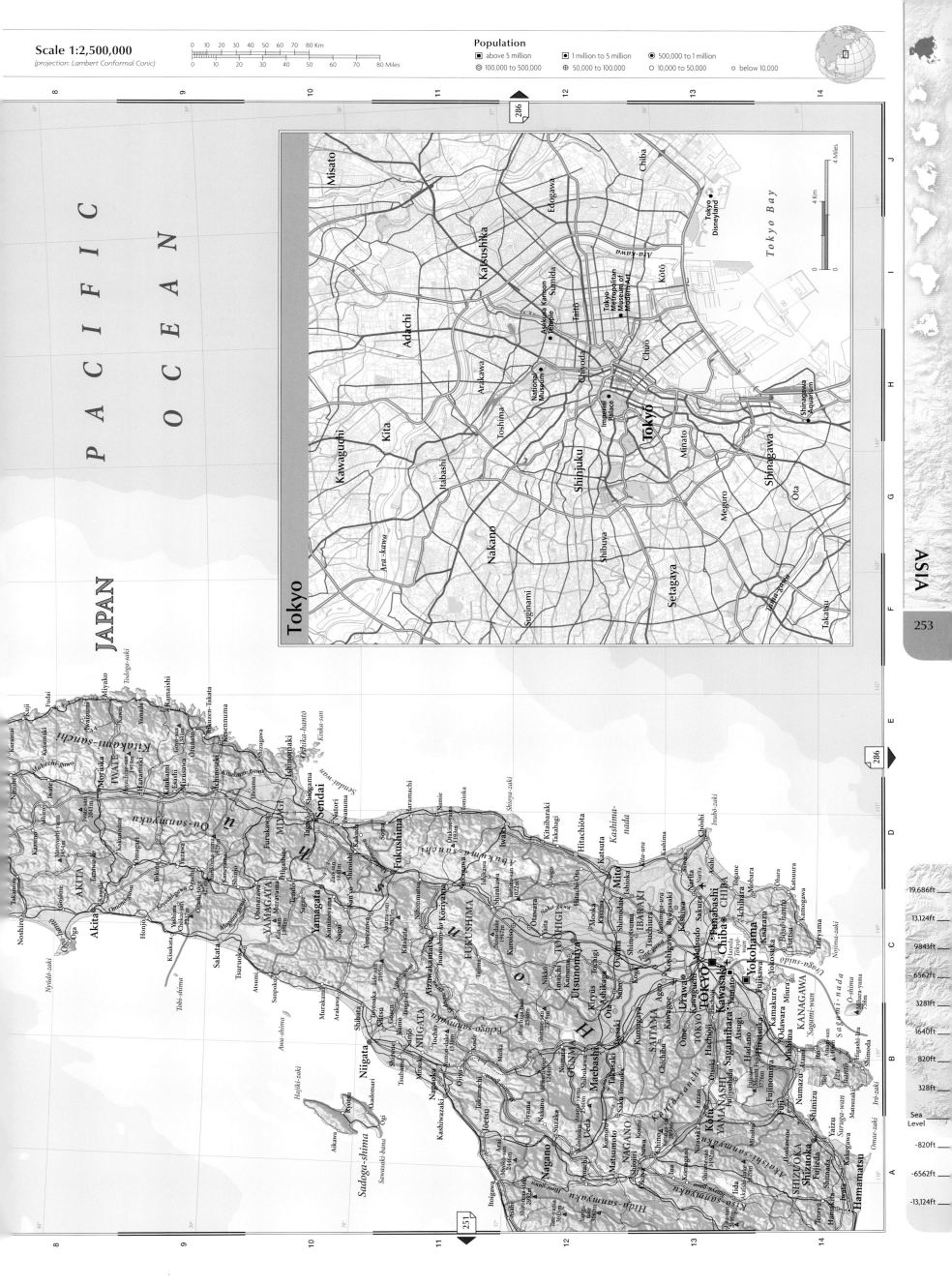

239

234

289

Map labels:

Himalayas · *CHINA*

Lhasa · Nangxian · Mainling · Rawu · Zigong · Neijiang · Chongqing · Zhangjiajie · Yueyang · Changde · Nanchang · Jingdezhen · Lanxi · Jinhua

Xigazê · Gyangzê · Xichang · Yibin · Luzhou · Zhishou · Yiyang · Changsha · Xiangtan · Zhuzhou · Liling · Pingxiang · Yong'an · Fuzhou · Shangrao

Mount Everest 8848m · Gangtok · Kunming · Guiyang · Kaili · Duyun · Guilin · Liuzhou · Hezhou · Shaoguan · Meizhou · Xiamen

THIMPHU · BHUTAN · Darjiling · Nanning · Guangzhou · Dongguan · Kowloon · Hong Kong (Special Administrative Region) · Gaoxiong

BANGLADESH · DHAKA · Khulna · INDIA · Kolkata · Chittagong

MYANMAR (BURMA) · Mandalay · NAY PYI TAW · LAOS · HA NOI · Hai Phong

Bay of Bengal · Sittwe · Chiang Mai · VIANGCHAN (VIENTIANE) · Vinh · Gulf of Tongking · Hainan Dao

SOUTH CHINA SEA

Yangon (Rangoon) · Gulf of Mottama · THAILAND · KRUNG THEP (BANGKOK) · VIETNAM · Huê · Đà Nẵng · PARACEL ISLANDS (disputed)

Andaman Islands (to India) · Andaman Sea · Gulf of Thailand · CAMBODIA · PHNUM PENH (PHNOM PENH) · Hồ Chí Minh · Nha Trang · Cam Ranh · SPRATLY ISLANDS (disputed)

Nicobar Islands (to India) · Phuket · George Town · Kuala Terengganu · Kota Kinabalu

Strait of Malacca · Medan · MALAYSIA · BRUNEI · BANDAR SERI BEGAWAN · Borneo

KUALA LUMPUR · PUTRAJAYA · SINGAPORE · Kuching · Kalimantan

INDIAN OCEAN · Sumatera (Sumatra) · Palembang · INDONESIA · Java Sea (Laut Jawa) · Makassar

JAKARTA · Bandung · Semarang · Surabaya · Jawa (Java) · Bali · Nusa Tenggara

Elevation scale:

6000m · 4000m · 3000m · 2000m · 1000m · 500m · 250m · 100m · Sea Level · -250m · -2000m · -4000m

Scale 1:15,500,000
(projection: Mercator)

0 50 100 150 200 250 300 350 400 Km
0 50 100 150 200 250 300 400 Miles

Population
■ above 5 million
□ 1 million to 5 million
◉ 500,000 to 1 million
◎ 100,000 to 500,000
⊕ 50,000 to 100,000
○ 10,000 to 50,000
∘ below 10,000

ASIA

255

Taipei

Wuku
Shihlin
Luchou
Martyrs Shrine
Nei Hu
Kuku
Confucius Temple
Keelung
Sanchung
Datung
Hsingtien Temple
T'aipei Songshan Airport
Tiding
Sinzhuang
Sanchong
Taipei (Taibei)
Sungshan
Taï Shan
Wanhua
Zhongcheng
Sinyi
Shinjuang
Lungshan Temple
National Theatre
Daan
Linguang
Banqiao
Hsin Chuang
National Museum of History
Banchiao
Shu Lin
Zhongher
Yungho
Wantang
Tucheng
Fang Liao
Jhonghe
Wunshan
T'aipei Zoo
Sindian

0 ___ Km
2 Miles

East China Sea
Nansei-shotō
Naze
Amami-ō-shima
Okinawa-shotō
Okinawa
Naha
Senkaku-shotō
Sakishima-shotō
Miyake-jima
Ishigaki-jima
Iriomote-jima

Huangyan
Wenzhou
Jilong
TAIBEI (TAIPEI)
Hualian
TAIWAN
Gaoxiong

PACIFIC
OCEAN

Tropic of Cancer

Philippine
Sea

Luzon
Tuguegarao
Ilagan
Baguio
Dagupan
Cabanatuan
Angeles
MANILA
Lucena
Batangas
Naga
Catanduanes Island
Legazpi City
Mindoro
Sibuyan Sea
Calbayog
Samar
Roxas City
Panay Island
Tacloban
Leyte
PHILIPPINES
Iloilo
Cadiz
Cebu
Negros
Bohol Sea
Butuan
Iligan
Cagayan de Oro
Bislig
Moro Gulf
Zamboanga
Lebak
Mindanao
Davao
Davao Gulf
General Santos
Sulu Archipelago

Babuyan Islands
Babuyan Channel

Yap
COLONIA

Mariana Islands

HAGÅTÑA (AGANA)
GUAM
(to USA)

MICRONESIA

Chuuk Islands

Babeldaob
MELEKEOK
PALAU

Celebes Sea
Kepulauan Sangir
Kepulauan Talaud
Manado
Gorontalo
Pulau Morotai
Ternate
Pulau Halmahera
Pulau Waigeo
Pulau Misool
Sorong
Jazirah Doberai
Pulau Biak
Pulau Yapen
Teluk Cenderawasih
Jayapura
Vanimo
Ninigo Group
Hermit Islands
Admiralty Islands
Manus Island
Lorengau
St. Matthias Group
New Hanover
Kavieng
Lihir Group
New Ireland
Taron

Molucca Sea
(Laut Maluku)
Laut Halmahera
Selat Dampier
Pulau Waigeo
Teluk Berau
Fakfak
Wahai
Pulau Seram
Waflia
Sulawesi (Celebes)
Kepulauan Banggai
Danau Towuti
Kendari
Pulau Buton
Ambon
Pulau Buru
Maluku (Moluccas)
Pulau Sula
Kepulauan Sula
Laut Seram
Puncak Jaya 5040m
Tembagapura
Amamapare
Pegunungan Maoke
New Guinea
Lumi
Green River
Sepik
Wewak
Angoram
Bogia
Karkar Island
Madang
Gloucester
Kimbe
Anepmete
New Britain
Bismarck Archipelago
Bismarck Sea
Rabaul
Witu Islands
Pomio
Toriu

INDONESIA

Banda Sea
(Laut Banda)
Kepulauan Tukangbesi
Kepulauan Bonerate
Kepulauan Alor
Pulau Wetar
Kepulauan Leti
DILI
EAST TIMOR
Timor
Lesser Sunda Islands
Nikiniki
Kupang
Pulau Roti
Savu Sea
Pulau Sawu

Pulau Kai
Kepulauan Aru
Pulau Yamdena
Kepulauan Tanimbar
Pulau Yos Sudarso
Sungai Digul
Sungai Mamberamo
Tabubil
Kiunga
Lake Murray
Weam
Emeti
Oriomo
Daru
Kiwai Island
Mari
Torres Strait

Central Range
Mount Wilhelm 4509m
Mendi
Mount Hagen
Goroka
Lae
Vitiaz Strait
Sialum
Finschhafen
Huon Gulf
Solomon Sea
PAPUA NEW GUINEA
Kerema
Hisiu
PORT MORESBY
Owen Stanley Range
Mount Suckling 3676m
Popondetta
Tufi
Kupiano
Magarida
Alotau
D'Entrecasteaux Islands
Kiriwina Islands
Woodlark Island
Guasopa
Louisiade Archipelago
Tagula Island

Arafura Sea

Timor Sea
Melville Island
Croker Island
Bathurst Island
Van Diemen Gulf
Darwin
Adelaide River
South Goulburn Island
Arnhem Land
Nhulunbuy
Gulf of Carpentaria
Wessel Islands
Moa Island
Prince of Wales Island
Cape York
Cape York Peninsula
Coral Sea

AUSTRALIA

Equator

19,686ft
13,124ft
9843ft
6562ft
3281ft
1640ft
820ft
328ft
Sea Level
-820ft
-6562ft
-13,124ft

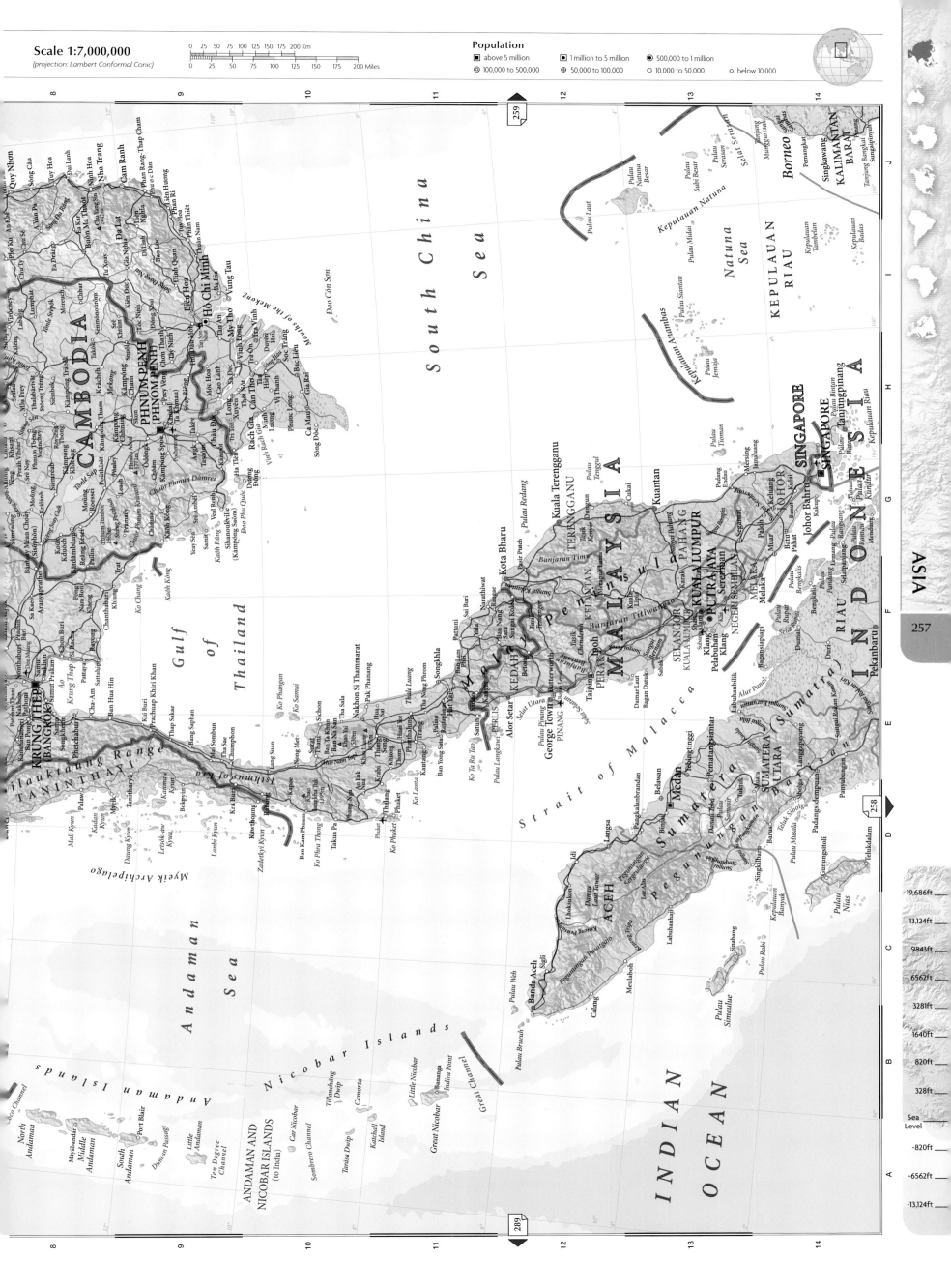

Western Maritime Southeast Asia

Andaman Sea

Nicobar Islands (to India)

Tarāsa Dwip
Camorta
Katchall Island
Little Nicobar
Great Nicobar
Bananga
Indira Point
Great Channel

THAILAND

SOUTH

MAL

MAL

Ao Luk Nua
Khao Luang
Pak Phanang
Krabi
Thung Song
Nakhon Si Thammarat
Hua Sai
Phuket
Ko Phuket
Thalang
Phuket
Khlong Thom
Huai Yot
Phatthalung
Ko Lanta
Trang
Palian
Thale Luang
Tha Nong Phrom
Songkhla
Kantang
Ban Yong Sata
Ko Ta Ru Tao
Satun
Hat Yai
Pattani
Sai Buri
Sadao
Ban Lam Phai
Yala
Narathiwat
Kangar
Ban Nang Sata
Rangae
Sungai Kolok
Pasir Puteh
Pulau Langkawi
Alor Setar
PERLIS
Betong
Kota Bharu
Pulau Pinang
Pulau Weh
Pulau Brueuh
Banda Aceh
Sigli
Butterworth
George Town
KEDAH
Tasik Temengor
KELANTAN
TERENGGANU
Kuala Terengganu
PINANG
Bayan Lepas
Selat Selat
Tasik Chenderoh
Dungun
Pulau Tenggul
Idi
Lhoksukon
ACEH
Calang
Taiping
Ipoh
PERAK
Kuala Lipis
Cukai
Langsa
Danau Laut Tawar
Damar Laut
PAHANG
Kuantan
Meulaboh
Pangkalanbrandan
Bagan Datuk
Sungai Pahang
Karak
Labuhanhaji
Belawan
Sabak
SELANGOR
Binjai
Medan
Tebingtinggi
KUALA LUMPUR
KUALA LUMPUR
PUTRAJAYA
Pulau Tioman
Klang
Shah Alam
Kepulauan Anambas
Pulau Siantan
Pematangsiantar
Pelabuhan Klang
Seremban
NEGERI SEMBILAN
Segamat
Padang Endau
Pulau Jemaja
Pulau Midai
Samosir
Danau Toba
MELAKA
Mersing
Tuktuk
Labuhanbilik
Melaka
JOHOR
Pulau Rabi
Sibolga
Sungai Kuala
Muara
Paloh
Keluang
Natuna Sea
Singkilbaru
Barus
Teluk Sibolga
Langgapayung
Muar
Batu Pahat
Pulau Rupat
Jamaluang
Pulau Musala
Kepulauan Banyak
Padangsidempuan
Benut
Kulai
Dumai
Bengkalis
Johor Bahru
SINGAPORE
Gunungsitoli
SUMATERA UTARA
Panyabungan
Duri
Kukup
SINGAPORE
Pulau Bintan
Pulau Nias
Pekanbaru
Selatpanjang
Batam
Tanjungpinang
KEPULAUAN RIAU
Telukdalam
Bangkinang
Sungai Kampar
Mendung
Kundur
Kepulauan Riau
Natal
Airbangis
RIAU
Kepulauan Tambelan
Pulau Simeulue
Bawa Ofuloa
Pulau Pini
Pulau Tanahmasa
Taluk
Rengat
Sapat
Pulau Pejantan
Kepulauan Batu Lambak
Bukittinggi
Sungai Indragiri
Tungkal
Kepulauan Badas
Padangpanjang
Danau Maninjau
Danau Singkarak
Sungai Kuantan
Kualatungkal
Tiku
Kepulauan Lingga
Pulau Lingga
Pulau Singkep
Padang
Solok
Sungaidareh
Kota Baru
Selat Berhala
Pulau Siberut
Muarasigep
Sungaipenuh
Labu
Pulau Singkep
Painan
Tarusan
JAMBI
Selat Karimata
Muarabungo
Muaratembesi
Jambi
Selat Mentawai
Taileleu
SUMATERA BARAT
Gunung Kerinci
3804m
Bangko
Belinyu
Teluk Kampa
Pulau Sipura
Pasirganting
Danau Kerinci
Merangin
Sarolangun
Mentok
Tanjung Raya
Sungai Tembesi
Pangkalpinang
Pulau Bangka
Pasaput
Pulau Pagai Utara
Babat
Sungsang
Koba
BANGKA-BELITUNG
Pulau Pagai Selatan
Surulangun
SUMATERA
Tanjungpandan
Tiop
Lubuklinggau
Muarabeliti
Air Musi
Palembang
Pulau Belitung
Selat Sanding
SELATAN
Perabumulih
Teluk Kait
Pulau Lepar
Tebingtinggi
Lahat
Muaraenim
Toboali
Pulau Gaspar
Bengkulu
BENGKULU
Air Ogan
Sungaibuntu
Tanjung Lumut
Danau Ranau
Bukitkemuning
Greater
Kotabumi
Pulau Enggano
Krui
LAMPUNG
Metro
Way Sekampung
Bandarlampung
Kepulauan Seribu
Soekarno-Hatta
JAKARTA
Pulau Rakata
Serang
JAKARTA RAY
Pulau Sangiang
Tangerang
Bekasi
Karawang
Rangkasbitung
Citeureup
Purwakarta
Pulau Panaitan
BANTEN
Bogor
Danau Subang
Cikawung
Sukabumi
Cianjur
Cipanas
JAWA BARAT
Pelabuhan Ratu
Garut
Genteng
Taraj
Cikal

Strait of Malacca

Pegunungan Barisan

Equator

INDIAN OCEAN

Selat Johor
Selat Johor

South China Sea

Christmas Island (to Australia)

Singapore

Zoological Gardens
Upper Peirce Reservoir
Central Catchment Nature Reserve
Ang Mo Kio
Buangkok
Tampines
Bukit Timah Nature Reserve
MacRitchie Reservoir
Kallang
Chia Keng
Jurong East
Joa Payoh
Tai Seng
Tan Tock Seng
K.G. Potong Pasir
Bedok
Bukit Timah
Raffles Park
Kandang Kerbau
Geylang Serai
Clementi
University of Singapore
Queenstown
National Stadium
National Museum
Cathedral
City Hall
Raffles Hotel
Pasir Panjang
Singapore
Marina South
Buona Vista
Telok Blangah
Cable Car
Pulau Brani
Keppel Harbour
Straits of Singapore
Sentosa Island
Palau Bukum
Palau Sakijang Bendera
Palau Tembakul

0   3 Km
0   3 Miles

6000m
4000m
3000m
2000m
1000m
500m
250m
100m
Sea Level
-250m
-2000m
-4000m

Scale 1:7,000,000

(projection: Mercator)

0 25 50 75 100 125 150 175 200 Km
0 25 50 75 100 125 150 175 200 Miles

Population

- ■ above 5 million
- ▣ 1 million to 5 million
- ◉ 500,000 to 1 million
- ◎ 100,000 to 500,000
- ⊕ 50,000 to 100,000
- ○ 10,000 to 50,000
- ∘ below 10,000

263

274

260

C H I N A   S E A

M A L A Y S I A

Sulu Sea

PHILIPPINES

Mindanao

Sindangan
Labason
Kabasalan Pagadian
Liloy
Siocon Tungawan
Dumagasa Point
Zamboanga
Isabela Lamitan
Moro Gulf

Balabac Island
Balabac Strait
Cagayan de Tawi Tawi
Pangutaran Group
Samales Group
Jolo Jolo
Tapul Group

Pulau Balambangan
Pulau Banggi
Kudat
Tiga Tarok
Teluk Paitan
Kanibongan

Tuaran
Gunung Kinabalu 4101m
Kota Kinabalu
Teluk Kimanis
Ranau
Sungai Labuk
Tambunan
SABAH
Keningau
Tenom
Kuala Penyu
Sungai Kinabatangan
Sandakan
Lahad Datu
Teluk Lahad Datu
Tawitawi
Balimbing
Tawitawi Group
Sibutu Passage
Sibutu

LABUAN
Pulau Labuan
Labuan
Brunei Bay
BANDAR SERI BEGAWAN
BRUNEI
Kuala Belait
Miri
Batang Baram

Sungai Sugut
Banjaran Crocker
Banjaran Brassey
Tawau
Pulau Timbun Mata
Pulau Sebatik
Pulau Bum Bum

Tanjung Payong
Loagan Bunut
Batang Tatau
Batang Baram
KALIMANTAN UTARA
Sungai Sembakung
Teluk Sebuku
Bunyu
Pulau Mandul
Pulau Bunyu
Tarakan
Pulau Tarakan
Pulau Mapat

C e l e b e s   S e a

Sulu Archipelago

Bintulu
Tanjung Budu
Kampung Sirik
Pulau Bruit
Tanjung Pasir
Mukah
Matu
SARAWAK
Balui
Belaga
Sungai Perindua
Sungai Sesayap
Tanjungbatu
Tanjung Selor
Teluk Pantai
Tanjungredeb
Sungai Kayan
Sungai Bahau
Pulau Maratua

Sibu
Sarikei
Kanowit
Batang Rajang
Batang Baleh
Metulang
Sungai Kayan
Sungai Keai
Peguungan Sambaliung
Teluk Sangkulirang

Sematan
Tanjung Datu
Teluk Datu
Kuching
Bau
Serian
Sri Aman
Batang Lupar
B o r n e o
Kapuas Mountains
Gunung Menyapa 2000m
Muarawahau
Sangkulirang
Sepasu
Gunung Antu 750m
Salumpaga
Oan
Teluk Bilang
Teluk Kwandang
Tolitoli
Leok
Teluk Paleleh

Singkawang
Bengkayang
Perigi
Sidas
Ngaipinyuh
Sungai Sai
Danau Luar
Danau Genali
Semitau
Kualakeriau
KALIMANTAN TIMUR
Peguunungan Muller
Pegunungan Schwaner
Gunung Malino 2499m
Tompo
Teluk Dampal
Lanu
GORONTALO
Danau Limboto
Kuandang
Gorontalo

Pontianak
Tanjung Putus
Sungai Landak
Sungai Kapuas
Sanggau
Sintang
K a l i m a n t a n
Nangapinoh
Nangaserawai
Longiram
Danau Melintang
Danau Semayang
Tenggarong
Tanjung Ayu
Molosipat
Tate
Towera
Donggala
Equator
Kepulauan Togian
Pulau Batudaka
Selat Walea
Maliku
T o m i n i   T e l u k

Pulau Subi Besar
Pulau Serasan
Selat Serasan
Tanjung Mungguresak
Pulau Maya
Pulau Karimata
Ketapang
Bukit Raya 2278m
Muarajuloi
Kunyi
Muaratewe
Tumbangsenamang
Nangatayap
Kualakuayan
Bawan
Memala
Muarakaman
Samarinda
Danau Jempang
Lohjanan
Sangasanga
Tanjung Bayur
Balikpapan
Waru
Teluk Balikpapan
Karosa
Palu
Lambogo
Pakuli
Danau Lindu
Poso
Pandiri
Pompanga
Tentena
Danau Poso
Baturebe
SULAWESI TENGAH
Kembani
Pulau Peleng
Pelek
Luwuk
Selat Peleng
Kepulauan Banggai

Kendawangan
Pulau Bawal
Pulau Gelam
Kotawaringin
Pangkalanbuun
Pegunungan Meratus
KALIMANTAN TENGAH
Kasongan
Kuala
Palangkaraya
Tanjung
Amuntai
SULAWESI BARAT
Mamuju
Babana
Gimpu
Tamba
Pompanga
Masamba
Danau Matana
Danau Towuti
Mahalona
Teluk Towori
Kepulauan Salabangka
Pulau Manui

Sampit
Danau Sembuu
Negara
Rantau
Kandangan
Kotabaru
Malunda
Wotu
Kolaka
Wawonii
Pulau Wowoni

I N D O N E S I A

Teluk Kumai
Teluk Sampit
Teluk Sebangan
Banjarmasin
Martapura
Pelaihari
Karambu
Pulau Sebuku
Pulau Laut
SULAWESI SELATAN
Majene
Parepare
Polewali
Enrekang
Danau Sidenreng
Danau Tempe
Singkang
Anabanua
Watampone
Rantepao
Asera
Kendari
SULAWESI TENGGARA
Kakea
Selat Staring

S u n d a   I s l a n d s

J a v a   S e a   (L a u t   J a w a)

Pulau Karimunjawa
Pulau Bawean
Pulau Masalembo Besar
Pulau Karamain
Kepulauan Laut Kecil
Teluk Lebani
Sulawesi (Celebes)
Kepulauan Pabbiring
Maros
Makassar
Takalar
Bulukumba
Jeneponto
Benteng
Pulau Kabia
Pulau Muna
Baubau
Kamaru
Selat Tioro
Selat Kabaena
Pulau Kabaena
Lasihao
Bondeipu

J a w a   (J a v a)

Cirebon
Pemalang
Brebes
Tegal
Pekalongan
Kudus
Pati
Tayu
Tuban
Pulau Madura
Ambunten
Sumenep
Kepulauan Kangean
Pulau Kangean
Kepulauan Sabalana
Pulau Tanahjampea
Pulau Kalao
Pulau Bonerate
Kepulauan Bonerate
Pulau Batuata

Batang
Semarang
Purwodadi
Blora
Cepu
Bojonegoro
Bangkalan
Surabaya
Pulau Sapudi
Kepulauan Tengah
Kepulauan Kalaotoa

B a l i   S e a   (L a u t   B a l i)

F l o r e s   S e a   (L a u t   F l o r e s)

JAWA TENGAH
Magelang
Salatiga
Bawen
Purwokerto
Cilacap
Purworejo
Yogyakarta
YOGYAKARTA
Bantul
Surakarta
Madiun
Kediri
Klaten
Ponorogo
Blitar
Tulungagung
Popoh
JAWA TIMUR
Jombang
Mojokerto
Malang
Pasuruan
Probolinggo
Bondowoso
Gunung Raung 3332m
Situbondo
Banyuwangi
Jember
Gunung Semeru 3676m
Lumajang
Teluk Grajagan
Nusa Barung
Grajakan
Negara
Singaraja
Tejakula
Bali
Karangasem
Denpasar
Kuta
Nusa Penida
Ngurah Rai
Tumajang
Selat Bali
Tabanan
Teluk Tawang
Teluk Penyu

N U S A   T E N G G A R A   B A R A T
Pulau Moyo
Kubu
Bayan
Alas
Sumbawabesar
Dompu
Pulau Sangeang
Raba
Pulau Komodo
Lubuhanbajo
Ruteng
Maumere
Endeh
Kepulauan Solor
Larantuka
Bima
Mataram
Pulau Lombok
Taliwang
Sumbawa
Gunung Tambora 2821m
Gunung Takan 1400m
Lunyuk
Teluk Saleh
Teluk Sanggar
Gunung Api 1949m
Pota
Gerampi
Bajawa
Selat Geliting
Selat Alas
Selat Sumbawa

N u s a   T e n g g a r a   (L e s s e r   S u n d a   I s l a n d s)

Bondokodi
Waikabubak
Waingapu
NUSA TENGGARA TIMUR
Pulau Sumba
Baing
Selat Sumba
S a v u   S e a
Kepulauan Sawu
Pulau Sawu
Selat Roti
Pulau Roti
Baa
Pulau Semau
Selat Raijua
Pulau Raijua

19,686ft
13,124ft
9843ft
6562ft
3281ft
1640ft
820ft
328ft
Sea Level
-820ft
-6562ft
-13,124ft

Makassar Strait (Selat Makassar)

Teluk Bone

Flores

Eastern Maritime Southeast Asia

A B C D E F G

PHILIPPINES
Mindanao
Palimbang · Mount Busa · Surallah · Malita
Parker Volcano · General Santos
Kiamba · Glan · Jose Abad Santos
Tinaca Point · Cape San Agustin
Sarangani Islands

Kota Kinabalu · Gunung Kinabalu 4101m
Ranau · Sungai Sugut · Sandakan
MALAYSIA · Tambunan · Sungai Labuk
LABUAN · Keningau · Teluk Labuk
Labuan · **SABAH** · Lahad Datu
Pulau Labuan · Tenom · Teluk Lahad Datu
Kuala Penyu · Sungai Segama
Bandar Seri Begawan · Pulau Timbun Mata
Kuala Belait · Tawau · Pulau Bum Bun
BANDAR SERI BEGAWAN · Pulau Sebatik
BRUNEI · Teluk Sebuku · Pulau Mandul
Miri · Sungai Baram · Pulau Bunyu
Sungai Sembakung · Tarakan
Celebes Sea
Tawitawi · Balimbing · Tawitawi Group
Sibutu · Sibutu Passage
Sulu Archipelago
Jolo · Jolo · Samales Group
Pangutaran Group · Tapul Group

Kepulauan Kawio
Kepulauan Nanusa
Pulau Karakelong · Kepulauan Talaud
Melanguane · Pulau Kaburuang
Pulau Salibabu · Damau

Loagan Bunut · Sungai Kayan
SARAWAK · **KALIMANTAN UTARA**
Metulang · Tanjung Selor
Borneo · Tanjungbatu · Pulau Maratua
Gunung Menyapa 2000m
Muarawahau · Sangkulirang
KALIMANTAN TIMUR · Sepasu · Gunung Antu 750m
Tahuna · Pulau Salibabu
Pulau Sangihe
Kepulauan Sangir
Selat Bangka · Pulau Bangka
Ulu · Pulau Siau
Pulau Tahulandang
Kepulauan Loloda Utara
Galela · Tobelo
Tanjung Sopi · Pulau Morotai
Sabatai · Tanjung Lelai
Bobopayo · Iga · Akelamo · Dodaga
Pediwang · Buli · Teluk Buli
Ternate · Pulau Ternate · Pulau Tidore · Bicol
Soasiu · Patani
MALUKU UTARA · Pulau Makian · Teluk Weda
Pulau Halmahera
Mafa · **Laut Halmahe**

Equator · Kalimantan
Muarajuloi · Kunyi · Longiram · Danau Semayang
Danau Melintang · Danau Jempang
Samarinda · Tenggarong · Tanjung Ayu
Lohjanan · Sangasanga · Tanjung Bayur
KALIMANTAN TENGAH · Waru
Muaratewe · Muarakaman · Balikpapan
Teluk Balikpapan · Teluk Adang
Bawan · Dayu
Palangkaraya · Sungai Barito · Tanjung
Amuntai · Kotabaru
Selat Makassar
Salumpaga · Oan
Tolitoli · Leok · Lanu
Tompo · **GORONTALO** · Gunung Malino 2499m
Teluk Dampal · Dondo · Danau Limboto
Teluk Tomini · **Gorontalo**
Bubaa · Teluk Gorontalo
Molosipat · Molibagu
SULAWESI UTARA
Manado · Serai · Bitung
Tomohon · Airmadidi
Amurang · Tondano · Danau Tondano
Kotamobagu · Gunung Bulawa 1970m

Tomini Teluk
Towera · Pulau Batudaka
Donggala · Pulau Togian
Palu · Lambogo
Pakuli · Tambarana
Danau Lindu · Gimpu · Tobamawi
Pandiri · Poso · Baturebe
Karosa · Tentena · Taripa · Danau Poso
SULAWESI BARAT · Mamuju
Sabana · Wotu
Malunda · **Sulawesi (Celebes)**
Masamba · Danau Towuti
Teluk Mamuju · Rantepao · Danau Matana
Majene · Polewali · Saroako · Mahalona
Teluk Mandar · Enrekang · Asera
Parepare · Singkang · Kolaka
Danau Tempe · Anabanua · **Kendari**
Sengkang · **SULAWESI TENGGARA**
SULAWESI SELATAN · Watampone
Makassar · Maros · Watulimo
Takalar · Bulukumba
Jeneponto · Selat Selayar
Tomini Teluk

Teluk Tomini
Molucca Sea (Laut Maluku)
Pulau Kasiruta · Kepulauan Bacan
Pulau Mandioli · Selat Obi
Pulau Bisa · Pulau Obi
Pulau Bacan · Gani
Pulau Damar
Selat Obi · Sesepe
Pulau Gomumu
Ceram Sea (Laut Seram)
Tanjung Nan · Lasahata · Pitu
Waflia · Namlea · Pulau Boano
Gunung Kaubalatmada 2729m
Danau Rana · Kelang · Amaha
Pulau Buru · Saparua
Tifu · Pulau Manipa · Watawa · Halong
Elara · **Ambon** · Pulau Ambon · Sapu
Ambelau · Kepulauan Lease
MALUKU
Teluk Tolo
Teluk Towori · Pulau Manui
Teluk Bone
Pulau Wowoni · Kakea
Pulau Padamarang · Honi
Bugingkalo · Bonelipu
Selat Tioro · Tampo · Pulau Muna
Lasthao · Pising · Kolowanawatobo
Pulau Kabaena · Raha · Kamaru
Baubau · Kepulauan Langkesi

INDONES
Kepulauan Laut Kecil
Pulau Karamain
Pulau Masalembo-besar
Pulau Kaledupa
Banda Sea (Laut Banda)
Kepulauan Tukangbesi
Pulau Binongko
Pulau Batuata
Kepulauan Kangean
Ambunten · Sumenep · Pulau Kangean
Pulau Sapudi
Bali Sea (Laut Bali)
Jawa (Java) · Situbondo
Bondowoso · Gunung Raung 3390m
JAWA TIMUR · Singaraja · Banyuwangi
Grajagan · Selat Bali · **Bali**
Teluk Grajagan · Tejakula
Bayan · Karangasem
Denpasar · Lombok
Negara · Ngurah Rai · Nusa Penida
Kuta · **Mataram**
NUSA TENGGARA BARAT
Pulau Moyo · Gunung Tambora 2821m
Teluk Saleh · Sumbawabesar · Dompu · Raba
Alas · Taliwang · **Sumbawa** · Gerampi
Lunyuk · Gunung Tukan 1400m
Nusa Tenggara (Lesser Sunda Islands)
Bondokodi · Pulau Sumba · Waingapu
Waikabubak · Baing
Savu Sea
Kepulauan Sabalana
Pulau Tengah
Kepulauan Tanahjampea
Pulau Kalao · Pulau Bonerate
Pulau Kalaotoa
Flores Sea (Laut Flores)
Kepulauan Bonerate
Pulau Sangeang
Pulau Palu · Larantuka
Labuhanbajo · Pota · Ruteng · Maumere
Komodo · **Flores** · Endeh
Bajawa
Teluk Sindeh
NUSA TENGGARA TIMUR
Pulau Lomblen
Pulau Alor · Pulau Alor
Kepulauan Alor · Kabir · Kalabahi
Labala · **DILI**
Pante Makasar (Part of East Timor)
Kefamenanu · **EAST TIMOR**
Gunung Kekneno 2070m · Atambua · Maliana
Sulamu · Lospalos
Kupang · Soe · Niktiniki · Suai
Toineke
Pulau Semau · Pulau Sawu
Pulau Roti · Selat Roti · Baa
Kepulauan Sawu · Selat Rajua
Timor Sea
Pulau Wetar · Selat Romang
Pulau Romang
Kepulauan Alor
Pulau Kambing · Manatuto
Pulau Moa · Pulau Leti
Kepulauan Damar
Pulau Damar
Tutuala · Pulau Serm

INDIAN OCEAN

6000m · 4000m · 3000m · 2000m · 1000m · 500m · 250m · 100m · Sea Level · -250m · -2000m · -4000m

259

South China Sea & the Philippines

MYANMAR (BURMA)

CHINA
YUNNAN

SHAN STATE

Shan Plateau

KAYAH STATE

KAYIN STATE

Tenasserim Range

MON STATE

THAILAND

LAOS

VIANGCHAN (VIENTIANE)

Khorat Plateau

Annamite Mountains

Bilauktaung Range

TANINTHAYI

Myeik Archipelago

Isthmus of Kra

Gulf of Thailand

KRUNG THEP (BANGKOK)

CAMBODIA

Tonlé Sap

Phnum Dângrêk

PHNUM PÉNH (PHNOM PENH)

VIETNAM

Gulf of Tonkin

HA NỘI

Hai Phong

GUANGXI ZHUANGZU ZIZHIQU

Nanning

HAINAN

Haikou

Hainan Dao

PARACEL ISLANDS (disputed)

Amphitrite Group

Crescent Group

Triton Island

Passu Keah

Đà Nẵng

Hồ Chí Minh

South China Sea

Spratly Island

MALAYSIA

George Town

Kuala Terengganu

Kota Bharu

Ipoh

PINANG

PERLIS

KEDAH

KELANTAN

TERENGGANU

PERAK

PAHANG

INDONESIA

ACEH

240
288
258

Sea Level
6000m
4000m
3000m
2000m
1000m
500m
250m
100m
Sea Level
−250m
−2000m
−4000m

Scale 1:7,000,000
(projection: Mercator)

0 25 50 75 100 125 150 175 200 Km
0 25 50 75 100 125 150 175 200 Miles

Population
- ■ above 5 million
- ■ 1 million to 5 million
- ● 500,000 to 1 million
- ◎ 100,000 to 500,000
- ⊕ 50,000 to 100,000
- ⊙ 10,000 to 50,000
- ○ below 10,000

243

H I J K L M N

GUANGDONG
Guangzhou
Foshan
Huizhou
Dongguan
Haifeng
Jiangmen
Zhongshan
Shenzhen
Zhuhai
Macau
(SAR)
Chek Lap Kok
Kowloon
Hong Kong
(Special Administrative Region)
Baiyun
Jiangmen
Lufeng
Puning
Shantou
Chaoyang
Nan'ao Dao

Shangchuan Dao

Lincoln Island

Tungsha Tao

Jiayi
Xinying
Tainan
TAIWAN
Pingdong
Gaoxing
Gaoxiong
Fangshan
Taodong
Lu Dao
Hengchun
Eluan Pi
Lan Yu

Tropic of Cancer

Bashi Channel

Batan Islands
Batan Island

Luzon Strait

Balintang Channel
Babuyan Island

Babuyan Islands

Babuyan Channel

Mayraira Point
Claveria
Aparri
Escarpada Point
Laoag
Mount Cagua 1133m
Cabugao
Dingras
Bangued
Tuao
Tuguegarao
Vigan
Bontoc
Tabuk
Candon
Ilagan
Bangar
Cauayan
San Fernando
Lagawe
Echague
Bauang
La Trinidad
Bayombong
Bolinao
Baguio
Sierra Madre
Cordillera Central
Abra
Cagayan

P h i l i p p i n e

Luzon

S e a

Lingayen
San Carlos
San Jose City
Baler
Dagupan
Lingayen Gulf
San Ildefonso Peninsula
Camiling
Tarlac
Cabanatuan
Masinloc
Iba
High Peak 2037m
Angeles
Mount Pinatubo 1485m
San Fernando
Olongapo
Malolos
Caloocan
Quezon City
Balanga
Pasig
MANILA
Imus
Laguna de Bay
Lamon Bay
Corregidor Island
Tagaytay
Ninoy Aquino
San Pablo
Labo
Daet
Nasugbu
Lipa
Lake Taal
Lucena
Calauag
Naga
Caramoan
Catanduanes Island
Lubang Island
Batangas
Catanauan
Iriga
Pili
Virac
Cape Calavite
Calapan
Boac
San Francisco
Tabaco
Mayon Volcano 2421m
Mamburao
Marinduque
San Pascual
Ligao
Legazpi City
Mindoro
Pinamalayan
Sorsogon
Mount Baco 2488m
Burias Island
Donsol
Sablayan
Roxas
Tablas Island
Odiongan
Bulan
Sibuyan Sea
Catarman
Laoang
San Jose
Sibuyan Island
Masbate
Calbayog
Busuanga Island
Cajidiocan
Balud
Masbate
Samar
Coron
Ibajay
Kalibo
Placer
Jintotolo Channel
Cajbayog
Borongan
Calamian Group
Biliran Island
Catbalogan
Culion Island
Roxas City
Visayan Sea
Naval
Calbiga
Linapacan Island
Culasi
Passi
Carigara
Tacloban
El Nido
Panay Island
Bogo
Ormoc
Leyte Gulf
Guiuan
SPRATLY ISLANDS
(disputed)
Northeast Cay
Southwest Cay
West York Island
Taytay
San Jose de Buenavista
Iloilo
Silay
Sagay
Cebu
Baybay
Abuyog
Sandy Cay
Thitu Island
Flat Island
Cuyo West Pass
Cuyo East Pass
Bacolod
Leyte
Loaita Island
Nanshan Island
Patnongon
San Carlos City
Danao
Sogod
Itu Aba Island
Sand Cay
Bago
Toledo
Camotes Sea
Maasin
Namyit Island
La Carlota
Canlaon Volcano 2465m
Lapu-Lapu
Dinagat Island
P H I L I P P I N E S
Himamaylan
Ubay
Dinagat
Sin Cowe Island
Sin Cowe East Island
Panay Gulf
Cebu
Siargao Island
Lansdowne Reef
Negros
Argao
Bohol
Surigao
"Cagayan Islands"
Sipalay
Siquijor Island
Jagna
Puerto Princesa
Bais
Tagbilaran
Camiguin Island
Quezon
Bayawan
Dumaguete
Bohol Sea
Cabadbaran
Tandag
Palawan
Siaton Point
Siaton
Butuan
Brooke's Point
Dipolog
Dapitan
Oroquieta
Cagayan de Oro
Gingoog
Tagoloan
Lianga
Prosperidad
Surigao Mountains
Agusan
Hinatuan
Mount Malindang 2425m
Iligan
Bislig
Sulu Sea
Labason
Sindangan
Iligan Bay
Ozamiz
Iligan
Malaybalay
Monkayo
Tubod
Tangub
Marawi
Maramag
Kabasalan
Lake Lanao
Siocon
Karomatan
Malabang
Nabunturan
Baganga
Tungawan
Pagadian
Pulangi
Tagum
Balabac Island
Sultan Kudarat
Midsayap
Pantukan
Manay
Pulau Balambangan
Cotabato
Mindanao
Davao
Balabac Strait
Zamboanga
Moro Gulf
Kidapawan
Mount Apo 2954m
Lupon
Kudat
Isabela
Lamitan
Mount Katanglad
Tagum
Mati
Pulau Banggi
Teluk Marudu
Tiga Tarok
Teluk Paitan
Kanibongan
Dumagasa Point
Basilan
Tacurong
Davao Gulf
Governor Generoso
M A L A Y S I A
Tuaran
Gunung Kinabalu 4101m
Ranau
Cagayan de Tawi Tawi
Pangutaran Group
Lebak
Isulan 2083m
Digos
Koronadal
Malita
Kota Kinabalu
Sandakan
Palimbang
Parker Volcano 1842m
Surallah
Cape San Agustin
Teluk Kimanis
SABAH
Jolo
Jolo
Samales Group
Kiamba
General Santos
Glan
Jose Abad Santos
LABUAN
Sungai Sugut
Tapul Group
Tinaca Point
Pulau Labuan
Labuan
Keningau
Sungai Labuk
Sungai Segama
Tawitawi
Balimbing
Sarangani Islands
BRUNEI
Bandar Seri Begawan
Brunei Bay
Tambunan
Tenom
Lahad Datu
Sibutu Passage
Kepulauan Nanusa
BANDAR SERI BEGAWAN
Banjaran Crocker
Banjaran Brassey
Teluk Lahad Datu
Sibutu
Sulu Archipelago
Kepulauan Kawio
Pulau Karakelong
Miri
Kuala Belait
Tawau
Pulau Tumbun Mata
Pulau Bum Bum
Sibutu
C e l e b e s S e a
Kepulauan Talaud
SARAWAK
Sebatik
Melanguane

260

Tropic of Cancer

19,686ft
13,124ft
9843ft
6562ft
3281ft
1640ft
820ft
328ft
Sea Level
-820ft
-6562ft
-13,124ft

286

ASIA

ASIA

Baghdad

Tigris
Shaala
Quds
Zahrā
Tunis
Maghreb
Sadr City
Al'Azamiyah
Rusāfa
Adel
Arbataash
Shaikh
Aomar
Baghdād
Karkh
Khansā'
Amin
Baghdadi
Museum
Iraqi National
Museum
Al-Shaab
Stadium
Muthana
Khudrā
Aalām
Liberation
Monument
Riyad
Al-Rasheed
Airport
Hamrā
Tishriyaa
Karrādah
Firdows
University
New
Baghdād
Baghdād
Intl. Airport
Jihād
Amal Qadisiya
Jizira
Dōra
Tigris
Qanat Al Jaysh
Diyālā

0   4 Km
0   4 Miles

Bangkok

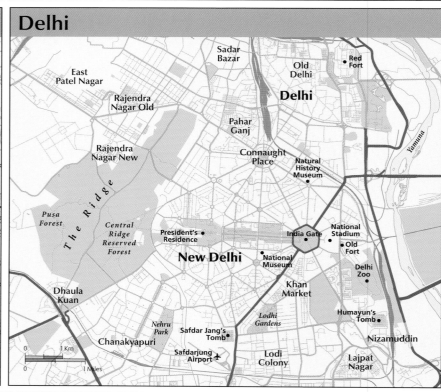

Nonthaburi
Bangkhen
Bangsu
Lad
Phrao
Chatuchak
Dusit
Phaya
Thai
Huay
Khwang
Chitralanda
Palace
Bangkok
Noi
National
Museum
Bang Kapi
Wat Phra Kaeo & Grand Palace
Jim Thomson's
House
Wat Arun
Khlong
Toey
Phasi
Charoen
Khlong
Bangkok
(Krung Thep)
Thonburi
Sathorn
Chom
Thong
Bang
Kholaem
Yannawa
Chao Phraya
Phra
Khanong
Phra
Pradaeng
Ratburana
Samut
Prakan

0   5 Km
0   5 Miles

Beijing

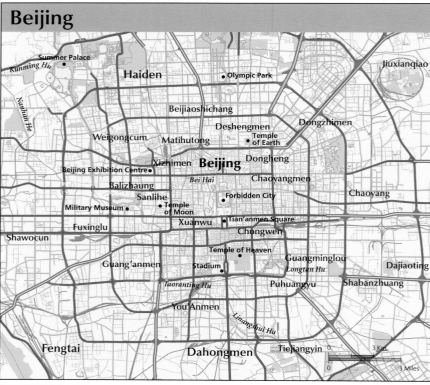

Summer Palace
Olympic Park
Jiuxianqiao
Kunming Hu
Haiden
Beijiaoshichang
Dongzhimen
Nanhai He
Weigongcum
Matihutong
Deshengmen
Temple
of Earth
Xizhimen
Dongcheng
Beijing Exhibition Centre
Beijing
Chaoyangmen
Balizhuang
Bei Hai
Chaoyang
Sanlihe
Temple
of Moon
Forbidden City
Military Museum
Fuxinglu
Xuanwu
Tian'anmen Square
Shawocun
Chongwen
Guangminglou
Dajiaoting
Temple of Heaven
Guang'anmen
Stadium
Longtan Hu
Shabanzhuang
Taoranting Hu
Puhuangyu
You'Anmen
Liangshui Hu
Fengtai
Dahongmen
Tiejiangyin

0   3 Km
0   3 Miles

Delhi

Sadar
Bazar
East
Patel Nagar
Old
Delhi
Red
Fort
Delhi
Rajendra
Nagar Old
Pahar
Ganj
Rajendra
Nagar New
Connaught
Place
Natural
History
Museum
Pusa
Forest
The Ridge
Central
Ridge
Reserved
Forest
President's
Residence
India Gate
National
Stadium
Old
Fort
New Delhi
National
Museum
Delhi
Zoo
Dhaula
Kuan
Khan
Market
Humayun's
Tomb
Nehru
Park
Safdar Jang's
Tomb
Lodhi
Gardens
Nizamuddin
Chanakyapuri
Safdarjung
Airport
Lodi
Colony
Lajpat
Nagar
Yamuna

0   1 Km
0   1 Miles

Dhaka

Ultra
Model
Town
Turag
Zia International
Airport
National
Zoo
Pallabi
Cantonment
Mirpur
Kafrul
Banani
Lake
Gulshan
Air Force
Museum
Dhaka
Tejgaon
Mohammadpur
National
Assembly Hall
Army Museum
Khilgaon
Hazaribag
Ramna
Bangladesh
National Museum
Shabujbag
Dhanmandi
Lalbag
Supreme Court
Buriganga
Kamrangirchar
Madaripur
Kotwali
Demra
Keraniganj
Keraniganj
Sutrapur
Shyampur
Grandaria
Dhaleshwari
Buriganga

0   3 Km
0   3 Miles

Kolkata

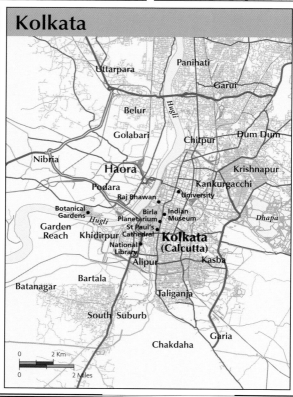

Panihati
Uttarpara
Garui
Belur
Hugli
Dum Dum
Golabari
Chitpur
Nibria
Krishnapur
Haora
Kankurgacchi
Podara
Raj bhawan
University
Dhapa
Botanical
Gardens
Hugli
Birla
Planetarium
Indian
Museum
Garden
Reach
Khidirpur
St Paul's
Cathedral
National
Library
Kolkata
(Calcutta)
Alipur
Kasba
Batanagar
Bartala
Taliganja
South Suburb
Chakdaha
Garia

0   2 Km
0   2 Miles

Kabul

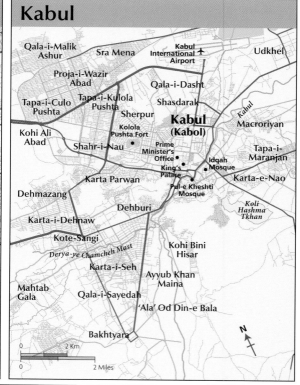

Qala-i-Malik
Ashur
Sra Mena
Kabul
International
Airport
Udkhel
Proja-i-Wazir
Abad
Qala-i-Dasht
Tapa-i-Culo
Pushta
Tapa-i-Kulola
Pushta
Shasdarak
Kohi Ali
Abad
Kolola
Pushta Fort
Sherpur
Kabul
(Kabol)
Macroriyan
Shahr-i-Nau
Prime
Minister's
Office
Kabul
Karta Parwan
King's
Palace
Idgah
Mosque
Tapa-i-
Maranjan
Dehmazang
Pul-e Kheshti
Mosque
Karta-e-Nao
Karta-i-Dehnaw
Dehburi
Koli
Hashma
Tkhan
Kote-Sangi
Derya-ye Chamcheh Mast
Kohi Bini
Hisar
Karta-i-Seh
Ayyub Khan
Maina
Mahtab
Gala
Qala-i-Sayedah
'Ala' Od Din-e Bala
Bakhtyara

N

0   2 Km
0   2 Miles

Hong Kong

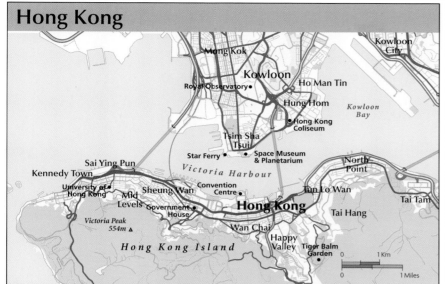

Istanbul

Kuala Lumpur

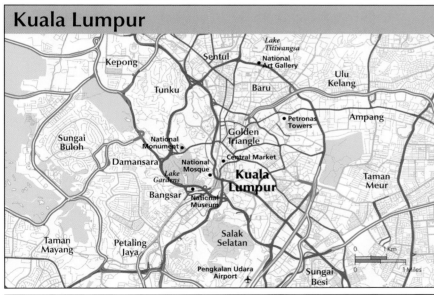

Ulan Bator

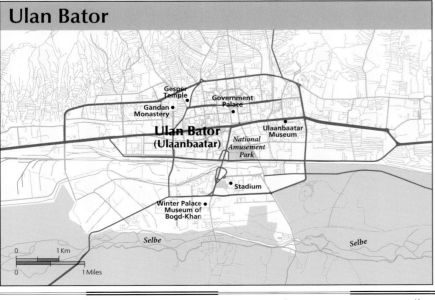

Islamabad

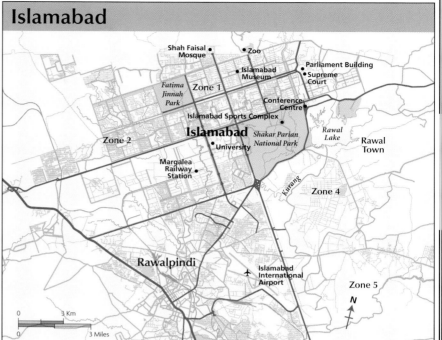

Jakarta

Manila

Australasia and Oceania with a total land area of
3,285,048 sq miles (8,508,238 sq km), takes in
14 countries including the continent of Australia,
New Zealand, Papua New Guinea, and many island
groups scattered across the Pacific Ocean.

FACTFILE

N **Most Northerly Point:** Eastern Island, Midway Islands 28° 15′ N

S **Most Southerly Point:** Macquarie Island, Australia 54° 30′ S

E **Most Easterly Point:** Clipperton Island, 109° 12′ W

W **Most Westerly Point:** Cape Inscription, Australia 112° 57′ E

Largest Lakes:
1 Lake Eyre, Australia 3430 sq miles (8884 sq km)
2 Lake Torrens, Australia 2200 sq miles (5698 sq km)
3 Lake Gairdner, Australia 1679 sq miles (4349 sq km)
4 Lake Mackay, Australia 1349 sq miles (3494 sq km)
5 Lake Argyle, Australia 800 sq miles (2072 sq km)

Longest Rivers:
1 Murray-Darling, Australia 2330 miles (3750 km)
2 Cooper Creek, Australia 880 miles (1420 km)
3 Warburton-Georgina, Australia 870 miles (1400 km)
4 Sepik, Indonesia/Papua New Guinea 700 miles (1126 km)
5 Fly, Indonesia/Papua New Guinea 652 miles (1050 km)

Largest Islands:
1 New Guinea, 312,000 sq miles (808,000 sq km)
2 South Island, New Zealand 56,308 sq miles (145,836 sq km)
3 North Island, New Zealand 43,082 sq miles (111,583 sq km)
4 Tasmania, Australia 24,911 sq miles (64,519 sq km)
5 New Britain, Papua New Guinea 13,570 sq miles (35,145 sq km)

Highest Points:
1 Mount Wilhelm, Papua New Guinea 14,793 ft (4509 m)
2 Mount Giluwe, Papua New Guinea 14,331 ft (4368 m)
3 Mount Herbert, Papua New Guinea 13,999 ft (4267 m)
4 Mount Bangeta, Papua New Guinea 13,520 ft (4121 m)
5 Mount Victoria, Papua New Guinea 13,360 ft (4072 m)

Lowest Point:
▼ Lake Eyre, Australia -53 ft (-16 m) below sea level

Highest recorded temperature:
⊕ Bourke, Australia 128°F (53°C)

Lowest recorded temperature:
⊖ Canberra, Australia -8°F (-22°C)

Wettest Place:
≋ Bellenden Ker, Australia 443 in (11,251 mm)

Driest Place:
⊖ Mulka Bore, Australia 4.05 in (102.8 mm)

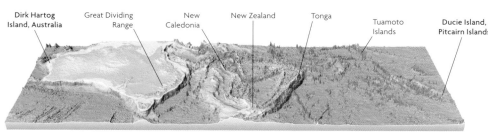

Cross-section from Dirk Hartog Island, Australia to Ducie Island, Pitcairn Islands

line of cross-section

0   500   1000 1500 Km
0   500   1000   1500 Miles

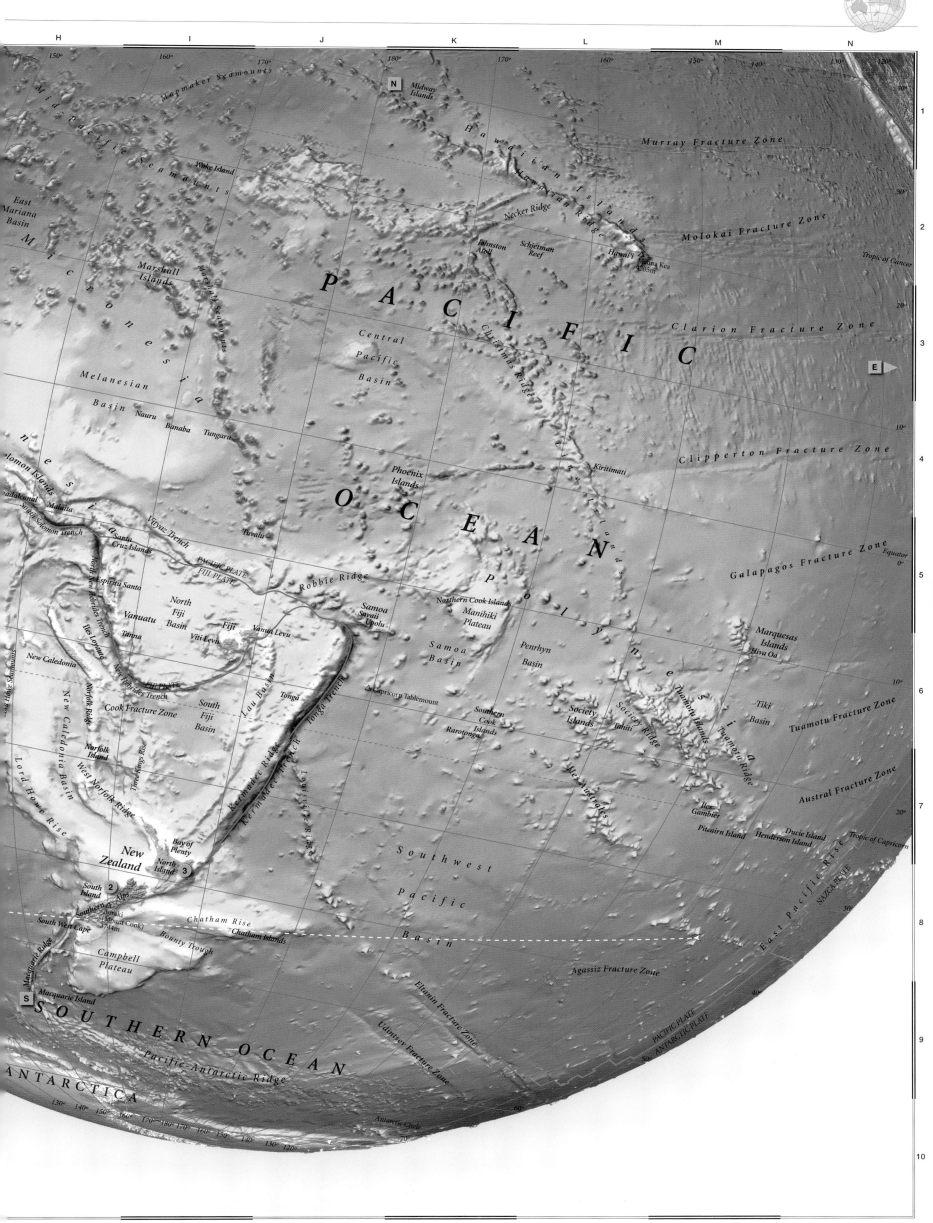

H I J K L M N

N Midway Islands

Mapmaker Seamounts

Mid-Pacific Seamounts

Wake Island

Murray Fracture Zone

Hawaiian Islands

Hawaiian Ridge

Necker Ridge

Molokai Fracture Zone

East Mariana Basin

Johnston Atoll

Schjetman Reef

Hawai'i · Mauna Kea 4205m

Tropic of Cancer

Marshall Islands

Marshall Seamounts

Central Pacific Basin

Clarion Fracture Zone

P A C I F I C

Melanesian

Basin   Nauru

Banaba   Tungaru

Christmas Ridge

Clipperton Fracture Zone

Phoenix Islands

Kiritimati

O C E A N

Solomon Islands

Guadalcanal Malaita

South Solomon Trench

Santa Cruz Islands

Vityaz Trench

Tuvalu

Line Islands

Galapagos Fracture Zone

Equator 0°

North Espiritu Santo

PACIFIC PLATE

FIJI PLATE

Robbie Ridge

Northern Cook Islands

Manihiki Plateau

Marquesas Islands

Hiva Oa

New Caledonia

Iles Loyauté

North Fiji Basin

Vanuatu

Tanna

Fiji

Viti Levu

Vanua Levu

Samoa

Savaii

Upolu

Samoa Basin

Penrhyn Basin

Tiki Basin

P o l y n e s i a

New Hebrides Trench

FIJI PLATE

Capricorn Tablemount

Southern Cook Islands

Rarotonga

Society Islands

Tahiti

Society Ridge

Tuamotu Islands

Tuamotu Fracture Zone

New Caledonia Basin

Norfolk Ridge

Cook Fracture Zone

South Fiji Basin

Lau Basin

Tonga

Kermadec Ridge

Kermadec Trench

Tonga Trench

Louisville Ridge

Iles Australes

Iles Gambier

Austral Fracture Zone

Lord Howe Rise

West Norfolk Ridge

Three Kings Rise

Norfolk Island

Bay of Plenty

Pitcairn Island

Ducie Island

Henderson Island

Tropic of Capricorn

New Zealand

North Island **3**

South Island **2**

Southern Alps

Aoraki (Mount Cook) 3744m

Chatham Rise

Chatham Islands

S o u t h w e s t

P a c i f i c

B a s i n

East Pacific Rise

NAZCA PLATE

South West Cape

Bounty Trough

Agassiz Fracture Zone

Campbell Plateau

Macquarie Ridge

S Macquarie Island

Elianin Fracture Zone

PACIFIC PLATE

ANTARCTIC PLATE

S O U T H E R N   O C E A N

Udintsev Fracture Zone

Pacific-Antarctic Ridge

A N T A R C T I C A

Antarctic Circle

H I J K L M N

Political

Vast expanses of ocean separate this geographically fragmented realm, characterized more by each country's isolation than by any political unity. Australia's and New Zealand's traditional ties with the United Kingdom, as members of the Commonwealth, are now being called into question as Australasian and Oceanian nations are increasingly looking to forge new relationships with neighboring Asian countries like Japan. External influences have featured strongly in the politics of the Pacific Islands; the various territories of Micronesia were largely under US control until the late 1980s, and France, New Zealand, the USA and the UK still have territories under colonial rule in Polynesia. Nuclear weapons-testing by Western superpowers was widespread during the Cold War period, but has now been discontinued.

Population

- ■ above 5 million
- ▣ 1 million to 5 million
- ◉ 500,000 to 1 million
- ◎ 100,000 to 500,000
- ⊕ 50,000 to 100,000
- ○ 10,000 to 50,000
- ○ below 10,000
- ● Country capital
- ◉ State capital

Borders

- full international border
- indication of maritime country extent
- indication of maritime dependent territory extent
- state border

Communications

- major roads
- major railroads

Scale 1:32,000,000
(projection: Lambert Azimuthal Equal Area)

Languages

English is spoken throughout Australia and New Zealand. In Australia, English has been superimposed on a mosaic of Aboriginal languages. In New Zealand, the indigenous language, Maori, is the official language besides English. In Papua New Guinea, Melanesian Pidgin has become a *lingua franca* alongside several hundred indigenous languages. Across the region, the indigenous languages can be grouped into (1) the Aboriginal languages of Australia, (2) the Papuan languages spoken mostly inland in Papua New Guinea, and (3) the widely dispersed Austronesian, which includes coastal languages of Papua New Guinea, New Zealand Maori, and languages of Oceania.

Language groups

- Australian
- Papuan
- Indo-European
- Austronesian

Population

Density of settlement in the region is generally low. Australia is one of the least densely populated countries on Earth with over 80% of its population living within 25 miles (40 km) of the coast — mostly in the southeast of the country. New Zealand, and the island groups of Melanesia, Micronesia and Polynesia, are much more densely populated, although many of the smaller islands remain uninhabited.

Population density
(people per sq mile)

- below 10
- 10-62
- 63-130
- 131-259
- 260-519
- 520-780
- above 780

Standard of living

In marked contrast to its neighbor, Australia, with one of the world's highest life expectancies and standards of living, Papua New Guinea is one of the world's least developed countries. In addition, high population growth and urbanization rates throughout the Pacific islands contribute to overcrowding. The Aboriginal and Maori people of Australia and New Zealand have been isolated for many years. Recently, their traditional land ownership rights have begun to be legally recognized in an effort to ease their social and economic isolation, and to improve living standards.

Standard of living
(UN human development index)

- low
- high
- figures unavailable

Transportation

While sea travel remains of paramount importance throughout the continent, well-developed regional and international air travel has reduced the region's global isolation. Internal air travel is particularly important in Australia, where distances are great and road systems are poorly developed or in some areas nonexistent. Australia's rail system, still operating on three different gauges, a legacy of its piecemeal development, is being upgraded, particularly in the north-south links.

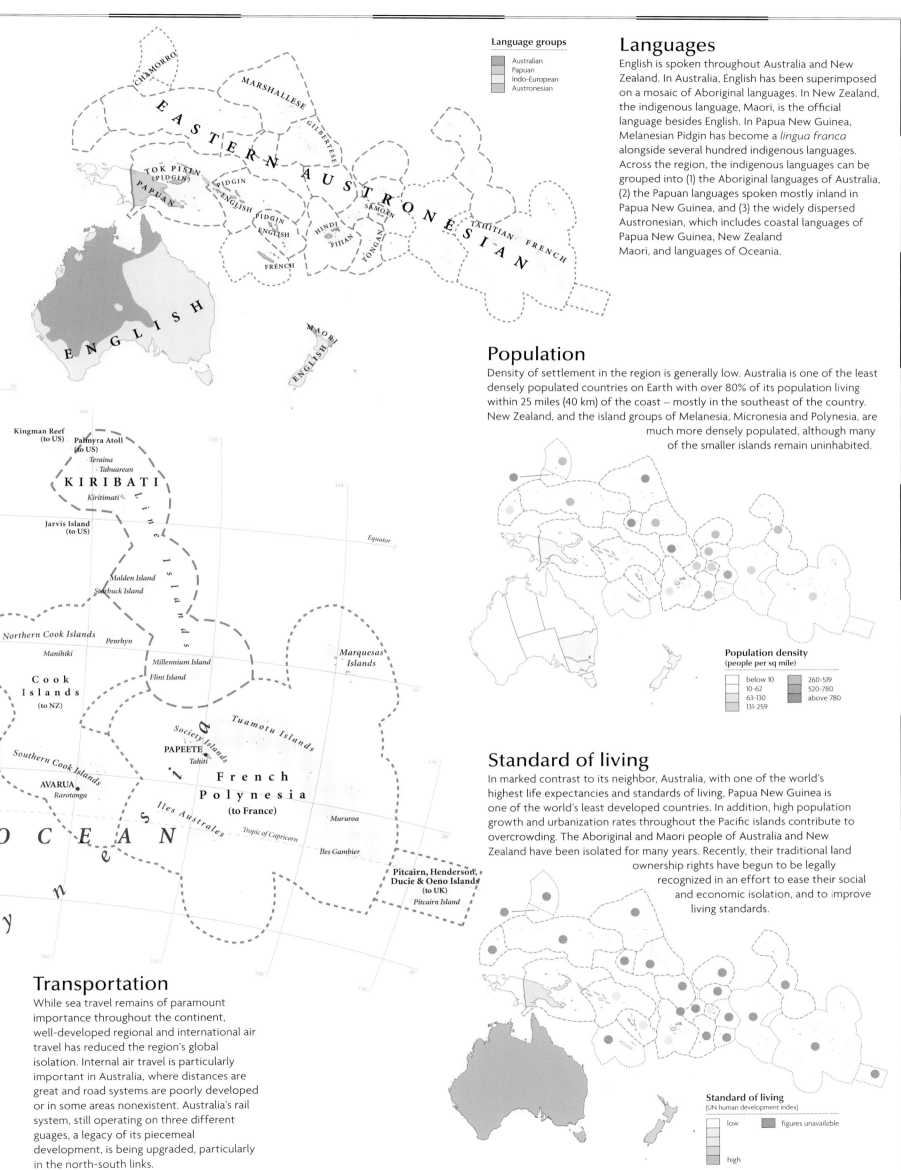

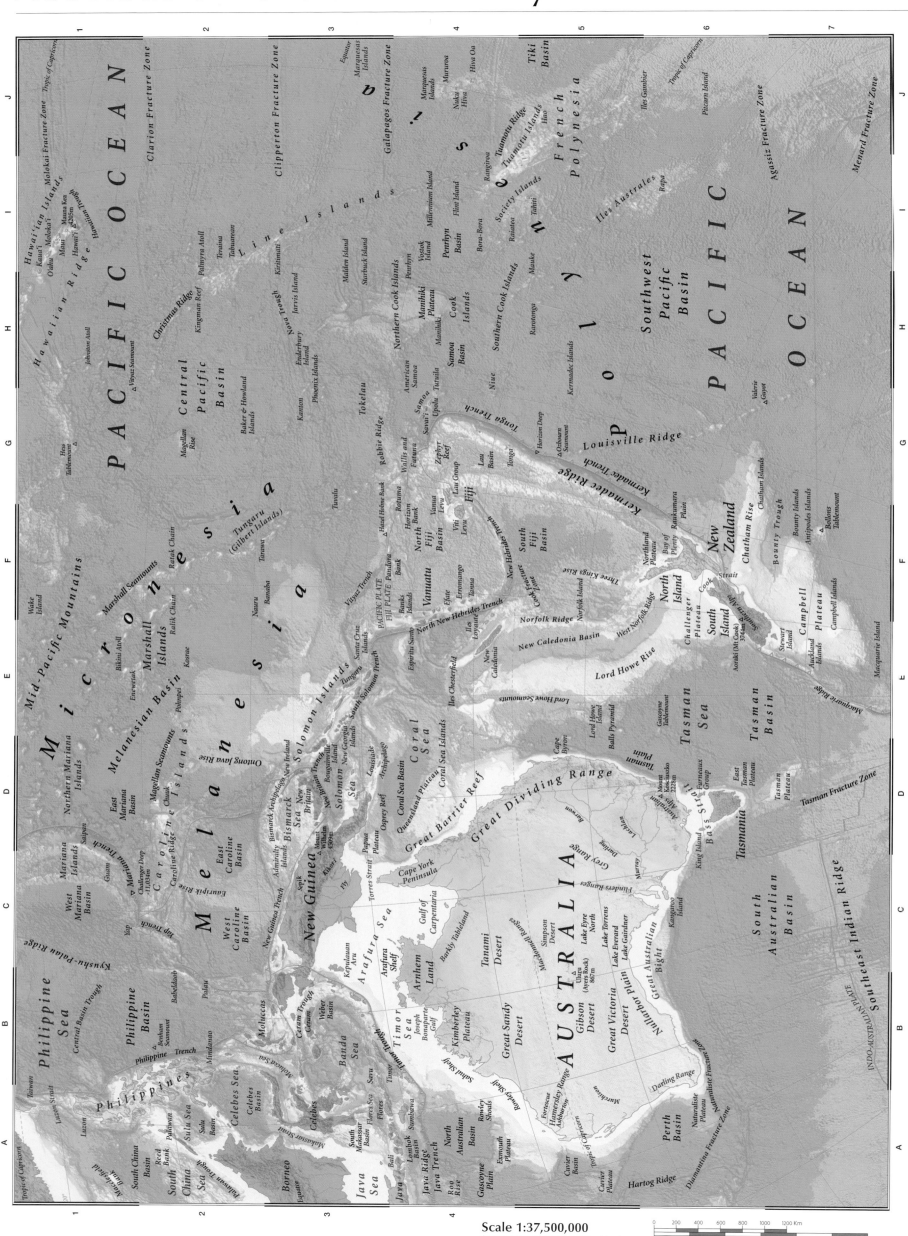

Scale 1:37,500,000
(projection: Lambert Azimuthal Equal Area)

0 200 400 600 800 1000 1200 Km
0 200 400 600 800 1000 1200 Miles

Climate

Surrounded by water, the climate of most areas is profoundly affected by the moderating effects of the oceans. Australia, however, is the exception. Its dry continental interior remains isolated from the ocean; temperatures soar during the day, and droughts are common. The coastal regions, where most people live, are cooler and wetter. The numerous islands scattered across the Pacific are generally hot and humid, subject to the different air circulation patterns and ocean currents that affect the area, including the El Niño ocean current anomaly, which produces extreme aridity.

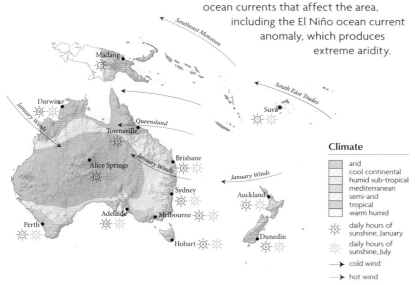

Climate

- arid
- cool continental
- humid sub-tropical
- mediterranean
- semi-arid
- tropical
- warm humid
- ☼ daily hours of sunshine, January
- ☼ daily hours of sunshine, July
- → cold wind
- → hot wind

Average Rainfall

January rainfall *July rainfall*

Rainfall

- 0–1 in (0–25 mm)
- 1–2 in (25–50 mm)
- 2–4 in (50–100 mm)
- 4–8 in (100–200 mm)
- 8–12 in (200–300 mm)
- 12–16 in (300–400 mm)
- 16–20 in (400–500 mm)
- more than 20 in (500 mm)

Average Temperature

January temperature *July temperature*

Temperature

- below -22°F (-30°C)
- -22 to -4°F (-30 to -20°C)
- -4 to 14°F (-20 to -10°C)
- 14 to 32°F (-10 to 0°C)
- 32 to 50°F (0 to 10°C)
- 50 to 68°F (10 to 20°C)
- 68 to 86°F (20 to 30°C)
- above 86°F (30°C)

Environmental issues

The prospect of rising sea levels poses a threat to many low-lying islands in the Pacific. Nuclear weapons-testing, once common throughout the region, was finally discontinued in 1996. Australia's ecological balance has been irreversibly altered by the introduction of alien species. Although it has the world's largest underground water reserve, the Great Artesian Basin, the availability of fresh water in Australia remains critical. Periodic droughts combined with over-grazing lead to desertification and increase the risk of devastating bush fires, and occasional flash floods.

☢ **PACIFIC TEST SITES**
Eniwetok Atoll, Marshall Islands
Bikini Atoll, Marshall Islands
Johnston Atoll
Mururoa Atoll, French Polynesia
Fangatau Atoll, French Polynesia
Christmas Island, Kiribati

Environmental issues

- national parks
- tropical forest
- forest destroyed
- desert
- desertification
- polluted rivers
- ☢ radioactive contamination
- marine pollution
- heavy marine pollution
- • poor urban air quality

Land use

Much of the region's industry is resource-based: sheep farming for wool and meat in Australia and New Zealand; mining in Australia and Papua New Guinea and fishing throughout the Pacific islands. Manufacturing is mainly limited to the large coastal cities in Australia and New Zealand, like Sydney, Adelaide, Melbourne, Brisbane, Perth, and Auckland, although small-scale enterprises operate in the Pacific islands, concentrating on processing of fish and foods. Tourism continues to provide revenue to the area—in Fiji it accounts for 15 percent of GNP.

Using the land and sea

- barren land
- cropland
- desert
- forest
- mountain region
- pasture
- 🐑 sheep
- 🌴 coconuts
- ☕ coffee
- 🎣 fishing
- 🍇 fruit
- 🦪 shellfish
- 🌾 sugar cane
- 🍇 vineyards
- ⚓ whaling
- 🌾 wheat

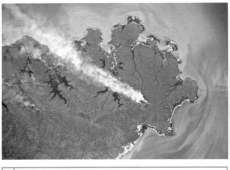

1 MELVILLE ISLAND, NORTHERN TERRITORY, AUSTRALIA
Lying off Australia's north coast, the island is sparsely populated consisting of sandy soils and mangrove swamps.

2 ANATAHAN, NORTHERN MARIANA ISLANDS
The volcano on Anatahan is one of 12 in the Mariana Islands and erupted on a large scale in April 2005.

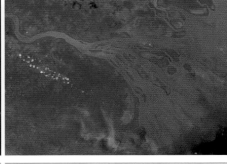

3 FLY RIVER, PAPUA NEW GUINEA
Flowing down from New Guinea's Central Range, the river carries a heavy load of sediment which it deposits in the Gulf of Papua, sometimes forming new islands.

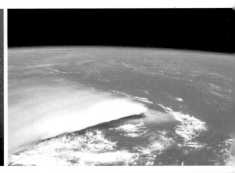

4 RABAUL VOLCANO, NEW BRITAIN, PAPUA NEW GUINEA
After erupting in 1994, this image shows how the highest particles blew west causing condensation of water vapor over a wide area.

9 ULURU/AYERS ROCK, NORTHERN TERRITORY, AUSTRALIA
This enormous sandstone rock occupies Australia's heart, both physically and emotionally.

10 JAMES RANGES, NORTHERN TERRITORY, AUSTRALIA
A series of low ridges, these hills lie at the geographical center of Australia.

11 LAKE EYRE, SOUTH AUSTRALIA, AUSTRALIA
This great salt lake consists of north and south sections, joined by a narrow channel, Lake Eyre South being the smaller, elongated saltflat at the bottom of the image.

12 NEWCASTLE, NEW SOUTH WALES, AUSTRALIA
The industrial seaport of Newcastle lies on the south bank of Hunter river.

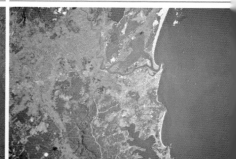

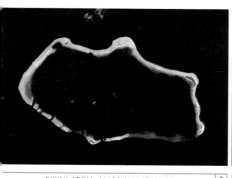

BIKINI ATOLL, MARSHALL ISLANDS `5`
This atoll was the site of 23 atomic bomb tests in the 1940s and 1950s, involving the intentional sinking of at least 13 naval vessels in the shallow lagoon.

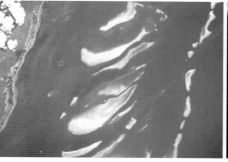

GREAT BARRIER REEF, QUEENSLAND, AUSTRALIA `6`
The world's largest reef system is made up of 3000 individual reefs and 900 islands and stretches for 1600 miles (2600 km).

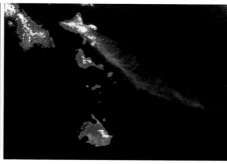

AMBRYM, VANUATU `7`
Mount Marum, a 4166 ft (1270 m) volcano, erupted in April 2004 producing an extensive plume of ash.

KIRITIMATI, KIRIBATI `8`
Kiritimati is the largest atoll in the Pacific Ocean, its interior lagoon filled in with coral growth.

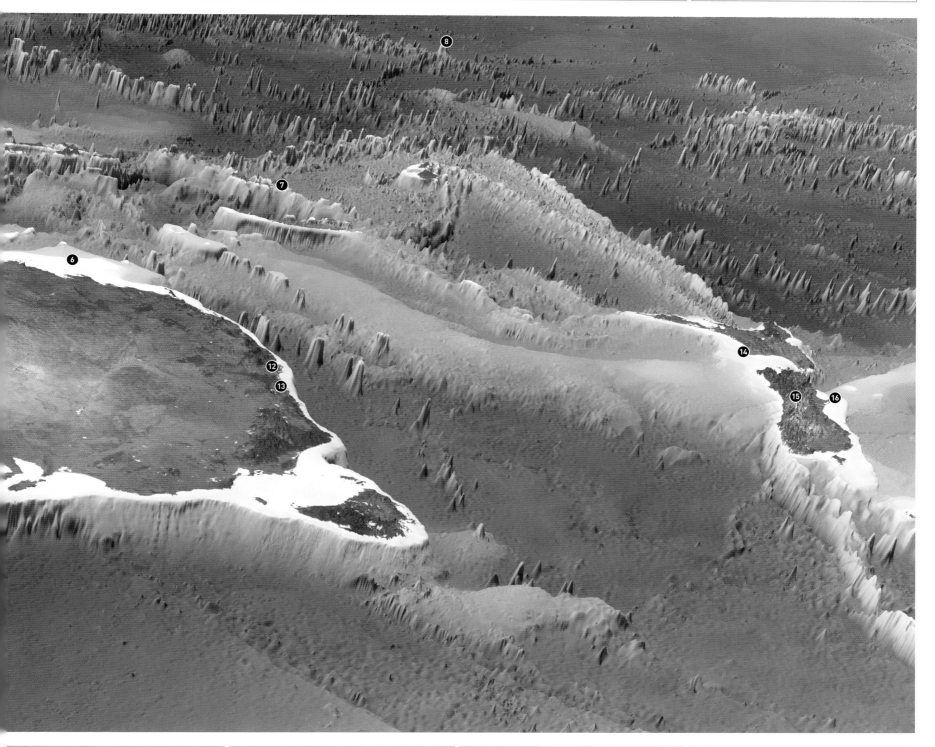

SYDNEY, NEW SOUTH WALES, AUSTRALIA `13`
Expanding outward from the inlet of Port Jackson, Australia's largest city was founded in 1788.

MOUNT TARANAKI, NORTH ISLAND, NEW ZEALAND `14`
This dormant 2518 m (8261 ft) volcano is one of the most symmetrical in the world.

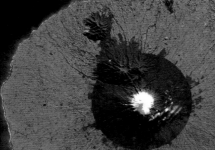

AORAKI/MOUNT COOK, SOUTH ISLAND, NEW ZEALAND `15`
New Zealand's highest peak rises 12,238 ft (3744 m) and is surrounded by permanent ice fields.

BANKS PENINSULA, SOUTH ISLAND, NEW ZEALAND `16`
With a circular drainage pattern typical of eroded volcanoes, this is the only recognizably volcanic feature on New Zealand's South Island.

Australia

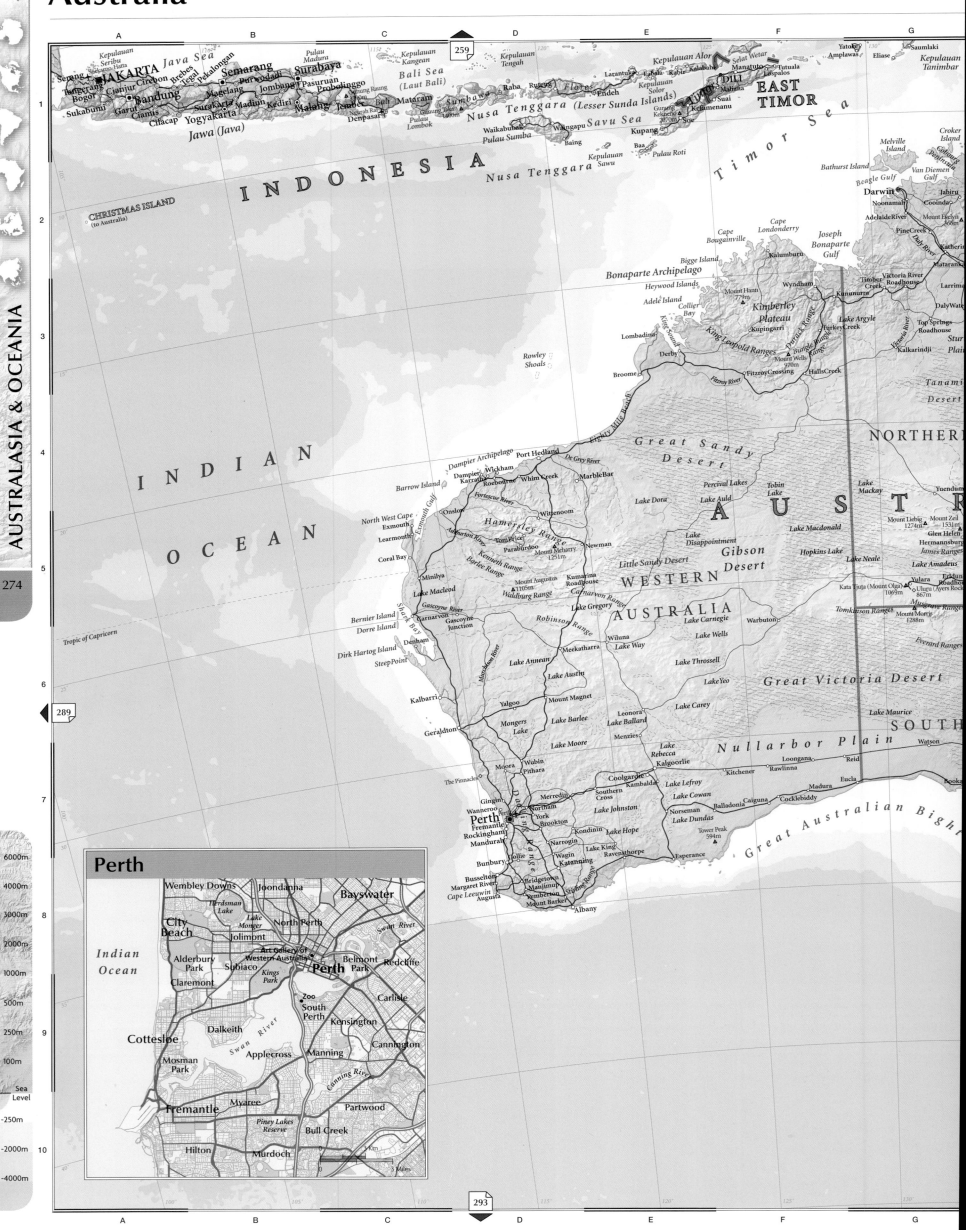

Scale 1:13,000,000
(projection: Lambert Conformal Conic)

0 50 100 150 200 250 300 350 400 Km
0 50 100 150 200 250 300 350 400 Miles

Population
■ above 5 million
■ 1 million to 5 million
◉ 500,000 to 1 million
◉ 100,000 to 500,000
⊕ 50,000 to 100,000
○ 10,000 to 50,000
○ below 10,000

Map labels

Arafura Sea
Gulf of Carpentaria
PAPUA NEW GUINEA
Solomon Sea
SOLOMON ISLANDS
HONIARA *Guadalcanal*
Bougainville Island
New Georgia Islands
PORT MORESBY
Torres Strait
Cape York
Cape York Peninsula
Gulf of Papua
NEW CALEDONIA (to France)
Coral Sea
CORAL SEA ISLANDS (to Australia)
Great Barrier Reef
Iles Chesterfield
Grand Passage
Tropic of Capricorn

QUEENSLAND
Great Artesian Basin
Cairns
Townsville
Charters Towers
Mackay
Rockhampton
Gladstone
Bundaberg
Hervey Bay
Fraser Island
Gympie
Sunshine Coast
Maroochydore-Mooloolaba
Caloundra
Toowoomba
Brisbane
Ipswich
Gold Coast
Surfers Paradise

Simpson Desert
Lake Eyre Basin
Lake Eyre North
Lake Eyre South
Sturt Stony Desert
Tirari Desert
Alice Springs
Tennant Creek
Mount Isa
Cloncurry
Coober Pedy

NEW SOUTH WALES
Darling River
Murray River
Broken Hill
Dubbo
Newcastle
SYDNEY
Wollongong
Parramatta
Penrith
Campbelltown
CANBERRA
AUSTRALIAN CAPITAL TERRITORY
JERVIS BAY TERRITORY
Coffs Harbour
Port Macquarie
Tamworth
Armidale
Grafton
Lord Howe Island (to Australia)

SOUTH AUSTRALIA
Adelaide
Port Augusta
Port Lincoln
Whyalla
Port Pirie
Spencer Gulf
Kangaroo Island
Eyre Peninsula
Lake Torrens
Lake Gairdner
Lake Frome

VICTORIA
Melbourne
Geelong
Ballarat
Bendigo
Mildura
Wodonga
Wagga Wagga
Albury
Port Phillip Bay
Bass Strait
King Island
Flinders Island

TASMANIA
Hobart
Launceston
Devonport
Burnie
Great Lake
Maria Island
South East Cape

PACIFIC OCEAN

Brisbane (inset)

Chermside
Everton Park
The Gap
Red Hill
Lutwyche
Clayfield
Toombul
Brisbane Airport
Myrtletown
Wynnum
Newstead
Hawthorne
Tingalpa
Manly
Brisbane
Queensland Art Gallery
Botanical Gardens
Woolloongabba
Indooroopilly
Greenslopes
Carina Heights
Belmont
Corinda
Mount Gravatt
Burbank
Brisbane River
Tingalpa Reservoir

Elevation scale
19,686ft
13,124ft
9843ft
6562ft
3281ft
1640ft
820ft
328ft
Sea Level
-820ft
-6562ft
-13,124ft

280
286
293

Southeast Australia

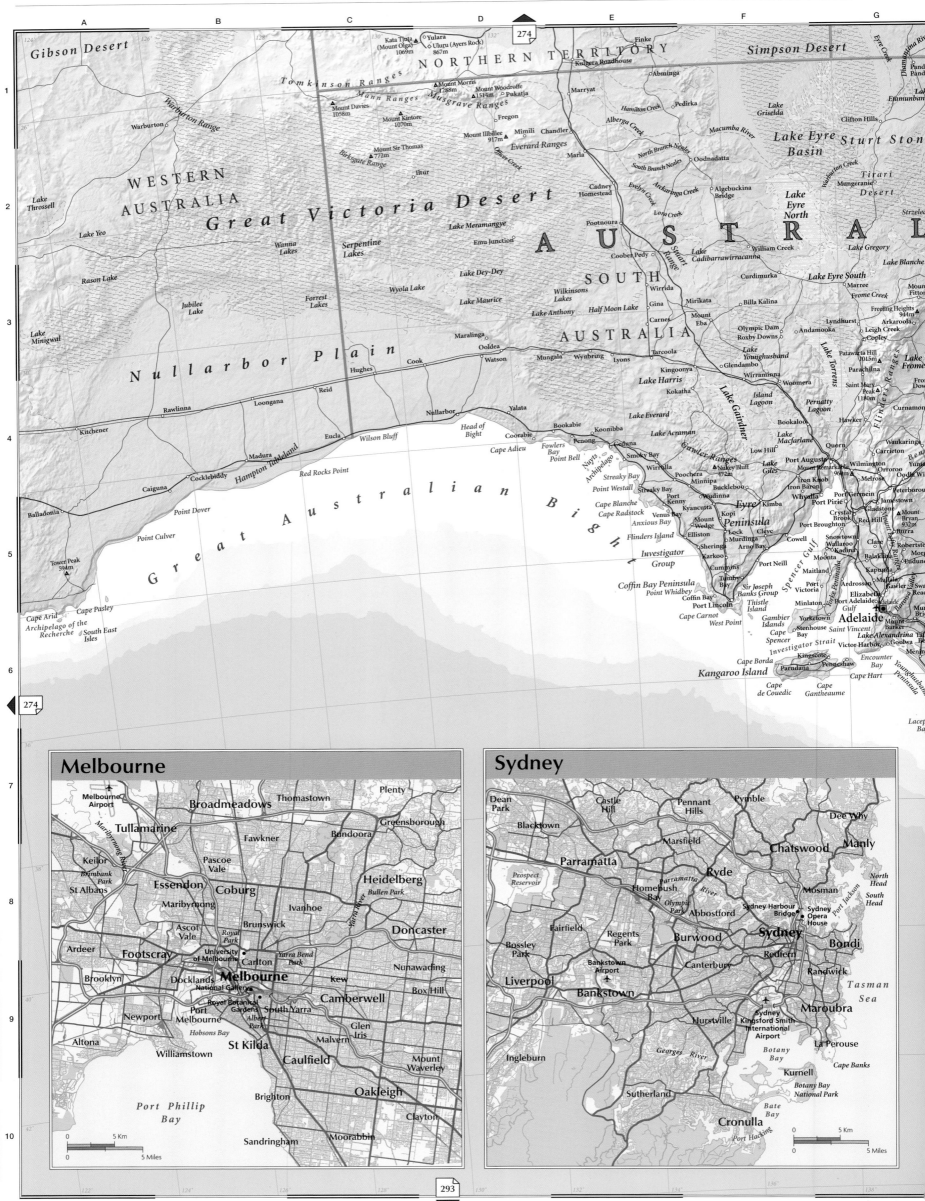

Scale 1:6,500,000
(projection: Lambert Conformal Conic)

```
0  25 50 75 100 125 150 175 200 Km
0  25   50   75   100  125  150  175  200 Miles
```

Population

■ above 5 million   ■ 1 million to 5 million   ◉ 500,000 to 1 million
◉ 100,000 to 500,000   ⊕ 50,000 to 100,000   ○ 10,000 to 50,000   ○ below 10,000

275
278
293

QUEENSLAND

NEW SOUTH WALES

VICTORIA

Tasman Sea

Bass Strait

TASMANIA

Tasmania

Brisbane • Ipswich • Toowoomba • Warwick • Gold Coast • Tweed Heads • Surfers Paradise • Hervey Bay • Maryborough • Gympie • Noosa Heads • Maroochydore-Mooloolaba • Caloundra • Bribie Island • Moreton Island • Fraser Island • Rainbow Beach • Nanango • Gayndah • Mundubbera • Murgon • Kingaroy • Nambour • Caboolture • Esk • Beaudesert • Nerang • Casino • Lismore • Ballina • Byron Bay • Cape Byron • Evans Head • Wooded Bluff • Yamba • Maclean • Grafton • Woolgoolga • Coffs Harbour • Sawtell • Urunga • Bellingen • Dorrigo • Nambucca Heads • Macksville • Kempsey • Smoky Cape • Korogoro Point • Point Plomer • Port Macquarie • Wauchope • Taree • Crowdy Head • Forster-Tuncurry • Gloucester • Myall Lake • Bulahdelah • Nelson Bay • Raymond Terrace • Maitland • Cessnock • Newcastle • Lake Macquarie • Morisset • Budgewoi Lake • Wyong • Gosford • Broken Bay • Hornsby • Penrith • Richmond • Parramatta • Sydney • Kingsford Smith • Botany Bay • Campbelltown • Camden • Picton • Wollongong • Port Kembla • Kiama • Shoalhaven • Nowra-Bomaderry • Jervis Bay • Ulladulla • Batemans Bay • Moruya • Narooma • Bermagui • Tathra • Merimbula • Bombala • Mallacoota

CANBERRA • **AUSTRALIAN CAPITAL TERRITORY** • **JERVIS BAY TERRITORY**

Melbourne • Geelong • Ballarat • Bendigo • Dandenong • Werribee • Sunbury • Bacchus Marsh • Sale • Traralgon • Morwell • Moe • Warragul • Leongatha • Wonthaggi • Phillip Island • Cape Otway • Apollo Bay • Lorne • Torquay • Warrnambool • Port Campbell • Colac • Camperdown • Portland • Port Fairy • Hamilton • Horsham • Ararat • Stawell • Mildura • Swan Hill • Echuca • Shepparton • Wangaratta • Wodonga • Albury • Wagga Wagga • Tumut • Cooma • Jindabyne • Mount Kosciuszko 2228m • Snowy Mountains

Broken Hill • Wilcannia • Cobar • Bourke • Brewarrina • Walgett • Moree • Narrabri • Gunnedah • Tamworth • Armidale • Inverell • Glen Innes • Tenterfield • Dubbo • Parkes • Orange • Bathurst • Lithgow • Goulburn • Yass • Young • Cowra • Forbes • Wellington • Mudgee • Muswellbrook • Singleton • Scone • Gilgandra • Coonabarabran • Coonamble • Bogan Gate

Riverina

Deniliquin • Hay • Griffith • Leeton • Narrandera • Finley • Tocumwal • Corowa • Holbrook

Hobart • Launceston • Devonport • Burnie • Ulverstone • Wynyard • Smithton • George Town • Scottsdale • Saint Helens • Bicheno • Swansea • Oatlands • Bridgewater • Sorell • New Norfolk • Kingston • Huonville • Geeveston • King Island • Currie • Grassy • Flinders Island • Whitemark • Lady Barron • Cape Barren Island • Clarke Island • Furneaux Group

Great Dividing Range • **New England Range**

Cooper Creek • Lake Yamma Yamma • Cordillo Downs • Eromanga • Quilpie • Thylungra • Charleville • Cunnamulla • Thargomindah • Tibooburra • Mount Sturt 288m • Milparinka • Packsaddle • White Cliffs • Menindee • Mount Arrowsmith 293m • Darling River • Murray River • Murrumbidgee River • Lachlan River • Macquarie River

Fraser Island • **Moreton Island** • **North Stradbroke Island** • **South Stradbroke Island**

New Zealand

NEW ZEALAND

North Island

Auckland

Elevation scale:
6000m
4000m
3000m
2000m
1000m
500m
250m
100m
Sea Level
-250m
-2000m
-4000m

North Island labels

Three Kings Islands
North Cape
Cape Reinga
Cape Maria van Diemen
Parengarenga Harbour
Great Exhibition Bay
Ninety Mile Beach
Te Kao
Rangaunu Bay
Cape Karikari
Doubtless Bay
Mangonui
Awanui
Kaitaia
Ahipara
Tauroa Point
Hokianga Harbour
Omapere
Kaikohe
Kawakawa
Russell
Okaihau
Kerikeri
Bay of Islands
Cape Brett
Whangaruru Harbour
Cavalli Islands
Poor Knights Islands
Kaiwi
Whangarei
Hikurangi
Bream Head
Bream Bay
Hen and Chickens
Mokohinau Islands
Portland
Maungaturoto
Waiotira
Dargaville
Ruawai
Kaihu
Kaipara Harbour
Paparoa
North Head
Wellsford
Helensville
Muriwai Beach
Warkworth
Orewa
Leigh
Cape Rodney
Kawau Island
Little Barrier Island
Great Barrier Island
Port Fitzroy
Coromandel Channel
Colville Channel
Cape Colville
Mercury Islands
Great Mercury Island
The Aldermen Islands
Mayor Island
Motiti Island
Mount Maunganui
White Island
Lottin Point
Hicks Bay
East Cape
Te Araroa
Tikitiki
Tokomaru Bay
Mawhai Point
Tolaga Bay
Whangara
GISBORNE
Gisborne
Poverty Bay
Young Nicks Head
Portland Island
Mahia Peninsula
Table Cape
Nuhaka
Long Point
Wairoa
Napier
Hastings
Havelock North
Cape Kidnappers
Hawke Bay
HAWKE'S BAY
Cape Turnagain
Porangahau
Dannevirke
Woodville
Pahiatua
Masterton
Carterton
Castlepoint
WELLINGTON
Wellington
Paraparaumu
Paekakariki
Kapiti Island
Otaki
Levin
Foxton
Shannon
Palmerston North
Feilding
Marton
Bulls
Wanganui
MANAWATU
WANGANUI
Waverley
Patea
Waitotara
Hawera
Kaponga
Eltham
Stratford
TARANAKI
New Plymouth
Mount Taranaki (Mount Egmont) 2518m
Cape Egmont
Opunake
Manaia
South Taranaki Bight
North Taranaki Bight
Mokau
Awakino
Urenui
Te Kuiti
Otorohanga
Te Awamutu
Cambridge
Hamilton
WAIKATO
Huntly
Ngaruawahia
Raglan
Kawhia Harbour
Kawhia
Aotea Harbour
Waitomo Caves
Piopio
Taumarunui
National Park
Turangi
Lake Taupo
Taupo
Mangakino
Tokoroa
Putaruru
Tirau
Matamata
Morrinsville
Te Aroha
Paeroa
Waihi
Katikati
Tauranga
Te Puke
Whakatane
Opotiki
BAY OF PLENTY
Bay of Plenty
Matata
Kawerau
Lake Rotorua
Rotorua
Murupara
Lake Waikaremoana
Wairoa
Coromandel Peninsula
Coromandel
Whitianga
Whangamata
Whangapoua
Thames
Firth of Thames
Kaiaua
Pokeno
Pukekohe
Waiuku
Tuakau
Papakura
Manukau
Manurewa
Takapuna
Auckland
AUCKLAND
Waiheke Island
Rangitoto Island
Hauraki Gulf
Kaimai Range
Raukumara Range
Kaweka Range
Ruahine Range
Tararua Range
Rimutaka Range
Kaimanawa Mountains
Ruapehu 2797m
Ngauruhoe
Tongariro
Coromandel Range
Hunua Range
Hapuakohe Range
NORTHLAND

Tasman Sea

T a s m a n S e a

Auckland inset labels

Motutapu Island
Motuihe Island
Browns Island
Rangitoto Island
Waitemata Harbour
Karaka Bay
Buckland Beach
Howick
Pakuranga
Otara
Otahuhu
Papatoetoe
Clover Park
Manukau
Auckland Intl. Airport
Manukau Harbour
Mangere
Onehunga
Ambury Park
Blockhouse Bay
Green Bay
Avondale
Te Atatu
Point Chevalier
Chelsea Park
Lake Pupuke
Takapuna
North Shore
Northcote
Kauri Park
Highland Park
Pakuranga
Glen Innes
Mission Bay
Kohimarama Bay
Devonport
Maritime Museum
Auckland
Skytower
Grafton
Remuera
Ellerslie
Royal Oak
Mount Wellington
St Johns Park
Tamaki River
Eden Park
Mount Eden
Mount Roskill
One Tree Hill
Cornwall Park
Stardome & Auckland Observatory
Auckland Museum
Auckland Zoo
Huntington Park

Scale:
3 Km
3 Miles

Scale 1:3,200,000
(projection: Lambert Conformal Conic)

0 20 40 60 80 100 Km
0 20 40 60 80 100 Miles

Population
- ■ above 5 million
- ■ 1 million to 5 million
- ● 500,000 to 1 million
- ◉ 100,000 to 500,000
- ⊕ 50,000 to 100,000
- ○ 10,000 to 50,000
- ○ below 10,000

286

275 | 293 | 275

Wellington

Chartwell · Wilton · Northland · Botanic Gardens · Karori · Kelburn · Thorndon · Parliament Buildings & Beehive · Lambton · Museum of New Zealand · Lambton Harbour · Wellington · Te Aro · Mount Victoria · Oriental Bay · Roseneath · Hataitai · Mount Crawford · Scorching Bay · Karaka Bay · Kau Bay · Worser Bay · Seatoun · Miramar · Strathmore Park · Point Dorset · Breaker Bay · Evans Bay · Kilbirnie · Rongotai · Wellington Int. Airport · Lyall Bay · Melrose · Wellington Zoo · Newtown · Mornington · Southgate · Houghton Bay · Mitchelltown · Brooklyn · Government House · Wellington South · Kowhai Park · Highbury · Kingston · Happy Valley · Island Bay · Owhiro Bay · Owhiro Bay

Wellington Harbour (Port Nicholson)

Point Halswell

South Island

PACIFIC OCEAN

WELLINGTON · MARLBOROUGH · TASMAN · WEST COAST · CANTERBURY · OTAGO · SOUTHLAND

Cape Palliser · Cape Campbell · Blenheim · Kaikoura · Christchurch · Banks Peninsula · Pegasus Bay · Greymouth · Hokitika · Timaru · Oamaru · Dunedin · Invercargill · Queenstown · Lake Wakatipu · Lake Wanaka · Lake Te Anau · Lake Manapouri · Milford Sound · Stewart Island · Foveaux Strait · Canterbury Bight · Canterbury Plains · Southern Alps

Mount Cook 3754m

19,686ft
13,124ft
9843ft
6562ft
3281ft
1640ft
820ft
328ft
Sea Level
-820ft
-6562ft
-13,124ft

Papua New Guinea & Melanesia

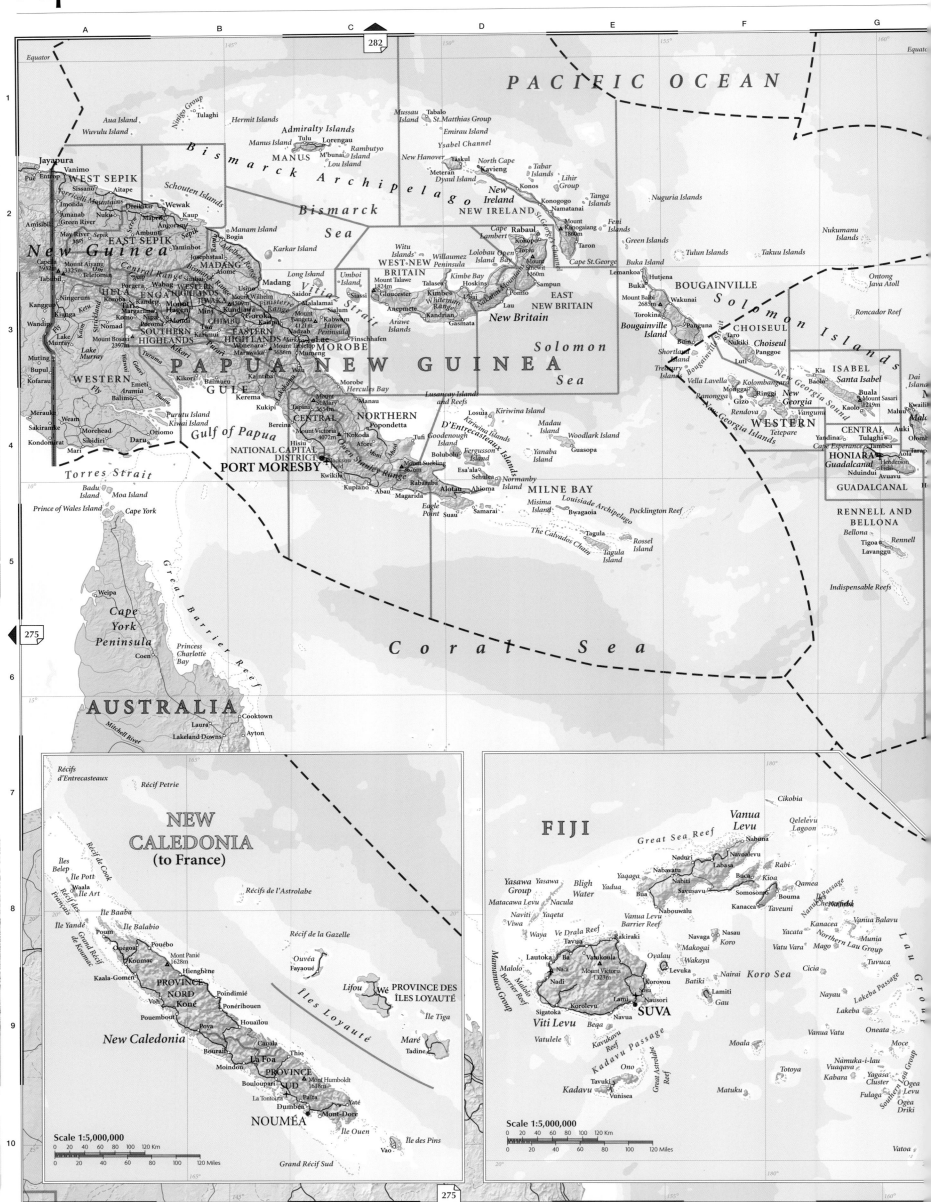

282
275
275

PACIFIC OCEAN

Equator

Ninigo Group
Tulaghi
Hermit Islands
Admiralty Islands
Manus Island   Tulu
MANUS   Lorengau
M'bunai   Rambutyo
Lou Island
Mussau Island   Tabalo
St. Matthias Group
Emirau Island
Ysabel Channel
Taskul   North Cape
Kavieng
Tabar Islands
Lihir Group
Konos   Kavieng
New Hanover
Meteran   Konos
Dyaul Island
Namatanai
New Ireland
NEW IRELAND
Konogogo
Tanga Islands
Feni Islands
Nuguria Islands
Nukumanu Islands

Aua Island
Wuvulu Island

Jayapura
Vanimo
Pué   Entrop
WEST SEPIK
Sissano   Aitape
Torricelli Mountains
Imonda
Amanab   Green River
Amisibil
May River   Sepik
Nuku
Wandji
Tabubil
Kanggup
Kiunga
Muting
Bupul
Kofarau
Merauke
Sakiramke
Kondomirat
Weam
Morehead
Sibidiri
Mari
Daru
Oriomo

New Guinea
Mount Aiyang 3932m
Capella 3932m   3325m
HELA
ENGA HIGHLANDS
Porgera   Wabag
Koroba   Kandep
Tari   Margarima
Komo   Nipa
Ialibu   Poroma
Mount Bosavi 2397m
SOUTHERN HIGHLANDS
Kikori
WESTERN
Kiunga   Ketu
Balimo
Aramia
Lake Murray
Kamusi
Kukipi
Kerema
GULF
Baimuru
Puruti Island
Kiwai Island

Bismarck Sea

Manam Island
Bogia
Karkar Island
Saidor
Madang
MADANG
Usino
Bundi
Mount Wilhelm 4509m
WESTERN HIGHLANDS
Hagen   Minj
Mount Hagen
JIWAKA
CHIMBU
Kundiawa   Goroka
Kaiapit
EASTERN HIGHLANDS
Karimui
Marawaka

Long Island
Umboi Island
Vitiaz Strait
Malalamai
Sialum
Bangeta
Kabwum
Wonenara
Mount Tabletop 3686m
Markham
Lae   Nadzab
MOROBE
Finschhafen
Huon Peninsula
Wau   Mumeng
Morobe
Hercules Bay
Menyamya

Witu Islands
Willaumez Peninsula
WEST NEW BRITAIN
Gloucester
Talasea
Kimbe Bay
Anepmete   Hoskins
Kimbe
Whiteman Range
Nakanai Mountains
Arawe Islands
Pomio
Kandrian   Gasmata

Mussau
Cape Lambert
Rabaul
Kokopo
Toru
Taron
EAST NEW BRITAIN
Lobaou Bay
Open Bay
Sampun
Mount Shewut
Mount Talawe 1824m

New Britain

Cape St. George
Buka Island
Lemankoa
Buka   Hutjena
Mount Balbi 2685m   Wakunai
BOUGAINVILLE
Bougainville Island
Panguna
Bougainville Strait
Buin
Shortland Island
Treasury Islands

Solomon Sea

Solomon Islands

Green Islands
Ontong Java Atoll

Tulun Islands
Takuu Islands

Roncador Reef

CHOISEUL
Taro
Nukiki   Choiseul
Panggoe
Luti
Kia
New Georgia Sound
Vella Lavella
Ranongga
Gizo   Kolombangara
Monggga   New Georgia
Ringgi   Rendova
Vangunu
Tetepare
New Georgia Islands
WESTERN

ISABEL
Santa Isabel
Buala
Mount Sasari 1219m
Kaolo
CENTRAL
Yandina   Tulaghi
Cape Esperance   Tambea
HONIARA
Guadalcanal
Henderson Field
Nduindui
Avuavu
GUADALCANAL

Dai Island
Malu'u
Auki
Aola
Kwaii

RENNELL AND BELLONA
Bellona
Tigoa   Rennell
Lavanggu

Indispensable Reefs

PAPUA NEW GUINEA

Kikori
Bereina
CENTRAL
Tapini
Mount Victoria 4072m
NATIONAL CAPITAL DISTRICT
PORT MORESBY
Kwikila
Abau
Kupiano
Magarida
Eagle Point
Suau   Samarai

Jackson Field
Mount St. Mary
NORTHERN
Manau
Kokoda
Popondetta
Afore
Tufi
Mori
Owen Stanley Range
Rabaraba
Alotau
Ahioma
MILNE BAY
Misima
Magarida

Lusancay Islands and Reefs
Losuia
Kiriwina Island
Kiriwina Islands
D'Entrecasteaux Islands
Goodenough Island
Bolubolu
Fergusson Island
Esa'ala
Schulea
Normanby Island
Mount Suckling 3676m

Madau Island
Woodlark Island
Yanaba Island
Guasopa

Louisiade Archipelago
Bwagaoia
Pocklington Reef
The Calvados Chain
Tagula
Rossel Island
Tagula Island

Coral Sea

Torres Strait
Badu Island
Moa Island
Prince of Wales Island
Cape York

AUSTRALIA
Weipa
Cape York Peninsula
Coen
Laura
Cooktown
Lakeland Downs
Ayton
Mitchell River
Princess Charlotte Bay
Great Barrier Reef

Cikobia

Inset: NEW CALEDONIA (to France)

Récifs d'Entrecasteaux
Récif Petrie
Récif de Cook
Îles Belep
Île Pott
Waala   Île Art
Récif Huon
Récifs Français
Île Baaba
Île Yandé
Poum
Ouégoua   Île Balabio
Pouébo
Koumac
Mont Panié 1628m
Hienghène
Kaala-Gomen
PROVINCE NORD
Voh   Koné
Poindimié
Pouembout   Ponérihouen
Poya   Houaïlou
New Caledonia
Bourail
La Foa   Thio
Moindou
Canala
PROVINCE SUD
Boulouparis   Mont Humboldt 1618m
Paita
La Tontouta   Yaté
Dumbéa   Mont-Dore
NOUMÉA
Île Ouen
Récif de l'Astrolabe
Récif de la Gazelle
Ouvéa
Fayaoué
Lifou   Wé
PROVINCE DES ÎLES LOYAUTÉ
Île Tiga
Îles Loyauté
Maré
Tadine
Île des Pins
Vao
Grand Récif Sud

Scale 1:5,000,000
0 20 40 60 80 100 120 Km
0 20 40 60 80 100 120 Miles

Inset: FIJI

Vanua Levu
Great Sea Reef
Nabuna
Yasawa Group   Yasawa
Naduri
Nabavatu   Navoalevu   Rabi
Yaqaga   Labasa   Buca   Kioa
Yadua   Bua   Savusavu   Qamea
Matacawa Levu   Nacula   Nabouwalu   Somosomo
Naviti   Yaqeta   Kanacea
Viwa   Vanua Levu Barrier Reef   Taveuni
Waya   Ve Drala Reef
Tavua   Navaga   Nasau
Rakiraki   Makogai   Koro
Lautoka   Ba   Vatukoula   Oyalau
Nadi   Mount Victoria 1323m   Wakaya
Nadi   Levuka
Malolo   Korovou
Malolo Barrier Reef   Nairai   Koro Sea
Mamanuca Group   Batiki
Korolevu   Lami   Lamiti
Sigatoka   Lami   Gau
Viti Levu   Nausori
SUVA
Beqa   Navua
Vatulele   Kavukavu
Kadavu Passage   Moala
Ono   Tavuki
Great Astrolabe Reef
Kadavu   Vunisea   Matuku

Cikobia
Qelelevu Lagoon
Namuka Passage
Kanacea
Vanua Balavu
Yacata   Mago
Vatu Vara   Northern Lau Group
Cicia   Munia
Tuvuca
Nayau   Lakeba Passage
Lakeba
Vanua Vatu
Oneata
Moce
Namuka-i-lau   Vuaqava
Kabara   Yagasa Cluster
Totoya   Southern Lau Group
Fulaga   Ogea Driki
Vatoa

Scale 1:5,000,000
0 20 40 60 80 100 120 Km
0 20 40 60 80 100 120 Miles

Elevation scale
6000m
4000m
3000m
2000m
1000m
500m
250m
100m
Sea Level
-250m
-2000m
-4000m

Side tab
AUSTRALASIA & OCEANIA
280

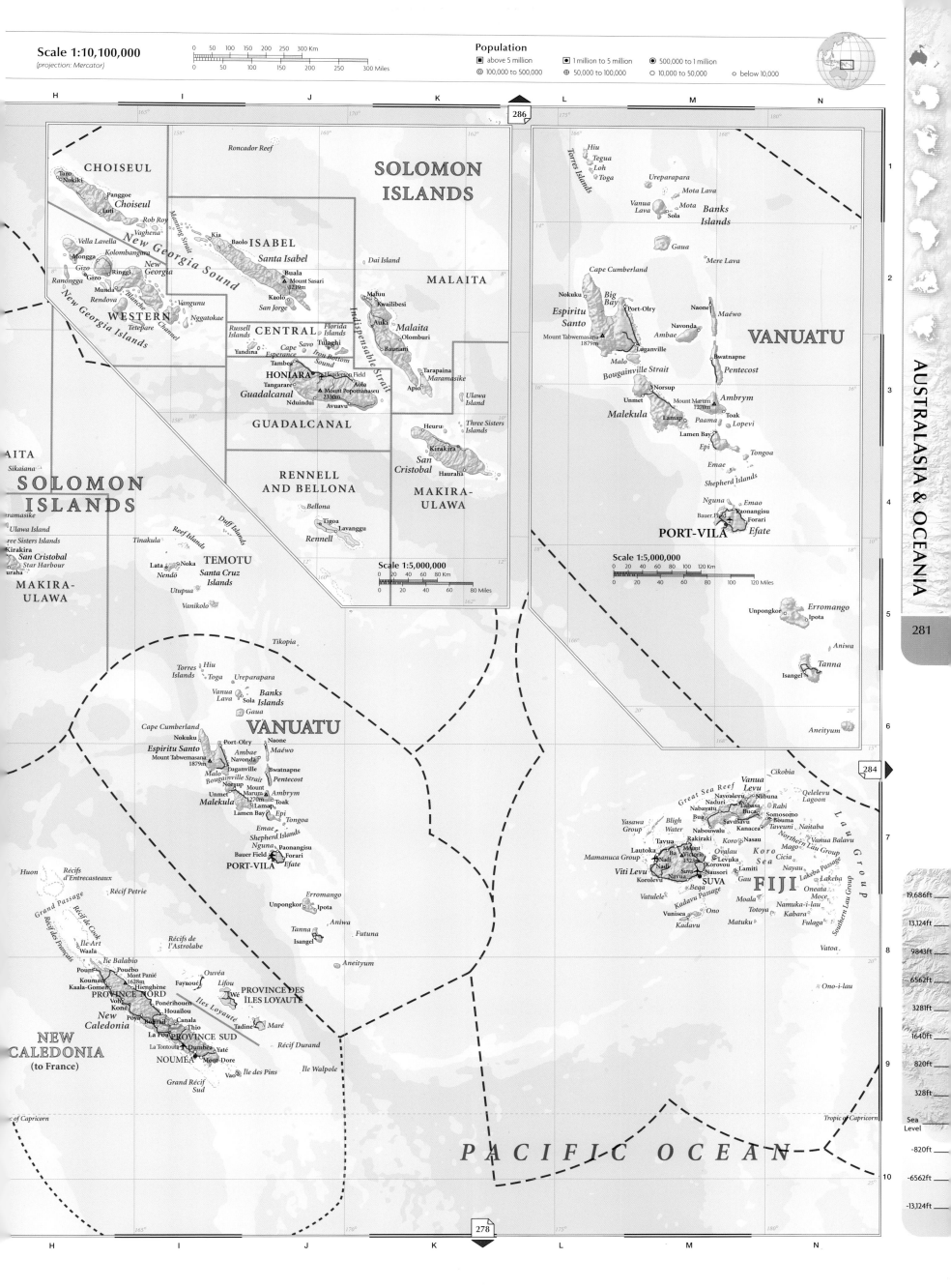

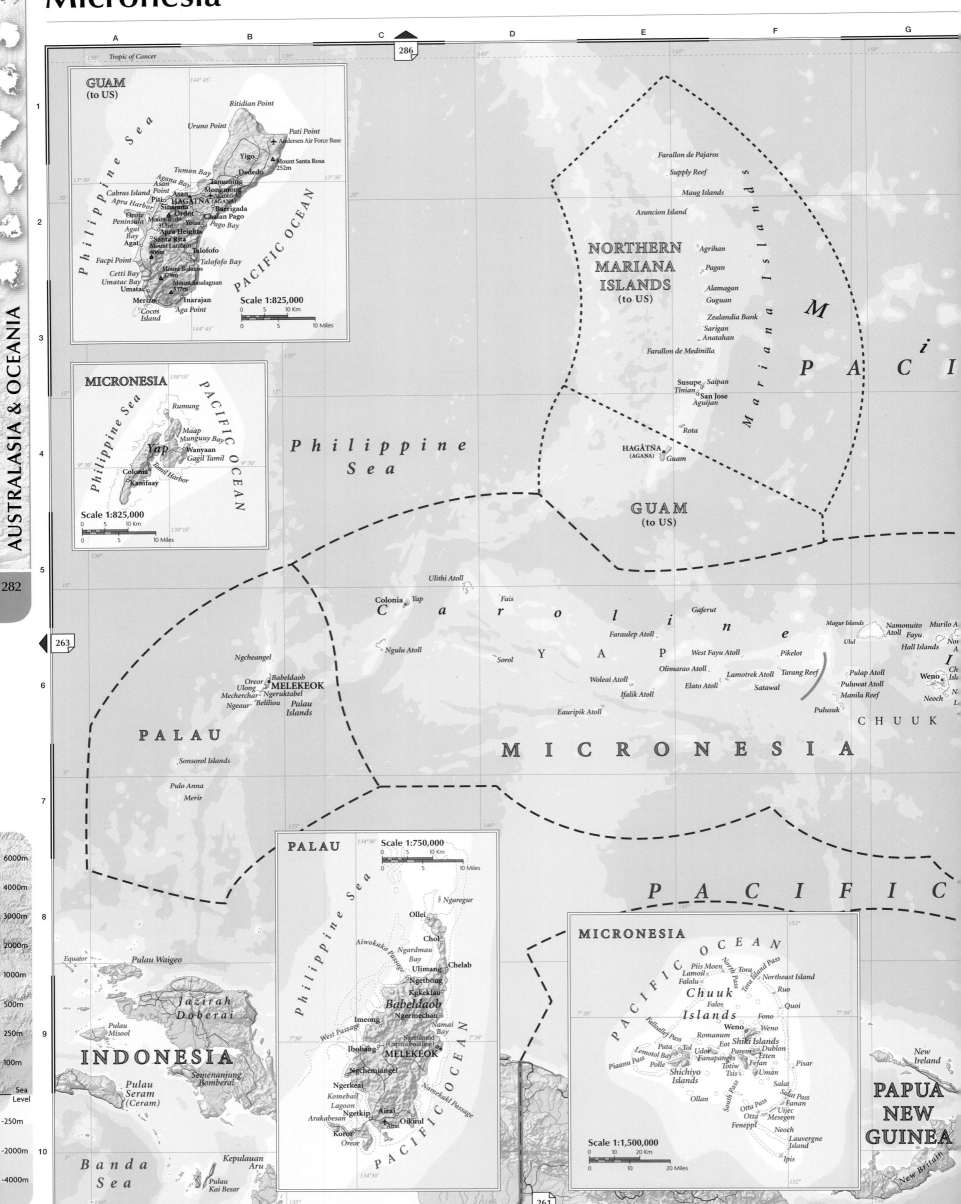

GUAM
(to US)

Ritidian Point

Uruno Point

Pati Point

Andersen Air Force Base

Yigo

Mount Santa Rosa
252m

Dededo

Tumon Bay

Tamuning
Mongmong

Agana Bay
Asan
Agana
Cabras Island
Point
Piti
HAGÅTÑA (AGANA)
Apra Harbor
Sinajana
Ordot
Barrigada
Orote
Mount Tenjo
Chalan Pago
Peninsula
313m
Yona
Pugo Bay
Agat
Apra Heights
Bay
Santa Rita
Agat
Mount Lamlam
406m
Julofofo

Facpi Point
Mount Bolanos

Talofofo Bay

Cetti Bay
Umatac Bay
Mount Sasalaguan
Umatac
Inarajan
Merizo
Aga Point
Cocos
Island

Philippine Sea

PACIFIC OCEAN

Scale 1:825,000
0   5   10 Km
0   5   10 Miles

MICRONESIA

PACIFIC OCEAN

Rumung

Maap
Munguuy Bay
Yap
Wanyaan
Gagil Tamil
Colonia
Tamil Harbor
Kanifaay

Philippine Sea

Scale 1:825,000
0   5   10 Km
0   5   10 Miles

Farallon de Pajaros

Supply Reef

Maug Islands

NORTHERN
MARIANA
ISLANDS
(to US)

Asuncion Island

Agrihan

Pagan

Alamagan
Guguan

Zealandia Bank
Sarigan
Anatahan

Farallon de Medinilla

Susupe   Saipan
Tinian
San Jose
Aguijan

Rota

HAGÅTÑA
(AGANA)
Guam

GUAM
(to US)

Mariana Islands

M
PACI

Philippine
Sea

Ulithi Atoll

Colonia   Yap

Fais

Gaferut

Magur Islands   Namonuito   Murilo A
Ulul   Atoll   Fayu
Hall Islands   Nor
A

C a r o l i n e

Faraulep Atoll

West Fayu Atoll   Pikelot

Ngulu Atoll

Sorol

Y   A   P

Olimarao Atoll   Lamotrek Atoll   Tarang Reef

Weno   Ch
I
Is

Ngcheangel

Woleai Atoll   Elato Atoll   Satawal

Pulap Atoll
Puluwat Atoll
Manila Reef
Neoch   La

Oreor   Babeldaob
Ulong   Ngeruktabel
Mecherchar
MELEKEOK
Ngeaur   Beliliou
Palau
Islands

Ifalik Atoll

Eauripik Atoll

Pulusuk

CHUUK

PALAU

Sonsorol Islands

M I C R O N E S I A

Pulo Anna

Merir

PALAU

Scale 1:750,000
0   5   10 Km
0   5   10 Miles

Ngaregur

Ollei

Chol

Aiwokako Passage
Ngardmau
Bay
Ulimang   Chelab
Ngetbong
Kgkeklau

Babeldaob
Imeong
Ngermechau
Namai
Bay
West Passage
Ngetulmud
(Capitol building)
Ibobang
MELEKEOK
Ngchemiangel
Namekakl Passage
Ngerkeai
Komebail
Lagoon   Airai
Arakabesan
Ngetkip   Oikiul
Koror   Airai
Oreor

Philippine Sea

PACIFIC OCEAN

PACIFIC

P A C I F I C

MICRONESIA

PACIFIC OCEAN

Piis Moen   Tora
Lamoil   North
Falalu   Pass   Tonoas   Tonom Island Pass
Chuuk   Falos   Northeast Island
Islands   Weno   Ruo
Fono
Romanum   Weno
Fallaelei Pass   Eot   Shiki Islands   Quoi
Lemotol Bay   Tol   Fanapanges   Parem   Dublon
Piaanu Pass   Pata   Udot   Fefan   Etten
Polle   Totiw   Uman
Shichiyo   Tsis   Pisar
Islands
Salat
Ollan   Salat Pass
South Pass   Fanan
Otta Pass   Mesegon
Otta
Neoch
Feneppi   Lauvergne
Island
Ipis

Scale 1:1,500,000
0   10   20 Km
0   10   20 Miles

Equator

Pulau Waigeo

Jazirah
Doberai

Pulau Misool

INDONESIA

Pulau
Seram
(Ceram)

Semenanjung
Bomberai

PAPUA
NEW
GUINEA

New
Ireland

New Britain

Banda
Sea

Kepulauan
Aru

Pulau
Kai Besar

6000m
4000m
3000m
2000m
1000m
500m
250m
100m
Sea
Level
-250m
-2000m
-4000m

286

263

261

Tropic of Cancer

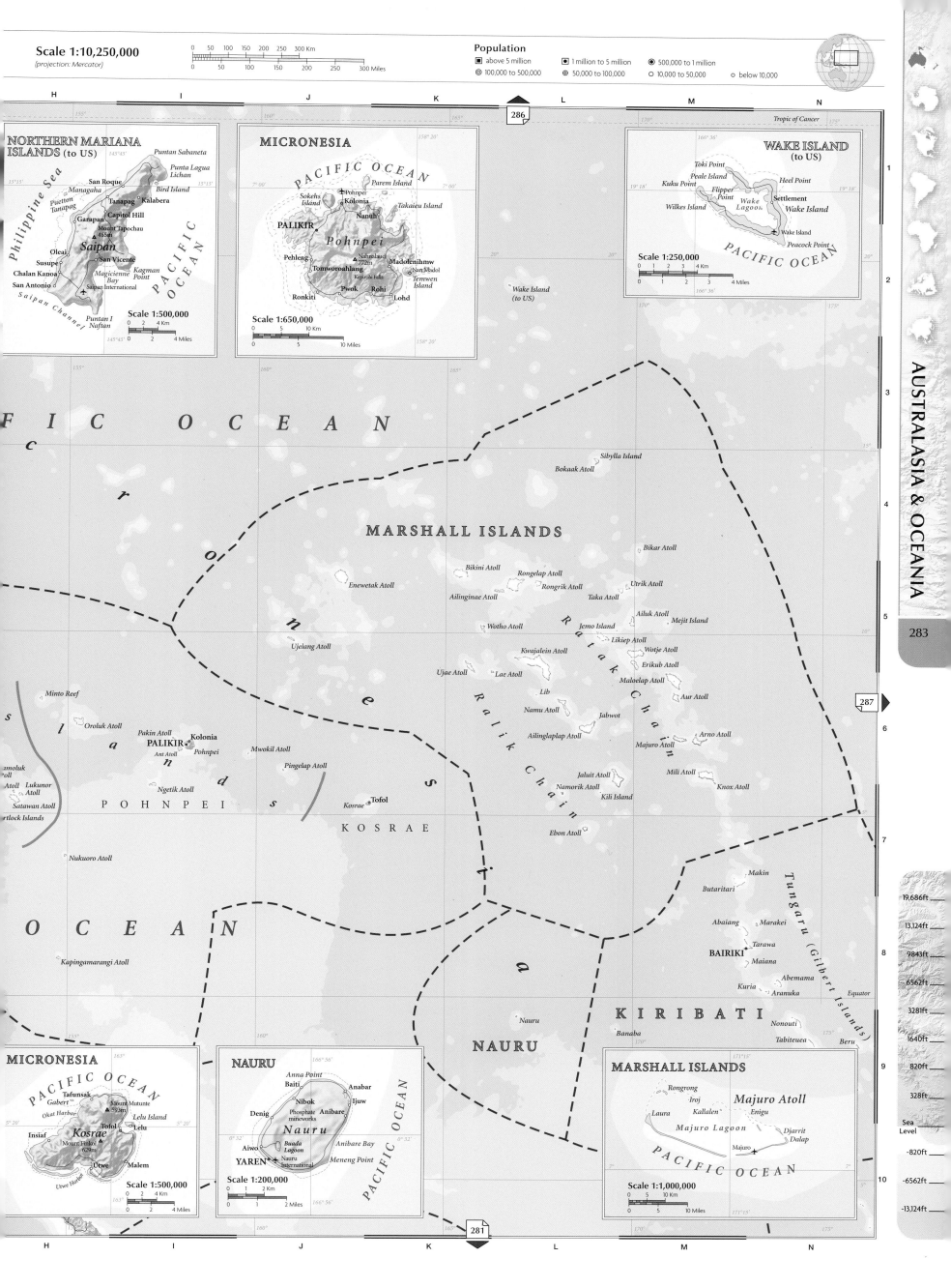

Polynesia

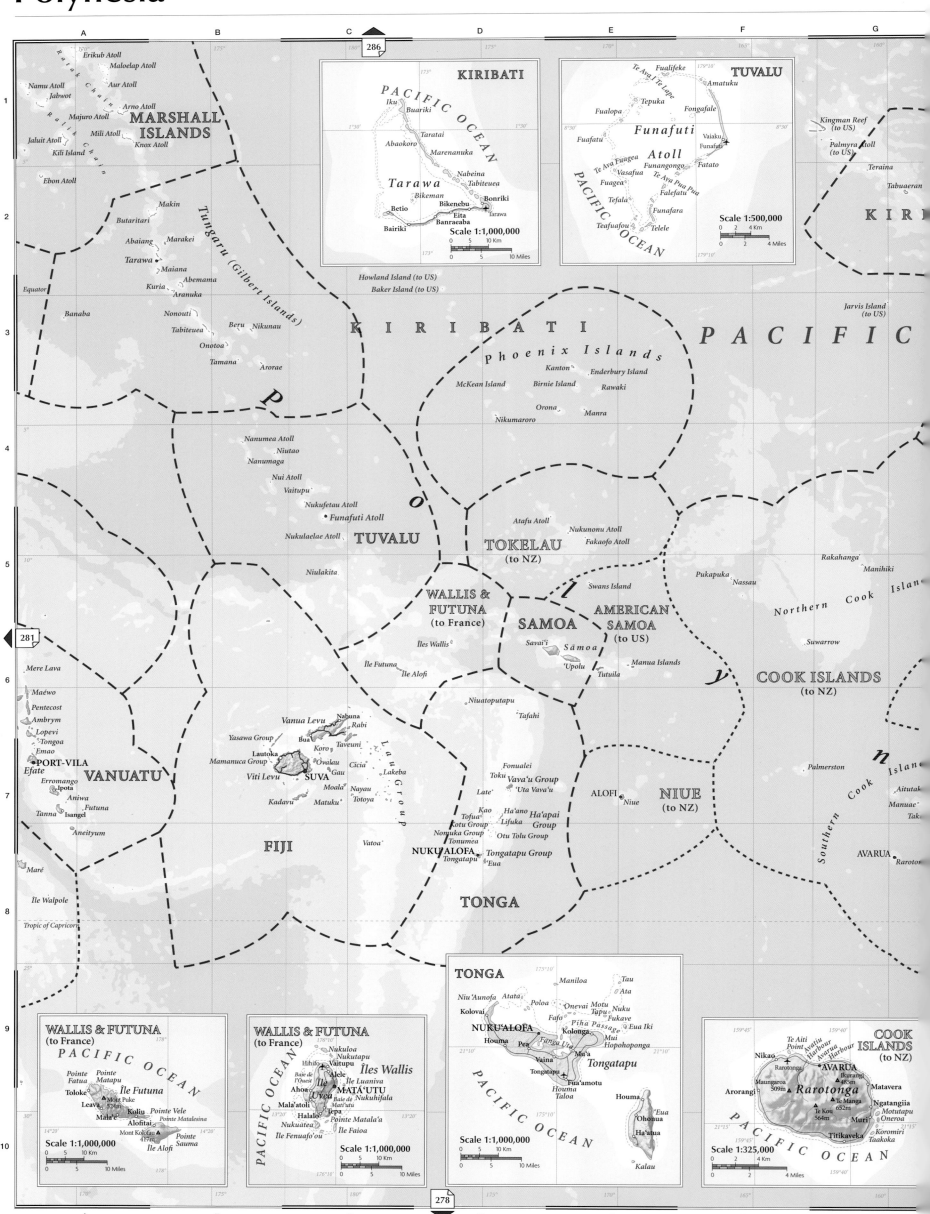

286

281

278

AUSTRALASIA & OCEANIA

KIRIBATI

PACIFIC OCEAN

Iku
Buariki
Taratai
Abaokoro
Marenanuka
Tarawa
Nabeina
Tabiteuea
Bikeman
Bonriki
Betio
Eita
Banraeaba Tarawa
Bairiki

Scale 1:1,000,000

TUVALU

Te Ava Ite Lagu
Fualifeke
Amatuku
Fualopa
Tepuka
Fongafale
Fuafatu
Fatato
Funafuti
Atoll
Vaiaku Funafuti
Funangongo
Vasafua
Te Ava Fuagea
Te Ava Pua Pua
Fuagea
Falefatu
Tefala
Funafara
Teafuafou
Telele

Scale 1:500,000

Howland Island (to US)
Baker Island (to US)

Kingman Reef (to US)
Palmyra Atoll (to US)
Teraina
Tabuaeran
KIRI

MARSHALL ISLANDS
Erikub Atoll
Maloelap Atoll
Namu Atoll
Aur Atoll
Jabwot
Arno Atoll
Majuro Atoll
Mili Atoll
Knox Atoll
Jaluit Atoll
Kili Island
Ebon Atoll

Rarik Chain
Ralik Chain

Makin
Butaritari
Marakei
Abaiang
Tarawa
Maiana
Kuria
Abemama
Aranuka
Equator
Banaba
Nonouti
Tabiteuea
Beru
Nikunau
Onotoa
Tamana
Arorae

Tungaru (Gilbert Islands)

K I R I B A T I

Phoenix Islands
Kanton
McKean Island
Birnie Island
Enderbury Island
Rawaki
Orona
Nikumaroro
Manra

P A C I F I C

Jarvis Island (to US)

Nanumea Atoll
Niutao
Nanumaga
Nui Atoll
Vaitupu
Nukufetau Atoll
Funafuti Atoll
TUVALU
Nukulaelae Atoll

Atafu Atoll
Nukunonu Atoll
Fakaofo Atoll
TOKELAU (to NZ)

Rakahanga
Manihiki

Niulakita

Swans Island
Pukapuka
Nassau

Northern Cook Islands

WALLIS & FUTUNA (to France)
Îles Wallis

SAMOA
AMERICAN SAMOA (to US)

Suwarrow

Île Futuna
Île Alofi
Savai'i
Sāmoa
'Upolu
Manua Islands
Tutuila

COOK ISLANDS (to NZ)

Mere Lava
Maéwo
Pentecost
Ambrym
Lopevi
Tongoa
Emao
PORT-VILA
Efate
Erromango
Ipota
Aniwa
Tanna
Futuna
Isangel
Aneityum

VANUATU

Yasawa Group
Vanua Levu
Nabuna
Rabi
Bua
Koro
Taveuni
Lautoka
Mamanuca Group
Owalau
Cicia
Viti Levu
SUVA
Gau
Moala
Nayau
Lakeba
Kadavu
Matuku
Totoya
Vatoa

Lau Group

FIJI

Niuatoputapu
Tafahi

Fonualei
Toku
Vava'u Group
Late
'Uta Vava'u

Fuavea
Kao
Ha'ano
Ha'apai Group
Tofua
Kotu Group
Lifuka
Nomuka Group
Otu Tolu Group
Tonumea
NUKU'ALOFA
Tongatapu Group
Tongatapu
'Eua

TONGA

ALOFI
Niue
NIUE (to NZ)

Palmerston

Southern Cook Islands

AVARUA
Rarotonga
Aitutaki
Manuae

Maré
Île Walpole

Tropic of Capricorn

WALLIS & FUTUNA (to France)
PACIFIC OCEAN
Pointe Fatua
Pointe Matapu
Toloke
Île Futuna
Mont Puke 574m
Leava
Koliu
Pointe Vele
Mala'e
Alofitai
Pointe Matalesina
Mont Kolofau 417m
Pointe Sauma
Île Alofi

Scale 1:1,000,000

WALLIS & FUTUNA (to France)
PACIFIC OCEAN
Nukuloa
Nukutapu
Hihifo
Vaitupu
Baie de l'Ouest
Île
Alele
Ahoa
Île Luaniva
MATÁ'UTU
Baie de Nukuhifala
Halalo
Tepa
Nukuatea
Pointe Matala'a
Mala'atoli
Île Faioa
Île Fenuafo'ou

Îles Wallis
'Uvea

Scale 1:1,000,000

TONGA
Maniloa
Tau
Niu 'Aunofa
Atatá
Ata
Poloa
Kolovai
Fafo
Onevai Motu
Tapu
Nuku
Houma
Kolonga
Fukave
'Eua Iki
Pea
Piha Passage
Mu'a
Hopohoponga
Fanga 'Uta
Vaina
Tongatapu
Fua'amotu
Houma
Taloa
Houma
'Ohonua
'Eua
Ha'atua
Kalau

NUKU'ALOFA

PACIFIC OCEAN

Scale 1:1,000,000

COOK ISLANDS (to NZ)
Te Aiti Point
Avatiu
Harbour
Avarua
Harbour
Nikao
AVARUA
Ikurangi
Matavera
Maungaroa 509m
Te Manga 652m
Arorangi
Rarotonga
Te Kou 564m
Ngatangiia
Motutapu
Oneroa
Muri
Titikaveka
Koromiri
Taakoka

Scale 1:325,000

PACIFIC OCEAN

6000m
4000m
3000m
2000m
1000m
500m
250m
100m
Sea Level
-250m
-2000m
-4000m

Scale 1:15,500,000
(projection: Mercator)

0 50 100 150 200 250 300 350 400 Km
0 50 100 150 200 250 300 350 400 Miles

Population
- ■ above 5 million
- □ 1 million to 5 million
- ◉ 500,000 to 1 million
- ◎ 100,000 to 500,000
- ⊕ 50,000 to 100,000
- ⊙ 10,000 to 50,000
- ○ below 10,000

287

SAMOA (inset)

Scale 1:3,000,000

0 20 40 Km
0 20 40 Miles

Savai'i
Fagamālo
Falealupo
Sataua
Cape Puava
Fālelima
Mauga Silisili 1858m
Tuasivi
Pu'apu'a
Salelologa
Sala'ilua
Satupa'iteau
Cape Asuisui
Taga
SAMOA
Palauli Bay
Apolima Strait
Fagaloa Bay
'Upolu
ĀPIA
Feleolo
Matautu
Mauga Fito
Mauga
Lotofaga
Fasito'o
Poutasi
Ti'avea
Safata Bay
Salani
S ā m o a

AMERICAN SAMOA (to US)

PAGO PAGO
Cape Matātula
Manu'a Islands
Cape Taputapu
Steps Point
Tutuila
'Aunu'u Island
Ofu
Olosega
Luma
Ta'ū

P A C I F I C   O C E A N

KIRIBATI (inset)

Scale 1:1,175,000

0 5 10 Km
0 5 10 Miles

PACIFIC OCEAN
KIRIBATI
Northwest Point
Cape Manning
London
Banana
Northeast Point
Cook Island
Saint Stanislas
Kiritimati
Paris
Manulu Lagoon
Kiritimati (Christmas Island)
Poland
South West Point
Vaskess Bay
Isles Lagoon
Joe's Hill
Bay of Wrecks
Azur Lagoon
Aeon Point
Pelican Lagoon
South East Point

Equator

FRENCH POLYNESIA (inset)

FRENCH POLYNESIA (to France)

Scale 1:1,000,000

0 5 10 Km
0 5 10 Miles

Baie d'Opunohu
Baie de Cook
Pointe Aroa
Papetoai
Mont Matotea 714m
Paopao
Moorea
Afareaitu
Mont Tohiea 1207m
Haapiti
Pointe Nuupere
Pointe Nuuroa

Îles du Vent
Baie de Matavai
Pointe Vénus
Mahina
Papenoo
PAPEETE
Pirea
Tiarei
Faaa
Faaa
Mont Aorai 2066m
Hitiaa
Punaauia
Mont Orohena 2241m
Tahiti
Passe Tamotoe
Baie de Taravao
Paea
Mont Tetufera 1799m
Faaone
Maraa
Taravao
Isthme de Taravao
Pointe Maraa
Papara
Mataiea
Afaahiti
Toahotu
Tautira
Récif Tepaee
Vairao
Presqu'île de Taiarapu
Teahupoo
Mont Rooniu 1332m

Main map

P A C I F I C   O C E A N

Malden Island
-buck Island
-hyn
Millennium Island
Vostok Island
Flint Island

Îles Marquises
Hatutu
Eiao
Nuku Hiva
Taiohae
Ua Huka
Ua Pu
Atuona
Hiva Oa
Tahuata
Motane
Fatu Hiva
Omoa

Kiritimati (Christmas Island)

Îles Sous le Vent
Motu One
Manuae
Maupiti
Tupai
Bora-Bora
Maupihaa
Tahaa
Fare
Maiao
Maupiti
Raiatea
Huahine
Moorea
Maiao
PAPEETE
Tahiti
Mehetia
Îles du Vent
Archipel de la Société

Îles du Roi Georges
Îles du Désappointement
Mataiva
Tikehau
Ahe
Manihi
Takapoto
Takaroa
Tepoto
Napuka
Rangiroa
Tikei
Pukapuka
Îles Palliser
Aratika
Niau
Toau
Kauehi
Takume
Fagatau
Fakarava
Raraka
Katiu
Fakahina
Faaite
Makemo
Raroia
Tahanea
Nihiru
Tehuata
Marutea
Anaa
Haraiki
Hikueru
Tauere
Amanu
Reitoru
Marokau
Hao
Akiaki
Ravahere
Pukarua
Negonego
Vahitahi
Reao
Manuhagi
Paraoa
Vairaatea
Pinaki
Hereheretue
Îles du Duc de Gloucester
'Ahunui
Vanavana
Tureia
Groupe Actéon
Maria
Tenarara
Marutea
Rimatara
Rurutu
Moruroa
Maria
Tematagi
Fagataufa
Tubuai
Îles Gambier
Magareva
Temoe
Raevavae
Rapa Iti
Marotiri
Îles Australes

P A C I F I C   O C E A N

FRENCH POLYNESIA (to France)

Tropic of Capricorn

PITCAIRN, HENDERSON DUCIE & OENO ISLANDS (to UK)
Oeno Island
Henderson Island
Ducie Island
Pitcairn Island

287

NIUE (inset)

NIUE (to NZ)

Scale 1:1,000,000

0 5 10 Km
0 5 10 Miles

Hikutavake
Toi
Mutalau
Makefu
Tuapa
Lakepa
Makapu Point
Alofi Bay
ALOFI
Niue
Liku
Halagigie Point
Hanan
Tamakautoga
Avatele
Hakupu
Tepa Point
Mata Point

PACIFIC OCEAN

PITCAIRN ISLAND (inset)

PITCAIRN ISLAND (to UK)

Scale 1:125,000

0 0.5 1 Km
0 0.5 1 Miles

Young's Rock
Bounty Bay
ADAMSTOWN
Pitcairn Island
Adam's Rock
Point Christian
St Paul's Point

PACIFIC OCEAN

P A C I F I C   O C E A N

Elevation scale:
19,686ft
13,124ft
9843ft
6562ft
3281ft
1640ft
820ft
328ft
Sea Level
-820ft
-6562ft
-13,124ft

Pacific Ocean

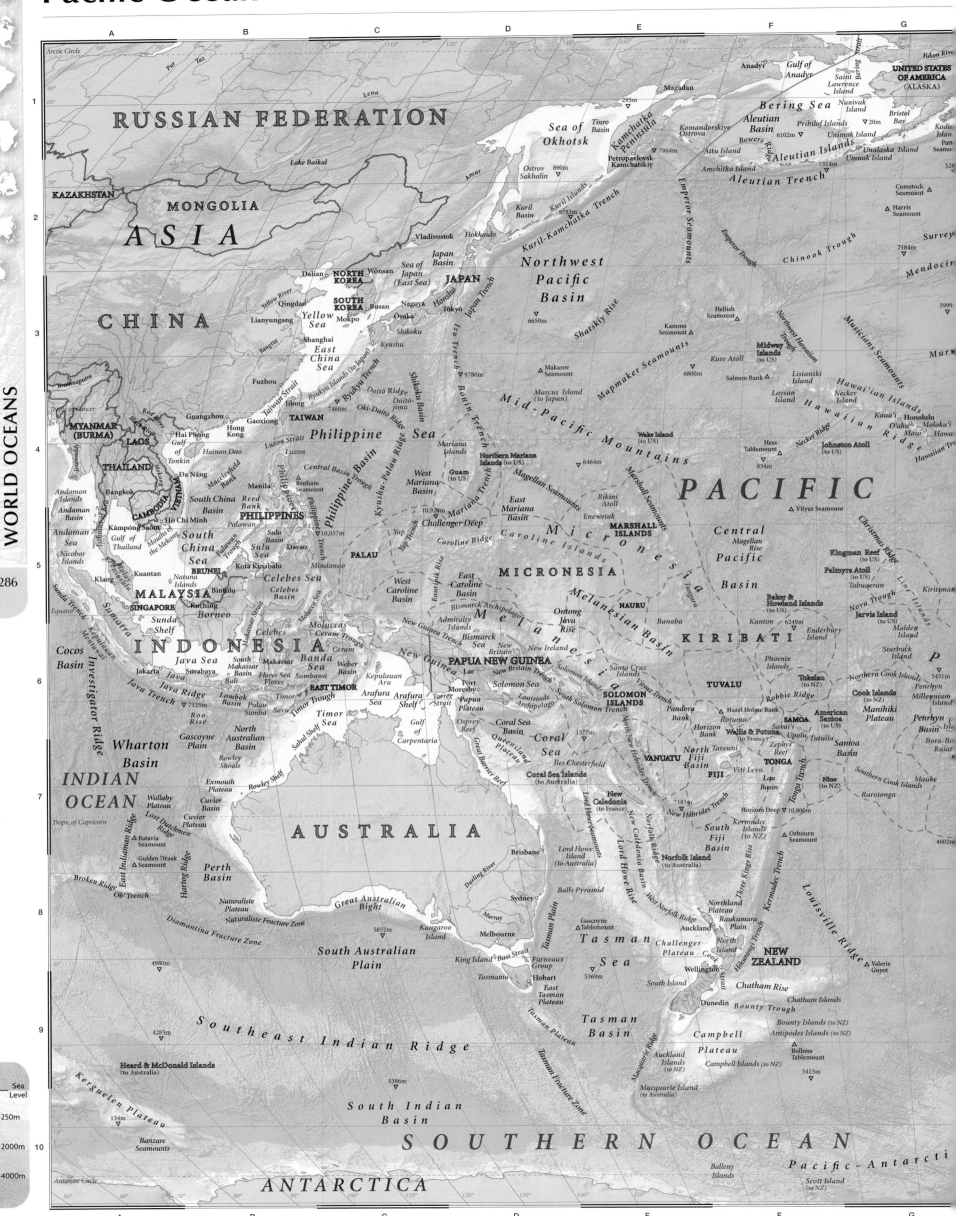

RUSSIAN FEDERATION

KAZAKHSTAN

MONGOLIA

ASIA

CHINA

Lake Baikal

Arctic Circle

Sea of Okhotsk

Bering Sea

Aleutian Islands

UNITED STATES OF AMERICA (ALASKA)

Aleutian Trench

Kamchatka Peninsula

Kuril Islands

Kuril-Kamchatka Trench

Northwest Pacific Basin

Emperor Seamounts

Chinook Trough

NORTH KOREA

SOUTH KOREA

JAPAN

Sea of Japan (East Sea)

Japan Trench

Shatskiy Rise

Musicians Seamounts

Midway Islands (to US)

Hawaiian Islands

PACIFIC

MYANMAR (BURMA)

LAOS

THAILAND

VIETNAM

CAMBODIA

TAIWAN

Philippine Sea

Mid-Pacific Mountains

Marshall Seamounts

MARSHALL ISLANDS

Central Pacific Basin

Mariana Trench

Challenger Deep

MICRONESIA

NAURU

KIRIBATI

PHILIPPINES

PALAU

South China Sea

MALAYSIA

SINGAPORE

BRUNEI

INDONESIA

Borneo

Celebes Sea

Banda Sea

PAPUA NEW GUINEA

SOLOMON ISLANDS

TUVALU

SAMOA

American Samoa (to US)

Cook Islands

INDIAN OCEAN

Wharton Basin

AUSTRALIA

Coral Sea

VANUATU

FIJI

TONGA

Niue (to NZ)

Perth Basin

Great Australian Bight

Sydney

Melbourne

Tasman Sea

NEW CALEDONIA (to France)

NEW ZEALAND

Chatham Rise

Tasmania

Tasman Basin

Campbell Plateau

Kerguelen Plateau

South Indian Basin

SOUTHERN OCEAN

ANTARCTICA

Sea Level

−250m

−2000m

−4000m

Scale 1:62,500,000
(projection: Robinson)

500 1000 1500 2000 Km
500 1000 1500 2000 Miles

Map labels:

Great Bear Lake
Great Slave Lake
Foxe Basin
Foxe Channel
Hudson Strait
Ungava Bay
Greenland (to Denmark)
Denmark Strait
ICELAND
Iceland
Norwegian Basin
Labrador Sea
Reykjanes Basin
Imatsusuak Channel
Reykjanes Ridge
Iceland Basin
Hatton Ridge
3300m
Anchorage
Gulf of Alaska
Pratt Seamount
Alaska Plain
Welker Seamount
Queen Charlotte Islands
Labrador Basin
Erik Ridge
Northwest Atlantic Mid-Ocean Canyon
Charlie-Gibbs Fracture Zone
West Thulean Rise
East Thulean Rise
Edoras Bank
Rockall Bank
Rockall Trough
ufts Plain
Gilbert Seamounts
Vancouver Island
Vancouver
Seattle
Columbia
Fraser
CANADA
Hamilton Bank
Newfoundland
NORTH AMERICA
Lake Superior
Lake Huron
Gulf of St Lawrence
St Lawrence
Nova Scotia
13m
Flemish Cap
Grand Banks of Newfoundland
Newfoundland Seamounts
Milne Seamounts
Kings Trough
Cascadia Basin
Cascadia
fracture Zone
San Francisco
Lake Michigan
Lake Ontario
Lake Erie
Georges Bank
69m
6492m
Newfoundland Ridge
Newfoundland Basin
ioneer Fracture Zone
UNITED STATES OF AMERICA
New England Seamounts
Corner Seamounts
Oceanographer Fracture Zone
fracture Zone
5561m
Fisberling Seamount
Channel Escarpment
Colorado
5464m
Sohm Plain
Atlantis Fracture Zone
Moonless Mountains
Guadalupe (to Mexico)
Long Beach
Channel Islands
Mississippi
Rio Grande
Texas-Louisiana Shelf
Hatteras Plain
Bermuda (to UK)
Bermuda Rise
Nashville Seamount
ATLANTIC
Azores (to Portugal)
lokai Fracture Zone
Cedros Trench
Gulf of California
West Florida Shelf
Blake-Bahama Ridge
Blake Plateau
Sargasso Sea
Kane Fracture Zone
Tropic of Cancer
OCEAN
MEXICO
Gulf of Mexico
Mexico Basin
Puerto Vallarta
Straits of Florida
THE BAHAMAS
CUBA
Nares Plain
Revillagigedo Islands (to Mexico)
Mathematicians Seamounts
Middle America Trench
Cayman Trench
West Indies
Windward Passage
Puerto Rico Trench
Greater Antilles
Leeward Islands
Mid-Atlantic Ridge
OCEAN
Alphecca Seamount
East Pacific Rise
GUATEMALA
BELIZE
HONDURAS
Puerto San José
EL SALVADOR
NICARAGUA
Acajutla
Corinto
Caribbean Sea
Venezuelan Basin
Lesser Antilles
TRINIDAD & TOBAGO
Vema Fracture Zone
Barracuda Fracture Zone
Doldrums Fracture Zone
Clarion Fracture Zone
Clipperton Island (to France)
6662m
3806m
Guatemala Basin
COSTA RICA
Caldera
PANAMA
Gulf of Honduras
Gulf of Darien
Panama Canal
Panama City
Colombian Basin
Orinoco
VENEZUELA
GUYANA
FRENCH GUIANA (to France)
SURINAME
Demerara Plateau
Demerara Plain
Ceara Ridge
pperton Fracture Zone
Cocos Ridge
Colón Ridge
Buenaventura
Panama Basin
COLOMBIA
Tumaco
Magdalena
Amazon Fan
4567m
apagos Fracture Zone
Isla San Cristóbal
Isla Isabela
Galápagos Islands (to Ecuador)
Carnegie Ridge
Esmeraldas
ECUADOR
Guayaquil
Amazon
Ceara Plain
Equator
Gallego Rise
Bauer Basin
Grijalva Ridge
Paita
BRAZIL
SOUTH
5852m
Galápagos Rise
Peru-Chile Trench
PERU
Callao
AMERICA
Mendaña Fracture Zone
Nazca Ridge
BOLIVIA
Hotspur Seamount
Nuku Hiva
Marquesas Islands
Hiva Oa
Peru Basin
Ilha da Trindade
Marquesas Fracture Zone
Tuamotu Fracture Zone
Yupanqui Basin
8069m
PARAGUAY
Tropic of Capricorn
Tiki Basin
Austral Fracture Zone
Sala y Gomez (to Chile)
Islas de los Desventurados (to Chile)
Antofagasta
Santos Plateau
Henderson Island
Ducie Island
Easter Island (to Chile)
Sala y Gomez Ridge
Easter Fracture Zone
Isla San Ambrosio
Isla San Félix
ARGENTINA
Pitcairn Island
Pitcairn, Henderson, Ducie & Oeno Islands (to UK)
Chile Basin
636m
Iles Gambier
Rio Grande Gap
Rio Grande Rise
Rapa
Roggeveen Basin
Islas Juan Fernández (to Chile)
URUGUAY
Agassiz Fracture Zone
Challenger Fracture Zone
Isla Alejandro Selkirk
Isla Robinson Crusoe
Valparaiso
Selkirk Rise
Talcahuano
Argentine Basin
1426m
East Pacific Rise
Chile Rise
Mocha Fracture Zone
Zapiola Ridge
Guafo Fracture Zone
Argentine Plain
Falkland Escarpment
Gulf of San Jorge
outhwest Pacific Basin
Menard Fracture Zone
Mornington Abyssal Plain
6034m
Chile Trench
Punta Arenas
Falkland Islands (to UK)
Burdwood Bank
Falkland Plateau
Maurice Ewing Bank
Islas Orcadas Rise
Eltanin Fracture Zone
Cape Horn
West Scotia Ridge
South Georgia
8325m
South Sandwich Trench
Udintsev Fracture Zone
Yaghan Basin
Drake Passage
South Shetland Trough
South Shetland Islands
South Orkney Islands
Scotia Sea
5576m
South Scotia Basin
7152m
America-Antarctica Ridge
Southeast Pacific Basin
Bellingshausen Plain
De Gerlache Seamounts
Bellingshausen Sea
Antarctic Peninsula
SOUTHERN OCEAN
Amundsen Plain
Marie Byrd Seamount
Peter I Island (to Norway)
Weddell Plain
Antarctic Circle

Sea Level
-820ft
-6562ft
-13,124ft

RUSSIAN FEDERATION

ASIA

CHINA

MONGOLIA

KAZAKHSTAN

EUROPE

NORWAY

SWEDEN

FINLAND

DENMARK

ESTONIA

LATVIA

LITHUANIA

RUSS. FED.

POLAND

BELARUS

UKRAINE

MOLDOVA

ROMANIA

BULGARIA

SLOVAKIA

HUNGARY

CZECH REPUBLIC

AUSTRIA

SLOVENIA

CROATIA

BOZ & HERZ.

SERBIA

MONTENEGRO KOS.

MACEDONIA

ALBANIA

GREECE

TURKEY

GEORGIA

ARMENIA

AZERBAIJAN

SYRIA

LEBANON

ISRAEL

JORDAN

IRAQ

KUWAIT

SAUDI ARABIA

BAHRAIN

QATAR

U.A.E.

OMAN

YEMEN

IRAN

AFGHANISTAN

PAKISTAN

TURKMENISTAN

UZBEKISTAN

TAJIKISTAN

KYRGYZSTAN

INDIA

NEPAL

BHUTAN

BANGLADESH

MYANMAR (BURMA)

THAILAND

LAOS

VIETNAM

CAMBODIA

MALAYSIA

SINGAPORE

BRUNEI

PHILIPPINES

TAIWAN

NORTH KOREA

SOUTH KOREA

JAPAN

SRI LANKA

MALDIVES

EGYPT

LIBYA

CHAD

SUDAN

SOUTH SUDAN

CENTRAL AFRICAN REPUBLIC

ERITREA

DJIBOUTI

ETHIOPIA

SOMALIA

AFRICA

Laptev Sea

Kara Sea

Barents Sea

Lena

Yenisey

Ob

Irtysh

Tobol

Ishim

Pechora

Northern Dvina

Volga

Don

Kama

Ural

Lake Baikal

Lake Zaysan

Lake Balkhash

Aral Sea

Caspian Sea

Black Sea

Mediterranean Sea

Ionian Sea

Adriatic Sea

Baltic Sea

Crete

Cyprus

Sinai

Red Sea

Nile

White Nile

Blue Nile

Sudd

Lake Tana

Lake Turkana

Lake Albert

Mogadishu

Shebeli

Juba

Persian Gulf

Gulf of Oman

Gulf of Aden

Arabian Sea

Arabian Basin

Carlsberg Ridge

Owen Fracture Zone

Socotra

Bay of Bengal

Ganges Fan

Indus Fan

Indus

Ganges

Brahmaputra

Mouths of the Ganges

Andaman Sea

Andaman Islands (to India)

Nicobar Islands (to India)

Laccadive Islands (to India)

Maldive Plateau

Sunda Trench

Ninetyeast Ridge

South China Sea

South China Basin

East China Sea

Yellow Sea

Sea of Japan (East Sea)

Korea Strait

Gulf of Tonkin

Gulf of Thailand

Strait of Malacca

Philippine Sea

Philippine Trench

Sulu Sea

Celebes Sea

Banda Sea

Luzon Strait

Taiwan Strait

Yangtze

Yellow River

Mekong

Salween

Irrawaddy

Arctic Circle

Tropic of Cancer

Sea Level

−250m

−2000m

−4000m

Scale 1:32,000,000
(projection: Robinson)

0 200 400 600 800 1000 1200 Km
0 200 400 600 800 1000 1200 Miles

Sea Level
-820ft
-6562ft
-13,124ft

INDIAN OCEAN

SOUTHERN OCEAN

AUSTRALIA

INDONESIA

EAST TIMOR

MADAGASCAR

SOUTH AFRICA

Banda Sea
Java Sea
Timor Sea
Savu Sea
Celebes
Makassar
Sumba
Sumbawa
Bali
Lombok
Java
Sumatra
Flores
Sunda Shelf

Timor Trough
Timor
Pulau Sumba
Lombok Basin
Java-Java Ridge
7125m
Roo Rise
Java Trench
4464m
Christmas Island (to Australia)
Vening Meinesz Seamounts
Cocos Islands (to Australia)
5759m

Ashmore & Cartier Islands (to Australia)
Sahul Shelf
Wyndham
Broome
Port Hedland
Rowley Shoals
Rowley Shelf
Exmouth Plateau
North Australian Basin
Gascoyne Plain
5678m

Cuvier Basin
Cuvier Plateau
Wallaby Plateau
Lost Dutchmen Ridge
Wharton Basin
4025m
Batavia Seamount
Gulden Draak Seamount
East Indiaman Ridge
Hartog Ridge
Broken Ridge
Ob' Trench
Geraldton
Perth Basin
Fremantle
Bunbury
Albany
Naturaliste Plateau
Naturaliste Fracture Zone
Diamantina Fracture Zone
Great Australian Bight
South Australian Basin
5657m
5386m
4980m
4285m

Southeast Indian Ridge

South Indian Basin

Investigator Ridge
Cocos Basin
Ninetyeast Ridge
Mid-Indian Basin
Chagos Archipelago
British Indian Ocean Territory (to UK)
Chagos-Laccadive Ridge
Chagos Trench
Diego Garcia
Mid-Indian Ridge
Osborn Plateau
5614m
4023m

Amsterdam Fracture Zone
Amsterdam Island
St Paul Island

Kerguelen Plateau
Heard & McDonald Islands (to Australia)
184m
Banzare Seamounts
French Southern & Antarctic Lands (to France)
Kerguelen
4684m
5386m

Prydz Bay

Enderby Plain

Mascarene Plateau
Mascarene Basin
Mascarene Plain
Mascarene Islands
Saya de Malha Bank
Nazareth Bank
Cargados Carajos Bank
Seychelles Bank
Mahé
SEYCHELLES
Amirante Islands
Amirante Basin
Amirante Ridge
Amirante Trench
Fred Seamount
Bardin Seamount
Farquhar Group
Agalega Islands
Aldabra Group
3658m
2078m
7023m
Egeria Fracture Zone
Vema Fracture Zone
Marie Celeste Fracture Zone
Argo Fracture Zone
Rodrigues (to Mauritius)
MAURITIUS
Réunion (to France)
Mauritius Trench

Southwest Indian Ridge

Crozet Basin
Crozet Plateau
Crozet Islands
Del Cano Rise
Prince Edward Islands (to South Africa)
Indomed Fracture Zone
Prince Edward Fracture Zone
Walters Shoal
4996m
4968m
Ob' Tablemount
Lena Tablemount
5380m

Atlantic-Indian Basin
Atlantic-Indian Ridge

Matingley Rise
Comoros
COMOROS
Mayotte (to France)
Comoro
Moheli
Giraud Seamount
Davie Ridge
Mozambique Channel
Madagascar Basin
Madagascar Plateau
Natal Basin
Natal Valley
Mozambique Plateau
Mozambique Escarpment
Transkei Basin
Agulhas Plateau
Agulhas Basin
Africana Seamount
Protea Seamount
Agulhas Bank
5819m
Toamasina
198m
69m
497m

DEM. REP. OF CONGO
BURUNDI
TANZANIA
MALAWI
ZAMBIA
ZIMBABWE
MOZAMBIQUE
BOTSWANA
SWAZILAND
LESOTHO
SOUTH AFRICA

Lake Victoria
Lake Tanganyika
Lake Rukwa
Lake Nyasa
Lake Mweru
Lake Cahora Bassa
Lake Kariba
Mombasa
Pemba
Zanzibar
Tanga
Dar es Salaam
Mafia
Cabo Delgado
Nacala
Rovuma
Lurio
Quelimane
Beira
Bassas da India
Îte Europa
Jaguar Seamount
Juan de Nova
Zambezi
Limpopo
Maputo
Drakensberg
Tugela
Durban
East London
Port Elizabeth
Mosselbaai
Cape Town
Cape of Good Hope
Cape Agulhas
Orange River
Tropic of Capricorn
Antarctic Circle

Atlantic Ocean

Sea Level
−250m
−2000m
−4000m

Oceans and Seas
Barents Sea
Norwegian Sea
Greenland Sea
Iceland Sea
North Sea
Baltic Sea
Labrador Sea
Baffin Bay
Hudson Bay
Davis Strait
Denmark Strait
Gulf of St Lawrence
Bay of Biscay
Celtic Sea
Mediterranean Sea
Sargasso Sea
Caribbean Sea
Gulf of Mexico
Gulf of Guinea
West Indies
ARCTIC OCEAN
ATLANTIC OCEAN

Land
CANADA
NORTH AMERICA
UNITED STATES OF AMERICA
MEXICO
GUATEMALA
BELIZE
HONDURAS
EL SALVADOR
NICARAGUA
COSTA RICA
PANAMA
COLOMBIA
VENEZUELA
GUYANA
SURINAME
FRENCH GUIANA
CUBA
JAMAICA
HAITI
DOMINICAN REPUBLIC
THE BAHAMAS
BARBADOS
TRINIDAD & TOBAGO
Greenland (to Denmark)
ICELAND
Reykjavik
UNITED KINGDOM
IRELAND
FINLAND
SWEDEN
NORWAY
Scandinavia
ESTONIA
LATVIA
LITHUANIA
RUS. FED.
BELARUS
POLAND
UKRAINE
DENMARK
NETH.
BELGIUM
GERMANY
CZECH REPUBLIC
SLOVAKIA
AUSTRIA
HUNGARY
ROMANIA
SLOVENIA
CROATIA
BOS. & HERZ.
SERBIA
MONTENEGRO
KOS.
MACEDONIA
ALBANIA
GREECE
ITALY
SWITZ.
FRANCE
SPAIN
PORTUGAL
Sahara
ALGERIA
LIBYA
CHAD
TUNISIA
MOROCCO
Western Sahara (occupied by Morocco)
MAURITANIA
MALI
NIGER
AFRICA
NIGERIA
BENIN
TOGO
GHANA
IVORY COAST
BURKINA FASO
LIBERIA
SIERRA LEONE
GUINEA
GUINEA-BISSAU
GAMBIA
SENEGAL
CAPE VERDE
CAMEROON
CENTRAL AFRICAN REPUBLIC
CONGO

Ocean Floor Features
Mid-Atlantic Ridge
Reykjanes Ridge
Charlie-Gibbs Fracture Zone
Azores-Biscay Rise
Azores Fracture Zone
East Azores Fracture Zone
Oceanographer Fracture Zone
Atlantis Fracture Zone
Pico Fracture Zone
Kane Fracture Zone
Vema Fracture Zone
Barracuda Fracture Zone
Doldrums Fracture Zone
Four North Fracture Zone
Jan Mayen Fracture Zone
Jan Mayen Ridge
Faraday Fracture Zone
Maxwell Fracture Zone
Akademik Kurchatov Fracture Zone
Greenland-Iceland Rise
Kolbeinsey Ridge
Faroe-Iceland Ridge
Iceland Plateau
Iceland Basin
Greenland Basin
Reykjanes Basin
Labrador Basin
Newfoundland Basin
Sohm Plain
Nares Plain
Hatteras Plain
Demerara Plain
Madeira Plain
Iberian Plain
Tagus Plain
Biscay Plain
Cape Verde Plain
Canary Basin
Cape Verde Basin
Gambia Plain
Sierra Leone Basin
Guatemala Basin
Venezuelan Basin
Colombian Basin
Baffin Basin
Foxe Basin
Bermuda Rise
New England Seamounts
Corner Seamounts
Nashville Seamount
Great Meteor Tablemount
Cruiser Tablemount
Madeira Tablemount
Charrat Seamounts
Seamounts
Dacia Seamount
Agadir Canyon
Goban Spur
Porcupine Bank
Rockall Bank
Hatton Bank
Rockall
Porcupine Plain
Porcupine Bank
Galicia Bank
Bissau Plain
Northwest Atlantic Mid-Ocean Canyon
Grand Banks of Newfoundland
Newfoundland Ridge
Newfoundland Seamounts
Flemish Cap
Georges Bank
Blake Plateau
Blake-Bahama Ridge
Bermuda (to UK)
Canary Islands (to Spain)
Madeira (to Portugal)
Azores (to Portugal)
Cape Verde Terrace
Researcher Seamount
Puerto Rico Trench
Middle America Trench
Cayman Trench

Cities / Places
Nuuk
Halifax
Boston
New York
Baltimore
Montreal
Jacksonville
Savannah
New Orleans
Houston
Corpus Christi
Mobile
Tampico
Veracruz
Mexico City
Belize City
San José
Bluefields
Corinto
Limón
Cristobal
Panama City
Maracaibo
Barranquilla
Cartagena
Georgetown
Paramaribo
Cayenne
La Guaira
Reykjavik
Belfast
Cork
Southampton
Milford Haven
Nantes
Bordeaux
Bilbao
Gijón
Lisboa
Leixões
Casablanca
Safi
Nouadhibou
Nouakchott
Dakar
Banjul
Bissau
Conakry
Freetown
Monrovia
Abidjan
Accra
Lomé
Cotonou
Lagos
Porto-Novo
Douala
Port Harcourt

Great Lakes
Lake Superior
Lake Michigan
Lake Huron
Lake Erie
Lake Ontario
Mississippi
Amazon Fan
Ceará Ridge
Cocos Ridge

Scale 1:34,400,000
(projection: Robinson)

0 200 400 600 800 1000 1200 Km
0 200 400 600 800 1000 1200 Miles

Sea Level

-820ft

-6562ft

-13,124ft

GABON
CONGO
DEM. REP.
ANGOLA (Cabinda)
Matadi
Pointe-Noire
Luanda
Lobito
ANGOLA
Namibe
NAMIBIA
Walvis Bay
Lüderitz
Namib Desert
Tropic of Capricorn
Orange
SOUTH AFRICA
Cape Town
Cape of Good Hope
Protea Seamount

Congo Fan
Pierre Brazza Seamounts
Basin
Angola Basin
Zubov Seamount
5042m
Dampier Seamount
6039m
Namibia Plain
Orange Fan
Walvis Ridge
Cape Basin
Vema Seamount
5115m
Cape Rise
Schmidt-Ott Seamount

Romanche F.Z.
Chain Fracture Zone
6308m
Pernambuco Basin
Ascension Fracture Zone
Ascension Island (to UK)
Bode Verde Fracture Zone
570m
Saint Helena
(to UK)
Bonaparte Seamount
Saint Helena Fracture Zone
Rio Grande Fracture Zone
Tristan da Cunha Fracture Zone
Tristan da Cunha (to UK)
1799m
Gough Fracture Zone
Gough Island
Discovery Tablemount
Meteor Rise
Simmons Seamounts
Davis Seamount
Atlantic-Indian Ridge
Bouvet Island (to Norway)
Atlantic-Indian Basin
Maud Rise
Astrid Ridge

SOUTHERN OCEAN

ANTARCTICA
Lazarev Sea
Riiser-Larsen Sea
Antarctic Circle

Atlantic Ridge
Mid-Atlantic Ridge
America-Antarctica Ridge

Parnaíba Ridge
Fernando de Noronha (to Brazil)
Brazil Basin
Pernambuco Seamounts
Stocks Seamount
Fernz Ridge
Ilhas Martin Vaz
Ilha da Trindade
636m
Rio Grande Rise
Zapiola Seamount
Islas Orcadas Rise
1748m
8325m
South Sandwich Trench
South Sandwich Fracture Zone

Belém Ridge
Recife
Hotspur Seamount
Rio Grande Gap
Santos Plateau
Argentine Basin
Zapiola Ridge
South Georgia Rise
3667m
South Georgia & the South Sandwich Islands (to UK)
East Scotia Ridge
East Scotia Basin
Weddell Plain

BRAZIL
SOUTH AMERICA
Ceará Plain
São Francisco
Vitória
Rio de Janeiro
Santos
Paranaguá
Montevideo
URUGUAY
PARAGUAY
Río de la Plata
Buenos Aires
Bahía Blanca
Gulf of San Matías
Gulf of San Jorge
ARGENTINA
Patagonia
Patagonian Shelf
Falkland Islands (to UK)
Falkland Plateau
Falkland Escarpment
Argentine Plain
Maurice Ewing Bank
West Scotia Ridge
South Georgia Ridge
Tehuelche Fracture Zone
Endurance Fracture Zone
Quest Fracture Zone
Burdwood Bank
Yaghan Basin
Protector Basin
Scotia Sea
South Scotia Ridge
South Orkney Islands
5576m
South Shetland Islands
Bransfield
Weddell Sea

Tocantins
Paraná
Uruguay
Cape Horn
Punta Arenas
Tierra del Fuego
Drake Passage
South Shetland Trough
Antarctic Peninsula
Ronne Ice Shelf

BOLIVIA
PERU
Callao
Paita
Guayaquil
Galápagos Islands (to Ecuador)
CHILE
Antofagasta
Valparaíso
Talcahuano
Peru-Chile Trench
Chile Trench
Chile Basin
8069m
Nazca Ridge
Peru Basin
Yupanqui Basin
Bauer Basin
Carnegie Ridge
Grijalva Ridge
Mendaña Fracture Zone
5,885m
Sala y Gómez Ridge
Easter Fracture Zone
Islas de los Desventurados (to Chile)
Isla San Félix
Isla San Ambrosio
Islas Juan Fernández (to Chile)
Isla Robinson Crusoe
Isla Alejandro Selkirk
Selkirk Rise
Tropic of Capricorn
Chile Rise
Chile Rise
6003m
Mocha Fracture Zone
Guafo Fracture Zone
Mornington Abyssal Plain
De Gerlache Seamounts
Peter I Island (to Norway)
Bellingshausen Plain
Bellingshausen Sea

PACIFIC OCEAN
Roggeveen Basin
Challenger Fracture Zone
Menard Fracture Zone
Eltanin Fracture Zone
Southeast Pacific Basin
Antarctic Circle

SOUTHERN OCEAN
ANTARCTICA
Amundsen Sea

Antarctica

ATLANTIC OCEAN

PACIFIC OCEAN

SOUTHERN OCEAN

Scotia Sea

Drake Passage

Weddell Sea

Bellingshausen Sea

Amundsen Sea

Research stations on King George Island

Arctowski (to Poland)
Ártigas (to Uruguay)
Bellingshausen (to Russian Federation)
Comandante Ferraz (to Brazil)
Great Wall (to China)
Jubany (to Argentina)
King Sejong (to South Korea)
Teniente Rodolfo Marsh (to Chile)

FALKLAND ISLANDS
(to UK)
STANLEY
East Falkland
West Falkland
Mount Adam 700m
Cape Meredith
Cabo de Hornos (Cape Horn)

Tierra del Fuego
Ushuaia
Porvenir
Punta Arenas

CHILE

Ronne Ice Shelf
Larsen Ice Shelf
Ellsworth Land
Marie Byrd Land
West Antarctica

Vinson Massif 4897m
Ellsworth Mountains
Mount Seelig 3022m
Mount Sidley 4181m
Mount Siple 3100m

Peter I Øy (to Norway)

Antarctic Peninsula
Palmer Land
Graham Land

TERRITORIAL CLAIMS

Argentinian claim
Brazilian zone of interest
British claim
Norwegian undefined limit
Australian claim
Chilean claim
French claim
Australian claim
New Zealand claim

6000m
4000m
3000m
2000m
1000m
500m
250m
100m
Sea Level
-250m
-2000m
-4000m

The Arctic

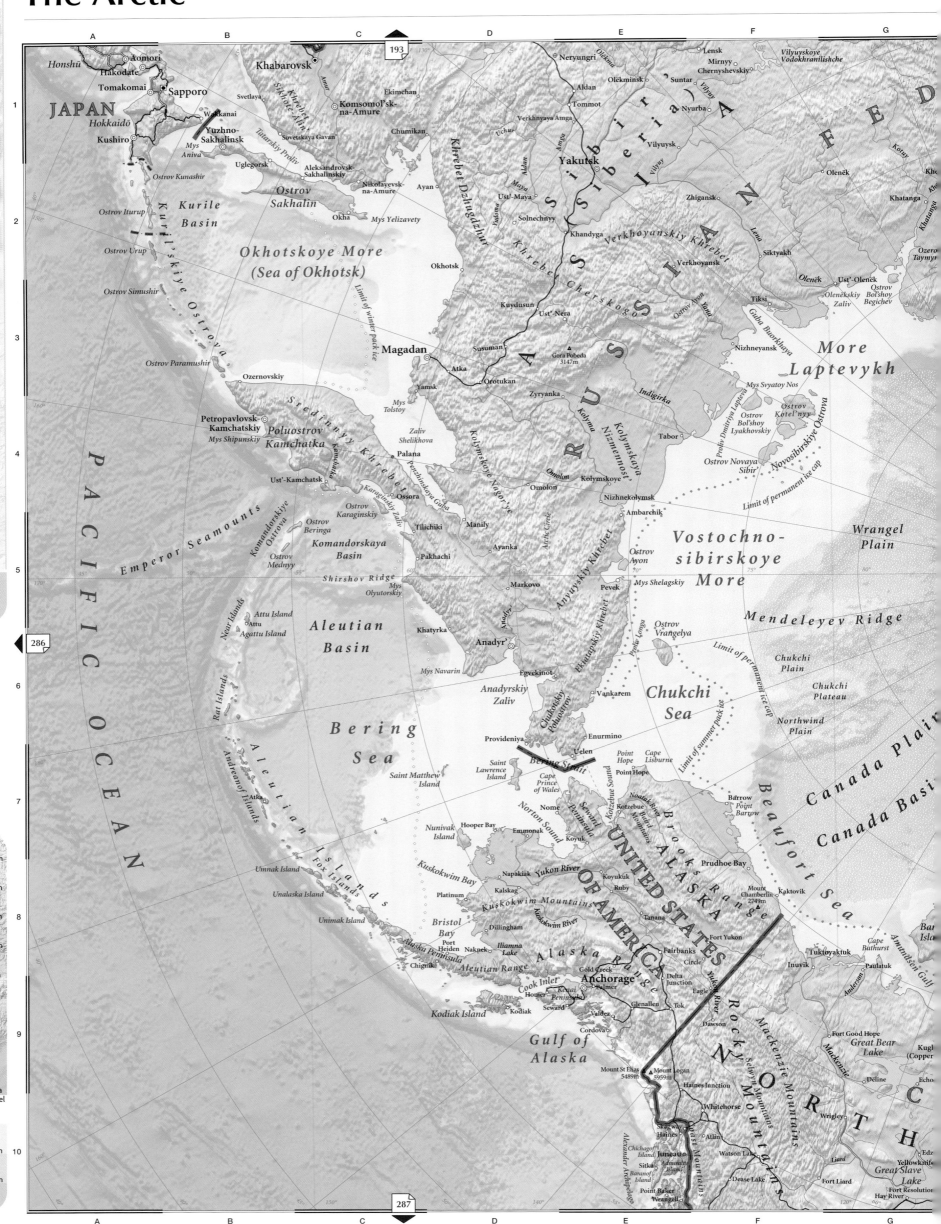

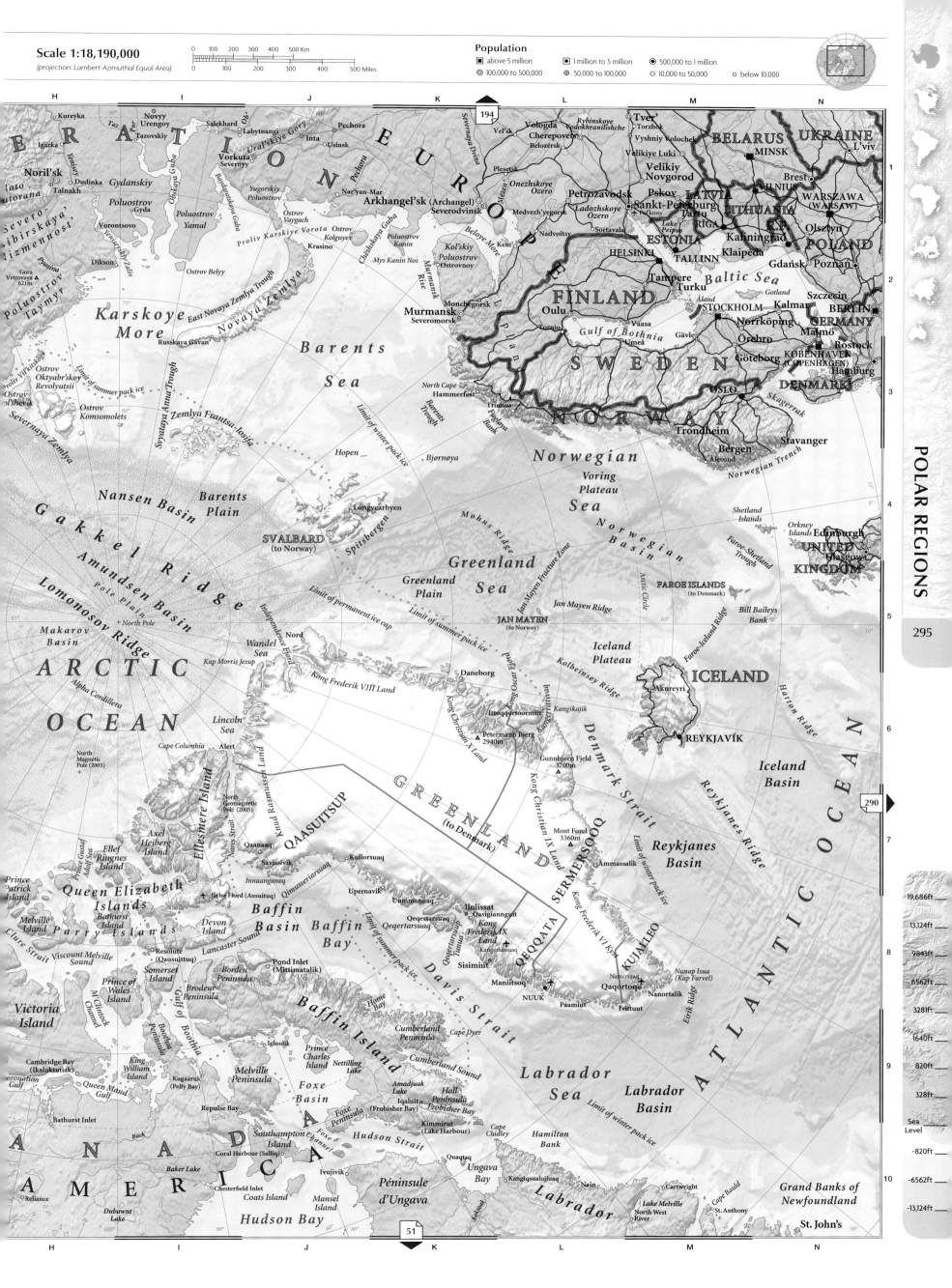

Geographical comparisons

Largest countries

Russian Federation	6,592,735 sq miles	(17,075,200 sq km)
Canada	3,855,171 sq miles	(9,984,670 sq km)
USA	3,794,100 sq miles	(9,826,675 sq km)
China	3,705,386 sq miles	(9,596,960 sq km)
Brazil	3,286,470 sq miles	(8,511,965 sq km)
Australia	2,967,893 sq miles	(7,686,850 sq km)
India	1,269,339 sq miles	(3,287,590 sq km)
Argentina	1,068,296 sq miles	(2,766,890 sq km)
Kazakhstan	1,049,150 sq miles	(2,717,300 sq km)
Algeria	919,590 sq miles	(2,381,740 sq km)

Smallest countries

Vatican City	0.17 sq miles	(0.44 sq km)
Monaco	0.75 sq miles	(1.95 sq km)
Nauru	8.2 sq miles	(21.2 sq km)
Tuvalu	10 sq miles	(26 sq km)
San Marino	24 sq miles	(61 sq km)
Liechtenstein	62 sq miles	(160 sq km)
Marshall Islands	70 sq miles	(181 sq km)
St. Kitts & Nevis	101 sq miles	(261 sq km)
Maldives	116 sq miles	(300 sq km)
Malta	124 sq miles	(320 sq km)

Largest islands

		To the nearest 1000 – or 100,000 for the largest
Greenland	849,400 sq miles	(2,200,000 sq km)
New Guinea	312,000 sq miles	(808,000 sq km)
Borneo	292,222 sq miles	(757,050 sq km)
Madagascar	229,300 sq miles	(594,000 sq km)
Sumatra	202,300 sq miles	(524,000 sq km)
Baffin Island	183,800 sq miles	(476,000 sq km)
Honshu	88,800 sq miles	(230,000 sq km)
Britain	88,700 sq miles	(229,800 sq km)
Victoria Island	81,900 sq miles	(212,000 sq km)
Ellesmere Island	75,700 sq miles	(196,000 sq km)

Richest countries

	GNI per capita, in US$
Monaco	186,950
Liechtenstein	136,770
Norway	102,610
Switzerland	90,760
Qatar	86,790
Luxembourg	69,900
Australia	65,390
Sweden	61,760
Denmark	61,680
Singapore	54,040

Poorest countries

	GNI per capita, in US$
Burundi	260
Malawi	270
Somalia	288
Central African Republic	320
Niger	400
Liberia	410
Dem. Rep. Congo	430
Madagascar	440
Guinea	460
Ethiopia	470
Eritrea	490
Gambia	500

Most populous countries

China	1,393,800,000
India	1,267,400,000
USA	322,600,000
Indonesia	252,800,000
Brazil	202,120,000
Pakistan	185,100,000
Nigeria	178,500,000
Bangladesh	159,000,000
Russian Federation	142,500,000
Japan	127,000,000

Least populous countries

Vatican City	842
Nauru	9488
Tuvalu	10,782
Palau	21,186
San Marino	32,742
Monaco	36,950
Liechtenstein	37,313
St Kitts & Nevis	51,538
Marshall Islands	70,983
Dominica	73,449
Andorra	85,458
Antigua & Barbuda	91,295

Most densely populated countries

Monaco	49,267 people per sq mile	(18,949 per sq km)
Singapore	23,305 people per sq mile	(9016 per sq km)
Vatican City	4953 people per sq mile	(1914 per sq km)
Bahrain	4762 people per sq mile	(1841 per sq km)
Maldives	3448 people per sq mile	(1333 per sq km)
Malta	3226 people per sq mile	(1250 per sq km)
Bangladesh	3066 people per sq mile	(1184 per sq km)
Taiwan	1879 people per sq mile	(725 per sq km)
Barbados	1807 people per sq mile	(698 per sq km)
Mauritius	1671 people per sq mile	(645 per sq km)

Most sparsely populated countries

Mongolia	5 people per sq mile	(2 per sq km)
Namibia	7 people per sq mile	(3 per sq km)
Australia	8 people per sq mile	(3 per sq km)
Suriname	8 people per sq mile	(3 per sq km)
Iceland	8 people per sq mile	(3 per sq km)
Botswana	9 people per sq mile	(4 per sq km)
Libya	9 people per sq mile	(4 per sq km)
Mauriania	10 people per sq mile	(4 per sq km)
Canada	10 people per sq mile	(4 per sq km)
Guyana	11 people per sq mile	(4 per sq km)

Most widely spoken languages

1. Chinese (Mandarin)	6. Arabic
2. English	7. Bengali
3. Hindi	8. Portuguese
4. Spanish	9. Malay-Indonesian
5. Russian	10. French

Largest conurbations

	Urban area population
Tokyo	37,800,000
Jakarta	30,500,000
Manila	24,100,000
Delhi	24,000,000
Karachi	23,500,000
Seoul	23,500,000
Shanghai	23,400,000
Beijing	21,000,000
New York City	20,600,000
Guangzhou	20,600,000
São Paulo	20,300,000
Mexico City	20,000,000
Mumbai	17,700,000
Osaka	17,400,000
Lagos	17,000,000
Moscow	16,100,000
Dhaka	15,700,000
Lahore	15,600,000
Los Angeles	15,000,000
Bangkok	15,000,000
Kolkatta	14,700,000
Buenos Aires	14,100,000
Tehran	13,500,000
Istanbul	13,300,000
Shenzhen	12,000,000

Countries with the most land borders

14: China	(Afghanistan, Bhutan, India, Kazakhstan, Kyrgyzstan, Laos, Mongolia, Myanmar (Burma), Nepal, North Korea, Pakistan, Russian Federation, Tajikistan, Vietnam)
14: Russian Federation	(Azerbaijan, Belarus, China, Estonia, Finland, Georgia, Kazakhstan, Latvia, Lithuania, Mongolia, North Korea, Norway, Poland, Ukraine)
10: Brazil	(Argentina, Bolivia, Colombia, French Guiana, Guyana, Paraguay, Peru, Suriname, Uruguay, Venezuela)
9: Congo, Dem. Rep.	(Angola, Burundi, Central African Republic, Congo, Rwanda, South Sudan, Tanzania, Uganda, Zambia)
9: Germany	(Austria, Belgium, Czech Republic, Denmark, France, Luxembourg, Netherlands, Poland, Switzerland)
8: Austria	(Czech Republic, Germany, Hungary, Italy, Liechtenstein, Slovakia, Slovenia, Switzerland)
8: France	(Andorra, Belgium, Germany, Italy, Luxembourg, Monaco, Spain, Switzerland)
8: Tanzania	(Burundi. Dem. Rep. Congo, Kenya, Malawi, Mozambique, Rwanda, Uganda, Zambia)
8: Turkey	(Armenia, Azerbaijan, Bulgaria, Georgia, Greece, Iran, Iraq, Syria)
8: Zambia	(Angola, Botswana, Dem. Rep.Congo, Malawi, Mozambique, Namibia, Tanzania, Zimbabwe)

Longest rivers

Nile (NE Africa)	4160 miles	(6695 km)
Amazon (South America)	4049 miles	(6516 km)
Yangtze (China)	3915 miles	(6299 km)
Mississippi/Missouri (USA)	3710 miles	(5969 km)
Ob'-Irtysh (Russian Federation)	3461 miles	(5570 km)
Yellow River (China)	3395 miles	(5464 km)
Congo (Central Africa)	2900 miles	(4667 km)
Mekong (Southeast Asia)	2749 miles	(4425 km)
Lena (Russian Federation)	2734 miles	(4400 km)
Mackenzie (Canada)	2640 miles	(4250 km)
Yenisey (Russian Federation)	2541 miles	(4090km)

Highest mountains

	Height above sea level	
Everest	29,029 ft	(8848 m)
K2	28,253 ft	(8611 m)
Kangchenjunga I	28,210 ft	(8598 m)
Makalu I	27,767 ft	(8463 m)
Cho Oyu	26,907 ft	(8201 m)
Dhaulagiri I	26,796 ft	(8167 m)
Manaslu I	26,783 ft	(8163 m)
Nanga Parbat I	26,661 ft	(8126 m)
Annapurna I	26,547 ft	(8091 m)
Gasherbrum I	26,471 ft	(8068 m)

Largest bodies of inland water

	With area and depth	
Caspian Sea	143,243 sq miles (371,000 sq km)	3215 ft (980 m)
Lake Superior	31,151 sq miles (83,270 sq km)	1289 ft (393 m)
Lake Victoria	26,828 sq miles (69,484 sq km)	328 ft (100 m)
Lake Huron	23,436 sq miles (60,700 sq km)	751 ft (229 m)
Lake Michigan	22,402 sq miles (58,020 sq km)	922 ft (281 m)
Lake Tanganyika	12,703 sq miles (32,900 sq km)	4700 ft (1435 m)
Great Bear Lake	12,274 sq miles (31,790 sq km)	1047 ft (319 m)
Lake Baikal	11,776 sq miles (30,500 sq km)	5712 ft (1741 m)
Great Slave Lake	10,981 sq miles (28,440 sq km)	459 ft (140 m)
Lake Erie	9,915 sq miles (25,680 sq km)	197 ft (60 m)

Deepest ocean features

Challenger Deep, Mariana Trench (Pacific)	35,827 ft	(10,920 m)
Vityaz III Depth, Tonga Trench (Pacific)	35,704 ft	(10,882 m)
Vityaz Depth, Kuril-Kamchatka Trench (Pacific)	34,588 ft	(10,542 m)
Cape Johnson Deep, Philippine Trench (Pacific)	34,441 ft	(10,497 m)
Kermadec Trench (Pacific)	32,964 ft	(10,047 m)
Ramapo Deep, Japan Trench (Pacific)	32,758 ft	(9984 m)
Milwaukee Deep, Puerto Rico Trench (Atlantic)	30,185 ft	(9200 m)
Argo Deep, Torres Trench (Pacific)	30,070 ft	(9165 m)
Meteor Depth, South Sandwich Trench (Atlantic)	30,000 ft	(9144 m)
Planet Deep, New Britain Trench (Pacific)	29,988 ft	(9140 m)

Greatest waterfalls

	Mean flow of water	
Boyoma (Dem. Rep. Congo)	600,400 cu. ft/sec	(17,000 cu.m/sec)
Khône (Laos/Cambodia)	410,000 cu. ft/sec	(11,600 cu.m/sec)
Niagara (USA/Canada)	195,000 cu. ft/sec	(5500 cu.m/sec)
Grande, Salto (Uruguay)	160,000 cu. ft/sec	(4500 cu.m/sec)
Paulo Afonso (Brazil)	100,000 cu. ft/sec	(2800 cu.m/sec)
Urubupungā, Salto do (Brazil)	97,000 cu. ft/sec	(2750 cu.m/sec)
Iguaçu (Argentina/Brazil)	62,000 cu. ft/sec	(1700 cu.m/sec)
Maribondo, Cachoeira do (Brazil)	53,000 cu. ft/sec	(1500 cu.m/sec)
Victoria (Zimbabwe)	39,000 cu. ft/sec	(1100 cu.m/sec)
Murchison Falls (Uganda)	42,000 cu. ft/sec	(1200 cu.m/sec)
Churchill (Canada)	35,000 cu. ft/sec	(1000 cu.m/sec)
Kaveri Falls (India)	33,000 cu. ft/sec	(900 cu.m/sec)

Highest waterfalls

	* Indicates that the total height is a single leap	
Angel (Venezuela)	3212 ft	(979 m)
Tugela (South Africa)	3110 ft	(948 m)
Utigard (Norway)	2625 ft	(800 m)
Mongefossen (Norway)	2539 ft	(774 m)
Mtarazi (Zimbabwe)	2500 ft	(762 m)
Yosemite (USA)	2425 ft	(739 m)
Ostre Mardola Foss (Norway)	2156 ft	(657 m)
Tyssestrengane (Norway)	2119 ft	(646 m)
*Cuquenan (Venezuela)	2001 ft	(610 m)
Sutherland (New Zealand)	1903 ft	(580 m)
*Kjellfossen (Norway)	1841 ft	(561 m)

Largest deserts

	NB – Most of Antarctica is a polar desert, with only 50mm of precipitation annually	
Sahara	3,450,000 sq miles	(9,065,000 sq km)
Gobi	500,000 sq miles	(1,295,000 sq km)
Ar Rub al Khali	289,600 sq miles	(750,000 sq km)
Great Victorian	249,800 sq miles	(647,000 sq km)
Sonoran	120,000 sq miles	(311,000 sq km)
Kalahari	120,000 sq miles	(310,800 sq km)
Kara Kum	115,800 sq miles	(300,000 sq km)
Takla Makan	100,400 sq miles	(260,000 sq km)
Namib	52,100 sq miles	(135,000 sq km)
Thar	33,670 sq miles	(130,000 sq km)

Hottest inhabited places

Djibouti (Djibouti)	86° F	(30 °C)
Tombouctou (Mali)	84.7° F	(29.3 °C)
Tirunelveli (India)		
Tuticorin (India)		
Nellore (India)	84.5° F	(29.2 °C)
Santa Marta (Colombia)		
Aden (Yemen)	84° F	(28.9 °C)
Madurai (India)		
Niamey (Niger)		
Hodeida (Yemen)	83.8° F	(28.8 °C)
Ouagadougou (Burkina Faso)		
Thanjavur (India)		
Tiruchchirappalli (India)		

Driest inhabited places

Aswân (Egypt)	0.02 in	(0.5 mm)
Luxor (Egypt)	0.03 in	(0.7 mm)
Arica (Chile)	0.04 in	(1.1 mm)
Ica (Peru)	0.1 in	(2.3 mm)
Antofagasta (Chile)	0.2 in	(4.9 mm)
Al Minya (Egypt)	0.2 in	(5.1 mm)
Asyut (Egypt)	0.2 in	(5.2 mm)
Callao (Peru)	0.5 in	(12.0 mm)
Trujillo (Peru)	0.55 in	(14.0 mm)
Al Fayyum (Egypt)	0.8 in	(19.0 mm)

Wettest inhabited places

Mawsynram (India)	467 in	(11,862 mm)
Mount Waialeale (Hawaii, USA)	460 in	(11,684 mm)
Cherrapunji (India)	450 in	(11,430 mm)
Cape Debundsha (Cameroon)	405 in	(10,290 mm)
Quibdo (Colombia)	354 in	(8892 mm)
Buenaventura (Colombia)	265 in	(6743 mm)
Monrovia (Liberia)	202 in	(5131 mm)
Pago Pago (American Samoa)	196 in	(4990 mm)
Mawlamyine (Myanmar [Burma])	191 in	(4852 mm)
Lae (Papua New Guinea)	183 in	(4645 mm)

Countries of the World

There are currently 196 independent countries in the world – more than at any previous time – and almost 60 dependencies. Antarctica is the only land area on Earth that is not officially part of, and does not belong to, any single country.

In 1950, the world comprised 82 countries. In the decades following, many more states came into being as they achieved independence from their former colonial rulers. Most recent additions were caused by the breakup of the former Soviet Union in 1991, and the former Yugoslavia in 1992, which swelled the ranks of independent states. In July 2011, South Sudan became the latest country to be formed after declaring independence from Sudan.

Country factfile key

Formation Date of independence / date current borders were established
Population Total population / population density – based on total *land* area
Languages An asterisk (*) denotes the official language(s)
Calorie consumption Average number of calories consumed daily per person

AFGHANISTAN
Central Asia

Official name Islamic Republic of Afghanistan
Formation 1919 / 1919
Capital Kabul
Population 31.3 million / 124 people per sq mile (48 people per sq km)
Total area 250,000 sq. miles (647,500 sq. km)
Languages Pashtu*, Tajik, Dari*, Farsi, Uzbek, Turkmen
Religions Sunni Muslim 80%, Shi'a Muslim 19%, Other 1%
Ethnic mix Pashtun 38%, Tajik 25%, Hazara 19%, Uzbek and Turkmen 15%, Other 3%
Government Nonparty system
Currency Afghani = 100 puls
Literacy rate rate 32%
Calorie consumption 2090 kilocalories

ALBANIA
Southeast Europe

Official name Republic of Albania
Formation 1912 / 1921
Capital Tirana
Population 3.2 million / 302 people per sq mile (117 people per sq km)
Total area 11,100 sq. miles (28,748 sq. km)
Languages Albanian*, Greek
Religions Sunni Muslim 70%, Albanian Orthodox 20%, Roman Catholic 10%
Ethnic mix Albanian 98%, Greek 1%, Other 1%
Government Parliamentary system
Currency Lek = 100 qindarka (qintars)
Literacy rate 97%
Calorie consumption 3023 kilocalories

ALGERIA
North Africa

Official name People's Democratic Republic of Algeria
Formation 1962 / 1962
Capital Algiers
Population 39.9 million / 43 people per sq mile (17 people per sq km)
Total area 919,590 sq. miles (2,381,740 sq. km)
Languages Arabic*, Tamazight (Kabyle, Shawia, Tamashek), French
Religions Sunni Muslim 99%, Christian and Jewish 1%
Ethnic mix Arab 75%, Berber 24%, European and Jewish 1%
Government Presidential system
Currency Algerian dinar = 100 centimes
Literacy rate 73%
Calorie consumption 3296 kilocalories

ANDORRA
Southwest Europe

Official name Principality of Andorra
Formation 1278 / 1278
Capital Andorra la Vella
Population 85,485 / 475 people per sq mile (184 people per sq km)
Total area 181 sq. miles (468 sq. km)
Languages Spanish, Catalan*, French, Portuguese
Religions Roman Catholic 94%, Other 6%
Ethnic mix Spanish 46%, Andorran 28%, Other 18%, French 8%
Government Parliamentary system
Currency Euro = 100 cents
Literacy rate 99%
Calorie consumption Not available

ANGOLA
Southern Africa

Official name Republic of Angola
Formation 1975 / 1975
Capital Luanda
Population 22.1 million / 46 people per sq mile (18 people per sq km)
Total area 481,351 sq. miles (1,246,700 sq. km)
Languages Portuguese*, Umbundu, Kimbundu, Kikongo
Religions Roman Catholic 68%, Protestant 20%, Indigenous beliefs 12%
Ethnic mix Ovimbundu 37%, Kimbundu 25%, Other 25%, Bakongo 13%
Government Presidential system
Currency Readjusted kwanza = 100 lwei
Literacy rate 71%
Calorie consumption 2473 kilocalories

ANTIGUA & BARBUDA
West Indies

Official name Antigua and Barbuda
Formation 1981 / 1981
Capital St. John's
Population 91,295 / 537 people per sq mile (207 people per sq km)
Total area 170 sq. miles (442 sq. km)
Languages English*, English patois
Religions Anglican 45%, Other Protestant 42%, Roman Catholic 10%, Other 2%, Rastafarian 1%
Ethnic mix Black African 95%, Other 5%
Government Parliamentary system
Currency East Caribbean dollar = 100 cents
Literacy rate 99%
Calorie consumption 2396 kilocalories

ARGENTINA
South America

Official name Argentine Republic
Formation 1816 / 1816
Capital Buenos Aires
Population 41.8 million / 40 people per sq mile (15 people per sq km)
Total area 1,068,296 sq. miles (2,766,890 sq. km)
Languages Spanish*, Italian, Amerindian languages
Religions Roman Catholic 70%, Other 18%, Protestant 9%, Muslim 2%, Jewish 1%
Ethnic mix Indo-European 97%, Mestizo 2%, Amerindian 1%
Government Presidential system
Currency Argentine peso = 100 centavos
Literacy rate 98%
Calorie consumption 3155 kilocalories

ARMENIA
Southwest Asia

Official name Republic of Armenia
Formation 1991 / 1991
Capital Yerevan
Population 3 million / 261 people per sq mile (101 people per sq km)
Total area 11,506 sq. miles (29,800 sq. km)
Languages Armenian*, Azeri, Russian
Religions Armenian Apostolic Church (Orthodox) 88%, Armenian Catholic Church 6%, Other 6%
Ethnic mix Armenian 98%, Other 1%, Yezidi 1%
Government Parliamentary system
Currency Dram = 100 luma
Literacy rate 99%
Calorie consumption 2809 kilocalories

AUSTRALIA
Australasia & Oceania

Official name Commonwealth of Australia
Formation 1901 / 1901
Capital Canberra
Population 23.6 million / 8 people per sq mile (3 people per sq km)
Total area 2,967,893 sq. miles (7,686,850 sq. km)
Languages English*, Italian, Cantonese, Greek, Arabic, Vietnamese, Aboriginal languages
Religions Roman Catholic 26%, Nonreligious 19%, Anglican 19%, Other 17%, Other Christian 13%, United Church 6%
Ethnic mix European origin 50%, Australian 25.5%, other 19%, Asian 5%, Aboriginal 0.5%
Government Parliamentary system
Currency Australian dollar = 100 cents
Literacy rate 99%
Calorie consumption 3265 kilocalories

AUSTRIA
Central Europe

Official name Republic of Austria
Formation 1918 / 1919
Capital Vienna
Population 8.5 million / 266 people per sq mile (103 people per sq km)
Total area 32,378 sq. miles (83,858 sq. km)
Languages German*, Croatian, Slovenian, Hungarian (Magyar)
Religions Roman Catholic 78%, Nonreligious 9%, Other (including Jewish and Muslim) 8%, Protestant 5%
Ethnic mix Austrian 93%, Croat, Slovene, and Hungarian 6%, Other 1%
Government Parliamentary system
Currency Euro = 100 cents
Literacy rate 99%
Calorie consumption 3784 kilocalories

AZERBAIJAN
Southwest Asia

Official name Republic of Azerbaijan
Formation 1991 / 1991
Capital Baku
Population 9.5 million / 284 people per sq mile (110 people per sq km)
Total area 33,436 sq. miles (86,600 sq. km)
Languages Azeri*, Russian
Religions Shi'a Muslim 68%, Sunni Muslim 26%, Russian Orthodox 3%, Armenian Apostolic Church (Orthodox) 2%, Other 1%
Ethnic mix Azeri 91%, Other 3%, Lazs 2%, Armenian 2%, Russian 2%
Government Presidential system
Currency New manat = 100 gopik
Literacy rate 99%
Calorie consumption 2952 kilocalories

THE BAHAMAS
West Indies

Official name Commonwealth of The Bahamas
Formation 1973 / 1973
Capital Nassau
Population 400,000 / 103 people per sq mile (40 people per sq km)
Total area 5382 sq. miles (13,940 sq. km)
Languages English*, English Creole, French Creole
Religions Baptist 32%, Anglican 20%, Roman Catholic 19%, Other 17%, Methodist 6%, Church of God 6%
Ethnic mix Black African 85%, European 12%, Asian and Hispanic 3%
Government Parliamentary system
Currency Bahamian dollar = 100 cents
Literacy rate 96%
Calorie consumption 2575 kilocalories

BAHRAIN
Southwest Asia

Official name Kingdom of Bahrain
Formation 1971 / 1971
Capital Manama
Population 1.3 million / 4762 people per sq mile (1841 people per sq km)
Total area 239 sq. miles (620 sq. km)
Languages Arabic*
Religions Muslim (mainly Shi'a) 99%, Other 1%
Ethnic mix Bahraini 63%, Asian 19%, Other Arab 10%, Iranian 8%
Government Mixed monarchical–parliamentary system
Currency Bahraini dinar = 1000 fils
Literacy rate 95%
Calorie consumption Not available

BANGLADESH
South Asia

Official name People's Republic of Bangladesh
Formation 1971 / 1971
Capital Dhaka
Population 159 million / 3066 people per sq mile (1184 people per sq km)
Total area 55,598 sq. miles (144,000 sq. km)
Languages Bengali*, Urdu, Chakma, Marma (Magh), Garo, Khasi, Santhali, Tripuri, Mro
Religions Muslim (mainly Sunni) 88%, Hindu 11%, Other 1%
Ethnic mix Bengali 98%, Other 2%
Government Parliamentary system
Currency Taka = 100 poisha
Literacy rate 59%
Calorie consumption 2450 kilocalories

BARBADOS
West Indies

Official name Barbados
Formation 1966 / 1966
Capital Bridgetown
Population 300,000 / 1807 people per sq mile (698 people per sq km)
Total area 166 sq. miles (430 sq. km)
Languages Bajan (Barbadian English), English*
Religions Anglican 40%, Other 24%, Nonreligious 17%, Pentecostal 8%, Methodist 7%, Roman Catholic 4%
Ethnic mix Black African 92%, White 3%, Other 3%, Mixed race 2%
Government Parliamentary system
Currency Barbados dollar = 100 cents
Literacy rate 99%
Calorie consumption 3047 kilocalories

BELARUS
Eastern Europe

Official name Republic of Belarus
Formation 1991 / 1991
Capital Minsk
Population 9.3 million / 116 people per sq mile (45 people per sq km)
Total area 80,154 sq. miles (207,600 sq. km)
Languages Belarussian*, Russian*
Religions Orthodox Christian 80%, Roman Catholic 14%, Other 4%, Protestant 2%
Ethnic mix Belarussian 81%, Russian 11%, Polish 4%, Ukrainian 2%, Other 2%
Government Presidential system
Currency Belarussian rouble = 100 kopeks
Literacy rate 99%
Calorie consumption 3253 kilocalories

BELGIUM
Northwest Europe

Official name Kingdom of Belgium
Formation 1830 / 1919
Capital Brussels
Population 11.1 million / 876 people per sq mile (338 people per sq km)
Total area 11,780 sq. miles (30,510 sq. km)
Languages Dutch*, French*, German*
Religions Roman Catholic 88%, Other 10%, Muslim 2%
Ethnic mix Fleming 58%, Walloon 33%, Other 6%, Italian 2%, Moroccan 1%
Government Parliamentary system
Currency Euro = 100 cents
Literacy rate 99%
Calorie consumption 3793 kilocalories

BELIZE
Central America

Official name Belize
Formation 1981 / 1981
Capital Belmopan
Population 300,000 / 34 people per sq mile (13 people per sq km)
Total area 8867 sq. miles (22,966 sq. km)
Languages English Creole, Spanish, English*, Mayan, Garifuna (Carib)
Religions Roman Catholic 62%, Other 13%, Anglican 12%, Methodist 6%, Mennonite 4%, Seventh-day Adventist 3%
Ethnic mix Mestizo 49%, Creole 25%, Maya 11%, Garifuna 6%, Other 6%, Asian Indian 3%
Government Parliamentary system
Currency Belizean dollar = 100 cents
Literacy rate 75%
Calorie consumption 2751 kilocalories

BENIN
West Africa

Official name Republic of Benin
Formation 1960 / 1960
Capital Porto-Novo
Population 10.6 million / 248 people per sq mile (96 people per sq km)
Total area 43,483 sq. miles (112,620 sq. km)
Languages Fon, Bariba, Yoruba, Adja, Houeda, Somba, French*
Religions Indigenous beliefs and Voodoo 50%, Christian 30%, Muslim 20%
Ethnic mix Fon 41%, Other 21%, Adja 16%, Yoruba 12%, Bariba 10%
Government Presidential system
Currency CFA franc = 100 centimes
Literacy rate 29%
Calorie consumption 2594 kilocalories

BHUTAN
South Asia

Official name Kingdom of Bhutan
Formation 1656 / 1865
Capital Thimphu
Population 800,000 / 44 people per sq mile (17 people per sq km)
Total area 18,147 sq. miles (47,000 sq. km)
Languages Dzongkha*, Nepali, Assamese
Religions Mahayana Buddhist 75%, Hindu 25%
Ethnic mix Drukpa 50%, Nepalese 35%, Other 15%
Government Mixed monarchical–parliamentary system
Currency Ngultrum = 100 chetrum
Literacy rate 53%
Calorie consumption Not available

BOLIVIA
South America

Official name Plurinational State of Bolivia
Formation 1825 / 1938
Capital La Paz (administrative); Sucre (judicial)
Population 10.8 million / 26 people per sq mile (10 people per sq km)
Total area 424,162 sq. miles (1,098,580 sq. km)
Languages Aymara*, Quechua*, Spanish*
Religions Roman Catholic 93%, Other 7%
Ethnic mix Quechua 37%, Aymara 32%, Mixed race 13%, European 10%, Other 8%
Government Presidential system
Currency Boliviano = 100 centavos
Literacy rate 94%
Calorie consumption 2254 kilocalories

BOSNIA & HERZEGOVINA
Southeast Europe

Official name Bosnia and Herzegovina
Formation 1992 / 1992
Capital Sarajevo
Population 3.8 million / 192 people per sq mile (74 people per sq km)
Total area 19,741 sq. miles (51,129 sq. km)
Languages Bosnian*, Serbian*, Croatian*
Religions Muslim (mainly Sunni) 40%, Orthodox Christian 31%, Roman Catholic 15%, Other 10%, Protestant 4%
Ethnic mix Bosniak 48%, Serb 34%, Croat 16%, Other 2%
Government Parliamentary system
Currency Marka = 100 pfeninga
Literacy rate 98%
Calorie consumption 3130 kilocalories

BOTSWANA
Southern Africa

Official name Republic of Botswana
Formation 1966 / 1966
Capital Gaborone
Population 2 million / 9 people per sq mile (4 people per sq km)
Total area 231,803 sq. miles (600,370 sq. km)
Languages Setswana, English*, Shona, San, Khoikhoi, isiNdebele
Religions Christian (mainly Protestant) 70%, Nonreligious 20%, Traditional beliefs 6%, Other (including Muslim) 4%
Ethnic mix Tswana 79%, Kalanga 11%, Other 10%
Government Presidential system
Currency Pula = 100 thebe
Literacy rate 87%
Calorie consumption 2285 kilocalories

BRAZIL
South America

Official name Federative Republic of Brazil
Formation 1822 / 1828
Capital Brasília
Population 202 million / 62 people per sq mile (24 people per sq km)
Total area 3,286,470 sq. miles (8,511,965 sq. km)
Languages Portuguese*, German, Italian, Spanish, Polish, Japanese, Amerindian languages
Religions Roman Catholic 74%, Protestant 15%, Atheist 7%, Other 3%, Afro-American Spiritist 1%
Ethnic mix White 54%, Mixed race 38%, Black 6%, Other 2%
Government Presidential system
Currency Real = 100 centavos
Literacy rate 91%
Calorie consumption 3263 kilocalories

BRUNEI
Southeast Asia

Official name Brunei Darussalam
Formation 1984 / 1984
Capital Bandar Seri Begawan
Population 400,000 / 197 people per sq mile (76 people per sq km)
Total area 2228 sq. miles (5770 sq. km)
Languages Malay*, English, Chinese
Religions Muslim (mainly Sunni) 66%, Buddhist 14%, Other 10%, Christian 10%
Ethnic mix Malay 67%, Chinese 16%, Other 11%, Indigenous 6%
Government Monarchy
Currency Brunei dollar = 100 cents
Literacy rate 95%
Calorie consumption 2949 kilocalories

BULGARIA
Southeast Europe

Official name Republic of Bulgaria
Formation 1908 / 1947
Capital Sofia
Population 7.2 million / 169 people per sq mile (65 people per sq km)
Total area 42,822 sq. miles (110,910 sq. km)
Languages Bulgarian*, Turkish, Romani
Religions Bulgarian Orthodox 83%, Muslim 12%, Other 4%, Roman Catholic 1%
Ethnic mix Bulgarian 84%, Turkish 9%, Roma 5%, Other 2%
Government Parliamentary system
Currency Lev = 100 stotinki
Literacy rate 98%
Calorie consumption 2877 kilocalories

BURKINA FASO
West Africa

Official name Burkina Faso
Formation 1960 / 1960
Capital Ouagadougou
Population 17.4 million / 165 people per sq mile (64 people per sq km)
Total area 105,869 sq. miles (274,200 sq. km)
Languages Mossi, Fulani, French*, Tuare g, Dyula, Songhai
Religions Muslim 55%, Christian 25%, Traditional beliefs 20%
Ethnic mix Mossi 48%, Other 21%, Peul 10%, Lobi 7%, Bobo 7%, Mandé 7%
Government Transitional regime
Currency CFA franc = 100 centimes
Literacy rate 29%
Calorie consumption 2720 kilocalories

BURUNDI
Central Africa

Official name Republic of Burundi
Formation 1962 / 1962
Capital Bujumbura
Population 10.5 million / 1060 people per sq mile (409 people per sq km)
Total area 10,745 sq. miles (27,830 sq. km)
Languages Kirundi*, French*, Kiswahili
Religions Roman Catholic 62%, Traditional beliefs 23%, Muslim 10%, Protestant 5%
Ethnic mix Hutu 85%, Tutsi 14%, Twa 1%
Government Presidential system
Currency Burundian franc = 100 centimes
Literacy rate 87%
Calorie consumption 1604 kilocalories

CAMBODIA
Southeast Asia

Official name Kingdom of Cambodia
Formation 1953 / 1953
Capital Phnom Penh
Population 15.4 million / 226 people per sq mile (87 people per sq km)
Total area 69,900 sq. miles (181,040 sq. km)
Languages Khmer*, French, Chinese, Vietnamese, Cham
Religions Buddhist 93%, Muslim 6%, Christian 1%
Ethnic mix Khmer 90%, Vietnamese 5%, Other 4%, Chinese 1%
Government Parliamentary system
Currency Riel = 100 sen
Literacy rate 74%
Calorie consumption 2411 kilocalories

CAMEROON
Central Africa

Official name Republic of Cameroon
Formation 1960 / 1961
Capital Yaoundé
Population 22.8 million / 127 people per sq mile (49 people per sq km)
Total area 183,567 sq. miles (475,400 sq. km)
Languages Bamileke, Fang, Fulani, French*, English*
Religions Roman Catholic 35%, Traditional beliefs 25%, Muslim 22%, Protestant 18%
Ethnic mix Cameroon highlanders 31%, Other 21%, Equatorial Bantu 19%, Kirdi 11%, Fulani 10%, Northwestern Bantu 8%
Government Presidential system
Currency CFA franc = 100 centimes
Literacy rate 71%
Calorie consumption 2586 kilocalories

CANADA
North America

Official name Canada
Formation 1867 / 1949
Capital Ottawa
Population 35.5 million / 10 people per sq mile (4 people per sq km)
Total area 3,855,171 sq, miles (9,984,670 sq. km)
Languages English*, French*, Chinese, Italian, German, Ukrainian, Portuguese, Inuktitut, Cree
Religions Roman Catholic 44%, Protestant 29%, Other and nonreligious 27%
Ethnic mix European origin 66%, other 27%, Asian 5%, Amerindian 2%
Government Parliamentary system
Currency Canadian dollar = 100 cents
Literacy rate 99%
Calorie consumption 3419 kilocalories

CAPE VERDE
Atlantic Ocean

Official name Republic of Cape Verde
Formation 1975 / 1975
Capital Praia
Population 500,000 / 321 people per sq mile (124 people per sq km)
Total area 1557 sq. miles (4033 sq. km)
Languages Portuguese Creole, Portuguese*
Religions Roman Catholic 97%, Other 2%, Protestant (Church of the Nazarene) 1%
Ethnic mix Mestiço 71%, African 28%, European 1%
Government Mixed presidential–parliamentary system
Currency Escudo = 100 centavos
Literacy rate 85%
Calorie consumption 2716 kilocalories

CENTRAL AFRICAN REPUBLIC
Central Africa

Official name Central African Republic
Formation 1960 / 1960
Capital Bangui
Population 4.7 million / 20 people per sq mile (8 people per sq km)
Total area 240,534 sq. miles (622,984 sq. km)
Languages Sango, Banda, Gbaya, French*
Religions Traditional beliefs 35%, Roman Catholic 25%, Protestant 25%, Muslim 15%
Ethnic mix Baya 33%, Banda 27%, Other 17%, Mandjia 13%, Sara 10%
Government Transitional regime
Currency CFA franc = 100 centimes
Literacy rate 37%
Calorie consumption 2154 kilocalories

CHAD
Central Africa

Official name Republic of Chad
Formation 1960 / 1960
Capital N'Djaména
Population 13.2 million / 27 people per sq mile (10 people per sq km)
Total area 495,752 sq. miles (1,284,000 sq. km)
Languages French*, Sara, Arabic*, Maba
Religions Muslim 51%, Christian 35%, Animist 7%, Traditional beliefs 7%
Ethnic mix Other 30%, Sara 28%, Mayo-Kebbi 12%, Arab 12%, Ouaddai 9%, Kanem-Bornou 9%
Government Presidential system
Currency CFA franc = 100 centimes
Literacy rate 37%
Calorie consumption 2110 kilocalories

CHILE
South America

Official name Republic of Chile
Formation 1818 / 1883
Capital Santiago
Population 17.8 million / 62 people per sq mile (24 people per sq km)
Total area 292,258 sq. miles (756,950 sq. km)
Languages Spanish*, Amerindian languages
Religions Roman Catholic 89%, Other and nonreligious 11%
Ethnic mix Mestizo and European 90%, Other Amerindian 9%, Mapuche 1%
Government Presidential system
Currency Chilean peso = 100 centavos
Literacy rate 99%
Calorie consumption 2989 kilocalories

CHINA
East Asia

Official name People's Republic of China
Formation 960 / 1999
Capital Beijing
Population 1.39 billion / 387 people per sq mile (149 people per sq km)
Total area 3,705,386 sq. miles (9,596,960 sq. km)
Languages Mandarin*, Wu, Cantonese, Hsiang, Min, Hakka, Kan
Religions Nonreligious 59%, Traditional beliefs 20%, Other 13%, Buddhist 6%, Muslim 2%
Ethnic mix Han 92%, Other 4%, Hui 1%, Miao 1%, Manchu 1%, Zhuang 1%
Government One-party state
Currency Renminbi (known as yuan) = 10 jiao = 100 fen
Literacy rate 95%
Calorie consumption 3108 kilocalories

COLOMBIA
South America

Official name Republic of Colombia
Formation 1819 / 1903
Capital Bogotá
Population 48.9 million / 122 people per sq mile (47 people per sq km)
Total area 439,733 sq, miles (1,138,910 sq. km)
Languages Spanish*, Wayuu, Páez, and other Amerindian languages
Religions Roman Catholic 95%, Other 5%
Ethnic mix Mestizo 58%, White 20%, European–African 14%, African 4%, African–Amerindian 3%, Amerindian 1%
Government Presidential system
Currency Colombian peso = 100 centavos
Literacy rate 94%
Calorie consumption 2804 kilocalories

COMOROS
Indian Ocean

Official name Union of the Comoros
Formation 1975 / 1975
Capital Moroni
Population 800,000 / 929 people per sq mile (359 people per sq km)
Total area 838 sq. miles (2170 sq. km)
Languages Arabic*, Comoran*, French*
Religions Muslim (mainly Sunni) 98%, Other 1%, Roman Catholic 1%
Ethnic mix Comoran 97%, Other 3%
Government Presidential system
Currency Comoros franc = 100 centimes
Literacy rate 76%
Calorie consumption 2139 kilocalories

CONGO
Central Africa

Official name Republic of the Congo
Formation 1960 / 1960
Capital Brazzaville
Population 4.6 million / 35 people per sq mile (13 people per sq km)
Total area 132,046 sq. miles (342,000 sq. km)
Languages Kongo, Teke, Lingala, French*
Religions Traditional beliefs 50%, Roman Catholic 35%, Protestant 13%, Muslim 2%
Ethnic mix Bakongo 51%, Teke 17%, Other 16%, Mbochi 11%, Mbédé 5%
Government Presidential system
Currency CFA franc = 100 centimes
Literacy rate 79%
Calorie consumption 2195 kilocalories

CONGO, DEM. REP.
Central Africa

Official name Democratic Republic of the Congo
Formation 1960 / 1960
Capital Kinshasa
Population 69.4 million / 79 people per sq mile (31 people per sq km)
Total area 905,563 sq. miles (2,345,410 sq. km)
Languages Kiswahili, Tshiluba, Kikongo, Lingala, French*
Religions Roman Catholic 50%, Protestant 20%, Traditional beliefs and other 10%, Muslim 10%, Kimbanguist 10%
Ethnic mix Other 55%, Mongo, Luba, Kongo, and Mangbetu-Azande 45%
Government Presidential system
Currency Congolese franc = 100 centimes
Literacy rate 61%
Calorie consumption 1585 kilocalories

COSTA RICA
Central America

Official name Republic of Costa Rica
Formation 1838 / 1838
Capital San José
Population 4.9 million / 249 people per sq mile (96 people per sq km)
Total area 19,730 sq. miles (51,100 sq. km)
Languages Spanish*, English Creole, Bribri, Cabecar
Religions Roman Catholic 71%, Evangelical 14%, Nonreligious 11%, Other 4%
Ethnic mix Mestizo and European 94%, Black 3%, Other 1%, Chinese 1%, Amerindian 1%
Government Presidential system
Currency Costa Rican colón = 100 céntimos
Literacy rate 97%
Calorie consumption 2898 kilocalories

CROATIA
Southeast Europe

Official name Republic of Croatia
Formation 1991 / 1991
Capital Zagreb
Population 4.3 million / 197 people per sq mile (76 people per sq km)
Total area 21,831 sq. miles (56,542 sq. km)
Languages Croatian*
Religions Roman Catholic 88%, Other 7%, Orthodox Christian 4%, Muslim 1%
Ethnic mix Croat 90%, Other 5%, Serb 5%
Government Parliamentary system
Currency Kuna = 100 lipa
Literacy rate 99%
Calorie consumption 3052 kilocalories

CUBA
West Indies

Official name Republic of Cuba
Formation 1902 / 1902
Capital Havana
Population 11.3 million / 264 people per sq mile (102 people per sq km)
Total area 42,803 sq. miles (110,860 sq. km)
Languages Spanish*
Religions Nonreligious 49%, Roman Catholic 40%, Atheist 6%, Other 4%, Protestant 1%
Ethnic mix Mulatto (mixed race) 51%, White 37%, Black 11%, Chinese 1%
Government One-party state
Currency Cuban peso = 100 centavos
Literacy rate 99%
Calorie consumption 3277 kilocalories

CYPRUS
Southeast Europe

Official name Republic of Cyprus
Formation 1960 / 1960
Capital Nicosia
Population 1.2 million / 336 people per sq mile (130 people per sq km)
Total area 3571 sq. miles (9250 sq. km)
Languages Greek*, Turkish*
Religions Orthodox Christian 78%, Muslim 18%, Other 4%
Ethnic mix Greek 81%, Turkish 11%, Other 8%
Government Presidential system
Currency Euro = 100 cents; (TRNC: new Turkish lira = 100 kurus)
Literacy rate 99%
Calorie consumption 2661 kilocalories

CZECH REPUBLIC
Central Europe

Official name Czech Republic
Formation 1993 / 1993
Capital Prague
Population 10.7 million / 351 people per sq mile (136 people per sq km)
Total area 30,450 sq. miles (78,866 sq. km)
Languages Czech*, Slovak, Hungarian (Magyar)
Religions Roman Catholic 39%, Atheist 38%, Other 18%, Protestant 3%, Hussite 2%
Ethnic mix Czech 90%, Moravian 4%, Other 4%, Slovak 2%
Government Parliamentary system
Currency Czech koruna = 100 haleru
Literacy rate 99%
Calorie consumption 3292 kilocalories

DENMARK
Northern Europe

Official name Kingdom of Denmark
Formation 950 / 1944
Capital Copenhagen
Population 5.6 million / 342 people per sq mile (132 people per sq km)
Total area 16,639 sq. miles (43,094 sq. km)
Languages Danish*
Religions Evangelical Lutheran 95%, Roman Catholic 3%, Muslim 2%
Ethnic mix Danish 96%, Other (including Scandinavian and Turkish) 3%, Faeroese and Inuit 1%
Government Parliamentary system
Currency Danish krone = 100 øre
Literacy rate 99%
Calorie consumption 3363 kilocalories

DJIBOUTI
East Africa

Official name Republic of Djibouti
Formation 1977 / 1977
Capital Djibouti
Population 900,000 / 101 people per sq mile (39 people per sq km)
Total area 8494 sq. miles (22,000 sq. km)
Languages Somali, Afar, French*, Arabic*
Religions Muslim (mainly Sunni) 94%, Christian 6%
Ethnic mix Issa 60%, Afar 35%, Other 5%
Government Presidential system
Currency Djibouti franc = 100 centimes
Literacy rate 70%
Calorie consumption 2526 kilocalories

DOMINICA
West Indies

Official name Commonwealth of Dominica
Formation 1978 / 1978
Capital Roseau
Population 73,449 / 253 people per sq mile (98 people per sq km)
Total area 291 sq. miles (754 sq. km)
Languages French Creole, English*
Religions Roman Catholic 77%, Protestant 15%, Other 8%
Ethnic mix Black 87%, Mixed race 9%, Carib 3%, Other 1%
Government Parliamentary system
Currency East Caribbean dollar = 100 cents
Literacy rate 88%
Calorie consumption 3047 kilocalories

DOMINICAN REPUBLIC
West Indies

Official name Dominican Republic
Formation 1865 / 1865
Capital Santo Domingo
Population 10.5 million / 562people per sq mile (217 people per sq km)
Total area 18,679 sq. miles (48,380 sq. km)
Languages Spanish*, French Creole
Religions Roman Catholic 95%, Other and nonreligious 5%
Ethnic mix Mixed race 73%, European 16%, Black African 11%
Government Presidential system
Currency Dominican Republic peso = 100 centavos
Literacy rate 91%
Calorie consumption 2614 kilocalories

EAST TIMOR
Southeast Asia

Official name Democratic Republic of Timor-Leste
Formation 2002 / 2002
Capital Dili
Population 1.2 million / 213 people per sq mile (82 people per sq km)
Total area 5756 sq. miles (14,874 sq. km)
Languages Tetum (Portuguese/Austronesian)*, Bahasa Indonesia, Portuguese*
Religions Roman Catholic 95%, Other (including Muslim and Protestant) 5%
Ethnic mix Papuan groups approx 85%, Indonesian approx 13%, Chinese 2%
Government Parliamentary system
Currency US dollar = 100 cents
Literacy rate 58%
Calorie consumption 2083 kilocalories

ECUADOR
South America

Official name Republic of Ecuador
Formation 1830 / 1942
Capital Quito
Population 16 million / 150 people per sq mile (58 people per sq km)
Total area 109,483 sq. miles (283,560 sq. km)
Languages Spanish*, Quechua, other Amerindian languages
Religions Roman Catholic 95%, Protestant, Jewish, and Other 5%
Ethnic mix Mestizo 77%, White 11%, Amerindian 7%, Black African 5%
Government Presidential system
Currency US dollar = 100 cents
Literacy rate 93%
Calorie consumption 2477 kilocalories

EGYPT
North Africa

Official name Arab Republic of Egypt
Formation 1936 / 1982
Capital Cairo
Population 83.4 million / 217 people per sq mile (84 people per sq km)
Total area 386,660 sq. miles (1,001,450 sq. km)
Languages Arabic*, French, English, Berber
Religions Muslim (mainly Sunni) 90%, Coptic Christian and other 9%, Other Christian 1%
Ethnic mix Egyptian 99%, Nubian, Armenian, Greek, and Berber 1%
Government Transitional regime
Currency Egyptian pound = 100 piastres
Literacy rate 74%
Calorie consumption 3557 kilocalories

EL SALVADOR
Central America

Official name Republic of El Salvador
Formation 1841 / 1841
Capital San Salvador
Population 6.4 million / 800 people per sq mile (309 people per sq km)
Total area 8124 sq. miles (21,040 sq. km)
Languages Spanish*
Religions Roman Catholic 80%, Evangelical 18%, Other 2%
Ethnic mix Mestizo 90%, White 9%, Amerindian 1%
Government Presidential system
Currency Salvadorean colón = 100 centavos; and US dollar = 100 cents
Literacy rate 86%
Calorie consumption 2513 kilocalories

EQUATORIAL GUINEA
Central Africa

Official name Republic of Equatorial Guinea
Formation 1968 / 1968
Capital Malabo
Population 800,000 / 74 people per sq mile (29 people per sq km)
Total area 10,830 sq. miles (28,051 sq. km)
Languages Spanish*, Fang, Bubi, French*
Religions Roman Catholic 90%, Other 10%
Ethnic mix Fang 85%, Other 11%, Bubi 4%
Government Presidential system
Currency CFA franc = 100 centimes
Literacy rate 94%
Calorie consumption Not available

ERITREA
East Africa

Official name State of Eritrea
Formation 1993 / 2002
Capital Asmara
Population 6.5 million / 143 people per sq mile (55 people per sq km)
Total area 46,842 sq. miles (121,320 sq. km)
Languages Tigrinya*, English*, Tigre, Afar, Arabic*, Saho, Bilen, Kunama, Nara, Hadareb
Religions Christian 50%, Muslim 48%, Other 2%
Ethnic mix Tigray 50%, Tigre 31%, Other 9%, Afar 5%, Saho 5%
Government Mixed presidential–parliamentary system
Currency Nakfa = 100 cents
Literacy rate 70%
Calorie consumption 1640 kilocalories

ESTONIA
Northeast Europe

Official name Republic of Estonia
Formation 1991 / 1991
Capital Tallinn
Population 1.3 million / 75 people per sq mile (29 people per sq km)
Total area 17,462 sq. miles (45,226 sq. km)
Languages Estonian*, Russian
Religions Evangelical Lutheran 56%, Orthodox Christian 25%, Other 19%
Ethnic mix Estonian 69%, Russian 25%, Other 4%, Ukrainian 2%
Government Parliamentary system
Currency Euro = 100 cents
Literacy rate 99%
Calorie consumption 3214 kilocalories

ETHIOPIA
East Africa

Official name Federal Democratic Republic of Ethiopia
Formation 1896 / 2002
Capital Addis Ababa
Population 96.5 million / 225 people per sq mile (87 people per sq km)
Total area 435,184 sq. miles (1,127,127 sq. km)
Languages Amharic*, Tigrinya, Galla, Sidamo, Somali, English, Arabic
Religions Orthodox Christian 40%, Muslim 40%, Traditional beliefs 15%, Other 5%
Ethnic mix Oromo 40%, Amhara 25%, Other 13%, Sidama 9%, Tigray 7%, Somali 6%
Government Parliamentary system
Currency Birr = 100 cents
Literacy rate 39%
Calorie consumption 2131 kilocalories

FIJI
Australasia & Oceania

Official name Republic of Fiji
Formation 1970 / 1970
Capital Suva
Population 900,000 / 128 people per sq mile (49 people per sq km)
Total area 7054 sq. miles (18,270 sq. km)
Languages Fijian, English*, Hindi, Urdu, Tamil, Telugu
Religions Hindu 38%, Methodist 37%, Roman Catholic 9%, Muslim 8%, Other 8%
Ethnic mix Melanesian 51%, Indian 44%, Other 5%
Government Parliamentary system
Currency Fiji dollar = 100 cents
Literacy rate 94%
Calorie consumption 2930 kilocalories

FINLAND
Northern Europe

Official name Republic of Finland
Formation 1917 / 1947
Capital Helsinki
Population 5.4 million / 46 people per sq mile (18 people per sq km)
Total area 130,127 sq. miles (337,030 sq. km)
Languages Finnish*, Swedish*, Sámi
Religions Evangelical Lutheran 83%, Other 15%, Orthodox Christian 1%, Roman Catholic 1%
Ethnic mix Finnish 93%, Other (including Sámi) 7%
Government Parliamentary system
Currency Euro = 100 cents
Literacy rate 99%
Calorie consumption 3285 kilocalories

FRANCE
Western Europe

Official name French Republic
Formation 987 / 1919
Capital Paris
Population 64.6 million / 304 people per sq mile (117 people per sq km)
Total area 211,208 sq. miles (547,030 sq. km)
Languages French*, Provençal, German, Breton, Catalan, Basque
Religions Roman Catholic 88%, Muslim 8%, Protestant 2%, Buddhist 1%, Jewish 1%
Ethnic mix French 90%, North African (mainly Algerian) 6%, German (Alsace) 2%, Breton 1%, Other (including Corsicans) 1%
Government Mixed presidential–parliamentary system
Currency Euro = 100 cents
Literacy rate 99%
Calorie consumption 3524 kilocalories

GABON
Central Africa

Official name Gabonese Republic
Formation 1960 / 1960
Capital Libreville
Population 1.7 million / 17 people per sq mile (7 people per sq km)
Total area 103,346 sq. miles (267,667 sq. km)
Languages Fang, French*, Punu, Sira, Nzebi, Mpongwe
Religions Christian (mainly Roman Catholic) 55%, Traditional beliefs 40%, Other 4%, Muslim 1%
Ethnic mix Fang 26%, Shira-punu 24%, Other 16%, Foreign residents 15%, Nzabi-duma 11%, Mbédé-Teke 8%
Government Presidential system
Currency CFA franc = 100 centimes
Literacy rate 82%
Calorie consumption 2781 kilocalories

GAMBIA
West Africa

Official name Republic of the Gambia
Formation 1965 / 1965
Capital Banjul
Population 1.9 million / 492 people per sq mile (190 people per sq km)
Total area 4363 sq. miles (11,300 sq. km)
Languages Mandinka, Fulani, Wolof, Jola, Soninke, English*
Religions Sunni Muslim 90%, Christian 8%, Traditional beliefs 2%
Ethnic mix Mandinka 42%, Fulani 18%, Wolof 16%, Jola 10%, Serahuli 9%, Other 5%
Government Presidential system
Currency Dalasi = 100 butut
Literacy rate 52%
Calorie consumption 2849 kilocalories

GEORGIA
Southwest Asia

Official name Georgia
Formation 1991 / 1991
Capital Tbilisi
Population 4.3 million / 160 people per sq mile (62 people per sq km)
Total area 26,911 sq. miles (69,700 sq. km)
Languages Georgian*, Russian, Azeri, Armenian, Mingrelian, Ossetian, Abkhazian* (in Abkhazia)
Religions Georgian Orthodox 74%, Muslim 10%, Russian Orthodox 10%, Armenian Apostolic Church (Orthodox) 4%, Other 2%
Ethnic mix Georgian 84%, Azeri 6%, Armenian 6%, Russian 2%, Ossetian 1%, Other 1%
Government Presidential system
Currency Lari = 100 tetri
Literacy rate 99%
Calorie consumption 2731 kilocalories

GERMANY
Northern Europe

Official name Federal Republic of Germany
Formation 1871 / 1990
Capital Berlin
Population 82.7 million / 613 people per sq mile (237 people per sq km)
Total area 137,846 sq. miles (357,021 sq. km)
Languages German*, Turkish
Religions Protestant 34%, Roman Catholic 33%, Other 30%, Muslim 3%
Ethnic mix German 92%, Other European 3%, Other 3%, Turkish 2%
Government Parliamentary system
Currency Euro = 100 cents
Literacy rate 99%
Calorie consumption 3539 kilocalories

GHANA
West Africa

Official name Republic of Ghana
Formation 1957 / 1957
Capital Accra
Population 26.4 million / 297 people per sq mile (115 people per sq km)
Total area 92,100 sq. miles (238,540 sq. km)
Languages Twi, Fanti, Ewe, Ga, Adangbe, Gurma, Dagomba (Dagbani), English*
Religions Christian 69%, Muslim 16%, Traditional beliefs 9%, Other 6%
Ethnic mix Akan 49%, Mole-Dagbani 17%, Ewe 13%, Other 9%, Ga and Ga-Adangbe 8%, Guan 4%
Government Presidential system
Currency Cedi = 100 pesewas
Literacy rate 72%
Calorie consumption 3003 kilocalories

GREECE
Southeast Europe

Official name Hellenic Republic
Formation 1829 / 1947
Capital Athens
Population 11.1 million / 220 people per sq mile (85 people per sq km)
Total area 50,942 sq. miles (131,940 sq. km)
Languages Greek*, Turkish, Macedonian, Albanian
Religions Orthodox Christian 98%, Muslim 1%, Other 1%
Ethnic mix Greek 98%, Other 2%
Government Parliamentary system
Currency Euro = 100 cents
Literacy rate 97%
Calorie consumption 3433 kilocalories

GRENADA
West Indies

Official name Grenada
Formation 1974 / 1974
Capital St. George's
Population 110,152 / 841 people per sq mile (324 people per sq km)
Total area 131 sq. miles (340 sq. km)
Languages English*, English Creole
Religions Roman Catholic 68%, Anglican 17%, Other 15%
Ethnic mix Black African 82%, Mulatto (mixed race) 13%, East Indian 3%, Other 2%
Government Parliamentary system
Currency East Caribbean dollar = 100 cents
Literacy rate 96%
Calorie consumption 2453 kilocalories

GUATEMALA
Central America

Official name Republic of Guatemala
Formation 1838 / 1838
Capital Guatemala City
Population 15.9 million / 380 people per sq mile (147 people per sq km)
Total area 42,042 sq. miles (108,890 sq. km)
Languages Quiché, Mam, Cakchiquel, Kekchí, Spanish*
Religions Roman Catholic 65%, Protestant 33%, Other and nonreligious 2%
Ethnic mix Amerindian 60%, Mestizo 30%, Other 10%
Government Presidential system
Currency Quetzal = 100 centavos
Literacy rate 78%
Calorie consumption 2419 kilocalories

GUINEA
West Africa

Official name Republic of Guinea
Formation 1958 / 1958
Capital Conakry
Population 12 million / 126 people per sq mile (49 people per sq km)
Total area 94,925 sq. miles (245,857 sq. km)
Languages Pulaar, Malinké, Soussou, French*
Religions Muslim 85%, Christian 8%, Traditional beliefs 7%
Ethnic mix Peul 40%, Malinké 30%, Soussou 20%, Other 10%
Government Presidential system
Currency Guinea franc = 100 centimes
Literacy rate 25%
Calorie consumption 2553 kilocalories

GUINEA-BISSAU
West Africa

Official name Republic of Guinea-Bissau
Formation 1974 / 1974
Capital Bissau
Population 1.7 million / 157 people per sq mile (60 people per sq km)
Total area 13,946 sq. miles (36,120 sq. km)
Languages Portuguese Creole, Balante, Fulani, Malinké, Portuguese*
Religions Traditional beliefs 50%, Muslim 40%, Christian 10%
Ethnic mix Balante 30%, Fulani 20%, Other 16%, Mandyako 14%, Mandinka 13%, Papel 7%
Government Presidential system
Currency CFA franc = 100 centimes
Literacy rate 57%
Calorie consumption 2304 kilocalories

GUYANA
South America

Official name Cooperative Republic of Guyana
Formation 1966 / 1966
Capital Georgetown
Population 800,000 / 11 people per sq mile (4 people per sq km)
Total area 83,000 sq. miles (214,970 sq. km)
Languages English Creole, Hindi, Tamil, Amerindian languages, English*
Religions Christian 57%, Hindu 28%, Muslim 10%, Other 5%
Ethnic mix East Indian 43%, Black African 30%, Mixed race 17%, Amerindian 9%, Other 1%
Government Presidential system
Currency Guyanese dollar = 100 cents
Literacy rate 85%
Calorie consumption 2648 kilocalories

HAITI
West Indies

Official name Republic of Haiti
Formation 1804 / 1844
Capital Port-au-Prince
Population 10.5 million / 987 people per sq mile (381 people per sq km)
Total area 10,714 sq. miles (27,750 sq. km)
Languages French Creole*, French*
Religions Roman Catholic 55%, Protestant 28%, Other (including Voodoo) 16%, Nonreligious 1%
Ethnic mix Black African 95%, Mulatto (mixed race) and European 5%
Government Presidential system
Currency Gourde = 100 centimes
Literacy rate 49%
Calorie consumption 2091 kilocalories

HONDURAS
Central America

Official name Republic of Honduras
Formation 1838 / 1838
Capital Tegucigalpa
Population 8.3 million / 192 people per sq mile (74 people per sq km)
Total area 43,278 sq. miles (112,090 sq. km)
Languages Spanish*, Garífuna (Carib), English Creole
Religions Roman Catholic 97%, Protestant 3%
Ethnic mix Mestizo 90%, Black African 5%, Amerindian 4%, White 1%
Government Presidential system
Currency Lempira = 100 centavos
Literacy rate 85%
Calorie consumption 2651 kilocalories

HUNGARY
Central Europe

Official name Hungary
Formation 1918 / 1947
Capital Budapest
Population 9.9 million / 278 people per sq mile (107 people per sq km)
Total area 35,919 sq. miles (93,030 sq. km)
Languages Hungarian (Magyar)*
Religions Roman Catholic 52%, Calvinist 16%, Other 15%, Nonreligious 14%, Lutheran 3%
Ethnic mix Magyar 90%, Roma 4%, German 3%, Serb 2%, Other 1%
Government Parliamentary system
Currency Forint = 100 fillér
Literacy rate 99%
Calorie consumption 2968 kilocalories

ICELAND
Northwest Europe

Official name Republic of Iceland
Formation 1944 / 1944
Capital Reykjavík
Population 300,000 / 8 people per sq mile (3 people per sq km)
Total area 39,768 sq. miles (103,000 sq. km)
Languages Icelandic*
Religions Evangelical Lutheran 84%, Other (mostly Christian) 10%, Roman Catholic 3%, Nonreligious 3%
Ethnic mix Icelandic 94%, Other 5%, Danish 1%
Government Parliamentary system
Currency Icelandic króna = 100 aurar
Literacy rate 99%
Calorie consumption 3339 kilocalories

INDIA
South Asia

Official name Republic of India
Formation 1947 / 1947
Capital New Delhi
Population 1.27 billion / 1104 people per sq mile (426 people per sq km)
Total area 1,269,339 sq. miles (3,287,590 sq. km)
Languages Hindi*, English*, Urdu, Bengali, Marathi, Telugu, Tamil, Bihari, Gujarati, Kanarese
Religions Hindu 81%, Muslim 13%, Christian 2%, Sikh 2%, Buddhist 1%, Other 1%
Ethnic mix Indo-Aryan 72%, Dravidian 25%, Mongoloid and other 3%
Government Parliamentary system
Currency Indian rupee = 100 paise
Literacy rate 63%
Calorie consumption 2459 kilocalories

INDONESIA
Southeast Asia

Official name Republic of Indonesia
Formation 1949 / 1999
Capital Jakarta
Population 253 million / 364 people per sq mile (141 people per sq km)
Total area 741,096 sq. miles (1,919,440 sq. km)
Languages Javanese, Sundanese, Madurese, Bahasa Indonesia*, Dutch
Religions Sunni Muslim 86%, Protestant 6%, Roman Catholic 3%, Hindu 2%, Other 2%, Buddhist 1%
Ethnic mix Javanese 41%, Other 29%, Sundanese 15%, Coastal Malays 12%, Madurese 3%
Government Presidential system
Currency Rupiah = 100 sen
Literacy rate 93%
Calorie consumption 2777 kilocalories

IRAN
Southwest Asia

Official name Islamic Republic of Iran
Formation 1502 / 1990
Capital Tehran
Population 78.5 million / 124 people per sq mile (48 people per sq km)
Total area 636,293 sq. miles (1,648,000 sq. km)
Languages Farsi*, Azeri, Luri, Gilaki, Mazanderani, Kurdish, Turkmen, Arabic, Baluchi
Religions Shi'a Muslim 89%, Sunni Muslim 9%, Other 2%
Ethnic mix Persian 51%, Azari 24%, Other 10%, Lur and Bakhtiari 8%, Kurdish 7%
Government Islamic theocracy
Currency Iranian rial = 100 dinars
Literacy rate 84%
Calorie consumption 3058 kilocalories

IRAQ
Southwest Asia

Official name Republic of Iraq
Formation 1932 / 1990
Capital Baghdad
Population 34.8 million / 206 people per sq mile (80 people per sq km)
Total area 168,753 sq. miles (437,072 sq. km)
Languages Arabic*, Kurdish*, Turkic languages, Armenian, Assyrian
Religions Shi'a Muslim 60%, Sunni Muslim 35%, Other (including Christian) 5%
Ethnic mix Arab 80%, Kurdish 15%, Turkmen 3%, Other 2%
Government Parliamentary system
Currency New Iraqi dinar = 1000 fils
Literacy rate 79%
Calorie consumption 2489 kilocalories

IRELAND
Northwest Europe

Official name Ireland
Formation 1922 / 1922
Capital Dublin
Population 4.7 million / 177 people per sq mile (68 people per sq km)
Total area 27,135 sq. miles (70,280 sq. km)
Languages English*, Irish*
Religions Roman Catholic 87%, Other and nonreligious 10%, Anglican 3%
Ethnic mix Irish 99%, Other 1%
Government Parliamentary system
Currency Euro = 100 cents
Literacy rate 99%
Calorie consumption 3591 kilocalories

ISRAEL
Southwest Asia

Official name State of Israel
Formation 1948 / 1994
Capital Jerusalem (not internationally recognized)
Population 7.8 million / 994 people per sq mile (384 people per sq km)
Total area 8019 sq. miles (20,770 sq. km)
Languages Hebrew*, Arabic*, Yiddish, German, Russian, Polish, Romanian, Persian
Religions Jewish 76%, Muslim (mainly Sunni) 16%, Other 4%, Druze 2%, Christian 2%
Ethnic mix Jewish 76%, Arab 20%, Other 4%
Government Parliamentary system
Currency Shekel = 100 agorot
Literacy rate 98%
Calorie consumption 3619 kilocalories

ITALY
Southern Europe

Official name Italian Republic
Formation 1861 / 1947
Capital Rome
Population 61.1 million / 538 people per sq mile (208 people per sq km)
Total area 116,305 sq. miles (301,230 sq. km)
Languages Italian*, German, French, Rhaeto-Romanic, Sardinian
Religions Roman Catholic 85%, Other and nonreligious 13%, Muslim 2%
Ethnic mix Italian 94%, Other 4%, Sardinian 2%
Government Parliamentary system
Currency Euro = 100 cents
Literacy rate 99%
Calorie consumption 3539 kilocalories

IVORY COAST
West Africa

Official name Republic of Côte d'Ivoire
Formation 1960 / 1960
Capital Yamoussoukro
Population 20.8 million / 169 people per sq mile (65 people per sq km)
Total area 124,502 sq. miles (322,460 sq. km)
Languages Akan, French*, Krou, Voltaique
Religions Muslim 38%, Traditional beliefs 25%, Roman Catholic 25%, Other 6%, Protestant 6%
Ethnic mix Akan 42%, Voltaique 18%, Mandé du Nord 17%, Krou 11%, Mandé du Sud 10%, Other 2%
Government Presidential system
Currency CFA franc = 100 centimes
Literacy rate 41%
Calorie consumption 2799 kilocalories

JAMAICA
West Indies

Official name Jamaica
Formation 1962 / 1962
Capital Kingston
Population 2.8 million / 670 people per sq mile (259 people per sq km)
Total area 4243 sq. miles (10,990 sq. km)
Languages English Creole, English*
Religions Other and nonreligious 45%, Other Protestant 20%, Church of God 18%, Baptist 10%, Anglican 7%
Ethnic mix Black 91%, Mulatto (mixed race) 7%, European and Chinese 1%, East Indian 1%
Government Parliamentary system
Currency Jamaican dollar = 100 cents
Literacy rate 88%
Calorie consumption 2746 kilocalories

JAPAN
East Asia

Official name Japan
Formation 1590 / 1972
Capital Tokyo
Population 127 million / 874 people per sq mile (337 people per sq km)
Total area 145,882 sq. miles (377,835 sq. km)
Languages Japanese*, Korean, Chinese
Religions Shinto and Buddhist 76%, Buddhist 16%, Other (including Christian) 8%
Ethnic mix Japanese 99%, Other (mainly Korean) 1%
Government Parliamentary system
Currency Yen = 100 sen
Literacy rate 99%
Calorie consumption 2719 kilocalories

JORDAN
Southwest Asia

Official name Hashemite Kingdom of Jordan
Formation 1946 / 1967
Capital Amman
Population 7.5 million / 218 people per sq mile (84 people per sq km)
Total area 35,637 sq. miles (92,300 sq. km)
Languages Arabic*
Religions Sunni Muslim 92%, Christian 6%, Other 2%
Ethnic mix Arab 98%, Circassian 1%, Armenian 1%
Government Monarchy
Currency Jordanian dinar = 1000 fils
Literacy rate 98%
Calorie consumption 3149 kilocalories

KAZAKHSTAN
Central Asia

Official name Republic of Kazakhstan
Formation 1991 / 1991
Capital Astana
Population 16.6 million / 16 people per sq mile (6 people per sq km)
Total area 1,049,150 sq. miles (2,717,300 sq. km)
Languages Kazakh*, Russian, Ukrainian, German, Uzbek, Tatar, Uighur
Religions Muslim (mainly Sunni) 47%, Orthodox Christian 44%, Other 7%, Protestant 2%
Ethnic mix Kazakh 57%, Russian 27%, Other 8%, Uzbek 3%, Ukrainian 3%, German 2%
Government Presidential system
Currency Tenge = 100 tiyn
Literacy rate 99%
Calorie consumption 3107 kilocalories

KENYA
East Africa

Official name Republic of Kenya
Formation 1963 / 1963
Capital Nairobi
Population 45.5 million / 208 people per sq mile (80 people per sq km)
Total area 224,961 sq. miles (582,650 sq. km)
Languages Kiswahili*, English*, Kikuyu, Luo, Kalenjin, Kamba
Religions Christian 80%, Muslim 10%, Traditional beliefs 9%, Other 1%
Ethnic mix Other 28%, Kikuyu 22%, Luo 14%, Luhya 14%, Kalenjin 11%, Kamba 11%
Government Presidential system
Currency Kenya shilling = 100 cents
Literacy rate 72%
Calorie consumption 2206 kilocalories

KIRIBATI
Australasia & Oceania

Official name Republic of Kiribati
Formation 1979 / 1979
Capital Tarawa Atoll
Population 104,488 / 381 people per sq mile (147 people per sq km)
Total area 277 sq. miles (717 sq. km)
Languages English*, Kiribati
Religions Roman Catholic 55%, Kiribati Protestant Church 36%, Other 9%
Ethnic mix Micronesian 99%, Other 1%
Government Presidential system
Currency Australian dollar = 100 cents
Literacy rate 99%
Calorie consumption 3022 kilocalories

KOSOVO (not yet recognised)
Southeast Europe

Official name Republic of Kosovo
Formation 2008 / 2008
Capital Pristina
Population 1.9 million / 451 people per sq mile (174 people per sq km)
Total area 4212 sq. miles (10,908 sq. km)
Languages Albanian*, Serbian*, Bosniak, Gorani, Roma, Turkish
Religions Muslim 92%, Roman Catholic 4%, Orthodox Christian 4%
Ethnic mix Albanian 92%, Serb 4%, Bosniak and Gorani 2%, Turkish 1%, Roma 1%
Government Parliamentary system
Currency Euro = 100 cents
Literacy rate 92%
Calorie consumption Not available

KUWAIT
Southwest Asia

Official name State of Kuwait
Formation 1961 / 1961
Capital Kuwait City
Population 3.5 million / 509 people per sq mile (196 people per sq km)
Total area 6880 sq. miles (17,820 sq. km)
Languages Arabic*, English
Religions Sunni Muslim 45%, Shi'a Muslim 40%, Christian, Hindu, and other 15%
Ethnic mix Kuwaiti 45%, Other Arab 35%, South Asian 9%, Other 7%, Iranian 4%
Government Monarchy
Currency Kuwaiti dinar = 1000 fils
Literacy rate 96%
Calorie consumption 3471 kilocalories

KYRGYZSTAN
Central Asia

Official name Kyrgyz Republic
Formation 1991 / 1991
Capital Bishkek
Population 5.6 million / 73 people per sq mile (28 people per sq km)
Total area 76,641 sq. miles (198,500 sq. km)
Languages Kyrgyz*, Russian*, Uzbek, Tatar, Ukrainian
Religions Muslim (mainly Sunni) 70%, Orthodox Christian 30%
Ethnic mix Kyrgyz 69%, Uzbek 14%, Russian 9%, Other 6%, Dungan 1%, Uighur 1%
Government Presidential system
Currency Som = 100 tyiyn
Literacy rate 99%
Calorie consumption 2828 kilocalories

LAOS
Southeast Asia

Official name Lao People's Democratic Republic
Formation 1953 / 1953
Capital Vientiane
Population 6.9 million / 77 people per sq mile (30 people per sq km)
Total area 91,428 sq. miles (236,800 sq. km)
Languages Lao*, Mon-Khmer, Yao, Vietnamese, Chinese, French
Religions Buddhist 65%, Other (including animist) 34%, Christian 1%
Ethnic mix Lao Loum 66%, Lao Theung 30%, Lao Soung 2%, Other 2%
Government One-party state
Currency Kip = 100 at
Literacy rate 73%
Calorie consumption 2356 kilocalories

LATVIA
Northeast Europe

Official name Republic of Latvia
Formation 1991 / 1991
Capital Riga
Population 2 million / 80 people per sq mile (31 people per sq km)
Total area 24,938 sq. miles (64,589 sq. km)
Languages Latvian*, Russian
Religions Other 43%, Lutheran 24%, Roman Catholic 18%, Orthodox Christian 15%
Ethnic mix Latvian 62%, Russian 27%, Other 4%, Belarussian 3%, Ukrainian 2%, Polish 2%
Government Parliamentary system
Currency Euro = 100 cents
Literacy rate 99%
Calorie consumption 3293 kilocalories

LEBANON
Southwest Asia

Official name Lebanese Republic
Formation 1941 / 1941
Capital Beirut
Population 5 million / 1266 people per sq mile (489 people per sq km)
Total area 4015 sq. miles (10,400 sq. km)
Languages Arabic*, French, Armenian, Assyrian
Religions Muslim 60%, Christian 39%, Other 1%
Ethnic mix Arab 95%, Armenian 4%, Other 1%
Government Parliamentary system
Currency Lebanese pound = 100 piastres
Literacy rate 90%
Calorie consumption 3181 kilocalories

LESOTHO
Southern Africa

Official name Kingdom of Lesotho
Formation 1966 / 1966
Capital Maseru
Population 2.1 million / 179 people per sq mile (69 people per sq km)
Total area 11,720 sq. miles (30,355 sq. km)
Languages English*, Sesotho*, isiZulu
Religions Christian 90%, Traditional beliefs 10%
Ethnic mix Sotho 99%, European and Asian 1%
Government Parliamentary system
Currency Loti = 100 lisente; and South African rand = 100 cents
Literacy rate 76%
Calorie consumption 2595 kilocalories

LIBERIA
West Africa

Official name Republic of Liberia
Formation 1847 / 1847
Capital Monrovia
Population 4.4 million / 118 people per sq mile (46 people per sq km)
Total area 43,000 sq. miles (111,370 sq. km)
Languages Kpelle, Vai, Bassa, Kru, Grebo, Kissi, Gola, Loma, English*
Religions Christian 40%, Traditional beliefs 40%, Muslim 20%
Ethnic mix Indigenous tribes (12 groups) 49%, Kpellé 20%, Bassa 16%, Gio 8%, Krou 7%
Government Presidential system
Currency Liberian dollar = 100 cents
Literacy rate 43%
Calorie consumption 2251 kilocalories

LIBYA
North Africa

Official name State of Libya
Formation 1951 / 1951
Capital Tripoli
Population 6.3 million / 9 people per sq mile (4 people per sq km)
Total area 679,358 sq. miles (1,759,540 sq. km)
Languages Arabic*, Tuareg
Religions Muslim (mainly Sunni) 97%, Other 3%
Ethnic mix Arab and Berber 97%, Other 3%
Government Transitional regime
Currency Libyan dinar = 1000 dirhams
Literacy rate 90%
Calorie consumption 3211 kilocalories

LIECHTENSTEIN
Central Europe

Official name Principality of Liechtenstein
Formation 1719 / 1719
Capital Vaduz
Population 37,313 / 602 people per sq mile (233 people per sq km)
Total area 62 sq. miles (160 sq. km)
Languages German*, Alemannish dialect, Italian
Religions Roman Catholic 79%, Other 13%, Protestant 8%
Ethnic mix Liechtensteiner 66%, Other 12%, Swiss 10%, Austrian 6%, German 3%, Italian 3%
Government Parliamentary system
Currency Swiss franc = 100 rappen/centimes
Literacy rate 99%
Calorie consumption Not available

LITHUANIA
Northeast Europe

Official name Republic of Lithuania
Formation 1991 / 1991
Capital Vilnius
Population 3 million / 119 people per sq mile (46 people per sq km)
Total area 25,174 sq. miles (65,200 sq. km)
Languages Lithuanian*, Russian
Religions Roman Catholic 77%, Other 17%, Russian Orthodox 4%, Protestant 1%, Old believers 1%
Ethnic mix Lithuanian 85%, Polish 7%, Russian 6%, Belarussian 1%, Other 1%
Government Parliamentary system
Currency Euro = 100 cents
Literacy rate 99%
Calorie consumption 3463 kilocalories

LUXEMBOURG
Northwest Europe

Official name Grand Duchy of Luxembourg
Formation 1867 / 1867
Capital Luxembourg-Ville
Population 500,000 / 501 people per sq mile (193 people per sq km)
Total area 998 sq. miles (2586 sq. km)
Languages Luxembourgish*, German*, French*
Religions Roman Catholic 97%, Protestant, Orthodox Christian, and Jewish 3%
Ethnic mix Luxembourger 62%, Foreign residents 38%
Government Parliamentary system
Currency Euro = 100 cents
Literacy rate 99%
Calorie consumption 3568 kilocalories

MACEDONIA
Southeast Europe

Official name Republic of Macedonia
Formation 1991 / 1991
Capital Skopje
Population 2.1 million / 212 people per sq mile (82 people per sq km)
Total area 9781 sq. miles (25,333 sq. km)
Languages Macedonian*, Albanian*, Turkish, Romani, Serbian
Religions Orthodox Christian 65%, Muslim 29%, Roman Catholic 4%, Other 2%
Ethnic mix Macedonian 64%, Albanian 25%, Turkish 4%, Roma 3%, Serb 2%, Other 2%
Government Mixed presidential–parliamentary system
Currency Macedonian denar = 100 deni
Literacy rate 98%
Calorie consumption 2923 kilocalories

MADAGASCAR
Indian Ocean

Official name Republic of Madagascar
Formation 1960 / 1960
Capital Antananarivo
Population 23.6 million / 105 people per sq mile (41 people per sq km)
Total area 226,656 sq. miles (587,040 sq. km)
Languages Malagasy*, French*, English*
Religions Traditional beliefs 52%, Christian (mainly Roman Catholic) 41%, Muslim 7%
Ethnic mix Other Malay 46%, Merina 26%, Betsimisaraka 15%, Betsileo 12%, Other 1%
Government Mixed presidential–parliamentary system
Currency Ariary = 5 iraimbilanja
Literacy rate 64%
Calorie consumption 2052 kilocalories

MALAWI
Southern Africa

Official name Republic of Malawi
Formation 1964 / 1964
Capital Lilongwe
Population 16.8 million / 463 people per sq mile (179 people per sq km)
Total area 45,745 sq. miles (118,480 sq. km)
Languages Chewa, Lomwe, Yao, Ngoni, English*
Religions Protestant 55%, Roman Catholic 20%, Muslim 20%, Traditional beliefs 5%
Ethnic mix Bantu 99%, Other 1%
Government Presidential system
Currency Malawi kwacha = 100 tambala
Literacy rate 61%
Calorie consumption 2334 kilocalories

MALAYSIA
Southeast Asia

Official name Malaysia
Formation 1963 / 1965
Capital Kuala Lumpur; Putrajaya (administrative)
Population 30.2 million / 238 people per sq mile (92 people per sq km)
Total area 127,316 sq. miles (329,750 sq. km)
Languages Bahasa Malaysia*, Malay, Chinese, Tamil, English
Religions Muslim (mainly Sunni) 61%, Buddhist 19%, Christian 9%, Hindu 6%, Other 5%
Ethnic mix Malay 53%, Chinese 26%, Indigenous tribes 12%, Indian 8%, Other 1%
Government Parliamentary system
Currency Ringgit = 100 sen
Literacy rate 93%
Calorie consumption 2855 kilocalories

MALDIVES
Indian Ocean

Official name Republic of Maldives
Formation 1965 / 1965
Capital Male'
Population 400,000 / 3448 people per sq mile (1333 people per sq km)
Total area 116 sq. miles (300 sq. km)
Languages Dhivehi (Maldivian), Sinhala, Tamil, Arabic
Religions Sunni Muslim 100%
Ethnic mix Arab–Sinhalese–Malay 100%
Government Presidential system
Currency Rufiyaa = 100 laari
Literacy rate 98%
Calorie consumption 2722 kilocalories

MALI
West Africa

Official name Republic of Mali
Formation 1960 / 1960
Capital Bamako
Population 15.8 million / 34 people per sq mile (13 people per sq km)
Total area 478,764 sq. miles (1,240,000 sq. km)
Languages Bambara, Fulani, Senufo, Soninke, French*
Religions Muslim (mainly Sunni) 90%, Traditional beliefs 6%, Christian 4%
Ethnic mix Bambara 52%, Other 14%, Fulani 11%, Saracolé 7%, Soninka 7%, Tuareg 5%, Mianka 4%
Government Presidential system
Currency CFA franc = 100 centimes
Literacy rate 34%
Calorie consumption 2833 kilocalories

MALTA
Southern Europe

Official name Republic of Malta
Formation 1964 / 1964
Capital Valletta
Population 400,000 / 3226 people per sq mile (1250 people per sq km)
Total area 122 sq. miles (316 sq. km)
Languages Maltese*, English*
Religions Roman Catholic 98%, Other and nonreligious 2%
Ethnic mix Maltese 96%, Other 4%
Government Parliamentary system
Currency Euro = 100 cents
Literacy rate 92%
Calorie consumption 3389 kilocalories

MARSHALL ISLANDS
Australasia & Oceania

Official name Republic of the Marshall Islands
Formation 1986 / 1986
Capital Majuro
Population 70,983 / 1014 people per sq mile (392 people per sq km)
Total area 70 sq. miles (181 sq. km)
Languages Marshallese*, English*, Japanese, German
Religions Protestant 90%, Roman Catholic 8%, Other 2%
Ethnic mix Micronesian 90%, Other 10%
Government Presidential system
Currency US dollar = 100 cents
Literacy rate 91%
Calorie consumption Not available

MAURITANIA
West Africa

Official name Islamic Republic of Mauritania
Formation 1960 / 1960
Capital Nouakchott
Population 4 million / 10 people per sq mile (4 people per sq km)
Total area 397,953 sq. miles (1,030,700 sq. km)
Languages Arabic*, Hassaniyah Arabic, Wolof, French
Religions Sunni Muslim 100%
Ethnic mix Maure 81%, Wolof 7%, Tukolor 5%, Other 4%, Soninka 3%
Government Presidential system
Currency Ouguiya = 5 khoums
Literacy rate 46%
Calorie consumption 2791 kilocalories

MAURITIUS
Indian Ocean

Official name Republic of Mauritius
Formation 1968 / 1968
Capital Port Louis
Population 1.2 million / 1671 people per sq mile (645 people per sq km)
Total area 718 sq. miles (1860 sq. km)
Languages French Creole, Hindi, Urdu, Tamil, Chinese, English*, French
Religions Hindu 48%, Roman Catholic 24%, Muslim 17%, Protestant 9%, Other 2%
Ethnic mix Indo-Mauritian 68%, Creole 27%, Sino-Mauritian 3%, Franco-Mauritian 2%
Government Parliamentary system
Currency Mauritian rupee = 100 cents
Literacy rate 89%
Calorie consumption 3055 kilocalories

MEXICO
North America

Official name United Mexican States
Formation 1836 / 1848
Capital Mexico City
Population 124 million / 168 people per sq mile (65 people per sq km)
Total area 761,602 sq. miles (1,972,550 sq. km)
Languages Spanish*, Nahuatl, Mayan, Zapotec, Mixtec, Otomi, Totonac, Tzotzil, Tzeltal
Religions Roman Catholic 77%, Other 14%, Protestant 6%, Nonreligious 3%
Ethnic mix Mestizo 60%, Amerindian 30%, European 9%, Other 1%
Government Presidential system
Currency Mexican peso = 100 centavos
Literacy rate 94%
Calorie consumption 3072 kilocalories

MICRONESIA
Australasia & Oceania

Official name Federated States of Micronesia
Formation 1986 / 1986
Capital Palikir (Pohnpei Island)
Population 105,681 / 390 people per sq mile (151 people per sq km)
Total area 271 sq. miles (702 sq. km)
Languages Trukese, Pohnpeian, Kosraean, Yapese, English*
Religions Roman Catholic 50%, Protestant 47%, Other 3%
Ethnic mix Chuukese 49%, Pohnpeian 24%, Other 14%, Kosraean 6%, Yapese 5%, Asian 2%
Government Nonparty system
Currency US dollar = 100 cents
Literacy rate 81%
Calorie consumption Not available

MOLDOVA
Southeast Europe

Official name Republic of Moldova
Formation 1991 / 1991
Capital Chisinau
Population 3.5 million / 269 people per sq mile (104 people per sq km)
Total area 13,067 sq. miles (33,843 sq. km)
Languages Moldovan*, Ukrainian, Russian
Religions Orthodox Christian 93%, Other 6%, Baptist 1%
Ethnic mix Moldovan 84%, Ukrainian 7%, Gagauz 5%, Russian 2%, Bulgarian 1%, Other 1%
Government Parliamentary system
Currency Moldovan leu = 100 bani
Literacy rate 99%
Calorie consumption 2837 kilocalories

MONACO
Southern Europe

Official name Principality of Monaco
Formation 1861 / 1861
Capital Monaco-Ville
Population 36,950 / 49,267 people per sq mile (18,949 people per sq km)
Total area 0.75 sq. miles (1.95 sq. km)
Languages French*, Italian, Monégasque, English
Religions Roman Catholic 89%, Protestant 6%, Other 5%
Ethnic mix French 47%, Other 21%, Italian 16%, Monégasque 16%
Government Mixed monarchical–parliamentary system
Currency Euro = 100 cents
Literacy rate 99%
Calorie consumption Not available

MONGOLIA
East Asia

Official name Mongolia
Formation 1924 / 1924
Capital Ulan Bator
Population 2.9 million / 5 people per sq mile (2 people per sq km)
Total area 604,247 sq. miles (1,565,000 sq. km)
Languages Khalkha Mongolian, Kazakh, Chinese, Russian
Religions Tibetan Buddhist 50%, Nonreligious 40%, Shamanist and Christian 6%, Muslim 4%
Ethnic mix Khalkh 95%, Kazakh 4%, Other 1%
Government Mixed presidential–parliamentary system
Currency Tugrik (tögrög) = 100 möngö
Literacy rate 98%
Calorie consumption 2463 kilocalories

MONTENEGRO
Southeast Europe

Official name Montenegro
Formation 2006 / 2006
Capital Podgorica
Population 600,000 / 113 people per sq mile (43 people per sq km)
Total area 5332 sq. miles (13,812 sq. km)
Languages Montenegrin*, Serbian, Albanian, Bosniak, Croatian
Religions Orthodox Christian 74%, Muslim 18%, Roman Catholic 4%, Other 4%
Ethnic mix Montenegrin 43%, Serb 32%, Other 12%, Bosniak 8%, Albanian 5%
Government Parliamentary system
Currency Euro = 100 cents
Literacy rate 98%
Calorie consumption 3568 kilocalories

MOROCCO
North Africa

Official name Kingdom of Morocco
Formation 1956 / 1969
Capital Rabat
Population 35.5 million / 194 people per sq mile (75 people per sq km)
Total area 172,316 sq. miles (446,300 sq. km)
Languages Arabic*, Tamazight (Berber), French, Spanish
Religions Muslim (mainly Sunni) 99%, Other (mostly Christian) 1%
Ethnic mix Arab 70%, Berber 29%, European 1%
Government Mixed monarchical–parliamentary system
Currency Moroccan dirham = 100 centimes
Literacy rate 67%
Calorie consumption 3334 kilocalories

MOZAMBIQUE
Southern Africa

Official name Republic of Mozambique
Formation 1975 / 1975
Capital Maputo
Population 26.5 million / 88 people per sq mile (34 people per sq km)
Total area 309,494 sq. miles (801,590 sq. km)
Languages Makua, Xitsonga, Sena, Lomwe, Portuguese*
Religions Traditional beliefs 56%, Christian 30%, Muslim 14%
Ethnic mix Makua Lomwe 47%, Tsonga 23%, Malawi 12%, Shona 11%, Yao 4%, Other 3%
Government Presidential system
Currency New metical = 100 centavos
Literacy rate 51%
Calorie consumption 2283 kilocalories

MYANMAR (BURMA)
Southeast Asia

Official name Republic of the Union of Myanmar
Formation 1948 / 1948
Capital Nay Pyi Taw
Population 53.7 million / 212 people per sq mile (82 people per sq km)
Total area 261,969 sq. miles (678,500 sq. km)
Languages Myanmar (Burmese)*, Shan, Karen, Rakhine, Chin, Yangbye, Kachin, Mon
Religions Buddhist 89%, Christian 4%, Muslim 4%, Other 2%, Animist 1%
Ethnic mix Burman (Bamah) 68%, Other 12%, Shan 9%, Karen 7%, Rakhine 4%
Government Presidential system
Currency Kyat = 100 pyas
Literacy rate 93%
Calorie consumption 2571 kilocalories

NAMIBIA
Southern Africa

Official name Republic of Namibia
Formation 1990 / 1994
Capital Windhoek
Population 2.3 million / 7 people per sq mile (3 people per sq km)
Total area 318,694 sq. miles (825,418 sq. km)
Languages Ovambo, Kavango, English*, Bergdama, German, Afrikaans
Religions Christian 90%, Traditional beliefs 10%
Ethnic mix Ovambo 50%, Other tribes 22%, Kavango 9%, Damara 7%, Herero 7%, Other 5%
Government Presidential system
Currency Namibian dollar = 100 cents; and South African rand = 100 cents
Literacy rate 76%
Calorie consumption 2086 kilocalories

NAURU
Australasia & Oceania

Official name Republic of Nauru
Formation 1968 / 1968
Capital None
Population 9488 / 1171 people per sq mile (452 people per sq km)
Total area 8.1 sq. miles (21 sq. km)
Languages Nauruan*, Kiribati, Chinese, Tuvaluan, English
Religions Nauruan Congregational Church 60%, Roman Catholic 35%, Other 5%
Ethnic mix Nauruan 93%, Chinese 5%, European 1%, Other Pacific islanders 1%
Government Nonparty system
Currency Australian dollar = 100 cents
Literacy rate 95%
Calorie consumption Not available

NEPAL
South Asia

Official name Federal Democratic Republic of Nepal
Formation 1769 / 1769
Capital Kathmandu
Population 28.1 million / 532 people per sq mile (205 people per sq km)
Total area 54,363 sq. miles (140,800 sq. km)
Languages Nepali*, Maithili, Bhojpuri
Religions Hindu 81%, Buddhist 11%, Muslim 4%, Other (including Christian) 4%
Ethnic mix Other 52%, Chhetri 16%, Hill Brahman 13%, Tharu 7%, Magar 7%, Tamang 5%
Government Transitional regime
Currency Nepalese rupee = 100 paisa
Literacy rate 57%
Calorie consumption 2673 kilocalories

NETHERLANDS
Northwest Europe

Official name Kingdom of the Netherlands
Formation 1648 / 1839
Capital Amsterdam; The Hague (administrative)
Population 16.8 million / 1283 people per sq mile (495 people per sq km)
Total area 16,033 sq. miles (41,526 sq. km)
Languages Dutch*, Frisian
Religions Roman Catholic 36%, Other 34%, Protestant 27%, Muslim 3%
Ethnic mix Dutch 82%, Other 12%, Surinamese 2%, Turkish 2%, Moroccan 2%
Government Parliamentary system
Currency Euro = 100 cents
Literacy rate 99%
Calorie consumption 3147 kilocalories

NEW ZEALAND
Australasia & Oceania

Official name New Zealand
Formation 1947 / 1947
Capital Wellington
Population 4.6 million / 44 people per sq mile (17 people per sq km)
Total area 103,737 sq. miles (268,680 sq. km)
Languages English*, Maori*
Religions Anglican 24%, Other 22%, Presbyterian 18%, Nonreligious 16%, Roman Catholic 15%, Methodist 5%
Ethnic mix European 75%, Maori 15%, Other 7%, Samoan 3%
Government Parliamentary system
Currency New Zealand dollar = 100 cents
Literacy rate 99%
Calorie consumption 3170 kilocalories

NICARAGUA
Central America

Official name Republic of Nicaragua
Formation 1838 / 1838
Capital Managua
Population 6.2 million / 135 people per sq mile (52 people per sq km)
Total area 49,998 sq. miles (129,494 sq. km)
Languages Spanish*, English Creole, Miskito
Religions Roman Catholic 80%, Protestant Evangelical 17%, Other 3%
Ethnic mix Mestizo 69%, White 17%, Black 9%, Amerindian 5%
Government Presidential system
Currency Córdoba oro = 100 centavos
Literacy rate 78%
Calorie consumption 2564 kilocalories

NIGER
West Africa

Official name Republic of Niger
Formation 1960 / 1960
Capital Niamey
Population 18.5 million / 38 people per sq mile (15 people per sq km)
Total area 489,188 sq. miles (1,267,000 sq. km)
Languages Hausa, Djerma, Fulani, Tuareg, Teda, French*
Religions Muslim 99%, Other (including Christian) 1%
Ethnic mix Hausa 53%, Djerma and Songhai 21%, Tuareg 11%, Fulani 7%, Kanuri 6%, Other 2%
Government Presidential system
Currency CFA franc = 100 centimes
Literacy rate 16%
Calorie consumption 2546 kilocalories

NIGERIA
West Africa

Official name Federal Republic of Nigeria
Formation 1960 / 1961
Capital Abuja
Population 179 million / 508 people per sq mile (196 people per sq km)
Total area 356,667 sq. miles (923,768 sq. km)
Languages Hausa, English*, Yoruba, Ibo
Religions Muslim 50%, Christian 40%, Traditional beliefs 10%
Ethnic mix Other 29%, Hausa 21%, Yoruba 21%, Ibo 18%, Fulani 11%
Government Presidential system
Currency Naira = 100 kobo
Literacy rate 51%
Calorie consumption 2700 kilocalories

NORTH KOREA
East Asia

Official name Democratic People's Republic of Korea
Formation 1948 / 1953
Capital Pyongyang
Population 25 million / 538 people per sq mile (208 people per sq km)
Total area 46,540 sq. miles (120,540 sq. km)
Languages Korean*
Religions Atheist 100%
Ethnic mix Korean 100%
Government One-party state
Currency North Korean won = 100 chon
Literacy rate 99%
Calorie consumption 2094 kilocalories

NORWAY
Northern Europe

Official name Kingdom of Norway
Formation 1905 / 1905
Capital Oslo
Population 5.1 million / 43 people per sq mile (17 people per sq km)
Total area 125,181 sq. miles (324,220 sq. km)
Languages Norwegian* (Bokmål "book language" and Nynorsk "new Norsk"), Sámi
Religions Evangelical Lutheran 88%, Other and nonreligious 8%, Muslim 2%, Pentecostal 1%, Roman Catholic 1%
Ethnic mix Norwegian 93%, Other 6%, Sámi 1%
Government Parliamentary system
Currency Norwegian krone = 100 øre
Literacy rate 99%
Calorie consumption 3484 kilocalories

OMAN
Southwest Asia

Official name Sultanate of Oman
Formation 1951 / 1951
Capital Muscat
Population 3.9 million / 48 people per sq mile (18 people per sq km)
Total area 82,031 sq. miles (212,460 sq. km)
Languages Arabic*, Baluchi, Farsi, Hindi, Punjabi
Religions Ibadi Muslim 75%, Other Muslim and Hindu 25%
Ethnic mix Arab 88%, Baluchi 4%, Persian 3%, Indian and Pakistani 3%, African 2%
Government Monarchy
Currency Omani rial = 1000 baisa
Literacy rate 87%
Calorie consumption 3143 kilocalories

PAKISTAN
South Asia

Official name Islamic Republic of Pakistan
Formation 1947 / 1971
Capital Islamabad
Population 185 million / 622 people per sq mile (240 people per sq km)
Total area 310,401 sq. miles (803,940 sq. km)
Languages Punjabi, Sindhi, Pashtu, Urdu*, Baluchi, Brahui
Religions Sunni Muslim 77%, Shi'a Muslim 20%, Hindu 2%, Christian 1%
Ethnic mix Punjabi 56%, Pathan (Pashtun) 15%, Sindhi 14%, Mohajir 7%, Baluchi 4%, Other 4%
Government Parliamentary system
Currency Pakistani rupee = 100 paisa
Literacy rate 55%
Calorie consumption 2440 kilocalories

PALAU
Australasia & Oceania

Official name Republic of Palau
Formation 1994 / 1994
Capital Melekeok
Population 21,186 / 108 people per sq mile (42 people per sq km)
Total area 177 sq. miles (458 sq. km)
Languages Palauan*, English*, Japanese, Angaur, Tobi, Sonsorolese
Religions Christian 66%, Modekngei 34%
Ethnic mix Palauan 74%, Filipino 16%, Other 6%, Chinese and other Asian 4%
Government Nonparty system
Currency US dollar = 100 cents
Literacy rate 99%
Calorie consumption Not available

PANAMA
Central America

Official name Republic of Panama
Formation 1903 / 1903
Capital Panama City
Population 3.9 million / 133 people per sq mile (51 people per sq km)
Total area 30,193 sq. miles (78,200 sq. km)
Languages English Creole, Spanish*, Amerindian languages, Chibchan languages
Religions Roman Catholic 84%, Protestant 15%, Other 1%
Ethnic mix Mestizo 70%, Black 14%, White 10%, Amerindian 6%
Government Presidential system
Currency Balboa = 100 centésimos; and US dollar = 100 cents
Literacy rate 94%
Calorie consumption 2733 kilocalories

PAPUA NEW GUINEA
Australasia & Oceania

Official name Independent State of Papua New Guinea
Formation 1975 / 1975
Capital Port Moresby
Population 7.5 million / 43 people per sq mile (17 people per sq km)
Total area 178,703 sq. miles (462,840 sq. km)
Languages Pidgin English, Papuan, English*, Motu, 800 (est.) native languages
Religions Protestant 60%, Roman Catholic 37%, Other 3%
Ethnic mix Melanesian and mixed race 100%
Government Parliamentary system
Currency Kina = 100 toea
Literacy rate 63%
Calorie consumption 2193 kilocalories

PARAGUAY
South America

Official name Republic of Paraguay
Formation 1811 / 1938
Capital Asunción
Population 6.9 million / 45 people per sq mile (17 people per sq km)
Total area 157,046 sq. miles (406,750 sq. km)
Languages Guaraní*, Spanish*, German
Religions Roman Catholic 90%, Protestant (including Mennonite) 10%
Ethnic mix Mestizo 91%, Other 7%, Amerindian 2%
Government Presidential system
Currency Guaraní = 100 céntimos
Literacy rate 94%
Calorie consumption 2589 kilocalories

PERU
South America

Official name Republic of Peru
Formation 1824 / 1941
Capital Lima
Population 30.8 million / 62 people per sq mile (24 people per sq km)
Total area 496,223 sq. miles (1,285,200 sq. km)
Languages Spanish*, Quechua*, Aymara
Religions Roman Catholic 81%, Other 19%
Ethnic mix Amerindian 45%, Mestizo 37%, White 15%, Other 3%
Government Presidential system
Currency New sol = 100 céntimos
Literacy rate 94%
Calorie consumption 2700 kilocalories

PHILIPPINES
Southeast Asia

Official name Republic of the Philippines
Formation 1946 / 1946
Capital Manila
Population 100 million / 870 people per sq mile (336 people per sq km)
Total area 115,830 sq. miles (300,000 sq. km)
Languages Filipino*, English*, Tagalog, Cebuano, Ilocano, Hiligaynon, many other local languages
Religions Roman Catholic 81%, Protestant 9%, Muslim 5%, Other (including Buddhist) 5%
Ethnic mix Other 34%, Tagalog 28%, Cebuano 13%, Ilocano 9%, Hiligaynon 8%, Bisaya 8%
Government Presidential system
Currency Philippine peso = 100 centavos
Literacy rate 95%
Calorie consumption 2570 kilocalories

POLAND
Northern Europe

Official name Republic of Poland
Formation 1918 / 1945
Capital Warsaw
Population 38.2 million / 325 people per sq mile (125 people per sq km)
Total area 120,728 sq. miles (312,685 sq. km)
Languages Polish*
Religions Roman Catholic 93%, Other and nonreligious 5%, Orthodox Christian 2%
Ethnic mix Polish 98%, Other 2%
Government Parliamentary system
Currency Zloty = 100 groszy
Literacy rate 99%
Calorie consumption 3485 kilocalories

PORTUGAL
Southwest Europe

Official name Portuguese Republic
Formation 1139 / 1640
Capital Lisbon
Population 10.6 million / 299 people per sq mile (115 people per sq km)
Total area 35,672 sq. miles (92,391 sq. km)
Languages Portuguese*
Religions Roman Catholic 92%, Protestant 4%, Nonreligious 3%, Other 1%
Ethnic mix Portuguese 98%, African and other 2%
Government Parliamentary system
Currency Euro = 100 cents
Literacy rate 94%
Calorie consumption 3456 kilocalories

QATAR
Southwest Asia

Official name State of Qatar
Formation 1971 / 1971
Capital Doha
Population 2.3 million / 542 people per sq mile (209 people per sq km)
Total area 4416 sq. miles (11,437 sq. km)
Languages Arabic*
Religions Muslim (mainly Sunni) 95%, Other 5%
Ethnic mix Qatari 20%, Indian 20%, Other Arab 20%, Nepalese 13%, Filipino 10%, Other 10%, Pakistani 7%
Government Monarchy
Currency Qatar riyal = 100 dirhams
Literacy rate 97%
Calorie consumption Not available

ROMANIA
Southeast Europe

Official name Romania
Formation 1878 / 1947
Capital Bucharest
Population 21.6 million / 243 people per sq mile (94 people per sq km)
Total area 91,699 sq. miles (237,500 sq. km)
Languages Romanian*, Hungarian (Magyar), Romani, German
Religions Romanian Orthodox 87%, Protestant 5%, Roman Catholic 5%, Greek Orthodox 1%, Greek Catholic (Uniate) 1%, Other 1%
Ethnic mix Romanian 89%, Magyar 7%, Roma 3%, Other 1%
Government Presidential system
Currency New Romanian leu = 100 bani
Literacy rate 99%
Calorie consumption 3363 kilocalories

RUSSIAN FEDERATION
Europe / Asia

Official name Russian Federation
Formation 1480 / 1991
Capital Moscow
Population 143 million / 22 people per sq mile (8 people per sq km)
Total area 6,592,735 sq. miles (17,075,200 sq. km)
Languages Russian*, Tatar, Ukrainian, Chavash, various other national languages
Religions Orthodox Christian 75%, Muslim 14%, Other 11%
Ethnic mix Russian 80%, Other 12%, Tatar 4%, Ukrainian 2%, Bashkir 1%, Chavash 1%
Government Mixed Presidential–Parliamentary system
Currency Russian rouble = 100 kopeks
Literacy rate 99%
Calorie consumption 3358 kilocalories

RWANDA
Central Africa

Official name Republic of Rwanda
Formation 1962 / 1962
Capital Kigali
Population 12.1 million / 1256 people per sq mile (485 people per sq km)
Total area 10,169 sq. miles (26,338 sq. km)
Languages Kinyarwanda*, French*, Kiswahili, English*
Religions Christian 94%, Muslim 5%, Traditional beliefs 1%
Ethnic mix Hutu 85%, Tutsi 14%, Other (including Twa) 1%
Government Presidential system
Currency Rwanda franc = 100 centimes
Literacy rate 66%
Calorie consumption 2148 kilocalories

ST KITTS & NEVIS
West Indies

Official name Federation of Saint Christopher and Nevis
Formation 1983 / 1983
Capital Basseterre
Population 51,538 / 371 people per sq mile (143 people per sq km)
Total area 101 sq. miles (261 sq. km)
Languages English*, English Creole
Religions Anglican 33%, Methodist 29%, Other 22%, Moravian 9%, Roman Catholic 7%
Ethnic mix Black 95%, Mixed race 3%, White 1%, Other and Amerindian 1%
Government Parliamentary system
Currency East Caribbean dollar = 100 cents
Literacy rate 98%
Calorie consumption 2507 kilocalories

ST LUCIA
West Indies

Official name Saint Lucia
Formation 1979 / 1979
Capital Castries
Population 200,000 / 847 people per sq mile (328 people per sq km)
Total area 239 sq. miles (620 sq. km)
Languages English*, French Creole
Religions Roman Catholic 90%, Other 10%
Ethnic mix Black 83%, Mulatto (mixed race) 13%, Asian 3%, Other 1%
Government Parliamentary system
Currency East Caribbean dollar = 100 cents
Literacy rate 95%
Calorie consumption 2629 kilocalories

ST VINCENT & THE GRENADINES
West Indies

Official name Saint Vincent and the Grenadines
Formation 1979 / 1979
Capital Kingstown
Population 102,918 / 786 people per sq mile (303 people per sq km)
Total area 150 sq. miles (389 sq. km)
Languages English*, English Creole
Religions Anglican 47%, Methodist 28%, Roman Catholic 13%, Other 12%
Ethnic mix Black 66%, Mulatto (mixed race) 19%, Other 12%, Carib 2%, Asian 1%
Government Parliamentary system
Currency East Caribbean dollar = 100 cents
Literacy rate 88%
Calorie consumption 2960 kilocalories

SAMOA
Australasia & Oceania

Official name Independent State of Samoa
Formation 1962 / 1962
Capital Apia
Population 200,000 / 183 people per sq mile (71 people per sq km)
Total area 1104 sq. miles (2860 sq. km)
Languages Samoan*, English*
Religions Christian 99%, Other 1%
Ethnic mix Polynesian 91%, Euronesian 7%, Other 2%
Government Parliamentary system
Currency Tala = 100 sene
Literacy rate 99%
Calorie consumption 2872 kilocalories

SAN MARINO
Southern Europe

Official name Republic of San Marino
Formation 1631 / 1631
Capital San Marino
Population 32,742 / 1364 people per sq mile (537 people per sq km)
Total area 23.6 sq. miles (61 sq. km)
Languages Italian*
Religions Roman Catholic 93%, Other and nonreligious 7%
Ethnic mix Sammarinese 88%, Italian 10%, Other 2%
Government Parliamentary system
Currency Euro = 100 cents
Literacy rate 99%
Calorie consumption Not available

SAO TOME & PRINCIPE
West Africa

Official name Democratic Republic of Sao Tome and Principe
Formation 1975 / 1975
Capital São Tomé
Population 200,000 / 539 people per sq mile (208 people per sq km)
Total area 386 sq. miles (1001 sq. km)
Languages Portuguese Creole, Portuguese*
Religions Roman Catholic 84%, Other 16%
Ethnic mix Black 90%, Portuguese and Creole 10%
Government Presidential system
Currency Dobra = 100 céntimos
Literacy rate 70%
Calorie consumption 2676 kilocalories

SAUDI ARABIA
Southwest Asia

Official name Kingdom of Saudi Arabia
Formation 1932 / 1932
Capital Riyadh
Population 29.4 million / 36 people per sq mile (14 people per sq km)
Total area 756,981 sq. miles (1,960,582 sq. km)
Languages Arabic*
Religions Sunni Muslim 85%, Shi'a Muslim 15%
Ethnic mix Arab 72%, Foreign residents (mostly south and southeast Asian) 20%, Afro-Asian 8%
Government Monarchy
Currency Saudi riyal = 100 halalat
Literacy rate 94%
Calorie consumption 3122 kilocalories

SENEGAL
West Africa

Official name Republic of Senegal
Formation 1960 / 1960
Capital Dakar
Population 14.5 million / 195 people per sq mile (75 people per sq km)
Total area 75,749 sq. miles (196,190 sq. km)
Languages Wolof, Pulaar, Serer, Diola, Mandinka, Malinké, Soninké, French*
Religions Sunni Muslim 95%, Christian (mainly Roman Catholic) 4%, Traditional beliefs 1%
Ethnic mix Wolof 43%, Serer 15%, Peul 14%, Other 14%, Toucouleur 9%, Diola 5%
Government Presidential system
Currency CFA franc = 100 centimes
Literacy rate 52%
Calorie consumption 2426 kilocalories

SERBIA
Southeast Europe

Official name Republic of Serbia
Formation 2006 / 2008
Capital Belgrade
Population 9.5 million / 318 people per sq mile (123 people per sq km)
Total area 29,905 sq. miles (77,453 sq. km)
Languages Serbian*, Hungarian (Magyar)
Religions Orthodox Christian 85%, Roman Catholic 6%, Other 6%, Muslim 3%
Ethnic mix Serb 83%, Other 10%, Magyar 4%, Bosniak 2%, Roma 1%
Government Parliamentary system
Currency Serbian dinar = 100 para
Literacy rate 98%
Calorie consumption 2724 kilocalories

SEYCHELLES
Indian Ocean

Official name Republic of Seychelles
Formation 1976 / 1976
Capital Victoria
Population 91,650 / 881 people per sq mile (339 people per sq km)
Total area 176 sq. miles (455 sq. km)
Languages French Creole*, English*, French*
Religions Roman Catholic 82%, Anglican 6%, Other (including Muslim) 6%, Other Christian 3%, Hindu 2%, Seventh-day Adventist 1%
Ethnic mix Creole 89%, Indian 5%, Other 4%, Chinese 2%
Government Presidential system
Currency Seychelles rupee = 100 cents
Literacy rate 92%
Calorie consumption 2426 kilocalories

SIERRA LEONE
West Africa

Official name Republic of Sierra Leone
Formation 1961 / 1961
Capital Freetown
Population 6.2 million / 224 people per sq mile (87 people per sq km)
Total area 27,698 sq. miles (71,740 sq. km)
Languages Mende, Temne, Krio, English*
Religions Muslim 60%, Christian 30%, Traditional beliefs 10%
Ethnic mix Mende 35%, Temne 32%, Other 21%, Limba 8%, Kuranko 4%
Government Presidential system
Currency Leone = 100 cents
Literacy rate 44%
Calorie consumption 2333 kilocalories

SINGAPORE
Southeast Asia

Official name Republic of Singapore
Formation 1965 / 1965
Capital Singapore
Population 5.5 million / 23,305 people per sq mile (9016 people per sq km)
Total area 250 sq. miles (648 sq. km)
Languages Mandarin*, Malay*, Tamil*, English*
Religions Buddhist 55%, Taoist 22%, Muslim 16%, Hindu, Christian, and Sikh 7%
Ethnic mix Chinese 74%, Malay 14%, Indian 9%, Other 3%
Government Parliamentary system
Currency Singapore dollar = 100 cents
Literacy rate 96%
Calorie consumption Not available

SLOVAKIA
Central Europe

Official name Slovak Republic
Formation 1993 / 1993
Capital Bratislava
Population 5.5 million / 290 people per sq mile (112 people per sq km)
Total area 18,859 sq. miles (48,845 sq. km)
Languages Slovak*, Hungarian (Magyar), Czech
Religions Roman Catholic 69%, Nonreligious 13%, Other 13%, Greek Catholic (Uniate) 4%, Orthodox Christian 1%
Ethnic mix Slovak 86%, Magyar 10%, Roma 2%, Czech 1%, Other 1%
Government Parliamentary system
Currency Euro = 100 cents
Literacy rate 99%
Calorie consumption 2902 kilocalories

SLOVENIA
Central Europe

Official name Republic of Slovenia
Formation 1991 / 1991
Capital Ljubljana
Population 2.1 million / 269 people per sq mile (104 people per sq km)
Total area 7820 sq. miles (20,253 sq. km)
Languages Slovenian*
Religions Roman Catholic 58%, Other 28%, Atheist 10%, Orthodox Christian 2%, Muslim 2%
Ethnic mix Slovene 83%, Other 12%, Serb 2%, Croat 2%, Bosniak 1%
Government Parliamentary system
Currency Euro = 100 cents
Literacy rate 99%
Calorie consumption 3173 kilocalories

SOLOMON ISLANDS
Australasia & Oceania

Official name Solomon Islands
Formation 1978 / 1978
Capital Honiara
Population 600,000 / 56 people per sq mile (21 people per sq km)
Total area 10,985 sq. miles (28,450 sq. km)
Languages English*, Pidgin English, Melanesian Pidgin, 120 (est.) native languages
Religions Church of Melanesia (Anglican) 34%, Roman Catholic 19%, South Seas Evangelical Church 17%, Methodist 11%, Seventh-day Adventist 10%, Other 9%
Ethnic mix Melanesian 93%, Polynesian 4%, Micronesian 2%, Other 1%
Government Parliamentary system
Currency Solomon Islands dollar = 100 cents
Literacy rate 77%
Calorie consumption 2473 kilocalories

SOMALIA
East Africa

Official name Federal Republic of Somalia
Formation 1960 / 1960
Capital Mogadishu
Population 10.8 million / 45 people per sq mile (17 people per sq km)
Total area 246,199 sq. miles (637,657 sq. km)
Languages Somali*, Arabic*, English, Italian
Religions Sunni Muslim 99%, Christian 1%
Ethnic mix Somali 85%, Other 15%
Government Non-party system
Currency Somali shilin = 100 senti
Literacy rate 24%
Calorie consumption 1696 kilocalories

SOUTH AFRICA
Southern Africa

Official name Republic of South Africa
Formation 1934 / 1994
Capital Pretoria; Cape Town; Bloemfontein
Population 53.1 million / 113 people per sq mile (43 people per sq km)
Total area 471,008 sq. miles (1,219,912 sq. km)
Languages English, isiZulu, isiXhosa, Afrikaans, Sepedi, Setswana, Sesotho, Xitsonga, siSwati, Tshivenda, isiNdebele
Religions Christian 68%, Traditional beliefs and animist 29%, Muslim 2%, Hindu 1%
Ethnic mix Black 80%, Mixed race 9%, White 9%, Asian 2%
Government Presidential system
Currency Rand = 100 cents
Literacy rate 94%
Calorie consumption 3007 kilocalories

SOUTH KOREA
East Asia

Official name Republic of Korea
Formation 1948 / 1953
Capital Seoul; Sejong City (administrative)
Population 49.5 million / 1299 people per sq mile (501 people per sq km)
Total area 38,023 sq. miles (98,480 sq. km)
Languages Korean*
Religions Mahayana Buddhist 47%, Protestant 38%, Roman Catholic 11%, Confucianist 3%, Other 1%
Ethnic mix Korean 100%
Government Presidential system
Currency South Korean won = 100 chon
Literacy rate 99%
Calorie consumption 3329 kilocalories

SOUTH SUDAN
East Africa

Official name Republic of South Sudan
Formation 2011 / 2011
Capital Juba
Population 11.7 million / 47 people per sq mile (18 people per sq km)
Total area 248,777 sq. miles (644,329 sq. km)
Languages Arabic, Dinka, Nuer, Zande, Bari, Shilluk, Lotuko, English*
Religions Over half of the population follow Christian or traditional beliefs.
Ethnic mix Dinka 40%, Nuer 15%, Bari 10%, Shilluk/Anwak 10%, Azande 10%, Arab 10%, Other 5%
Government Transitional regime
Currency South Sudan pound = 100 piastres
Literacy rate 37%
Calorie consumption Not available

SPAIN
Southwest Europe

Official name Kingdom of Spain
Formation 1492 / 1713
Capital Madrid
Population 47.1 million / 244 people per sq mile (94 people per sq km)
Total area 194,896 sq. miles (504,782 sq. km)
Languages Spanish*, Catalan*, Galician*, Basque*
Religions Roman Catholic 96%, Other 4%
Ethnic mix Castilian Spanish 72%, Catalan 17%, Galician 6%, Basque 2%, Other 2%, Roma 1%
Government Parliamentary system
Currency Euro = 100 cents
Literacy rate 98%
Calorie consumption 3183 kilocalories

SRI LANKA
South Asia

Official name Democratic Socialist Republic of Sri Lanka
Formation 1948 / 1948
Capital Colombo; Sri Jayewardenapura Kotte
Population 21.4 million / 856 people per sq mile (331 people per sq km)
Total area 25,332 sq. miles (65,610 sq. km)
Languages Sinhala*, Tamil*, Sinhala-Tamil, English
Religions Buddhist 69%, Hindu 15%, Muslim 8%, Christian 8%
Ethnic mix Sinhalese 74%, Tamil 18%, Moor 7%, Other 1%
Government Mixed presidential–parliamentary system
Currency Sri Lanka rupee = 100 cents
Literacy rate 91%
Calorie consumption 2539 kilocalories

SUDAN
East Africa

Official name Republic of the Sudan
Formation 1956 / 2011
Capital Khartoum
Population 38.8 million / 54 people per sq mile (21 people per sq km)
Total area 718,722 sq. miles (1,861,481 sq. km)
Languages Arabic, Nubian, Beja, Fur
Religions Nearly the whole population is Muslim (mainly Sunni)
Ethnic mix Arab 60%, Other 18%, Nubian 10%, Beja 8%, Fur 3%, Zaghawa 1%
Government Presidential system
Currency New Sudanese pound = 100 piastres
Literacy rate 73%
Calorie consumption 2346 kilocalories

SURINAME
South America

Official name Republic of Suriname
Formation 1975 / 1975
Capital Paramaribo
Population 500,000 / 8 people per sq mile (3 people per sq km)
Total area 63,039 sq. miles (163,270 sq. km)
Languages Sranan (creole), Dutch*, Javanese, Sarnami Hindi, Saramaccan, Chinese, Carib
Religions Hindu 27%, Protestant 25%, Roman Catholic 23%, Muslim 20%, Traditional beliefs 5%
Ethnic mix East Indian 27%, Creole 18%, Black 15%, Javanese 15%, Mixed race 13%, Other 6%, Amerindian 4%, Chinese 2%
Government Mixed presidential–parliamentary system
Currency Surinamese dollar = 100 cents
Literacy rate 95%
Calorie consumption 2727 kilocalories

SWAZILAND
Southern Africa

Official name Kingdom of Swaziland
Formation 1968 / 1968
Capital Mbabane
Population 1.3 million / 196 people per sq mile (76 people per sq km)
Total area 6704 sq. miles (17,363 sq. km)
Languages English*, siSwati*, isiZulu, Xitsonga
Religions Traditional beliefs 40%, Other 30%, Roman Catholic 20%, Muslim 10%
Ethnic mix Swazi 97%, Other 3%
Government Monarchy
Currency Lilangeni = 100 cents
Literacy rate 83%
Calorie consumption 2275 kilocalories

SWEDEN
Northern Europe

Official name Kingdom of Sweden
Formation 1523 / 1921
Capital Stockholm
Population 9.6 million / 60 people per sq mile (23 people per sq km)
Total area 173,731 sq. miles (449,964 sq. km)
Languages Swedish*, Finnish, Sámi
Religions Evangelical Lutheran 75%, Other 13%, Muslim 5%, Other Protestant 5%, Roman Catholic 2%
Ethnic mix Swedish 86%, Foreign-born or first-generation immigrant 12%, Finnish and Sámi 2%
Government Parliamentary system
Currency Swedish krona = 100 öre
Literacy rate 99%
Calorie consumption 3160 kilocalories

SWITZERLAND
Central Europe

Official name Swiss Confederation
Formation 1291 / 1857
Capital Bern
Population 8.2 million / 534 people per sq mile (206 people per sq km)
Total area 15,942 sq. miles (41,290 sq. km)
Languages German*, Swiss-German, French*, Italian*, Romansch
Religions Roman Catholic 42%, Protestant 35%, Other and nonreligious 19%, Muslim 4%
Ethnic mix German 64%, French 20%, Other 9.5%, Italian 6%, Romansch 0.5%
Government Parliamentary system
Currency Swiss franc = 100 rappen/centimes
Literacy rate 99%
Calorie consumption 3487 kilocalories

SYRIA
Southwest Asia

Official name Syrian Arab Republic
Formation 1941 / 1967
Capital Damascus
Population 22 million / 310 people per sq mile (120 people per sq km)
Total area 71,498 sq. miles (184,180 sq. km)
Languages Arabic*, French, Kurdish, Armenian, Circassian, Turkic languages, Assyrian, Aramaic
Religions Sunni Muslim 74%, Alawi 12%, Christian 10%, Druze 3%, Other 1%
Ethnic mix Arab 90%, Kurdish 9%, Armenian, Turkmen, and Circassian 1%
Government Presidential system
Currency Syrian pound = 100 piastres
Literacy rate 85%
Calorie consumption 3106 kilocalories

TAIWAN
East Asia

Official name Republic of China (ROC)
Formation 1949 / 1949
Capital Taibei (Taipei)
Population 23.4 million / 1879 people per sq mile (725 people per sq km)
Total area 13,892 sq. miles (35,980 sq. km)
Languages Amoy Chinese, Mandarin Chinese*, Hakka Chinese
Religions Buddhist, Confucianist, and Taoist 93%, Christian 5%, Other 2%
Ethnic mix Han Chinese (pre-20th-century migration) 84%, Han Chinese (20th-century migration) 14%, Aboriginal 2%
Government Presidential system
Currency Taiwan dollar = 100 cents
Literacy rate 98%
Calorie consumption 2997 kilocalories

TAJIKISTAN
Central Asia

Official name Republic of Tajikistan
Formation 1991 / 1991
Capital Dushanbe
Population 8.4 million / 152 people per sq mile (59 people per sq km)
Total area 55,251 sq. miles (143,100 sq. km)
Languages Tajik*, Uzbek, Russian
Religions Sunni Muslim 95%, Shi'a Muslim 3%, Other 2%
Ethnic mix Tajik 80%, Uzbek 15%, Other 3%, Russian 1%, Kyrgyz 1%
Government Presidential system
Currency Somoni = 100 diram
Literacy rate 99%
Calorie consumption 2101 kilocalories

TANZANIA
East Africa

Official name United Republic of Tanzania
Formation 1964 / 1964
Capital Dodoma
Population 50.8 million / 148 people per sq mile (57 people per sq km)
Total area 364,898 sq. miles (945,087 sq. km)
Languages Kiswahili*, Sukuma, Chagga, Nyamwezi, Hehe, Makonde, Yao, Sandawe, English*
Religions Christian 63%, Muslim 35%, Other 2%
Ethnic mix Native African (over 120 tribes) 99%, European, Asian, and Arab 1%
Government Presidential system
Currency Tanzanian shilling = 100 cents
Literacy rate 68%
Calorie consumption 2208 kilocalories

THAILAND
Southeast Asia

Official name Kingdom of Thailand
Formation 1238 / 1907
Capital Bangkok
Population 67.2 million / 341 people per sq mile (132 people per sq km)
Total area 198,455 sq. miles (514,000 sq. km)
Languages Thai*, Chinese, Malay, Khmer, Mon, Karen, Miao
Religions Buddhist 95%, Muslim 4%, Other (including Christian) 1%
Ethnic mix Thai 83%, Chinese 12%, Malay 3%, Khmer and Other 2%
Government Transitional regime
Currency Baht = 100 satang
Literacy rate 96%
Calorie consumption 2784 kilocalories

TOGO
West Africa

Official name Togolese Republic
Formation 1960 / 1960
Capital Lomé
Population 7 million / 333 people per sq mile (129 people per sq km)
Total area 21,924 sq. miles (56,785 sq. km)
Languages Ewe, Kabye, Gurma, French*
Religions Christian 47%, Traditional beliefs 33%, Muslim 14%, Other 6%
Ethnic mix Ewe 46%, Other African 41%, Kabye 12%, European 1%
Government Presidential system
Currency CFA franc = 100 centimes
Literacy rate 60%
Calorie consumption 2366 kilocalories

TONGA
Australasia & Oceania

Official name Kingdom of Tonga
Formation 1970 / 1970
Capital Nuku'alofa
Population 106,440 / 383 people per sq mile (148 people per sq km)
Total area 289 sq. miles (748 sq. km)
Languages English*, Tongan*
Religions Free Wesleyan 41%, Other 17%, Roman Catholic 16%, Church of Jesus Christ of Latter-day Saints 14%, Free Church of Tonga 12%
Ethnic mix Tongan 98%, Other 2%
Government Monarchy
Currency Pa'anga (Tongan dollar) = 100 seniti
Literacy rate 99%
Calorie consumption Not available

TRINIDAD & TOBAGO
West Indies

Official name Republic of Trinidad and Tobago
Formation 1962 / 1962
Capital Port-of-Spain
Population 1.3 million / 656 people per sq mile (253 people per sq km)
Total area 1980 sq. miles (5128 sq. km)
Languages English Creole, English*, Hindi, French, Spanish
Religions Roman Catholic 26%, Hindu 23%, Other and nonreligious 23%, Anglican 8%, Baptist 7%, Pentecostal 7%, Muslim 6%
Ethnic mix East Indian 40%, Black 38%, Mixed race 20%, White and Chinese 1%, other 1%
Government Parliamentary system
Currency Trinidad and Tobago dollar = 100 cents
Literacy rate 99%
Calorie consumption 2889 kilocalories

TUNISIA
North Africa

Official name Tunisian Republic
Formation 1956 / 1956
Capital Tunis
Population 11.1 million / 185 people per sq mile (71 people per sq km)
Total area 63,169 sq. miles (163,610 sq. km)
Languages Arabic*, French
Religions Muslim (mainly Sunni) 98%, Christian 1%, Jewish 1%
Ethnic mix Arab and Berber 98%, Jewish 1%, European 1%
Government Mixed presidential–parliamentary system
Currency Tunisian dinar = 1000 millimes
Literacy rate 80%
Calorie consumption 3362 kilocalories

TURKEY
Asia / Europe

Official name Republic of Turkey
Formation 1923 / 1939
Capital Ankara
Population 75.8 million / 255 people per sq mile (98 people per sq km)
Total area 301,382 sq. miles (780,580 sq. km)
Languages Turkish*, Kurdish, Arabic, Circassian, Armenian, Greek, Georgian, Ladino
Religions Muslim (mainly Sunni) 99%, Other 1%
Ethnic mix Turkish 70%, Kurdish 20%, Other 8%, Arab 2%
Government Parliamentary system
Currency Turkish lira = 100 kurus
Literacy rate 95%
Calorie consumption 3680 kilocalories

TURKMENISTAN
Central Asia

Official name Turkmenistan
Formation 1991 / 1991
Capital Ashgabat
Population 5.3 million / 28 people per sq mile (11 people per sq km)
Total area 188,455 sq. miles (488,100 sq. km)
Languages Turkmen*, Uzbek, Russian, Kazakh, Tatar
Religions Sunni Muslim 89%, Orthodox Christian 9%, Other 2%
Ethnic mix Turkmen 85%, Other 6%, Uzbek 5%, Russian 4%
Government Presidential system
Currency New manat = 100 tenge
Literacy rate 99%
Calorie consumption 2883 kilocalories

TUVALU
Australasia & Oceania

Official name Tuvalu
Formation 1978 / 1978
Capital Funafuti Atoll
Population 10,782 / 1078 people per sq mile (415 people per sq km)
Total area 10 sq. miles (26 sq. km)
Languages Tuvaluan, Kiribati, English*
Religions Church of Tuvalu 97%, Baha'i 1%, Seventh-day Adventist 1%, Other 1%
Ethnic mix Polynesian 96%, Micronesian 4%
Government Nonparty system
Currency Australian dollar = 100 cents; and Tuvaluan dollar = 100 cents
Literacy rate 95%
Calorie consumption Not available

UGANDA
East Africa

Official name Republic of Uganda
Formation 1962 / 1962
Capital Kampala
Population 38.8 million / 504 people per sq mile (194 people per sq km)
Total area 91,135 sq. miles (236,040 sq. km)
Languages Luganda, Nkole, Chiga, Lango, Acholi, Teso, Lugbara, English*
Religions Christian 85%, Muslim (mainly Sunni) 12%, Other 3%
Ethnic mix Other 50%, Baganda 17%, Banyakole 10%, Basoga 9%, Iteso 7%, Bakiga 7%
Government Presidential system
Currency Uganda shilling = 100 cents
Literacy rate 74%
Calorie consumption 2279 kilocalories

UKRAINE
Eastern Europe

Official name Ukraine
Formation 1991 / 1991
Capital Kiev
Population 44.9 million / 193 people per sq mile (74 people per sq km)
Total area 223,089 sq. miles (603,700 sq. km)
Languages Ukrainian*, Russian, Tatar
Religions Christian (mainly Orthodox) 95%, Other 5%
Ethnic mix Ukrainian 78%, Russian 17%, Other 5%
Government Presidential system
Currency Hryvna = 100 kopiykas
Literacy rate 99%
Calorie consumption 3142 kilocalories

UNITED ARAB EMIRATES
Southwest Asia

Official name United Arab Emirates
Formation 1971 / 1972
Capital Abu Dhabi
Population 9.4 million / 291 people per sq mile (112 people per sq km)
Total area 32,000 sq. miles (82,880 sq. km)
Languages Arabic*, Farsi, Indian and Pakistani languages, English
Religions Muslim (mainly Sunni) 96%, Christian, Hindu, and other 4%
Ethnic mix Asian 60%, Emirian 25%, Other Arab 12%, European 3%
Government Monarchy
Currency UAE dirham = 100 fils
Literacy rate 90%
Calorie consumption 3215 kilocalories

UNITED KINGDOM
Northwest Europe

Official name United Kingdom of Great Britain and Northern Ireland
Formation 1707 / 1922
Capital London
Population 63.5 million / 681 people per sq mile (263 people per sq km)
Total area 94,525 sq. miles (244,820 sq. km)
Languages English*, Welsh*, Scottish Gaelic, Irish
Religions Anglican 45%, Other and nonreligious 36%, Roman Catholic 9%, Presbyterian 4%, Muslim 3%, Methodist 2%, Hindu 1%
Ethnic mix English 80%, Scottish 9%, West Indian, Asian, and other 5%, Northern Irish 3%, Welsh 3%
Government Parliamentary system
Currency Pound sterling = 100 pence
Literacy rate 99%
Calorie consumption 3414 kilocalories

UNITED STATES
North America

Official name United States of America
Formation 1776 / 1959
Capital Washington D.C.
Population 323 million / 91 people per sq mile (35 people per sq km)
Total area 3,794,100 sq. miles (9,826,675 sq. km)
Languages English*, Spanish, Chinese, French, German, Tagalog, Vietnamese, Italian, Korean, Russian, Polish
Religions Protestant 52%, Roman Catholic 25%, Other and nonreligious 20%, Jewish 2%, Muslim 1%
Ethnic mix White 60%, Hispanic 17%, Black American/African 14%, Asian 6%, American Indians & Alaksa Natives 2%, Pacific Islanders 1%
Government Presidential system
Currency US dollar = 100 cents
Literacy rate 99%
Calorie consumption 3639 kilocalories

URUGUAY
South America

Official name Oriental Republic of Uruguay
Formation 1828 / 1828
Capital Montevideo
Population 3.4 million / 50 people per sq mile (19 people per sq km)
Total area 68,039 sq. miles (176,220 sq. km)
Languages Spanish*
Religions Roman Catholic 66%, Other and nonreligious 30%, Jewish 2%, Protestant 2%
Ethnic mix White 90%, Mestizo 6%, Black 4%
Government Presidential system
Currency Uruguayan peso = 100 centésimos
Literacy rate 98%
Calorie consumption 2939 kilocalories

UZBEKISTAN
Central Asia

Official name Republic of Uzbekistan
Formation 1991 / 1991
Capital Tashkent
Population 29.3 million / 170 people per sq mile (65 people per sq km)
Total area 172,741 sq. miles (447,400 sq. km)
Languages Uzbek*, Russian, Tajik, Kazakh
Religions Sunni Muslim 88%, Orthodox Christian 9%, Other 3%
Ethnic mix Uzbek 80%, Russian 6%, Other 6%, Tajik 5%, Kazakh 3%
Government Presidential system
Currency Som = 100 tiyin
Literacy rate 99%
Calorie consumption 2675 kilocalories

VANUATU
Australasia & Oceania

Official name Republic of Vanuatu
Formation 1980 / 1980
Capital Port Vila
Population 300,000 / 64 people per sq mile (25 people per sq km)
Total area 4710 sq. miles (12,200 sq. km)
Languages Bislama (Melanesian pidgin)*, English*, French*, other indigenous languages
Religions Presbyterian 37%, Other 19%, Anglican 15%, Roman Catholic 15%, Traditional beliefs 8%, Seventh-day Adventist 6%
Ethnic mix ni-Vanuatu 94%, European 4%, Other 2%
Government Parliamentary system
Currency Vatu = 100 centimes
Literacy rate 83%
Calorie consumption 2820 kilocalories

VATICAN CITY
Southern Europe

Official name State of the Vatican City
Formation 1929 / 1929
Capital Vatican City
Population 842 / 4953 people per sq mile (1914 people per sq km)
Total area 0.17 sq. miles (0.44 sq. km)
Languages Italian*, Latin*
Religions Roman Catholic 100%
Ethnic mix The current pope is Argentinian, though most popes for the last 500 years have been Italian. Cardinals are from many nationalities, but Italians form the largest group. Most of the resident lay persons are Italian.
Government Papal state
Currency Euro = 100 cents
Literacy rate 99%
Calorie consumption Not available

VENEZUELA
South America

Official name Bolivarian Republic of Venezuela
Formation 1830 / 1830
Capital Caracas
Population 30.9 million / 91 people per sq mile (35 people per sq km)
Total area 352,143 sq. miles (912,050 sq. km)
Languages Spanish*, Amerindian languages
Religions Roman Catholic 96%, Protestant 2%, Other 2%
Ethnic mix Mestizo 69%, White 20%, Black 9%, Amerindian 2%
Government Presidential system
Currency Bolívar fuerte = 100 céntimos
Literacy rate 96%
Calorie consumption 2880 kilocalories

VIETNAM
Southeast Asia

Official name Socialist Republic of Vietnam
Formation 1976 / 1976
Capital Hanoi
Population 92.5 million / 736 people per sq mile (284 people per sq km)
Total area 127,243 sq. miles (329,560 sq. km)
Languages Vietnamese*, Chinese, Thai, Khmer, Muong, Nung, Miao, Yao, Jarai
Religions Other 74%, Buddhist 14%, Roman Catholic 7%, Cao Dai 3%, Protestant 2%
Ethnic mix Vietnamese 86%, Other 8%, Muong 2%, Tay 2%, Thai 2%
Government One-party state
Currency Đông = 10 hao = 100 xu
Literacy rate 94%
Calorie consumption 2745 kilocalories

YEMEN
Southwest Asia

Official name Republic of Yemen
Formation 1990 / 1990
Capital Sana
Population 25 million / 115 people per sq mile (44 people per sq km)
Total area 203,849 sq. miles (527,970 sq. km)
Languages Arabic*
Religions Sunni Muslim 55%, Shi'a Muslim 42%, Christian, Hindu, and Jewish 3%
Ethnic mix Arab 99%, Afro-Arab, Indian, Somali, and European 1%
Government Transitional regime
Currency Yemeni rial = 100 fils
Literacy rate 66%
Calorie consumption 2223 kilocalories

ZAMBIA
Southern Africa

Official name Republic of Zambia
Formation 1964 / 1964
Capital Lusaka
Population 15 million / 52 people per sq mile (20 people per sq km)
Total area 290,584 sq. miles (752,614 sq. km)
Languages Bemba, Tonga, Nyanja, Lozi, Lala-Bisa, Nsenga, English*
Religions Christian 63%, Traditional beliefs 36%, Muslim and Hindu 1%
Ethnic mix Bemba 34%, Other African 26%, Tonga 16%, Nyanja 14%, Lozi 9%, European 1%
Government Presidential system
Currency New Zambian kwacha = 100 ngwee
Literacy rate 61%
Calorie consumption 1930 kilocalories

ZIMBABWE
Southern Africa

Official name Republic of Zimbabwe
Formation 1980 / 1980
Capital Harare
Population 14.6 million / 98 people per sq mile (38 people per sq km)
Total area 150,803 sq. miles (390,580 sq. km)
Languages Shona, isiNdebele, English*
Religions Syncretic (Christian/traditional beliefs) 50%, Christian 25%, Traditional beliefs 24%, Other (including Muslim) 1%
Ethnic mix Shona 71%, Ndebele 16%, Other African 11%, White 1%, Asian 1%
Government Presidential system
Currency US $, South African rand, Euro, UK £, Botswana pula, Australian $, Chinese yuan, Indian rupee, and Japanese yen are legal tender
Literacy rate 84%
Calorie consumption 2110 kilocalories

Geographical names

The following glossary lists all geographical terms occurring on the maps and in main-entry names in the Index-Gazetteer. These terms may precede, follow or be run together with the proper element of the name; where they precede it the term is reversed for indexing purposes - thus Poluostrov Yamal is indexed as Yamal, Poluostrov.

Key

Geographical term
Language, Term

A

Å *Danish, Norwegian*, River
Āb *Persian*, River
Adrar *Berber*, Mountains
Agía, Ágios *Greek*, Saint
Air *Indonesian*, River
Ákra *Greek*, Cape, point
Alpen *German*, Alps
Alt- *German*, Old
Altiplanicie *Spanish*, Plateau
Älve, -älven *Swedish*, River
-ån *Swedish*, River
Anse *French*, Bay
'Aqabat *Arabic*, Pass
Archipiélago *Spanish*, Archipelago
Arcipelago *Italian*, Archipelago
Arquipélago *Portuguese*, Archipelago
Arrecife(s) *Spanish*, Reef(s)
Aru *Tamil*, River
Augstiene *Latvian*, Upland
Aukštuma *Lithuanian*, Upland
Aust- *Norwegian*, Eastern
Avtonomnyy Okrug *Russian*, Autonomous district
Āw *Kurdish*, River
'Ayn *Arabic*, Spring, well
'Ayoûn *Arabic*, Wells

B

Baelt *Danish*, Strait
Bahía *Spanish*, Bay
Baḩr *Arabic*, River
Baía *Portuguese*, Bay
Baie *French*, Bay
Bañado *Spanish*, Marshy land
Bandao *Chinese*, Peninsula
Banjaran *Malay*, Mountain range
Barajı *Turkish*, Dam
Barragem *Portuguese*, Reservoir
Bassin *French*, Basin
Batang *Malay*, Stream
Beinn, Ben *Gaelic*, Mountain
-berg *Afrikaans, Norwegian*, Mountain
Besar *Indonesian, Malay*, Big
Birkat, Birket *Arabic*, Lake, well,
Boğazı *Turkish*, Lake
Boka *Serbo-Croatian*, Bay
Bol'sh-aya, -iye, -oy, -oye *Russian*, Big
Botigh(i) *Uzbek*, Depression basin
-bre(en) *Norwegian*, Glacier
Bredning *Danish*, Bay
Bucht *German*, Bay
Bugt(en) *Danish*, Bay
Buḩayrat *Arabic*, Lake, reservoir
Buḩeiret *Arabic*, Lake
Bukit *Malay*, Mountain
-bukta *Norwegian*, Bay
bukten *Swedish*, Bay
Bulag *Mongolian*, Spring
Bulak *Uighur*, Spring
Burnu *Turkish*, Cape, point
Buuraha *Somali*, Mountains

C

Cabo *Portuguese*, Cape
Caka *Tibetan*, Salt lake
Canal *Spanish*, Channel
Cap *French*, Cape
Capo *Italian*, Cape, headland
Cascada *Portuguese*, Waterfall
Cayo(s) *Spanish*, Islet(s), rock(s)
Cerro *Spanish*, Hill
Chaîne *French*, Mountain range
Chapada *Portuguese*, Hills, upland
Chau *Cantonese*, Island
Chāy *Turkish*, River
Chhâk *Cambodian*, Bay
Chhu *Tibetan*, River
-chŏsuji *Korean*, Reservoir
Chott *Arabic*, Depression, salt lake
Chŭli *Uzbek*, Grassland, steppe
Ch'ün-tao *Chinese*, Island group
Chuŏr Phnum *Cambodian*, Mountains
Ciudad *Spanish*, City, town
Co *Tibetan*, Lake
Colline(s) *French*, Hill(s)
Cordillera *Spanish*, Mountain range
Costa *Spanish*, Coast
Côte *French*, Coast
Coxilha *Portuguese*, Mountains
Cuchilla *Spanish*, Mountains

D

Daban *Mongolian, Uighur*, Pass
Dağı *Azerbaijani, Turkish*, Mountain
Dağları *Azerbaijani, Turkish*, Mountains
-dake *Japanese*, Peak
-dal(en) *Norwegian*, Valley
Danau *Indonesian*, Lake
Dao *Chinese*, Island
Đao *Vietnamese*, Island
Daryā *Persian*, River
Daryācheh *Persian*, Lake
Dasht *Persian*, Desert, plain
Dawḩat *Arabic*, Bay
Denizi *Turkish*, Sea
Dere *Turkish*, Stream
Desierto *Spanish*, Desert
Dili *Azerbaijani*, Spit
-do *Korean*, Island
Dooxo *Somali*, Valley
Düzü *Azerbaijani*, Steppe
-dwīp *Bengali*, Island

E

-eilanden *Dutch*, Islands
Embalse *Spanish*, Reservoir
Ensenada *Spanish*, Bay
Erg *Arabic*, Dunes
Estany *Catalan*, Lake
Estero *Spanish*, Inlet
Estrecho *Spanish*, Strait
Étang *French*, Lagoon, lake
-ey *Icelandic*, Island
Ezero *Bulgarian, Macedonian*, Lake
Ezers *Latvian*, Lake

F

Feng *Chinese*, Peak
Fjord *Danish*, Fjord
-fjord(en) *Danish, Norwegian, Swedish*, fjord
-fjördhur *Icelandic*, Fjord
Fleuve *French*, River
Fliegu *Maltese*, Channel
-fljór *Icelandic*, River
-flói *Icelandic*, Bay
Forêt *French*, Forest

G

-gan *Japanese*, Rock
-gang *Korean*, River
Ganga *Hindi, Nepali, Sinhala*, River
Gaoyuan *Chinese*, Plateau
Garagumy *Turkmen*, Sands
-gawa *Japanese*, River
Gebel *Arabic*, Mountain
-gebirge *German*, Mountain range
Ghadīr *Arabic*, Well
Ghubbat *Arabic*, Bay
Gjiri *Albanian*, Bay
Gol *Mongolian*, River
Golfe *French*, Gulf
Golfo *Italian, Spanish*, Gulf
Göl(ü) *Turkish*, Lake
Golyam, -a *Bulgarian*, Big
Gora *Russian, Serbo-Croatian*, Mountain
Góra *Polish*, mountain
Gory *Russian*, Mountain
Gryada *Russian*, ridge
Guba *Russian*, Bay
-gundo *Korean*, island group
Gunung *Malay*, Mountain

H

Ḩadd *Arabic*, Spit
-haehyŏp *Korean*, Strait
Haff *German*, Lagoon
Hai *Chinese*, Bay, lake, sea
Haixia *Chinese*, Strait
Hamada *Arabic*, Plateau
Ḩammādat *Arabic*, Plateau
Hāmūn *Persian*, Lake
-hantō *Japanese*, Peninsula
Har, Haré *Hebrew*, Mountain
Ḩarrat *Arabic*, Lava-field
Hav(et) *Danish*, Swedish, Sea
Hawr *Arabic*, Lake
Hāyk' *Amharic*, Lake
He *Chinese*, River
-hegység *Hungarian*, Mountain range
Heide *German*, Heath, moorland
Helodrano *Malagasy*, Bay
Higashi- *Japanese*, East(ern)
Ḩişā' *Arabic*, Well
Hka *Burmese*, River
-ho *Korean*, Lake
Ḩolot *Hebrew*, Dunes
Hora *Belarussian, Czech*, Mountain
Hrada *Belarussian*, Mountain, ridge
Hsi *Chinese*, River
Hu *Chinese*, Lake
Huk *Danish*, Point

I

Île(s) *French*, Island(s)
Ilha(s) *Portuguese*, Island(s)
Ilhéu(s) *Portuguese*, Islet(s)
Imeni *Russian*, In the name of
Inish- *Gaelic*, Island
Insel(n) *German*, Island(s)
Irmağı, Irmak *Turkish*, River
Isla(s) *Spanish*, Island(s)
Isola (Isole) *Italian*, Island(s)

J

Jabal *Arabic*, Mountain
Jāl *Arabic*, Ridge
-järv *Estonian*, Lake
-järvi *Finnish*, Lake
Jazā'ir *Arabic*, Islands
Jazīrat *Arabic*, Island
Jazīreh *Persian*, Island
Jebel *Arabic*, Mountain
Jezero *Serbo-Croatian*, Lake
Jezioro *Polish*, Lake
Jiang *Chinese*, River
-jima *Japanese*, Island
Jižní *Czech*, Southern
-jõgi *Estonian*, River
-joki *Finnish*, River
-jökull *Icelandic*, Glacier
Jūn *Arabic*, Bay
Juzur *Arabic*, Islands

K

Kaikyō *Japanese*, Strait
-kaise *Lappish*, Mountain
Kali *Nepali*, River
Kalnas *Lithuanian*, Mountain
Kalns *Latvian*, Mountain
Kang *Chinese*, Harbour
Kangri *Tibetan*, Mountain(s)
Kaôh *Cambodian*, Island
Kapp *Norwegian*, Cape
Káto *Greek*, Lower
Kavīr *Persian*, Desert
K'edi *Georgian*, Mountain range
Kediet *Arabic*, Mountain
Kepi *Albanian*, Cape, point
Kepulauan *Indonesian, Malay*, Island group
Khalīg, Khalīj *Arabic*, Gulf
Khawr *Arabic*, Inlet
Khola *Nepali*, River
Khrebet *Russian*, Mountain range
Ko *Thai*, Island
-ko *Japanese*, Inlet, lake
Kólpos *Greek*, Bay
-kopf *German*, Peak
Körfäzi *Azerbaijani*, Bay
Körfezi *Turkish*, Bay
Kõrgustik *Estonian*, Upland
Kosa *Russian, Ukrainian*, Spit
Koshi *Nepali*, River
Kou *Chinese*, River-mouth
Kowtal *Persian*, Pass
Kray *Russian*, Region, territory
Kryazh *Russian*, Ridge
Kuduk *Uighur*, Well
Kūh(hā) *Persian*, Mountain(s)
-kul' *Russian*, Lake
Kŭl(i) *Tajik, Uzbek*, Lake
-kundo *Korean*, Island group
-kysten *Norwegian*, Coast
Kyun *Burmese*, Island

L

Laaq *Somali*, Watercourse
Lac *French*, Lake
Lacul *Romanian*, Lake
Lagh *Somali*, Stream
Lago *Italian, Portuguese, Spanish*, Lake
Lagoa *Portuguese*, Lagoon
Laguna *Italian, Spanish*, Lagoon, lake
Laht *Estonian*, Bay
Laut *Indonesian*, Bay
Lembalemba *Malagasy*, Plateau
Lerr *Armenian*, Mountain
Lerrnashght'a *Armenian*, Mountain range
Les *Czech*, Forest
Lich *Armenian*, Lake
Liehtao *Chinese*, Island group
Liqeni *Albanian*, Lake
Límni *Greek*, Lake
Ling *Chinese*, Mountain range
Llano *Spanish*, Plain, prairie
Lumi *Albanian*, River
Lyman *Ukrainian*, Estuary

M

Madīnat *Arabic*, City, town
Mae Nam *Thai*, River
-mägi *Estonian*, Hill
Maja *Albanian*, Mountain
Mal *Albanian*, Mountains
Mal-aya, -oye, -yy, *Russian*, Small
-man *Korean*, Bay
Mar *Spanish*, Sea
Marios *Lithuanian*, Lake
Massif *French*, Mountains
Meer *German*, Lake
-meer *Dutch*, Lake
Melkosopochnik *Russian*, Plain
-meri *Estonian*, Sea
Mifraz *Hebrew*, Bay
Minami- *Japanese*, South(ern)
-misaki *Japanese*, Cape, point
Monkhafad *Arabic*, Depression
Montagne(s) *French*, Mountain(s)
Montañas *Spanish*, Mountains
Mont(s) *French*, Mountain(s)
Monte *Italian, Portuguese*, Mountain
More *Russian*, Sea
Mörön *Mongolian*, River
Mys *Russian*, Cape, point

N

-nada *Japanese*, Open stretch of water
Nagor'ye *Russian*, Upland
Naḩal *Hebrew*, River
Nahr *Arabic*, River
Nam *Laotian*, River
Namakzār *Persian*, Salt desert
Né-a, -on, -os *Greek*, New
Nedre- *Norwegian*, Lower
-neem *Estonian*, Cape, point
Nehri *Turkish*, River
-nes *Norwegian*, Cape, point
Nevado *Spanish*, Snow-capped
Nieder- *German*, Lower
Nishi- *Japanese*, West(ern)
-nísi *Greek*, Island
Nisoi *Greek*, Islands
Nizhn-eye, -iy, -iye, -yaya *Russian*, Lower
Nizmennost' *Russian*, Lowland, plain
Nord *Danish, French, German*, North
Norte *Portuguese, Spanish*, North
Nos *Bulgarian*, Point, spit
Nosy *Malagasy*, Island
Nov-a, -i, *Bulgarian, Serbo-Croatian*, New
Nov-aya, -o, -oye, -yy, -yye *Russian*, New
Now-a, -e, -y *Polish*, New
Nur *Mongolian*, Lake
Nuruu *Mongolian*, Mountains
Nuur *Mongolian*, Lake
Nyzovyna *Ukrainian*, Lowland, plain

O

-ø *Danish*, Island
Ober- *German*, Upper
Oblast' *Russian*, Province
Órmos *Greek*, Bay
Orol(i) *Uzbek*, Island
Øster- *Norwegian*, Eastern
Ostrov(a) *Russian*, Island(s)
Otok *Serbo-Croatian*, Island
Oued *Arabic*, Watercourse
-oy *Faeroese*, Island
-øy(a) *Norwegian*, Island
Oya *Sinhala*, River
Ozero *Russian, Ukrainian*, Lake

P

Passo *Italian*, Pass
Pegunungan *Indonesian, Malay*, Mountain range
Pélagos *Greek*, Sea
Pendi *Chinese*, Basin
Penisola *Italian*, Peninsula
Pertuis *French*, Strait
Peski *Russian*, Sands
Phanom *Thai*, Mountain
Phou *Laotian*, Mountain
Pi *Chinese*, Point
Pic *Catalan, French*, Peak
Pico *Portuguese, Spanish*, Peak
-piggen *Danish*, Peak
Pik *Russian*, Peak
Pivostriv *Ukrainian*, Peninsula
Planalto *Portuguese*, Plateau
Planina, Planini *Bulgarian, Macedonian, Serbo-Croatian*, Mountain range
Plato *Russian*, Plateau
Ploskogor'ye *Russian*, Upland
Poluostrov *Russian*, Peninsula
Ponta *Portuguese*, Point
Porthmós *Greek*, Strait
Pótamos *Greek*, River
Presa *Spanish*, Dam
Prokhod *Bulgarian*, Pass
Proliv *Russian*, Strait
Pulau *Indonesian, Malay*, Island
Pulu *Malay*, Island
Punta *Spanish*, Point
Pushcha *Belorussian*, Forest
Puszcza *Polish*, Forest

Q

Qā' *Arabic*, Depression
Qalamat *Arabic*, Well
Qatorkŭh(i) *Tajik*, Mountain
Qiuling *Chinese*, Hills
Qolleh *Persian*, Mountain
Qu *Tibetan*, Stream
Quan *Chinese*, Well
Qulla(i) *Tajik*, Peak
Qundao *Chinese*, Island group

R

Raas *Somali*, Cape
-rags *Latvian*, Cape
Ramlat *Arabic*, Sands
Ra's *Arabic*, Cape, headland, point
Ravnina *Bulgarian, Russian*, Plain
Récif *French*, Reef
Recife *Portuguese*, Reef
Reka *Bulgarian*, River
Represa (Rep.) *Portuguese, Spanish*, Reservoir
Reshteh *Persian*, Mountain range
Respublika *Russian*, Republic, first-order administrative division
Respublika(si) *Uzbek*, Republic, first-order administrative division
-retsugan *Japanese*, Chain of rocks
-rettō *Japanese*, Island chain
Riacho *Spanish*, Stream
Riban' *Malagasy*, Mountains
Rio *Portuguese*, River
Río *Spanish*, River
Riu *Catalan*, River
Rivier *Dutch*, River
Rivière *French*, River
Rowd *Pashtu*, River
Rt *Serbo-Croatian*, Point
Rūd *Persian*, River
Rūdkhāneh *Persian*, River
Rudohorie *Slovak*, Mountains
Ruisseau *French*, Stream

S

-saar *Estonian*, Island
-saari *Finnish*, Island
Sabkhat *Arabic*, Salt marsh
Sāgar(a) *Hindi*, Lake, reservoir
Şaḩrā' *Arabic*, Desert
Saint, Sainte *French*, Saint
Salar *Spanish*, Salt-pan
Salto *Portuguese, Spanish*, Waterfall
Samudra *Sinhala*, Reservoir
-san *Japanese, Korean*, Mountain
-sanchi *Japanese*, Mountains
-sandur *Icelandic*, Beach
Sankt *German, Swedish*, Saint
-sanmaek *Korean*, Mountain range
-sanmyaku *Japanese*, Mountain range
San, Santa, Santo *Italian, Portuguese, Spanish*, Saint
São *Portuguese*, Saint
Sarīr *Arabic*, Desert
Sebkha, Sebkhet *Arabic*, Depression, salt marsh
Sedlo *Czech*, Pass
See *German*, Lake
Selat *Indonesian*, Strait
Selatan *Indonesian*, Southern
-selkä *Finnish*, Lake, ridge
Selseleh *Persian*, Mountain range
Serra *Portuguese*, Mountain
Serranía *Spanish*, Mountain
-seto *Japanese*, Channel, strait
Sever-naya, -noye, -nyy, -o *Russian*, Northern
Sha'īb *Arabic*, Watercourse
Shākh *Kurdish*, Mountain
Shamo *Chinese*, Desert
Shan *Chinese*, Mountain(s)
Shankou *Chinese*, Pass
Shanmo *Chinese*, Mountain range
Shaţţ *Arabic*, Distributary
Shet' *Amharic*, River
Shi *Chinese*, Municipality
-shima *Japanese*, Island
Shiqqat *Arabic*, Depression
-shotō *Japanese*, Group of islands
Shuiku *Chinese*, Reservoir
Shūrkhog(i) *Uzbek*, Salt marsh
Sierra *Spanish*, Mountains
Sint *Dutch*, Saint
-sjø(en) *Norwegian*, Lake
-sjön *Swedish*, Lake
Solonchak *Russian*, Salt lake
Solonchakovyye Vpadiny *Russian*, Salt basin, wetlands
Sơn *Vietnamese*, Mountain
Sông *Vietnamese*, River
Sør- *Norwegian*, Southern
-spitze *German*, Peak
Star-á, -é *Czech*, Old
Star-aya, -oye, -yy, -yye *Russian*, Old
Stenó *Greek*, Strait
Step' *Russian*, Steppe
Štít *Slovak*, Peak
Stœng *Cambodian*, River
Stolovaya Strana *Russian*, Plateau
Stredné *Slovak*, Middle
Střední *Czech*, Middle
Stretto *Italian*, Strait
Su Anbarı *Azerbaijani*, Reservoir
-suidō *Japanese*, Channel, strait
Sund *Swedish*, Sound, strait
Sungai *Indonesian, Malay*, River
Suu *Turkish*, River

T

Tal *Mongolian*, Plain
Tandavan' *Malagasy*, Mountain range
Tangorombohitr' *Malagasy*, Mountain massif
Tanjung *Indonesian, Malay*, Cape, point
Tao *Chinese*, Island
Ţaraq *Arabic*, Hills
Tassili *Berber*, Mountain, plateau
Tau *Russian*, Mountain(s)
Taungdan *Burmese*, Mountain range
Techníti Límni *Greek*, Reservoir
Tekojärvi *Finnish*, Reservoir
Teluk *Indonesian, Malay*, Bay
Tengah *Indonesian*, Middle
Terara *Amharic*, Mountain
Timur *Indonesian*, Eastern
-tind(an) *Norwegian*, Peak
Tizma(si) *Uzbek*, Mountain range, ridge
-tō *Japanese*, island
Tog *Somali*, Valley
-tōge *Japanese*, pass
Togh(i) *Uzbek*, mountain
Tônlé *Cambodian*, Lake
Top *Dutch*, Peak
-tunturi *Finnish*, Mountain
Ţurāq *Arabic*, hills
Tur'at *Arabic*, Channel

U

Udde(n) *Swedish*, Cape, point
'Uqlat *Arabic*, Well
Utara *Indonesian*, Northern
Uul *Mongolian*, Mountains

V

Väin *Estonian*, Strait
Vallée *French*, Valley
Varful *Romanian*, Peak
-vatn *Icelandic*, Lake
-vatnet *Norwegian*, Lake
Velayat *Turkmen*, Province
-vesi *Finnish*, Lake
Vestre- *Norwegian*, Western
-vidda *Norwegian*, Plateau
-vík *Icelandic*, Bay
-viken *Swedish*, Bay, inlet
Vinh *Vietnamese*, Bay
Víztárloló *Hungarian*, Reservoir
Vodaskhovishcha *Belarussian*, Reservoir
Vodokhranilishche (Vdkhr.) *Russian*, Reservoir
Vodoskhovyshche (Vdskh.) *Ukrainian*, Reservoir
Volcán *Spanish*, Volcano
Vostochn-o, yy *Russian*, Eastern
Vozvyshennost' *Russian*, Upland, plateau
Vozyera *Belarussian*, Lake
Vpadina *Russian*, Depression
Vrchovina *Czech*, Mountains
Vrh *Croat, Slovene*, Peak
Vychodné *Slovak*, Eastern
Vysochyna *Ukrainian*, Upland
Vysočina *Czech*, Upland

W

Waadi *Somali*, Watercourse
Wādī *Arabic* Watercourse
Wāḩat, Wâhat *Arabic*, Oasis
Wald *German*, Forest
Wan *Chinese*, Bay
Way *Indonesian*, River
Webi *Somali*, River
Wenz *Amharic*, River
Wiloyat(i) *Uzbek*, Province
Wyżyna *Polish*, Upland
Wzgórza *Polish*, Upland
Wzvyshsha *Belarussian*, Upland

X

Xé *Laotian*, River
Xi *Chinese*, Stream

Y

-yama *Japanese*, Mountain
Yanchi *Chinese*, Salt lake
Yanhu *Chinese*, Salt lake
Yarımadası *Azerbaijani, Turkish*, Peninsula
Yaylası *Turkish*, Plateau
Yazovir *Bulgarian*, Reservoir
Yoma *Burmese*, Mountains
Ytre- *Norwegian*, Outer
Yü *Chinese*, Island
Yunhe *Chinese*, Canal
Yuzhn-o, -yy *Russian*, Southern

Z

-zaki *Japanese*, Cape, point
Zaliv *Bulgarian, Russian*, Bay
-zan *Japanese*, Mountain
Zangbo *Tibetan*, River
Zapadn-aya, -o, -yy *Russian*, Western
Západné *Slovak*, Western
Západní *Czech*, Western
Zatoka *Polish, Ukrainian*, Bay
-zee *Dutch*, Sea
Zemlya *Russian*, Earth, land
Zizhiqu *Chinese*, Autonomous region

100 Mile House - Acerrae

INDEX

306

INDEX

GLOSSARY OF ABBREVIATIONS

This glossary provides a comprehensive guide to the abbreviations used in this Atlas, and in the Index.

A
abbrev. abbreviated
AD Anno Domini
Afr. Afrikaans
Alb. Albanian
Amh. Amharic
anc. ancient
approx. approximately
Ar. Arabic
Arm. Armenian
ASEAN Association of South East Asian Nations
ASSR Autonomous Soviet Socialist Republic
Aust. Australian
Az. Azerbaijani
Azerb. Azerbaijan

B
Basq. Basque
BC before Christ
Bel. Belarussian
Ben. Bengali
Ber. Berber
B-H Bosnia-Herzegovina
bn billion (one thousand million)
BP British Petroleum
Bret. Breton
Brit. British
Bul. Bulgarian
Bur. Burmese

C
C central
C. Cape
°C degrees Centigrade
CACM Central America Common Market
Cam. Cambodian
Cant. Cantonese
CAR Central African Republic
Cast. Castilian
Cat. Catalan
CEEAC Central America Common Market
Chin. Chinese
CIS Commonwealth of Independent States
cm centimetre(s)
Cro. Croat
Cz. Czech
Czech Rep. Czech Republic

D
Dan. Danish
Div. Divehi
Dom. Rep. Dominican Republic
Dut. Dutch

E
E east
EC *see* EU
EEC *see* EU
ECOWAS Economic Community of West African States
ECU European Currency Unit
EMS European Monetary System
Eng. English
est estimated
Est. Estonian
EU European Union (previously European Community [EC], European Economic Community [EEC])

F
°F degrees Fahrenheit
Faer. Faeroese
Fij. Fijian
Fin. Finnish
Fr. French
Fris. Frisian
ft foot/feet
FYROM Former Yugoslav Republic of Macedonia

G
g gram(s)
Gael. Gaelic
Gal. Galician
GDP Gross Domestic Product (the total value of goods and services produced by a country excluding income from foreign countries)
Geor. Georgian
Ger. German
Gk Greek
GNP Gross National Product (the total value of goods and services produced by a country)

H
Heb. Hebrew
HEP hydro-electric power
Hind. Hindi
hist. historical
Hung. Hungarian

I
I. Island
Icel. Icelandic
in inch(es)
In. Inuit (Eskimo)
Ind. Indonesian
Intl International
Ir. Irish
Is Islands
It. Italian

J
Jap. Japanese

K
Kaz. Kazakh
kg kilogram(s)
Kir. Kirghiz
km kilometre(s)
km^2 square kilometre (singular)
Kor. Korean
Kurd. Kurdish

L
L. Lake
LAIA Latin American Integration Association
Lao. Laotian
Lapp. Lappish
Lat. Latin
Latv. Latvian
Liech. Liechtenstein
Lith. Lithuanian
Lux. Luxembourg

M
m million/metre(s)
Mac. Macedonian
Maced. Macedonia
Mal. Malay
Malg. Malagasy
Malt. Maltese
mi. mile(s)
Mong. Mongolian
Mt. Mountain
Mts Mountains

N
N north
NAFTA North American Free Trade Agreement
Nep. Nepali
Neth. Netherlands
Nic. Nicaraguan
Nor. Norwegian
NZ New Zealand

P
Pash. Pashtu
PNG Papua New Guinea
Pol. Polish
Poly. Polynesian
Port. Portuguese
prev. previously

R
Rep. Republic
Res. Reservoir
Rmsch Romansch
Rom. Romanian
Rus. Russian
Russ. Fed. Russian Federation

S
S south
SADC Southern Africa Development Community
SCr. Serbo-Croatian
Sinh. Sinhala
Slvk Slovak
Slvn. Slovene
Som. Somali
Sp. Spanish
St., St Saint
Strs Straits
Swa. Swahili
Swe. Swedish
Switz. Switzerland

T
Taj. Tajik
Th. Thai
Thai. Thailand
Tib. Tibetan
Turk. Turkish
Turkm. Turkmenistan

U
UAE United Arab Emirates
Uigh. Uighur
UK United Kingdom
Ukr. Ukrainian
UN United Nations
Urd. Urdu
US/USA United States of America
USSR Union of Soviet Socialist Republics
Uzb. Uzbek

V
var. variant
Vdkhr. Vodokhranilishche (Russian for reservoir)
Vdskh. Vodoskhovyshche (Ukrainian for reservoir)
Vtn. Vietnamese

W
W west
Wel. Welsh

Y
Yugo. Yugoslavia

THIS INDEX LISTS all the placenames and features shown on the regional and continental maps in this Atlas. Placenames are referenced to the largest scale map on which they appear. The policy followed throughout the Atlas is to use the local spelling or local name at regional level; commonly-used English language names may occasionally be added (in parentheses) where this is an aid to identification e.g. Firenze (Florence). English names, where they exist, have been used for all international features e.g. oceans and country names; they are also used on the continental maps and in the introductory World section; these are then fully cross-referenced to the local names found on the regional maps. The index also contains commonly-found alternative names and variant spellings, which are also fully cross-referenced.

All main entry names are those of settlements unless otherwise indicated by the use of italicized definitions or representative symbols, which are keyed at the foot of each page.

1

56 *E6* **100 Mile House** *var.* Hundred Mile House. British Columbia, SW Canada *51°39′N 121°19′W*
115 *H9* **25 de Agosto** Florida, Uruguay *34°25′S 56°24′W*
118 *G9* **25 de Mayo** La Pampa, Argentina *37°48′S 67°41′W*
25 de Mayo *see* Veinticinco de Mayo
26 Bakinskikh Komissarov *see* Häsänabad
26 Baku Komissarlary Adyndaky *see* Uzboý

A

Aa *see* Gauja
155 *D13* **Aabenraa** *var.* Åbenrå, *Ger.* Apenrade. Syddanmark, SW Denmark *55°03′N 09°26′E*
155 *D10* **Aabybro** *var.* Åbybro. Nordjylland, N Denmark *57°09′N 09°32′E*
181 *A10* **Aachen** *Dut.* Aken, *Fr.* Aix-la-Chapelle; *anc.* Aquae Grani, Aquisgranum. Nordrhein-Westfalen, W Germany *50°47′N 06°06′E*
218 *F4* **Aadchît** Lebanon *33°20′N 35°25′E*
218 *F4* **Aaïtaït** Lebanon *33°33′N 35°40′E*
Aaiún *see* Laâyoune
178 *J3* **Aakirkeby** *var.* Åkirkeby. Bornholm, E Denmark *55°04′N 14°56′E*
218 *G1* **Aakkâr el Aatîga** Lebanon
155 *D11* **Aalborg** *var.* Ålborg, Ålborg-Nørresundby; *anc.* Alburgum. Nordjylland, N Denmark *57°03′N 09°56′E*
Aalborg Bugt *see* Ålborg Bugt
179 *E12* **Aalen** Baden-Württemberg, S Germany *48°50′N 10°06′E*
155 *D11* **Aalestrup** *var.* Ålestrup. Midtjylland, NW Denmark *56°42′N 09°31′E*
218 *F3* **Aaley** Lebanon *33°48′N 35°35′E*
162 *E6* **Aalsmeer** Noord-Holland, C Netherlands *52°17′N 04°43′E*
163 *D10* **Aalst** Oost-Vlaanderen, C Belgium *50°57′N 04°03′E*
162 *F7* **Aalst** *Fr.* Alost. Noord-Brabant, S Netherlands *51°23′N 05°29′E*
162 *I7* **Aalten** Gelderland, E Netherlands *51°56′N 06°35′E*
163 *C9* **Aalter** Oost-Vlaanderen, NW Belgium *51°05′N 03°28′E*
Aanaar *see* Inari
Aanaarjävri *see* Inarijärvi
141 *H5* **Aandster** North West, South Africa *27°25′S 25°10′E*
153 *H8* **Äänekoski** Keski-Suomi, W Finland *62°34′N 25°45′E*
218 *G3* **Aanjar** *var.* ‘Anjar. C Lebanon *33°45′N 35°56′E*
218 *G3* **Aanjar** Lebanon *33°43′N 35°55′E*
138 *E7* **Aansluit** Northern Cape, N South Africa *26°41′S 22°24′E*
218 *G2* **Aaqoûra** Lebanon
218 *G2* **Aaqoûra** Lebanon *34°07′N 35°54′E*
Aar *see* Aare
176 *D4* **Aarau** Aargau, N Switzerland *47°22′N 08°00′E*
176 *C4* **Aarberg** Bern, W Switzerland *47°19′N 07°54′E*
163 *C9* **Aardenburg** Zeeland, SW Netherlands *51°16′N 03°27′E*
174 *B3* **Aare** *var.* Aar. 〰 W Switzerland
174 *B2* **Aargau** *Fr.* Argovie. ⬗ *canton* N Switzerland
Aarhus *see* Århus
Aarlen *see* Arlon
155 *D11* **Aars** *var.* Års. Nordjylland, N Denmark *56°49′N 09°32′E*
163 *E10* **Aarschot** Vlaams Brabant, C Belgium *50°59′N 04°50′E*
Aassi, Nahr el *see* Orontes
Aat *see* Ath
218 *F3* **Aayoûn es Sîmâne** Lebanon *34°00′N 35°49′E*
239 *K7* **Aba** *prev.* Ngawa. Sichuan, C China *32°51′N 101°46′E*
134 *J6* **Aba** Orientale, NE Dem. Rep. Congo *03°52′N 30°14′E*
133 *K8* **Aba** Abia, S Nigeria *05°06′N 07°22′E*
220 *D3* **Abā al Qazāz, Bi’r** *well* NW Saudi Arabia
Abā as Su‘ūd *see* Najrān
107 *H4* **Abacaxis, Rio** 〰 NW Brazil
Abaco Island *see* Great Abaco/Little Abaco
Abaco Island *see* Great Abaco, N Bahamas
222 *D6* **Ābādān** Khūzestān, SW Iran *30°24′N 48°18′E*
228 *D7* **Abadan** *prev.* Bezmein, Büzmeýin, *Rus.* Byuzmeyin. Ahal Welaýaty, C Turkmenistan *38°08′N 57°53′E*
222 *F6* **Ābādeh** Fārs, C Iran *31°06′N 52°40′E*
130 *G4* **Abadla** W Algeria *31°04′N 02°39′W*
110 *E1* **Abaeté** Minas Gerais, SE Brazil *19°10′S 45°24′W*
113 *H5* **Abaí** Caazapá, S Paraguay *25°58′S 55°54′W*
Abai *see* Blue Nile
284 *B2* **Abaiang** *var.* Apia; *prev.* Charlotte Island. *atoll* Tungaru, W Kiribati
Abaj *see* Abay
133 *K7* **Abaji** Federal Capital District, C Nigeria *08°35′N 06°54′E*
79 *J5* **Abajo Peak** ▲ Utah, W USA *37°51′N 109°28′W*
133 *K8* **Abakaliki** Ebonyi, SE Nigeria *06°18′N 08°07′E*
192 *G8* **Abakan** Respublika Khakasiya, S Russian Federation *53°43′N 91°25′E*
227 *N1* **Abakan** 〰 S Russian Federation
133 *I4* **Abala** Tillabéri, SW Niger *14°55′N 03°27′E*
133 *J4* **Abalak** Tahoua, C Niger *15°28′N 06°18′E*
191 *H8* **Abalyanka** *Rus.* Obolyanka. 〰 N Belarus
192 *G7* **Aban** Krasnoyarskiy Kray, S Russian Federation *56°41′N 96°04′E*
222 *G6* **Āb Anbār-e Kān Sorkh** Yazd, C Iran *31°22′N 53°38′E*
105 *F8* **Abancay** Apurímac, SE Peru *13°37′S 72°52′W*
173 *K6* **Abanilla** Murcia, Spain *38°12′N 1°03′W*
284 *D1* **Abaokoro** *atoll* Tungaru, W Kiribati
Abariringa *see* Kanton
222 *G6* **Abarkūh** Yazd, C Iran *31°07′N 53°17′E*
252 *G3* **Abashiri** *var.* Abasiri. Hokkaidō, NE Japan *44°N 144°15′E*
252 *G3* **Abashiri-gawa** 〰 Hokkaidō, NE Japan
252 *G3* **Abashiri-ko** ◎ Hokkaidō, NE Japan
Abasiri *see* Abashiri
87 *K8* **Abasolo** Chiapas, Mexico *16°48′N 92°10′W*
85 *K5* **Abasolo** Guanajuato, Mexico
85 *M7* **Abasolo** Tamaulipas, C Mexico *24°02′N 98°18′W*
87 *H8* **Abasolo del Valle** Veracruz-Llave, Mexico *17°46′N 95°30′W*
280 *C4* **Abau** Central, S Papua New Guinea *10°04′S 148°34′E*
227 *I4* **Abay** *var.* Abaj. Karaganda, C Kazakhstan *49°38′N 72°50′E*
136 *D5* **Ābaya Hāyk’** *Eng.* Lake Margherita, *It.* Abbaia. ◎ SW Ethiopia
Ābay Wenz *see* Blue Nile
192 *G8* **Abaza** Respublika Khakasiya, S Russian Federation *52°40′N 89°58′E*
Abbaia *see* Ābaya Hāyk’
222 *G8* **Āb Bārīk** Fārs, S Iran
175 *B10* **Abbasanta** Sardegna, Italy, C Mediterranean Sea *40°08′N 08°49′E*
Abbatis Villa *see* Abbeville
72 *D4* **Abbaye, Point** *headland* Michigan, N USA *46°58′N 88°08′W*
Abbazia *see* Opatija
Abbé, Lake *see* Abhe, Lake
165 *H2* **Abbeville** *anc.* Abbatis Villa. Somme, N France *50°06′N 01°50′E*
69 *I3* **Abbeville** Alabama, S USA *31°35′N 85°16′W*
69 *K2* **Abbeville** Georgia, SE USA *31°58′N 83°18′W*
68 *C4* **Abbeville** Louisiana, S USA *29°58′N 92°08′W*
67 *H8* **Abbeville** South Carolina, SE USA *34°10′N 82°23′W*
157 *B10* **Abbeyfeale** *Ir.* Mainistir na Féile. SW Ireland *52°24′N 09°21′W*
160 *A2* **Abbeyleix** Laois, Ireland *52°54′N 7°21′W*
176 *E7* **Abbiategrasso** Lombardia, NW Italy *45°24′N 08°55′E*
154 *J1* **Abborrträsk** Norrbotten, N Sweden *65°24′N 19°33′E*
292 *F5* **Abbot Ice Shelf** *ice shelf* Antarctica
160 *G8* **Abbotsbury** United Kingdom *50°40′N 2°36′W*
140 *D9* **Abbotsdale** Western Cape, South Africa *33°29′S 18°40′E*
76 *C2* **Abbotsford** British Columbia, SW Canada *49°02′N 122°18′W*
72 *C5* **Abbotsford** Wisconsin, N USA *44°57′N 90°19′W*
231 *I4* **Abbottābād** Khyber Pakhtunkhwa, NW Pakistan *34°12′N 73°15′E*
191 *H9* **Abchuha** *Rus.* Obchuga. Minskaya Voblasts’, NW Belarus *54°30′N 29°22′E*
162 *F6* **Abcoude** Utrecht, C Netherlands *52°17′N 04°59′E*
216 *F2* **‘Abd al ‘Azīz, Jabal** ⛰ NE Syria
221 *I9* **‘Abd al Kūrī** *island* SE Yemen
197 *K3* **Abdulino** Orenburgskaya Oblast’, W Russian Federation *53°37′N 53°39′E*
134 *F2* **Abéché** *var.* Abécher, Abeshr. Ouaddaï, SE Chad *13°49′N 20°49′E*
Abécher *see* Abéché
223 *I5* **Āb-e Garm va Sard** Khorāsān-e Janūbī, E Iran
133 *I2* **Abeïbara** Kidal, NE Mali *19°07′N 01°52′E*
171 *H3* **Abejar** Castilla y León, N Spain *41°48′N 02°47′W*
102 *B5* **Abejorral** Antioquia, W Colombia *05°48′N 75°28′W*
Abela *see* Ávila
141 *K3* **Abel Erasmuspas** *pass* Limpopo, South Africa
Abellinum *see* Avellino
152 *C5* **Abeløya** *island* Kong Karls Land, E Svalbard
136 *D4* **Ābeltī** Oromīya, C Ethiopia *08°09′N 37°31′E*
284 *B3* **Abemama** *var.* Apamama; *prev.* Roger Simpson Island. *atoll* Tungaru, W Kiribati
261 *L7* **Abemaree** *var.* Abermarre. Papua, E Indonesia *07°03′S 140°10′E*
181 *J13* **Abenberg** Bayern, Germany *49°15′N 10°58′E*
132 *G8* **Abengourou** E Ivory Coast *06°42′N 03°27′W*
172 *G5* **Abenójar** Castilla-La Manacha, Spain *38°53′N 4°21′W*
Åbenrå *see* Aabenraa
179 *G12* **Abens** 〰 SE Germany
133 *I7* **Abeokuta** Ogun, SW Nigeria *07°07′N 03°21′E*
160 *E4* **Aberaeron** SW Wales, United Kingdom *52°15′N 04°15′W*
Aberbrothock *see* Arbroath
Abercorn *see* Mbala
74 *E3* **Abercrombie** North Dakota, N USA *46°25′N 96°42′W*
160 *F6* **Aberdare** United Kingdom *51°43′N 3°27′W*
160 *D3* **Aberdaron** United Kingdom *52°49′N 4°42′W*
277 *L4* **Aberdeen** New South Wales, SE Australia *32°09′S 150°55′E*
57 *M6* **Aberdeen** Saskatchewan, S Canada *52°15′N 106°19′W*
138 *F9* **Aberdeen** Eastern Cape, S South Africa *32°30′S 24°00′E*
156 *G5* **Aberdeen** *anc.* Devana. NE Scotland, United Kingdom *57°10′N 02°04′W*
64 *E9* **Aberdeen** Maryland, NE USA *39°28′N 76°09′W*
66 *C8* **Aberdeen** Mississippi, S USA *33°49′N 88°32′W*
67 *J7* **Aberdeen** North Carolina, SE USA *35°07′N 79°25′W*
74 *D4* **Aberdeen** South Dakota, N USA *45°27′N 98°29′W*
76 *B4* **Aberdeen** Washington, NW USA *46°57′N 123°48′W*
140 *G8* **Aberdeen Kendrew** Eastern Cape, South Africa *32°33′S 24°33′E*
55 *I3* **Aberdeen Lake** ◎ Nunavut, NE Canada
140 *G9* **Aberdeen Road** Eastern Cape, South Africa *32°45′S 24°19′E*
160 *E3* **Aberdyfi** United Kingdom *52°33′N 4°02′W*
159 *H1* **Aberfeldy** C Scotland, United Kingdom *56°38′N 03°49′W*
160 *E2* **Aberffraw** United Kingdom *53°11′N 4°27′W*
158 *G2* **Aberfoyle** United Kingdom *56°11′N 4°23′W*
160 *G5* **Abergavenny** *anc.* Gobannium. SE Wales, United Kingdom *51°50′N 03°W*
160 *E5* **Abergorlech** United Kingdom *51°59′N 4°04′W*
Abergwaun *see* Fishguard
159 *I3* **Aberlady** United Kingdom *56°00′N 2°51′W*
Abermarre *see* Abemaree
70 *D3* **Abernathy** Texas, SW USA *33°49′N 101°50′W*
159 *I2* **Abernethy** C Scotland, United Kingdom
160 *E4* **Aberporth** United Kingdom *52°08′N 4°33′W*
Abersee *see* Wolfgangsee
160 *E3* **Abersoch** United Kingdom *52°49′N 4°30′W*
Abertawe *see* Swansea
Aberteifi *see* Cardigan
160 *G6* **Abertillery** United Kingdom *51°44′N 3°08′W*
76 *D8* **Abert, Lake** ◎ Oregon, NW USA
160 *E4* **Aberystwyth** W Wales, United Kingdom *52°25′N 04°05′W*
Abeshr *see* Abéché
Ábeskovvu *see* Abisko
176 *G9* **Abetone** Toscana, C Italy *44°09′N 10°42′E*
195 *L4* **Abez’** Respublika Komi, NW Russian Federation *66°32′N 61°41′E*
222 *E3* **Āb Garm** Qazvin, N Iran
220 *F7* **Abhā** ‘Asīr, SW Saudi Arabia *18°16′N 42°32′E*
222 *E3* **Abhar** Zanjān, NW Iran *36°05′N 49°18′E*
Abhé Bad/Ābhē Bid Hāyk’ *see* Abhe, Lake
136 *F3* **Abhe, Lake** *var.* Lake Abbé, *Amh.* Ābhē Bid Hāyk’, *Som.* Abhé Bad. ◎ Djibouti/Ethiopia
133 *J7* **Abia** ⬗ *state* SE Nigeria
217 *K6* **‘Abīd ‘Alī** Wāsiṭ, E Iraq *32°20′N 45°58′E*
191 *I10* **Abidavichy** *Rus.* Obidovichi. Mahilyowskaya Voblasts’, E Belarus *53°20′N 30°25′E*
187 *J3* **Abide** Çanakkale, NW Turkey *40°04′N 26°13′E*
132 *F8* **Abidjan** S Ivory Coast *05°19′N 04°01′W*
140 *E5* **Abierkwasputs** *salt lake* Northern Cape, South Africa
Āb-i-Istāda *see* Īstādeh-ye Moqor, Āb-e-
218 *F6* **Abila** Jordan
75 *E9* **Abilene** Kansas, C USA *38°55′N 97°14′W*
70 *F4* **Abilene** Texas, SW USA *32°27′N 99°44′W*
Abindonia *see* Abingdon
161 *I6* **Abingdon** *anc.* Abindonia. S England, United Kingdom *51°41′N 01°17′W*
73 *B10* **Abingdon** Illinois, N USA *40°48′N 90°24′W*
67 *H5* **Abingdon** Virginia, NE USA *36°42′N 81°59′W*
Abingdon *see* Pinta, Isla
65 *M3* **Abington** Massachusetts, USA *42°06′N 70°57′W*
64 *F7* **Abington** Pennsylvania, NE USA *40°06′N 75°05′W*
196 *F8* **Abinsk** Krasnodarskiy Kray, SW Russian Federation *44°51′N 38°12′E*
79 *L6* **Abiquiu Reservoir** ⊞ New Mexico, SW USA
Āb-i-safed *see* Sefīd, Darya-ye
152 *F5* **Abisko** *Lapp.* Ábeskovvu. Norrbotten, N Sweden *68°21′N 18°50′E*
51 *J8* **Abitibi** 〰 Ontario, S Canada
58 *F7* **Abitibi, Lac** ◎ Ontario/Québec, S Canada
136 *E2* **Ābīy Ādī** Tigray, N Ethiopia *13°40′N 38°57′E*
190 *E5* **Abja-Paluoja** Viljandimaa, S Estonia *58°08′N 25°20′E*
Abkhazia *see* Apkhazeti
173 *I8* **Abla** Andalucía, Spain *37°08′N 2°47′W*
276 *E1* **Abminga** South Australia *26°07′S 134°49′E*
129 *I4* **Abnūb** *var.* Abnûb. C Egypt *27°18′N 31°09′E*
Abnûb *see* Abnūb
Åbo *see* Turku
232 *D4* **Abohar** Punjab, N India *30°11′N 74°14′E*
132 *G8* **Aboisso** SE Ivory Coast *05°26′N 03°13′W*
133 *N1* **Abo, Massif d’** ⛰ NW Chad
133 *I7* **Abomey** S Benin *07°14′N 02°00′E*
167 *M10* **Abondance** Rhône-Alpes, France *46°17′N 6°44′E*
134 *C6* **Abong Mbang** Est, SE Cameroon *03°58′N 13°10′E*
183 *G12* **Abony** Pest, C Hungary *47°10′N 20°00′E*
134 *E3* **Abou-Déïa** Salamat, SE Chad *11°30′N 19°18′E*
Aboudouhour *see* Abū aḍ Ḍuhūr
Abou Kémal *see* Abū Kamāl
Abou Simbel *see* Abū Sunbul
215 *K5* **Abovyan** C Armenia *40°16′N 44°33′E*
263 *K4* **Abra** 〰 Luzon, N Philippines
129 *N9* **Abrād, Wādī** *seasonal river* W Yemen
Abraham Bay *see* The Carlton
118 *C6* **Abranquil** Maule, Chile *35°45′S 71°33′W*
172 *C4* **Abrantes** *var.* Abrántes. Santarém, C Portugal *39°28′N 08°12′W*
112 *D3* **Abra Pampa** Jujuy, N Argentina *22°47′S 65°41′W*
Abrashlare *see* Brezovo
111 *J3* **Abre Campo** Minas Gerais, Brazil *20°18′S 42°29′W*
102 *C4* **Abrego** Norte de Santander, N Colombia *08°08′N 73°14′W*
Abrene *see* Pytalovo
84 *C6* **Abreojos, Punta** *headland* NW Mexico *26°43′N 113°36′W*
169 *M3* **Abriés** Provence-Alpes-Côte d’Azur, France *44°47′N 6°56′E*
115 *J4* **Abrojal** Rivera, Uruguay *31°45′S 55°01′W*
98 *G5* **Abrolhos Bank** *undersea feature* W Atlantic Ocean *18°30′S 38°45′W*
191 *E11* **Abrova** *Rus.* Obrovo. Brestskaya Voblasts’, SW Belarus *52°30′N 25°34′E*
188 *C7* **Abrud** *Ger.* Gross-Schlatten, *Hung.* Abrudbánya. Alba, SW Romania *46°16′N 23°05′E*
Abrudbánya *see* Abrud
190 *C5* **Abruka** *island* SW Estonia
175 *F8* **Abruzzese, Appennino** ⛰ C Italy
175 *G8* **Abruzzo** ⬗ *region* C Italy
220 *F8* **‘Abs** *var.* Sūq ‘Abs. W Yemen *16°42′N 42°55′E*
77 *J6* **Absaroka Range** ⛰ Montana/Wyoming, NW USA
64 *G9* **Absecon** New Jersey, USA *39°26′N 74°30′W*
215 *N4* **Abşeron Yarımadası** *Rus.* Apsheronskiy Poluostrov. *peninsula* E Azerbaijan
222 *F4* **Āb Shīrīn** Eşfahān, C Iran *34°17′N 51°17′E*
217 *L7* **Abtān** Maysān, SE Iraq *31°37′N 47°06′E*
177 *I3* **Abtenau** Salzburg, NW Austria *47°33′N 13°21′E*
232 *C7* **Ābu** Rājasthān, N India *24°41′N 72°50′E*
250 *D5* **Abu** Yamaguchi, Honshū, SW Japan *34°30′N 131°26′E*
216 *D3* **Abū aḍ Ḍuhūr** *Fr.* Aboudouhour. Idlib, NW Syria *35°30′N 37°00′E*
221 *J4* **Abū al Abyaḍ** *island* C United Arab Emirates
218 *H3* **Abū al ‘Aṭā, Jabal** ⛰ Syria
216 *E6* **Abū al Ḩuşayn, Khabrat** ◎ N Jordan
217 *I5* **Abū al Jīr** Al Anbār, C Iraq *33°16′N 42°55′E*
217 *M8* **Abū al Khaşīb** *var.* Abul Khasib. Al Başrah, SE Iraq *30°26′N 48°00′E*
217 *K8* **Abū at Tubrah, Thaqb** *well* S Iraq
219 *B11* **Abu Aweigila** Egypt *30°50′N 34°07′E*
Abu Balâs *see* Abu Ballās
129 *H5* **Abu Ballās** *var.* Abu Balâs. ▲ SW Egypt *24°28′N 27°36′E*
Abu Dhabi *see* Abū Ẓabī
217 *I5* **Abū Farūkh** Al Anbār, C Iraq *33°06′N 43°18′E*
134 *H3* **Abu Gabra** Eastern Darfur, W Sudan *11°02′N 26°50′E*
217 *H6* **Abū Ghār, Sha‘īb** *dry watercourse* S Iraq
129 *J8* **Abu Hamed** River Nile, N Sudan *19°32′N 33°20′E*
216 *G4* **Abū Ḩardān** *var.* Hajîne. Dayr az Zawr, E Syria *34°45′N 40°49′E*
217 *J5* **Abū Ḩasāwīyah** Diyālá, E Iraq *33°52′N 44°47′E*
216 *E6* **Abū Ḩifnah, Wādī** *dry watercourse* N Jordan
133 *K7* **Abuja** ● (Nigeria) Federal Capital District, C Nigeria *09°04′N 07°28′E*
217 *I6* **Abū Jahaf, Wādī** *dry watercourse* C Iraq
104 *E5* **Abujao, Río** 〰 E Peru
217 *J8* **Abū Jasrah** Al Muthanná, S Iraq *30°43′N 44°50′E*
219 *F12* **Abū Jurdhān** Jordan
216 *G4* **Abū Kamāl** *Fr.* Abou Kémal. Dayr az Zawr, E Syria *34°29′N 40°56′E*
260 *D5* **Abuki, Pegunungan** ⛰ Sulawesi, C Indonesia
253 *D11* **Abukuma-gawa** 〰 Honshū, C Japan
253 *D11* **Abukuma-sanchi** ⛰ Honshū, C Japan
Abula *see* Ávila
Abul Khasib *see* Abū al Khaşīb
134 *F6* **Abumombazi** *var.* Abumonbazi. Equateur, N Dem. Rep. Congo *03°43′N 22°06′E*
Abumonbazi *see* Abumombazi
106 *E6* **Abunã** Rondônia, W Brazil *09°41′S 65°20′W*
106 *D7* **Abunã, Rio** *var.* Río Abuná. 〰 Bolivia/Brazil
219 *G8* **Abū Nuşayr** *var.* Abu Nuseir. ‘Ammān, W Jordan *32°03′N 35°58′E*
219 *G8* **Abū Nuşayr** Jordan *32°05′N 35°52′E*
Abu Nuseir *see* Abū Nuşayr
217 *J8* **Abū Qabr** Al Muthanná, S Iraq *31°03′N 44°34′E*
218 *I2* **Abu Raḩbah** Syria *34°26′N 37°12′E*
216 *E4* **Abū Raḩbah, Jabal** ⛰ C Syria
217 *I4* **Abū Rajāsh** Şalāḩ ad Dīn, N Iraq *34°47′N 43°36′E*
217 *K8* **Abū Raqrāq, Ghadīr** *well* S Iraq
232 *C7* **Ābu Road** Rājasthān, N India *24°29′N 72°47′E*
136 *E1* **Abu Shagara, Ras** *headland* NE Sudan *18°04′N 38°31′E*
129 *I6* **Abu Simbel** *var.* Abu Sūnbul. *headland* Egypt
Abu Simbel *see* Abū Sunbul
217 *K8* **Abū Sudayrah** Al Muthanná, S Iraq *30°55′N 44°58′E*
217 *J7* **Abū Şukhayr** Al Qādisīyah, S Iraq *31°54′N 44°27′E*
Abu Sūnbul *see* Abu Simbel
Abū Sunbul *see* Abū Sunbul
252 *D5* **Abuta** Hokkaidō, NE Japan *42°34′N 140°44′E*
219 *G12* **Abū Ţarafah, Wādī** *dry watercourse* Jordan
279 *C9* **Abut Head** *headland* South Island, New Zealand *43°06′S 170°16′E*
136 *A1* **Abu ‘Urug** Northern Kordofan, C Sudan *15°52′N 30°25′E*
136 *E4* **Ābuyē Mēda** ▲ C Ethiopia *10°28′N 39°44′E*
263 *M7* **Abuyog** Leyte, C Philippines *10°45′N 124°58′E*
134 *J2* **Abu Zabad** Western Kordofan, C Sudan *12°21′N 29°16′E*
221 *J4* **Abū Ẓabī** *var.* Abū Ẓabī, *Eng.* Abu Dhabi. ● (United Arab Emirates) Abū Ẓaby, C United Arab Emirates *24°30′N 54°20′E*
Abū Ẓabī *see* Abū Ẓabī
129 *J3* **Abu Zenīma** E Egypt *29°01′N 33°08′E*
155 *H9* **Åby** Östergötland, S Sweden *58°40′N 16°10′E*
Abyaḍ, Al Baḩr al *see* White Nile
Åbybro *see* Aabybro
134 *I3* **Abyei** Southern Kordofan, S Sudan *09°35′N 28°28′E*
134 *I3* **Abyei Area** ⬗ *disputed region* Western Kordofan, S Sudan
Abyla *see* Ávila
Abymes *see* les Abymes
Abyssinia *see* Ethiopia
Açâba *see* Assaba
102 *C6* **Acacias** Meta, C Colombia *03°59′N 73°46′W*
55 *L3* **Acadia, Cape** *headland* Nunavut, C Canada
111 *I3* **Acaiaca** Minas Gerais, Brazil *20°21′S 43°09′W*
108 *C4* **Açailândia** Maranhão, E Brazil *04°51′S 47°26′W*
Acaill *see* Achill Island
88 *C5* **Acajutla** Sonsonate, W El Salvador *13°34′N 89°50′W*
172 *E7* **Acalá del Río** Andalucía, Spain *37°31′N 5°59′W*
134 *A7* **Acalayong** SW Equatorial Guinea *01°05′N 09°34′E*
86 *E6* **Acámbaro** Guanajuato, C Mexico *20°01′N 100°42′W*
86 *E6* **Acambay** México, Mexico *19°57′N 99°51′W*
102 *A4* **Acandí** Chocó, NW Colombia *08°32′N 77°20′W*
170 *C3* **A Cañiza** *var.* La Cañiza. Galicia, NW Spain *42°13′N 08°16′W*
86 *B3* **Acaponeta** Nayarit, C Mexico *22°30′N 105°21′W*
85 *I8* **Acaponeta, Río de** 〰 C Mexico
86 *E8* **Acapulco** *var.* Acapulco de Juárez. Guerrero, S Mexico *16°51′N 99°53′W*
Acapulco de Juárez *see* Acapulco
103 *J7* **Acarai Mountains** *Sp.* Serra Acaraí. ⛰ Brazil/Guyana
Acaraí, Serra *see* Acarai Mountains
108 *G3* **Acaraú** Ceará, NE Brazil *04°35′S 37°37′W*
102 *E3* **Acarigua** Portuguesa, N Venezuela *09°35′N 69°12′W*
170 *D1* **A Carreira** Galicia, NW Spain *43°21′N 08°12′W*
86 *F5* **Acatepec** Puebla, Mexico
86 *F7* **Acatepec** Puebla, Mexico *19°02′N 98°17′W*
85 *M7* **Acatlán** Jalisco, W Mexico *23°58′N 99°08′W*
87 *H7* **Acatlán** Oaxaca, Mexico *18°32′N 96°37′W*
86 *F7* **Acatlán** *var.* Acatlán de Osorio. Puebla, S Mexico *18°12′N 98°02′W*
86 *C5* **Acatlán de Juárez** Jalisco, Mexico *20°25′N 103°35′W*
Acatlán de Osorio *see* Acatlán
87 *I7* **Acayucan** *var.* Acayucán. Veracruz-Llave, E Mexico *17°59′N 94°58′W*
Accho *see* Akko
67 *M4* **Accomac** Virginia, NE USA *37°43′N 75°41′N*
168 *D6* **Accous** Aquitaine, France *42°59′N 0°36′W*
133 *H8* **Accra** ● (Ghana)SE Ghana *05°33′N 00°15′W*
159 *J9* **Accrington** NW England, United Kingdom *53°46′N 02°21′W*
114 *B7* **Acebal** Santa Fe, C Argentina *33°14′S 60°50′W*
115 *K4* **Aceguá** Rio Grande du Sol, S Brazil *31°52′S 54°12′W*
115 *K4* **Acegua** Cerro Largo, Uruguay *31°48′S 54°18′W*
258 *C3* **Aceh** *off.* Daerah Istimewa Aceh, *var.* Acheen, Achin, Atchin, Atjeh. ⬗ *autonomous district* NW Indonesia
175 *H9* **Acerenza** Basilicata, S Italy *40°46′N 15°51′E*
184 *A8* **Acerra** *anc.* Acerrae. Campania, S Italy *40°56′N 14°22′E*
Acerrae *see* Acerra

◆ Country
● Country Capital
◇ Dependent Territory
○ Dependent Territory Capital
⬗ Administrative Regions
✈ International Airport
▲ Mountain
⛰ Mountain Range
Volcano
〰 River
◎ Lake
⊞ Reservoir

◆ Country ◇ Dependent Territory ◇ Administrative Regions ▲ Mountain ▲ Volcano ◎ Lake
● Country Capital ○ Dependent Territory Capital ✈ International Airport ▲ Mountain Range ◆ River ▣ Reservoir

◆ Country ● Country Capital ◇ Dependent Territory ○ Dependent Territory Capital ◇ Administrative Regions ✈ International Airport ▲ Mountain ▲ Mountain Range ☐ Volcano ☐ River ☐ Lake ☐ Reservoir

◆ Country
◆ Country Capital
◇ Dependent Territory
◇ Dependent Territory Capital
◆ Administrative Regions
✈ International Airport
ᴧ Mountain
▲ Mountain Range
▲ Volcano
ᛈ River
ᴏ Lake
◆ Reservoir

◆ Country   ◇ Dependent Territory   ▲ Mountain   ✕ Volcano   ⊗ Lake
● Country Capital   ◇ Dependent Territory Capital   ◆ Administrative Regions   ▲ Mountain Range   ✍ River   ⊠ Reservoir
✕ International Airport

◆ Country ◇ Dependent Territory ▲ Mountain ▲ Mountain Range ≈ River ⊘ Lake
◇ Country Capital ◇ Dependent Territory Capital ◆ Administrative Regions ✕ International Airport ⊠ Reservoir

◆ Country   ◇ Dependent Territory   ◆ Administrative Regions   ▲ Mountain   ☼ Volcano   ☒ Lake
● Country Capital   ○ Dependent Territory Capital   ✈ International Airport   ▲ Mountain Range   ☒ River   ☒ Reservoir

◆ Country　　◇ Dependent Territory　　▲ Administrative Regions　　▲ Mountain　　◆ Volcano　　◎ Lake
● Country Capital　　○ Dependent Territory Capital　　✕ International Airport　　▲▲ Mountain Range　　♒ River　　⊞ Reservoir

| ◆ Country | ◇ Dependent Territory | ✈ Administrative Regions | ▲ Mountain | ☎ Volcano | ◎ Lake |
| ● Country Capital | ○ Dependent Territory Capital | ✈ International Airport | ▲ Mountain Range | ♣ River | ⊠ Reservoir |

◆ Country   ◇ Dependent Territory   ◈ Administrative Regions   ▲ Mountain   ☈ Volcano   ☒ Lake
● Country Capital   ○ Dependent Territory Capital   ✈ International Airport   ▲ Mountain Range   ☇ River   ☒ Reservoir

◆ Country ◇ Dependent Territory ◆ Administrative Regions ▲ Mountain ✖ Volcano ◦ Lake
● Country Capital ○ Dependent Territory Capital ✖ International Airport ▲ Mountain Range ≈ River ◦ Reservoir

◆ Country   ◇ Dependent Territory   ◈ Administrative Regions   ▲ Mountain   ◊ Volcano   ◎ Lake
● Country Capital   ○ Dependent Territory Capital   ✈ International Airport   ▲ Mountain Range   ≈ River   ■ Reservoir

F

285 M3 **Faaa** Tahiti, W French Polynesia 17°32´S 149°36´W
285 M3 **Faaa** ✈ (Papeete) Tahiti, W French Polynesia
155 D13 **Faaborg** var. Fåborg. Syddtjylland, C Denmark 55°06´N 10°15´E
235 C11 **Faadhippolhu Atoll** var. Fadiffolu, Lhaviyani Atoll. atoll N Maldives
285 J8 **Faaite** atoll Îles Tuamotu, C French Polynesia
285 M4 **Faaone** Tahiti, W French Polynesia 17°39´S 149°18´W
154 F5 **Fåberg** Oppland, S Norway 61°15´N 10°21´E
52 D9 **Faber Lake** ☒ Northwest Territories, W Canada
 Fåborg see Faaborg
177 I10 **Fabriano** Marche, C Italy 43°20´N 12°54´E
227 K7 **Fabrichnoye** prev. Fabrichnyy. Almaty, SE Kazakhstan
195 M8 **Fabrichnoye** Sverdlovskaya Oblast', Russian Federation
 Fabrichnyy see Fabrichnoye
102 G5 **Facatativá** Cundinamarca, C Colombia 04°49´N 74°22´W
133 L3 **Fachi** Agadez, C Niger 18°01´N 11°36´E
172 F13 **Facinas** Andalucía, Spain 36°08´N 5°42´W
282 A2 **Fayu/Faiyel Island** var. Fayaulep. atoll Caroline Islands, C Micronesia
64 E4 **Factoryville** Pennsylvania, NE USA 41°34´N 75°45´W
134 C6 **Fada** Ennedi-Ouest, E Chad 17°14´N 21°32´E
172 E4 **Fada** Enugu State, Nigeria 07°23´W
133 I5 **Fada-Ngourma** E Burkina Faso 12°N 00°26´E
193 I3 **Faddeya, Zaliv** bay N Russian Federation
193 I3 **Faddeyevskiy, Poluostrov** island Novosibirskiye Ostrova, NE Russian Federation
221 K7 **Fadli** Yemen 13°51´N 46°22´E
177 H8 **Faenza** anc. Faventia. Emilia-Romagna, N Italy 44°17´N 11°53´E
 Faeroe-Iceland Ridge see Faroe-Iceland Ridge
 Faeroe Islands see Faroe Islands
 Færøerne see Faroe Islands
 Faeroe-Shetland Trough see Faroe-Shetland Trough
170 G3 **Fafe** island Tongatapu Group, S Tonga
136 G4 **Fafen Shet'** ✍ E Ethiopia
284 D9 **Fafo** island Tongatapu Group, S Tonga
285 J3 **Fagaloa Bay** bay Upolu, E Samoa
285 J4 **Fagamalo** Savai'i, N Samoa 13°27´S 172°22´W
188 E4 **Făgăraş** Ger. Fogarasch, Hung. Fogaras. Braşov, C Romania 45°50´N 24°59´E
57 F6 **Fagatau** prev. Fangataufa. atoll Îles Tuamotu, C French Polynesia
285 K9 **Fagataufa** prev. Fangataufa. island Îles Tuamotu, SE French Polynesia
155 H10 **Fagerhult** Sweden 57°07´N 15°40´E
155 G8 **Fagernes** Oppland, S Norway 60°59´N 09°14´E
154 I7 **Fagersta** Västmanland, C Sweden 59°59´N 15°49´E
133 L5 **Faggo** var. Foggo. Bauchi, N Nigeria 11°22´N 09°55´E
117 C12 **Fagnano, Lago** ☒ S Argentina
163 E11 **Fagne** hill range S Belgium
132 E3 **Faguibine, Lac** var. Lake Fagibina. ☒ NW Mali
 Fahaheel see Al Fuḥayḥīl
 Fahlun see Falun
172 C3 **Faia** var. Faiã. Guarda, Portugal 40°18´N 07°30´E
170 A8 **Faial** Madeira, Portugal, NE Atlantic Ocean
172 B9 **Faial** var. Ilha do Faial. island Azores, Portugal, NE Atlantic Ocean
 Faial Island see Faylaka
284 C10 **Faioa, Île** island N Wallis and Futuna
275 J3 **Fairbairn Reservoir** ☒ Queensland, E Australia
55 J4 **Fairbanks** Alaska, USA 64°48´N 147°47´W
67 K7 **Fair Bluff** North Carolina, SE USA 34°19´N 79°02´W
73 G10 **Fairborn** Ohio, N USA 39°48´N 84°03´W
73 D10 **Fairbury** Illinois, N USA 40°45´N 88°30´W
74 F7 **Fairbury** Nebraska, C USA 40°08´N 97°10´W
80 C2 **Fairfax** California, USA 37°59´N 122°35´W
75 F9 **Fairfax** Missouri, C USA 40°19´N 95°23´W
75 F10 **Fairfax** Oklahoma, C USA 36°34´N 96°42´W
67 K3 **Fairfax** South Carolina, SE USA 32°57´N 81°14´W
79 N5 **Fairfax** Virginia, NE USA 38°50´N 77°18´W
65 G9 **Fairfield** Connecticut, USA 41°08´N 73°22´W
63 I10 **Fairfield** Idaho, NW USA 43°20´N 114°45´W
73 C12 **Fairfield** Illinois, N USA 38°22´N 88°21´W
74 H7 **Fairfield** Iowa, C USA 41°00´N 91°57´W
62 J2 **Fairfield** Montana, NW USA 47°37´N 111°59´W
57 G11 **Fairfield** Ohio, N USA 39°21´N 84°34´W
70 H5 **Fairfield** Texas, SW USA 31°44´N 96°10´W
161 J5 **Fairford** United Kingdom 51°42´N 1°47´W
59 K4 **Fair Grove** Missouri, C USA 37°22´N 93°09´W
65 H1 **Fair Haven** Massachusetts, NE USA 41°38´N 70°52´W
75 C10 **Fair Head Ir. An Fhaiodh.** headland N Northern Ireland, United Kingdom
68 C4 **Fairhope** Alabama, S USA 30°31´N 87°54´W
54 C3 **Fair Isle** island NE Scotland, United Kingdom
278 D10 **Fairlie** Canterbury, South Island, New Zealand 44°06´S 170°50´E
75 G10 **Fairland** Oklahoma, C USA 36°45´N 94°51´W
74 F7 **Fairmont** Minnesota, N USA 43°39´N 94°27´W
74 E6 **Fairmont** Nebraska, C USA 40°38´N 97°35´W
62 E5 **Fairmont** West Virginia, NE USA 39°28´N 80°08´W
79 L3 **Fairmount** Colorado, C USA
79 J4 **Fairview** Alberta, W Canada 56°05´N 118°28´W
74 C7 **Fairview** Michigan, N USA
79 L3 **Fairview** Montana, NW USA 47°51´N 104°03´W
75 E9 **Fairview** Oklahoma, C USA 36°16´N 98°29´W
79 H4 **Fairview** Utah, W USA 39°37´N 111°26´W

◆ Country
● Country Capital
◇ Dependent Territory
○ Dependent Territory Capital
◆ Administrative Regions
✕ International Airport
▲ Mountain
▲ Mountain Range
▲ Volcano
✍ River
☒ Lake
☒ Reservoir

◆ Country
● Country Capital
◇ Dependent Territory
○ Dependent Territory Capital
◈ Administrative Regions
✕ International Airport
▲ Mountain
▲▲ Mountain Range
▲ Volcano
♒ River
☒ Lake
☒ Reservoir

◆ Country   ◇ Dependent Territory   ◆ Administrative Regions   ▲ Mountain   ☒ Volcano   ◎ Lake
● Country Capital   ○ Dependent Territory Capital   ✈ International Airport   ▲ Mountain Range   ☞ River   ⊡ Reservoir

Ghadāmis - Gongyi
INDEX
344

128 B3 **Ghadāmis** *var.* Ghadamès, Rhadames. W Libya 30°08′N 09°30′E
221 K6 **Ghadan** E Oman 20°20′N 57°58′E
128 C4 **Ghaddūwah** C Libya 26°36′N 14°26′E
229 I6 **Ghafurov** *Rus.* Gafurov; *prev.* Sovetabad. NW Tajikistan 40°13′N 69°42′E
233 H6 **Ghāghara** ≈ S Asia
230 G8 **Ghaibi Dero** Sind, SE Pakistan 27°35′N 67°42′E
221 L5 **Ghalat** E Oman 21°06′N 58°51′E
217 L7 **Ghamūkah, Hawr** ◎ S Iraq
132 G7 **Ghana** *off.* Republic of Ghana. ◆ *republic* W Africa
221 K6 **Ghānah** *spring/well* S Oman 18°35′N 56°34′E
Ghanongga *see* Ranongga
Ghansi/Ghansiland *see* Ghanzi
138 E5 **Ghanzi** *var.* Khanzi. Ghanzi, W Botswana 21°39′S 21°38′E
138 E5 **Ghanzi** *var.* Ghansi, Ghansiland, Khanzi. ◈ *district* C Botswana
121 K8 **Ghanzi** *var.* Knanzi. ≈ Botswana/South Africa
Ghap'an *see* Kapan
219 E12 **Gharandal** Al'Aqabah, SW Jordan 30°12′N 35°18′E
217 K9 **Gharbīyah, Sha'īb al** ≈ S Iraq
Gharbt, Jabal al *see* Liban, Jebel
131 I3 **Ghardaïa** N Algeria 32°30′N 03°44′E
175 A13 **Ghardimaou** Tunisia
218 G6 **Ghārīyat ash Sharqīyah** Syria 32°40′N 36°16′E
229 J7 **Gharm** *Rus.* Garm. C Tajikistan 39°03′N 70°25′E
230 G10 **Gharo** Sind, SE Pakistan 24°44′N 67°35′E
217 L7 **Gharrāf, Shaṭṭ al** ≈ S Iraq
Gharvān *see* Gharyān
128 C2 **Gharyān** *var.* Gharvān. NW Libya 32°10′N 13°01′E
128 A5 **Ghāt** *var.* Gat. SW Libya 24°58′N 10°11′E
Ghawdex *see* Gozo
221 I4 **Ghayathi** Abū Ẓaby, W United Arab Emirates 23°51′N 53°01′E
Ghazāl, Baḥr al *see* Ghazal, Bahr el
133 N4 **Ghazal, Bahr el** *var.* Soro. *seasonal river* C Chad
136 A4 **Ghazal, Bahr el** *var.* Baḥr al Ghazāl. ≈ N South Sudan
229 I5 **Ghazalkent** Toshkent Viloyati, E Uzbekistan 41°30′N 69°46′E
130 G2 **Ghazaouet** NW Algeria 35°08′N 01°50′W
232 E5 **Ghāziābād** Uttar Pradesh, N India 28°42′N 77°28′E
233 H7 **Ghāzīpur** Uttar Pradesh, N India 25°36′N 83°36′E
230 G4 **Ghaznī** *var.* Ghazni. Ghaznī, E Afghanistan 33°31′N 68°24′E
230 G4 **Ghaznī** ◈ *province* SE Afghanistan
Ghazzah *see* Gaza
218 F4 **Ghazzé** Lebanon 33°40′N 35°49′E
Gheel *see* Geel
219 A13 **Gheita, Wâdi** Egypt
Ghelîzâne *see* Relizane
Ghent *see* Gent
Gheorghe Braţul *see* Sfântu Gheorghe, Braţul
Gheorghe Gheorghiu-Dej *see* Oneşti
188 D7 **Gheorgheni** *prev.* Gheorghieni, Sîn-Miclăuş, *Ger.* Niklasmarkt, *Hung.* Gyergyószentmiklós. Harghita, C Romania 46°43′N 25°36′E
Gheorghieni *see* Gheorgheni
188 C7 **Gherla** *Ger.* Neuschliss, *Hung.* Szamosújvár; *prev.* Armenierstadt. Cluj, NW Romania 47°02′N 23°55′E
Gheweifat *see* Ghuwayfāt
228 G6 **Ghijduwon** Buxoro Viloyati, C Uzbekistan 40°06′N 64°39′E
Ghilan *see* Gīlān
175 B10 **Ghilarza** Sardegna, Italy, C Mediterranean Sea 40°09′N 08°50′E
Ghilizane *see* Relizane
Ghimbi *see* Gīmbī
Ghiriş *see* Câmpia Turzii
175 C8 **Ghisonaccia** Corse, France, C Mediterranean Sea 42°00′N 09°25′E
Ghizo *see* Gizo
159 H1 **Ghlo, Beinn a'** ▲ United Kingdom 56°50′N 3°43′W
229 I6 **Ghonchí** *Rus.* Ganchi. NW Tajikistan 39°57′N 69°10′E
233 K7 **Ghoraghat** Rajshahi, NW Bangladesh 25°18′N 89°20′E
230 D3 **Ghōrīān** *prev.* Ghūrīān. Herāt, W Afghanistan 34°20′N 61°26′E
231 H7 **Ghotki** Sind, SE Pakistan 28°00′N 69°21′E
Ghowr *see* Gōwr
171 J10 **Ghriss** Algeria
229 K7 **Ghŭdara** *var.* Gudara, *Rus.* Kudara. SE Tajikistan 38°28′N 72°39′E
233 J7 **Ghugri** ≈ N India
229 K7 **Ghund** *Rus.* Gunt. ≈ SE Tajikistan
Ghurābīyah, Sha'īb al *see* Gharbīyah, Sha'īb al
Ghurdaqah *see* Al Ghurdaqah
Ghūrīān *see* Ghōrīān
221 I4 **Ghuwayfāt** *var.* Gheweifat. Abū Ẓaby, W United Arab Emirates 24°06′N 51°40′E
140 G9 **Ghwarriepoort pas** Eastern Cape, South Africa
186 G5 **Giáltra** Évvoia, C Greece 38°21′N 22°58′E
Giamame *see* Jamaame
257 I9 **Gia Nghia** *var.* Đak Nông. Đăc Lăc, S Vietnam 11°58′N 107°42′E
186 G3 **Giannitsá** *var.* Yiannitsá. Kentrikí Makedonía, N Greece 40°49′N 22°24′E
175 D8 **Giannutri, Isola di** *island* Archipelago Toscano, C Italy
158 D5 **Giant's Causeway** *Ir.* Clochán an Aifir. *lava flow* N Northern Ireland, United Kingdom
257 H10 **Gia Rai** Minh Hai, S Vietnam 09°14′N 105°28′E
175 G12 **Giarre** Sicilia, Italy, C Mediterranean Sea 37°44′N 15°12′E
169 H1 **Giat** Auvergne, France 45°48′N 2°29′E
169 M3 **Giaveno** Piemonte, NW Italy 45°02′N 07°21′E
90 F4 **Gibara** Holguín, E Cuba 21°09′N 76°11′W
75 D8 **Gibbon** Nebraska, C USA 40°45′N 98°50′W
76 E5 **Gibbon** Oregon, NW USA 45°40′N 118°22′W
77 H5 **Gibbonsville** Idaho, NW USA 45°33′N 113°55′W
67 M10 **Gibbs Hill** *hill* S Bermuda
140 C3 **Gibeon** Hardap, Namibia 25°08′S 17°46′E
152 F4 **Gibostad** Troms, N Norway 69°21′N 18°01′E
170 D8 **Gibraleón** Andalucía, S Spain 37°23′N 06°58′W
170 E9 **Gibraltar** ○ (Gibraltar) S Gibraltar 36°08′N 05°21′W
130 G2 **Gibraltar** ◇ *UK dependent territory* SW Europe
Gibraltar, Détroit de/Gibraltar, Estrecho de *see* Gibraltar, Strait of
170 E9 **Gibraltar, Strait of** *Fr.* Détroit de Gibraltar, *Sp.* Estrecho de Gibraltar. *strait* Atlantic Ocean/Mediterranean Sea
73 H9 **Gibsonburg** Ohio, N USA 41°22′N 83°19′W
73 D10 **Gibson City** Illinois, N USA 40°27′N 88°24′W
276 A1 **Gibson Desert** *desert* Western Australia
56 D8 **Gibsons** British Columbia, SW Canada 49°24′N 123°32′W
230 F7 **Gīdār** Baluchistān, SW Pakistan 28°16′N 66°00′E
234 F6 **Giddalūr** Andhra Pradesh, E India 15°24′N 78°54′E
71 H7 **Giddings** Texas, SW USA 30°12′N 96°59′W
75 J11 **Gideon** Missouri, C USA 36°27′N 89°55′W
219 A13 **Gidil, Wâdi Abu** Egypt
136 D6 **Gīdolē** Southern Nationalities, S Ethiopia 05°31′N 37°26′E
218 E6 **Gidona** Israel 32°32′N 35°21′E
181 H13 **Giebelstadt** Bayern, Germany 49°39′E 9°57′N
Giebnegáisi *see* Kebnekaise
181 I8 **Gieboldehausen** Niedersachsen, Germany 51°37′E 10°13′N
191 E8 **Giedraičiai** Utena, E Lithuania 55°05′N 25°16′E
165 H4 **Gien** Loiret, C France 47°40′N 02°37′E
169 L6 **Giens** Provence-Alpes-Côte d'Azur, France 43°02′N 6°08′E
140 G7 **Giesenskraal** Northern Cape, South Africa 30°32′S 23°18′E
181 F10 **Giessen** Hessen, W Germany 50°35′N 08°41′E
181 J10 **Giessübel** Thüringen, Germany 50°32′E 10°55′N
162 I4 **Gieten** Drenthe, NE Netherlands 53°00′N 06°43′E
158 G3 **Giffnock** United Kingdom 55°48′N 4°17′W
159 I3 **Gifford** United Kingdom 55°54′N 2°44′W
69 N7 **Gifford** Florida, SE USA 27°40′N 80°24′W
53 I7 **Gifford** ≈ Baffin Island, Nunavut, NE Canada
180 I5 **Gifhorn** Niedersachsen, N Germany 52°28′N 10°33′E
57 H3 **Gift Lake** Alberta, W Canada 55°49′N 115°57′W
Giftokastro *see* Tsigansko Gradishte
251 J4 **Gifu** *var.* Gihu. Gifu, Honshū, SW Japan 35°24′N 136°46′E
251 J3 **Gifu** *off.* Gifu-ken, *var.* Gihu. ◈ *prefecture* Honshū, SW Japan
Gifu-ken *see* Gifu
196 G7 **Gigant** Rostovskaya Oblast', SW Russian Federation 46°29′N 41°18′E
84 E6 **Giganta, Sierra de la** ▲▲ NW Mexico
102 B7 **Gigante** Huila, S Colombia 02°24′N 75°34′W
185 J5 **Gigen** Pleven, N Bulgaria 43°40′N 24°31′E
Giggiga *see* Jijiga
159 J8 **Giggleswick** United Kingdom 54°03′N 2°16′W
158 E4 **Gigha Island** *island* SW Scotland, United Kingdom
158 E4 **Gigha, Sound of** *strait* W Scotland, United Kingdom
175 D8 **Giglio, Isola del** *island* Archipelago Toscano, C Italy
Gihu *see* Gifu
250 B4 **Gijang** *prev.* Kijang. 35°14′N 129°12′E
228 G6 **G'ijduvon** *Rus.* Gizhduvon. Buxoro Viloyati, C Uzbekistan 40°06′N 64°38′E
170 E1 **Gijón** *var.* Xixón. Asturias, NW Spain 43°32′N 05°40′W
137 A9 **Gikongoro** SW Rwanda 02°30′S 29°32′E
79 H9 **Gila Bend** Arizona, SW USA 32°57′N 112°43′W
79 H9 **Gila Bend Mountains** ▲▲ Arizona, SW USA
79 J9 **Gila Mountains** ▲▲ Arizona, SW USA
78 G9 **Gila Mountains** ▲▲ Arizona, SW USA
222 E2 **Gīlān** *off.* Ostān-e Gīlān, *var.* Ghilan, Guilan. ◈ *province* NW Iran
Gīlān, Ostān-e *see* Gīlān
79 H9 **Gila River** ≈ Arizona, SW USA
114 D6 **Gilbert** Entre Ríos, Argentina 32°32′S 58°56′W
74 H3 **Gilbert** Minnesota, N USA 47°29′N 92°27′W
Gilbert Islands *see* Tungaru
56 D7 **Gilbert, Mount** ▲ British Columbia, SW Canada 50°49′N 124°03′W
275 I3 **Gilbert River** ≈ Queensland, NE Australia
42 B4 **Gilbert Seamounts** *undersea feature* NE Pacific Ocean 52°50′N 150°10′W
159 H6 **Gilcrux** United Kingdom 54°43′N 3°22′W
180 C6 **Gildehaus** Niedersachsen, Germany 52°18′E 7°07′N
77 I3 **Gildford** Montana, NW USA 48°34′N 110°21′W
139 K2 **Gilé** Zambézia, NE Mozambique 16°10′S 28°17′E
141 J2 **Gilead** Limpopo, South Africa 23°39′S 28°52′E
72 C4 **Gile Flowage** ◎ Wisconsin, N USA
276 F4 **Giles, Lake** *salt lake* South Australia
Gilf Kebir Plateau *see* Haḍabat al Jilf al Kabīr
158 D7 **Gilford** United Kingdom 54°22′N 6°20′W
277 K4 **Gilgandra** New South Wales, SE Australia 31°43′S 148°39′E
Gîlgău *see* Gâlgău
137 D8 **Gilgil** Nakuru, SW Kenya 0°29′S 36°19′E
231 J2 **Gilgit** Jammu and Kashmir, NE Pakistan 35°54′N 74°20′E
231 I2 **Gilgit** ≈ N Pakistan
55 J7 **Gillam** Manitoba, C Canada 56°25′N 94°45′W
155 F12 **Gilleleje** Hovedstaden, E Denmark 56°05′N 12°17′E
181 C11 **Gillenfeld** Rheinland-Pfalz, Germany 50°07′E 6°54′N
73 C11 **Gillespie** Illinois, N USA 39°07′N 89°49′W
75 I13 **Gillett** Arkansas, C USA 34°07′N 91°22′W
77 L6 **Gillette** Wyoming, C USA 44°17′N 105°30′W
53 K7 **Gillian, Lake** ◎ Nunavut, NE Canada
161 L6 **Gillingham** SE England, United Kingdom 51°24′N 00°33′E
158 A7 **Gill, Lough** ◎ Ireland
293 L4 **Gillock Island** *island* Antarctica
137 I10 **Gillot** ✈ (St-Denis) N Réunion 20°53′S 55°31′E
132 G10 **Gill Point** *headland* E Saint Helena 15°59′S 05°38′W
73 D10 **Gilman** Illinois, N USA 40°44′N 87°58′W
71 I4 **Gilmer** Texas, SW USA 32°44′N 94°58′W
159 H2 **Gilmerton** United Kingdom 56°23′N 3°48′W
55 M4 **Gilmour Island** *Island* Nunavut, C Canada
Gilolo *see* Halmahera, Pulau
136 C5 **Gīlo Wenz** ≈ SW Ethiopia
80 B4 **Gilroy** California, W USA 37°00′N 121°34′W
261 N7 **Giluwe, Mount** ▲ W Papua New Guinea 06°03′S 143°52′E
193 J7 **Gilyuy** ≈ SE Russian Federation
163 F8 **Gilze** Noord-Brabant, S Netherlands 51°33′N 04°56′E
251 H9 **Gima** Okinawa, Kume-jima, SW Japan
136 D4 **Gīmbī** *It.* Ghimbi. Oromīya, C Ethiopia 09°13′N 35°39′E
248 C6 **Gimcheon** *prev.* Kimch'ŏn. C South Korea 36°08′N 128°06′E
248 C7 **Gimhae** *prev.* Kim Hae. ✈ (Busan) SE South Korea 35°10′N 128°57′E
91 J3 **Gimie, Mount** ▲ C Saint Lucia 13°51′N 61°00′W
55 J9 **Gimli** Manitoba, S Canada 50°39′N 97°00′W
Gimma *see* Jīma
154 I7 **Gimo** Uppsala, C Sweden 60°11′N 18°12′E
171 J1 **Gimone** ≈ S France
168 F5 **Gimont** Midi-Pyrénées, France 43°38′N 0°52′E
Gimpoe *see* Gimpu
260 C4 **Gimpu** *prev.* Gimpoe. Sulawesi, C Indonesia 01°38′S 120°00′E
276 E3 **Gina** South Australia 29°56′S 134°33′E
Ginevra *see* Genève
163 F10 **Gingelom** Limburg, NE Belgium 50°46′N 05°09′E
274 D7 **Gingin** Western Australia 31°22′S 115°51′E
141 L6 **Gingindlovu** KwaZulu-Natal, South Africa 29°01′S 31°35′E
Gingindlovu *see* KwaGingindlovu
263 M8 **Gingoog** Mindanao, S Philippines 08°47′N 125°05′E
136 F5 **Gīnīr** Oromīya, C Ethiopia 07°12′N 40°43′E
218 F6 **Ginnosar** Israel 32°50′N 35°31′E
Giohar *see* Jawhar
175 I9 **Gióia del Colle** Puglia, SE Italy 40°47′N 16°56′E
175 H12 **Gioia, Golfo di** *gulf* S Italy
Giona *see* Gkióna
187 H4 **Gioúra** *island* Vóreies Sporádes, Greece, Aegean Sea
175 I9 **Giovinazzo** Puglia, SE Italy 41°11′N 16°40′E
Gipeswic *see* Ipswich
171 H2 **Gipuzkoa** *Cast.* Guipúzcoa. ◈ *province* País Vasco, N Spain
219 D13 **Girâfi, Wâdi** Egypt
Giran *see* Ilan
73 C11 **Girard** Illinois, N USA 39°27′N 89°46′W
75 G10 **Girard** Kansas, C USA 37°30′N 94°50′W
70 E4 **Girard** Texas, SW USA 33°18′N 100°38′W
102 C6 **Girardot** Cundinamarca, C Colombia 04°19′N 74°47′W
289 C9 **Giraud Seamount** *undersea feature* SW Indian Ocean 09°57′S 46°55′E
135 B13 **Giraul** ≈ SW Angola
156 G5 **Girdle Ness** *headland* NE Scotland, United Kingdom 57°09′N 02°04′W
215 H5 **Giresun** *var.* Kerasunt; *anc.* Cerasus, Pharnacia. Giresun, NE Turkey 40°55′N 38°35′E
215 H5 **Giresun** *var.* Kerasunt. ◈ *province* NE Turkey
215 H5 **Giresun Dağları** ▲▲ N Turkey
Girga *see* Jirjā
Girgeh *see* Jirjā
Girgenti *see* Agrigento
233 I8 **Girīdīh** Jhārkhand, NE India 24°10′N 86°20′E
277 J4 **Girilambone** New South Wales, SE Australia 31°19′S 146°57′E
Girin *see* Jilin
218 C2 **Girne** *Gk.* Kerýneia, Kyrenia. N Cyprus 35°20′N 33°20′E
167 M7 **Giromagny** Franche-Comté, France 47°45′N 6°50′E
Giron *see* Kiruna
171 L3 **Girona** *var.* Gerona; *anc.* Gerunda. Cataluña, NE Spain 41°59′N 02°49′E
171 L3 **Girona** *var.* Gerona. ◈ *province* Cataluña, NE Spain
164 F7 **Gironde** ◈ *department* SW France
164 F6 **Gironde** *estuary* SW France
171 K3 **Gironella** Cataluña, NE Spain 42°02′N 01°53′E
165 H8 **Girou** ≈ S France
158 F5 **Girvan** W Scotland, United Kingdom 55°14′N 04°53′W
70 D6 **Girvin** Texas, SW USA 31°05′N 102°24′W
278 J5 **Gisborne** Gisborne, North Island, New Zealand 38°41′S 178°01′E
278 I5 **Gisborne** *off.* Gisborne District. ◈ *unitary authority* North Island, New Zealand
Gisborne District *see* Gisborne
159 J8 **Gisburn** United Kingdom 53°56′N 2°16′W
Giseifu *see* Uijeongbu
Gisenye *see* Gisenyi
137 A8 **Gisenyi** *var.* Gisenye. NW Rwanda 01°42′S 29°18′E
155 F10 **Gislaved** Jönköping, S Sweden 57°19′N 13°30′E
165 H3 **Gisors** Eure, N France 49°18′N 01°46′E
Gissar *see* Hisor
229 I7 **Gissar Range** *Rus.* Gissarskiy Khrebet. ▲▲ Tajikistan/Uzbekistan
Gissarskiy Khrebet *see* Gissar Range
163 B9 **Gistel** West-Vlaanderen, W Belgium 51°09′N 02°58′E
176 D4 **Giswil** Obwalden, C Switzerland 46°49′N 08°11′E
186 E4 **Gitánes** *ancient monument* Ípeiros, W Greece
137 A9 **Gitarama** C Rwanda 02°05′S 29°45′E
137 A9 **Gitega** C Burundi 03°20′S 29°56′E
Githio *see* Gýtheio
180 I7 **Gittelde** Niedersachsen, Germany 51°48′E 10°12′N
176 E5 **Giubiasco** Ticino, S Switzerland 46°11′N 09°01′E
174 F7 **Giulianova** Abruzzi, C Italy 42°45′N 13°58′E
Giulie, Alpi *see* Julian Alps
Giumri *see* Gyumri
188 F9 **Giurgeni** Ialomiţa, SE Romania 44°45′N 27°48′E
188 E10 **Giurgiu** Giurgiu, S Romania 43°54′N 25°58′E
188 E10 **Giurgiu** ◈ *county* SE Romania
218 D7 **Giv'at Hayyim** *var.* Giv'at Khaim. Central, C Israel 32°23′N 34°56′E
Giv'at Khaim *see* Giv'at Hayyim
155 C12 **Give** Syddanmark, C Denmark 55°51′N 09°15′E
166 G5 **Giverny** Haute-Normandie, France 49°04′N 1°32′E
167 J3 **Givet** Ardennes, N France 50°08′N 04°50′E
165 J6 **Givors** Rhône, E France 45°35′N 04°47′E
167 K5 **Givry-en-Argonne** Champagne-Ardenne, France 48°57′N 4°53′E
141 K2 **Giyani** Limpopo, NE South Africa 23°20′S 30°37′E
136 E4 **Giyon** Oromīya, C Ethiopia 08°31′N 37°56′E
129 I3 **Giza** *var.* Al Jīzah, El Gîza, Gizeh. N Egypt 30°01′N 31°13′E
129 I3 **Giza, Pyramids of** *ancient monument* N Egypt
Gizhduvon *see* G'ijduvon
193 M5 **Gizhiga** Magadanskaya Oblast', E Russian Federation 61°58′N 160°16′E
193 M5 **Gizhiginskaya Guba** *bay* E Russian Federation
281 H2 **Gizo** Gizo, NW Solomon Islands 08°03′S 156°49′E
281 H2 **Gizo** *var.* Ghizo. *island* NW Solomon Islands
182 H4 **Giżycko** *Ger.* Lötzen. Warmińsko-Mazurskie, NE Poland 54°03′N 21°48′E
Gízymałów *see* Hrymayliv
184 G7 **Gjakovë** *Serb.* Đakovica. W Kosovo 42°22′N 20°30′E
154 D5 **Gjende** ◎ S Norway
184 F6 **Gjeravicë** *Serb.* Đeravica. ▲ S Serbia 42°33′N 20°08′E
155 C8 **Gjerstad** Aust-Agder, S Norway 58°54′N 09°03′E
184 G6 **Gjilan** *Serb.* Gnjilane. E Kosovo 42°27′N 21°28′E
Gjinokastër *see* Gjirokastër
184 F10 **Gjirokastër** *var.* Gjirokastra; *prev.* Gjinokastër, *Gk.* Argyrokastron, *It.* Argirocastro. Gjirokastër, S Albania 40°04′N 20°09′E
184 F9 **Gjirokastër** ◈ *district* S Albania
Gjirokastra *see* Gjirokastër
53 H8 **Gjoa Haven** *var.* Uqsuqtuuq. King William Island, Nunavut, NW Canada 68°38′N 95°57′W
154 E6 **Gjøvik** Oppland, S Norway 60°47′N 10°40′E
184 E9 **Gjuhëzës, Kepi i** *headland* SW Albania 40°25′N 19°19′E
Gjurgjevac *see* Đurđevac
186 G5 **Gkióna** *var.* Giona. ▲▲ C Greece
218 D2 **Gkréko, Akrotíri** *var.* Cape Greco, Pidálion. *cape* E Cyprus
163 F10 **Glabbeek-Zuurbemde** Vlaams Brabant, C Belgium 50°54′N 04°58′E
59 K8 **Glace Bay** Cape Breton Island, Nova Scotia, SE Canada 46°12′N 59°57′W
56 G7 **Glacier** British Columbia, SW Canada 51°12′N 117°33′W
83 L7 **Glacier Bay** *inlet* Alaska, USA
76 D3 **Glacier Peak** ▲ Washington, NW USA 48°06′N 121°06′W
238 G8 **Gladaindong Feng** ▲ C China 33°24′N 91°00′E
181 C8 **Gladbeck** Nordrhein-Westfalen, Germany 51°34′E 6°59′N
141 J2 **Gladdeklipkop** Limpopo, South Africa 24°09′S 29°29′E
67 H5 **Glade Spring** Virginia, NE USA 36°47′N 81°46′W
160 G4 **Gladestry** United Kingdom 52°11′N 3°08′W
71 I4 **Gladewater** Texas, SW USA 32°32′N 94°57′W
275 K5 **Gladstone** Queensland, E Australia 23°52′S 151°16′E
276 G5 **Gladstone** South Australia 33°16′S 138°21′E
55 I9 **Gladstone** Manitoba, S Canada 50°12′N 98°56′W
72 E5 **Gladstone** Michigan, N USA 45°51′N 87°01′W
72 G7 **Gladwin** Michigan, N USA 43°58′N 84°29′W
155 F8 **Glafsfjorden** ◎ C Sweden
152 B2 **Gláma** *physical region* NW Iceland
154 E6 **Gláma** *var.* Glommen. ≈ S Norway
159 I1 **Glamis** United Kingdom 56°36′N 3°00′W
184 C4 **Glamoč** Federacija Bosne I Hercegovine, NE Boznia and Herzegovina 44°01′N 16°51′E
157 F11 **Glamorgan** *cultural region* S Wales, United Kingdom
155 D13 **Glamsbjerg** Syddtjylland, C Denmark 55°17′N 10°07′E
263 M10 **Glan** Mindanao, S Philippines 05°49′N 125°11′E
177 J4 **Glan** ≈ SE Austria
181 D12 **Glan** ≈ W Germany
155 H9 **Glan** ◎ S Sweden
160 E5 **Glanamman** United Kingdom 51°48′N 3°56′W
181 D13 **Glan-Münchweiler** Rheinland-Pfalz, Germany 49°28′E 7°26′N
Glaris *see* Glarus
176 E4 **Glarner Alpen** *Eng.* Glarus Alps. ▲▲ E Switzerland
176 E4 **Glarus** Glarus, E Switzerland 47°03′N 09°04′E
174 C3 **Glarus** *Fr.* Glaris. ◈ *canton* C Switzerland
Glarus Alps *see* Glarner Alpen
75 E9 **Glasco** Kansas, C USA 39°21′N 97°50′W
158 G3 **Glasgow** S Scotland, United Kingdom 55°53′N 04°15′W
64 E8 **Glasgow** Delaware, USA 39°36′N 75°45′W
66 E5 **Glasgow** Kentucky, S USA 37°00′N 85°54′W
75 H9 **Glasgow** Missouri, C USA 39°13′N 92°51′W
77 K3 **Glasgow** Montana, NW USA 48°12′N 106°37′W
67 J4 **Glasgow** Virginia, NE USA 37°37′N 79°27′W
156 F6 **Glasgow** ✈ W Scotland, United Kingdom 55°52′N 04°27′W
57 L5 **Glaslyn** Saskatchewan, S Canada 53°20′N 108°18′W
64 F8 **Glassboro** New Jersey, NE USA 39°40′N 75°05′W
158 G6 **Glasserton** United Kingdom 54°42′N 4°27′W
70 C6 **Glass Mountains** ▲▲ Texas, SW USA
160 G7 **Glastonbury** SW England, United Kingdom 51°09′N 02°43′W
65 J4 **Glastonbury** Connecticut, USA 41°43′N 72°36′W
Glatz *see* Kłodzko
179 H9 **Glauchau** Sachsen, E Germany 50°48′N 12°32′E
Glavn'a Morava *see* Velika Morava
Glavnik *see* Gllamnik
195 J9 **Glazov** Udmurtskaya Respublika, NW Russian Federation 58°06′N 52°38′E
Głda *see* Gwda
177 K4 **Gleinalpe** ▲▲ SE Austria
177 L4 **Gleisdorf** Steiermark, SE Austria 47°07′N 15°43′E
Gleiwitz *see* Gliwice
158 E4 **Glenacardoch Point** *headland* United Kingdom 55°35′N 5°43′W
83 J6 **Glenallen** Alaska, USA 62°06′N 145°33′W
158 A9 **Glenamaddy** Galway, Ireland 53°36′N 8°33′W
164 D4 **Glénan, Îles** *island group* NW France
158 E5 **Glenariff** United Kingdom 55°03′N 6°04′W
158 E6 **Glenarm** United Kingdom 54°58′N 5°58′W
278 D11 **Glenavy** Canterbury, South Island, New Zealand 44°53′S 171°04′E
158 E7 **Glenavy** United Kingdom 54°35′N 6°13′W
54 B2 **Glenboyle** Yukon, NW Canada 63°55′N 138°43′W
64 D9 **Glen Burnie** Maryland, NE USA 39°09′N 76°37′W
79 I5 **Glen Canyon** *canyon* Utah, W USA
79 I5 **Glen Canyon Dam** *dam* Arizona, SW USA
159 H6 **Glencaple** United Kingdom 55°00′N 3°35′W
73 B12 **Glen Carbon** Illinois, N USA 38°45′N 89°58′W
62 B6 **Glencoe** Ontario, S Canada 42°44′N 81°42′W
139 H7 **Glencoe** KwaZulu/Natal, E South Africa 28°10′S 30°15′E
74 G5 **Glencoe** Minnesota, N USA 44°46′N 94°09′W
156 E5 **Glen Coe** *valley* N Scotland, United Kingdom
158 A6 **Glencolumbkille** Donegal, Ireland 54°42′N 8°43′W
141 H9 **Glenconnor** Eastern Cape, South Africa 33°24′S 25°10′E
64 I6 **Glen Cove** New York, NE USA 40°51′N 73°38′W
79 H8 **Glendale** Arizona, SW USA 33°32′N 112°11′W
81 D10 **Glendale** California, W USA 34°09′N 118°20′W
276 F3 **Glendambo** South Australia 30°59′S 135°45′E
159 H2 **Glendevon** United Kingdom 56°13′N 3°37′W
77 M4 **Glendive** Montana, NW USA 47°08′N 104°42′W
77 M8 **Glendo** Wyoming, C USA 42°27′N 105°01′W
81 E10 **Glendora** California, USA 34°08′N 117°52′W
103 J6 **Glendor Mountains** C Guyana
158 H2 **Gleneagles** C Scotland, United Kingdom
277 H7 **Glenelg River** ≈ South Australia/Victoria, SE Australia
159 H2 **Glenfarg** United Kingdom 56°16′N 3°24′W
74 D3 **Glenfield** North Dakota, N USA 47°25′N 98°33′W
158 F1 **Glenfinnan** United Kingdom 56°52′N 5°27′W
71 H7 **Glen Flora** Texas, SW USA 29°22′N 96°12′W
158 D5 **Glengad Head** *headland* N Ireland
274 G5 **Glen Helen** Northern Territory, N Australia 23°45′S 132°46′E
277 L3 **Glen Innes** New South Wales, SE Australia 29°42′S 151°45′E
72 F6 **Glen Lake** ◎ Michigan, N USA
158 F6 **Glenluce** United Kingdom 54°52′N 4°50′W
54 B3 **Glenlyon Peak** ▲ Yukon, W Canada 62°32′N 134°51′W
64 D10 **Glenn Dale** Maryland, USA 38°59′N 76°49′W
79 J10 **Glenn, Mount** ▲ Arizona, SW USA 31°55′N 110°00′W
76 G8 **Glenns Ferry** Idaho, NW USA 42°57′N 115°18′W
81 E8 **Glennville** California, USA 35°44′N 118°42′W
69 L2 **Glennville** Georgia, SE USA 31°56′N 81°55′W
54 B5 **Glenora** British Columbia, W Canada 57°52′N 131°16′W
277 I7 **Glenorchy** Victoria, SE Australia 36°56′S 142°39′E
277 M3 **Glenreagh** New South Wales, SE Australia 30°04′S 153°00′E
77 L8 **Glenrock** Wyoming, C USA 42°51′N 105°52′W
159 I2 **Glenrothes** E Scotland, United Kingdom 56°11′N 03°09′W
63 H5 **Glens Falls** New York, NE USA 43°18′N 73°38′W
64 F7 **Glenside** Pennsylvania, USA 40°06′N 75°09′W
158 B6 **Glenties** *Ir.* Na Gleannta. Donegal, NW Ireland 54°47′N 08°17′W
74 B3 **Glen Ullin** North Dakota, N USA 46°49′N 101°49′W
67 I3 **Glenville** West Virginia, NE USA 38°57′N 80°51′W
75 H13 **Glenwood** Arkansas, C USA 34°19′N 93°33′W
75 F8 **Glenwood** Iowa, C USA 41°03′N 95°44′W
74 F4 **Glenwood** Minnesota, N USA 45°39′N 95°23′W
79 H4 **Glenwood** Utah, W USA 38°45′N 111°59′W
72 A5 **Glenwood City** Wisconsin, N USA 45°04′N 92°11′W
79 K3 **Glenwood Springs** Colorado, C USA 39°33′N 107°21′W
180 I1 **Gleschendorf** Schleswig-Holstein, Germany 54°02′E 10°40′N
176 D5 **Gletsch** Valais, S Switzerland 46°34′N 08°21′E
Glevum *see* Gloucester
184 C3 **Glina** *var.* Banijska Palanka. Sisak-Moslavina, NE Croatia 45°19′N 16°07′E
191 J8 **Glinka** Smolenskaya Oblast', Russian Federation
154 C5 **Glittertind** ▲ S Norway 61°24′N 08°19′E
183 F8 **Gliwice** *Ger.* Gleiwitz. Śląskie, S Poland 50°19′N 18°49′E
184 G6 **Gllamnik** *Serb.* Glavnik. N Kosovo 42°53′N 21°10′E
79 I9 **Globe** Arizona, SW USA 33°24′N 110°47′W
Globino *see* Hlobyne
179 F14 **Glockturm** ▲ SW Austria 46°54′N 10°42′E
188 F6 **Glodeni** *Rus.* Glodyany. N Moldova 47°47′N 27°33′E
Glodyany *see* Glodeni
Glogau *see* Głogów
177 L3 **Gloggnitz** Niederösterreich, E Austria 47°41′N 15°57′E
182 D6 **Głogów** *Ger.* Glogau, Glogow. Dolnośląskie, SW Poland 51°40′N 16°04′E
Glogow *see* Głogów
183 E8 **Głogówek** *Ger.* Oberglogau. Opolskie, S Poland 50°21′N 17°51′E
152 E5 **Glomfjord** Nordland, C Norway 66°49′N 14°00′E
Glomma *see* Gláma
Glommen *see* Gláma
154 J1 **Glommersträsk** Norrbotten, N Sweden 65°17′N 19°40′E
139 M4 **Glorieuses, Îles** *Eng.* Glorioso Islands. *island* (to France) N Madagascar
Glorioso Islands *see* Glorieuses, Îles
117 I11 **Glorious Hill** *hill* East Falkland, Falkland Islands
82 E6 **Glory of Russia Cape** *headland* Saint Matthew Island, Alaska, USA 60°36′N 172°57′W
159 J10 **Glossop** United Kingdom 53°25′N 1°54′W
68 D3 **Gloster** Mississippi, S USA 31°12′N 91°01′W
277 M4 **Gloucester** New South Wales, SE Australia 32°01′S 152°00′E
280 C3 **Gloucester** New Britain, E Papua New Guinea 05°30′S 148°30′E
161 H5 **Gloucester** *hist.* Caer Glou, *Lat.* Glevum. C England, United Kingdom 51°53′N 02°14′W
65 M2 **Gloucester** Massachusetts, NE USA 42°36′N 70°36′W
67 M4 **Gloucester** Virginia, NE USA 37°26′N 76°33′W
64 F8 **Gloucester City** New Jersey, USA 39°54′N 75°07′W
161 H5 **Gloucestershire** *cultural region* C England, United Kingdom
73 I11 **Glouster** Ohio, N USA 39°30′N 82°04′W
88 E2 **Glovers Reef** *reef* E Belize
65 H1 **Gloversville** New York, NE USA 43°03′N 74°20′W
182 G6 **Głowno** Łódź, C Poland 51°58′N 19°43′E
183 E8 **Głubczyce** *Ger.* Leobschütz. Opolskie, S Poland 50°13′N 17°50′E
196 G6 **Glubokiy** Rostovskaya Oblast', SW Russian Federation 48°34′N 40°16′E
227 L3 **Glubokoye** Vostochnyy Kazakhstan, E Kazakhstan 50°08′N 82°16′E
Glubokoye *see* Hlybokaye
183 E8 **Głuchołazy** *Ger.* Ziegenhais. Opolskie, S Poland 50°20′N 17°23′E
180 G2 **Glückstadt** Schleswig-Holstein, N Germany 53°47′N 09°26′E
Glukhov *see* Hlukhiv
159 J8 **Glusburn** United Kingdom 53°54′N 2°00′W
Glushkevichi *see* Hlushkavichy
Glusk/Glussk *see* Hlusk
Glybokaya *see* Hlyboka
160 G2 **Glyn-Ceiriog** United Kingdom 52°56′N 3°11′W
160 F2 **Glyn-Dyfrdwy** United Kingdom 52°58′N 3°16′W
155 C11 **Glyngøre** Midtjylland, NW Denmark 56°45′N 08°55′E
197 I5 **Gmelinka** Volgogradskaya Oblast', SW Russian Federation 50°50′N 46°51′E
177 J4 **Gmünd** Kärnten, S Austria 46°56′N 13°32′E
177 K1 **Gmünd** Niederösterreich, N Austria 48°47′N 14°59′E
Gmünd *see* Schwäbisch Gmünd
177 J3 **Gmunden** Oberösterreich, N Austria 47°56′N 13°48′E
Gmundner See *see* Traunsee
154 I5 **Gnarp** Gävleborg, C Sweden 62°03′N 17°19′E
177 L4 **Gnas** Steiermark, SE Austria 46°53′N 15°48′E
Gnaviyani *see* Fuammulah
Gnesen *see* Gniezno
155 I8 **Gnesta** Södermanland, C Sweden 59°05′N 17°20′E
182 E5 **Gniezno** *Ger.* Gnesen. Weilkopolskie, C Poland 52°33′N 17°35′E
Gnjilane *see* Gjilan
161 H3 **Gnosall** United Kingdom 52°47′N 2°15′W
155 G10 **Gnosjö** Jönköping, S Sweden 57°22′N 13°44′E
234 C6 **Goa** *prev.* Old Goa, Vela Goa, Velha Goa. Goa, W India 15°31′N 73°56′E
234 C6 **Goa** *var.* Old Goa. ◈ *state* W India
Goabddális *see* Kåbdalis
140 C4 **Goageb** Karas, Namibia 26°45′S 17°14′E
87 N10 **Goascorán, Río** ≈ El Salvador/Honduras
132 G8 **Goaso** *var.* Gawso. W Ghana 06°49′N 02°27′W
158 F4 **Goatfell** ▲ United Kingdom 55°37′N 5°11′W
136 E5 **Goba** Oromīya, C Ethiopia 07°02′N 39°58′E
140 A2 **Gobabed** Erongo, W Namibia 23°36′S 15°03′E
140 D1 **Gobabis** Omaheke, E Namibia 22°25′S 18°58′E
Gobannium *see* Abergavenny
290 H3 **Goban Spur** *undersea feature* NW Atlantic Ocean
118 G9 **Gobernador Ayala** Mendoza, Argentina 37°33′S 68°05′W
114 B4 **Gobernador Candioti** Santa Fe, Argentina 31°24′S 60°45′W
114 C8 **Gobernador Castro** Buenos Aires, Argentina 33°39′S 59°53′W
118 G3 **Gobernador Civit** Mendoza, Argentina 33°20′S 67°58′W
114 B2 **Gobernador Crespo** Santa Fe, Argentina 30°18′S 60°24′W
117 C11 **Gobernador Gregores** Santa Cruz, S Argentina 48°43′S 70°21′W
113 H6 **Gobernador Ingeniero Virasoro** Corrientes, NE Argentina 28°06′S 56°00′W
114 E10 **Gobernador Udaondo** Buenos Aires, Argentina 35°18′S 58°36′W
239 L3 **Gobi** *desert* China/Mongolia
251 H6 **Gobō** Wakayama, Honshū, SW Japan 33°52′N 135°09′E
Gobolka Awdal *see* Awdal
Gobolka Sahil *see* Sahil
Gobolka Sool *see* Sool
180 B7 **Goch** Nordrhein-Westfalen, W Germany 51°41′N 06°10′E
140 D3 **Gochas** Hardap, S Namibia 24°54′S 18°43′E
181 I12 **Gochsheim** Bayern, Germany 50°01′E 10°17′N
161 J7 **Godalming** United Kingdom 51°11′N 0°36′W
234 G5 **Godāvari** *var.* Godavari. ≈ C India
Godavari *see* Godāvari
234 H6 **Godāvari, Mouths of the** *delta* E India
59 I7 **Godbout** Québec, SE Canada 49°19′N 67°37′W
75 E10 **Goddard** Kansas, C USA 37°39′N 97°34′W
181 F9 **Goddelsheim** Hessen, Germany 51°12′E 8°49′N
62 B5 **Goderich** Ontario, S Canada 43°43′N 81°43′W
166 E4 **Goderville** Haute-Normandie, France 49°39′N 0°22′E
Godhavn *see* Qeqertarsuaq
232 C8 **Godhra** Gujarāt, W India 22°49′N 73°40′E
Göding *see* Hodonín
183 G11 **Gödöllő** Pest, N Hungary 47°36′N 19°20′E
118 F3 **Godoy Cruz** Mendoza, W Argentina 32°59′S 68°49′W
55 K6 **Gods** ≈ Manitoba, C Canada
55 J7 **Gods Lake** ◎ Manitoba, C Canada
55 J7 **Gods Lake Narrows** Manitoba, C Canada 54°29′N 94°21′W
55 K3 **Gods Mercy, Bay of** *coastal sea feature* Nunavut, NE Canada
Godthaab/Godthåb *see* Nuuk
Godwin Austen, Mount *see* K2
Goede Hoop, Kaap de *see* Good Hope, Cape of
Goedgegun *see* Nhlangano
Goeie Hoop, Kaap die *see* Good Hope, Cape of
59 I4 **Goélands, Lac aux** ◎ Québec, SE Canada
162 D7 **Goeree** *island* SW Netherlands
163 D8 **Goes** Zeeland, SW Netherlands 51°30′N 03°55′E
250 A1 **Goesan** *prev.* Koesan. Ch'ungch'ŏng-bukto, South Korea 36°49′N 127°48′E
Goettingen *see* Göttingen
81 I11 **Goffs** California, USA 34°55′N 115°04′W
65 L1 **Goffstown** New Hampshire, NE USA 43°01′N 71°34′W
58 E7 **Gogama** Ontario, S Canada 47°42′N 81°44′W
250 E4 **Gō-gawa** ≈ Honshū, SW Japan
72 C4 **Gogebic, Lake** ◎ Michigan, N USA
72 C4 **Gogebic Range** *hill range* Michigan/Wisconsin, N USA
Gogi Lerr *see* Gogi, Mount
215 L5 **Gogi, Mount** *Arm.* Gogi Lerr, *Az.* Küküdağ. ▲ Armenia/Azerbaijan 39°33′N 45°35′E
194 C8 **Gogland, Ostrov** *island* NW Russian Federation
183 E8 **Gogolin** Opolskie, S Poland 50°28′N 18°04′E
Gogonou *see* Gogounou
133 I6 **Gogounou** *var.* Gogonou. N Benin 10°50′N 02°50′E
232 E5 **Gohāna** Haryāna, N India 29°06′N 76°43′E
111 L1 **Goiabeira** Minas Gerais, Brazil 19°00′S 41°18′W
111 I5 **Goianà** Minas Gerais, Brazil 21°32′S 43°12′W
109 B9 **Goianésia** Goiás, C Brazil 15°21′S 49°02′W
109 B10 **Goiânia** *prev.* Goyania. *state capital* Goiás, C Brazil 16°43′S 49°18′W
109 B9 **Goiás** Goiás, C Brazil 15°57′S 50°07′W
109 C9 **Goiás** *off.* Estado de Goiás; *prev.* Goiaz, Goyaz. ◈ *state* C Brazil
Goiás, Estado de *see* Goiás
Goiaz *see* Goiás
Goidhoo Atoll *see* Horsburgh Atoll
158 F3 **Goil, Loch** *inlet* W Scotland, United Kingdom
113 I4 **Goio-Erê** Paraná, SW Brazil 24°08′S 53°07′W
163 F8 **Goirle** Noord-Brabant, S Netherlands 51°31′N 05°04′E
172 C3 **Góis** Coimbra, N Portugal 40°10′N 08°06′W
251 I5 **Gojō** *var.* Gozyô. Nara, Honshū, SW Japan 34°21′N 135°42′E
253 C8 **Gojōme** Akita, Honshū, NW Japan 39°55′N 140°07′E
231 I5 **Gojra** Punjab, E Pakistan 31°10′N 72°43′E
250 D7 **Gokase-gawa** ≈ Kyūshū, SW Japan
214 A5 **Gökçeada** *var.* Imroz Adasī, *Gk.* Imbros. *island* NW Turkey
Gökçeada *see* İmroz
228 D7 **Gökdepe** *Rus.* Gëkdepe, Geok-Tepe. Ahal Welaýaty, C Turkmenistan 38°05′N 58°08′E
214 E4 **Gökırmak** ≈ N Turkey
Goklenkuy, Solonchak *see* Geklengkui, Solonchak
214 B7 **Gökova Körfezi** *gulf* SW Turkey
214 F7 **Göksu** ≈ S Turkey
214 G7 **Göksun** Kahramanmaraş, C Turkey 38°03′N 36°30′E
214 E8 **Göksu Nehri** ≈ S Turkey
138 G3 **Gokwe** Midlands, NW Zimbabwe 18°13′S 28°55′E
154 D6 **Gol** Buskerud, S Norway 60°42′N 08°57′E
233 M6 **Golāghāt** Assam, NE India 26°31′N 93°54′E
158 A5 **Gola Island** *island* Donegal, Ireland
182 E5 **Gołańcz** Wielkopolskie, C Poland 52°57′N 17°17′E
218 F5 **Golan Heights** ▲▲ Syria
218 F5 **Golan Heights** *Ar.* Al Jawlān, *Heb.* HaGolan. ▲▲ SW Syria
Golārā *see* Ārān-va-Bidgol
Golaya Pristan *see* Hola Prystan'
223 I7 **Golbāf** Kermān, C Iran 29°51′N 57°44′E
214 G7 **Gölbaşı** Adıyaman, S Turkey 37°46′N 37°40′E
179 H14 **Gölbner** ▲ SW Austria 46°51′N 12°31′E
73 C13 **Golconda** Illinois, N USA 37°20′N 88°29′W
80 J1 **Golconda** Nevada, W USA 40°56′N 117°29′W
80 J1 **Golconda Summit** ▲ Nevada, USA 40°55′N 117°23′W
214 C5 **Gölcük** Kocaeli, NW Turkey 40°44′N 29°50′E
64 B3 **Gold** Pennsylvania, USA 41°52′N 77°50′W
182 I3 **Gołdap** *Ger.* Goldap. Warmińsko-Mazurskie, NE Poland 54°19′N 22°23′E
76 A8 **Gold Beach** Oregon, NW USA 42°25′N 124°27′W
Goldberg *see* Złotoryja
277 M2 **Gold Coast** *cultural region* Queensland, E Australia
124 B5 **Gold Coast** *coastal region* S Ghana
83 I5 **Gold Creek** Alaska, USA 62°48′N 149°40′W
57 H7 **Golden** British Columbia, SW Canada 51°19′N 116°58′W
79 L3 **Golden** Colorado, C USA 39°40′N 105°12′W
278 F7 **Golden Bay** *bay* South Island, New Zealand
75 G11 **Golden City** Missouri, C USA 37°23′N 94°05′W
76 D5 **Goldendale** Washington, NW USA 45°49′N 120°49′W
Goldener Tisch *see* Zlatý Stôl
90 G8 **Golden Grove** E Jamaica 17°56′N 76°17′W
62 E3 **Golden Lake** ◎ Ontario, SE Canada
68 E5 **Golden Meadow** Louisiana, S USA 29°22′N 90°15′W
Golden Sands *see* Zlatni Pyasatsi
Golden State, The *see* California
139 H3 **Golden Valley** Mashonaland West, N Zimbabwe 18°11′S 29°50′E
114 D9 **Goldey** Buenos Aires, Argentina 34°37′S 59°18′W
80 H6 **Goldfield** Nevada, W USA 37°42′N 117°15′W
Goldingen *see* Kuldīga
Goldmarkt *see* Zlatna
80 H6 **Gold Point** Nevada, USA 37°21′N 117°22′W
56 C8 **Gold River** Vancouver Island, British Columbia, SW Canada 49°41′N 126°05′W
80 E1 **Gold Run** California, USA 39°11′N 120°51′W
67 L6 **Goldsboro** North Carolina, SE USA 35°23′N 78°00′W
70 D5 **Goldsmith** Texas, SW USA 31°58′N 102°36′W
70 G5 **Goldthwaite** Texas, SW USA 31°28′N 98°35′W
215 J5 **Göle** Ardahan, NE Turkey 40°47′N 42°36′E
Golema Ada *see* Ostrovo
185 I6 **Golema Planina** ▲▲ W Bulgaria
185 H6 **Golemi Vrah** *var.* Golemi Vrŭkh. ▲ W Bulgaria 42°41′N 22°38′E
Golemi Vrŭkh *see* Golemi Vrah
182 C4 **Goleniów** *Ger.* Gollnow. Zachodnio-pomorskie, NW Poland 53°34′N 14°48′E
223 H2 **Golestān** *off.* Ostān-e Golestān. ◈ *province* N Iran
Golestān, Ostān-e *see* Golestān
81 B9 **Goleta** California, W USA 34°26′N 119°50′W
89 I9 **Golfito** Puntarenas, SE Costa Rica 08°42′N 83°10′W
168 G10 **Golfo de San Jorge** NE Spain
187 M7 **Golgeli Daglar** ▲▲ Denizli, Turkey
187 N7 **Gölhisar** Burdur, Turkey 37°09′N 29°42′E
70 G8 **Goliad** Texas, SW USA 28°40′N 97°26′W
184 F5 **Golija** ▲▲ SW Serbia
Golinka *see* Gongbo'gyamda
185 H6 **Goljak** ▲▲ SE Serbia
214 G5 **Gölköy** Ordu, N Turkey 40°42′N 37°37′E
Gollel *see* Lavumisa
177 L2 **Göllersbach** ≈ NE Austria
181 J8 **Göllingen** Thüringen, Germany 51°21′E 11°01′N
Gollnow *see* Goleniów
187 L5 **Gölmarmara** Manisa, Turkey 38°43′N 27°55′E
Golmo *see* Golmud
239 I6 **Golmud** *var.* Ge'e'mu, Golmo, *Chin.* Ko-erh-mu. Qinghai, C China 36°23′N 94°56′E
174 C7 **Golo** ≈ Corse, France, C Mediterranean Sea
Golovanevsk *see* Holovanivs'k
Golovchin *see* Halowchyn
82 G5 **Golovin** Alaska, USA 64°33′N 162°54′W
222 E5 **Golpāyegān** *var.* Gulpaigan. Eşfahān, W Iran 33°23′N 50°18′E
Golshan *see* Ţabas
Gol'shany *see* Hal'shany
156 F4 **Golspie** N Scotland, United Kingdom 57°59′N 03°56′W
184 G4 **Golubac** Serbia, NE Serbia 44°38′N 21°36′E
182 F5 **Golub-Dobrzyń** Kujawski-pomorskie, C Poland 53°07′N 19°03′E
227 J2 **Golubovka** Pavlodar, N Kazakhstan 53°07′N 74°11′E
135 C11 **Golungo Alto** Kwanza Norte, NW Angola 09°10′S 14°45′E
185 L5 **Golyama Kamchia** *var.* Golyama Kamchiya. ≈ E Bulgaria
Golyama Kamchiya *see* Golyama Kamchia
185 L5 **Golyama Reka** ≈ N Bulgaria
Golyama Syutka *see* Golyama Syutkya
185 J7 **Golyama Syutkya** *var.* Golyama Syutka. ▲ SW Bulgaria 41°55′N 24°03′E
185 J7 **Golyam Perelik** ▲ S Bulgaria 41°37′N 24°34′E
185 J7 **Golyam Persenk** ▲ S Bulgaria 41°50′N 24°33′E
191 I8 **Golynki** Smolenskaya Oblast', Russian Federation
135 J8 **Goma** Nord-Kivu, NE Dem. Rep. Congo 01°36′S 29°08′E
251 H5 **Gomadan-zan** ▲ Honshū, SW Japan 34°03′N 135°34′E
168 B9 **Gómara** Castilla y León, Spain 41°37′N 2°13′W
233 H7 **Gomati** *var.* Gumti. ≈ N India
133 L6 **Gombe** Gombe, E Nigeria 10°19′N 11°02′E
187 N8 **Gömbe** Antalya, Turkey 36°33′N 29°40′E
121 L6 **Gombe** *var.* Igombe. ≈ E Tanzania
133 M6 **Gombi** Adamawa, E Nigeria 10°07′N 12°45′E
Gombroon *see* Bandar-e 'Abbās
Gomel' *see* Homyel'
Gomel'skaya Oblast' *see* Homyel'skaya Voblasts'
170 A10 **Gomera** *island* Islas Canarias, Spain, NE Atlantic Ocean
85 J9 **Gómez** Tabasco, Mexico
84 G4 **Gómez Farías** Chihuahua, N Mexico 29°25′N 107°46′W
85 L7 **Gómez Farías** Coahuila, Mexico 24°57′N 101°02′W
85 M8 **Gómez Farías** Tamaulipas, Mexico 23°03′N 99°09′W
85 J6 **Gómez Palacio** Durango, C Mexico 25°39′N 103°30′W
238 F7 **Gomo** Xizang Zizhiqu, W China 33°37′N 86°40′E
141 K3 **Gompies** Limpopo, South Africa 24°27′S 29°25′E
260 G5 **Gomumu, Pulau** *island* E Indonesia
223 I4 **Gonābād** *var.* Gunabad. Khorāsān-e Razavī, NE Iran 36°30′N 59°18′E
90 G5 **Gonaïves** *var.* Les Gonaïves. N Haiti 19°26′N 72°41′W
193 K7 **Gonam** ≈ NE Russian Federation
141 L1 **Gonarezhou National Park** Zimbabwe
90 G6 **Gonâve, Canal de la** *var.* Canal de Sud. *channel* N Caribbean Sea
90 G5 **Gonâve, Golfe de la** *gulf* N Caribbean Sea
Gonāveh *see* Bandar-e Gonāveh
90 G6 **Gonâve, Île de la** *island* C Haiti
Gonbadān *see* Do Gonbadān
223 H3 **Gonbad-e Kāvūs** *var.* Gunbad-i-Qawus. Golestán, N Iran 37°15′N 55°11′E
110 E7 **Gonçalves** Minas Gerais, Brazil 22°40′S 45°51′W
169 L2 **Goncelin** Rhône-Alpes, France 45°20′N 5°59′E
232 G6 **Gonda** Uttar Pradesh, N India 27°08′N 81°58′E
Gondar *see* Gonder
181 F14 **Gondelsheim** Baden-Württemberg, Germany 49°04′E 8°40′N
136 D3 **Gonder** *var.* Gondar. Āmara, NW Ethiopia 12°36′N 37°27′E
181 D11 **Gondershausen** Rheinland-Pfalz, Germany 50°09′E 7°30′N
134 E4 **Gondey** Moyen-Chari, S Chad 09°07′N 19°10′E
234 G3 **Gondia** Mahārāshtra, C India 21°27′N 80°12′E
172 B1 **Gondomar** Porto, NW Portugal 41°10′N 08°35′W
167 K6 **Gondrecourt-le-Château** Lorraine, France 48°31′N 5°30′E
168 E5 **Gondrin** Midi-Pyrénées, France 43°53′N 0°15′E
218 F5 **Gonén** Israel 33°07′N 35°38′E
214 B5 **Gönen** Balıkesir, W Turkey 40°06′N 27°39′E
214 B5 **Gönen Çayı** ≈ NW Turkey
242 G3 **Gong'an** Hubei, China 30°02′N 112°08′E
239 H9 **Gongbo'gyamda** *var.* Golinka. Xizang Zizhiqu, W China 30°03′N 93°10′E
Gongchang *see* Longxi
242 F8 **Gongcheng** Guangxi, China 24°31′N 110°29′E
243 K6 **Gongchuan** Fujian, SE China 26°05′N 117°26′E
238 G9 **Gonggar** *var.* Gyixong. Xizang Zizhiqu, W China 29°18′N 90°56′E
240 C4 **Gongga Shan** ▲ C China 29°50′N 101°55′E
239 J6 **Gonghe** *var.* Qabqa. Qinghai, C China 36°20′N 100°46′E
Gongjiang *see* Yudu
238 E3 **Gongliu** *var.* Tokkuztara. Xinjiang Uygur Zizhiqu, NW China 43°29′N 82°16′E
133 M6 **Gongola** ≈ E Nigeria
Gongoleh State *see* Jonglei
277 J3 **Gongolgon** New South Wales, SE Australia 30°19′S 146°57′E
239 I4 **Gongpoquan** Gansu, N China 41°45′N 100°27′E
Gongquan *see* Gongxian
243 J7 **Gong Shui** ≈ Jiangxi, China
Gongtang *see* Damxung
242 B4 **Gongxian** *var.* Gongquan, Gong Xian. Sichuan, C China 28°25′N 104°51′E
Gong Xian *see* Gongxian
245 H7 **Gongyi** Henan, China 34°28′N 112°35′E

◆ Country
● Country Capital
◇ Dependent Territory
○ Dependent Territory Capital
◈ Administrative Regions
✈ International Airport
▲ Mountain
▲▲ Mountain Range
⛰ Volcano
≈ River
◎ Lake
⊟ Reservoir

Gudermes - Ḩalbūn

197 I9 Gudermes Chechenskaya Respublika, SW Russian Federation 43°23′N 46°06′E
180 I3 Gudow Schleswig-Holstein, Germany 53°33′E 10°47′N
234 F7 Gūdūr Andhra Pradesh, E India 14°10′N 79°51′E
228 B7 Gudurolum Balkan Welaýaty, W Turkmenistan 37°28′N 54°30′E
154 B6 Gudvangen Sogn Og Fjordane, S Norway 60°54′N 06°49′E
167 M7 Guebwiller Haut-Rhin, NE France 47°55′N 07°13′E
Guéckédou see Guékédou
132 D7 Guékédou var. Guéckédou. Guinée-Forestière, S Guinea 08°33′N 10°08′W
87 H8 Guelatao Oaxaca, SE Mexico
Guelders see Gelderland
134 D3 Guélengdeng Mayo-Kébbi Est, W Chad 10°55′N 15°31′E
131 J1 Guelma var. Gâlma. NE Algeria 36°29′N 07°25′E
130 D4 Guelmime var. Goulimime. SW Morocco 28°59′N 10°10′W
62 C5 Guelph Ontario, S Canada 43°34′N 80°16′W
166 C7 Gueméné-Penfao Loire-Atlantique, NW France 47°37′N 01°49′W
166 A6 Guémené-sur-Scorff Bretagne, France 48°04′N 3°12′W
171 N9 Guenzet Algeria
164 F4 Guer Morbihan, NW France 47°54′N 02°07′W
134 E3 Guéra off. Région du Guéra. ⬖ region S Chad
164 E4 Guérande Loire-Atlantique, NW France 47°20′N 02°25′W
Guéra, Région du see Guéra
134 F2 Guéréda Wadi Fira, E Chad 14°30′N 22°05′E
165 H6 Guéret Creuse, C France 46°10′N 01°52′E
167 I9 Guérigny Bourgogne, France 47°05′N 3°12′E
80 B1 Guerneville California, USA 38°30′N 123°00′W
Guernica/Guernica y Lumo see Gernika-Lumo
80 D6 Guernsey California, USA 36°13′N 119°38′W
77 M8 Guernsey Wyoming, C USA 42°16′N 104°44′W
198 D1 Guernsey ◇ British Crown Dependency Channel Islands, NW Europe
166 B4 Guernsey island Channel Islands, NW Europe
132 C3 Guérou Assaba, S Mauritania 16°48′N 11°40′W
70 F9 Guerra Texas, SW USA 26°54′N 98°53′W
85 L4 Guerrero Coahuila, Mexico 28°18′N 100°23′W
86 E4 Guerrero San Luis Potosí, C Mexico 21°33′N 99°48′W
85 M9 Guerrero Tamaulipas, NE Mexico 21°33′N 99°48′W
86 E7 Guerrero ⬖ state S Mexico
84 C5 Guerrero Negro Baja California Sur, NW Mexico 27°56′N 114°04′W
114 B8 Guerrico Buenos Aires, Argentina 33°40′S 60°24′W
165 I5 Gueugnon Saône-et-Loire, C France 46°36′N 04°03′E
132 E8 Guéyo S Ivory Coast 05°25′N 06°04′W
243 H5 Gugang Jiangxi, SE China 28°17′N 113°45′E
175 G8 Guglionesi Molise, C Italy 41°54′N 14°54′E
282 E3 Guguan island C Northern Mariana Islands
Guhrau see Góra
Gui see Guangxi Zhuangzu Zizhiqu
172 B3 Guia Leiria, Portugal 39°57′N 8°47′W
Guiana see French Guiana
95 L3 Guiana Basin undersea feature W Atlantic Ocean 11°00′N 52°00′W
98 D2 Guiana Highlands var. Macizo de las Guayanas. ▲▲ N South America
Guiba see Juba
164 F4 Guichen Ille-et-Vilaine, NW France 47°57′N 01°47′W
243 K2 Guichi prev. Guichi. Anhui, SE China 30°39′N 117°29′E
Guichi see Guichi
114 G5 Guichón Paysandú, W Uruguay 32°30′S 57°13′W
133 K5 Guidan-Roumji Maradi, S Niger 13°40′N 06°41′E
Guidder see Guider
239 K6 Guide var. Heyin. Qinghai, C China 36°06′N 101°25′E
134 C3 Guider var. Guidder. Nord, N Cameroon 09°55′N 13°59′E
132 C4 Guidimaka ⬖ region S Mauritania
133 L5 Guidimouni Zinder, S Niger 13°40′N 09°31′E
242 C6 Guiding Guizhou, China 26°20′N 107°08′E
111 I5 Guidoval Minas Gerais, Brazil 21°09′S 42°48′W
132 B3 Guier, Lac de var. Lac de Guiers. ⊚ N Senegal
Guiers, Lac de see Guier, Lac de
242 E9 Guigang var. Guixian, Gui Xian. Guangxi Zhuangzu Zizhiqu, S China 23°06′N 109°36′E
132 E8 Guiglo W Ivory Coast 06°33′N 07°29′W
167 H6 Guignes Île-de-France, France 48°38′N 2°48′E
102 F3 Güigüe Carabobo, N Venezuela 10°05′N 67°48′W
139 I6 Guijá Gaza, S Mozambique 24°31′S 33°02′E
88 C4 Güija, Lago de ⊚ El Salvador/Guatemala
242 F9 Gui Jiang var. Gui Shui. ∿ S China
243 M3 Guiji Shan ▲▲ Zhejiang, China
170 E4 Guijuelo Castilla y León, N Spain 40°34′N 05°40′W
Guilan see Gīlān
161 J7 Guildford SE England, United Kingdom 51°14′N 00°35′W
63 K3 Guildford Maine, NE USA 45°10′N 69°22′W
63 I4 Guildhall Vermont, NE USA 44°34′N 71°36′W
159 H2 Guildtown United Kingdom 56°28′N 3°24′W
65 J5 Guilford Connecticut, USA 41°17′N 72°41′W
165 J7 Guilherand Ardèche, E France 44°57′N 04°49′E
242 F7 Guilin var. Kuei-lin, Kweilin. Guangxi Zhuangzu Zizhiqu, S China 25°15′N 110°16′E
55 N5 Guillaume-Delisle, Lac ⊚ Québec, NE Canada
169 M4 Guillaumes Provence-Alpes-Côte d'Azur, France 44°05′N 6°51′E
84 D3 Guillermo Prieto Durango, Mexico 30°26′N 112°40′W
85 I7 Guillermo Prieto Durango, Mexico 24°52′N 105°0′W
165 K7 Guillestre Hautes-Alpes, SE France 44°41′N 06°39′E
160 G3 Guilsfield United Kingdom 52°41′N 3°09′W
170 C3 Guimarães var. Guimaráes. Braga, N Portugal 41°26′N 08°19′W
Guimaráes see Guimarães
102 G8 Guimarães Rosas, Pico ▲ NW Brazil
110 C1 Guimarânia Minas Gerais, Brazil 18°51′S 46°47′W
245 K7 Guimeng Ding ▲ Shandong, China 35°20′N 117°30′E
66 C8 Guin Alabama, S USA 33°58′N 87°54′W
Güina see Wina
80 C1 Guinda California, USA 38°50′N 122°12′W
132 D6 Guinea off. Republic of Guinea, var. Guinée; prev. French Guinea, People's Revolutionary Republic of Guinea. ◆ republic W Africa
291 I8 Guinea Basin undersea feature E Atlantic Ocean 0°00′N 05°00′W
132 A5 Guinea-Bissau off. Republic of Guinea-Bissau, Fr. Guinée-Bissau, Port. Guiné-Bissau; prev. Portuguese Guinea. ◆ republic W Africa
Guinea-Bissau, Republic of see Guinea-Bissau
120 F4 Guinea Fracture Zone tectonic feature E Atlantic Ocean
133 H9 Guinea, Gulf of Fr. Golfe de Guinée. gulf E Atlantic Ocean
Guinea, People's Revolutionary Republic of see Guinea
Guinea, Republic of see Guinea
Guiné-Bissau see Guinea-Bissau
Guinée see Guinea
Guinée-Bissau see Guinea-Bissau
Guinée, Golfe de see Guinea, Gulf of
61 L10 Güines La Habana, W Cuba 22°50′N 82°02′W
166 G1 Guînes Nord-Pas-de-Calais, France 50°52′N 1°52′E
164 E3 Guingamp Côtes d'Armor, NW France 48°34′N 03°09′W
242 E9 Guiping Guangxi, China 23°14′N 110°02′E
Guipúzcoa see Gipuzkoa
90 C3 Güira de Melena La Habana, W Cuba 22°47′N 82°33′W
130 G4 Guir, Hamada du desert Algeria/Morocco
103 I2 Güiria Sucre, NE Venezuela 10°37′N 62°21′W
111 J5 Guiricema Minas Gerais, Brazil 21°00′S 42°43′W
159 L7 Guisborough United Kingdom 54°32′N 1°09′W
167 I3 Guise Picardie, France 49°54′N 3°38′E
159 K8 Guiseley United Kingdom 53°52′N 1°43′W
242 F8 Gui Shui ∿ Guang Zhuangzu Zizhiqu, China
Gui Shui see Gui Jiang
170 D1 Guitiriz Galicia, NW Spain 43°10′N 07°52′W
132 F8 Guitri S Ivory Coast 05°31′N 05°14′W
263 M7 Guiuan Samar, C Philippines 11°02′N 125°45′E
243 K4 Guixi prev. Xiongshi. Jiangxi, SE China 28°17′N 117°11′E
Gui Xian/Guixian see Guigang
242 C6 Guiyang var. Kuei-Yang, Kuei-yang, Kueyang, Kweiyang; prev. Kweichu. province capital Guizhou, S China 26°33′N 106°45′E
242 G8 Guiyang Hunan, China 24°26′N 112°26′E
243 H9 Guizhou Guangdong, SE China 22°46′N 113°15′E
242 C6 Guizhou var. Guizhou Sheng, Kuei-chou, Kweichow, Qian. ⬖ province S China
Guizhou Sheng see Guizhou
168 C3 Gujan-Mestras Gironde, SW France 44°39′N 01°04′W
232 B8 Gujarāt var. Gujerat. ⬖ state W India
231 J4 Gūjar Khān Punjab, E Pakistan 33°19′N 73°23′E
Gujerat see Gujarāt
243 I5 Gujiang Jiangxi, SE China 27°11′N 114°47′E
244 G5 Gujiao Shanxi, China 37°32′N 112°05′E
231 J5 Gujrānwāla Punjab, NE Pakistan 32°11′N 74°09′E
231 J5 Gujrāt Punjab, E Pakistan 32°34′N 74°04′E
228 B5 Gulandag Rus. Gory Kulandag. ▲▲ Balkan Welaýaty, W Turkmenistan
244 A5 Gulang Gansu, C China 37°31′N 102°55′E
277 K4 Gulargambone New South Wales, SE Australia 31°19′S 148°31′E
234 E5 Gulbarga Karnātaka, C India 17°22′N 76°47′E
190 F6 Gulbene Ger. Alt-Schwanenburg. NE Latvia 57°10′N 26°44′E
229 K6 Gul'cha Kir. Gülchö. Oshskaya Oblast', SW Kyrgyzstan 40°16′N 73°27′E
Gülchö see Gul'cha
289 H10 Gulden Draak Seamount undersea feature E Indian Ocean 33°45′S 101°00′E
214 F7 Gülek Boğazı var. Cilician Gates. pass S Turkey
280 B4 Gulf ⬖ province S Papua New Guinea
68 G4 Gulf Breeze Florida, SE USA 30°21′N 87°09′W
Gulf of Liaotung see Liaodong Wan
69 K7 Gulfport Florida, SE USA 27°45′N 82°42′W
68 F4 Gulfport Mississippi, S USA 30°22′N 89°06′W
68 G4 Gulf Shores Alabama, S USA 30°15′N 87°40′W
277 K4 Gulgong New South Wales, SE Australia 32°22′S 149°31′E
242 B4 Gulin Sichuan, C China 28°06′N 105°47′E
261 I6 Gulir Pulau Kasiui, E Indonesia 04°27′S 131°41′E
Gulistan see Guliston
229 I6 Guliston Rus. Gulistan. Sirdaryo Viloyati, E Uzbekistan 40°29′N 68°46′E
Gulja see Yining
83 J6 Gulkana Alaska, USA 62°17′N 145°25′W
159 I3 Gullane United Kingdom 56°02′N 2°49′W
57 L8 Gull Lake Saskatchewan, S Canada 50°05′N 108°30′W
73 F8 Gull Lake ⊚ Michigan, N USA
74 G3 Gull Lake ⊚ Minnesota, N USA
243 J6 Gullonggang Jiangxi, SE China 26°26′N 115°42′E
155 G8 Gullspång Västra Götaland, S Sweden 58°58′N 14°04′E
214 B7 Güllük Körfezi prev. Akbük Limanı. bay W Turkey
232 D2 Gulmarg Jammu and Kashmir, NW India 34°04′N 74°25′E
Gulpaigan see Golpāyegān
163 H10 Gulpen Limburg, SE Netherlands 50°48′N 05°53′E
Gul'shad see Gul'shat
227 J6 Gul'shat var. Gul'shad. Karaganda, E Kazakhstan 46°37′N 74°22′E
136 B7 Gulu N Uganda 02°46′N 32°21′E
Gŭlŭbovo see Galabovo
185 J5 Gulyantsi Pleven, N Bulgaria 43°37′N 24°40′E
Gulyaypole see Hulyaypole
Guma see Pishan
Gümai see Darlag
134 F6 Gumba Equateur, NW Dem. Rep. Congo 02°58′N 21°23′E
Gumbinnen see Gusev
137 D12 Gumbiro Ruvuma, S Tanzania 10°19′S 35°40′E
228 B6 Gumdag prev. Kum-Dag. Balkan Welaýaty, W Turkmenistan 39°13′N 54°35′E
133 L5 Gumel Jigawa, N Nigeria 12°37′N 09°23′E
250 A2 Gumi prev. Kumi. 36°07′N 128°20′E
170 G3 Gumiel de Hizán Castilla y León, N Spain 41°46′N 03°42′W
233 I8 Gumla Jhārkhand, N India 23°03′N 84°36′E
Gumma see Gunma
181 D9 Gummersbach Nordrhein-Westfalen, W Germany 51°01′N 07°34′E
133 J5 Gummi Zamfara, NW Nigeria 12°07′N 05°07′E
181 I10 Gumpelstadt Thüringen, Germany 50°50′E 10°18′N
Gumpolds see Humpolec
Gumti see Gomati
141 I6 Gumtree Free State, South Africa 27°27′S 27°52′E
Gümülcine/Gümüljina see Komotiní
Gümüşane see Gümüşhane
215 H5 Gümüşhane var. Gümüşane, Gumushkhane. Gümüşhane, NE Turkey 40°31′N 39°27′E
215 H5 Gümüşhane var. Gümüşane, Gumushkhane. ⬖ province NE Turkey
Gumushkhane see Gümüşhane
261 J6 Gumzai Pulau Kola, E Indonesia 05°27′S 134°38′E
232 E7 Guna Madhya Pradesh, C India 24°39′N 77°18′E
Gunabad see Gonābād
Gunan see Qijiang
Gunbad-i-Qawus see Gonbad-e Kāvūs
277 J5 Gunbar New South Wales, SE Australia 34°03′S 145°32′E
277 K6 Gundagai New South Wales, SE Australia 35°06′S 148°03′E
181 G13 Gundelsheim Baden-Württemberg, Germany 49°17′E 9°10′N
134 F6 Gundji Equateur, N Dem. Rep. Congo 02°03′N 21°31′E
235 E8 Gundlupet Karnātaka, W India 11°48′N 76°42′E
214 D8 Gündoğmuş Antalya, S Turkey 36°50′N 32°07′E
187 M5 Guney Kütahya, Turkey 38°51′N 29°23′E
215 I6 Güney Doğu Toroslar ▲▲ SE Turkey
135 E9 Gungu Bandundu, SW Dem. Rep. Congo 05°43′S 19°20′E
197 J9 Gunib Respublika Dagestan, SW Russian Federation 42°24′N 46°55′E
184 E3 Gunja Vukovar-Srijem, E Croatia 44°53′N 18°51′E
73 F8 Gun Lake ⊚ Michigan, N USA
253 B12 Gunma off. Gunma-ken, var. Gumma. ⬖ prefecture Honshū, S Japan
Gunma-ken see Gunma
295 L6 Gunnbjørn Fjeld var. Gunnbjörns Bjerge. ▲ C Greenland 69°03′N 29°36′W
Gunnbjörns Bjerge see Gunnbjørn Fjeld
181 E8 Günne Nordrhein-Westfalen, Germany 51°30′E 8°02′N
277 L4 Gunnedah New South Wales, SE Australia 30°59′S 150°15′E
137 G10 Gunner's Quoin var. Coin de Mire. island N Mauritius
79 K4 Gunnison Colorado, C USA 38°33′N 106°55′W
79 H4 Gunnison Utah, W USA 39°09′N 111°49′W
79 J4 Gunnison River ∿ Colorado, C USA
67 L2 Gunpowder River ∿ Maryland, NE USA
Güns see Kőszeg
248 B6 Gunsan var. Gunsan, Jap. Gunzan; prev. Kunsan. W South Korea 35°58′N 126°42′E
Gunsan see Gunsan
177 J2 Gunskirchen Oberösterreich, N Austria 48°07′N 13°54′E
Gunt see Ghund
234 E6 Guntakal Andhra Pradesh, C India 15°11′N 77°24′E
181 E12 Guntersblum Rheinland-Pfalz, Germany 49°48′E 8°21′N
66 E8 Guntersville Alabama, S USA 34°21′N 86°17′W
66 D8 Guntersville Lake ⊠ Alabama, S USA
234 G6 Guntūr var. Guntur. Andhra Pradesh, SE India 16°20′N 80°27′E
258 C4 Gunungsitoli Pulau Nias, W Indonesia 01°11′N 97°35′E
234 H5 Gunupur Odisha, E India 19°04′N 83°52′E
160 C10 Gunwalloe United Kingdom 50°02′N 5°16′W
250 B2 Gunwi prev. Kunwi. Kyŏngsang-bukto, South Korea 36°14′N 128°34′E
179 E13 Günz ∿ S Germany
Gunzan see Gunsan
179 E12 Günzburg Bayern, S Germany 48°26′N 10°18′E
181 J14 Gunzenhausen Bayern, S Germany 49°07′N 10°45′E
244 B6 Guochengyi Gansu, China 36°08′N 104°33′E
245 J9 Guo He ∿ Anhui/Henan, C China
Guolüezhen see Lingbao
Guovdageaidnu see Kautokeino
245 J8 Guoyang Anhui, E China 33°30′N 116°12′E
245 K8 Gupei Jiangsu, E China 34°07′N 117°53′E
188 B7 Gurahonţ Hung. Honctő. Arad, W Romania 46°16′N 22°21′E
Gurahumora see Gura Humorului
188 E6 Gura Humorului Ger. Gurahumora. Suceava, NE Romania 47°31′N 26°00′E
228 E5 Gurbansoltan Eje prev. Ýylanly, Rus. Il'yaly. Daşoguz Welaýaty, N Turkmenistan 41°57′N 59°42′E
238 F3 Gurbantünggüt Shamo desert W China
232 E3 Gurdāspur Punjab, N India 32°04′N 75°28′E
75 H13 Gurdon Arkansas, C USA 33°55′N 93°09′W
Gurdzhaani see Gurjaani
190 J2 Gurenichi Leningradskaya Oblast', Russian Federation
Gurgan see Gorgān
232 E5 Gurgaon Haryāna, N India 28°27′N 77°01′E
108 E6 Gurguéia, Rio ∿ NE Brazil
103 I4 Guri, Embalse de ⊠ E Venezuela
215 L4 Gurjaani Rus. Gurdzhaani. E Georgia 41°42′N 45°47′E
177 J4 Gurk Kärnten, S Austria 46°52′N 14°17′E
177 J4 Gurk Slvn. Krka. ∿ S Austria
Gurkfeld see Krško
185 K6 Gurkovo prev. Kolupchii. Stara Zagora, C Bulgaria 42°42′N 25°46′E
177 J4 Gurktaler Alpen ▲▲ S Austria
228 E5 Gurlan Rus. Gurlen. Xorazm Viloyati, W Uzbekistan 41°54′N 60°18′E
Gurlen see Gurlan
139 I3 Guro Manica, C Mozambique 17°28′S 33°18′E
214 G6 Gürün Sivas, C Turkey 38°44′N 37°15′E
108 B7 Gurupi Tocantins, C Brazil 11°44′S 49°01′W
107 N3 Gurupi, Rio ∿ NE Brazil
219 C11 Gurûr, Wâdi el Egypt
232 C7 Guru Sikhar ▲ NW India 24°45′N 72°51′E
239 I2 Gurvanbulag var. Höviyn Am. Bayanhongor, C Mongolia 47°08′N 98°41′E
239 K1 Gurvanbulag var. Avdzaga. Bulgan, C Mongolia 47°43′N 103°30′E
239 J3 Gurvantes var. Urt. Ömnögovĭ, S Mongolia 43°16′N 101°00′E
Gur'yev/Gur'yevskaya Oblast' see Atyrau
250 C3 Guryongpo prev. Kuryongp'o. Kyŏngsang-bukto, South Korea 35°59′N 129°33′E
133 J5 Gusau Zamfara, NW Nigeria 12°18′N 06°27′E
191 C9 Gusev Ger. Gumbinnen. Kaliningradskaya Oblast', W Russian Federation 54°36′N 22°14′E
245 N2 Gushan Liaoning, China 39°32′N 123°20′E
228 F9 Gushgy Rus. Kushka. ∿ Mary Welaýaty, S Turkmenistan
Gush Ḥalav see Jīsh
243 I1 Gushi Henan, China 32°06′N 115°25′E
Gushiago see Gushiegu
133 H6 Gushiegu var. Gushiago. NE Ghana 09°54′N 00°12′W
251 I10 Gushikawa Okinawa, Okinawa, SW Japan 26°21′N 127°50′E
184 F6 Gusinje E Montenegro 42°34′N 19°51′E
191 I8 Gusino Smolenskaya Oblast', Russian Federation
193 I8 Gusinoozersk Respublika Buryatiya, S Russian Federation 51°18′N 106°28′E
196 G2 Gus'-Khrustal'nyy Vladimirskaya Oblast', W Russian Federation 55°39′N 40°42′E
175 B10 Guspini Sardegna, Italy, C Mediterranean Sea 39°33′N 08°39′E
177 L4 Güssing Burgenland, SE Austria 47°03′N 16°19′E
177 K3 Gusswerk Steiermark, E Austria 47°43′N 15°18′E
152 B5 Gustav Adolf Land physical region NE Svalbard
293 L3 Gustav Bull Mountains ▲▲ Antarctica
84 D2 Gustavo Sotelo Sonora, Mexico 31°33′N 113°34′W
83 L7 Gustavus Alaska, USA 58°24′N 135°44′W
152 B4 Gustav V Land physical region NE Svalbard
80 C4 Gustine California, W USA 37°14′N 121°00′W
70 G5 Gustine Texas, SW USA 31°51′N 98°24′W
178 G5 Güstrow Mecklenburg-Vorpommern, NE Germany 53°48′N 12°12′E
155 H9 Gusum Östergötland, S Sweden 58°15′N 16°30′E
Guta/Gúta see Kolárovo
Gutenstein see Ravne na Koroškem
180 E7 Gütersloh Nordrhein-Westfalen, W Germany 51°54′N 08°23′E
75 E12 Guthrie Oklahoma, C USA 35°53′N 97°26′W
70 E3 Guthrie Texas, SW USA 33°38′N 100°21′W
74 G7 Guthrie Center Iowa, C USA 41°40′N 94°30′W
243 L6 Gutian Fujian, China 26°20′N 118°26′E
243 L6 Gutian Shuiku ⊠ Fujian, China
86 G5 Gutiérrez Zamora Veracruz-Llave, E Mexico 20°29′N 97°07′W
Guting see Yutai
Gutta see Kolárovo
74 I6 Guttenberg Iowa, C USA 42°47′N 91°06′W
Guttentag see Dobrodzień
Guttstadt see Dobre Miasto
239 I2 Guulin Govĭ-Altay, C Mongolia 46°33′N 97°21′E
233 L6 Guwāhāti prev. Gauhāti. Assam, NE India 26°09′N 91°42′E
217 I2 Guwēr var. Al Kuwayr, Al Quwayr, Quwair. Arbīl, N Iraq 36°03′N 43°30′E
228 A5 Guwlumaýak Rus. Kuuli-Mayak. Balkan Welaýaty, NW Turkmenistan 40°14′N 52°43′E
103 J5 Guyana off. Co-operative Republic of Guyana; prev. British Guiana. ◆ republic N South America
Guyana, Co-operative Republic of see Guyana
67 H3 Guyandotte River ∿ West Virginia, NE USA
Guyane see French Guiana
244 F2 Guyang Inner Mongolia, China 41°01′N 110°02′E
161 K3 Guyhirn United Kingdom 52°37′N 0°04′E
Guyi see Sanjiang
75 B11 Guymon Oklahoma, C USA 36°42′N 101°30′W
228 F7 Guynuk Lebap Welaýaty, NE Turkmenistan 39°18′N 63°00′E
Guyong see Jiangle
66 G6 Guyot, Mount ▲ North Carolina/Tennessee, SE USA 35°42′N 83°15′W
277 L3 Guyra New South Wales, SE Australia 30°13′S 151°42′E
245 I1 Guyuan Hebei, China 41°24′N 115°25′E
244 C6 Guyuan Ningxia, N China 35°57′N 106°13′E
Guzar see G'uzor
218 B2 Güzelyurt Gk. Kólpos Mórfu, Morphou. W Cyprus 35°12′N 33°E
218 B2 Güzelyurt Körfezi var. Morfou Bay, Morphou Bay, Gk. Kólpos Mórfou. bay W Cyprus
245 K9 Guzhen Anhui, China 38°11′N 117°11′E
Guzhou see Rongjiang
84 G2 Guzmán Chihuahua, N Mexico 31°13′N 107°27′W
84 G2 Guzmán, Laguna de ⊚ Chihuahua, Mexico
229 H7 G'uzor Rus. Guzar. Qashqadaryo Viloyati, S Uzbekistan 38°41′N 66°12′E
191 B9 Gvardeysk Ger. Tapaiu. Kaliningradskaya Oblast', W Russian Federation 54°39′N 21°02′E
Gvardeyskoye see Hvardiys'ke
277 K3 Gwabegar New South Wales, SE Australia 30°34′S 148°58′E
230 D9 Gwādar var. Gwadur. Baluchistān, SW Pakistan 25°09′N 62°21′E
230 D9 Gwādar East Bay bay SW Pakistan
230 D9 Gwādar West Bay bay SW Pakistan
Gwadur see Gwādar
138 G3 Gwai Matabeleland North, W Zimbabwe 19°17′S 27°37′E
160 E2 Gwalchmai United Kingdom 53°15′N 4°25′W
232 F6 Gwalior Madhya Pradesh, C India 26°16′N 78°12′E
138 G4 Gwanda Matabeleland South, SW Zimbabwe 20°56′S 29°E
134 H5 Gwane Orientale, N Dem. Rep. Congo 04°40′N 25°51′E
248 B7 Gwangju off. Kwangju-gwangyŏksi, var. Guangju, Kwangchu, Jap. Kōshū; prev. Kwangju. SW South Korea 35°09′N 126°53′E
250 A1 Gwangju prev. Kwangju. Kyŏnggi-do, South Korea 37°25′N 127°16′E
250 A4 Gwangyang prev. Kwangyang. 34°58′N 127°35′E
138 G3 Gwayi ∿ W Zimbabwe
182 E4 Gwda var. Głda, Ger. Küddow. ∿ NW Poland
156 B7 Gweebarra Bay Ir. Béal an Bheara. inlet W Ireland
158 B5 Gweedore Ir. Gaoth Dobhair. Donegal, NW Ireland 55°03′N 08°14′W
Gwelo see Gweru
157 G11 Gwent cultural region S Wales, United Kingdom
139 H4 Gweru prev. Gwelo. Midlands, C Zimbabwe 19°27′S 29°49′E
74 E4 Gwinner North Dakota, N USA 46°10′N 97°42′W
133 M6 Gwoza Borno, NE Nigeria 11°07′N 13°40′E
Gwy see Wye
160 F2 Gwyddelwern United Kingdom 53°00′N 3°23′W
277 L3 Gwydir River ∿ New South Wales, SE Australia
157 F10 Gwynedd var. Gwyneth. cultural region NW Wales, United Kingdom
Gwyneth see Gwynedd
167 L8 Gy Franche-Comté, France 47°24′N 5°49′E
239 H9 Gyaca var. Ngarrab. Xizang Zizhiqu, W China 29°06′N 92°37′E
Gya'gya see Saga
Gyaijêpozhanggê see Zhidoi
Gyaisi see Jiulong
187 K8 Gyalí var. Yialí. island Dodekánisa, Greece, Aegean Sea
Gyamotang see Dêngqên
Gyandzha see Gäncä
Gyangkar see Dinggyê
238 G9 Gyangzê Xizang Zizhiqu, W China 28°50′N 89°38′E
238 F8 Gyaring Co ⊚ W China
239 I7 Gyaring Hu ⊚ C China
187 I7 Gyáros var. Yioúra. island Kykládes, Greece, Aegean Sea
192 G4 Gyda Yamalo-Nenetskiy Avtonomnyy Okrug, N Russian Federation 70°55′N 78°34′E
192 G4 Gydanskiy Poluostrov Eng. Gyda Peninsula. peninsula N Russian Federation
Gyda Peninsula see Gydanskiy Poluostrov
171 I10 Gydel Algeria
140 D9 Gydo Pass pass Western Cape, South Africa
Gyêgu see Yushu
250 A1 Gyeonggi-do prev. Kyŏnggi-do. ⬖
248 B5 Gyeonggi-man prev. Kyŏnggi-man. bay NW South Korea
248 C6 Gyeongju Jap. Keishū; prev. Kyŏngju. SE South Korea 35°49′N 129°09′E
250 B3 Gyeongsan prev. Kyŏngsan. 35°47′N 128°43′E
250 B2 Gyeongsangbuk-do prev. Kyŏngsangbuk-do. ⬖
250 A3 Gyeongsangnam-Do prev. Kyŏngsangnam-do. ⬖
Gyéres see Câmpia Turzii
Gyergyószentmiklós see Gheorgheni
Gyergyótölgyes see Tulgheş
Gyertyámos see Cărpiniş
Gyeva see Detva
Gyigang see Zayü
Gyixong see Gonggar
178 G2 Gyldenløveshøy hill range C Denmark
277 M1 Gympie Queensland, E Australia 26°05′S 152°40′E
256 C6 Gyobingauk Bago, SW Myanmar (Burma) 18°14′N 95°39′E
183 H12 Gyomaendrőd Békés, SE Hungary 46°56′N 20°50′E
Gyömbér see Ďumbier
183 G11 Gyöngyös Heves, NE Hungary 47°44′N 19°49′E
183 E11 Győr Ger. Raab, Lat. Arrabona. Győr-Moson-Sopron, NW Hungary 47°41′N 17°40′E
183 E11 Győr-Moson-Sopron off. Győr-Moson-Sopron Megye. ⬖ county NW Hungary
Győr-Moson-Sopron Megye see Győr-Moson-Sopron
54 F4 Gypsum Point headland Northwest Territories, NW Canada
55 I9 Gypsumville Manitoba, S Canada 51°47′N 98°38′W
59 H2 Gyrfalcon Islands island group Northwest Territories, NE Canada
154 I7 Gysinge Gävleborg, C Sweden 60°16′N 16°55′E
186 G8 Gýtheio var. Githio; prev. Yíthion. Pelopónnisos, S Greece 36°46′N 22°34′E
228 G7 Gyuichbirleshik Lebap Welaýaty, E Turkmenistan 38°10′N 64°33′E
183 H12 Gyula Rom. Jula. Békés, SE Hungary 46°39′N 21°17′E
Gyulafehérvár see Alba Iulia
Gyulovo see Roza
215 K5 Gyumri var. Giumri, Rus. Kumayri; prev. Aleksandropol', Leninakan. W Armenia 40°48′N 43°51′E
228 C7 Gyunuzyndag, Gora ▲ Balkan Welaýaty, W Turkmenistan 38°15′N 56°25′E
228 F8 Gyzylbaydak Rus. Krasnoye Znamya. Mary Welaýaty, S Turkmenistan 36°51′N 62°24′E
Gyzyletrek see Etrek
228 C5 Gyzylgaýa Rus. Kizyl-Kaya. Balkan Welaýaty, NW Turkmenistan 40°37′N 55°15′E
228 A6 Gyzylsuw Rus. Kizyl-Su. Balkan Welaýaty, W Turkmenistan 39°49′N 53°00′E
Gyzyrlabat see Serdar
Gzhatsk see Gagarin

H

233 K6 Ha W Bhutan 27°17′N 89°22′E
Haabai see Ha'apai Group
163 E10 Haacht Vlaams Brabant, C Belgium 50°58′N 04°38′E
177 J2 Haag Niederösterreich, NE Austria 48°07′N 14°32′E
292 F5 Haag Nunataks ▲▲ Antarctica
141 J2 Haakdoring Limpopo, South Africa 24°26′S 28°49′E
152 A5 Haakon VII Land physical region NW Svalbard
162 I6 Haaksbergen Overijssel, E Netherlands 52°09′N 06°45′E
163 C8 Haamstede Zeeland, SW Netherlands 51°43′N 03°45′E
284 D7 Ha'ano island Ha'apai Group, C Tonga
284 D7 Ha'apai Group var. Haabai. island group C Tonga
152 H7 Haapajärvi Pohjois-Pohjanmaa, C Finland 63°45′N 25°20′E
153 H9 Haapamäki Pirkanmaa, C Finland 62°11′N 24°32′E
152 H7 Haapavesi Pohjois-Pohjanmaa, C Finland 64°09′N 25°25′E
285 L3 Haapiti Moorea, W French Polynesia 17°33′S 149°52′W
190 D4 Haapsalu Ger. Hapsal. Läänemaa, W Estonia 58°58′N 23°32′E
Ha'Arava see 'Arabah, Wādī al
155 D13 Haarby var. Hårby. Syddtjylland, C Denmark 55°13′N 10°07′E
181 F8 Haaren Nordrhein-Westfalen, Germany 51°34′E 8°44′N
162 E6 Haarlem prev. Harlem. Noord-Holland, W Netherlands 52°23′N 04°39′E
278 C10 Haast West Coast, South Island, New Zealand 43°53′S 169°02′E
278 C10 Haast ∿ South Island, New Zealand
278 C10 Haast Pass pass South Island, New Zealand
284 E10 Ha'atua 'Eau, E Tonga 21°23′S 174°57′W
230 F9 Hab ∿ SW Pakistan
221 J4 Haba var. Al Haba. Dubayy, NE United Arab Emirates 25°01′N 55°37′E
238 F1 Habahe var. Kaba. Xinjiang Uygur Zizhiqu, NW China 48°04′N 86°20′E
221 J7 Ḩabarūt var. Habrut. SW Oman 17°19′N 52°45′E
136 E7 Habaswein Isiolo, NE Kenya 01°01′N 39°27′E
163 G13 Habay-la-Neuve Luxembourg, SE Belgium 49°43′N 05°38′E
217 I5 Ḩabbānīyah, Buḩayrat ⊚ C Iraq
218 F4 Habbouch Lebanon 33°24′N 35°29′E
Habelschwerdt see Bystrzyca Kłodzka
233 L7 Habiganj Sylhet, NE Bangladesh 24°23′N 91°25′E
245 I1 Habirag Nei Mongol Zizhiqu, N China 42°18′N 115°40′E
155 G10 Habo Västra Götaland, S Sweden 57°55′N 14°05′E
252 J4 Habomai Islands island group Kuril'skiye Ostrova, SE Russian Federation
218 D6 HaBonim Israel 32°38′N 34°56′E
252 E3 Haboro Hokkaidō, NE Japan 44°19′N 141°42′E
161 K1 Habrough United Kingdom 53°36′N 0°15′W
Habrut see Ḩabarūt
221 J4 Ḩabshān Abū Z̧aby, C United Arab Emirates 23°51′N 53°34′E
102 B8 Hacha Putumayo, S Colombia 0°02′S 75°30′W
251 M7 Hachijō-jima island Izu-shotō, SE Japan
251 J3 Hachiman Gifu, Honshū, SW Japan 35°46′N 136°57′E
253 C8 Hachimori Akita, Honshū, C Japan 40°22′N 139°59′E
252 E7 Hachinohe Aomori, Honshū, C Japan 40°30′N 141°29′E
251 M8 Hachiōji Tōkyō, Hachijō-jima, SE Japan 35°40′N 139°20′E
253 B13 Hachiōji Tōkyō, Honshū, S Japan 35°40′N 139°20′E
86 F2 Hacienda de la Mesa Tamaulipas, Mexico 24°14′N 99°35′W
81 D10 Hacienda Heights California, USA 34°00′N 117°58′W
215 M5 Hacıqabal prev. Qazimämmäd. SE Azerbaijan 40°03′N 48°56′E
154 G4 Hackås Jämtland, C Sweden 62°55′N 14°31′E
65 H6 Hackensack New Jersey, NE USA 40°51′N 73°57′W
64 G6 Hackettstown New Jersey, USA 40°51′N 74°50′W
128 G6 Ḩadabat al Jilf al Kabīr var. Gilf Kebir Plateau. plateau SW Egypt
Hadama see Nazrēt
253 B13 Hadano Kanagawa, Honshū, S Japan 35°22′N 139°14′E
221 J7 Ḩadbaram S Oman 17°27′N 55°13′E
218 G2 Hadchit Lebanon
218 G2 Hadchit Lebanon 34°15′N 35°59′E
217 J8 Ḩaddānīyah well S Iraq
159 I3 Haddington SE Scotland, United Kingdom 55°59′N 02°46′W
161 M3 Haddiscoe United Kingdom 52°31′N 1°35′E
221 L5 Ḩadd, Ra's al headland NE Oman 22°28′N 59°58′E
Haded see Xadeed
133 L5 Hadejia Jigawa, N Nigeria 12°22′N 10°02′E
133 L5 Hadejia ∿ N Nigeria
218 D7 Ḫadera Israel 32°26′N 34°55′E
218 D7 Hadera var. Khadera; prev. Ḫadera. Haifa, N Israel 32°26′N 34°55′E
Ḫadera see Hadera
Hadersleben see Haderslev
155 D13 Haderslev Ger. Hadersleben. Syddanmark, SW Denmark 55°15′N 09°30′E
235 C13 Hadhdhunmathi Atoll atoll S Maldives
221 J9 Hadīboh Suquţrā, SE Yemen 12°38′N 54°05′E
238 F6 Hadilik Xinjiang Uygur Zizhiqu, W China 37°51′N 86°10′E
214 D7 Hadım Konya, S Turkey 36°58′N 32°27′E
220 D4 Hadīyah Al Madīnah, W Saudi Arabia 25°36′N 38°31′E
134 D2 Hadjer-Lamis off. Région du Hadjer-Lamis. ⬖ region SW Chad
Hadjer-Lamis, Région du see Hadjer-Lamis
171 L9 Hadjout Algeria
161 L6 Hadleigh United Kingdom 51°32′N 0°36′E
161 H3 Hadley United Kingdom 52°42′N 2°29′W
52 F6 Hadley Bay bay Victoria Island, Nunavut, N Canada
180 J7 Hadmersleben Sachsen-Anhalt, Germany 51°59′E 11°18′N
160 G3 Hadnall United Kingdom 52°46′N 2°43′W
256 H5 Ha Đông var. Hadong. Ha Tây, N Vietnam 20°58′N 105°46′E
Hadong see Ha Đông
Hadramaut see Ḩaḑramawt
136 I2 Ḩaḑramawt Eng. Hadramaut. ▲▲ S Yemen
Hadria see Adria
Hadrianopolis see Edirne
159 J5 Hadrian's Wall ancient wall N England, United Kingdom
Hadria Picena see Apricena
155 D11 Hadsten Midtjylland, C Denmark 56°19′N 10°03′E
155 D11 Hadsund Nordjylland, N Denmark 56°43′N 10°08′E
189 J3 Hadyach Rus. Gadyach. Poltavs'ka Oblast', NE Ukraine 50°21′N 34°00′E
185 M6 Hadzhiyska Reka var. Khadzhiyska Reka. ∿ E Bulgaria
184 E5 Hadžići Federacija Bosne I Hercegovine, SE Bosnia and Herzegovina 43°49′N 18°12′E
248 B5 Haeju S North Korea 38°04′N 125°40′E
Haerbin/Haerhpin/Ha-erh-pin see Harbin
220 G3 Ḩafar al Bāţin Ash Sharqīyah, N Saudi Arabia 28°25′N 45°59′E
180 I1 Haffkrug Schleswig-Holstein, Germany 54°03′E 10°45′N
57 M5 Hafford Saskatchewan, S Canada 52°43′N 107°19′W
214 G5 Hafik Sivas, N Turkey 39°53′N 37°24′E
219 F13 Ḩafīr, Wādī dry watercourse Jordan
231 J5 Ḩāfizābād Punjab, E Pakistan 32°03′N 73°42′E
152 B3 Hafnarfjörður Höfuðborgarsvæðið, W Iceland 64°03′N 21°57′W
Hafnia see Denmark
Hafnia see København
Hafren see Severn
Hafun see Xaafuun
Hafun, Ras see Xaafuun, Raas
136 C2 Hag 'Abdullah Sinnar, E Sudan 13°59′N 33°35′E
137 F8 Hagadera Garissa, E Kenya 0°06′N 40°23′E
218 E5 HaGalil Eng. Galilee. ▲▲ N Israel
62 C2 Hagar Ontario, S Canada 46°27′N 80°22′W
234 E7 Hagari var. Vedāvati. ∿ W India
282 A2 Hagåtña , var. Agaña. O (Guam) NW Guam 13°27′N 144°45′E
180 D2 Hage Niedersachsen, Germany 53°37′E 7°16′N
178 G7 Hagelberg hill NE Germany
82 G7 Hagemeister Island island Alaska, USA
181 D8 Hagen Nordrhein-Westfalen, W Germany 51°22′N 07°27′E
180 J3 Hagenow Mecklenburg-Vorpommern, N Germany 53°27′N 11°10′E
56 C5 Hagensborg British Columbia, SW Canada 52°24′N 126°24′W
136 E4 Hāgere Hiywet var. Agere Hiywet, Ambo. Oromīya, C Ethiopia 09°00′N 37°55′E
76 G8 Hagerman Idaho, NW USA 42°48′N 114°53′W
79 M9 Hagerman New Mexico, SW USA 33°07′N 104°19′W
64 B8 Hagerstown Maryland, NE USA 39°39′N 77°44′W
62 C6 Hagersville Ontario, S Canada 42°58′N 80°03′W
164 F8 Hagetmau Landes, SW France 43°40′N 00°36′W
154 G7 Hagfors Värmland, C Sweden 60°03′N 13°45′E
154 G3 Häggenås Jämtland, C Sweden 63°24′N 14°53′E
250 D5 Hagi Yamaguchi, Honshū, SW Japan 34°25′N 131°22′E
256 G4 Ha Giang Ha Giang, N Vietnam 22°50′N 104°58′E
Hagios Evstrátios see Ágios Efstrátios
HaGolan see Golan Heights
165 K3 Hagondange Moselle, NE France 49°16′N 06°06′E
157 B10 Hag's Head Ir. Ceann Caillí. headland W Ireland 52°56′N 09°29′W
166 C3 Hague, Cap de la headland N France 49°43′N 01°56′W
165 L3 Haguenau Bas-Rhin, NE France 48°49′N 07°47′E
251 N9 Hahajima-rettō island group SE Japan
139 I9 Hahaya ✈ (Moroni) Grande Comore, NW Comoros
181 D9 Hahn Nordrhein-Westfalen, Germany 51°01′E 7°27′N
180 I7 Hahndorf Niedersachsen, Germany 51°58′E 10°26′N
68 E4 Hahnville Louisiana, S USA 29°58′N 90°24′W
140 D5 Haib Karas, S Namibia 28°12′S 18°19′E
Haibak see Aibak
230 F9 Haibo ∿ SW Pakistan
Haibowan see Wuhai
245 N2 Haicheng Liaoning, NE China 40°53′N 122°45′E
Haicheng see Haifeng
Haicheng see Haiyuan
Haida see Nový Bor
Haidarabad see Hyderābād
Haidenschaft see Ajdovščina
256 H5 Hai Dương Hai Hưng, N Vietnam 20°56′N 106°21′E
218 D6 Haifa ⬖ district NW Israel
Haifa see Hefa
Haifa, Bay of see Mifrats Hefa
243 I9 Haifeng var. Haicheng. Guangdong, S China 22°56′N 115°19′E
Haifong see Hai Phong
245 J4 Hai He ∿ E China
Haikang see Leizhou
240 F9 Haikou var. Hai-k'ou, Hoihow, Fr. Hoï-Hao. province capital Hainan, S China 20°N 110°17′E
Hai-k'ou see Haikou
220 E3 Ḩā'il Ḩā'il, NW Saudi Arabia 27°N 42°50′E
220 E3 Ḩā'il off. Minţaqah Ḩā'il. ⬖ province N Saudi Arabia
247 J3 Hailar He ∿ NE China
76 G7 Hailey Idaho, NW USA 43°31′N 114°18′W
62 D1 Haileybury Ontario, S Canada 47°27′N 79°39′W
248 E1 Hailin Heilongjiang, NE China 44°37′N 129°24′E
Ḩā'il, Minţaqah see Ḩā'il
Hailong see Meihekou
161 L8 Hailsham United Kingdom 50°52′N 0°16′E
247 L3 Hailun Heilongjiang, NE China 48°16′N 126°29′E
152 H7 Hailuoto Swe. Karlö. island W Finland
Haima see Haymā'
243 J9 Haimen Guangdong, SE China 23°12′N 116°37′E
243 M1 Haimen Jiangsu, China 31°32′N 121°05′E
Haimen see Taizhou
240 F9 Hainan var. Hainan Sheng, Qiong. ⬖ province S China
240 F9 Hainan Dao island S China
Hainan Sheng see Hainan
Hainan Strait see Qiongzhou Haixia
Hainasch see Ainaži
Hainau see Chojnów
163 D11 Hainaut ⬖ province SW Belgium
Hainburg see Hainburg an der Donau
177 M2 Hainburg an der Donau var. Hainburg. Niederösterreich, NE Austria 48°09′N 16°57′E
83 L6 Haines Alaska, USA 59°13′N 135°27′W
76 E6 Haines Oregon, NW USA 44°53′N 117°56′W
69 L6 Haines City Florida, SE USA 28°06′N 81°37′W
54 A3 Haines Junction Yukon, W Canada 60°45′N 137°30′W
177 L2 Hainfeld Niederösterreich, NE Austria 48°03′N 15°47′E
179 H9 Hainichen Sachsen, E Germany 50°58′N 13°08′E
243 M2 Haining Zhejiang, China 30°19′N 120°25′E
Hai Ninh see Mong Cai
256 H5 Hai Phong var. Haifong, Haiphong. N Vietnam 20°50′N 106°41′E
Haiphong see Hai Phong
243 M7 Haitan Dao island SE China
90 G5 Haiti off. Republic of Haiti. ◆ republic C West Indies
Haiti, Republic of see Haiti
80 F7 Haiwee Reservoir ⊠ California, W USA
129 K8 Haiya Red Sea, NE Sudan 18°17′N 36°21′E
239 J6 Haiyan var. Sanjiaocheng. Qinghai, W China 36°55′N 100°54′E
243 M2 Haiyan Zhejiang, E China 30°31′N 120°56′E
245 M5 Haiyang prev. Dongcun. Shandong, China 34°28′N 121°06′E
Haiyang see Xiuning
245 N3 Haiyang Dao island Liaoning, China
242 F7 Haiyang Shan ▲▲ S China
244 C6 Haiyuan Ningxia, N China 36°32′N 105°31′E
245 L7 Haizhou Wan bay Jiangsu, China
Hajda see Nový Bor
183 H11 Hajdú-Bihar off. Hajdú-Bihar Megye. ⬖ county E Hungary
Hajdú-Bihar Megye see Hajdú-Bihar
183 H11 Hajdúböszörmény Hajdú-Bihar, E Hungary 47°39′N 21°32′E
183 I11 Hajdúhadház Hajdú-Bihar, E Hungary 47°40′N 21°40′E
183 H11 Hajdúnánás Hajdú-Bihar, E Hungary 47°50′N 21°26′E
183 H11 Hajdúszoboszló Hajdú-Bihar, E Hungary 47°27′N 21°24′E
175 B14 Hajeb El Ayoun Tunisia
217 J1 Ḩājī Ebrāhīm, Kūh-e ▲ Iran/Iraq 36°53′N 44°56′E
253 B10 Hajiki-zaki headland Sado, C Japan 38°19′N 138°28′E
Hajîne see Abū Ḩardān
233 I7 Hājīpur Bihār, N India 25°41′N 85°13′E
220 F8 Ḩajjah W Yemen 15°43′N 43°33′E
217 K7 Ḩajjama Al Muthanná, S Iraq 31°24′N 45°20′E
223 H8 Ḩājjīābād Hormozgān, C Iran
217 J9 Ḩājj, Thaqb al well S Iraq
184 F6 Hajla ▲▲ E Montenegro
182 J5 Hajnówka Ger. Hermhausen. Podlaskie, NE Poland 52°45′N 23°32′E
Haka see Hakha
Hakapehi see Punaauia
Hakâri see Hakkâri
219 D11 HaKatan, HaMakhtesh prev. HaMakhtesh HaQatan. ▲▲ S Israel
180 J6 Hakenstedt Sachsen-Anhalt, Germany 52°11′E 11°16′N
256 B4 Hakha var. Haka. Chin State, W Myanmar (Burma) 22°42′N 93°41′E
215 K7 Hakkâri var. Çölemerik, Hakâri. Hakkâri, SE Turkey 37°36′N 43°45′E
215 K7 Hakkâri var. Hakkari. ⬖ province SE Turkey
Hakkari see Hakkâri
152 G5 Hakkas Norrbotten, N Sweden 66°53′N 21°36′E
251 I5 Hakken-zan ▲ Honshū, SW Japan 34°11′N 135°57′E
252 D7 Hakkōda-san ▲ Honshū, C Japan 40°40′N 140°49′E
252 F2 Hako-dake ▲ Hokkaidō, NE Japan 44°40′N 142°22′E
252 D6 Hakodate Hokkaidō, NE Japan 41°46′N 140°43′E
140 E4 Hakskeenpan salt lake Northern Cape, South Africa
251 J2 Hakui Ishikawa, Honshū, SW Japan 36°55′N 136°46′E
285 I10 Hakupu SE Niue 19°06′S 169°50′E
251 J3 Haku-san ▲ Honshū, SW Japan 36°07′N 136°45′E
Hakusan see Mattō
Hal see Halle
230 G9 Hāla Sind, SE Pakistan 25°47′N 68°28′E
216 D2 Ḩalab Eng. Aleppo, Fr. Alep; anc. Beroea. Ḩalab, NW Syria 36°14′N 37°10′E
216 D2 Ḩalab off. Muḩāfaz̧at Ḩalab, var. Aleppo, Halab. ⬖ governorate NW Syria
216 D2 Ḩalab ✈ Ḩalab, NW Syria 36°12′N 37°10′E
Halab see Ḩalab
220 F5 Ḩalabān var. Halibān. Ar Riyāḑ, C Saudi Arabia 23°29′N 44°20′E
Ḩalabja see Hełebce
Ḩalabjah see Hełebce
Ḩalab, Muḩāfaz̧at see Ḩalab
228 G7 Halaç Rus. Khalach. Lebap Welaýaty, E Turkmenistan 38°05′N 64°46′E
87 L5 Halachó Yucatán, Mexico 20°29′N 90°05′W
285 H10 Halagigie Point headland W Niue
129 K6 Halaib SE Egypt 22°10′N 36°33′E
129 K6 Hala'ib Triangle ⬖ disputed region S Egypt / N Sudan
284 C10 Halalo Île Uvea, N Wallis and Futuna 13°21′S 176°11′W
256 I7 Ha Lam Quang Nam-Đa Năng, C Vietnam 15°42′N 108°24′E
Halandri see Chalándri
221 K7 Ḩalāniyāt, Juzur al var. Jazā'ir Bin Ghalfān, Eng. Kuria Muria Islands. island group S Oman
221 K7 Ḩalānīyāt, Khalīj al Eng. Kuria Muria Bay. bay S Oman
Halas see Kiskunhalas
218 F7 Ḩalāwah Jordan 32°23′N 35°39′E
218 G1 Halba Lebanon
Halban see Tsetserleg
180 J7 Halberstadt Sachsen-Anhalt, C Germany 51°54′N 11°04′E
218 G3 Ḩalbūn Syria 33°40′N 36°15′E

◆ Country
● Country Capital
◇ Dependent Territory
○ Dependent Territory Capital
⬖ Administrative Regions
✈ International Airport
▲ Mountain
▲▲ Mountain Range
⛰ Volcano
∿ River
⊚ Lake
⊠ Reservoir

INDEX

◆ Country   ◇ Dependent Territory   ✕ Administrative Regions   ★ International Airport   ▲ Mountain   ▲ Mountain Range   ⧩ Volcano   ≈ River   ◎ Lake   ▦ Reservoir
● Country Capital   ○ Dependent Territory Capital

India - Iténez, Río
INDEX
353

India see Inđija
62 D8 **Indiana** Pennsylvania, NE USA 40°37′N 79°09′W
73 F10 **Indiana** off. State of Indiana, also known as Hoosier State. ◐ state N USA
73 F11 **Indianapolis** state capital Indiana, N USA 39°46′N 86°09′W
54 E5 **Indian Cabins** Alberta, W Canada 59°51′N 117°06′W
88 E1 **Indian Church** Orange Walk, N Belize 17°47′N 88°39′W
Indian Desert see Thar Desert
72 E5 **Indian Lake** ◎ Michigan, N USA
62 G5 **Indian Lake** ◎ New York, NE USA
73 H10 **Indian Lake** ▣ Ohio, N USA
289 F10 **Indian Ocean** ocean
74 G7 **Indianola** Iowa, C USA 41°21′N 93°33′W
66 A8 **Indianola** Mississippi, S USA 33°27′N 90°39′W
110 B1 **Indianópolis** Minas Gerais, Brazil 19°02′S 47°55′W
78 G4 **Indian Peak** ▲ Utah, W USA 38°18′N 113°52′W
69 M6 **Indian River** lagoon Florida, SE USA
81 I8 **Indian Springs** Nevada, W USA 36°33′N 115°40′W
69 N7 **Indiantown** Florida, SE USA 27°01′N 80°29′W
Indian Union see India
109 B10 **Indiara** Goiás, S Brazil 17°12′S 50°09′W
India, Republic of see India
India, Union of see India
195 I3 **Indiga** Nenetskiy Avtonomnyy Okrug, NW Russian Federation 67°40′N 49°01′E
193 K4 **Indigirka** ≈ NE Russian Federation
184 F3 **Inđija** Hung. India; prev. Indjija. Vojvodina, N Serbia 45°03′N 20°04′E
81 G12 **Indio** California, W USA 33°42′N 116°13′W
89 H7 **Indio, Río** ≈ SE Nicaragua
232 E5 **Indira Gandhi** ✈ (Delhi) Delhi, N India
280 G5 **Indispensable Reefs** reef Central, S Solomon Islands
281 J2 **Indispensable Strait** strait C Solomon Islands
Indjija see Inđija
205 J8 **Indo-Australian Plate** tectonic feature
289 C11 **Indomed Fracture Zone** tectonic feature SW Indian Ocean
254 G8 **Indonesia** off. Republic of Indonesia, Ind. Republik Indonesia; prev. Dutch East Indies, Netherlands East Indies, United States of Indonesia. ◆ republic SE Asia
Indonesian Borneo see Kalimantan
Indonesia, Republic of see Indonesia
Indonesia, Republik see Indonesia
Indonesia, United States of see Indonesia
232 D8 **Indore** Madhya Pradesh, C India 22°42′N 75°51′E
258 E5 **Indragiri, Sungai** var. Batang Kuantan, Inderagiri. ≈ Sumatera, W Indonesia
Indramajoe/Indramaju see Indramayu
259 H8 **Indramayu** prev. Indramajoe, Indramaju. Jawa, C Indonesia 06°22′S 108°20′E
234 G5 **Indrāvati** ≈ S India
165 H5 **Indre** ◐ department C France
165 H5 **Indre** ≈ C France
154 B7 **Indre Ålvik** Hordaland, S Norway 60°26′N 06°27′E
164 G5 **Indre-et-Loire** ◐ department C France
Indreville see Châteauroux
230 G8 **Indus** Chin. Yindu He; prev. Yin-tu Ho. ≈ S Asia
Indus Cone see Indus Fan
288 E5 **Indus Fan** var. Indus Cone. undersea feature N Arabian Sea 16°00′N 66°30′E
230 G10 **Indus, Mouths of the** delta S Pakistan
138 G9 **Indwe** Eastern Cape, SE South Africa 31°28′S 27°20′E
214 E4 **İnebolu** Kastamonu, N Turkey 41°57′N 33°45′E
132 G2 **I-n-Échaï** oasis C Mali
185 M8 **İnecik** Tekirdağ, NW Turkey 40°55′N 27°16′E
214 C5 **İnegöl** Bursa, NW Turkey 40°06′N 29°31′E
114 B9 **Inés Indart** Buenos Aires, Argentina 34°24′S 60°33′W
Inessa see Biancavilla
188 B7 **Ineu** Hung. Borosjenő; prev. Inău. Arad, W Romania 46°26′N 21°51′E
Ineul/Ineu, Vîrful see Ineu, Vârful
188 D6 **Ineu, Vârful** var. Ineul; prev. Vîrful Ineu. ▲ N Romania 47°31′N 24°52′E
67 H4 **Inez** Kentucky, S USA 37°53′N 82°33′W
130 E4 **Inezgane** ✈ (Agadir) W Morocco 30°35′N 09°27′W
87 I9 **Inferior, Laguna** lagoon S Mexico
85 L6 **Infiernillo** Michoacán, S Mexico 26°02′N 99°55′W
86 D7 **Infiernillo** Michoacán, Mexico 18°17′N 101°55′W
86 D7 **Infiernillo, Presa del** ▣ S Mexico
Infiesto see L'Infiestu
153 H10 **Ingå** Fin. Inkoo. Uusimaa, S Finland 60°01′N 24°05′E
133 K3 **Ingal** var. I-n-Gall. Agadez, C Niger 16°52′N 06°57′E
I-n-Gall see Ingal
161 L6 **Ingatestone** United Kingdom 51°40′N 0°22′E
181 H13 **Ingelfingen** Baden-Württemberg, Germany 49°18′E 9°39′N
163 B10 **Ingelmunster** West-Vlaanderen, W Belgium 50°12′N 03°15′E
134 E7 **Ingende** Equateur, W Dem. Rep. Congo 0°15′S 18°58′E
181 E14 **Ingenheim** Rheinland-Pfalz, Germany 49°08′E 8°05′N
118 G3 **Ingeniero Giagnoni** Mendoza, Argentina 33°07′S 68°25′W
112 E4 **Ingeniero Guillermo Nueva Juárez** Formosa, N Argentina 23°55′S 61°50′W
118 G2 **Ingeniero Gustavo André** Mendoza, Argentina 32°42′S 68°19′W
116 C7 **Ingeniero Jacobacci** Río Negro, C Argentina 41°18′S 69°35′W
114 D5 **Ingeniero Miguel Sajaroff** Entre Ríos, Argentina 31°57′S 58°51′W
114 C8 **Ingeniero Moneta** Buenos Aires, Argentina 33°55′S 59°45′W
118 C2 **Ingeniero Santa María** Valparaíso, Chile 32°14′S 71°28′W
62 C5 **Ingersoll** Ontario, S Canada 43°03′N 80°53′W
Ingettolgoy see Selenge
275 J4 **Ingham** Queensland, NE Australia 18°35′S 146°12′E
161 L4 **Ingham** United Kingdom 52°18′N 0°43′E
229 H6 **Ingichka** Samarqand Viloyati, C Uzbekistan 39°46′N 65°56′E
159 J8 **Ingleborough** ▲ N England, United Kingdom 54°07′N 02°22′W
71 H9 **Ingleside** Texas, SW USA 27°52′N 97°12′W
159 J8 **Ingleton** N England, United Kingdom 54°09′N 02°30′W
277 L2 **Inglewood** Queensland, Australia
278 G6 **Inglewood** Taranaki, North Island, New Zealand 39°07′S 174°13′E
81 D10 **Inglewood** California, W USA 33°57′N 118°21′W
193 I8 **Ingoda** ≈ S Russian Federation
141 K5 **Ingogo** KwaZulu-Natal, South Africa 27°34′S 29°54′E
159 N10 **Ingoldmells** E England, United Kingdom 53°12′N 00°18′E
161 L2 **Ingoldmells** E England, United Kingdom 53°12′N 00°18′E
179 F12 **Ingolstadt** Bayern, S Germany 48°46′N 11°26′E
77 K4 **Ingomar** Montana, NW USA 46°34′N 107°21′W
59 K8 **Ingonish Beach** Cape Breton Island, Nova Scotia, SE Canada 46°42′N 60°22′W
233 J7 **Ingrāj Bāzār** prev. English Bazar. West Bengal, NE India 25°00′N 88°10′E
70 F7 **Ingram** Texas, SW USA 30°04′N 99°14′W
166 D8 **Ingrandes** Pays de la Loire, France 47°24′N 0°55′W
293 L4 **Ingrid Christensen Coast** physical region Antarctica
131 J9 **I-n-Guezzam** S Algeria 19°35′N 05°49′E
Ingulets see Inhulets'
Inguri see Enguri
Ingushetia/Ingushetiya, Respublika see Ingushetiya, Respublika
197 I9 **Ingushetiya, Respublika** var. Respublika Ingushetiya, Eng. Ingushetia. ◐ autonomous republic SW Russian Federation
141 L5 **Ingwavuma** KwaZulu-Natal, South Africa 27°08′S 31°59′E
167 M5 **Ingwiller** Alsace, France 48°52′N 7°29′E
139 J6 **Inhambane** Inhambane, SE Mozambique 23°52′S 35°31′E
139 I5 **Inhambane** off. Província de Inhambane. ◐ province S Mozambique
Inhambane, Província de see Inhambane
139 J3 **Inhaminga** Sofala, C Mozambique 18°24′S 35°00′E
111 J2 **Inhapim** Minas Gerais, Brazil 19°33′S 42°07′W
139 J6 **Inharrime** Inhambane, SE Mozambique 24°29′S 35°01′E
139 J4 **Inhassoro** Inhambane, E Mozambique 21°32′S 35°13′E
110 G2 **Inhaúme** Minas Gerais, Brazil 19°29′S 44°22′W
189 J6 **Inhulets'** Rus. Ingulets. Dnipropetrovs'ka Oblast', E Ukraine 47°43′N 33°16′E
189 I7 **Inhulets'** Rus. Ingulets. ≈ S Ukraine
171 H6 **Iniesta** Castilla-La Mancha, C Spain 39°27′N 01°45′W
I-ning see Yining
102 E7 **Inírida, Río** ≈ E Colombia
Inis see Ennis
Inis Ceithleann see Enniskillen
Inis Córthaidh see Enniscorthy
Inis Díomáin see Ennistimon
157 A9 **Inishbofin** Ir. Inis Bó Finne. island W Ireland
158 A7 **Inishcrone** Sligo, Ireland 54°13′N 9°06′W
157 B9 **Inisheer** var. Inishere, Ir. Inis Oírr. island W Ireland
Inishere see Inisheer
157 A9 **Inishmaan** Ir. Inis Meáin. island W Ireland
157 B9 **Inishmore** Ir. Árainn. island W Ireland
158 A7 **Inishmurray** island Sligo, Ireland
158 C5 **Inishowen** peninsula N Ireland
158 D5 **Inishowen Head** headland N Ireland
158 C4 **Inishtrahull** Ir. Inis Trá Tholl. island NW Ireland
157 A9 **Inishturk** Ir. Inis Toirc. island W Ireland
160 A4 **Inistioge** Kilkenny, Ireland 52°29′N 7°04′W
277 K1 **Injune** Queensland, Australia
161 H4 **Inkberrow** United Kingdom 52°12′N 1°58′W
Inkoo see Ingå
279 F8 **Inland Kaikoura Range** ▲▲ South Island, New Zealand
Inland Sea see Seto-naikai
84 E3 **Inmaculada** Sonora, Mexico 29°55′N 111°48′W
67 H7 **Inman** South Carolina, SE USA 35°03′N 82°05′W
295 J7 **Innaanganeq** var. Kap York. headland NW Greenland 75°54′N 66°27′W
277 H2 **Innamincka** South Australia 27°47′S 140°45′E
154 F6 **Innbygda** ≈ S Norway
152 E5 **Inndyr** Nordland, C Norway 67°01′N 14°00′E
88 E2 **Inner Channel** inlet SE Belize
156 D6 **Inner Hebrides** island group W Scotland, United Kingdom
137 I8 **Inner Islands** var. Central Group. island group NE Seychelles
159 I4 **Innerleithen** United Kingdom 55°37′N 3°04′W
Inner Mongolia/Inner Mongolian Autonomous Region see Nei Mongol Zizhiqu
176 E4 **Inner Rhoden** former canton Appenzell. ◐ NW Switzerland
156 D5 **Inner Sound** strait NW Scotland, United Kingdom
180 H6 **Innerste** ≈ C Germany
158 G1 **Innerwick** United Kingdom 56°36′N 4°18′W
275 J3 **Innisfail** Queensland, NE Australia 17°29′S 146°03′E
57 I6 **Innisfail** Alberta, SW Canada 52°01′N 113°59′W
Inniskilling see Enniskillen
83 H6 **Innoko River** ≈ Alaska, USA
250 F5 **Innoshima** var. Innosima. Hiroshima, SW Japan 34°18′N 133°09′E
Innosima see Innoshima
Innsbruch see Innsbruck
176 G4 **Innsbruck** var. Innsbruch. Tirol, W Austria 47°17′N 11°25′E
135 E8 **Inongo** Bandundu, W Dem. Rep. Congo 01°55′S 18°20′E
Inoucdjouac see Inukjuak
Inowrazlaw see Inowrocław
182 F5 **Inowrocław** Ger. Hohensalza; prev. Inowrazlaw. Kujawski-pomorskie, C Poland 52°47′N 18°15′E
106 D10 **Inquisivi** La Paz, W Bolivia 16°55′S 67°10′W
Inrin see Yuanlin
130 G9 **I-n-Sâkâne, 'Erg** desert N Mali
132 G2 **I-n-Sâkâne, 'Erg** desert N Mali
131 I5 **I-n-Salah** var. In Salah. C Algeria 27°11′N 02°31′E
197 H3 **Insar** Respublika Mordoviya, W Russian Federation 53°52′N 44°26′E
283 H10 **Insiaf** Kosrae, E Micronesia
154 G6 **Insjön** Dalarna, C Sweden 60°40′N 15°05′E
Insterburg see Chernyakhovsk
Insula see Lille
188 F9 **Însurăţei** Brăila, SE Romania 44°55′N 27°40′E
195 K4 **Inta** Respublika Komi, NW Russian Federation 66°00′N 60°10′E
133 I3 **I-n-Tebezas** Kidal, E Mali 17°58′N 01°51′E
Interamna see Teramo
Interamna Nahars see Terni
74 B5 **Interior** South Dakota, N USA 43°42′N 101°57′W
176 D5 **Interlaken** Bern, SW Switzerland 46°41′N 07°51′E
74 G2 **International Falls** Minnesota, N USA 48°38′N 93°26′W
256 D6 **Inthanon, Doi** ▲ NW Thailand 18°33′N 98°29′E
88 E4 **Intibucá** ◐ department SW Honduras
88 E5 **Intipucá** La Unión, SE El Salvador 13°10′N 88°03′W
112 F6 **Intiyaco** Santa Fe, C Argentina 28°43′S 60°04′W
188 E8 **Întorsura Buzăului** Ger. Bozau, Hung. Bodzafordulő. Covasna, E Romania 45°40′N 26°02′E
68 C4 **Intracoastal Waterway** inland waterway system Louisiana, S USA
71 I8 **Intracoastal Waterway** inland waterway system Texas, SW USA
176 E5 **Intragna** Ticino, S Switzerland 46°12′N 08°42′E
253 D13 **Inubō-zaki** headland Honshū, S Japan 35°42′N 140°51′E
250 D7 **Inukai** Ōita, Kyūshū, SW Japan 33°05′N 131°37′E
58 F3 **Inukjuak** var. Inoucdjouac; prev. Port Harrison. Québec, NE Canada 58°28′N 77°58′W
52 E8 **Inulik Lake** ◎ Nunavut, NW Canada
117 D13 **Inútil, Bahía** bay S Chile
Inuuvik see Inuvik
52 B6 **Inuvik** var. Inuuvik. Northwest Territories, NW Canada 68°25′N 133°35′W
251 J4 **Inuyama** Aichi, Honshū, SW Japan 35°23′N 136°56′E
104 F7 **Inuya, Río** ≈ E Peru
195 K8 **In'va** ≈ NW Russian Federation
158 B6 **Inver** Donegal, Ireland 54°39′N 8°17′W
158 F2 **Inveraray** W Scotland, United Kingdom 56°13′N 05°05′W
158 G2 **Inverarnan** United Kingdom 56°19′N 4°43′W
159 J1 **Inverbervie** United Kingdom 56°51′N 2°16′W
278 B12 **Invercargill** Southland, South Island, New Zealand 46°25′S 168°22′E
277 L3 **Inverell** New South Wales, SE Australia 29°46′S 151°10′E
156 F4 **Invergordon** N Scotland, United Kingdom 57°42′N 04°02′W
159 I2 **Invergowrie** United Kingdom 56°27′N 3°03′W
159 I1 **Inverkeilor** United Kingdom 56°38′N 2°32′W
159 H3 **Inverkeithing** United Kingdom 56°02′N 3°23′W
57 H8 **Invermere** British Columbia, SW Canada 50°30′N 116°00′W
118 D6 **Invernada, Laguna de la** ◎ Maule, Chile
118 D6 **Invernada, Río de la** ≈ Maule, Chile
59 K8 **Inverness** Cape Breton Island, Nova Scotia, SE Canada 46°14′N 61°19′W
156 F5 **Inverness** N Scotland, United Kingdom 57°27′N 04°15′W
80 A2 **Inverness** California, USA 38°06′N 122°51′W
69 L6 **Inverness** Florida, SE USA 28°50′N 82°19′W
156 E5 **Inverness** cultural region NW Scotland, United Kingdom
158 F1 **Inversanda** United Kingdom 56°41′N 5°22′W
156 G5 **Inverurie** NE Scotland, United Kingdom 57°14′N 02°14′W
276 E5 **Investigator Group** island group South Australia
289 H9 **Investigator Ridge** undersea feature E Indian Ocean 11°30′S 98°10′E
276 F6 **Investigator Strait** strait South Australia
74 F6 **Inwood** Iowa, C USA 43°16′N 96°25′W
192 F8 **Inya** Respublika Altay, S Russian Federation 50°27′N 86°45′E
193 L5 **Inya** ≈ E Russian Federation
Inyanga see Nyanga
139 I3 **Inyangani** ▲ NE Zimbabwe 18°22′S 32°57′E
138 G4 **Inyathi** Matabeleland North, SW Zimbabwe 19°39′S 28°54′E
81 F8 **Inyokern** California, W USA 35°37′N 117°48′W
80 F6 **Inyo Mountains** ▲▲ California, W USA
197 I3 **Inza** Ul'yanovskaya Oblast', W Russian Federation 53°51′N 46°21′E
197 M2 **Inzer** Respublika Bashkortostan, W Russian Federation 54°11′N 57°37′E
197 H4 **Inzhavino** Tambovskaya Oblast', W Russian Federation 52°18′N 42°28′E
186 F4 **Ioánnina** var. Janina, Yannina. Ípeiros, W Greece 39°39′N 20°52′E
250 C10 **Iō-jima** var. Iwojima. island Nansei-shotō, SW Japan
194 F3 **Iokan'ga** ≈ NW Russian Federation
75 F10 **Iola** Kansas, C USA 37°55′N 95°24′W
Iolcus see Iolkós
186 G4 **Iolkós** anc. Iolcus. site of ancient city Thessalía, C Greece
Iolotan' see Ýolöten
135 B14 **Iona** Namibe, SW Angola 16°54′S 12°39′E
158 D2 **Iona** island W Scotland, United Kingdom
188 F10 **Ion Corvin** Constanţa, SE Romania 44°07′N 27°50′E
80 D3 **Ione** California, W USA 38°21′N 120°55′W
80 I4 **Ione** Nevada, USA 38°57′N 117°35′W
188 C9 **Ioneşti** Vâlcea, SW Romania 44°52′N 24°12′E
73 G8 **Ionia** Michigan, N USA 42°59′N 85°04′W
Ionia Basin see Ionian Basin
148 D9 **Ionian Basin** var. Ionia Basin. undersea feature Ionian Sea, C Mediterranean Sea 36°00′N 20°00′E
186 E6 **Iónia Nisiá** var. Iónioi Nísoi, Eng. Ionian Islands. island group W Greece
Ionian Islands see Iónia Nisiá/Iónioi Nísoi
175 J13 **Ionian Sea** Gk. Iónio Pélagos, It. Mar Ionio. sea C Mediterranean Sea
186 E5 **Iónioi Nísoi** Eng. Ionian Islands. ◐ region W Greece
Iónioi Nísoi see Iónia Nisiá
Ionio, Mar/Iónio Pélagos see Ionian Sea
Iordan see Yordon
215 L4 **Iori** var. Qabırrı. ≈ Azerbaijan/Georgia
Iorrais, Ceann see Erris Head
187 J8 **Íos** var. Nio. island Kykládes, Greece, Aegean Sea
Íos see Chóra
251 J9 **Io-Tori-shima** prev. Tori-shima. island Izu-shotō, SE Japan
68 B4 **Iowa** Louisiana, S USA 30°12′N 93°00′W
74 G7 **Iowa** off. State of Iowa, also known as Hawkeye State. ◐ state C USA
74 I7 **Iowa City** Iowa, C USA 41°40′N 91°32′W
74 H6 **Iowa Falls** Iowa, C USA 42°31′N 93°15′W
70 G3 **Iowa Park** Texas, SW USA 33°57′N 98°40′W
74 H7 **Iowa River** ≈ Iowa, C USA
191 H11 **Ipa** ≈ SE Belarus
111 J2 **Ipaba** Minas Gerais, Brazil 19°23′S 42°25′W
111 K2 **Ipanema** Minas Gerais, Brazil 19°47′S 41°44′W
111 J2 **Ipatinga** Minas Gerais, SE Brazil 19°32′S 42°30′W
197 H8 **Ipatovo** Stavropol'skiy Kray, SW Russian Federation 45°40′N 42°51′E
186 E4 **Ípeiros** Eng. Epirus. ◐ region W Greece
110 B9 **Iperó** São Paulo, Brazil 23°21′S 47°41′W
181 I12 **Iphofen** Bayern, Germany 49°41′E 10°17′N
102 A8 **Ipiales** Nariño, SW Colombia 0°52′N 77°38′W
282 F10 **Ipis** atoll Chuuk Islands, C Micronesia
106 B5 **Ipixuna** Amazonas, W Brazil 06°57′S 71°42′W
258 D2 **Ipoh** Perak, Peninsular Malaysia 04°36′N 101°02′E
281 N5 **Ipota** Erromango, S Vanuatu 18°54′S 169°19′E
134 F5 **Ippy** Ouaka, C Central African Republic 06°17′N 21°13′E
214 A4 **İpsala** Edirne, NW Turkey 40°56′N 26°23′E
Ipsario see Ypsário
181 I13 **Ipsheim** Bayern, Germany 49°32′E 10°29′N
277 M2 **Ipswich** Queensland, E Australia 27°28′S 152°40′E
161 M4 **Ipswich** hist. Gipeswic. E England, United Kingdom 52°05′N 01°08′E
74 D4 **Ipswich** South Dakota, N USA 45°24′N 99°00′W
110 B4 **Ipuã** São Paulo, Brazil 20°27′S 48°02′W
110 D7 **Ipuiúna** Minas Gerais, Brazil 22°06′S 46°11′W
Iput' see Iputs'
191 I11 **Iputs'** Rus. Iput'. ≈ Belarus/Russian Federation
55 N1 **Iqaluit** prev. Frobisher Bay. province capital Baffin Island, Nunavut, NE Canada 63°44′N 68°28′W
Iqlid see Eqlīd
112 A2 **Iquique** Tarapacá, N Chile 20°15′S 70°08′W
104 F3 **Iquitos** Loreto, N Peru 03°51′S 73°13′W
70 D6 **Iraan** Texas, SW USA 30°52′N 101°52′W
134 F5 **Ira Banda** Haute-Kotto, E Central African Republic 05°57′N 22°05′E
250 G9 **Irabu-jima** island Miyako-shotō, SW Japan
110 B7 **Iracemápolis** São Paulo, Brazil 22°35′S 47°32′W
103 M5 **Iracoubo** N French Guiana 05°28′N 53°15′W
251 J5 **Irago-misaki** headland Honshū, SW Japan 34°35′N 137°00′E
113 I6 **Iraí** Rio Grande do Sul, S Brazil 27°15′S 53°17′W
110 B1 **Iraí de Minas** Minas Gerais, Brazil 18°59′S 47°28′W
187 H2 **Irákleia** Kentrikí Makedonía, N Greece 41°09′N 23°16′E
187 J8 **Irákleia** island Kykládes, Greece, Aegean Sea
187 J10 **Irákleio** var. Herakleion, Eng. Candia; prev. Iráklion. Kríti, Greece, E Mediterranean Sea 35°20′N 25°08′E
186 G4 **Irákleio** anc. Heracleum. castle Kentrikí Makedonía, N Greece
187 J10 **Irákleio** ✈ Kríti, Greece, E Mediterranean Sea 35°20′N 25°10′E
Iráklion see Irákleio
114 B10 **Irala** Buenos Aires, Argentina 34°46′S 60°41′W
222 G5 **Iran** off. Islamic Republic of Iran; prev. Persia. ◆ republic SW Asia
106 G3 **Iranduba** Amazonas, NW Brazil 03°19′S 60°09′W
145 H8 **Iranian Plate** tectonic feature
222 G6 **Iranian Plateau** var. Plateau of Iran. plateau N Iran
Iran, Islamic Republic of see Iran
Iran Mountains see Iran, Pegunungan
259 K4 **Iran, Pegunungan** var. Iran Mountains. ▲▲ Indonesia/Malaysia
Iran, Plateau of see Iranian Plateau
223 J8 **Īrānshahr** Sīstān va Balūchestān, SE Iran 27°14′N 60°40′E
103 I2 **Irapa** Sucre, NE Venezuela 10°37′N 62°35′W
86 D5 **Irapuato** Guanajuato, C Mexico 20°40′N 101°23′W
217 I2 **Iraq** off. Republic of Iraq, Ar. 'Irāq. ◆ republic SW Asia
'Irāq see Iraq
Iraq, Republic of see Iraq
113 J5 **Irati** Paraná, S Brazil 25°25′S 50°38′W
171 I2 **Irati** ≈ N Spain
168 C7 **Irati** ≈ Spain
195 J5 **Irayël'** Respublika Komi, NW Russian Federation 64°28′N 55°20′E
89 H8 **Irazú, Volcán** ⛰ C Costa Rica 09°57′N 83°52′W
Irbenskiy Zaliv/Irbes Šaurums see Irbe Strait
190 C5 **Irbe Strait** Est. Kura Kurk, Latv. Irbes Šaurums, Irbenskiy Zaliv; prev. Est. Irbe Väin. strait Estonia/Latvia
Irbe Väin see Irbe Strait
218 G6 **Irbid** Irbid, N Jordan 32°33′N 35°51′E
218 F7 **Irbid** off. Muḩāfaẓat Irbid. ◐ governorate N Jordan
Irbid, Muḩāfaẓat see Irbid
Irbīl see Arbīl
195 M9 **Irbit** Sverdlovskaya Oblast', C Russian Federation 57°37′N 63°10′E
177 J3 **Irdning** Steiermark, SE Austria 47°29′N 14°04′E
134 E7 **Irebu** Equateur, W Dem. Rep. Congo 0°32′S 17°44′E
168 A8 **Iregua** ≈ La Rioja, Spain
157 C10 **Ireland** off. Republic of Ireland, Ir. Éire. ◆ republic NW Europe
144 B6 **Ireland** Lat. Hibernia. island Ireland/United Kingdom
67 M10 **Ireland Island North** island W Bermuda
67 M10 **Ireland Island South** island W Bermuda
Ireland, Republic of see Ireland
195 K9 **Iren'** ≈ NW Russian Federation
278 B11 **Irene, Mount** ▲ South Island, New Zealand 45°04′S 167°24′E
Irgalem see Yirga 'Alem
Irgiz see Yrghyz
219 F10 **Irhāb** Jordan
219 F10 **Irhāb** Jordan 32°19′N 36°06′E
Irian see New Guinea
Irian Barat see Papua
Irian Jaya see Papua
Irian Jaya Barat see Papua Barat
Irian, Teluk see Cenderawasih, Teluk
114 A9 **Iriarte** Buenos Aires, Argentina 34°25′S 61°55′W
134 F1 **Iriba** Wadi Fira, NE Chad 15°10′N 22°11′E
263 L6 **Iriga** Luzon, N Philippines 13°26′N 123°24′E
114 A5 **Irigoyen** Santa Fe, Argentina 32°10′S 61°09′W
197 M4 **Iriklinskoye Vodokhranilishche** ▣ W Russian Federation
137 D11 **Iringa** Iringa, C Tanzania 07°49′S 35°39′E
137 D11 **Iringa** ◐ region S Tanzania
250 E10 **Iriomote-jima** island Sakishima-shotō, SW Japan
88 G3 **Iriona** Colón, NE Honduras 15°55′N 85°10′W
95 L4 **Iriri** ≈ N Brazil
107 K3 **Iriri, Rio** ≈ C Brazil
Iris see Yeşilırmak
80 J7 **Irish, Mount** ▲ Nevada, W USA 37°39′N 115°22′W
157 E9 **Irish Sea** Ir. Muir Éireann. sea C British Isles
217 K8 **Irjal ash Shaykhīyah** Al Muthanná, S Iraq 30°49′N 44°58′E
229 K6 **Irkeshtam** Oshskaya Oblast', SW Kyrgyzstan 39°39′N 73°49′E
193 H8 **Irkutsk** Irkutskaya Oblast', S Russian Federation 52°18′N 104°15′E
193 H7 **Irkutskaya Oblast'** ◐ province S Russian Federation
Irlir, Gora see Irlir Tog'i
228 F4 **Irlir Tog'i** var. Gora Irlir. ▲ N Uzbekistan 42°43′N 63°24′E
Irminger Basin see Reykjanes Basin
67 I8 **Irmo** South Carolina, SE USA 34°05′N 81°10′W
164 D3 **Iroise** sea NW France
283 M10 **Iroj** var. Eroj. island Ratak Chain, SE Marshall Islands
276 F4 **Iron Baron** South Australia 33°01′S 137°13′E
281 J3 **Iron Bottom Sound** sound C Solomon Islands
62 A2 **Iron Bridge** Ontario, S Canada 46°16′N 83°12′W
66 D7 **Iron City** Tennessee, S USA 35°01′N 87°34′W
62 D4 **Irondale** ≈ Ontario, SE Canada
276 F4 **Iron Knob** South Australia 32°46′S 137°08′E
158 C9 **Iron, Lough** ◎ Ireland
72 D5 **Iron Mountain** Michigan, N USA 45°51′N 88°03′W
158 B8 **Iron Mountains** ▲▲ N Ireland
72 D4 **Iron River** Michigan, N USA 46°05′N 88°38′W
72 B4 **Iron River** Wisconsin, N USA 46°34′N 91°22′W
75 J10 **Ironton** Missouri, C USA 37°37′N 90°40′W
73 I12 **Ironton** Ohio, N USA 38°32′N 82°40′W
72 C4 **Ironwood** Michigan, N USA 46°27′N 90°10′W
58 E7 **Iroquois Falls** Ontario, S Canada 48°47′N 80°41′W
73 E10 **Iroquois River** ≈ Illinois/Indiana, N USA
251 L5 **Irō-zaki** headland Honshū, S Japan 34°36′N 138°49′E
Irpen' see Irpin'
189 H3 **Irpin'** Rus. Irpen'. Kyyivs'ka Oblast', N Ukraine 50°31′N 30°16′E
189 H3 **Irpin'** Rus. Irpen'. ≈ N Ukraine
220 G9 **'Irqah** SW Yemen 13°42′N 47°21′E
256 C5 **Irrawaddy** var. Ayeyarwady. ≈ W Myanmar (Burma)
Irrawaddy see Ayeyawady
256 C7 **Irrawaddy, Mouths of the** delta SW Myanmar (Burma)
188 G3 **Irsha** ≈ N Ukraine
188 C5 **Irshava** Zakarpats'ka Oblast', W Ukraine 48°19′N 23°03′E
175 H9 **Irsina** Basilicata, S Italy 40°42′N 16°18′E
Irtish see Yertis
Irtysh see Yertis
Irtyshsk see Yertis
134 J7 **Irumu** Orientale, E Dem. Rep. Congo 01°27′N 29°52′E
171 H1 **Irun** Cast. Irún. País Vasco, N Spain 43°20′N 01°48′W
Irún see Irun
Iruña see Pamplona
111 K3 **Irupi** Espírito Santo, Brazil 20°21′S 41°38′W
171 H2 **Irurtzun** Navarra, N Spain 42°55′N 01°50′W
158 G4 **Irvine** W Scotland, United Kingdom 55°37′N 04°40′W
81 D11 **Irvine** California, USA 33°40′N 117°49′W
66 G4 **Irvine** Kentucky, S USA 37°42′N 83°59′W
158 C7 **Irvinestown** United Kingdom 54°28′N 7°38′W
71 H4 **Irving** Texas, SW USA 32°47′N 96°57′W
66 E4 **Irvington** Kentucky, S USA 37°52′N 86°16′W
250 C8 **Isa** prev. Ōkuchi, Ōkuti. Kagoshima, Kyūshū, SW Japan 32°04′N 130°36′E
Isaak see Iisaku
168 C7 **Isaba** Navarra, Spain 42°52′N 0°55′W
74 B4 **Isabel** South Dakota, N USA 45°21′N 101°25′W
281 I1 **Isabel** off. Isabel Province. ◐ province N Solomon Islands
263 L9 **Isabela** Basilan Island, SW Philippines 06°41′N 122°00′E
91 H7 **Isabela** W Puerto Rico 18°30′N 67°02′W
91 H5 **Isabela, Cabo** headland NW Dominican Republic 19°54′N 71°03′W
105 A10 **Isabela, Isla** var. Albemarle Island. island Galapagos Islands, Ecuador, E Pacific Ocean
85 H10 **Isabela, Isla** island C Mexico
88 G5 **Isabella, Cordillera** ▲▲ NW Nicaragua
81 E8 **Isabella Lake** ▣ California, W USA
72 E3 **Isabelle, Point** headland Michigan, N USA 47°20′N 87°56′W
Isabel Province see Isabel
Isabel Segunda see Vieques
188 F9 **Isaccea** Tulcea, E Romania 45°16′N 28°28′E
152 B1 **Ísafjarðardjúp** inlet NW Iceland
152 B1 **Ísafjarðardjúp** inlet NW Iceland
152 B1 **Ísafjörður** Vestfirðir, NW Iceland 66°04′N 23°09′W
250 C7 **Isahaya** Nagasaki, Kyūshū, SW Japan 32°51′N 130°02′E
231 I5 **Īsa Khel** Punjab, E Pakistan 32°39′N 71°20′E
190 J2 **Isakovo** Leningradskaya Oblast', Russian Federation
139 L9 **Isalo** var. Massif de L'Isalo. ▲▲ SW Madagascar
135 F8 **Isandja** Kasai-Occidental, C Dem. Rep. Congo 03°03′S 21°57′E
281 N5 **Isangel** Tanna, S Vanuatu 19°34′S 169°17′E
134 G7 **Isangi** Orientale, C Dem. Rep. Congo 0°46′N 24°15′E
176 G3 **Isar** ≈ Austria/Germany
179 G12 **Isar-Kanal** canal SE Germany
Isbarta see Isparta
Isca Damnoniorum see Exeter
175 F9 **Ischia** var. Isola d'Ischia; anc. Aenaria. Campania, S Italy 40°44′N 13°57′E
175 F9 **Ischia, Isola d'** island S Italy
102 A7 **Iscuandé** var. Santa Bárbara. Nariño, SW Colombia 02°32′N 78°00′W
251 J5 **Ise** Mie, Honshū, SW Japan 34°29′N 136°43′E
180 I5 **Ise** ≈ N Germany
155 E12 **Isefjord** fjord E Denmark
Iseghem see Izegem
180 I5 **Isenbüttel** Niedersachsen, Germany 52°26′E 10°35′N
Isenhof see Püssi
176 F6 **Iseo** Lombardia, N Italy 45°40′N 10°03′E
169 M2 **Iseran, Col de l'** pass E France
165 J7 **Isère** ◐ department E France
165 J7 **Isère** ≈ E France
181 D8 **Iserlohn** Nordrhein-Westfalen, W Germany 51°23′N 07°42′E
175 G8 **Isernia** var. Æsernia. Molise, C Italy 41°35′N 14°14′E
253 B12 **Isesaki** Gunma, Honshū, S Japan 36°19′N 139°11′E
205 J3 **Iset'** ≈ C Russian Federation
251 I4 **Ise-wan** bay S Japan
133 I7 **Iseyin** Oyo, W Nigeria 07°56′N 03°33′E
Isfahan see Eşfahān
229 I6 **Isfana** Batkenskaya Oblast', SW Kyrgyzstan 39°51′N 69°31′E
229 J6 **Isfara** N Tajikistan 40°06′N 70°34′E
230 F3 **Isfi Maidān** Gōwr, N Afghanistan 35°09′N 66°16′E
152 B5 **Isfjorden** fjord W Svalbard
Isgender see Kul'mach
Isha Baydhabo see Baydhabo
195 L7 **Isherim, Gora** ▲ NW Russian Federation 61°06′N 59°09′E
197 J3 **Isheyevka** Ul'yanovskaya Oblast', W Russian Federation 54°27′N 48°18′E
250 F10 **Ishigaki** Okinawa, Ishigaki-jima, SW Japan 24°20′N 124°09′E
250 F10 **Ishigaki-jima** island Sakishima-shotō, SW Japan
252 E4 **Ishikari** Hokkaidō, NE Japan 43°12′N 141°21′E
252 E4 **Ishikari-gawa** var. Isikari Gawa. ≈ Hokkaidō, NE Japan
252 D4 **Ishikari-wan** bay Hokkaidō, NE Japan
253 D11 **Ishikawa** Fukushima, Honshū, C Japan 37°08′N 140°26′E
251 J9 **Ishikawa** var. Isikawa. Okinawa, Okinawa, SW Japan 26°25′N 127°47′E
251 I2 **Ishikawa** off. Ishikawa-ken, var. Isikawa. ◐ prefecture Honshū, SW Japan
Ishikawa-ken see Ishikawa
192 E7 **Ishim** Tyumenskaya Oblast', C Russian Federation 56°13′N 69°25′E
197 L3 **Ishimbay** Respublika Bashkortostan, W Russian Federation 53°21′N 56°03′E
227 H3 **Ishimskoye** Akmola, C Kazakhstan 51°23′N 67°07′E
253 D10 **Ishinomaki** var. Isinomaki. Miyagi, Honshū, C Japan 38°26′N 141°17′E
253 C13 **Ishioka** var. Isioka. Ibaraki, Honshū, S Japan 36°11′N 140°16′E
250 F6 **Ishizuchi-san** ▲ Shikoku, SW Japan 33°44′N 133°07′E
231 H2 **Ishkamish** prev. Eshkamesh. Takhār, NE Afghanistan 36°25′N 69°11′E
231 I2 **Ishkāshim** prev. Eshkāshem. Badakhshān, NE Afghanistan 36°43′N 71°34′E
Ishkashim see Ishkoshim
Ishkashimskiy Khrebet see Ishkoshim, Qatorkŭhi
229 J8 **Ishkoshim** Rus. Ishkashim. S Tajikistan 36°46′N 71°35′E
229 J8 **Ishkoshim, Qatorkŭhi** Rus. Ishkashimskiy Khrebet. ▲▲ SE Tajikistan
72 E4 **Ishpeming** Michigan, N USA 46°29′N 87°40′W
229 H6 **Ishtixon** Rus. Ishtykhan. Samarqand Viloyati, C Uzbekistan 39°59′N 66°28′E
Ishtykhan see Ishtixon
Ishurdi see Iswardi
115 K5 **Isidoro Noblia** Cerro Largo, NE Uruguay 31°58′S 54°09′W
116 J3 **Isidoro Noblia** Treinta y tres, Uruguay 32°00′S 54°12′W
164 F2 **Isigny-sur-Mer** Calvados, N France 49°20′N 01°06′W
Isikari Gawa see Ishikari-gawa
Isikawa see Ishikawa
187 K3 **Işıklar Dağı** ▲▲ NW Turkey
175 B10 **Isili** Sardegna, Italy, C Mediterranean Sea 39°46′N 09°06′E
192 E7 **Isil'kul'** Omskaya Oblast', C Russian Federation 54°52′N 71°07′E
Isinomaki see Ishinomaki
Isioka see Ishioka
137 D8 **Isiolo** Isiolo, C Kenya 0°20′N 37°36′E
136 E7 **Isiolo** ◐ county C Kenya
134 I6 **Isiro** Orientale, NE Dem. Rep. Congo 02°51′N 27°47′E
152 C4 **Isispynten** headland NE Svalbard 79°51′N 26°44′E
193 J6 **Isit** Respublika Sakha (Yakutiya), NE Russian Federation 60°53′N 125°32′E
230 F2 **Iskabad Canal** canal N Afghanistan
229 I5 **Iskandar** Rus. Iskander. Toshkent Viloyati, E Uzbekistan 41°32′N 69°46′E
Iskander see Iskandar
185 J5 **Iskar** var. Iskăr, Iskŭr. ≈ NW Bulgaria
Iskăr see Iskar
185 I6 **Iskar, Yazovir** var. Yazovir Iskŭr; prev. Yazovir Stalin. ▣ W Bulgaria
218 D2 **İskele** var. Trikomo, Gk. Tríkomon. E Cyprus 35°16′N 33°54′E
214 F8 **İskenderun** Eng. Alexandretta. Hatay, S Turkey 36°34′N 36°10′E
214 F8 **İskenderun Körfezi** Eng. Gulf of Alexandretta. gulf S Turkey
214 F5 **İskilip** Çorum, N Turkey 40°45′N 34°28′E
Iski-Nauket see Nookat
192 F7 **Iskitim** Novosibirskaya Oblast', C Russian Federation 54°36′N 83°05′E
185 K7 **Iskra** prev. Popovo. Haskovo, S Bulgaria 41°55′N 25°12′E
Iskŭr see Iskar
Iskŭr, Yazovir see Iskar, Yazovir
87 H7 **Isla** Veracruz-Llave, SE Mexico 18°01′N 95°30′W
159 I1 **Isla** ≈ United Kingdom
87 K7 **Isla Aguada** Campeche, Mexico 18°47′N 91°28′W
191 F9 **Islach** Rus. Isloch'. ≈ C Belarus
170 D8 **Isla Cristina** Andalucía, S Spain 37°12′N 07°20′W
Isla de León see San Fernando
117 A9 **Isla Guafo** island Los Lagos, Chile
117 A9 **Isla Guaiteca** island Aisén, Chile
231 I4 **Islāmābād** ● (Pakistan) Federal Capital Territory Islāmābād, NE Pakistan 33°40′N 73°08′E
231 I4 **Islāmābād** ✈ Federal Capital Territory Islāmābād, NE Pakistan 33°40′N 73°08′E
Islamabad see Anantnāg
231 H10 **Islāmkot** Sind, SE Pakistan 24°37′N 70°04′E
69 N10 **Islamorada** Florida Keys, Florida, SE USA 24°55′N 80°37′W
234 I2 **Islāmpur** Bihār, N India 25°09′N 85°13′E
Islam Qala see Eslām Qal'eh
65 H8 **Island Beach** spit New Jersey, NE USA
63 L2 **Island Falls** Maine, NE USA 45°59′N 68°16′W
Island/Ísland see Iceland
276 F4 **Island Lagoon** ◎ South Australia
55 J8 **Island Lake** ◎ Manitoba, C Canada
74 H3 **Island Lake Reservoir** ▣ Minnesota, N USA
77 I6 **Island Park** Idaho, NW USA 44°27′N 111°21′W
140 C7 **Island Point** point Northern Cape, South Africa
63 I4 **Island Pond** Vermont, NE USA 44°48′N 71°51′W
278 G2 **Islands, Bay of** inlet North Island, New Zealand
165 J4 **Is-sur-Tille** Côte d'Or, C France 47°34′N 05°03′E
88 F2 **Islas de la Bahía** ◐ department N Honduras
291 F12 **Islas Orcadas Rise** undersea feature S Atlantic Ocean
158 D3 **Islay** island SW Scotland, United Kingdom
188 D10 **Islaz** Teleorman, S Romania 43°44′N 24°45′E
74 G4 **Isle** Minnesota, N USA 46°08′N 93°28′W
164 G6 **Isle** ≈ W France
158 G7 **Isle of Man** ◇ British Crown Dependency NW Europe
158 G6 **Isle of Whithorn** United Kingdom 54°42′N 4°22′W
67 L5 **Isle of Wight** Virginia, NE USA 36°54′N 76°41′W
161 I8 **Isle of Wight** cultural region S England, United Kingdom
285 N2 **Isles Lagoon** ◎ Kiritimati, E Kiribati
79 L7 **Isleta Pueblo** New Mexico, SW USA 34°54′N 106°40′W
80 C2 **Isleton** California, USA 38°10′N 121°37′W
Isloch' see Islach
114 G8 **Ismael Cortinas** Flores, S Uruguay 33°57′S 57°05′W
Ismailia see Al Ismā'īlīya
Ismâ'ilîya see Al Ismā'īlīya
Ismid see İzmit
213 M2 **Ismoili Somoní, Qullai** prev. Qullai Kommunizm. ▲ E Tajikistan
129 I5 **Isnā** var. Esna. SE Egypt 25°16′N 32°30′E
172 C3 **Isna** Castelo Branco, Portugal 39°50′N 7°52′W
172 C3 **Isna, Ribeira da** ≈ Portugal
153 G9 **Isojoki** Etelä-Pohjanmaa, W Finland 62°07′N 22°00′E
137 B12 **Isoka** Muchinga, NE Zambia 10°08′S 32°43′E
169 M4 **Isola** Provence-Alpes-Côte d'Azur, France 44°11′N 7°03′E
Isola d'Ischia see Ischia
Isola d'Istria see Izola
168 F8 **Isona** Cataluña, Spain 42°07′N 1°03′E
Isonzo see Soča
53 J7 **Isortoq River** ≈ Nunavut, NE Canada
214 C7 **Isparta** var. Isbarta. Isparta, SW Turkey 37°46′N 30°32′E
214 D7 **Isparta** var. Isbarta. ◐ province SW Turkey
185 L5 **Isperih** var. Isperikh; prev. Kemanlar. Razgrad, N Bulgaria 43°43′N 26°49′E
Isperikh see Isperih
175 G13 **Ispica** Sicilia, Italy, C Mediterranean Sea 36°47′N 14°55′E
230 D8 **Ispikān** Baluchistān, SW Pakistan 26°21′N 62°15′E
215 I5 **İspir** Erzurum, NE Turkey 40°29′N 41°02′E
219 D10 **Israel** off. State of Israel, var. Medinat Israel, Heb. Yisrael, Yisra'el. ◆ republic SW Asia
Israel, State of see Israel
190 G5 **Issa** Pskovskaya Oblast', Russian Federation
Issa see Vis
103 J5 **Issano** C Guyana 05°49′N 59°28′W
132 E8 **Issia** SW Ivory Coast 06°33′N 06°33′W
Issiq Köl see Issyk-Kul', Ozero
169 N1 **Issogne** Valle D'Aosta, NW Italy 45°39′N 07°41′E
165 I6 **Issoire** Puy-de-Dôme, C France 45°33′N 03°15′E
165 H5 **Issoudun** anc. Uxellodunum. Indre, C France 46°57′N 01°59′E
181 B8 **Issum** Nordrhein-Westfalen, Germany 51°32′E 6°26′N
137 C10 **Issuna** Singida, C Tanzania 05°24′S 34°48′E
167 K8 **Is-sur-Tille** Bourgogne, France 47°31′N 5°06′E
Issyk see Yesik
Issyk-Kul' see Balykchy
229 M4 **Issyk-Kul', Ozero** var. Issiq Köl, Kir. Ysyk-Köl. ◎ E Kyrgyzstan
229 M4 **Issyk-Kul'skaya Oblast'** Kir. Ysyk-Köl Oblasty. ◐ province E Kyrgyzstan
167 J9 **Issy-l'Évèque** Bourgogne, France 46°43′N 3°58′E
230 G5 **Īstādeh-ye Moqor, Āb-e-** var. Āb-i-Istāda. ◎ SE Afghanistan
187 M2 **İstanbul** Bul. Tsarigrad, Eng. Istanbul, prev. Constantinople; anc. Byzantium. Istanbul, NW Turkey 41°02′N 28°57′E
214 C4 **İstanbul** ◐ province NW Turkey
214 C4 **İstanbul Boğazı** var. Bosporus Thracius, Eng. Bosphorus, Bosporus, Turk. Karadeniz Boğazi. strait NW Turkey
Istarska Županija see Istra
187 H6 **Isthmía** Pelopónnisos, S Greece 37°55′N 23°02′E
187 H5 **Istiaía** Évvoia, C Greece 38°57′N 23°09′E
102 B5 **Istmina** Chocó, W Colombia 05°09′N 76°42′W
69 M7 **Istokpoga, Lake** ◎ Florida, SE USA
184 A2 **Istra** off. Istarska Županija. ◐ province NW Croatia
184 A3 **Istra** Eng. Istria, Ger. Istrien. cultural region NW Croatia
165 J8 **Istres** Bouches-du-Rhône, SE France 43°30′N 04°59′E
Istria/Istrien see Istra
263 M9 **Isulan** Mindanao, S Philippines 06°36′N 124°36′E
233 K7 **Iswardi** var. Ishurdi. Rajshahi, W Bangladesh 24°10′N 89°04′E
197 L3 **Isyangulovo** Respublika Bashkortostan, W Russian Federation 52°10′N 56°38′E
112 G5 **Itá** Central, S Paraguay 25°29′S 57°21′W
111 L5 **Itabapoana, Rio** ≈ Esperíto Santo, Brazil
109 G8 **Itaberaba** Bahia, E Brazil 12°34′S 40°21′W
111 I2 **Itabira** prev. Presidente Vargas. Minas Gerais, SE Brazil 19°39′S 43°14′W
111 H3 **Itabirito** Minas Gerais, Brazil 20°15′S 43°48′W
111 I8 **Itaboraí** Rio de Janeiro, Brazil 22°45′S 42°52′W
109 G9 **Itabuna** Bahia, E Brazil 14°48′S 39°18′W
107 K9 **Itacaiu** Mato Grosso, S Brazil 14°49′S 51°21′W
107 H3 **Itacoatiara** Amazonas, N Brazil 03°06′S 58°22′W
111 L3 **Itaguaçú** Espírito Santo, Brazil 19°48′S 40°51′W
111 H8 **Itaguaí** Rio de Janeiro, Brazil 22°52′S 43°47′W
110 G4 **Itaguara** Minas Gerais, Brazil 20°23′S 44°29′W
102 B5 **Itagüí** Antioquia, W Colombia 06°12′N 75°40′W
118 C5 **Itahue** Maule, Chile 35°09′S 71°21′W
112 G6 **Itá Ibaté** Corrientes, NE Argentina 27°27′S 57°24′W
113 I4 **Itaipú, Represa de** ▣ Brazil/Paraguay
107 I3 **Itaituba** Pará, NE Brazil 04°15′S 55°56′W
113 K6 **Itajaí** Santa Catarina, S Brazil 26°50′S 48°39′W
110 A6 **Itaju** São Paulo, Brazil 22°00′S 48°48′W
110 F7 **Itajubá** Minas Gerais, Brazil 22°30′S 45°30′W
84 E4 **Italia** Michoacán, Mexico
Italia/Italiana, Republica/Italian Republic, The see Italy
Italian Somaliland see Somalia
111 K5 **Italva** Rio de Janeiro, Brazil 21°25′S 41°42′W
71 H5 **Italy** Texas, SW USA 32°10′N 96°52′W
174 E7 **Italy** off. The Italian Republic, It. Italia, Repubblica Italiana. ◆ republic S Europe
109 G10 **Itamaraju** Bahia, E Brazil 16°58′S 39°32′W
106 C5 **Itamarati** Amazonas, W Brazil 06°13′S 68°17′W
111 I5 **Itamarati** Minas Gerais, Brazil 21°25′S 42°49′W
109 E11 **Itambé, Pico de** ▲ SE Brazil 18°23′S 43°21′W
251 H4 **Itami** ✈ (Ōsaka) Ōsaka, Honshū, SW Japan 34°47′N 135°24′E
110 C5 **Itamoji** Minas Gerais, Brazil 21°05′S 47°03′W
110 F7 **Itamonte** Minas Gerais, Brazil 22°17′S 44°53′W
187 H3 **Ítamos** ▲ N Greece 40°06′N 23°51′E
233 L6 **Itānagar** state capital Arunāchal Pradesh, NE India 27°02′N 93°38′E
110 D10 **Itanhaém** São Paulo, Brazil 24°11′S 46°47′W
110 F7 **Itanhandu** Minas Gerais, Brazil 22°18′S 44°57′W
111 K1 **Itanhomi** Minas Gerais, Brazil 19°10′S 41°52′W
Itany see Litani
109 F10 **Itaobim** Minas Gerais, SE Brazil 16°34′S 41°27′W
111 J6 **Itaocara** Rio de Janeiro, Brazil 21°41′S 42°04′W
108 H6 **Itaparica, Represa de** ▣ E Brazil
114 F3 **Itapebí** Salto, Uruguay 31°18′S 57°42′W
110 F4 **Itapecerica** Minas Gerais, Brazil 20°28′S 45°07′W
110 D9 **Itapecerica da Serra** São Paulo, Brazil 23°43′S 46°50′W
108 E3 **Itapecuru-Mirim** Maranhão, E Brazil 03°24′S 44°20′W
111 L5 **Itapemirim** Espírito Santo, Brazil 21°01′S 40°50′W
111 K5 **Itaperuna** Rio de Janeiro, SE Brazil 21°14′S 41°51′W
109 G9 **Itapetinga** Bahia, E Brazil 15°17′S 40°16′W
110 B9 **Itapetininga** São Paulo, S Brazil 23°36′S 48°07′W
110 A10 **Itapeva** São Paulo, S Brazil 23°58′S 48°54′W
110 C9 **Itapevi** São Paulo, Brazil 23°33′S 46°56′W
95 M4 **Itapicuru, Rio** ≈ NE Brazil
108 G3 **Itapipoca** Ceará, E Brazil 03°29′S 39°35′W
110 D7 **Itapira** São Paulo, S Brazil 22°25′S 46°46′W
110 A6 **Itápolis** São Paulo, Brazil 21°36′S 48°43′W
113 K4 **Itaporanga** São Paulo, S Brazil 23°43′S 49°28′W
113 H5 **Itapúa** off. Departamento de Itapúa. ◐ department SE Paraguay
Itapúa, Departamento de see Itapúa
106 F6 **Itapuã do Oeste** Rondônia, W Brazil 09°21′S 63°07′W
113 H7 **Itaqui** Rio Grande do Sul, S Brazil 29°10′S 56°28′W
111 L3 **Itarana** Espírito Santo, Brazil 19°51′S 40°52′W
113 K4 **Itararé** São Paulo, S Brazil 24°07′S 49°16′W
113 K4 **Itararé, Rio** ≈ S Brazil
110 C10 **Itariri** São Paulo, Brazil 24°18′S 47°10′W
232 E8 **Itārsi** Madhya Pradesh, C India 22°39′N 77°48′E
71 H5 **Itasca** Texas, SW USA 32°09′N 97°09′W
Itassi see Vieille Case
118 B7 **Itata, Río** ≈ Chile
112 G6 **Itatí** Corrientes, NE Argentina 27°16′S 58°15′W
110 G3 **Itatiaiucu** Minas Gerais, Brazil 20°12′S 44°25′W
110 C8 **Itatiba** São Paulo, Brazil 23°00′S 46°51′W
113 K4 **Itatinga** São Paulo, S Brazil 23°08′S 48°36′W
110 D4 **Itaú de Minas** Minas Gerais, Brazil 20°43′S 46°45′W
110 G3 **Itaúna** Minas Gerais, Brazil 20°04′S 44°34′W
111 H4 **Itaverava** Minas Gerais, Brazil 20°40′S 43°36′W
161 J7 **Itchen** ≈ United Kingdom
186 G6 **Itéas, Kólpos** gulf C Greece
106 F8 **Iténez, Río** var. Rio Guaporé. ≈ Bolivia/Brazil see also Rio Guaporé

◆ Country
● Country Capital
◇ Dependent Territory
○ Dependent Territory Capital
◐ Administrative Regions
✈ International Airport
▲ Mountain
▲▲ Mountain Range
⛰ Volcano
≈ River
◎ Lake
▣ Reservoir

J

Legend				
◆ Country	◇ Dependent Territory	▲ Mountain	✹ Volcano	◌ Lake
● Country Capital	○ Dependent Territory Capital	▲ Mountain Range	~ River	◌ Reservoir
	◇ Administrative Regions	✈ International Airport		

◆ Country   ◇ Dependent Territory   ◈ Administrative Regions   ▲ Mountain   ◊ Volcano   ⊚ Lake
● Country Capital   ○ Dependent Territory Capital   ✕ International Airport   ▲ Mountain Range   ≈ River   ⊟ Reservoir

◆ Country ◇ Dependent Territory ◈ Administrative Régions ▲ Mountain 🌋 Volcano ◎ Lake
● Country Capital ○ Dependent Territory Capital ✈ International Airport ▲ Mountain Range ◆ River ⬚ Reservoir

◆ Country
● Country Capital
◇ Dependent Territory
◇ Dependent Territory Capital
◆ Administrative Regions
✈ International Airport
▲ Mountain
▲ Mountain Range
☈ Volcano
~ River
◉ Lake
☐ Reservoir

◆ Country ◇ Dependent Territory ▲ Mountain ⋇ Volcano ⊚ Lake
● Country Capital ○ Dependent Territory Capital ✕ International Airport ▲ Mountain Range ♒ River ⊠ Reservoir
◊ Administrative Regions

◆ Country ◇ Dependent Territory ◆ Administrative Regions ▲ Mountain ◎ Lake
● Country Capital ○ Dependent Territory Capital ✈ International Airport ▲ Mountain Range ☙ River ▲ Volcano ■ Reservoir

Laurentian Highlands - Leslie
INDEX
366

Laurentian Highlands see Laurentian Mountains
63 I1 **Laurentian Mountains** var. Laurentian Highlands, Fr. Les Laurentides. plateau Newfoundland and Labrador/Québec, Canada
63 I1 **Laurentian Mountains** ▲▲ Quebec, SE Canada
63 H3 **Laurentides** Québec, SE Canada 45°51′N 73°49′W
Laurentides, Les see Laurentian Mountains
175 H10 **Lauria** Basilicata, S Italy 40°03′N 15°50′E
292 E1 **Laurie Island** island Antarctica
166 G10 **Lauriére** Limousin, France 46°05′N 1°29′E
159 H6 **Laurieston** United Kingdom 54°58′N 4°03′W
67 J7 **Laurinburg** North Carolina, SE USA 34°46′N 79°29′W
72 D3 **Laurium** Michigan, N USA 47°14′N 88°26′W
Lauru see Choiseul
176 C5 **Lausanne** It. Losanna. Vaud, SW Switzerland 46°32′N 06°39′E
179 J9 **Lausche** var. Luže. ▲ Czech Republic/Germany 50°52′N 14°39′E see also Luže
Lausche see Luže
182 C7 **Lausitzer Bergland** var. Lausitzer Gebirge, Cz. Gory Lużyckie, Lužické Hory', Eng. Lusatian Mountains. ▲▲ E Germany
Lausitzer Gebirge see Lausitzer Bergland
Lausitzer Neisse see Neisse
169 L3 **Lautaret, Col du** pass SE France
116 B6 **Lautaro** Araucanía, C Chile 38°30′S 71°30′W
181 E14 **Lauter** ≈ W Germany
181 G10 **Lauterbach** Hessen, C Germany 50°37′N 09°24′E
167 N9 **Lauterbrunnen** Bern, C Switzerland 46°36′N 07°52′E
181 J11 **Lautertal** Bayern, Germany 50°20′E 10°58′N
259 K7 **Laut Kecil, Kepulauan** island group N Indonesia
280 D9 **Lautoka** Viti Levu, W Fiji 17°36′S 177°28′E
259 K7 **Laut, Pulau** prev. Laoet. island Borneo, C Indonesia
258 G2 **Laut, Pulau** island Kepulauan Natuna, W Indonesia
168 G5 **Lautrec** Midi-Pyrénées, France 43°43′N 2°09′E
259 K6 **Laut, Selat** strait Borneo, C Indonesia
258 B2 **Laut Tawar, Danau** ◎ Sumatera, NW Indonesia
282 F10 **Lauvergne Island** island Chuuk, C Micronesia
162 H3 **Lauwers Meer** ◎ N Netherlands
162 H3 **Lauwersoog** Groningen, NE Netherlands 53°25′N 06°14′E
164 G8 **Lauzerte** Tarn-et-Garonne, S France 44°15′N 01°08′E
71 H8 **Lavaca Bay** bay Texas, SW USA
71 H8 **Lavaca River** ≈ Texas, SW USA
158 B6 **Lavagh More** ▲ N Ireland
63 H3 **Laval** Québec, SE Canada 45°32′N 73°44′W
164 F4 **Laval** Mayenne, NW France 48°04′N 00°46′W
171 I5 **La Vall d'Uixó** var. Vall D'Uxó. Valenciana, E Spain 39°49′N 00°15′W
118 F2 **Lavalle** Mendoza, Argentina 32°43′S 68°35′W
115 J8 **Lavalleja** ◈ department S Uruguay
63 H2 **Lavaltrie** Québec, SE Canada 45°56′N 73°14′W
281 J4 **Lavanggu** Rennell, S Solomon Islands 11°39′S 160°13′E
114 B8 **La Vanguardia** Buenos Aires, Argentina 33°44′S 60°48′W
114 B7 **La Vanguardia** Santa Fe, Argentina 33°18′S 60°36′W
222 G9 **Lāvān, Jazīreh-ye** island S Iran
177 K4 **Lavant** ≈ S Austria
118 A8 **Lavapie, Punta** point Bío-Bío, Chile
168 E4 **Lavardac** Aquitaine, France 44°11′N 0°18′E
190 D4 **Lavassaare** Ger. Lawassaar. Pärnumaa, SW Estonia 58°29′N 24°22′E
168 G5 **Lavaur** Midi-Pyrénées, France 43°42′N 1°49′E
170 F2 **La Vecilla de Curueño** Castilla y León, N Spain 42°51′N 05°24′W
118 D2 **La Vega** Valparaíso, Chile 32°13′S 70°53′W
91 H5 **La Vega** var. Concepción de la Vega. C Dominican Republic 19°15′N 70°33′W
La Vela see La Vela de Coro
102 E2 **La Vela de Coro** var. La Vela. Falcón, N Venezuela 11°30′N 69°33′W
165 H9 **Lavelanet** Ariège, S France 42°56′N 01°50′E
175 H9 **Lavello** Basilicata, S Italy 41°03′N 15°48′E
161 L4 **Lavenham** United Kingdom 52°06′N 0°48′E
84 F5 **La Ventana** Baja California Sur, NW Mexico 27°41′N 109°37′W
84 C2 **La Ventana** Baja California Norte, NW Mexico 31°43′N 115°04′W
79 H5 **La Verkin** Utah, W USA 37°12′N 113°16′W
75 C11 **Laverne** Oklahoma, C USA 36°42′N 99°53′W
70 G7 **La Vernia** Texas, SW USA 29°19′N 98°07′W
169 K2 **La Verpilliére** Rhône-Alpes, France 45°38′N 5°09′E
218 F6 **Lavi** Israel 32°47′N 35°26′E
190 C1 **Lavia** Satakunta, SW Finland 61°36′N 22°34′E
62 E2 **Lavieille, Lake** ◎ Ontario, SE Canada
154 A6 **Lavik** Sogn Og Fjordane, S Norway 61°06′N 05°25′E
La Vila Joíosa see Villajoyosa
169 J4 **Lavilledieu** Rhône-Alpes, France 44°34′N 4°28′E
168 G1 **La Villetelle** Limousin, France 45°55′N 2°21′E
77 J5 **Lavina** Montana, NW USA 46°18′N 108°55′W
168 F5 **Lavit** Midi-Pyrénées, France 43°58′N 0°55′E
292 E3 **Lavoisier Island** island Antarctica
66 G8 **Lavonia** Georgia, SE USA 34°26′N 83°06′W
165 J7 **la Voulte-sur-Rhône** Ardèche, E France 44°49′N 04°46′E
169 I2 **Lavoûte-Chilhac** Auvergne, France 45°09′N 3°24′E
110 F5 **Lavras** Minas Gerais, Brazil 21°14′S 45°00′W
115 K3 **Lavras do Sul** Rio Grande do Sul, Brazil 30°49′S 53°55′W
82 E4 **Lavrentiya** Chukotskiy Avtonomnyy Okrug, Russian Federation 65°30′N 171°00′E
110 F7 **Lavrinhas** São Paulo, Brazil 22°35′S 44°54′W
187 H7 **Lávrio** prev. Lávrion. Attikí, C Greece 37°43′N 24°03′E
Lávrion see Lávrio
190 F5 **Lavry** Pskovskaya Oblast', Russian Federation
139 H7 **Lavumisa** prev. Gollel. SE Swaziland 27°18′S 31°55′E
Lawak see Nanshan Island
231 I3 **Lawarai Pass** pass N Pakistan
Lawassaar see Lavassaare
220 G9 **Lawdar** SW Yemen 13°49′N 45°55′E
158 G1 **Lawers, Ben** ▲ United Kingdom 56°34′N 4°13′W
70 F5 **Lawn** Texas, SW USA 32°07′N 99°45′W
64 D7 **Lawnton** Pennsylvania, USA 40°16′N 76°48′W
293 L3 **Law Promontory** headland Antarctica
132 G6 **Lawra** NW Ghana 10°40′N 02°49′W
278 C12 **Lawrence** Otago, South Island, New Zealand 45°53′S 169°43′E
73 F11 **Lawrence** Indiana, N USA 39°49′N 86°01′W
75 F9 **Lawrence** Kansas, C USA 38°58′N 95°15′W
65 L1 **Lawrence** Massachusetts, NE USA 42°42′N 71°09′W
66 F4 **Lawrenceburg** Kentucky, S USA 38°02′N 84°53′W
66 D7 **Lawrenceburg** Tennessee, S USA 35°16′N 87°20′W
66 G8 **Lawrenceville** Georgia, SE USA 33°57′N 83°59′W
73 D12 **Lawrenceville** Illinois, N USA 38°43′N 87°40′W
64 G7 **Lawrenceville** New Jersey, USA 40°18′N 74°44′W
67 L5 **Lawrenceville** Virginia, NE USA 36°45′N 77°50′W
80 F5 **Laws** California, USA 37°24′N 118°21′W
75 G9 **Lawson** Missouri, C USA 39°26′N 94°12′W
75 D13 **Lawton** Oklahoma, C USA 34°35′N 98°20′W
220 C2 **Lawz, Jabal al** ▲ NW Saudi Arabia 28°45′N 35°20′E
155 G8 **Laxå** Örebro, C Sweden 59°00′N 14°37′E
158 G7 **Laxey** E Isle of Man
195 K4 **Laya** ≈ NW Russian Federation
105 G10 **La Yarada** Tacna, SW Peru 18°14′S 70°30′W
161 L5 **Layer de la Haye** United Kingdom 51°50′N 0°51′E
221 H8 **Layjūn** C Yemen 15°27′N 49°16′E
220 G5 **Laylā** var. Laila. Ar Riyāḍ, C Saudi Arabia 22°14′N 46°40′E
69 H1 **Lay Lake** ⊡ Alabama, S USA
91 L3 **Layou** Saint Vincent, Saint Vincent and the Grenadines 13°11′N 61°16′W
La Youne see El Ayoun
286 F4 **Laysan Island** island Hawaiian Islands, Hawai'i, USA
79 H2 **Layton** Utah, W USA 41°03′N 112°00′W
78 A3 **Laytonville** California, N USA 39°39′N 123°30′W
158 D9 **Laytown** Meath, Ireland 53°41′N 6°14′W
85 I6 **La Zarca** Durango, Mexico 25°50′N 104°44′W
137 I9 **Lazare, Pointe** headland Mahé, NE Seychelles 04°46′S 55°28′E
193 L7 **Lazarev** Khabarovskiy Kray, SE Russian Federation 52°11′N 141°18′E
184 F4 **Lazarevac** Serbia, C Serbia 44°25′N 20°17′E
291 H13 **Lazarev Sea** sea Antarctica
86 C7 **Lázaro Cárdenas** Michoacán, SW Mexico 17°56′N 102°13′W
87 I8 **Lázaro Cárdenas** Oaxaca, Mexico 16°44′N 94°52′W
191 D9 **Lazdijai** Alytus, S Lithuania 54°13′N 23°33′E
197 N8 **Lazerew Oroli** island NW Uzbekistan
190 I5 **Lazhiny** Novgorodskaya Oblast', Russian Federation
244 B8 **Lazikou** Gansu, China 34°01′N 103°32′E
175 E8 **Lazio** anc. Latium. ◈ region C Italy
179 H10 **Lázně Kynžvart** Ger. Bad Königswart. Karlovarský Kraj, W Czech Republic 50°00′N 12°40′E
114 D6 **Lazo** Entre Ríos, Argentina 32°52′S 59°26′W
159 I6 **Lazonby** United Kingdom 54°44′N 2°42′W
Lazovsk see Sîngerei
161 K5 **Lea** W England, United Kingdom
257 G9 **Leach** Poŭthĭsăt, W Cambodia 12°19′N 103°45′E
75 J12 **Leachville** Arkansas, C USA 35°56′N 90°15′W
74 A5 **Lead** South Dakota, N USA 44°21′N 103°45′W
159 I3 **Leadburn** United Kingdom 55°47′N 3°14′W
159 L10 **Leadenham** United Kingdom 53°03′N 0°35′W
57 L7 **Leader** Saskatchewan, S Canada 50°55′N 109°31′W
159 H4 **Leadhills** United Kingdom 55°24′N 3°46′W
63 L3 **Lead Mountain** ▲ Maine, NE USA 44°53′N 68°07′W
79 L3 **Leadville** Colorado, C USA 39°15′N 106°17′W
55 I7 **Leaf Rapids** Manitoba, C Canada 56°30′N 100°02′W
68 F3 **Leaf River** ≈ Mississippi, S USA
71 I7 **League City** Texas, SW USA 29°30′N 95°05′W
152 G2 **Leaibevuotna** Nor. Olderfjord. Finnmark, N Norway 70°29′N 24°58′E
68 F3 **Leakesville** Mississippi, S USA 31°09′N 88°33′W
70 F7 **Leakey** Texas, SW USA 29°44′N 99°48′W
Leal see Lihula
138 E2 **Lealui** Western, W Zambia 15°12′S 22°59′E
Leamhcán see Lucan
62 A6 **Leamington** Ontario, S Canada 42°03′N 82°35′W
Leamington/Leamington Spa see Royal Leamington Spa
Leammi see Lemmenjoki
243 J5 **Le'an** Jiangxi, China 27°16′N 115°29′E
70 G6 **Leander** Texas, SW USA 30°34′N 97°51′W
141 J4 **Leandra** Mpumalanga, South Africa 26°22′S 28°55′E
114 A9 **Leandro Alem** Buenos Aires, Argentina 34°30′S 61°24′W
110 F2 **Leandro Ferreira** Minas Gerais, Brazil 19°42′S 45°00′W
113 H6 **Leandro N. Alem** Misiones, NE Argentina 27°34′S 55°15′W
157 B10 **Leane, Lough** Ir. Loch Léin. ◎ SW Ireland
274 C5 **Learmonth** Western Australia 22°17′S 114°03′E
260 G6 **Leasi, Kepulauan** island group C Indonesia
161 J2 **Leasingham** United Kingdom 53°01′N 0°25′W
161 K7 **Leatherhead** United Kingdom 51°17′N 0°19′W
Leau see Zoutleeuw
L'Eau d'Heure see Plate Taille, Lac de la
284 A10 **Leava** Île Futuna, S Wallis and Futuna
Leavdnja see Lakselv
75 G9 **Leavenworth** Kansas, C USA 39°19′N 94°55′W
76 D4 **Leavenworth** Washington, NW USA 47°36′N 120°39′W
152 H3 **Leavvajohka** var. Levajok. Finnmark, N Norway 69°57′N 26°18′E
75 G9 **Leawood** Kansas, C USA 38°57′N 94°37′W
182 E3 **Łeba** Ger. Leba. Pomorskie, N Poland 54°45′N 17°32′E
182 E3 **Łeba** Ger. Leba. ≈ N Poland
Leba see Łeba
181 C13 **Lebach** Saarland, SW Germany 49°25′N 06°54′E
Łeba, Jezioro see Łebsko, Jezioro
263 M9 **Lebak** Mindanao, S Philippines 06°28′N 124°03′E
Lebanese Republic see Lebanon
260 C5 **Lebani,Teluk** bay Sulawesi, C Indonesia
73 E10 **Lebanon** Indiana, N USA 40°03′N 86°28′W
66 F4 **Lebanon** Kentucky, S USA 37°33′N 85°15′W
75 H10 **Lebanon** Missouri, C USA 37°40′N 92°40′W
63 I5 **Lebanon** New Hampshire, NE USA 43°40′N 72°15′W
76 B6 **Lebanon** Oregon, NW USA 44°32′N 122°54′W
64 D7 **Lebanon** Pennsylvania, NE USA 40°20′N 76°24′W
66 E6 **Lebanon** Tennessee, S USA 36°11′N 86°19′W
67 H5 **Lebanon** Virginia, NE USA 36°52′N 82°07′W
218 E4 **Lebanon** off. Lebanese Republic, Ar. Al Lubnān, Fr. Liban. ◆ republic SW Asia
66 E4 **Lebanon Junction** Kentucky, S USA 37°49′N 85°43′W
Lebanon, Mount see Liban, Jebel
228 F5 **Lebap** Lebapskiy Velayat, NE Turkmenistan 41°04′N 61°49′E
Lebapskiy Velayat see Lebap Welaýaty
228 F7 **Lebap Welaýaty** Rus. Lebapskiy Velayat; prev. Rus. Chardzhevskaya Oblast, Turkm. Chärjew Oblasty. ◈ province E Turkmenistan
169 H7 **Le Barcarés** Languedoc-Roussillon, France 42°47′N 3°02′E
Lebasee see Łebsko, Jezioro
163 D10 **Lebbeke** Oost-Vlaanderen, NW Belgium 51°00′N 04°08′E
169 L6 **Le Beausset** Provence-Alpes-Côte d'Azur, France 43°12′N 5°48′E
81 D9 **Lebec** California, W USA 34°51′N 118°52′W
Lebedin see Lebedyn
193 J7 **Lebedinyy** Respublika Sakha (Yakutiya), NE Russian Federation 58°23′N 125°24′E
196 G3 **Lebedyan'** Lipetskaya Oblast', W Russian Federation 53°00′N 39°11′E
189 J3 **Lebedyn** Rus. Lebedin. Sums'ka Oblast', NE Ukraine 50°36′N 34°30′E
58 F7 **Lebel-sur-Quévillon** Québec, SE Canada 49°01′N 76°56′W
152 H3 **Lebesby** Lapp. Davvesiida. Finnmark, N Norway 70°31′N 27°00′E
167 M10 **Le Biot** Rhône-Alpes, France 46°16′N 6°38′E
166 F9 **le Blanc** Indre, C France 46°38′N 01°04′E
169 I4 **Le Bleymard** Languedoc-Roussillon, France 44°29′N 3°44′E
134 G5 **Lebo** Orientale, N Dem. Rep. Congo 04°30′N 23°58′E
75 F10 **Lebo** Kansas, C USA 38°22′N 95°50′W
141 L4 **Lebombo Mountains** ▲▲ Swaziland
182 E3 **Lębork** var. Lębórk, Ger. Lauenburg, Lauenburg in Pommern. Pomorskie, N Poland 54°32′N 17°43′E
166 G6 **Le Boullay-Mivoye** Centre, France 48°39′N 1°24′E
165 I9 **le Boulou** Pyrénées-Orientales, S France 42°32′N 02°50′E
168 G3 **Le Bourg** Midi-Pyrénées, France 44°43′N 1°55′E
169 L3 **Le Bourg-d'Oisans** Rhône-Alpes, France 45°03′N 6°02′E
169 L1 **Le Bourget-du-Lac** Rhône-Alpes, France 45°39′N 5°52′E
141 K2 **Lebowakgomo** Limpopo, South Africa 24°12′S 29°30′E
176 B5 **Le Brassus** Vaud, W Switzerland 46°35′N 06°14′E
170 E8 **Lebrija** Andalucía, S Spain 36°55′N 06°04′W
182 E3 **Łebsko, Jezioro** Ger. Lebasee; prev. Jezioro Łeba. ◎ N Poland
116 A6 **Lebu** Bío Bío, C Chile 37°38′S 73°43′W
Lebyazh'ye see Akku
172 B1 **Leça da Palmeira** Porto, N Portugal 41°12′N 08°43′W
165 K8 **le Cannet** Alpes-Maritimes, SE France 43°35′N 07°E
Le Cap see Cap-Haïtien
169 I6 **Le Cap d'Agde** Languedoc-Roussillon, France 43°17′N 3°31′E
158 B9 **Lecarrow** Ireland 53°33′N 8°03′W
165 I2 **le Cateau-Cambrésis** Nord, N France 50°05′N 03°32′E
169 I5 **Le Caylar** Languedoc-Roussillon, France 43°51′N 3°18′E
175 J10 **Lecce** Puglia, SE Italy 40°23′N 18°11′E
176 E6 **Lecco** Lombardia, N Italy 45°51′N 09°23′E
176 F4 **Lech** Vorarlberg, W Austria 47°14′N 10°10′E
179 F13 **Lech** ≈ Austria/Germany
186 F6 **Lechainá** var. Lehena, Lekhainá. Dytikí Elláda, S Greece 37°57′N 21°16′E
243 H7 **Lechang** Guangdong, China 25°05′N 113°13′E
164 F6 **le Château d'Oléron** Charente-Maritime, W France 45°53′N 01°12′W
169 M1 **Le Châtelard** Rhône-Alpes, France 45°37′N 6°52′E
167 H10 **Le Châtelet** Limousin, France 46°12′N 2°27′E
165 J2 **le Chesne** Ardennes, N France 49°33′N 04°42′E
165 J7 **le Cheylard** Ardèche, E France 44°55′N 04°27′E
161 I6 **Lechlade** United Kingdom 51°42′N 1°42′W
176 F4 **Lechtaler Alpen** ▲▲ W Austria
168 D9 **Leciñena** Aragón, Spain 41°48′N 0°37′W
178 D3 **Leck** Schleswig-Holstein, N Germany 54°45′N 09°00′E
62 G1 **Lecointre, Lac** ◎ Québec, SE Canada
68 C3 **Lecompte** Louisiana, S USA 31°05′N 92°24′W
165 J5 **le Creusot** Saône-et-Loire, C France 46°48′N 04°27′E
166 B8 **Le Croisic** Pays de la Loire, France 47°18′N 2°31′W
166 G3 **Le Crotoy** Picardie, France 50°13′N 1°37′E
168 E5 **Lectoure** Midi-Pyrénées, France 43°56′N 0°37′E
Lecumberri see Lekunberri
182 I7 **Łęczna** Lubelskie, E Poland 51°20′N 22°52′E
182 F6 **Łęczyca** Ger. Lentschiza, Rus. Lenchitsa. Łódzkie, C Poland 52°04′N 19°10′E
180 D4 **Leda** ≈ NW Germany
161 H5 **Ledbury** United Kingdom 52°03′N 2°25′W
163 D10 **Lede** Oost-Vlaanderen, NW Belgium 50°58′N 03°59′E
170 E4 **Ledesma** Castilla y León, N Spain 41°05′N 06°00′W
91 N2 **le Diamant** SW Martinique 14°29′N 61°02′W
169 J5 **Lédignan** Languedoc-Roussillon, France 43°59′N 4°06′E
137 J8 **Le Digue** island Inner Islands, NE Seychelles
165 I6 **le Donjon** Allier, C France 46°19′N 03°50′E
164 G6 **le Dorat** Haute-Vienne, C France 46°14′N 01°05′E
Ledo Salinarius see Lons-le-Saunier
244 A5 **Ledu** Qinghai, C China 36°29′N 102°25′E
57 I5 **Leduc** Alberta, SW Canada 53°17′N 113°30′W
193 N4 **Ledyanaya, Gora** ▲ E Russian Federation 61°51′N 171°03′E
157 B11 **Lee** Ir. An Laoi. ≈ SW Ireland
160 G3 **Leebotwood** United Kingdom 52°35′N 2°47′W
74 G3 **Leech Lake** ◎ Minnesota, N USA
75 C12 **Leedey** Oklahoma, C USA 35°54′N 99°21′W
159 K9 **Leeds** N England, United Kingdom 53°50′N 01°35′W
66 D8 **Leeds** Alabama, S USA 33°33′N 86°32′W
74 D2 **Leeds** North Dakota, N USA 48°19′N 99°43′W
162 H3 **Leek** Groningen, NE Netherlands 53°10′N 06°24′E
159 J10 **Leek** United Kingdom 53°06′N 2°01′W
163 G9 **Leende** Noord-Brabant, SE Netherlands 51°21′N 05°34′E
180 D3 **Leer** Niedersachsen, NW Germany 53°14′N 07°26′E
162 F7 **Leerdam** Zuid-Holland, C Netherlands 51°54′N 05°06′E
162 G7 **Leersum** Utrecht, C Netherlands 52°01′N 05°26′E
69 L6 **Leesburg** Florida, SE USA 28°48′N 81°52′W
64 C9 **Leesburg** Virginia, NE USA 39°09′N 77°34′W
75 G9 **Lees Summit** Missouri, C USA 38°55′N 94°21′W
68 B3 **Leesville** Louisiana, S USA 31°08′N 93°15′W
70 G7 **Leesville** Texas, SW USA 29°22′N 97°45′W
73 J10 **Leesville Lake** ⊡ Ohio, N USA
Leesville Lake see Smith Mountain Lake
277 J5 **Leeton** New South Wales, SE Australia 34°33′S 146°24′E
140 G9 **Leeu** ≈ Eastern Cape, South Africa
141 H5 **Leeudoringstad** North-West, South Africa 27°14′S 26°14′E
140 F9 **Leeu-Gamka** Western Cape, South Africa 32°47′S 21°59′E
162 G3 **Leeuwarden** Fris. Ljouwert. Fryslân, N Netherlands 53°15′N 05°48′E
274 D8 **Leeuwin, Cape** headland Western Australia 34°18′S 115°03′E
80 F4 **Lee Vining** California, W USA 37°57′N 119°07′W
91 L5 **Leeward Islands** island group E West Indies
Leeward Islands see Sotavento, Ilhas de
Leeward Islands see Vent, Îles Sous le
180 I2 **Leezen** Schleswig-Holstein, Germany 53°52′E 10°15′N
135 D8 **Léfini** ≈ SE Congo
Léfka see Lefke
186 E5 **Lefkáda** prev. Levkás. Lefkáda, Iónia Nisiá, Greece, C Mediterranean Sea 38°50′N 20°42′E
186 E5 **Lefkáda** It. Santa Maura, prev. Levkás; anc. Leucas. island Iónia Nisiá, Greece, C Mediterranean Sea
187 H10 **Lefká Óri** ▲▲ Kríti, Greece, E Mediterranean Sea
218 B2 **Lefke** Gk. Léfka. W Cyprus 35°06′N 32°52′E
186 E4 **Lefkímmi** var. Levkímmi. Kérkyra, Iónia Nisiá, Greece, C Mediterranean Sea 39°26′N 20°05′E
Lefkonico/Lefkónikon see Geçitkale
Lefkosía/Lefkoşa see Nicosia
70 E2 **Lefors** Texas, SW USA 35°26′N 100°48′W
168 F6 **Le Fossat** Midi-Pyrénées, France 43°11′N 1°25′E
168 F6 **Le Fousseret** Midi-Pyrénées, France 43°17′N 1°04′E
91 N2 **le François** E Martinique 14°36′N 60°59′W
169 L3 **Le Freney-d'Oisans** Rhône-Alpes, France 45°02′N 6°07′E
53 I8 **Lefroy Bay** coastal sea feature Nunavut, NE Canada
274 E7 **Lefroy, Lake** salt lake Western Australia
141 H3 **Lefurutshane** North West, South Africa 25°13′S 26°24′E
Legaceaster see Chester
170 G5 **Leganés** Madrid, C Spain 40°20′N 03°46′W
Legaspi see Legazpi City
Legaspi see Legazpi City
263 M6 **Legazpi City** off. Legaspi. Luzon, N Philippines 13°07′N 123°44′E
159 M10 **Legbourne** United Kingdom 53°20′N 0°03′E
180 C6 **Legden** Nordrhein-Westfalen, Germany 52°02′E 7°06′N
166 C9 **Legé** Pays de la Loire, France 46°53′N 1°36′W
Leghorn see Livorno
182 H6 **Legionowo** Mazowieckie, C Poland 52°25′N 20°56′E
163 G13 **Léglise** Luxembourg, SE Belgium 49°48′N 05°31′E
176 G7 **Legnago** Lombardia, NE Italy 45°13′N 11°18′E
176 E6 **Legnano** Veneto, NE Italy 45°36′N 08°54′E
182 D7 **Legnica** Ger. Liegnitz. Dolnośląskie, SW Poland 51°12′N 16°11′E
168 E1 **Le Gond-Pontouvre** Poitou-Charentes, France 45°41′N 0°10′E
80 D5 **Le Grand** California, W USA 37°12′N 120°15′W
166 G10 **Le Grand-Bourg** Limousin, France 46°10′N 1°39′E
166 E7 **Le Grand-Lucé** Pays de la Loire, France 47°52′N 0°28′E
166 F9 **Le Grand-Pressigny** Centre, France 46°55′N 0°48′E
169 K2 **Le Grand Serre** Rhône-Alpes, France 45°16′N 5°06′E
165 I8 **le Grau-du-Roi** Gard, S France 43°32′N 04°10′E
168 F5 **Léguevin** Midi-Pyrénées, France 43°36′N 1°15′E
277 M2 **Legume** New South Wales, SE Australia 28°24′S 152°20′E
164 G2 **le Havre** Eng. Havre; prev. le Havre-de-Grâce. Seine-Maritime, N France 49°30′N 00°06′E
le Havre-de-Grâce see le Havre
Lehena see Lechainá
79 H2 **Lehi** Utah, W USA 40°23′N 111°51′W
64 F6 **Lehighton** Pennsylvania, NE USA 40°49′N 75°42′W
114 A3 **Lehmann** Santa Fe, Argentina 31°08′S 61°27′W
74 D3 **Lehr** North Dakota, N USA 46°15′N 99°21′W
181 I13 **Lehrberg** Bayern, Germany 49°20′E 10°31′N
180 I6 **Lehre** Niedersachsen, Germany 52°20′E 10°40′N
180 H6 **Lehrte** Niedersachsen, Germany 52°23′E 9°58′N
82 A1 **Lehua Island** island Hawaiian Islands, Hawai'i, USA
231 H6 **Leiāh** Punjab, NE Pakistan 30°59′N 70°58′E
177 K4 **Leibnitz** Steiermark, SE Austria 46°48′N 15°33′E
242 A4 **Leibo** Sichuan, C China 28°15′N 103°34′E
161 J3 **Leicester** Lat. Batae Coritanorum. C England, United Kingdom 52°38′N 01°05′W
161 I3 **Leicestershire** cultural region C England, United Kingdom
Leicheng see Leizhou
162 E6 **Leiden** prev. Leyden; anc. Lugdunum Batavorum. Zuid-Holland, W Netherlands 52°09′N 04°30′E
162 E6 **Leiderdorp** Zuid-Holland, W Netherlands 52°08′N 04°32′E
162 E6 **Leidschendam** Zuid-Holland, W Netherlands 52°05′N 04°24′E
163 C10 **Leie** Fr. Lys. ≈ Belgium/France
Leifear see Lifford
180 I6 **Leiferde** Niedersachsen, Germany 52°13′E 10°31′N
278 G3 **Leigh** Auckland, North Island, New Zealand 36°17′S 174°48′E
159 J9 **Leigh** NW England, United Kingdom 53°30′N 02°33′W
276 G3 **Leigh Creek** South Australia 30°27′S 138°23′E
66 D7 **Leighton** Alabama, S USA 34°42′N 87°31′W
161 J5 **Leighton Buzzard** E England, United Kingdom 51°55′N 00°41′W
Léim an Bhradáin see Leixlip
Léim An Mhadaidh see Limavady
Léime, Ceann see Loop Head, Ireland
Léime, Ceann see Slyne Head, Ireland
181 F13 **Leimen** Baden-Württemberg, SW Germany 49°21′N 08°40′E
180 H6 **Leine** ≈ NW Germany
181 I8 **Leinefelde** Thüringen, C Germany 51°22′N 10°19′E
Léin, Loch see Leane, Lough
157 D9 **Leinster** Ir. Cúige Laighean. cultural region E Ireland
160 A3 **Leinster, Mount** Ir. Stua Laighean. ▲ SE Ireland 52°36′N 06°45′W
160 G4 **Leintwardine** United Kingdom 52°22′N 2°52′W
191 D9 **Leipalingis** Alytus, S Lithuania 54°05′N 23°52′E
152 G5 **Leipojärvi** Norrbotten, N Sweden 67°03′N 21°15′E
73 G9 **Leipsic** Ohio, N USA 41°06′N 83°58′W
Leipsic see Leipzig
187 K7 **Leipsoí** island Dodekánisa, Greece, Aegean Sea
179 G8 **Leipzig** Pol. Lipsk, hist. Leipsic; anc. Lipsia. Sachsen, E Germany 51°19′N 12°24′E
179 G8 **Leipzig Halle** ✈ Sachsen, E Germany 51°26′N 12°14′E
172 B3 **Leiria** anc. Collipo. Leiria, C Portugal 39°45′N 08°49′W
172 B3 **Leiria** ◈ district C Portugal
154 A7 **Leirvik** Hordaland, S Norway 59°49′N 05°27′E
161 I3 **Leiscester** United Kingdom 52°38′N 1°08′W
242 D6 **Leishan** Guizhou, China 26°13′N 108°02′E
190 C4 **Leisi** Ger. Laisberg. Saaremaa, W Estonia 58°33′N 22°41′E
170 E2 **Leitariegos, Puerto de** pass NW Spain
66 E4 **Leitchfield** Kentucky, S USA 37°28′N 86°19′W
177 L2 **Leitha** Hung. Lajta. ≈ Austria/Hungary
54 E2 **Leith, Point** headland Northwest Territories, NW Canada
Leitir Ceanainn see Letterkenny
Leitmeritz see Litoměřice
Leitomischl see Litomyšl
158 B8 **Leitrim** Leitrim, Ireland 53°59′N 8°04′W
158 B8 **Leitrim** Ir. Liatroim. cultural region NW Ireland
168 B6 **Leitza** Span. Leiza. Navarra, Spain 43°05′N 1°55′W
158 D10 **Leixlip** Eng. Salmon Leap, Ir. Léim an Bhradáin. Kildare, E Ireland 53°23′N 06°32′W
290 H4 **Leixões** Porto, N Portugal 41°11′N 08°41′W
242 G6 **Leiyang** Hunan, S China 26°23′N 112°49′E
Leiza see Leitza
240 F9 **Leizhou** var. Haikang, Leicheng. Guangdong, S China 20°54′N 110°05′E
240 F9 **Leizhou Bandao** var. Luichow Peninsula. peninsula S China
162 E7 **Lek** ≈ SW Netherlands
187 I2 **Lekánis** ▲▲ NE Greece
139 I9 **Le Kartala** ▲ Grande Comore, NW Comoros
Le Kef see El Kef
168 A6 **Lekeitio** Pais Vasco, Spain 43°22′N 2°30′W
135 C8 **Lékéti, Monts de la** ▲▲ S Congo
141 I9 **Lekfontein** Eastern Cape, South Africa 33°01′S 26°55′E
Lekhainá see Lechainá
185 I5 **Lekhchevo** Montana, NW Bulgaria 43°32′N 23°31′E
140 C6 **Lekkersing** Northern Cape, South Africa 29°00′S 17°06′E
152 E5 **Leknes** Nordland, C Norway 68°07′N 13°36′E
135 C8 **Lékoumou** ◈ province SW Congo
154 G6 **Leksand** Dalarna, C Sweden 60°44′N 15°E
194 E6 **Leksozero, Ozero** ◎ NW Russian Federation
171 H2 **Lekunberri** var. Lecumberri. Navarra, N Spain 43°00′N 01°54′W
260 G3 **Lelai, Tanjung** headland Pulau Halmahera, N Indonesia 01°32′N 128°43′E
91 N2 **le Lamentin** var. Lamentin. C Martinique 14°37′N 61°01′W
72 F6 **Leland** Michigan, N USA 45°01′N 85°44′W
66 A8 **Leland** Mississippi, S USA 33°24′N 90°54′W
155 F8 **Lelång** var. Lelången. ◎ S Sweden
Lelången see Lelång
160 C9 **Lelant** United Kingdom 50°11′N 5°26′W
169 L4 **Le Lauzet-Ubaye** Provence-Alpes-Côte d'Azur, France 44°26′N 6°26′E
Lel'chitsy see Lyel'chytsy
le Léman see Geneva, Lake
Leli see Tianlin
70 E2 **Lelia Lake** Texas, SW USA 34°52′N 100°42′W
140 D7 **Leliefontein** Northern Cape, South Africa 30°18′S 18°05′E
184 E5 **Lelija** ▲ SE Bosnia and Herzegovina 43°25′N 18°31′E
245 J5 **Leling** Shandong, China 37°26′N 117°07′E
166 D7 **Le Lion-d'Angers** Pays de la Loire, France 47°38′N 0°43′W
176 C4 **Le Locle** Neuchâtel, W Switzerland 47°04′N 06°45′E
283 I10 **Lelu** Kosrae, E Micronesia
Lelu see Lelu Island
169 L6 **Le Luc** Provence-Alpes-Côte d'Azur, France 43°23′N 6°19′E
166 E7 **Le Lude** Pays de la Loire, France 47°39′N 0°09′E
282 I10 **Lelu Island** var. Lelu. island Kosrae, E Micronesia
103 L5 **Lelydorp** Wanica, N Suriname 05°36′N 55°04′W
162 G5 **Lelystad** Flevoland, C Netherlands 52°30′N 05°26′E
117 E14 **Le Maire, Estrecho de** strait S Argentina
169 I3 **Le Malzieu-Ville** Languedoc-Roussillon, France 44°51′N 3°21′E
258 E4 **Lemang** Pulau Rangsang, W Indonesia 01°04′N 102°44′E
280 E3 **Lemankoa** Buka Island, NE Papua New Guinea 05°06′S 154°23′E
Léman, Lac see Geneva, Lake
166 E7 **le Mans** Sarthe, NW France 48°N 00°12′E
74 F6 **Le Mars** Iowa, C USA 42°47′N 96°10′W
168 F6 **Le Mas-d'Azil** Midi-Pyrénées, France 43°05′N 1°22′E
177 J2 **Lembach im Mühlkreis** Oberösterreich, N Austria 48°28′N 13°53′E
179 D13 **Lemberg** ▲ SW Germany 48°09′N 08°47′E
Lemberg see L'viv
Lemdiyya see Médéa
110 C7 **Leme** São Paulo, Brazil 22°12′S 47°24′W
166 E6 **Le Mèle-sur-Sarthe** Basse-Normandie, France 48°31′N 0°21′E
166 E5 **Le Merlerault** Basse-Normandie, France 48°42′N 0°18′E
218 B2 **Lemesós** var. Limassol. SW Cyprus 34°41′N 33°02′E
180 E5 **Lemförde** Niedersachsen, Germany 52°28′E 8°23′N
180 F7 **Lemgo** Nordrhein-Westfalen, W Germany 52°02′N 08°54′E
77 H6 **Lemhi Range** ▲▲ Idaho, NW USA
53 M9 **Lemieux Islands** island group Nunavut, NE Canada
260 D3 **Lemito** Sulawesi, N Indonesia 0°34′N 121°31′E
152 H4 **Lemmenjoki** Lapp. Leammi. ≈ NE Finland
162 G4 **Lemmer** Fris. De Lemmer. Fryslân, N Netherlands 52°50′N 05°43′E
74 B4 **Lemmon** South Dakota, N USA 45°54′N 102°08′W
79 I9 **Lemmon, Mount** ▲ Arizona, SW USA 32°26′N 110°47′W
Lemnos see Límnos
140 E9 **Lemoenshoek** Western Cape, South Africa 33°51′S 20°51′E
169 H4 **Le Monastier** Languedoc-Roussillon, France 44°31′N 3°15′E
80 E6 **Lemoncove** California, USA 36°23′N 119°01′W
73 F11 **Lemon, Lake** ◎ Indiana, N USA
169 H2 **Le Mont-Dore** Auvergne, France 45°34′N 2°49′E
167 H10 **Le Montet** Auvergne, France 46°24′N 3°03′E
164 F3 **le Mont St-Michel** castle Manche, N France
80 D6 **Lemoore** California, W USA 36°16′N 119°48′W
282 E9 **Lemotol Bay** bay Chuuk Islands, C Micronesia
91 K1 **le Moule** var. Moule. Grande Terre, NE Guadeloupe 16°20′N 61°21′W
Lemovices see Limoges
Le Moyen-Ogooué see Moyen-Ogooué
59 H3 **le Moyne, Lac** ◎ Québec, E Canada
153 H9 **Lempäälä** Pirkanmaa, W Finland 61°14′N 23°47′E
169 I2 **Lempdes** Auvergne, France 45°23′N 3°17′E
88 D4 **Lempira** prev. Gracias. ◈ department SW Honduras
Lemsalu see Limbaži
175 H9 **Le Murge** ▲▲ SE Italy
195 L4 **Lemva** ≈ NW Russian Federation
155 C11 **Lemvig** Midtjylland, W Denmark 56°31′N 08°19′E
256 C6 **Lemyethna** Ayeyawady, SW Myanmar (Burma) 17°36′N 95°08′E
73 C8 **Lena** Illinois, N USA 42°22′N 89°49′W
205 L3 **Lena** ≈ NE Russian Federation
289 C12 **Lena Tablemount** undersea feature S Indian Ocean 51°06′S 56°54′E
Lenchitsa see Łęczyca
166 E9 **Lencloître** Poitou-Charentes, France 46°49′N 0°19′E
109 F8 **Lençóis** Bahia, E Brazil 12°36′S 41°24′W
110 A7 **Lençóis Paulista** São Paulo, S Brazil 22°35′S 48°51′W
158 F5 **Lendalfoot** United Kingdom 55°10′N 4°56′W
177 L5 **Lendava** Hung. Lendva, Ger. Unterlimbach; prev. Dolnja Lendava. NE Slovenia 46°33′N 16°27′E
140 E3 **Lendepas** Hardap, SE Namibia 24°41′S 19°58′E
194 D6 **Lendery** Finn. Lentiira. Respublika Kareliya, NW Russian Federation 63°20′N 31°18′E
181 D8 **Lendringsen** Nordrhein-Westfalen, Germany 51°25′E 7°50′N
Lendum see Lens
Lendva see Lendava
166 F5 **Le Neubourg** Haute-Normandie, France 49°09′N 0°55′E
75 G9 **Lenexa** Kansas, C USA 38°57′N 94°43′W
177 I2 **Lengau** Oberösterreich, N Austria 48°01′N 13°17′E
181 I8 **Lengefeld** Thüringen, Germany 51°15′E 10°23′N
181 I8 **Lengenfeld** Thuringen, Germany 51°15′N 10°23′E
227 I8 **Lenger** Yuzhnyy Kazakhstan, S Kazakhstan 42°10′N 69°54′E
180 D5 **Lengerich** Niedersachsen, Germany 52°33′E 7°31′N
180 E6 **Lengerich** Nordrhein-Westfalen, Germany 52°11′E 7°52′N
181 H12 **Lengfurt** Bayern, Germany 49°49′E 9°36′N
Lenghu see Lenghuzhen
239 H5 **Lenghuzhen** var. Lenghu. Qinghai, C China 38°50′N 93°25′E
244 A4 **Lenglong Ling** ▲ N China 37°40′N 102°13′E
176 C4 **Lengnau** Bern, W Switzerland 47°12′N 07°23′E
242 F5 **Lengshuijiang** Hunan, S China 27°42′N 111°26′E
Lengshuitan see Yongzhou
155 H11 **Lenhovda** Kronoberg, S Sweden 57°00′N 15°16′E
Lenīn see Uzynkol', Kazakhstan
Lenin see Akdepe, Turkmenistan
Leninabad see Khujand
Leninakan see Gyumri
Lenina, Pik see Lenin Peak
189 L8 **Lenine** Rus. Lenino. Avtonomna Respublika Krym, S Ukraine 45°18′N 35°47′E
Leninīgor see Leninogorsk
Leningrad see Sankt-Peterburg
Leningrad see Mu'minobod
196 G7 **Leningradskaya** Krasnodarskiy Kray, SW Russian Federation 46°19′N 39°23′E
293 J9 **Leningradskaya** Russian research station Antarctica 69°30′S 159°51′E
194 E8 **Leningradskaya Oblast'** ◈ province NW Russian Federation
Leningradskiy see Mu'minobod
Lenino see Lyenina, Belarus
Lenino see Lenine, Ukraine
Leninobod see Khujand
227 M3 **Leninogorsk** Kaz. Leninīgor. Vostochnyy Kazakhstan, E Kazakhstan 50°20′N 83°34′E
229 K6 **Lenin Peak** Rus. Pik Lenina, Taj. Qullai Lenin. ▲ Kyrgyzstan/Tajikistan 39°20′N 72°50′E
229 J4 **Leninpol'** Talasskaya Oblast', NW Kyrgyzstan 42°29′N 71°54′E
Lenin, Qullai see Lenin Peak
197 I6 **Leninsk** Volgogradskaya Oblast', SW Russian Federation 48°41′N 45°18′E
Leninsk see Baykonyr, Kazakhstan
Leninsk see Akdepe, Turkmenistan
Leninsk see Asaka, Uzbekistan
227 J2 **Leninskiy** Pavlodar, E Kazakhstan 52°13′N 76°50′E
192 F7 **Leninsk-Kuznetskiy** Kemerovskaya Oblast', S Russian Federation 54°42′N 86°16′E
195 I9 **Leninskoje** Kirovskaya Oblast', NW Russian Federation 58°19′N 47°03′E
Leninskoye see Uzynkol'
Lenin-Turkmenski see Türkmenabat
Leninváros see Tiszaújváros
Lenkoran' see Länkäran
181 D8 **Lenne** ≈ W Germany
181 E9 **Lennestadt** Nordrhein-Westfalen, W Germany 51°07′N 08°04′E
74 E6 **Lennox** South Dakota, N USA 43°21′N 96°53′W
117 E14 **Lennox, Isla** Eng. Lennox Island. island S Chile
Lennox Island see Lennox, Isla
67 I6 **Lenoir** North Carolina, SE USA 35°56′N 81°31′W
66 F6 **Lenoir City** Tennessee, S USA 35°48′N 84°15′W
176 C4 **Le Noirmont** Jura, NW Switzerland 47°14′N 06°57′E
62 F1 **Lenôtre, Lac** ◎ Québec, SE Canada
75 G8 **Lenox** Iowa, C USA 40°52′N 94°33′W
64 F4 **Lenox** Pennsylvania, USA 41°43′N 75°40′W
165 I1 **Lens** anc. Lendum, Lentium. Pas-de-Calais, N France 50°26′N 02°50′E
193 I6 **Lensk** Respublika Sakha (Yakutiya), NE Russian Federation 60°43′N 115°16′E
183 D12 **Lenti** Zala, SW Hungary 46°38′N 16°30′E
Lentia see Linz
152 I7 **Lentiira** Kainuu, E Finland 64°22′N 29°52′E
Lentiira see Lendery
175 G13 **Lentini** anc. Leontini. Sicilia, Italy, C Mediterranean Sea 37°17′N 15°00′E
Lentium see Lens
Lentschiza see Łęczyca
152 I7 **Lentua** ◎ E Finland
191 E9 **Lentvaris** Pol. Landwarów. Vilnius, SE Lithuania 24°39′N 24°58′E
81 F10 **Lenwood** California, USA 34°53′N 117°06′W
176 D3 **Lenzburg** Aargau, N Switzerland 47°23′N 08°11′E
177 I2 **Lenzing** Oberösterreich, N Austria 47°58′N 13°34′E
132 G6 **Léo** SW Burkina Faso 11°07′N 02°08′W
177 K3 **Leoben** Steiermark, C Austria 47°23′N 15°06′E
Leobschütz see Głubczyce
90 G6 **Léogâne** S Haiti 18°32′N 72°37′W
260 D3 **Leok** Sulawesi, N Indonesia 01°10′N 121°20′E
74 D4 **Leola** South Dakota, N USA 45°41′N 98°58′W
172 D2 **Leomil** Guarda, Portugal 40°38′N 6°58′W
160 G4 **Leominster** W England, United Kingdom 52°09′N 02°18′W
65 K2 **Leominster** Massachusetts, NE USA 42°29′N 71°43′W
164 F8 **Léon** Landes, SW France 43°54′N 01°17′W
86 D5 **León** var. León de los Aldamas. Guanajuato, C Mexico 21°05′N 101°43′W
88 G6 **León** León, NW Nicaragua 12°24′N 86°52′W
170 E2 **León** Castilla y León, NW Spain 42°34′N 05°34′W
75 G8 **Leon** Iowa, C USA 40°44′N 93°45′W
88 G6 **León** ◈ department W Nicaragua
170 E2 **León** ◈ province Castilla y León, NW Spain
León see Cotopaxi
71 H6 **Leona** Texas, SW USA 31°09′N 95°58′W
71 H4 **Leonard** Texas, SW USA 33°22′N 96°15′W
175 E8 **Leonardo da Vinci** prev. Fiumicino. ✈ (Roma) Lazio, C Italy 41°48′N 12°15′E
67 L3 **Leonardtown** Maryland, NE USA 38°17′N 76°35′W
140 D2 **Leonardville** Omaheke, Namibia 23°30′S 18°47′E
70 F8 **Leona River** ≈ Texas, SW USA
87 N5 **Leona Vicario** Quintana Roo, SE Mexico 20°57′N 87°06′W
179 D12 **Leonberg** Baden-Württemberg, SW Germany 48°48′N 09°01′E
169 K3 **Léoncel** Rhône-Alpes, France 44°54′N 5°12′E
112 F2 **León, Cerro** ▲ NW Paraguay 20°21′S 60°16′W
León de los Aldamas see León
177 J2 **Leonding** Oberösterreich, N Austria 48°17′N 14°15′E
174 F7 **Leonessa** Lazio, C Italy 42°36′N 12°56′E
175 G12 **Leonforte** Sicilia, Italy, C Mediterranean Sea 37°38′N 14°23′E
277 J7 **Leongatha** Victoria, SE Australia 38°30′S 145°56′E
86 C1 **León Guzman** Durango, Mexico 25°30′N 103°39′W
Leonídi see Leonídio
186 G7 **Leonídio** var. Leonídi. Pelopónnisos, S Greece 37°11′N 22°50′E
170 E2 **León, Montes de** ▲▲ NW Spain
274 E6 **Leonora** Western Australia 28°52′S 121°16′E
70 G5 **Leon River** ≈ Texas, SW USA
Leontini see Lentini
Léopold II, Lac see Mai-Ndombe, Lac
111 J5 **Leopoldina** Minas Gerais, Brazil 21°32′S 42°38′W
52 E3 **Leopold McClintock, Cape** headland Northwest Territories, NW Canada
163 F9 **Leopoldsburg** Limburg, NE Belgium 51°07′N 05°16′E
Léopoldville see Kinshasa
75 B10 **Leoti** Kansas, C USA 38°28′N 101°22′W
188 F7 **Leova** Rus. Leovo. SW Moldova 46°31′N 28°16′E
Leovo see Leova
164 E4 **le Palais** Morbihan, NW France 47°20′N 03°08′W
66 A6 **Lepanto** Arkansas, C USA 35°34′N 90°21′W
258 G6 **Lepar, Pulau** island W Indonesia
170 D8 **Lepe** Andalucía, S Spain 37°15′N 07°12′W
Lepel' see Lyepyel'
140 D8 **Lepelle** var. Elefantes; prev. Olifants. ≈ SW South Africa
166 C8 **Le Pellerin** Pays de la Loire, France 47°12′N 1°45′W
141 J2 **Lephalala** ≈ Limpopo, South Africa
141 H2 **Lephepe** var. Lephephe. Kweneng, SE Botswana 23°20′S 25°50′E
Lephephe see Lephepe
243 J4 **Leping** Jiangxi, S China 28°57′N 117°07′E
167 H5 **Le Plessis-Belleville** Picardie, France 49°06′N 2°46′E
166 C9 **Le Poiré-sur-Vie** Pays de la Loire, France 46°46′N 1°31′W
169 K2 **Le Pont-de-Beauvoisin** Rhône-Alpes, France 45°32′N 5°40′E
169 K2 **Le Pont-de-Claix** Rhône-Alpes, France 45°07′N 5°42′E
169 I4 **Le Pont-de-Montvert** Languedoc-Roussillon, France 44°22′N 3°45′E
168 E8 **Le Pont de Suert** prev. Pont de Suert. Cataluña, Spain 42°24′N 0°45′E
169 J5 **Le Pontet** Provence-Alpes-Côte d'Azur, France 43°58′N 4°51′E
Lépontiennes, Alpes/Lepontine, Alpi see Lepontine Alps
176 E5 **Lepontine Alps** Fr. Alpes Lépontiennes, It. Alpi Lepontine. ▲▲ Italy/Switzerland
135 D9 **Le Pool** ◈ province S Congo
137 I10 **Le Port** NW Réunion
165 H1 **le Portel** Pas-de-Calais, N France 50°42′N 01°35′E
169 J3 **Le Pouzin** Rhône-Alpes, France 44°45′N 4°45′E
153 I8 **Leppävirta** Pohjois-Savo, C Finland 62°30′N 27°50′E
91 M1 **le Prêcheur** NW Martinique 14°48′N 61°14′W
227 K6 **Lepsi** prev. Lepsy. Taldykorgan, SE Kazakhstan 46°14′N 78°56′E
227 K6 **Lepsi** prev. Lepsy. ≈ SE Kazakhstan
Lepsy see Lepsi
Le Puglie see Puglia
165 I7 **le Puy** prev. le Puy-en-Velay, hist. Anicium, Podium Anicensis. Haute-Loire, C France 45°03′N 03°53′E
169 I3 **Le Puy-en Velay** Auvergne, France 45°02′N 3°53′E
le Puy-en-Velay see le Puy
167 I3 **Le Quesnoy** Nord-Pas-de-Calais, France 50°15′N 3°38′E
91 J1 **le Raizet** var. Le Raizet. ✈ (Pointe-à-Pitre) Grande Terre, C Guadeloupe 16°16′N 61°31′W
175 F12 **Lercara Friddi** Sicilia, Italy, C Mediterranean Sea 37°45′N 13°37′E
85 H3 **Lerdo de Tejada** Veracruz-Llave, E Mexico 30°04′N 107°01′W
134 C3 **Léré** Mayo-Kébbi Ouest, SW Chad 09°41′N 14°17′E
167 H8 **Léré** Centre, France 47°28′N 2°52′E
Leribe see Hlotse
176 F9 **Lerici** Liguria, NW Italy 44°06′N 09°53′E
102 E8 **Lérida** Vaupés, SE Colombia 0°01′S 70°28′W
168 E9 **Lérida** Cataluña, Spain 41°37′N 0°37′E
171 J3 **Lérida** ◈ province Cataluña, NE Spain
Lérida see Lleida
87 L6 **Lerma** Campeche, Mexico 19°48′N 90°36′W
170 G3 **Lerma** Castilla y León, N Spain 42°02′N 03°46′W
86 C5 **Lerma, Río** ≈ C Mexico
Lerna see Lérni
186 G7 **Lérni** var. Lerna. prehistoric site Pelopónnisos, S Greece
91 N1 **le Robert** E Martinique 14°41′N 60°57′W
140 G3 **Lerolwane** Southern, Botswana 25°36′S 24°32′E
187 K7 **Léros** island Dodekánisa, Greece, Aegean Sea
73 C10 **Le Roy** Illinois, N USA 40°21′N 88°45′W
75 F10 **Le Roy** Kansas, C USA 38°04′N 95°37′W
74 H6 **Le Roy** Minnesota, N USA 43°30′N 92°30′W
64 B1 **Le Roy** New York, NE USA 42°58′N 77°58′W
Lerrnayin Gharabakh see Nagorno-Karabakh
155 F10 **Lerum** Västra Götaland, S Sweden 57°46′N 12°12′E
167 M8 **Le Russey** Franche-Comté, France 47°10′N 6°44′E
156 H1 **Lerwick** NE Scotland, United Kingdom 60°09′N 01°09′W
169 K2 **Les Abrets** Rhône-Alpes, France 45°32′N 5°35′E
91 J1 **les Abymes** var. Abymes. Grande Terre, C Guadeloupe 16°16′N 61°31′W
167 H8 **Les Aix-d'Angillon** Centre, France 47°12′N 2°34′E
les Albères see Albères, Chaîne des
165 H3 **les Andelys** Eure, N France 49°15′N 01°26′E
91 M2 **les Anses-d'Arlets** SW Martinique 14°29′N 61°05′W
170 F1 **Les Arriondes** prev. Arriondas. Asturias, N Spain 43°23′N 05°11′W
167 H7 **Les Bordes** Centre, France 47°49′N 2°24′E
171 J3 **Les Borges Blanques** var. Borjas Blancas. Cataluña, NE Spain 41°31′N 00°52′E
Lesbos see Lésvos
168 G7 **Les Cabannes** Midi-Pyrénées, France 42°47′N 1°40′E
Les Cayes see Cayes
72 G5 **Les Cheneaux Islands** island Michigan, N USA
169 M1 **Les Contamines-Montjoie** Rhône-Alpes, France 45°50′N 6°44′E
171 J5 **Les Coves de Vinromá** Cast. Cuevas de Vinromá. Valenciana, E Spain 40°18′N 00°07′E
169 L3 **les Écrins** ▲ E France 44°54′N 06°25′E
176 C5 **Le Sépey** Vaud, W Switzerland 46°21′N 07°04′E
59 I7 **Les Escoumins** Québec, SE Canada 48°21′N 69°26′W
166 C9 **Les Essarts** Pays de la Loire, France 46°46′N 1°14′W
167 M10 **Les Gets** Rhône-Alpes, France 46°09′N 6°40′E
Les Gonaïves see Gonaïves
242 A3 **Leshan** Sichuan, C China 29°42′N 103°43′E
176 D6 **Les Haudères** Valais, SW Switzerland 46°02′N 07°27′E
164 F5 **les Herbiers** Vendée, NW France 46°52′N 01°01′W
Lesh/Leshi see Lezhë
195 H5 **Leshukonskoye** Arkhangel'skaya Oblast', NW Russian Federation 64°54′N 45°48′E
Lesina see Hvar
175 H8 **Lesina, Lago di** ◎ SE Italy
187 J2 **Lesítse** ▲▲ NE Greece
154 D5 **Lesja** Oppland, S Norway 62°07′N 08°56′E
154 G7 **Lesjöfors** Värmland, C Sweden 59°57′N 14°12′E
183 I9 **Lesko** Podkarpackie, SE Poland 49°28′N 22°19′E
185 H6 **Leskovac** Serbia, SE Serbia 43°00′N 21°58′E
184 G9 **Leskovik** var. Leskoviku. Korçë, S Albania 40°09′N 20°39′E
Leskoviku see Leskovik
159 I2 **Leslie** United Kingdom 56°12′N 3°13′W
77 H7 **Leslie** Idaho, NW USA 43°51′N 113°28′W
73 G8 **Leslie** Michigan, N USA 42°27′N 84°25′W

◆ Country
● Country Capital
◇ Dependent Territory
○ Dependent Territory Capital
◈ Administrative Regions
✈ International Airport
▲ Mountain
▲▲ Mountain Range
Volcano
≈ River
◎ Lake
⊡ Reservoir

| ◆ Country | ◇ Dependent Territory | ✥ Administrative Regions | ▲ Mountain | ◉ Volcano | ◎ Lake |
| ● Country Capital | ○ Dependent Territory Capital | ✕ International Airport | ▲▲ Mountain Range | ↗ River | ⊟ Reservoir |

◆ Country ○ Dependent Territory ◆ Administrative Regions ▲ Mountain ☒ Volcano ◙ Lake
● Country Capital ○ Dependent Territory Capital ✈ International Airport ▲ Mountain Range ∿ River ☐ Reservoir

M

◆ Country ● Country Capital ◇ Dependent Territory ◇ Dependent Territory Capital ◇ Administrative Regions ✕ International Airport ▲ Mountain ▲ Mountain Range ▲ Volcano ≈ River ◉ Lake ◨ Reservoir

◆ Country
● Country Capital
◇ Dependent Territory
○ Dependent Territory Capital
◐ Administrative Regions
✈ International Airport
▲ Mountain
▲▲ Mountain Range
⋀ Volcano
≈ River
◎ Lake
⊡ Reservoir

◆ Country   ◇ Dependent Territory   ◈ Administrative Regions   ▲ Mountain   ☼ Volcano   ◎ Lake
● Country Capital   ○ Dependent Territory Capital   ✕ International Airport   ▲ Mountain Range   ♣ River   ◙ Reservoir

◆ Country
● Country Capital
◇ Dependent Territory
○ Dependent Territory Capital
✕ Administrative Regions
✕ International Airport
▲ Mountain
▲ Mountain Range
⧫ Volcano
♒ River
⊠ Lake
⊞ Reservoir

◆ Country
● Country Capital
◇ Dependent Territory
○ Dependent Territory Capital
◆ Administrative Regions
✈ International Airport
▲ Mountain
▲ Mountain Range
⊼ Volcano
∞ River
⊚ Lake
⊗ Reservoir

◆ Country   ◇ Dependent Territory   ◈ Administrative Regions   ▲ Mountain   ☒ Volcano   ◎ Lake
● Country Capital   ◉ Dependent Territory Capital   × International Airport   ▲ Mountain Range   ✎ River   ☒ Reservoir

◆ Country
◈ Country Capital
◇ Dependent Territory
○ Dependent Territory Capital
◆ Administrative Regions
✕ International Airport
▲ Mountain
▲ Mountain Range
☒ Volcano
♣ River
◉ Lake
⊞ Reservoir

◆ Country ◇ Dependent Territory ✶ Administrative Regions ▲ Mountain ☒ Volcano ⊚ Lake
● Country Capital ○ Dependent Territory Capital ✈ International Airport ▲ Mountain Range ≈ River ◲ Reservoir

Narbo Martius - Neuenstadt
INDEX
381

Narbo Martius see Narbonne
165 I9 **Narbonne** anc. Narbo Martius. Aude, S France 43°11′N 03°E
169 H6 **Narbonne-Plage** Languedoc-Roussillon, France 43°10′N 3°10′E
161 I3 **Narborough** United Kingdom 52°34′N 1°12′W
Narborough Island see Fernandina, Isla
170 E1 **Narcea** ≈ NW Spain
114 B3 **Naré** Santa Fe, Argentina 30°58′S 60°28′W
232 F4 **Narendranagar** Uttarakhand, N India 30°10′N 78°21′E
Nares Abyssal Plain see Nares Plain
290 D6 **Nares Plain** var. Nares Abyssal Plain. undersea feature NW Atlantic Ocean 23°30′N 63°00′W
Nares Stræde see Nares Strait
295 I7 **Nares Strait** Dan. Nares Stræde. strait Canada/Greenland
182 I5 **Narew** ≈ E Poland
234 D6 **Nargund** Karnātaka, W India 15°43′N 75°23′E
140 C2 **Narib** Hardap, S Namibia 24°11′S 17°46′E
140 C7 **Nariep** Northern Cape, South Africa 30°46′S 17°44′E
Narikrik see Knox Atoll
158 B6 **Narin** Donegal, Ireland 54°50′N 8°28′W
Narin Gol see Omon Gol
102 A7 **Nariño** off. Departamento de Narino. ◈ province SW Colombia
253 C13 **Narita** Chiba, Honshū, S Japan 35°46′N 140°20′E
253 C13 **Narita** ✈ (Tōkyō) Chiba, Honshū, S Japan 35°45′N 140°23′E
Narıya see An Nu'ayrīyah
246 C2 **Nariyn Gol** ≈ Mongolia/Russian Federation
239 J2 **Nariynteel** var. Tsagaan-Ovoo. Övörhangay, C Mongolia 45°57′N 101°25′E
232 F4 **Nārkanda** Himāchal Pradesh, NW India 31°14′N 77°27′E
152 H6 **Narkaus** Lappi, NW Finland 66°13′N 26°09′E
232 G8 **Narmada** var. Narbada. ≈ C India
232 E5 **Narnaul** var. Nārnaul. Haryāna, N India 28°04′N 76°10′E
175 F13 **Naro** Sicilia, Italy, C Mediterranean Sea 37°18′N 13°48′E
Narodichi see Narodychi
195 L5 **Narodnaya, Gora** ▲ NW Russian Federation 65°04′N 60°12′E
188 G2 **Narodychi** Rus. Narodichi. Zhytomyrs'ka Oblast', N Ukraine 51°11′N 29°01′E
196 F2 **Naro-Fominsk** Moskovskaya Oblast', W Russian Federation 55°25′N 36°41′E
137 D8 **Narok** Narok, SW Kenya 01°04′S 35°54′E
137 D8 **Narok** ◈ county SW Kenya
170 D1 **Narón** Galicia, NW Spain 43°31′N 08°08′W
277 L6 **Narooma** New South Wales, SE Australia 36°16′S 150°08′E
Narova see Narva
Narovlya see Narowlya
231 J5 **Nārowāl** Punjab, E Pakistan 32°04′N 74°54′E
191 H12 **Narowlya** Rus. Narovlya. Homyel'skaya Voblasts', SE Belarus 51°48′N 29°30′E
153 G8 **Närpes** Fin. Närpiö. Österbotten, W Finland 62°28′N 21°19′E
Närpiö see Närpes
277 L3 **Narrabri** New South Wales, SE Australia 30°21′S 149°48′E
65 L4 **Narragansett Pier** Rhode Island, USA 41°26′N 71°27′W
277 J5 **Narrandera** New South Wales, SE Australia 34°46′S 146°32′E
277 K3 **Narran Lake** ◎ New South Wales, SE Australia
274 D7 **Narrogin** Western Australia 32°53′S 117°17′E
277 K4 **Narromine** New South Wales, SE Australia 32°16′S 148°15′E
67 I4 **Narrows** Virginia, NE USA 37°19′N 80°48′W
64 G4 **Narrowsburg** New York, USA 41°37′N 75°04′W
295 M8 **Narsarsuaq** ✈ Kujalleo, S Greenland 61°07′N 45°03′W
232 F8 **Narsimhapur** Madhya Pradesh, C India 22°58′N 79°15′E
233 K7 **Narsingdi** var. Narsinghdi. Dhaka, C Bangladesh 23°56′N 90°40′E
Narsinghdi see Narsingdi
232 E8 **Narsinghgarh** Madhya Pradesh, C India 23°42′N 77°08′E
239 N2 **Nart** Nei Mongol Zizhiqu, N China 42°54′N 115°55′E
Nartës, Gjol i/Nartës, Laguna e see Nartës, Liqeni i
184 E9 **Nartës, Liqeni i** var. Gjol i Nartës, Laguna e Nartës. ◎ SW Albania
186 G5 **Nartháki** ▲ C Greece 39°12′N 22°24′E
197 H9 **Nartkala** Kabardino-Balkarskaya Respublika, SW Russian Federation 43°34′N 43°55′E
140 D4 **Narubis** Karas, Namibia 26°58′S 18°36′E
250 G5 **Naruto** Tokushima, Shikoku, SW Japan 34°11′N 134°37′E
194 C8 **Narva** Ida-Virumaa, NE Estonia 59°23′N 28°12′E
190 F4 **Narva** prev. Narova. ≈ Estonia/Russian Federation
190 F3 **Narva Bay** Est. Narva Laht, Ger. Narwa-Bucht, Rus. Narvskiy Zaliv. bay Estonia/Russian Federation
Narva Laht see Narva Bay
194 C8 **Narva Reservoir** Est. Narva Veehoidla, Rus. Narvskoye Vodokhranilishche. ⊠ Estonia/Russian Federation
Narva Veehoidla see Narva Reservoir
152 F4 **Narvik** Nordland, C Norway 68°26′N 17°24′E
Narvskiy Zaliv see Narva Bay
Narvskoye Vodokhranilishche see Narva Reservoir
Narwa-Bucht see Narva Bay
232 E4 **Narwāna** Haryāna, NW India 29°36′N 76°11′E
195 J3 **Nar'yan-Mar** prev. Beloshchel'ye, Dzerzhinskiy. Nenetskiy Avtonomnyy Okrug, NW Russian Federation 67°38′N 53°E
192 F6 **Narym** Tomskaya Oblast', C Russian Federation 58°59′N 81°20′E
Narymskiy Khrebet see Khrebet Naryn
229 L5 **Naryn** Narynskaya Oblast', C Kyrgyzstan 41°24′N 76°E
229 K5 **Naryn** ≈ Kyrgyzstan/Uzbekistan
238 D3 **Narynkol** Kaz. Narynqol. Almaty, SE Kazakhstan 42°45′N 80°12′E
Naryn Oblasty see Narynskaya Oblast'
Narynqol see Narynkol
229 L5 **Narynskaya Oblast'** Kir. Naryn Oblasty. ◈ province C Kyrgyzstan
Naryn Zhotasy see Khrebet Naryn
196 F3 **Naryshkino** Orlovskaya Oblast', W Russian Federation 53°00′N 35°41′E
169 N3 **Narzole** Piemonte, NW Italy 44°35′N 07°52′E
154 G7 **Nås** Dalarna, C Sweden 60°28′N 14°30′E
56 B2 **Nass** ≈ British Columbia, SW Canada
152 E6 **Nasafjellet** Lapp. Násávárre. ▲ C Norway 66°29′N 15°23′E
154 H3 **Näsåker** Västernorrland, C Sweden 63°27′N 16°55′E
280 F8 **Nasau** Koro, C Fiji 17°20′S 179°26′E
181 D11 **Nassau** Rheinland-Pfalz, Germany 50°19′E 7°48′N
284 F5 **Nassau** island N Cook Islands
188 D6 **Năsăud** Ger. Nussdorf, Hung. Naszód. Bistrița-Năsăud, N Romania 47°16′N 24°24′E
Násávárre see Nasafjellet
169 H3 **Nasbinals** Lozère, S France 44°40′N 03°03′E
Na Sceirí see Skerries
Nase see Naze
278 D11 **Naseby** Otago, South Island, New Zealand 45°02′S 170°09′E
161 J4 **Naseby** United Kingdom 52°23′N 0°59′W
223 H7 **Nāșerīyeh** Kermān, C Iran
75 G14 **Nash** Texas, SW USA 33°26′N 94°04′W
234 C4 **Nāshik** prev. Nāsik. Mahārāshtra, W India 20°05′N 73°48′E
104 E2 **Nashiño, Río** ≈ Ecuador/Peru
72 A7 **Nashua** Iowa, C USA 42°57′N 92°32′W
77 L3 **Nashua** Montana, NW USA 48°06′N 106°16′W
65 L1 **Nashua** New Hampshire, NE USA 42°45′N 71°26′W
75 G13 **Nashville** Arkansas, C USA 33°57′N 93°50′W
69 K3 **Nashville** Georgia, SE USA 31°12′N 83°15′W
73 C12 **Nashville** Illinois, N USA 38°20′N 89°22′W
73 F11 **Nashville** Indiana, N USA 39°13′N 86°15′W
67 L6 **Nashville** North Carolina, SE USA 35°58′N 78°00′W
66 D6 **Nashville** state capital Tennessee, S USA 36°11′N 86°48′W
66 D6 **Nashville** ✈ Tennessee, S USA 36°06′N 86°44′W
290 D5 **Nashville Seamount** undersea feature NW Atlantic Ocean 30°00′N 57°20′W
184 E2 **Našice** Osijek-Baranja, E Croatia 45°29′N 18°05′E
182 H5 **Nasielsk** Mazowieckie, C Poland 52°33′N 20°46′E
153 H9 **Näsijärvi** ◎ SW Finland
Nāsik see Nāshik
136 B4 **Nasir** Upper Nile, NE South Sudan 08°37′N 33°06′E
230 G7 **Nasīrābād** Baluchistān, SW Pakistan 28°25′N 68°29′E
230 D9 **Nasīrābād** Baluchistān, SW Pakistan 26°15′N 62°32′E
Nasir, Buhayrat/Nâşir, Buḥeiret see Nasser, Lake
Nāsiri see Ahvāz
Nasiriya see An Nāşirīyah
Nás na Ríogh see Naas
175 G12 **Naso** Sicilia, Italy, C Mediterranean Sea 38°07′N 14°46′E
Nasratabad see Zābol
133 K7 **Nassarawa** Nassarawa, C Nigeria 08°33′N 07°42′E
61 M9 **Nassau** ● (The Bahamas) New Providence, N The Bahamas 25°03′N 77°21′W
69 L4 **Nassau Sound** sound Florida, SE USA
176 G4 **Nassereith** Tirol, W Austria 47°19′N 10°51′E
129 J6 **Nasser, Lake** var. Buhayrat Nasir, Buḥayrat Nāşir, Buḥeiret Nâşir. ◎ Egypt/Sudan
155 G10 **Nässjö** Jönköping, S Sweden 57°39′N 14°40′E
163 F12 **Nassogne** Luxembourg, SE Belgium 50°08′N 05°19′E
58 G3 **Nastapoka Islands** island group Northwest Territories, C Canada
181 D11 **Nastätten** Rheinland-Pfalz, Germany 50°12′E 7°52′N
153 H9 **Nastola** Päijät-Häme, S Finland 60°57′N 25°56′E
253 C11 **Nasu-dake** ▲ Honshū, S Japan 37°07′N 139°57′E
263 K5 **Nasugbu** Luzon, N Philippines 14°03′N 120°39′E
190 H5 **Nasva** Pskovskaya Oblast', Russian Federation
154 H5 **Näsviken** Gävleborg, C Sweden 61°46′N 16°55′E
Naszód see Năsăud
138 F4 **Nata** Central, NE Botswana 20°11′S 26°10′E
102 C6 **Natagaima** Tolima, C Colombia 03°38′N 75°07′W
108 J5 **Natal** state capital Rio Grande do Norte, E Brazil 05°46′S 35°15′W
258 C5 **Natal** Sumatera, N Indonesia 0°32′N 99°07′E
Natal see KwaZulu/Natal
289 B10 **Natal Basin** var. Mozambique Basin. undersea feature W Indian Ocean 30°00′S 40°00′E
70 F7 **Natalia** Texas, SW USA 29°11′N 98°51′W
195 L10 **Natal'insk** Sverdlovskaya Oblast, Russian Federation
54 C7 **Natalkuz Lake** ◎ British Columbia, SW Canada
121 M9 **Natal Valley** undersea feature SW Indian Ocean 31°00′S 33°15′E
Natanya see Netanya
222 F5 **Naṭanz** Eşfahān, C Iran 33°31′N 51°55′E
59 K6 **Natashquan** Québec, E Canada 50°10′N 61°50′W
59 K6 **Natashquan** ≈ Newfoundland and Labrador/Québec, E Canada
68 D3 **Natchez** Mississippi, S USA 31°34′N 91°24′W
68 B2 **Natchitoches** Louisiana, S USA 31°45′N 93°05′W
110 E7 **Natércia** Minas Gerais, Brazil 22°07′S 45°30′W
167 N10 **Naters** Valais, S Switzerland 46°22′N 08°00′E
Nathanya see Netanya
152 B5 **Nathorst Land** physical region W Svalbard
Nathula see Nacula
280 B4 **National Capital District** ◈ province S Papua New Guinea
81 E13 **National City** California, W USA 32°40′N 117°06′W
278 G6 **National Park** Manawatu-Wanganui, North Island, New Zealand 39°11′S 175°22′E
54 D6 **Nation River** ≈ British Columbia, SW Canada
133 H6 **Natitingou** NW Benin 10°21′N 01°26′E
55 L3 **Native Bay** coastal sea feature Nunavut, NE Canada
111 K5 **Natividade** Rio de Janeiro, Brazil 21°03′S 41°59′W
110 F9 **Natividade** São Paulo, Brazil 23°24′S 45°26′W
84 B5 **Natividad, Isla** island NW Mexico
219 G9 **Natl** Jordan 31°39′N 35°52′E
159 I7 **Natland** United Kingdom 54°17′N 2°44′W
84 G4 **Nàtora** Sonora, Mexico 28°56′N 108°39′W
253 D10 **Natori** Miyagi, Honshū, C Japan 38°12′N 140°51′E
62 C8 **Natrona Heights** Pennsylvania, NE USA 40°37′N 79°42′W
137 D9 **Natron, Lake** ◎ Kenya/Tanzania
Natsrat see Natzrat
256 C6 **Nattalin** Bago, C Myanmar (Burma) 18°25′N 95°34′E
152 G6 **Nattavaara** Lapp. Nahtavárr. Norrbotten, N Sweden 66°45′N 20°58′E
177 J2 **Natternbach** Oberösterreich, N Austria 48°26′N 13°44′E
155 H11 **Nättraby** Blekinge, S Sweden 56°12′N 15°30′E
258 G3 **Natuna Besar, Pulau** island Kepulauan Natuna, W Indonesia
Natuna Islands see Natuna, Kepulauan
258 G3 **Natuna, Kepulauan** var. Natuna Islands. island group W Indonesia
258 G4 **Natuna, Laut** Eng. Natuna Sea. sea W Indonesia
Natuna Sea see Natuna, Laut
66 G4 **Natural Bridge** tourist site Kentucky, C USA
289 I11 **Naturaliste Fracture Zone** tectonic feature E Indian Ocean
266 E6 **Naturaliste Plateau** undersea feature E Indian Ocean
218 E6 **Natzrat** var. Natsrat, Ar. En Nazira, Eng. Nazareth; prev. Nazerat. Northern, N Israel 32°42′N 35°18′E
Nau see Nov
165 H8 **Naucelle** Aveyron, S France 44°10′N 02°19′E
140 B2 **Nauchas** Hardap, C Namibia 23°40′S 16°19′E
176 G4 **Nauders** Tirol, W Austria 46°52′N 10°31′E
140 G8 **Naudesbergpas** pass Eastern Cape, South Africa
141 I7 **Naudesnek** pass Eastern Cape, South Africa
Naugard see Nowogard
65 J4 **Naugatuck** Connecticut, USA 41°29′N 73°03′W
190 D7 **Naujamiestis** Panevėžys, C Lithuania 55°42′N 24°10′E
190 C7 **Naujoji Akmenė** Šiaulai, NW Lithuania 56°20′N 22°57′E
231 H9 **Naukot** var. Naokot. Sind, SE Pakistan 24°52′N 69°27′E
181 G8 **Naumburg** Hessen, Germany 51°15′E 9°10′N
179 G8 **Naumburg** var. Naumburg an der Saale. Sachsen-Anhalt, C Germany 51°09′N 11°48′E
Naumburg am Queis see Nowogrodziec
Naumburg an der Saale see Naumburg
118 B1 **Naunau** ancient monument Easter Island, Chile, E Pacific Ocean
118 E9 **Naunauco** Neuquén, Argentina 37°37′S 70°11′W
219 F8 **Nā'ūr** 'Ammān, W Jordan 31°52′N 35°50′E
219 F8 **Nāūr** Jordan 31°53′N 35°50′E
181 E11 **Naurod** Hessen, Germany 50°08′E 8°18′N
283 J10 **Nauru** off. Republic of Nauru; prev. Pleasant Island. ◆ republic W Pacific Ocean
267 I4 **Nauru** island W Pacific Ocean
283 J10 **Nauru International** ✈ S Nauru
Nauru, Republic of see Nauru
Nausari see Navsāri
65 N4 **Nauset Beach** beach Massachusetts, NE USA
Naushahra see Nowshera
230 G8 **Naushahro Fīroz** Sind, SE Pakistan 26°51′N 68°11′E
Naushara see Nowshera
280 E9 **Nausori** Viti Levu, W Fiji 18°01′S 178°31′E
104 F4 **Nauta** Loreto, N Peru 04°31′S 73°36′W
233 H6 **Nautanwa** Uttar Pradesh, N India 27°26′N 83°25′E
86 G6 **Nautla** Veracruz-Llave, E Mexico 20°15′N 96°45′W
Nauzad see Now Zād
85 L4 **Nava** Coahuila, NE Mexico 28°28′N 100°45′W
Navabad see Navobod
172 F2 **Navacepeda de Tormes** Castilla y León, Spain 40°22′N 5°15′W
170 F4 **Nava del Rey** Castilla y León, N Spain 41°19′N 05°04′W
233 J8 **Navadwīp** prev. Nabadwip. West Bengal, NE India 23°24′N 88°23′E
280 F8 **Navaga** Koro, W Fiji 17°21′S 179°22′E
170 F5 **Navahermosa** Castilla-La Mancha, C Spain 39°39′N 04°25′W
191 E10 **Navahrudak** Pol. Nowogródek, Rus. Novogrudok. Hrodzyenskaya Voblasts', W Belarus 53°36′N 25°50′E
191 E10 **Navahrudskaye Wzvyshsha** Rus. Novogrudskaya Vozvyshennost'. ▲▲ W Belarus
79 I5 **Navajo Mount** ▲ Utah, W USA 37°00′N 110°52′W
79 K5 **Navajo Reservoir** ⊠ New Mexico, SW USA
263 M7 **Naval** Biliran Island, C Philippines 11°32′N 124°26′E
172 G1 **Navalmanzano** Castilla y León, Spain 41°13′N 4°15′W
170 E5 **Navalmoral de la Mata** Extremadura, W Spain 39°54′N 05°33′W
172 G2 **Navalperal de Pinares** Castilla y León, Spain 40°35′N 4°24′W
172 F5 **Navalvillar de Pela** Extremadura, Spain 39°06′N 5°28′W
170 E6 **Navalvillar de Pelea** Extremadura, W Spain 39°05′N 05°27′W
158 D9 **Navan** Ir. An Uaimh. E Ireland 53°39′N 06°41′W
Navanagar see Jāmnagar
191 G8 **Navapolatsk** Rus. Novopolotsk. Vitsyebskaya Voblasts', N Belarus 55°34′N 28°35′E
230 G4 **Nāvar, Dasht-e** Pash. Dasht-i-Nawar. desert C Afghanistan
193 N3 **Navarin, Mys** headland NE Russian Federation 62°18′N 179°06′E
117 D14 **Navarino, Isla** island S Chile
171 H2 **Navarra** Eng./Fr. Navarre. ◈ autonomous community N Spain
Navarre see Navarra
168 D6 **Navarrenx** Aquitaine, France 43°20′N 0°45′W
171 H2 **Navarrete** La Rioja, N Spain 42°26′N 02°34′W
114 D10 **Navarro** Buenos Aires, E Argentina 35°00′S 59°15′W
168 C7 **Navascués** Navarra, Spain 42°43′N 1°07′W
172 D4 **Navas del Madroño** Extremadura, Spain 39°37′N 6°39′W
172 G1 **Navas de Oro** Castilla y León, Spain 41°12′N 4°26′W
170 G7 **Navas de San Juan** Andalucía, S Spain 38°11′N 03°19′W
172 D3 **Navasfrías** Castilla y León, Spain 40°18′N 6°49′W
71 H6 **Navasota** Texas, SW USA 30°23′N 96°05′W
71 H6 **Navasota River** ≈ Texas, SW USA
90 F6 **Navassa Island** ◇ US unincorporated territory C West Indies
191 G11 **Navasyolki** Rus. Novosëlki. Homyel'skaya Voblasts', SE Belarus 52°24′N 28°33′E
191 E10 **Navayel'nya** Pol. Nowojelnia, Rus. Novoyel'nya. Hrodzyenskaya Voblasts', W Belarus 53°28′N 25°35′E
172 D2 **Nave** Guarda, Portugal 40°24′N 6°58′W
159 M10 **Navenby** United Kingdom 53°06′N 0°31′W
261 L5 **Naver** Papua, E Indonesia 03°27′S 139°45′E
190 E4 **Navesti** ≈ C Estonia
170 E1 **Navia** Asturias, N Spain 43°33′N 06°43′W
170 E1 **Navia** ≈ NW Spain
113 I3 **Naviraí** Mato Grosso do Sul, SW Brazil 23°01′S 54°09′W
280 D8 **Naviti** island Yasawa Group, NW Fiji
196 E3 **Navlya** Bryanskaya Oblast', W Russian Federation 52°47′N 34°28′E
280 F8 **Navoalevu** Vanua Levu, N Fiji 16°22′S 179°28′E
229 J7 **Navobod** Rus. Navabad, Novabad. C Tajikistan 39°00′N 70°06′E
229 I7 **Navobod** Rus. Navabad. W Tajikistan 38°37′N 68°42′E
Navoi see Navoiy
228 G6 **Navoiy** Rus. Navoi. Navoiy Viloyati, C Uzbekistan 40°05′N 65°23′E
Navoiyskaya Oblast' see Navoiy Viloyati
228 G4 **Navoiy Viloyati** Rus. Navoiyskaya Oblast'. ◈ province N Uzbekistan
84 F5 **Navojoa** Sonora, NW Mexico 27°04′N 109°28′W
Navolat see Navolato
84 G7 **Navolato** var. Navolat. Sinaloa, C Mexico 24°46′N 107°42′W
281 M2 **Navonda** Ambae, C Vanuatu 15°21′S 167°58′E
Návpaktos see Náfpaktos
Návplion see Náfplio
133 H6 **Navrongo** N Ghana 10°51′N 01°03′W
232 C9 **Navsāri** var. Nausari. Gujarāt, W India 20°55′N 72°55′E
280 E9 **Navua** Viti Levu, W Fiji 18°15′S 178°10′E
53 I5 **Navy Board Inlet** coastal sea feature Nunavut, NE Canada
218 G5 **Nawá** Dar'ā, S Syria 32°53′N 36°03′E
218 G5 **Nawá** Syria 32°53′N 36°03′E
Nawabashah see Nawābshāh
233 J7 **Nawabganj** Rajshahi, NW Bangladesh 24°35′N 88°21′E
232 G6 **Nawābganj** Uttar Pradesh, N India 26°52′N 82°09′E
230 G9 **Nawābshāh** var. Nawabashah. Sind, S Pakistan 26°15′N 68°26′E
233 I7 **Nawāda** Bihār, N India 24°54′N 85°33′E
232 D5 **Nawalgarh** Rājasthān, N India 27°48′N 75°21′E
Nawar, Dasht-i- see Nāvar, Dasht-e
256 D4 **Nawnghkio** var. Nawngkio. Shan State, C Myanmar (Burma) 22°17′N 96°50′E
Nawngkio see Nawnghkio
215 L6 **Naxçıvan** Rus. Nakhichevan'. SW Azerbaijan 39°14′N 45°24′E
242 B4 **Naxi** Sichuan, C China 28°50′N 105°20′E
187 J7 **Náxos** var. Naxos. Náxos, Kykládes, Greece, Aegean Sea 36°07′N 25°24′E
187 J7 **Náxos** island Kykládes, Greece, Aegean Sea
168 D6 **Nay** Aquitaine, France 43°11′N 0°16′W
85 I9 **Nayar** Nayarit, Mexico 22°16′N 104°28′W
85 I9 **Nayarit** ◈ state C Mexico
280 G9 **Nayau** island Lau Group, E Fiji
223 I5 **Nāy Band** Khorāsān-e Janūbī, E Iran 32°26′N 57°30′E
161 L5 **Nayland** E England, United Kingdom 51°58′N 00°46′E
242 B6 **Nayong** Guizhou, China 26°16′N 105°13′E
252 F3 **Nayoro** Hokkaidō, NE Japan 44°22′N 142°27′E
254 C3 **Nay Pyi Taw** ● Nay Pyi Taw, prev. Pyinmana. C Myanmar (Burma) 19°44′N 96°16′E
172 B4 **Nazaré** var. Nazare. Leiria, C Portugal 39°36′N 09°04′W
Nazare see Nazaré
85 J7 **Nazareno** Durango, Mexico 25°23′N 103°25′W
64 F6 **Nazareth** Pennsylvania, USA 40°44′N 75°19′W
70 D3 **Nazareth** Texas, SW USA 34°32′N 102°06′W
Nazareth see Natzrat
289 D9 **Nazareth Bank** undersea feature W Indian Ocean
85 J7 **Nazas** Durango, C Mexico 25°15′N 104°06′W
85 I7 **Nazas, Río** ≈ Durango, Mexico
105 E9 **Nazca** Ica, S Peru 14°53′S 74°54′W
42 G10 **Nazca Plate** tectonic feature
287 L7 **Nazca Ridge** undersea feature E Pacific Ocean 22°00′S 82°00′W
251 K9 **Naze** var. Nase. Kagoshima, Amami-ōshima, SW Japan 28°21′N 129°30′E
218 E6 **Nazerat** Israel 32°42′N 35°17′E
Nazerat see Natzrat
215 J6 **Nazik Gölü** ◎ E Turkey
214 B7 **Nazilli** Aydın, SW Turkey 37°55′N 28°20′E
215 I6 **Nazımiye** Tunceli, E Turkey 39°12′N 39°51′E
192 F6 **Nazino** Tomskaya Oblast', C Russian Federation 60°02′N 78°51′E
Nazinon see Red Volta
190 I3 **Naziya** Leningradskaya Oblast', Russian Federation
56 D5 **Nazko** British Columbia, SW Canada 52°57′N 123°44′W
218 E7 **Nazlat Isā** West Bank 32°24′N 35°03′E
218 E7 **Nazlat Israelā** West Bank 32°24′N 35°03′E
197 I9 **Nazran'** Respublika Ingushetiya, SW Russian Federation 43°14′N 44°47′E
136 E4 **Nazrēt** var. Adama, Hadama. Oromīya, C Ethiopia 08°31′N 39°20′E
Nazwāh see Nizwa
192 E7 **Nazyvayevsk** Omskaya Oblast', C Russian Federation 55°35′N 71°13′E
138 G1 **Nchanga** Copperbelt, C Zambia 12°30′S 27°53′E
135 I11 **Nchelenge** Luapula, N Zambia 09°20′S 28°50′E
Ncheu see Ntcheu
141 I8 **Nciba** prev. Swart Kei. ≈ Eastern Cape, South Africa see also Swart Kei
138 G9 **Nciba** Eng. Great Kei; prev. Groot-Kei. ≈ S South Africa
Ndaghamcha, Sebkra de see Te-n-Dghâmcha, Sebkhet
137 C10 **Ndala** Tabora, C Tanzania 04°45′S 33°15′E
135 C11 **N'Dalatando** Port. Salazar, Vila Salazar. Kwanza Norte, NW Angola 09°19′S 14°48′E
141 K7 **Ndaleni** Kwazulu Natal, South Africa 29°55′S 30°19′E
133 I6 **Ndali** C Benin 09°50′N 02°46′E
137 A8 **Ndeke** SW Uganda 0°11′S 30°04′E
134 F4 **Ndélé** Bamingui-Bangoran, N Central African Republic 08°24′N 20°41′E
135 B8 **Ndendé** Ngounié, S Gabon 02°21′S 11°20′E
135 B9 **Ndindi** Nyanga, S Gabon 03°47′S 11°06′E
134 C2 **N'Djaména** var. Ndjamena; prev. Fort-Lamy. ● (Chad) Ville de N'Djaména, W Chad 12°08′N 15°02′E
134 C2 **N'Djaména** ✈ Ville de N'Djaména, W Chad 12°09′N 15°00′E
Ndjamena see N'Djaména
N'Djaména, Région de la Ville de see N'Djaména, Ville de
134 D2 **N'Djaména, Ville de** ◈ region SW Chad
134 B7 **Ndjolé** Moyen-Ogooué, W Gabon 0°07′S 10°45′E
138 G1 **Ndola** Copperbelt, C Zambia 12°59′S 28°35′E
Ndrhamcha, Sebkha de see Te-n-Dghâmcha, Sebkhet
134 G5 **Ndu** Orientale, N Dem. Rep. Congo 04°36′N 22°49′E
137 C9 **Nduguti** Singida, C Tanzania 04°19′S 34°40′E
281 J3 **Nduindui** Guadalcanal, C Solomon Islands 09°46′S 159°54′E
Nduke see Kolombangara
141 L5 **Ndumo** KwaZulu-Natal, South Africa 26°55′S 32°15′E
141 L6 **Ndundula** KwaZulu-Natal, South Africa 28°41′S 31°31′E
141 K6 **Ndwedwe** KwaZulu-Natal, South Africa 29°30′S 30°56′E
Ndzouani see Nzwani
186 G4 **Néa Anchiálos** var. Nea Anhialos, Néa Ankhíalos. Thessalía, C Greece 39°16′N 22°49′E
Nea Anhialos/Néa Ankhíalos see Néa Anchiálos
187 H5 **Néa Artáki** Évvoia, C Greece 38°31′N 23°39′E
158 D6 **Neagh, Lough** ◎ United Kingdom
157 D8 **Neagh, Lough** ◎ E Northern Ireland, United Kingdom
76 B3 **Neah Bay** Washington, NW USA 48°21′N 124°39′W
187 J8 **Nea Kaméni** island Kykládes, Greece, Aegean Sea
274 G5 **Neale, Lake** ◎ Northern Territory, C Australia
187 H3 **Néa Moudanía** var. Néa Moudhaniá. Kentrikí Makedonía, N Greece 40°14′N 23°17′E
Néa Moudhaniá see Néa Moudanía
188 E7 **Neamț** ◈ county NE Romania
Neapel see Napoli
186 F3 **Neápoli** prev. Neápolis. Dytikí Makedonía, N Greece 40°19′N 21°23′E
187 J10 **Neápoli** Kríti, Greece, E Mediterranean Sea 35°15′N 25°37′E
187 H8 **Neápoli** Pelopónnisos, S Greece 36°29′N 23°05′E
Neápolis see Neápoli, Greece
Neapolis see Napoli, Italy
Neapolis see Nablus, West Bank
82 A9 **Near Islands** island group Aleutian Islands, Alaska, USA
160 F6 **Neath** S Wales, United Kingdom 51°40′N 03°48′W
187 H2 **Néa Zíchni** var. Néa Zíkhni; prev. Néa Zíkhna. Kentrikí Makedonía, NE Greece 41°02′N 23°50′E
Néa Zíkhna/Néa Zíkhni see Néa Zíchni
88 C3 **Nebaj** Quiché, W Guatemala 15°25′N 91°05′W
132 G6 **Nebbou** S Burkina Faso 11°22′N 01°49′W
277 J2 **Nebine Creek** ≈ Queensland, SE Australia
Nebitdag see Balkanabat
102 G8 **Neblina, Pico da** ▲ NW Brazil 0°49′N 66°31′W
194 E8 **Nebolchi** Novgorodskaya Oblast', W Russian Federation 59°08′N 33°19′E
79 H3 **Nebo, Mount** ▲ Utah, W USA 39°47′N 111°46′W
74 C7 **Nebraska** off. State of Nebraska, also known as Blackwater State, Cornhusker State, Tree Planters State. ◈ state C USA
75 F8 **Nebraska City** Nebraska, C USA 40°38′N 95°52′W
175 G12 **Nebrodi, Monti** var. Monti Caronie. ▲▲ Sicilia, Italy, C Mediterranean Sea
56 D4 **Nechako** ≈ British Columbia, SW Canada
74 E1 **Neche** North Dakota, N USA 48°57′N 97°33′W
71 I5 **Neches** Texas, SW USA 31°51′N 95°28′W
71 I5 **Neches River** ≈ Texas, SW USA
181 G14 **Neckar** ≈ SW Germany
181 F13 **Neckargemünd** Baden-Württemberg, Germany 49°24′E 8°48′N
181 G13 **Neckargerach** Baden-Württemberg, Germany 49°24′E 9°04′N
181 G14 **Neckarsulm** Baden-Württemberg, SW Germany 49°12′N 09°13′E
286 G3 **Necker Island** island C British Virgin Islands
267 L2 **Necker Ridge** undersea feature N Pacific Ocean
116 H6 **Necochea** Buenos Aires, E Argentina 38°34′S 58°42′W
161 L3 **Necton** United Kingdom 52°39′N 0°46′E
170 D1 **Neda** Galicia, NW Spain 43°29′N 08°09′W
186 F7 **Néda** var. Nédas. ≈ S Greece
Nédas see Néda
71 J7 **Nederland** Texas, SW USA 29°58′N 93°59′W
Nederland see Netherlands
162 G7 **Neder Rijn** Eng. Lower Rhine. ≈ C Netherlands
163 G9 **Nederweert** Limburg, SE Netherlands 51°17′N 05°45′E
155 D8 **Nedre Tokke** ◎ S Norway
Nedrigaylov see Nedryhayliv
189 J2 **Nedryhayliv** Rus. Nedrigaylov. Sums'ka Oblast', NE Ukraine 50°51′N 33°54′E
162 I6 **Neede** Gelderland, E Netherlands 52°08′N 06°36′E
65 L2 **Needham** Massachusetts, USA 42°17′N 71°14′W
77 J7 **Needle Mountain** ▲ Wyoming, C USA 44°03′N 109°33′W
81 I11 **Needles** California, W USA 34°50′N 114°37′W
161 I8 **Needles Point** headland United Kingdom 50°40′N 1°35′W
157 H12 **Needles, The** rocks S England, United Kingdom
112 G5 **Ñeembucú** off. Departamento de Ñeembucú. ◈ department SW Paraguay
Ñeembucú, Departamento de see Ñeembucú
72 D6 **Neenah** Wisconsin, N USA 44°09′N 88°26′W
55 I9 **Neepawa** Manitoba, S Canada 50°14′N 99°29′W
53 J7 **Neergaard Lake** ◎ Nunavut, NE Canada
180 D3 **Neermoor** Niedersachsen, Germany 53°18′E 7°26′N
163 G9 **Neerpelt** Limburg, NE Belgium 51°13′N 05°26′E
180 I3 **Neetze** Niedersachsen, Germany 53°16′E 10°38′N
131 K2 **Nefta** ✈ W Tunisia 34°03′N 08°05′E
196 G8 **Neftegorsk** Krasnodarskiy Kray, SW Russian Federation 44°21′N 39°40′E
197 K1 **Neftekamsk** Respublika Bashkortostan, W Russian Federation 56°07′N 54°13′E
197 I8 **Neftekumsk** Stavropol'skiy Kray, SW Russian Federation 44°45′N 45°00′E
192 F6 **Nefteyugansk** Khanty-Mansiyskiy Avtonomnyy Okrug-Yugra, C Russian Federation 61°07′N 72°18′E
Neftezavodsk see Seÿdi
175 B13 **Nefza** Tunisia
135 D10 **Negage** var. N'Gage. Uíge, NW Angola 07°47′S 15°27′E
Negapatam/Negapattinam see Nāgappattinam
259 J9 **Negara** Bali, Indonesia 08°21′S 114°35′E
259 K6 **Negara** Borneo, C Indonesia 02°40′S 115°05′E
Negara Brunei Darussalam see Brunei
72 E4 **Negaunee** Michigan, N USA 46°30′N 87°36′W
219 D9 **Negba** Israel 31°40′N 34°41′E
136 E6 **Negēlē** var. Negelli, It. Neghelli. Oromīya, C Ethiopia 05°13′N 39°43′E
Negelli see Negēlē
Negeri Pahang Darul Makmur see Pahang
Negeri Selangor Darul Ehsan see Selangor
258 E3 **Negeri Sembilan** var. Negri Sembilan. ◈ state Peninsular Malaysia
152 B6 **Negerpynten** headland S Svalbard 77°15′N 22°40′E
Negev see HaNegev
Negev see HaNegev
Neghelli see Negēlē
188 D8 **Negoiu** var. Negoiul. ▲ S Romania 45°34′N 24°34′E
Negoiul see Negoiu
137 E12 **Negomane** var. Negomano. Cabo Delgado, N Mozambique 11°22′S 38°32′E
Negomano see Negomane
235 F10 **Negombo** Western Province, SW Sri Lanka 07°13′N 79°51′E
285 K7 **Negonego** prev. Nengonengo. atoll Îles Tuamotu, C French Polynesia
Negoreloye see Nyeharelaye
185 H4 **Negotin** Serbia, E Serbia 44°14′N 22°31′E
185 H8 **Negotino** C Macedonia 41°29′N 22°04′E
Negra, Punto headland NW Peru 06°03′S 81°08′W
170 C2 **Negreira** Galicia, NW Spain 42°54′N 08°46′W
168 F5 **Nègrepelisse** Midi-Pyrénées, France 44°04′N 1°31′E
188 F7 **Negrești** Vaslui, E Romania 46°50′N 27°28′E
Negrești see Negrești-Oaș
188 C6 **Negrești-Oaș** Hung. Avasfelsőfalu; prev. Negrești. Satu Mare, NE Romania 47°56′N 23°22′E
90 D7 **Negril** W Jamaica 18°16′N 78°21′W
Negri Sembilan see Negeri Sembilan
118 C1 **Negro, Ensenada del** bay Coquimbo, Chile
116 E6 **Negro, Río** ≈ E Argentina
112 F5 **Negro, Río** ≈ NE Argentina
106 F9 **Negro, Río** ≈ E Bolivia
98 D3 **Negro, Rio** ≈ N South America
115 J5 **Negro, Río** ≈ Brazil/Uruguay
118 E4 **Negro, Río** ≈ Región Metropolitana, Chile
112 G4 **Negro, Río** ≈ C Paraguay
Negro, Río see Chixoy, Río, Guatemala/Mexico
Negro, Río see Sico Tinto, Río, Honduras
263 L8 **Negros** island C Philippines
188 F10 **Negru Vodă** Constanța, SE Romania 43°49′N 28°12′E
63 N1 **Neguac** New Brunswick, SE Canada 47°16′N 65°04′W
72 G2 **Negwazu, Lake** ◎ Ontario, S Canada
Négyfalu see Săcele
219 D9 **NEgyptba** Israel 31°40′N 34°41′E
76 B5 **Nehalem** Oregon, NW USA 45°42′N 123°55′W
76 B5 **Nehalem River** ≈ Oregon, NW USA
Nehavend see Nahāvand
223 J6 **Nehbandān** Khorāsān-e Jonūbī, E Iran 31°00′N 60°00′E
247 K3 **Nehe** Heilongjiang, NE China 48°28′N 124°52′E
91 H6 **Neiba** var. Neyba. SW Dominican Republic 18°31′N 71°25′W
Néid, Carn Uí see Mizen Head
152 I3 **Neiden** Finnmark, N Norway 69°41′N 29°23′E
Neidín see Kenmare
Néifinn see Nephin
167 L10 **Neige, Crêt de la** ▲ E France 46°18′N 05°58′E
137 I10 **Neiges, Piton des** ▲ C Réunion 21°05′S 55°28′E
63 J1 **Neiges, Rivière des** ≈ Québec, SE Canada
242 B3 **Neijiang** Sichuan, C China 29°32′N 105°03′E
140 E6 **Neilersdrif** Northern Cape, South Africa 28°45′S 20°59′E
72 B6 **Neillsville** Wisconsin, N USA 44°34′N 90°36′W
Nei Monggol Zizhiqu/Nei Mongol see Nei Mongol Zizhiqu
247 I5 **Nei Mongol Gaoyuan** plateau NE China
244 F1 **Nei Mongol Zizhiqu** var. Nei Mongol, Eng. Inner Mongolia, Inner Mongolian Autonomous Region; prev. Nei Monggol Zizhiqu. ◈ autonomous region N China
245 I5 **Neiqiu** Hebei, E China 37°22′N 114°34′E
Neiriz see Neyrīz
179 J8 **Neisse** Cz. Lužická Nisa Pol. Nisa, Ger. Lausitzer Neisse, Nysa Łużycka. ≈ C Europe
Neisse see Nysa
102 B6 **Neiva** Huila, S Colombia 02°58′N 75°15′W
244 G9 **Neixiang** Henan, China 33°03′N 111°50′E
239 N7 **Neixiang** Henan, C China 33°08′N 111°50′E
Nejafabad see Najafābād
55 I5 **Nejanilini Lake** ◎ Manitoba, C Canada
87 H9 **Nejapa** Oaxaca, Mexico 16°37′N 95°59′W
Nejd see Najd
136 D4 **Nek'emtē** var. Lakemti, Nakamti. Oromīya, C Ethiopia 09°06′N 36°31′E
197 H5 **Nekhayevskaya** Volgogradskaya Oblast', SW Russian Federation 50°25′N 41°44′E
72 C6 **Nekoosa** Wisconsin, N USA 44°19′N 89°54′W
Neksø Bornholm see Nexø
172 C2 **Nelas** Viseu, N Portugal 40°32′N 07°52′W
194 D10 **Nelidovo** Tverskaya Oblast', W Russian Federation 56°13′N 32°45′E
74 E7 **Neligh** Nebraska, C USA 42°07′N 98°01′W
193 K6 **Nel'kan** Khabarovskiy Kray, E Russian Federation 57°44′N 136°09′E
152 H4 **Nellim** var. Nellimö, Lapp. Njellim. Lappi, N Finland 68°49′N 28°18′E
Nellimö see Nellim
234 F7 **Nellore** Andhra Pradesh, E India 14°29′N 80°E
141 K4 **Nelsbergpas** pass Mpumalanga, South Africa
114 B4 **Nelson** Santa Fe, C Argentina 31°16′S 60°45′W
56 G9 **Nelson** British Columbia, SW Canada 49°29′N 117°17′W
279 F8 **Nelson** Nelson, South Island, New Zealand 41°17′S 173°17′E
159 J8 **Nelson** NW England, United Kingdom 53°51′N 02°13′W
75 D8 **Nelson** Nebraska, C USA 40°12′N 98°04′W
81 J10 **Nelson** Nevada, USA 35°42′N 114°49′W
278 E7 **Nelson** ◈ unitary authority South Island, New Zealand
55 J7 **Nelson** ≈ Manitoba, C Canada
277 M5 **Nelson Bay** New South Wales, SE Australia 32°48′S 152°10′E
277 H7 **Nelson, Cape** headland Victoria, SE Australia 38°25′S 141°33′E
117 B12 **Nelson, Estrecho** strait SE Pacific Ocean
55 I7 **Nelson House** Manitoba, C Canada 55°49′N 98°51′W
72 B4 **Nelson Lake** ◎ Wisconsin, N USA
80 G7 **Nelson Range** ridge California, USA
73 I11 **Nelsonville** Ohio, N USA 39°27′N 82°13′W
75 G8 **Nelsoon River** ≈ Iowa/Missouri, C USA
140 F8 **Nelspoort** Western Cape, South Africa 32°07′S 23°00′E
141 K3 **Nelspruit** province capital Mpumalanga, NE South Africa
Nelspruit see Mbombela
132 E3 **Néma** Hodh ech Chargui, SE Mauritania 16°32′N 07°12′W
191 C8 **Neman** Ger. Ragnit. Kaliningradskaya Oblast', W Russian Federation 55°01′N 22°00′E
144 E5 **Neman** Bel. Nyoman, Ger. Memel, Lith. Nemunas, Pol. Niemen. ≈ NE Europe
Nemausus see Nîmes
186 G6 **Neméa** Pelopónnisos, S Greece 37°49′N 22°40′E
Německý Brod see Havlíčkův Brod
58 E7 **Nemegosenda** ≈ Ontario, S Canada
191 E8 **Nemencinė** Vilnius, SE Lithuania 54°50′N 25°29′E
Nemetocenna see Arras
Nemirov see Nemyriv
165 H4 **Nemours** Seine-et-Marne, N France 48°16′N 02°41′E
Nemunas see Neman
252 I4 **Nemuro** Hokkaidō, NE Japan 43°20′N 145°35′E
252 I4 **Nemuro-hantō** peninsula Hokkaidō, NE Japan
252 I3 **Nemuro-kaikyō** strait Japan/Russian Federation
252 H4 **Nemuro-wan** bay N Japan
188 C3 **Nemyriv** Rus. Nemirov. L'vivs'ka Oblast', NW Ukraine 50°08′N 23°28′E
188 G5 **Nemyriv** Rus. Nemirov. Vinnyts'ka Oblast', C Ukraine 48°58′N 28°50′E
157 C10 **Nenagh** Ir. An tAonach. Tipperary, C Ireland 52°52′N 08°12′W
83 I5 **Nenana** Alaska, USA 64°33′N 149°05′W
83 I5 **Nenana River** ≈ Alaska, USA
281 I5 **Nendö** var. Swallow Island. island Santa Cruz Islands, E Solomon Islands
180 F5 **Nendorf** Niedersachsen, Germany 52°30′E 8°59′N
161 K3 **Nene** ≈ United Kingdom
157 I10 **Nene** ≈ E England, United Kingdom
195 K3 **Nenetskiy Avtonomnyy Okrug** ◈ autonomous district Arkhangel'skaya Oblast', NW Russian Federation
Nengonengo see Negonego
193 K8 **Nenjiang** Heilongjiang, NE China 49°11′N 125°18′E
247 K3 **Nen Jiang** var. Nonni. ≈ NE China
181 E11 **Nentershausen** Rheinland-Pfalz, Germany 50°25′E 7°56′N
159 J6 **Nenthead** United Kingdom 54°46′N 2°20′W
282 F10 **Neoch** atoll Caroline Islands, C Micronesia
186 F6 **Neochóri** Dytikí Elláda, C Greece 38°23′N 21°14′E
75 F11 **Neodesha** Kansas, C USA 37°25′N 95°40′W
74 F7 **Neola** Iowa, C USA 41°27′N 95°40′W
186 G5 **Néo Monastíri** var. Néon Monastiri. Thessalía, C Greece 39°22′N 21°55′E
Néon Karlovasi/Néon Karlovásion see Karlovási
Néon Monastiri see Néo Monastíri
75 G11 **Neosho** Missouri, C USA 36°53′N 94°24′W
75 F10 **Neosho River** ≈ Kansas/Oklahoma, C USA
219 E10 **Ne'ot HaKikkar** Israel 30°57′N 35°22′E
219 E13 **Ne'ot Smadar** Israel
193 H7 **Nepa** ≈ C Russian Federation
233 I5 **Nepal** off. Nepal. ◆ monarchy S Asia
Nepal see Nepal
232 G5 **Nepālganj** Mid Western, SW Nepal 28°04′N 81°37′E
62 F3 **Nepean** Ontario, SE Canada 45°19′N 75°54′W
79 H3 **Nephi** Utah, W USA 39°43′N 111°50′W
157 B8 **Nephin** Ir. Néifinn. ▲ W Ireland 54°00′N 09°21′W
63 M1 **Nepisiguit** ≈ New Brunswick, SE Canada
121 K5 **Nepoko** ≈ NE Dem. Rep. Congo
110 F5 **Nepomuceno** Minas Gerais, Brazil 21°14′S 45°15′W
65 H7 **Neptune** New Jersey, NE USA 40°10′N 74°03′W
174 F7 **Nera** anc. Nar. ≈ C Italy
164 G8 **Nérac** Lot-et-Garonne, SW France 44°08′N 00°21′E
277 M2 **Nerang** Queensland, Australia
183 C8 **Neratovice** Ger. Neratowitz. Středocesky Kraj, C Czech Republic 50°16′N 14°31′E
Neratowitz see Neratovice
193 J8 **Nercha** ≈ S Russian Federation
193 J8 **Nerchinsk** Zabaykal'skiy Kray, S Russian Federation 52°01′N 116°25′E
194 G10 **Nerekhta** Kostromskaya Oblast', NW Russian Federation 57°27′N 40°33′E
190 E7 **Nereta** S Latvia 56°12′N 25°18′E
174 F7 **Nereto** Abruzzo, C Italy 42°49′N 13°50′E
184 D5 **Neretva** ≈ Bosnia and Herzegovina/Croatia
186 E5 **Nerikós** ruins Lefkáda, Iónia Nísiá, Greece, C Mediterranean Sea
135 F13 **Neriquinha** Kuando Kubango, SE Angola 15°44′S 21°34′E
191 D8 **Neris** Bel. Viliya, Pol. Wilia; prev. Pol. Wilja. ≈ Belarus/Lithuania
Neris see Viliya
167 H10 **Néris-les-Bains** Auvergne, France 46°17′N 2°40′E
170 G9 **Nerja** Andalucía, S Spain 36°45′N 03°35′W
194 F10 **Nerl'** ≈ W Russian Federation
195 L6 **Nerokhi** Khanty-Mansiyskiy Avtonomnyy Okrug-Yugra, Russian Federation
169 J1 **Néronde** Rhône-Alpes, France 45°50′N 4°14′E
261 I6 **Nerong, Selat** strait Kepulauan Kai, E Indonesia
171 H7 **Nerpio** Castilla-La Mancha, C Spain 38°08′N 02°18′W
118 C5 **Nerquihue** Libertador General Bernardo O'Higgins, Chile 34°40′S 71°34′W
170 E8 **Nerva** Andalucía, S Spain 37°40′N 06°31′W
193 J7 **Neryungri** Respublika Sakha (Yakutiya), NE Russian Federation 56°38′N 124°19′E
162 G3 **Nes** Fryslân, N Netherlands 53°28′N 05°46′E
154 D6 **Nesbyen** Buskerud, S Norway 60°36′N 09°35′E
65 I6 **Nesconset** New York, USA 40°51′N 73°09′W
185 M6 **Nesebar** var. Nesebŭr. Burgas, E Bulgaria 42°40′N 27°43′E
Nesebŭr see Nesebar
Neshcherdo, Ozero see Nyeshcharda, Vozyera
218 E6 **Nesher** Israel 32°45′N 35°03′E
152 E2 **Neskaupstaður** Austurland, E Iceland 65°08′N 13°45′W
152 D6 **Nesna** Nordland, C Norway 66°11′N 12°54′E
172 C3 **Nesperal** Castelo Branco, Portugal 39°49′N 8°10′W
75 C10 **Ness City** Kansas, C USA 38°27′N 99°54′W
Nesselsdorf see Kopřivnice
179 D14 **Nesslau** Sankt Gallen, NE Switzerland 47°13′N 09°12′E
156 E5 **Ness, Loch** ◎ N Scotland, United Kingdom
159 L7 **Ness Point** headland N England, United Kingdom
Nesterov see Zhovkva
159 I10 **Neston** United Kingdom 53°17′N 3°03′W
187 I2 **Néstos** Bul. Mesta, Turk. Kara Su. ≈ Bulgaria/Greece see also Mesta
Néstos see Mesta
Nes Tsiyona see Nes Ziyyona
154 A7 **Nesttun** Hordaland, S Norway 60°19′N 05°16′E
Nesvizh see Nyasvizh
219 D8 **Nes Ziyyona** var. Nes Tsiyona. Central, C Israel 31°55′N 34°48′E
218 D7 **Netanya** var. Natanya, Nathanya. Central, C Israel 32°20′N 34°51′E
162 H6 **Netherlands** off. Kingdom of the Netherlands, var. Holland, Dut. Koninkrijk der Nederlanden, Nederland. ◆ monarchy NW Europe
Netherlands East Indies see Indonesia
Netherlands Guiana see Suriname
Netherlands, Kingdom of the see Netherlands
Netherlands New Guinea see Papua
188 E3 **Netishyn** Khmel'nyts'ka Oblast', W Ukraine 50°20′N 26°38′E
219 D9 **Netivot** Southern, S Israel 31°26′N 34°36′E
175 H11 **Neto** ≈ S Italy
181 E9 **Netphen** Nordrhein-Westfalen, Germany 50°55′E 8°06′N
181 B8 **Nettetal** Nordrhein-Westfalen, Germany 51°19′E 6°17′N
53 L8 **Nettilling Fiord** coastal sea feature Nunavut, NE Canada
53 L8 **Nettilling Lake** ◎ Baffin Island, Nunavut, N Canada
74 G2 **Nett Lake** ◎ Minnesota, N USA
159 M10 **Nettleham** United Kingdom 53°16′N 0°29′W
180 H6 **Nettlingen** Niedersachsen, Germany 52°10′E 10°10′N
175 E9 **Nettuno** Lazio, C Italy 41°27′N 12°40′E
Netum see Noto
86 A2 **Netzahualcóyotl, Presa** ⊠ SE Mexico
Netze see Noteć
Neu Amerika see Puławy
Neubetsche see Novi Bečej
Neubidschow see Nový Bydžov
Neubistritz see Nová Bystřice
180 D4 **Neubörger** Niedersachsen, Germany 52°58′E 7°27′N
178 H5 **Neubrandenburg** Mecklenburg-Vorpommern, NE Germany 53°33′N 13°16′E
180 F4 **Neubruchhausen** Niedersachsen, Germany 52°50′E 8°50′N
181 H12 **Neubrunn** Bayern, Germany 49°44′E 9°40′N
180 J6 **Neu Büddenstedt** Niedersachsen, Germany 52°11′E 11°02′N
179 F12 **Neuburg an der Donau** Bayern, S Germany 48°43′N 11°10′E
176 C4 **Neuchâtel** Ger. Neuenburg. Neuchâtel, W Switzerland 46°59′N 06°55′E
174 B2 **Neuchâtel** Ger. Neuenburg. ◈ canton W Switzerland
176 C4 **Neuchâtel, Lac de** Ger. Neuenburger See. ◎ W Switzerland
181 G13 **Neudenau** Baden-Württemberg, Germany 49°18′E 9°16′N
Neudorf see Spišská Nová Ves
180 I5 **Neudorf-Platendorf** Niedersachsen, Germany 52°33′E 10°36′N
180 J4 **Neue Elde** canal N Germany
Neuenburg see Neuchâtel
Neuenburg an der Elbe see Nymburk
Neuenburger See see Neuchâtel, Lac de
180 C5 **Neuenhaus** Niedersachsen, Germany 52°30′E 6°58′N
180 D6 **Neuenkirchen** Nordrhein-Westfalen, Germany 52°15′E 7°22′N
180 F4 **Neuenland** ✈ (Bremen) Bremen, NW Germany 53°03′N 08°46′E
181 D8 **Neuenrade** Nordrhein-Westfalen, Germany 51°17′E 7°47′N
Neuenstadt see La Neuveville

◆ Country
● Country Capital
◇ Dependent Territory
○ Dependent Territory Capital
◈ Administrative Regions
✈ International Airport
▲ Mountain
▲▲ Mountain Range
🌋 Volcano
≈ River
◎ Lake
⊠ Reservoir

◆ Country   ◇ Dependent Territory   ✕ Administrative Regions   ▲ Mountain   ▲ Volcano   ☺ Lake
● Country Capital   ○ Dependent Territory Capital   ✈ International Airport   ▲ Mountain Range   ❖ River   ◩ Reservoir

◆ Country   ◇ Dependent Territory   ◈ Administrative Regions   ▲ Mountain   ◉ Volcano   ◎ Lake
● Country Capital   ○ Dependent Territory Capital   ✕ International Airport   ▲▲ Mountain Range   ⟷ River   ▢ Reservoir

◆ Country   ◇ Dependent Territory   ▲ Administrative Regions   ▲ Mountain   ⛰ Volcano   ⊚ Lake
● Country Capital   ○ Dependent Territory Capital   ✕ International Airport   ▲ Mountain Range   ≈ River   ⊡ Reservoir

◆ Country
● Country Capital
◇ Dependent Territory
○ Dependent Territory Capital
▲ Administrative Regions
✕ International Airport
▲ Mountain
▲ Mountain Range
▲ Volcano
☒ River
◎ Lake
◎ Reservoir

● Country ◇ Dependent Territory ◆ Administrative Regions ▲ Mountain ☒ Volcano ◎ Lake
○ Country Capital ○ Dependent Territory Capital ✈ International Airport ▲ Mountain Range ⌘ River ◙ Reservoir

⬦ Country
⬥ Country Capital
⬦ Dependent Territory
○ Dependent Territory Capital
◆ Administrative Regions
✈ International Airport
▲ Mountain
▲ Mountain Range
☉ Volcano
♒ River
☉ Lake
☉ Reservoir

◆ Country ◇ Dependent Territory ✈ Administrative Regions ▲ Mountain ▲ Volcano ☺ Lake
● Country Capital ◉ Dependent Territory Capital ✈ International Airport ▲ Mountain Range ↗ River ☐ Reservoir

| ◆ Country | ◇ Dependent Territory | ✈ Administrative Regions | ▲ Mountain | ▲ Volcano | ◉ Lake |
| ● Country Capital | ○ Dependent Territory Capital | ✈ International Airport | ▲ Mountain Range | ☒ River | ☒ Reservoir |

S

◆ Country ● Country Capital ◇ Dependent Territory ○ Dependent Territory Capital ✕ Administrative Regions ✈ International Airport ▲ Mountain ▲ Mountain Range ⮾ Volcano ⋙ River ⊚ Lake ⊠ Reservoir

	◆ Country	◇ Dependent Territory	◈ Administrative Regions	▲ Mountain	☒ Volcano	⊜ Lake
	● Country Capital	○ Dependent Territory Capital	✕ International Airport	▲ Mountain Range	↗ River	⊜ Reservoir

◆ Country	◇ Dependent Territory	◈ Administrative Regions	▲ Mountain	♒ Volcano	⊙ Lake
● Country Capital	◇ Dependent Territory Capital	✈ International Airport	▲ Mountain Range	♒ River	⊡ Reservoir

◆ Country　　○ Country Capital　　◇ Dependent Territory　　○ Dependent Territory Capital　　◆ Administrative Regions　　● Country Capital　　✕ International Airport　　▲ Mountain　　▲ Mountain Range　　✕ Volcano　　∿ River　　◎ Lake　　◎ Reservoir

---

◆ Country	◇ Dependent Territory	◉ Administrative Regions	▲ Mountain	⛰ Volcano	◎ Lake
● Country Capital	○ Dependent Territory Capital	✕ International Airport	▲ Mountain Range	✍ River	▢ Reservoir

◆ Country   ◇ Dependent Territory   ✦ Administrative Regions   ▲ Mountain   ◈ Volcano   ☉ Lake
● Country Capital   ◇ Dependent Territory Capital   ✈ International Airport   ▲ Mountain Range   ↔ River   ◈ Reservoir

◆ Country ◇ Dependent Territory ★ Administrative Regions ▲ Mountain 🌋 Volcano ☺ Lake
● Country Capital ○ Dependent Territory Capital ✈ International Airport ▲ Mountain Range ♒ River ▣ Reservoir

◆ Country
● Country Capital
◊ Dependent Territory
○ Dependent Territory Capital
◈ Administrative Regions
✕ International Airport
▲ Mountain
▲ Mountain Range
🌋 Volcano
♒ River
◎ Lake
⊟ Reservoir

◆ Country   ◇ Dependent Territory   ◇ Administrative Regions   ▲ Mountain   ☒ Volcano   ⊘ Lake
● Country Capital   ○ Dependent Territory Capital   ✕ International Airport   ▲ Mountain Range   ✦ River   ◻ Reservoir

◆ Country   ◇ Dependent Territory   ◈ Administrative Regions   ▲ Mountain   ⛰ Volcano   ◎ Lake
● Country Capital   ◇ Dependent Territory Capital   ✈ International Airport   ▲ Mountain Range   ∿ River   ▣ Reservoir

◆ Country   ◇ Dependent Territory   ◈ Administrative Regions   ▲ Mountain   ▲ Volcano   ◎ Lake
● Country Capital   ○ Dependent Territory Capital   ✈ International Airport   ▲▲ Mountain Range   ≈ River   ⬭ Reservoir

◆ Country   ◇ Dependent Territory   ▲ Administrative Regions   ▲ Mountain   ▲ Volcano   ◎ Lake
● Country Capital   ○ Dependent Territory Capital   ✈ International Airport   ▲ Mountain Range   ❧ River   ▣ Reservoir

◇ Country   ◆ Dependent Territory   ◆ Administrative Regions   ▲ Mountain   ▲ Volcano   ⊘ Lake
◆ Country Capital   ○ Dependent Territory Capital   ✈ International Airport   ▲ Mountain Range   ≈ River   ⊠ Reservoir

V

◆ Country
● Country Capital
◇ Dependent Territory
○ Dependent Territory Capital
◈ Administrative Regions
× International Airport
▲ Mountain
▲ Mountain Range
◣ Volcano
◆ River
◎ Lake
◪ Reservoir

◆ Country ◇ Dependent Territory ◈ Administrative Regions ▲ Mountain ⊠ Volcano ⊙ Lake
● Country Capital ○ Dependent Territory Capital ★ International Airport ▲ Mountain Range ➤ River ⊠ Reservoir

◆ Country	◇ Dependent Territory	◈ Administrative Regions	▲ Mountain	▲ Volcano	⊚ Lake
● Country Capital	○ Dependent Territory Capital	✕ International Airport	▲ Mountain Range	↗ River	⊡ Reservoir

◆ Country
● Country Capital
◇ Dependent Territory
◌ Dependent Territory Capital
◈ Administrative Regions
✕ International Airport
▲ Mountain
▲ Mountain Range
⧆ Volcano
∼ River
☐ Lake
⊡ Reservoir

Picture credits

T = top, B = bottom, A = above, L = left, R = right, C = center

Every effort has been made to trace the copyright holders and we apologize in advance for any unintentional omissions. We would be pleased to insert the appropriate acknowledgement in any subsequent edition of this publication.

Alamy Images: E.J. Baumeister Jr. 32br; blickwinkel 15fbr; Danita Delimont 15bc; Mike Goldwater 38cl; Jon Arnold Images 40crb; Jenny Matthews 31crb; Rob Niebrugge 14bl, 14tc; David Norton Photography 21cr; Panorama Media (Beijing) Ltd. 15fcla; Alex Segre 35bl; Jon Sparks 15cla; Keren Su / China Span 15cra; Maciej Wojtkowiak 26cb;

Corbis: Dave Amit / Reuters 31cb; Yann Arthus-Bertrand 30cla; Lloyd Cluff 14fcra; Najlah Feanny 32ca; Annie Griffiths Belt 15br; Danny Lehman 14cra; Reuters 30br; Galen Rowell 15bl; Chuck Savage 28tc; Scott T. Smith 15fcra; David Woods 30cb; **European Parliament Photolibrary (www.europarl.eu):** 26tr; **Getty Images:** Laurance B. Aiuppy /Photographer's Choice 21tl; Daniel H. Bailey / Veer / Photonica 21ftr; Pascal Crapet / Stone 14fbl; Diehm / Stone 20clb; Georgette Douwma / Image Bank 21cra; George F. Herben / National Geographic 14br; James Kerrick / Stone 15fbl; Roine Magnusson / Image Bank 21crb; Joanna McCarthy / Riser 20tc; Paul Nicklen / National Geographic 14fbr; Joe Raedle 28cb; Chad Slattery / Stone 34tr; Michael Townsend / Stone 21ftl; Joseph Van Os / Image Bank 20cla; Jeremy Walker / Stone 20cl;

NASA: Jesse Allen, Earth Observatory; based on data provided by the ASTER Science Team 23crb; Ron Beck, USGS Eros Data Center Satellite Systems Branch 24bc; JSC Gateway to Astronary Photography of Earth 22br; U.S. Geological Survey 8ca; U.S. Naval Observatory / Antonio Cidadao 9t; Image provided by the USGS EROS Data Center Satellite Systems Branch as part of the Earth as Art II image series 14fcla; **Science Photo Library:** NASA 23cr; **Still Pictures:** Fred Bruemmer 14cla; Das Fotoarchiv 27ca; Mark Edwards 23tr; NASA / UNEP 23bc, 23bl; Ray Pfortner 21tr; Michael Sewell 14bc; Sean Sprague 29bl **Jacket images:** Front: **Getty Images:** Buck Campbell

All other images © Dorling Kindersley.
For further information see: www.dkimages.com

Data for the bathymetric maps provided by Planetary Visions Limited based on ETOPO2 global relief data, SRTM30 land elevation data and the Generalised Bathymetric Chart of the Ocean.

ETOPO2 published by the U.S. Department of Commerce, National Oceanic and Atmospheric Administration, National Geophysical Data Center, 2001.

SRTM30 published by NASA and the National Geospatial Intelligence Agency, 2005, distributed by the U.S. Geological Survey.

GEBCO One Minute Grid reproduced from the GEBCO Digital Atlas published by the British Oceanographic Data Centre on behalf of the Intergovernmental Oceanographic Commission of UNESCO and the International Hydrographic Organisation, 2003.

Terrestrial Ecoregions Data: Olson, D. M, E. Dinerstein, E.D. Wikramanayake, N.D. Burgess, G.V.N. Powell, E.C. Underwood, J.A. D'amico, I. Itoua, H.E. Strand, J.C. Morrison, C.J. Loucks, T.F. Allnutt, T.H. Ricketts, Y. Kura, J.F. Lamoreux, W.W.Wettengel, P. Hedao, & K.R. Kassem. 2001. Terrestrial Ecoregions of the World: A New Map of Life on Earth. BioScience 51:933-938

Town plans derived from OpenStreetMap data © OpenStreetMap contributors

◆ Country	◇ Dependent Territory	⬦ Administrative Regions	▲ Mountain	🌋 Volcano	◎ Lake
● Country Capital	○ Dependent Territory Capital	✕ International Airport	⛰ Mountain Range	〜 River	▣ Reservoir

NORTH AMERICA

 CANADA

 UNITED STATES OF AMERICA

 MEXICO

 BELIZE

 COSTA RICA

 EL SALVADOR

 GUATEMALA

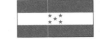 HONDURAS

SOUTH AMERICA

 GRENADA

 HAITI

 JAMAICA

 ST KITTS & NEVIS

 ST LUCIA

 ST VINCENT & THE GRENADINES

 TRINIDAD & TOBAGO

 COLOMBIA

AFRICA

 URUGUAY

 CHILE

 PARAGUAY

 ALGERIA

 EGYPT

 LIBYA

 MOROCCO

 TUNISIA

 LIBERIA

 MALI

 MAURITANIA

 NIGER

 NIGERIA

 SENEGAL

 SIERRA LEONE

 TOGO

 BURUNDI

 DJIBOUTI

 ERITREA

 ETHIOPIA

 KENYA

 RWANDA

 SOMALIA

 SUDAN

 NAMIBIA

 SOUTH AFRICA

 SWAZILAND

 ZAMBIA

 ZIMBABWE

 COMOROS

 MADAGASCAR

 MAURITIUS

 LUXEMBOURG

 NETHERLANDS

 GERMANY

 FRANCE

 MONACO

 ANDORRA

 PORTUGAL

 SPAIN

 POLAND

 SLOVAKIA

 ALBANIA

 BOSNIA & HERZEGOVINA

 CROATIA

 KOSOVO (disputed)

 MACEDONIA

 MONTENEGRO

ASIA

 LATVIA

 LITHUANIA

 CYPRUS

 MALTA

 RUSSIAN FEDERATION

 ARMENIA

 AZERBAIJAN

 GEORGIA

 TURKEY

 QATAR

 SAUDI ARABIA

 UNITED ARAB EMIRATES

 YEMEN

 IRAN

 KAZAKHSTAN

 KYRGYZSTAN

 TAJIKISTAN

 CHINA

MONGOLIA

NORTH KOREA

SOUTH KOREA

TAIWAN

JAPAN

MYANMAR (BURMA)

CAMBODIA

AUSTRALASIA & OCEANIA

SINGAPORE

MALDIVES

AUSTRALIA

NEW ZEALAND

PAPUA NEW GUINEA

FIJI

SOLOMON ISLANDS

VANUATU